Encyclopedia of
AGING

Encyclopedia of Aging

David J. Ekerdt, Editor in Chief

Copyright © by Macmillan Reference USA, an imprint of The Gale Group, Inc., a division of Thomson Learning.

Macmillan Reference USA™ and Thomson Learning™ are trademarks used herein under license.

For more information, contact
Macmillan Reference USA
An imprint of the Gale Group
300 Park Avenue South, 9th Floor
New York, NY 10010

Macmillan Reference USA
The Gale Group, Inc.
27500 Drake Rd.
Farmington Hills, MI 48331-3535

For permission to use material from this product, submit your request via Web at http://www.gale-edit.com/permissions, or you may download our Permissions Request form and submit your request by fax or mail to:

Permissions Department
The Gale Group, Inc.
27500 Drake Rd.
Farmington Hills, MI 48331-3535
Permissions hotline:
248-699-8006 or 800-877-4253, ext. 8006
Fax: 248-699-8074 or 800-762-4058

LIBRARY OF CONGRESS CATALOG-IN-PUBLICATION DATA

Encyclopedia of aging / David J. Ekerdt, editor.— 1st ed.
　　p. cm.
　　　　Includes bibliographical references and index.
　　　　ISBN 0-02-865472-2 (set : hardcover : alk. paper)
　　　　1. Gerontology—Encyclopedias. 2. Aged—Encyclopedias. 3. Aging—Encyclopedias. I. Ekerdt, David J. (David Joseph), 1949-

　　HQ1061 .E534 2002
　　305.26′03—dc21
　　　2002002596

ISBNs
Volume 1: 0-02-865468-4
Volume 2: 0-02-865469-2
Volume 3: 0-02-865470-6
Volume 4: 0-02-865471-4

Printed in the United States of America
10 9 8 7 6 5 4 3 2 1

CONTENTS

EDITORIAL AND PRODUCTION STAFF

Linda S. Hubbard, *Editorial Director*

Ray Abruzzi and Bradley J. Morgan, *Project Editors*

Jonathan Aretakis, Anne Davidson, Peter Jaskowiak, and Beth Wilson, *Copy Editors*

Anne Janette Johnson, Amy Lucas, Tracy Siddall, Matthew M. Totsky, *Proofreaders*

Linda K. Fetters, *Indexer*

Datapage Technologies International, Inc., *Typesetter*

GGS Information Services, *Art Program*

Smokey Mountain Computer Services, *Data Capture Contractor*

Robert Duncan, Leitha Etheridge-Sims, Lezlie Light, Michael Logusz, Kelley Quinn, *Imaging and Multimedia*

Lori Hines, *Permissions*

Mary Beth Trimper, *Composition Manager*

Evi Seoud, *Assistant Production Manager*

Rhonda Williams, *Buyer*

Pamela A. E. Galbreath, *Senior Art Director*

Gwendolyn S. Tucker, *Data Capture Project Administrator*

MACMILLAN REFERENCE USA

Frank Menchaca, *Vice President*

Hélène Potter, *Editor in Chief*

PREFACE

The scientific and scholarly study of aging gained great momentum over the last half of the twentieth century. With more people living longer lives, there were also great advances in the provision of clinical and social services to older people. An infusion of government support helped train a wider number of practitioners and researchers for the field. All of these efforts over the last several decades have generated a lot of new information and insights about aging.

This new knowledge has been shared mainly among professionals in aging, but the time has come to open this storehouse to a broad audience. We, the editors, have designed the Macmillan *Encyclopedia of Aging* to present advanced ideas about aging at an accessible level. We offer this encyclopedia so that readers, students in particular, can understand the progression of their own lives and the lives of their loved ones; the important questions that scientists and scholars pursue; the policies and practices that promote well-being for older people; the transformations that occur with an aging society; and perhaps the meaning of life's time.

What does an encyclopedia about aging encompass? One way to summarize the subject would be to put the contents under three general headings: the aged, aging, and age. (Bengtson, Rice, and Johnson) Knowledge about *the aged* concerns individuals and populations that have lived a long time—their characteristics, their impact on the community and on history, their status, and the way they are regarded. A great theme of this new century will be the increasing proportions of aged persons around the world and what this means for their respective societies. *Aging,* in turn, is about

change—change in structure, function, and behavior. Whether these changes are called development, growth, maturation, or senescence (the process of becoming old), the focus is on how and why change occurs. It is "the long way of thinking" about many biological, psychological, and social dimensions of life (Elder). *Age,* of course, is a count of time. But it is also a cultural shorthand signifying who people are and the probable roles that they occupy over a lifetime (Fry). Age is a basis for regulating social life, for extending and withdrawing privileges, and it is a fundamental way by which we define ourselves (I am sixteen; I am forty; I am one hundred years old!).

As this encyclopedia covers topics about age, aging, and the aged in more than 400 separate entries, it expresses some general propositions about the field:

All things age. We prize old wines but discard old tires. This encyclopedia concentrates on living things, and most entries are devoted to the human experience of aging. Yet aging occurs in all animals, both for whole organisms and also within single cells. Biologists are gaining important insights about aging by studying and even manipulating the life spans of short-lived species such as roundworms and fruit flies. At another level, if we collect people into groups, we can also observe the aging of such entities as families, birth cohorts (e.g., baby boomers), or entire populations.

Aging is lifelong. People typically think of aging as something that begins in midlife, and age sixty-five remains a widely used, though artificial, demarcation of old age.

Yet the explanation of age-related change requires frameworks that encompass the entire life span or biographical life course. As a result, entries in this encyclopedia freely embrace ideas about growth, development, and adaptation for all phases of life.

Lives are not bounded by birth and death. Each one of us is an expression of our ancestor's cell lines perpetuated over countless generations. As a species, then, our genetic inheritance for longevity and senescence is an evolutionary story playing out over millennia. As individuals, it is fascinating to realize that the egg from which we were born originated as our grandmother carried in her womb our own mother. At the end, individuals do die, but it comforts us that they can live on in memorials and legacies. They survive as ancestors in memory and in the persistence of culture down through the generations.

Aging is ancient. There have always been people who have lived long lives, though never as many as there are at the beginning of this new century. Far from being a modern fascination, observations about life change and longevity have been recorded across all of history. But it was not until longevity was "democratized" in the twentieth century that gerontology (the study of aging) and geriatrics (the care of older people) were formally organized as specialty fields.

People age in a specific time and place. Even as scientists search for the fundamental regularities of aging and formulate explanations for the longevity of living things, humans nonetheless age within history and culture. Who is "young" and who is "old," what people can expect of life, what the generations owe each other, what is an elder's place in society—these are matters that shift with the times and locale.

Aging seems to come as a surprise. With the passing of years, individuals try mightily to conserve a certain sameness about themselves. Ageless in their own minds, they are startled to see signs of aging in their faces and bodies. Entire societies, too, often remain blind to the realities of aging populations and must struggle to appreciate both the potential and needs of their elders.

We do not age alone. We can will ourselves to think that aging is an individual experience, but only by overlooking the contexts of human life. A changeable social convoy of family and friends accompanies us from cradle to grave. They support us and create a fabric of meaning for our lives; there is no person's biography that is not also the story of other people. With lives so intertwined, events that occur to others are consequential to us and can even redirect our life course.

Aging is a worldwide concern. When covering cultural, social, and political topics, this encyclopedia primarily focuses on the United States and Canada. However, we have also included information about general population processes in other regions. Throughout the world, as death rates decline and longevity increases, the size of a nation's older population can swell, creating pressure to adopt policies that address elders' health and economic well-being.

Research and scholarship proceed in many disciplines. Many view aging primarily as a biological or physical process that has consequences for health and well being. Economic issues, too, command attention. These fields, however, only begin to describe the scholarly interest in aging. For this work the editors have used a broad scope that includes contributions from the behavioral and social sciences, bioethics, humanities, fine arts, religion, journalism, law, and engineering.

Finally, there is a persistent question: *Are long lives the best lives?* Knowledge about aging is never far from feelings about aging, because the essential fact of our humanity is that we all grow older and die. The contemporary outlook about aging is profoundly ambiguous: we both celebrate and regret it, with no single emotional tone for this topic. Individuals try mightily to live long, full lives, but dislike the manifestations of aging. Whole societies organize efforts to guarantee the welfare and longevity of their citizens, but then resent the elders in their midst. Old age is at once wanted and unwanted, "long enough and far from being long enough" (Blythe, p. 29).

The contents of these four volumes rest upon the careful, thoughtful efforts of seven associate editors: Robert Applebaum, Miami University; Karen C. A. Holden, University of Wisconsin; Stephen G. Post, Case Western Reserve University; Kenneth Rockwood,

Dalhousie University; Richard Schulz, University of Pittsburgh; Richard L. Sprott, The Ellison Foundation; and Peter Uhlenberg, University of North Carolina. Each of these experts specializes in one or more areas of aging, which allowed them to work cooperatively to design the topics to be covered, identify and recruit authors, and evaluate first drafts of each article. They were patient and prompt as the need arose, and always good humored.

We were grateful to enlist contributions from an international cast of authors who are among the top scientists and scholars in aging. We thank them for their clear, authoritative presentation of this multidisciplinary subject matter. We thank Elly Dickason, former publisher at Macmillan Library Reference, for animating this project, and we are very grateful to editor Ray Abruzzi, who steered this complex work through the minutiae of publication without himself going too gray. For myself, much is owed to my elders, Jeremiah E. Silbert, Morton C. Creditor, and the late William G. Bartholome, who always maintained that, beyond one's own horizons, there is more to learn.

DAVID J. EKERDT

BIBLIOGRAPHY

Bengtson, Vern L.; Rice, Cara J.; and Johnson, Malcolm L. "Are Theories of Aging Important? Models and Explanations in Gerontology at the Turn of the Century." In *Handbook of Theories of Aging.* Edited by V. L. Bengtson and K. W. Schaie. New York: Springer Publishing Company, Inc., 1999. Pages 3–20.

Elder, Glen H. "The Life Course and Human Development." In *Handbook of Child Psychology, Volume 1: Theoretical Models of Human Development.* Edited by R. M. Lerner. New York: John Wiley & Sons, Inc., 1998. Pages 939–991.

Fry, Christine L. "Anthropological Theories of Age and Aging." In *Handbook of Theories of Aging.* Edited by V. L. Bengtson and K. W. Schaie. New York: Springer Publishing Company, Inc., 1999. Pages 271–286.

Blythe, Ronald. *The View in Winter: Reflections on Old Age.* New York: Harcourt Brace Jovanovich, 1979.

LIST OF ARTICLES

LIST OF AUTHORS

W. Andrew Achenbaum
University of Houston
College of Humanities
GERONTOCRACY

Rebecca G. Adams
University of North Carolina
at Greensboro
FRIENDSHIP

Virgil H. Adams III
University of Kansas
CULTURAL DIVERSITY

George J. Agich
Cleveland Clinic Foundation
AUTONOMY

Emily M. Agree
John Hopkins School of
Hygiene & Public Health
TECHNOLOGY AND AGING

Joann Ahrens
Visiting Nurse Service of
New York
HOME HEALTH THERAPIES

Steven M. Albert
Gertrude H. Sergievsky
Center, Columbia
University
QUALITY OF LIFE,
DEFINITION AND
MEASUREMENT

Donna M. Alfieri
New York College of
Podiatric Medicine
FOOT

James E. Allen
University of North Carolina
at Chapel Hill
NURSING HOME
ADMINISTRATION

Phil Allen
The University of Akron
REACTION TIME

R. G. Allen
The Sally Balin Medical
Center
CELLULAR AGING
CELLULAR AGING: BASIC
PHENOMENA

Duane Francis Alwin
University of Michigan
AGE-PERIOD-COHORT MODEL

Jeong Shin An
University of Missouri-
Columbia
DIVORCE

Georgia J. Anetzberger
Benjamin Rose Institute
ADULT PROTECTIVE
SERVICES

Robert A. Applebaum
Scripps Gerontology Center,
Miami University
LONG-TERM CARE, QUALITY
OF

Patricia A. Aréean
University of California
PROBLEM-SOLVING THERAPY

Wilbert S. Aronow
Hebrew Hospital Home
CHOLESTEROL

Rakesh C. Arora
Dalhousie University
SURGERY IN ELDERLY
PEOPLE
VASCULAR DISEASE

Jeffrey D. Astroth
University of Colorado
Health Sciences Center
DENTAL CARE

Robert C. Atchley
The Naropa Institute
SPIRITUALITY

Carol D. Austin
University of Calgary
CASE MANAGEMENT

Jan Baars
Tilburg University
WEST EUROPE

Ronet Bachman
University of Delaware
CRIMINAL VICTIMIZATION
OF THE ELDERLY

Daniel S. Bailis
HLHP Research Institute
HEALTH ATTITUDE

Francisco G. Barbeite
Georgia Institute of
Technology
JOB PERFORMANCE

Andrzej Bartke
Southern Illinois University
THEORIES OF BIOLOGICAL
AGING: PROGRAMMED
AGING

Amanda Smith Barusch
University of Utah
SOCIAL SERVICES

Scott A. Bass
University of Maryland
PRODUCTIVE AGING

Neeti Bathia
Duke University
*DIAGNOSTIC AND
STATISTICAL MANUAL OF
MENTAL DISORDERS-IV*

Margaret P. Battin
University of Utah
SUICIDE AND ASSISTED
SUICIDE, ETHICAL ASPECTS

Renée L. Beard
University of California, San
Francisco
MEDICALIZATION OF AGING

B. Lynn Beattie
Vancouver Hospital &
Health Sciences Centre
TREMOR
TWITCHES

Victoria Hilkeuitch Bedford
University of Indianapolis
SIBLING RELATIONSHIPS

Laurel Beedon
AARP
SUPPLEMENTAL SECURITY
INCOME

Howard Bergman
Jewish General Hospital
HOME VISITS

Mercedes Bern-Klug
University of Kansas
Medical Center
FUNERAL AND MEMORIAL
PRACTICES

Deepak Bhole
University of Southern
California
FRUIT FLIES, *DROSOPHILA*

Robert H. Binstock
Case Western Reserve
University
AGE-BASED RATIONING OF
HEALTH CARE
POLITICAL BEHAVIOR

Taranjeet K. Bird
CANADA, HEALTH CARE
COVERAGE FOR OLDER
PEOPLE

Fredda Blanchard-Fields
Georgia Tech
SOCIAL COGNITION

Béla John Bognár
Wright State University
GOVERNMENT ASSISTED
HOUSING
HOUSING: ALTERNATIVE
OPTIONS

Vilhelm Bohr
Gerontology Research
Center
DNA DAMAGE AND REPAIR

Stanley J. Bolanowski
Syracuse University
TOUCH, SENSE OF

Marvin O. Boluyt
University of Michigan
PHYSIOLOGICAL CHANGES,
ORGAN SYSTEMS:
CARDIOVASCULAR

Michael J. Borrie
University of Western
Ontario
URINARY INCONTINENCE

Dominique Broccoli
Fox Chase Cancer Center
CELLULAR AGING:
TELOMERES

John Brocklehurst
CONSTIPATION

Susan V. Brooks
University of Michigan
PHYSIOLOGICAL CHANGES,
ORGAN SYSTEMS: SKELETAL
MUSCLE

Antonin Bukovsky
University of Tennessee
Medical Center
IMMUNOLOGY: ANIMAL
MODELS

Louis D. Burgio
University of Alabama
BEHAVIOR MANAGEMENT
SUNDOWN SYNDROME

Robert N. Butler
Mt. Sinai School of Medicine
LIFE REVIEW

Sidney Callahan
Hudson House
PARENTAL OBLIGATIONS

Lori D. Campbell
McMaster University
KIN

Judith Campisi
Lawrence Berkeley National
Laboratory
CANCER, BIOLOGY
GENETICS: GENE
EXPRESSION
GENETICS: TUMOR
SUPPRESSION
PHYSIOLOGICAL CHANGES,
FIBROBLAST CELLS

Michael P. Cancro
University of Pennsylvania
IMMUNE SYSTEM

Arnold I. Caplan
Case Western Reserve
University
PHYSIOLOGICAL CHANGES:
STEM CELLS

Elwood Carlson
University of South Carolina
EAST EUROPE AND FORMER
USSR

Sara Carmel
ISRAEL

Francis G. Caro
University of Massachusetts
PERSONAL CARE
VOLUNTEER ACTIVITIES
AND PROGRAMS

Maria Cattell
SUB-SAHARAN AFRICA

Michael R. Caudle
University of Tennessee
Graduate School of
Medicine
IMMUNOLOGY: ANIMAL
MODELS

Judith G. Chipperfield
University of Manitoba
HEALTH ATTITUDE

John W. Church
CANADA, HEALTH CARE
COVERAGE FOR OLDER
PEOPLE

A. Mark Clarfield
Sarah Herzog Memorial
Hospital
HOME VISITS

Robert L. Clark
North Carolina State
University
RETIREMENT: EARLY
RETIREMENT INCENTIVES

Anna-Lisa Cohen
University of Victoria
PLASTICITY

Carl Cohen
SUNY Brooklyn
HOMELESSNESS

Harvey Jay Cohen
Duke University Medical
Center
CANCER, DIAGNOSIS AND
MANAGEMENT

Susan E. Coldwell
University of Washington
TASTE AND SMELL

Barbara J. Coleman
AARP Public Policy Institute
LONG-TERM CARE AND
WOMEN

Meredith Coley
Massachusetts Institute of
Technology
DRIVING ABILITY

Martin J. Connolly
Manchester Royal Infirmary
SMOKING

Fay Lomax Cook
Northwestern University
GENERATIONAL EQUITY

Susan G. Cooley
VA Medical Center
VETERANS CARE

Teresa M. Cooney
University of Missouri
DIVORCE

Rebecca B. Costello
National Institutes of Health
NUTRITION, DIETARY
SUPPLEMENTS

Joseph Coughlin
DRIVING ABILITY

Vincent J. Cristofalo
The Lankenau Institute for
Medical Research
CELLULAR AGING
CELLULAR AGING: BASIC
PHENOMENA

William H. Crown
The MEDSTAT Group
LIFE CYCLE THEORIES OF
SAVINGS AND
CONSUMPTION

Stephan Crystal
Rutgers University -
Institute for Health
POVERTY

Neal E. Cutler
Widener University
FINANCIAL PLANNING FOR
LONG-TERM CARE

Stephen J. Cutler
University of Vermont
GERONTOLOGY
LEISURE

Sara Czaja
University of Miami School
of Medicine
HUMAN FACTORS

Charles A. Czeisler
Harvard Medical School,
Brigham and Women's
Hospital
CIRCADIAN RHYTHMS

Dale Dannefer
University of Rochester
SOCIAL THEORIES OF AGING

Sultan Darvesh
QEII Health Sciences Centre
MULTIPLE SYSTEM ATROPHY
PARKINSONISM

Shawn Davis
Scripps Gerontology Center,
Miami University
LONG-TERM CARE, QUALITY
OF

Sharon A. DeVaney
Purdue University
CONSUMPTION AND AGE
ESTATE PLANNING

Susan De Vos
University of Wisconsin
LATIN AMERICA

Roger A. Dixon
University of Victoria
METAMEMORY
PLASTICITY

Pamela Doty
U.S. Dept. of Health and
Human Services
LONG-TERM CARE AROUND
THE GLOBE

Adam Drewnowski
University of Washington
TASTE AND SMELL

Jeanne F. Duffy
Harvard Medical School,
Brigham and Women's
General Clinical Research
Center
CIRCADIAN RHYTHMS

Burton Dunlop
Florida International
University
CRIMINAL BEHAVIOR

Joseph A. Durlak
Loyola University Chicago
DEATH ANXIETY

Robin Eastwood
International
Psychogeriatrics Association
PSYCHIATRIC DISEASE IN
RELATION TO PHYSICAL
ILLNESS

J. Kevin Eckert
University of Maryland B.C.
BOARD AND CARE HOMES

Autumn Edenfield
Duke University
PSYCHOTHERAPY

Rita B. Effros
UCLA School of Medicine
ESTROGEN

David Eggebeen
Pennsylvania State
University
INTERGENERATIONAL
EXCHANGES

David J. Ekerdt
Gerontology Center -
University of Kansas
CULTURAL DIVERSITY
RETIREMENT, TRANSITION

Timo Erkinjuntti
Hospital District of Helsinki
and Uusimaa
VASCULAR DEMENTIA

Carroll L. Estes
University of California at
San Francisco
MEDICALIZATION OF AGING

Catherine Exley
  St. James University
    Hospital
    SWALLOWING

Thomas J. Fairchild
  University of North Texas
    NURSING HOMES

John A. Faulkner
  University of Michigan
    PHYSIOLOGICAL CHANGES,
      ORGAN SYSTEMS: SKELETAL
      MUSCLE

Christiane Fauron
  University of Utah
    MITOCHONDRIA

Maria Fiatarone Singh
  School of Exercise & Sport
    Science
    EXERCISE

Robert C. Ficke
  Westat
    CONGREGATE AND HOME-
      DELIVERED MEALS

Susan Coombs Ficke
  Aging Health
    Communications
    CONGREGATE AND HOME-
      DELIVERED MEALS

Sigrun-Heide Filipp
  Universitat Trier
    MOTIVATION

Kimberly M. Firth
  THE NATIONAL INSTITUTE
    ON AGING/NATIONAL
    INSTITUTES OF HEALTH

Susan E. Fisher
  University of Alabama
    BEHAVIOR MANAGEMENT

Tobi Flewwelling
  QEII Health Sciences
    Centre
    OCCUPATIONAL THERAPY

Sarah Forbes
  University of Kansas
    PALLIATIVE CARE

Jonathan Barry Forman
  Oklahoma University
    EMPLOYEE RETIREMENT
      INCOME SECURITY ACT

Emile Franssen
  RETROGENESIS

Susan Freter
  Centre for Health Care of
    the Elderly
    REHABILITATION
    WALKING AIDS

Alexandra M. Freund
  Max Planck Institute for
    Human Development
    SELECTION, OPTIMIZATION,
    AND COMPENSATION: A
    MODEL OF SUCCESSFUL
    AGING

Robert B. Friedland
  Center on an Aging Society
    LONG-TERM CARE
    INSURANCE

James F. Fries
  Stanford University
    COMPRESSION OF
      MORBIDITY

Christine L. Fry
  Loloya University of Chicago
    AGE

Tamas Fürlöp
  Universitè de Sherbrooke
    DIABETES MELLITUS

Guarav Gandotra
  RETROGENESIS

Mary Ganguli
  University of Pittsburgh
    MENTAL STATUS
      EXAMINATION

Elizabeth M. Gardner
  MCP Hahnemann
    University
    IMMUNOLOGY, HUMAN

Rachel Garfield
  Henry J. Kaiser Family
    Foundation
    MEDICAID

Thesia I. Garner
  Bureau of Labor Statistics
    CONSUMER PRICE INDEX
      AND COLAS

Serge Gauthier
  McGill Centre for Studies in
    Aging
    ALZHEIMER'S DISEASE

Leonid A. Gavrilov
  University of Chicago
    EVOLUTION OF AGING
    GENETICS
    GENETICS: ETHNICITY

Natalia S. Gavrilova
  NORC/University of Chicago
    EVOLUTION OF AGING
    GENETICS
    GENETICS: ETHNICITY

Christopher L. Gentile
  NORC/University of Chicago
    NUTRITION

Scott Miyake Geron
  Boston University School of
    Social Work
    FUNCTIONAL ABILITY

George A. Gescheider
  Hamilton College
    TOUCH, SENSE OF

Linda S. Ghent
  Eastern Illinois University
    MEDICATION COSTS AND
      REIMBURSEMENTS

Grover C. Gilmore
  Case Western Reserve
    University
    VISION AND PERCEPTION

Norval D. Glenn
  University of Texas at Austin
    MARRIAGE AND REMARRIAGE

Susan Gold
  Jewish General Hospital
    HOME VISITS

Janet Gordon
  QEII Health Sciences Centre
    OSTEOPOROSIS

Sandra Gordon-Salant
  University of Maryland at
    College Park
    HEARING

Elise L. Gould, et al..
  University of Wiscsonsin-
    Madison
    HEALTH INSURANCE,
      NATIONAL APPROACHES

John Grantmyre
  QEII Health Sciences Centre
    ANDROPAUSE
    PROSTATE

Jaber F. Gubrium
  University of Florida
    QUALITATIVE RESEARCH
    NARRATIVE

Michael S. Gutter
University of Wiscsonsin-
Madison
INDIVIDUAL RETIREMENT
ACCOUNTS
RETIREMENT PLANNING

Carole Haber
University of Delaware
NURSING HOMES: HISTORY
PROLONGEVITY

Larissa Hachinski
STROKE

Vladimir Hachinski
London Health Sciences
Center
STROKE

Jennifer Kay Hackney
University of Kansas
PETS

William E. Haley
University of South Florida
LIFE EVENTS AND STRESS
STRESS AND COPING

Laura Haltzel
Social Security
Administration
SOCIAL SECURITY
ADMINISTRATION
SOCIAL SECURITY, AND THE
U.S. FEDERAL BUDGET

Jenifer Hamil-Luker
University of North Carolina
-Chapel Hill
AGE DISCRIMINATION

Barbara C. Hansen
UMB School of Medicine
NUTRITION, OBESITY

Melissa Hardy
Pepper Institute
COHORT CHANGE

Charles B. Hatcher
Iowa State University
ECONOMIC WELL-BEING

Betty Havens
University of Manitoba
CANADA

Jutta Heckhausen
School of Social Ecology
LIFE-SPAN THEORY OF
CONTROL
MIDLIFE CRISIS

Herbert Hendin, M. D.
American Suicide
Foundation
EUTHANASIA AND SENICIDE

Jon Hendricks
Oregon State University
GERONTOLOGY
LEISURE

Ruth E. Herman
University of Kansas
LANGUAGE COMPREHENSION

A. Regula Herzog
Institute for Social Research-
University of Michigan
PANEL STUDIES

James C. Hickman
University of Wisconsin
PENSIONS: FINANCING AND
REGULATION

Catherine Hill
Institute for Women's Policy
Research
RETIREMENT, DECISION
MAKING

Gregory A. Hinrichsen
Hillside Hospital
INTERPERSONAL
PSYCHOTHERAPY

Lynne Gershenson Hodgson
Quinnipiac University
GRANDPARENTHOOD

Karen Holden
University of Wisconsin-
Madison
DISABILITY: ECONOMIC
COSTS AND INSURANCE
PROTECTION
RISK MANAGEMENT AND
INSURANCE

Douglas Holmes
NURSING HOMES: SPECIAL
CARE UNITS

James A. Holstein
NARRATIVE
QUALITATIVE RESEARCH

Stephen Holzapfel
Women's College Hospital
MENOPAUSE

Nancy Hooyman
University of Washington
FEMINIST THEORY

Peter Hornsby
Bayor College of Medicine
MOLECULAR THERAPY

William J. Hoyer
Syracuse University
LIFE-SPAN DEVELOPMENT
MEMORY TRAINING

Margaret F. Hudson
University of North
Carolina-Chapel Hill
ELDER ABUSE AND NEGLECT

Robert B. Hudson
Boston University
ADMININISTRATION ON
AGING
FEDERAL AGENCIES ON
AGING
OLDER AMERICANS ACT

Robert A. Hummer
University of Texas, Austin
LIFE EXPECTANCY
LONGEVITY: SOCIAL ASPECTS

Sally Balch Hurme
AARP
CONSUMER PROTECTION

Charles Huyett
Sheperd's Centers of
America
INTERNET RESOURCES

Howard M. Iams
Social Security
Administration
SELF-EMPLOYMENT

Ellen L. Idler
Rutgers University
HEALTH, SOCIAL FACTORS
PERCEIVED HEALTH

Ivonne-Marie Indrikovs
University of Texas Medical
Branch
SOCIAL SUPPORT

Susan Jackson
University of Kansas Medical
Center
SPEECH

Michael Jakowec
University of Southern
California
NEUROTRANSMITTERS

Yuri Jang
University of South Florida
LIFE EVENTS AND STRESS
STRESS AND COPING

Pamela G. Jarrett
St. Joseph's Hospital
DISEASE PRESENTATION

Cynthia R. Jasper
University of Wisconsin
RETAILING AND OLDER
ADULTS

S. Michal Jazwinski
Louisiana State University
Medical Center
YEAST

Nancy S. Jecker
University of Washington
INTERGENERATIONAL
JUSTICE
REFUSING AND
WITHDRAWING MEDICAL
TREATMENT

Bruce Jennings
The Hastings Center
QUALITY OF LIFE,
PHILOSOPHICAL AND
ETHICAL DIMENSIONS

Thomas E. Johnson
University of Colorado
LIFE-SPAN EXTENSION
ROUNDWORMS:
CAENORHABDITIS ELEGANS

Thomas E. Joiner, Jr.
Florida State University
DEPRESSION

Pálmi V. Jónsson
Landspitali University
Hospital -Landakst
FAINTING

Arnold Kahn
UCSF Medical Center
DHEA
ENDOCRINE SYSTEM

Marshall B. Kapp
Wright State University
ADVANCE DIRECTIVES FOR
HEALTH CARE
AMERICANS WITH
DISABILITIES ACT
GUARDIANSHIP

Julia Kasl-Godley
U.S. Department of
Veterans Affairs
REALITY ORIENTATION

Alfred W. Kaszniak
University of Arizona
NEUROPSYCHOLOGY

Stephen Katz
Trent University
AGING

Gayle Kaufman
Davidson College
GENDER

Sharon R. Kaufman
University of California, San
Francisco, Institute for
Health and Aging
DEATH AND DYING

Lenard W. Kaye
University of Maine
HOME CARE AND HOME
SERVICES

Susan Kemper
University of Kansas
LANGUAGE COMPREHENSION

Sunnie Kennedy
RETROGENESIS

Andrew Kertesz
St. Joseph's Health Care
FRONTOTEMPORAL
DEMENTIA

Caroline J. Ketcham
Arizona State University
MOTOR PERFORMANCE

Suzanne L. Khalil
SUBJECTIVE WELL-BEING

Meeryoung Kim
WIDOWHOOD: ECONOMIC
ISSUES

Eric R. Kingson
Syracuse University
SOCIAL SECURITY, HISTORY
AND OPERATIONS

Susan A. Kirkland
Dalhousie University
EPIDEMIOLOGY

Jane Marie Kirschling
University of Southern
Maine
HOSPICE

Paul Kleyman
American Society on Aging
IMAGES OF AGING

Janice A. Knebl
NURSING HOMES

Bob G. Knight
University of Southern
California
COGNITIVE-BEHAVIORAL
THERAPY

Steven Kohama
ORTRC
GENETICS: PARENTAL
INFLUENCE

Joseph A. Koncelik
Georgia Tech College of
Architecture
HOUSING AND TECHNOLOGY

Sophie M. Korczyk
Analytical Services
PENSIONS, PUBLIC PENSIONS

John A. Krout
Ithaca College
SENIOR CENTERS

Patrick M. Krueger
University of Colorado,
Boulder
LIFE EXPECTANCY

Mark S. Lachs
Cornell Medical College
WORKFORCE ISSUES IN
LONG-TERM CARE

Edward G. Lakatta
Gerontology Research
Center
PHYSIOLOGICAL CHANGES,
ORGAN SYSTEMS:
CARDIOVASCULAR

Susan C. Lanspery
Brandeis University
AGING IN PLACE
CONGREGATE HOUSING

Jeff Lashbrook
SUNY Brockport
AGE NORMS

Raymond LeBlanc
QEII Health Sciences Centre
EYE, AGING-RELATED
DISEASES TE HOUSING

Chin Chin Lee
University of Miami School
of Medicine
HUMAN FACTORS

Gary R. Lee
  Bowling Green State
  University
  WIDOWHOOD

Philip E. Lee
  TREMOR
  TWITCHES

Margaret T. Lehman-Blake
  LANGUAGE DISORDERS

Eric Lenze
  Western Psychiatry Institute
  and Clinic
  ANXIETY

Jeff Levin
  RELIGION

Judith Levy
  University of Illinois at
  Chicago
  SEXUALITY

Phoebe S. Liebig
  University of Southern
  California
  PROFESSIONAL
  ORGANIZATIONS

Robert D. Lindeman
  University of New Mexico
  FLUID BALANCE

James Lindesay
  Leicester General Hospital
  DELIRIUM

Richard A. Lockshin
  St. John's University
  CELLULAR AGING: CELL
  DEATH

Robert Logan
  Council on Aging of South
  Western Ohio
  AREA AGENCIES ON AGING

Oscar Lopez
  Univerity of Pittsburgh
  School of Medicine
  MEMORY DYSFUNCTION,
  DRUG TREATMENT

Karyn Loscocco
  Center for Women in
  Government
  AGE INTEGRATION AND AGE
  SEGREGATION

Janet Huber Lowry
  Austin College Department
  of Sociology
  EDUCATION

Thomas R. Lynch
  Duke University Medical
  Center
  DIAGNOSTIC AND
  STATISTICAL MANUAL OF
  MENTAL DISORDERS-IV
  PSYCHOTHERAPY

Patricia Passuth Lynott
  Ithaca College
  CRITICAL GERONTOLOGY
  DISENGAGEMENT

Robert J. Lynott
  Ithaca College
  CRITICAL GERONTOLOGY
  DISENGAGEMENT

Paul MacDonald
  Cape Breton Regional
  Hospital
  HEART DISEASE
  REVASCULARIZATION:
  BYPASS SURGERY AND
  ANGIOPLASTY

Chris MacKnight
  Dalhousie University
  BALANCE AND MOBILITY
  CENTENARIANS
  CREUTZFELDT-JAKOB
  DISEASE

Diane J. Macunovich
  Barnard College, Columbia
  University
  BABY BOOMERS

Carol Magai
  Long Island University
  EMOTION

Laurie Herzig Mallery
  QEII Health Sciences Centre
  DIZZINESS
  PHYSICAL THERAPY FOR THE
  ELDERLY

William C. Mann
  College of Health
  Professionals, University of
  Florida
  HOME ADAPTATION AND
  EQUIPMENT

R. E. Mansel
  University of Wales College
  of Medicine
  BREAST

Jennifer Margrett
  Pennsylvania State
  University
  PROBLEM SOLVING,
  EVERYDAY

Thomas J. Marrie
  University of Alberta
  PNEUMONIA

Linda G. Martin
  Population Council
  JAPAN

Lisa Martin
  Case Western Reserve
  University
  CAREGIVING, INFORMAL

Lynn M. Martire
  University Center for Social
  and Urban Research,
  University of Pittsburgh
  INTERVENTIONS, PSYCHO-
  SOCIAL-BEHAVIORAL

Edward J. Masoro
  University of Texas Health
  Science Center
  NUTRITION, CALORIC
  RESTRICTION
  PHYSIOLOGICAL CHANGES

Christy Matsuoka
  University of Southern
  California
  HOUSING

Todd J. Maurer
  Georgia Institute of
  Technology
  JOB PERFORMANCE

Gerald E. McClearn
  Pennsylvania State
  University
  GENETICS: GENE-
  ENVIRONMENT
  INTERACTION

Robert W. McClelland
  University of Calgary
  CASE MANAGEMENT

Dayna McCrary
  ADULT DAY CARE

Laurence B. McCullough
  Baylor College of Medicine
  LONG-TERM CARE ETHICS

Kathryn B. McGrew
  Miami University
  MENTAL HEALTH SERVICES

Patrick L. McKee
  Colorado State University
  VISUAL ARTS AND AGING

Julie McLaughlin
Rutgers University
HEALTH, SOCIAL FACTORS
PERCEIVED HEALTH

Julie Ann McMullin
University of Western
Ontario
INEQUALITY

Tay K. McNamara
Boston College
WELFARE STATE

Shelly A. McNeil
QEII Health Science Centre
INFLUENZA
URINARY TRACT INFECTION

Thomas H. McNeill
Keck School of Medicine
NEUROTRANSMITTERS

Shahla Mehdizadeh
Scripps Gerontology Center
MIDDLE EASTERN
COUNTRIES

Mark F. Mehler
Albert Einstein College of
Medicine
NEUROBIOLOGY
NEURODEGENERATIVE
DISEASES

Graydon S. Meinelly
University of British
Columbia
DIABETES MELLITUS

Douglas K. Miller
St. Louis University
SURVEYS

W. Alan Miller
Purdue University
ESTATE PLANNING

Meredith Minear
University of Michigan
MEMORY, EVERYDAY

Jim Mitchell
ECU-Center on Aging
RURAL ELDERLY

Susan L. Mitchell
Harvard Medical Center
TUBE FEEDING

Lona Mody
University of Michigan
URINARY TRACT INFECTION

Robert Mollica
National Academy for State
Health Policy
ASSISTED LIVING

Cathy Ventrell Monsees
AGEISM

Marilyn Moon
The Urban Institute
MEDICARE

Irene Moore
University of Cincinnati
GERIATRIC ASSESSMENT
UNIT

Leslie A. Morgan
University of Maryland,
Baltimore County
BOARD AND CARE HOMES

Daniel K. Mroczek
Fordham University
PERSONALITY

Larry C. Mullins
Auburn University-
Montgomery
LONELINESS

Benoit H. Mulsant
University of Pittsburgh
Medical Center
ELECTROCONVULSIVE
THERAPY
GERIATRIC PSYCHIATRY

Alicia H. Munnell
Boston College
PENSIONS, PLAN TYPES AND
POLICY APPROACHES

Andrea Munroe
PHYSICAL THERAPY FOR THE
ELDERLY

Donna M. Murasko
MCP Hahnemann
University
IMMUNOLOGY, HUMAN

Jan E. Mutchler
University of Massachusetts,
Boston
EMPLOYMENT OF OLDER
WORKERS

Ian Nelson
Scripps Gerontology Center
CONTINUING CARE
RETIREMENT
COMMUNITIES

James Lindemann Nelson
Michigan State University
FILIAL OBLIGATIONS

Robert Newcomer
University of California, San
Francisco
HEALTH AND LONG-TERM
CARE PROGRAM
INTEGRATION

Nancy R. Nichols
Monash University
STRESS

Christy M. Nishita
University of Southern
California
LIVING ARRANGEMENTS

Thomas H. Norwood
University of Washington
CELLULAR AGING: DNA
POLYMORPHISMS

Frank Nuessel
University of Louisville
LANGUAGE ABOUT AGING

Shaun O'Keeffe
Merlin Park Regional
Hospital
DECONDITIONING

Morris A. Okun
Arizona State University
SUBJECTIVE WELL-BEING

S. Jay Olshansky
University of Chicago
MORTALITY

Barbara O'Neill
Rutgers University
RETIREMENT PLANNING
PROGRAMS

Angela M. O'Rand
Duke University
RETIREMENT, PATTERNS

David K. Orren
University of Kentucky,
Chandler Medical Center
ACCELERATED AGING:
HUMAN PROGEROID
SYNDROMES

Alberto Palloni
University of Wisconsin
LATIN AMERICA

Erdman B. Palmore
Duke University
SUCCESSFUL AGING

Lori Parham
Florida State University,
Pepper Institute on Aging
STATUS OF OLDER PEOPLE:
MODERNIZATION

Denise C. Park
University of Michigan
MEMORY, EVERYDAY

Tim G. Parkin
University of Canterbury,
New Zealand
STATUS OF OLDER PEOPLE:
THE ANCIENT AND
BIBLICAL WORLDS

Christopher J. Patterson
Hamilton Health Science
Corporation
PERIODIC HEALTH
EXAMINATION

Eliza Pavalko
Indiana University
LIFE COURSE

James R. Peacock
University of North
Carolina, Charlotte
GAY AND LESBIAN AGING

Jane L. Pearson
National Institutes of Mental
Health, Preventive
Intervention Program
SUICIDE

Rudolph G. Penner
Urban Institute
TAXATION

Marisol Perez
Florida State University
DEPRESSION

Raymond P. Perry
University of Manitoba
HEALTH ATTITUDE

David A. Peterson
University of Southern
California
CAREERS IN AGING

Jeremy W. Pettit
Florida State Univesity
DEPRESSION

Karl Pillemer
Cornell University
PARENT-CHILD
RELATIONSHIP
WORKFORCE ISSUES IN
LONG-TERM CARE

Eric T. Poehlman
UniversitÈ de MontrÈal
NUTRITION

Bruce G. Pollock
University of Pittsburgh
Medical Center
ANTIDEPRESSANTS

Stephen G. Post
Case Western Research
University
ANTI-AGING RESEARCH:
ETHICAL AND RELIGIOUS
PERSPECTIVES
DEMENTIA: ETHICAL ISSUES

Holly G. Prigerson
Yale University School of
Medicine
BEREAVEMENT

Jon Pynoos
University of Southern
California
HOUSING
LIVING ARRANGEMENTS

Nawab Qzilibash
Oxford University
EVIDENCE-BASED MEDICINE

S. Irudaya Rajan
Center for Development
Studies, Kerala, India
SOUTH ASIA

Carol Raphael
Visiting Nurse Service of
New York
HOME HEALTH THERAPIES

Anna M. Rappaport
William M. Mercer, Inc.
ANNUITIES
RISK MANAGEMENT AND
INSURANCE

Robert P. Rebelein
University of Cincinnati
BEQUESTS AND
INHERITANCES

Barry Reisberg
New York University School
of Medicine
RETROGENESIS

Elaine M. Replogle
Rutgers University
MARITAL RELATIONSHIPS

Thomas Rice
University of California, Los
Angeles
MEDIGAP

David R. Riddle
Wake Forest University
School of Medicine
NEUROCHEMISTRY

Anne-Sophie Rigaud
Assistance Publique,
Hùpitaux des Paris
HIGH BLOOD PRESSURE

Sara E. Rix
AARP, Public Policy Institute
CANADA, INCOME
PROTECTION FOR
RETIREES
INCOME SUPPORT FOR
NONWORKERS, NATIONAL
APPROACHES

Duncan Robertson
MULTIDISCIPLINARY TEAM

Gia S. Robinson
University of Southern
California
COGNITIVE-BEHAVIORAL
THERAPY

Kenneth Rockwood
Dalhousie University
ALCOHOLISM
ASSESSMENT
DEMENTIA
DEMENTIA WITH LEWY
BODIES
EVIDENCE-BASED MEDICINE
EYE, AGING-RELATED
DISEASES
FRAILTY
GERIATRIC MEDICINE
KIDNEY, AGING
PAIN MANAGEMENT
SURGERY IN ELDERLY
PEOPLE
VASCULAR DEMENTIA

Peter Rockwood
HIP FRACTURE

Rachel Rodriguez
The University of Alabama
SUNDOWN SYNDROME

Richard G. Rogers
University of Colorado
LIFE EXPECTANCY
LONGEVITY: SOCIAL ASPECTS

Carlos H. Rojas-Fernandez
Texas Tech University,
Health Sciences Center
DRUGS AND AGING

Barbara J. Rolls
Penn State University
TASTE AND SMELL

G. Alec Rooke
University of Washington
ANESTHESIA

Michael R. Rose
University of California,
Irvine
LONGEVITY:
REPRODUCTION
LONGEVITY: SELECTION

Carolyn Rosenthal
McMaster University,Center
for Gerontological Studies
KIN

Jane L. Ross
National Academy of
Sciences
SOCIAL SECURITY
ADMINISTRATION
SOCIAL SECURITY, AND THE
U.S. FEDERAL BUDGET

J. Barrie Ross
Dalhousie University
HAIR
PRESSURE ULCERS
SKIN

George S. Roth
National Institutes of Health
PRIMATES

Max B. Rothman
Florida International
University
CRIMINAL BEHAVIOR

Ronenn Roubenoff
Tufts University
SARCOPENIA

Diane Rowland
Henry J. Kaiser Family
Foundation
MEDICAID

Laura Rudkin
University of Texas Medical
Branch, Galveston
SOCIAL SUPPORT

Benjamin Rusak
Dalhousie University
SLEEP

Peggy Ruyak
Dalhousie University
SLEEP

Judith A. Salerno
National Institute on Aging
VETERANS CARE

Dallas Salisbury
Employee Benefit Research
Institute
SAVINGS

Marisa A. Scala
Center for Medicare
Education
CONSUMER DIRECTED CARE

K. Warner Schaie
The Pennsylvania State
University
INTELLIGENCE

James H. Schulz
Brandeis University
DIVORCE: ECONOMIC ISSUES

Richard Schulz
University of Pittsburgh
INTERVENTIONS, PSYCHO-
SOCIAL-BEHAVIORAL

David Scott
King's College University of
London, GTK School of
Medicine
ARTHRITIS

Colin Selman
University of Aberdeen,
Scotland
THE DISPOSABLE SOMA
THEORY OF AGING

Daniel L. Segal
University of Colorado at
Colorado Springs
PSYCHOLOGICAL
ASSESSMENT

Pearl H. Seo
Duke Medical Center
CANCER, DIAGNOSIS AND
MANAGEMENT

William J. Serow
Florida State University,
Center for the Study of
Population
THE OLDEST OLD

Amy R. Shannon
AARP
PENSIONS, HISTORY

Bryna Shatenstein
University of Montreal
MALNUTRITION

Lois Shaw
Institute for Women's Policy
Research
RETIREMENT, DECISION
MAKING

M. Katherine Shear
University of Pittsburgh
ANXIETY

Dena Shenk
University of North
Carolina, Charlotte
GAY AND LESBIAN AGING

Christine Short
Nova Scotia Rehabilitation
Center
WHEELCHAIRS

Gabriel K. Silverman
Program on Aging
BEREAVEMENT

Merril Silverstein
University of Southern
California
CORESIDENCE

Dean Keith Simonton
University of California-
Davis
CREATIVITY

David A. Sinclair
Harvard Medical School
GENETICS: LONGEVITY
ASSURANCE

Douglas E, Sinclair
QEII Health Sciences
Centre
EMERGENCY ROOM

Maria Fiatarone Singh
EXERCISE

Troy Sitland
QEII Health Sciences
Centre
ANDROPAUSE
PROSTATE

Anderson D. Smith
Georgia Institute of
Technology
MEMORY

Donna L. Smith
University of Alberta
CANADA, HEALTH CARE
COVERAGE FOR OLDER
PEOPLE

Jacqui Smith
Max Planck Institute for
Human Development
DEVELOPMENTAL
PSYCHOLOGY

James P. Smith
ASSETS AND WEALTH

Jay Sokolovsky
University of South Florida
STATUS OF OLDER PEOPLE:
TRIBAL SOCIETIES

LalithKumar K. Solai
ANTIDEPRESSANTS

William E. Sonntag
Wake Forest University
School of Medicine
GROWTH HORMONE
NEUROENDOCRINE SYSTEM

John R. Speakman
University of Aberdeen
THEORIES OF BIOLOGICAL
AGING: DISPOSABLE SOMA

Avron Spiro III
PERSONALITY

Richard L. Sprott
The Ellison Medical
Foundation
BIOLOGY OF AGING
BIOMARKERS OF AGING
RODENTS

Sidney M. Stahl
THE NATIONAL INSTITUTE
ON AGING/NATIONAL
INSTITUTES OF HEALTH

Ursula Staudinger
Technische Universitat
Dresden
WISDOM

George E. Stelmach
Arizona State University
MOTOR PERFORMANCE

Kenneth J. Stewart
United States Department of
Labor
CONSUMER PRICE INDEX
AND COLAS

Eleanor Palo Stoller
Case Western Reserve
University
CAREGIVING, INFORMAL

Robyn I. Stone
American Association of
Homes and Services for the
Aging
LONG-TERM CARE
FINANCING

Jane Karnes Straker
Miami University
NURSING HOMES:
CONSUMER INFORMATION

Debra Street
Florida State University
STATUS OF OLDER PEOPLE:
MODERNIZATION

Gordon F. Streib
University of Florida
RETIREMENT COMMUNITIES

Rita Strombeck
SEXUALITY

S. Sudha
SOUTH ASIA

J. Jill Suitor
Louisiana State University
PARENT-CHILD
RELATIONSHIP

Megan M. Sweeney
University of California, Los
Angeles
MARITAL RELATIONSHIPS

Toshio Takeda
Kyoto University
ACCELERATED AGING:
ANIMAL MODELS

Raymond C. Tallis
EPILEPSY

Jeanne A. Teresi
Columbia University
QUALITY OF LIFE,
DEFINITION AND
MEASUREMENT

Daniel Tessier
Sherbrooke Geriatric
Institute
DIABETES MELLITUS

Meera B. Thadani
University of Manitoba
Faculty of Pharmacy
DRUG REGULATION
HERBAL THERAPY
VITAMINS

Patricia M. Thane
University Sussex
STATUS OF OLDER PEOPLE:
PREINDUSTRIAL WEST

Connie A. Tompkins
University of Pittsburgh
LANGUAGE DISORDERS

John Tower
University of Southern
California
FRUIT FLIES, *DROSOPHILA*

Judith Treas
University of California at
Irvine
IMMIGRANTS

John A. Turner
PENSIONS, HISTORY
PENSIONS, PUBLIC PENSIONS

Irene Turpie
McMaster University
DAY HOSPITALS

Michael Tyler
University of California at
Irvine
IMMIGRANTS

Peter Uhlenberg
University of North Carolina
AGE DISCRIMINATION
FAMILY
MIGRATION AND
GEOGRAPHIC
DISTRIBUTION

Deborah A. Vandewater
GERONTOLOGICAL NURSING
NURSE PRACTITIONER

Jan Vijg
CTRC Research Foundation
MUTATION

Christine M. Vitt
Duke University Medical
Center
PSYCHOTHERAPY

Heather R. Walen
CONTROL, PERCEIVED

Dorothy Wambolt
QEII Health Science Center
SOCIAL WORK

Huber R. Warner
The National Institute on
Aging
MOLECULAR BIOLOGY OF
AGING

THEORIES OF BIOLOGICAL
  AGING: DNA DAMAGE
THEORIES OF BIOLOGICAL
  AGING: ERROR
  CATASTROPHE

John R. Weeks
  San Diego State University
  POPULATION AGING

David G. Wells
  Yale University
  NEUROPLASTICITY

Richard A. Wells
  Princess Margaret Hospital
  BLOOD

Heather White
  QEII Health Science Centre
  OCCUPATIONAL THERAPY

John B. Williamson
  Boston College
  WELFARE STATE

Sherry L. Willis
  Pennsylvania State
  University
  PROBLEM SOLVING,
    EVERYDAY

James Willott
  University of South Florida
  BRAIN

Andrea E. Willson
  Florida State University
  COHORT CHANGE

Kathryn Wilson
  Kent State University
  EMPLOYEE HEALTH
    INSURANCE

Frederic D. Wolinksy
  St. Louis University
  SURVEYS

Diana S. Woodruff-Pak
  Temple University
  LEARNING

Marjorie H. Woollacott
  University of Oregon
  BALANCE, SENSE OF

L. Randall Wray
  University of Missouri
  SOCIAL SECURITY: LONG-
    TERM FINANCING AND
    REFORM

Bernadette M. Wright
  AARP Public Policy Institute
  LONG-TERM CARE

Sophia Wright
  SOCIAL SECURITY
    ADMINISTRATION
  SOCIAL SECURITY, AND THE
    U.S. FEDERAL BUDGET

Carsten Wrosch
  Carnegie Mellon University
  DEVELOPMENTAL TASKS

Anne M. Wyatt-Brown
  University of Florida
  LITERATURE AND AGING

Frances Yang
  University of Southern
  California
  CORESIDENCE

Jean-Claude Yernault
  Hopital Erasme,
    Department of Respiratory
    Medicine
  LUNG, AGING

Zeng Yi
  Duke University
  CHINA

Stuart Younger
  Case Western Reserve
  University
  COMPETENCY

Zahra Zakeri
  Galveston College
  CELLULAR AGING: CELL
    DEATH

OUTLINE OF CONTENTS

The outline of articles that follows was compiled by the editors to provide readers with an overview of the encyclopedia's coverage of topics in aging. This systematic list is intended to be helpful in developing courses, pursuing research, or simply browsing in a particular area of gerontology or geriatrics. Readers seeking a particular topic should consult the index of this encyclopedia.

Many topics in aging cut across thematic and disciplinary lines. For example, "longevity" is a topic in biology, health care, and social science. "Family caregiving" draws scholars from health care, social services, and social and behavioral science. In the interest of economy, every article in this encyclopedia appears but once on the list. Rather than list a large number of topics under multiple headings, we have placed each article under its most appropriate heading. The entries themselves can also help the reader discover the interconnected knowledge base in aging, as we encourage them to follow the cross-references that are shown at the end of each article.

The headings below are *not* listed in alphabetical order. Rather, they are listed in an order of knowledge that is customary in the field of aging—the sequence will no doubt be familiar to specialists who work in the aging field. The consideration of age and aging tends to begin with demography so as to characterize the longevity of individuals and describe the nature of aging populations. In this way, cross-national, cultural, and historical perspectives establish aging as an enduring and universal concern. Next in the list of headings are the interests of various disciplines. An implicit order here focuses on the maturation and aging processes from the narrowest context up to the societal level, from topics in biological gerontology to issues in social policy and practice. It should be noted, however, that the order of headings does not suggest that one discipline is more important than another when it comes to understanding age and aging.

Because the list is not in alphabetical order, please consult the master list of headings that appears directly after this paragraph to locate the position of the heading you are consulting.

Interpersonal Psychotherapy
Interventions, Psycho-Social-Behavioral
Life Review
Memory Dysfunction, Drug Treatment
Mental Health Services
Problem-Solving Therapy
Psychotherapy

SOCIAL THEORIES OF AGING

Critical Gerontology
Disengagement
Feminist Theory
Narrative
Theories, Social

PATHS ACROSS THE LIFE COURSE

Age Discrimination
Age Integration and Age Segregation
Aging in Place
Consumption and Age
Coresidence
Criminal Behavior
Criminal Victimization
Education
Homelessness
Inequality
Leisure
Life Course
Life Events and Stress
Living Arrangements
Midlife Crisis   \
Productive Aging
Religion
Spirituality
Successful Aging
Volunteer Activities and Programs

RELATIONSHIPS

Bereavement
Caregiving, Informal
Divorce: Trends and Consequences
Family
Filial Obligations
Friendship
Grandparenthood
Intergenerational Exchanges
Kin
Marital Relationships
Marriage and Remarriage
Parental Obligations
Parent-Child Relationship
Pets
Sibling Relationships
Social Support
Widowhood

SELECTED POPULATION GROUPS

Baby Boomers
Centenarians
Gay and Lesbian Aging
Immigrants

Oldest Old
Rural Elderly

POLITICAL QUESTIONS

Generational Equity
Gerontocracy
Intergenerational Justice
Political Behavior
Welfare State

WORK AND RETIREMENT

Employment of Older Workers
Job Performance
Retirement Planning
Retirement, Decision Making
Retirement, Early Retirement Incentives
Retirement, Patterns
Retirement, Transition
Self-Employment

PENSIONS AND SOCIAL SECURITY

Income Support for Nonworkers, National
  Approaches
Pensions, Financing and Regulation
Pensions, History
Pensions, Plan Types and Policy Approaches
Pensions, Public
Retirement Planning Programs
Social Security, History and Operations
Social Security, Long-Term Financing and
  Reform
Social Security and the U.S. Federal Budget
Supplemental Security Income

HEALTH INSURANCE

Disability, Economic Costs and Insurance
  Protection
Employee Health Insurance
Health Insurance, National Approaches
Long-Term Care Insurance
Medicaid
Medicare
Medication Costs and Reimbursements
Medigap
Risk Management and Insurance

ECONOMICS AND FINANCES

Annuities
Assets and Wealth
Bequests and Inheritances
Consumer Price Index and COLAs
Consumer Protection
Divorce: Economic Issues
Economic Well-Being
Estate Planning
Financial Planning for Long-Term Care
Individual Retirement Accounts
Life Cycle Theories of Savings and Consumption
Poverty
Retail and Older Adults
Savings
Taxation
Widowhood, Economic Issues

ACCELERATED AGING: ANIMAL MODELS

Animal models have been used to study accelerated aging, accelerated senescence, premature aging, premature senescence, and progeria-like syndromes. These models may be grouped into four classes: (1) experimentally induced models, (2) gene-modified models, (3) selection models, and (4) spontaneous models. There has been much debate over the connection between accelerated aging and disease status in animal models. Investigators interested in the basic mechanisms of normal aging have had to be prudent in their choice of animal models because early diseases leading to reduced life spans usually result from certain defects unrelated to mechanisms associated with normal aging, as suggested by David E. Harrison. In actuality, however, it is fairly difficult to discriminate between accelerated aging due to acceleration of the normal aging process and that due to the manifestation of diseases or pathologies. Thus, it might be important to check the pathologies or diseases an animal model manifests throughout its lifetime. In this context, species such as the nematode and fruit fly have disadvantages, in spite of their usefulness for genetic studies, because of a scarcity of information on diseases and pathologies.

Experimentally induced models

Adult-thymectomized lab mice. When male mice are thymectomized (removal of the thymus), their mean life span is reduced, though they don't show any specific pathologies. The reduced life span is thought to be due to accelerated aging of the immune system; that is, an accelerated decline in spleen cell responsiveness to T-cell mitogens such as phytohemagglutinin and staphylococcal enterotoxin.

Dihydrotachysterol-treated rats. In laboratory tests, when young rats are given dihydrotachysterol (reduced form of tachysterol generated from irradiated ultraviolet) orally, their life span is greatly reduced. They show pathologies such as loss of body weight; atrophy of the liver, kidney, thymicolymphatic apparatus, and fat and connective tissue; generalized arteriosclerosis with calcification; and loss of elasticity of the skin. Hans Selye, et al. designated the changes induced by dihydrotachysterol a progeria-like syndrome (progeria is a condition characterized by retardation of growth, wrinkled skin, cataracts, osteoporosis, and premature senile manifestations, among other symptoms). However, cataracts are rarely observed, and osteosclerosis, not osteoporosis, occurs in the bone in dihydrotachysterol-treated rats. So, the progeria-like syndrome induced by dihydrotachysterol in rats cannot be considered an exact replica of premature senility in humans.

Radiation model. Beginning with the experiments of S. Russ and G. M. Scott, who reported an increased death rate in chronically irradiated rats, there has been repeated confirmation of the fact that sublethal total-body irradiation from an external source can increase the mortality rate or reduce the life span of mammals. In some of the experiments, the irradiated animals died prematurely with roughly the same diseases as those associated with death in the control groups. However, the diseases did not necessarily have the same incidence or order, and sometimes there were increases or decreases in the absolute incidence of certain diseases. Some diseases occurred in irradiated groups that were not observed in the control groups. A single exposure of mice to sublethal irradiation shortened life span at some doses by increasing the initial mortality rate (IMR)—the age-independent mortality rate calculated at the age of maturation—but without further accelerating the age-dependent mortality rate. The general increase of IMR without increase in the acceleration of mortality suggests that the rate of organismic senescence is not accelerated by life-shortening radiation, as discussed by Caleb E. Finch.

Gene-modified models

Mev-1 (kn 1). A methyl viologen–sensitive mutant of the nematode *Caenorhabditis elegans*, named *mev-1 (kn 1)*, was isolated after ethyl methanesulfonate mutagenesis. The herbicide methyl viologen, or paraquat, is a potent free-radical generator. The mutant *C. elegans* strain is about four times more sensitive to methyl viologen than the wild type (N2), and is also hypersensitive to oxygen. The mean life span of the mutant is remarkably reduced. The activity of superoxide dismutase, a scavenging enzyme for superoxide anion (O_2), is reduced in mev-1 (kn 1) by about half, compared to N2. (O_2 is also a free-radical generator.) In 1998, Naoaki Ishii et al. reported that mev-1 encodes a subunit of the enzyme succinate dehydrogenase cytochrome b, which is a component of complex II of the mitochondrial respiratory chain, and that the ability of complex II to catalyze electron transport from succinate to ubiquinone is compromised in the mutant. This defect may cause an indirect increase in superoxide levels, which in turn leads to oxygen hypersensitivity and accelerated aging.

D. melanogaster cSOD^n108. The role of copper/zinc-containing superoxide dismutase (cSOD) in metabolic defense against O_2 toxicity in the fruit fly, *Drosophila melanogaster*, has been examined through the properties of a mutant strain of *D. melanogaster* carrying cSOD-null mutation. The mutant, termed *cSOD^n108* confers recessive sensitivity to the paraquat. This indicates that the cSOD-null condition in fact leads to impaired O_2 metabolism. The mean adult life span of the mutant (11.8 days) is remarkably decreased compared to that of the control parental stocks (55.4–57.8 days). Furthermore, male mutants are completely sterile, and females are

nearly so. Thus, the primary biological consequence of the reduced O_2 dismutation capacity of cSOD^n108 is infertility and a reduction in life span.

B10. F mice. A congenic line of mice, called *B10. F,* was produced by introducing a segment of chromosome 17 (*H-2^n*) from the strain F/St on the background of the C57BL/10 of *H-2^b* by backcrossing. The congenic B10. F mice gray early, suffer severe weight loss, and have skin that becomes thin and fragile. The mean life span of the B10. F mice is reduced, with 90 percent of the mice dying within seventeen months. The survival curve also shows significantly accelerated aging in the B10. F mice. At twelve to fourteen months these mice have a capacity to produce plaques to red-blood cells of sheep (an antigen for immunization) that is 12 percent of the capacity at four months, as assessed as one aspect of the immune competence of the B10. F mice. Since the strain is a congenic line, the genetic difference (and possibly the basis for the degenerative signs and reduced life span) is amenable to analysis.

Klotho mice. The insertion of a mutated transgene in mice has been found to disrupt a new gene locus, termed *klotho*, resulting in the manifestation of various phenotypes resembling those in patients with premature-aging syndromes. Homozygous *klotho* mice show growth retardation and have a short life span—up to three to four weeks of age—and the mice grow normally but show growth retardation thereafter, gradually becoming inactive and marasmic (emaciated), and dying prematurely at eight to nine weeks of age. The average life span of klotho mice is 60.7 days. The pathological phenotypes are infertility, hypokinesis (decreased function of the left ventricle), atrophy of genital organs and the thymus, arteriosclerosis, ectopic calcification, osteoporosis, skin atrophy, emphysema, and abnormalities in the pituitary gland. The klotho gene encodes a membrane protein that shares a sequence similarity with the β-glucosidase enzymes and expresses mainly in kidney and brain. It is hoped that the study of klotho mice with a single gene mutation will help to clarify the molecular-genetic mechanisms of both premature aging and accelerated aging.

Selection models

L line. High (H) and low (L) antibody responder lines of mice have been separated by selective breeding, presenting a maximal interline difference in antibody response to sheep red-blood cells, which was reached after fifteen successive generations of selective breeding. The life span of the H line and L line is 612 days and 346 days, respectively. Interpopulation correlation between life span and antibody response has shown that the life span is correlated positively with 2-mercaptoethanol (a reducing agent)–resistant agglutinin response and negatively with 2-mercaptoethanol-sensitive agglutinin response. Pathological examinations have revealed that chronic nephritis and malignant lymphoma are cardinal phenotypes observed at death in both the H and L lines. Mortality due to an early incidence of chronic nephritis, with a reduced-sized kidney and an irregular scarring of the cortex contribute to the shorter life span of the L line. The L responder mice also show a significant increase in malignant lymphomas, compared to the H responder mice. Thus, chronic nephritis and malignant lymphomas should be considered as the two main diseases accounting for the reduced life span of the lower antibody responder L line.

Senescence-accelerated mouse. The senescence-accelerated mouse (SAM), which consists of fourteen senescence-prone inbred strains (SAMP) and four senescence-resistant inbred strains (SAMR), has been under development since 1970. The manifestation of senescence in SAMP does not occur in the developmental stage, but it occurs in an accelerated manner following normal development, though there is no evidence of growth retardation, malformation, limb palsy, or other neurological signs, such as tremors and convulsions. The life span of SAMP is about 40 percent shorter than that of SAMR. Thus, accelerated senescence is considered to be a characteristic feature common to all SAMP mice. Both SAMP and SAMR strains manifest various pathobiological phenotypes, which are often characteristic enough to differentiate the strains. These phenotypes include senile amyloidosis, impaired immune response, hyperinflation of the lungs, hearing impairment, deficits in learning and memory, cataracts, alveolar bone loss, degenerative joint disease, abnormality of circadian rhythms, emotional disorders, and brain atrophy.

Studies suggest that a hyperoxidative status due to mitochondrial dysfunction plays a pivotal role in the manifestation of accelerated senescence, as well as pathologic phenotypes, in SAMP. Genetic studies to identify the genes for accelerated senescence of SAMP mice and for pathological phenotypes such as senile osteoporosis of SAMP6 mice are underway.

S strain. By selection and inbreeding of Wistar rats (an ordinary strain of rats) for sensitivity to the cataractogenic effect of a galactose-rich diet, a sensitive (S) and a resistant (R) rat strain were developed. A heritable increase in cellular hexose uptake has been associated with an increased intracellular generation of hydroxy radicals, increased endogenous lipid peroxidation, mitochondrial dysfunction, numerous DNA rearrangements, and membrane fragility in the S rats. Age-related degenerative diseases such as emphysema, cataracts, myocardial alterations, spinal column deformations, and impaired retention of long-term memory also manifest in the S rats. The life span of S rats is more than 50 percent shorter than that of R rats. Because of high embryonic mortality, fertility is also lower in the S rats. It is reasonable to conclude that continuous oxidative damage results ultimately in premature aging and in early death of the S rats.

Spontaneous models

Belgian hares. A certain family of Belgian hares, part of a large breeding colony organized for the study of constitutional problems, developed premature senescence as a hereditary entity. From observations made on individuals representing twenty generations with the condition, two principal forms of the degenerative syndrome were recognized: acute and chronic (the essential difference between the two forms being the degree and rate of deterioration). However, there have been no reports on the aging characteristics and pathological findings, including histopathology, of the various degenerative lesions.

TOSHIO TAKEDA

See also GENETICS; LONGEVITY: SELECTION; MOLECULAR BIOLOGY OF AGING.

BIBLIOGRAPHY

COVELLI, V.; MOUTON, D.; MAJO, V. D.; BOUTHILLIER, Y.; BANGRAZI, C.; MEVEL, J.-C.; REBESSI, S.; DORIA, G.; and BIOZZI, G. "Inheritance of Immune Responsiveness, Life Span, and Disease Incidence in Interline Crosses of Mice Selected for High or Low Multispecific Antibody Production." *Journal of Immunology* 142 (1989): 1224–1234.

FINCH, C. E. *Longevity, Senescence, and the Genome.* Chicago: The University of Chicago Press, 1994.

HARRISON, D. E. "Potential Misinterpretations Using Models of Accelerated Aging." *Journal of Gerontology: Biological Sciences* 49 (1994): B245.

ISHII, N.; FUJII, M.; HARTMAN, P. S.; TSUDA, M.; YASUDA, K.; SENOO-MATSUDA, N.; YANASE, S.; AYUSAWA, D.; and SUZUKI, K. "A Mutation in Succinate Dehydrogenase Cytochrome *b* Causes Oxidative Stress and Ageing in Nematodes." *Nature* 394 (1998): 694–697.

JEEJEEBHOY, H. F. "Decreased Longevity of Mice Following Thymectomy in Adult Life." *Transplantation* 12 (1971): 525–527.

KURO-O, M.; MATSUMURA, Y.; AIZAWA, H.; KAWAGUCHI, H.; SUGA, T.; UTSUGI, T.; OHYAMA, Y.; KURABAYASHI, M.; KANAME, T.; KUME, E.; IWASAKI, H.; IIDA, A.; SHIRAKI-IIDA, T.; NISHIKAWA, S.; NAGAI, R.; and NABESHIMA, Y. "Mutation of the Mouse *klotho* Gene Leads to a Syndrome Resembling Ageing." *Nature* 390 (1997): 45–51.

PEARCE, L., and BROWN, W. H. "Hereditary Premature Senescence of the Rabbit I. Chronic Form; Genertal Features." *Journal of Experimental Medicine* 111 (1960): 485–504.

PHILLIPS, J. P.; CAMPBELL, S. D.; MICHAUD, D.; CHARBONNEAU, M.; and HILLIKER, A. J. "Null Mutation of Copper/Zinc Superoxide Dismutase in *Drosophila* Confers Hypersensitivity to Paraquat and Reduced Longevity." *Proceedings of the National Academy of Sciences, USA* 86 (1989): 2761–2765.

POPP, D. M. "Use of Congenic Mice to Study the Genetic Basis of Degenerative Disease." *Birth Defects: Original Article Series* 14 (1978): 261–279.

RUSS, S., and SCOTT, G. M. "Biological Effects of Gamma Irradiation." *British Journal of Radiology* 120 (1939): 440–441.

SALGANIK, R. I.; SOLOVYOVA, N. A.; DIKALOV, S. I.; GRISHAEVA, O. N.; SEMENOVA, L. A.; and POPOVSKY, A. V. "Inherited Enhancement of Hydroxyl Radical Generation and Lipid Peroxidation in the S Strain Rats Results in DNA Rearrangements, Degenerative Diseases, and Premature Aging." *Biochemical and Biophysical Research Communications* 199 (1994): 726–733.

SELYE, H.; STREBEL, R.; and MIKULAJ, L. "A Progeria-like Syndrome Produced by Dihydrotachysterol and Its Prevention by Methyltestosterone and Ferric Dextran." *Journal of the American Geriatric Society* 11 (1963): 1–16.

TAKEDA, T. "Senescence-Accelerated Mouse (SAM): A Biogerontological Resource in Aging Research." *Neurobiology of Aging* 20 (1999): 105–110.

ACCELERATED AGING: HUMAN PROGEROID SYNDROMES

Human aging is a complex process resulting from the interaction between a person's genetic makeup, their environment, and time. Individuals mature to adulthood, then undergo a gradual degenerative process that eventually results in death. Most of us go through these processes at roughly equivalent rates; indicating that a carefully controlled developmental program operates until adulthood. It is not clear, however, whether aging is also programmed or whether maturation is simply followed by random deterioration in the decades after our reproductive years. Such questions remain unresolved, although decreased performance of many body systems is directly related to increasing age—our bodies wrinkle and lose muscle, our hair turns gray and thins, our bones become brittle, and increasingly we succumb to age-related diseases, including cancer, diabetes, hypertension, atherosclerosis, and several neurological disorders.

Although most of us feel that we age too quickly, we should count ourselves lucky. Several human genetic diseases are noteworthy for their accelerated development of certain aging characteristics. Specifically, *accelerated aging* is defined as the earlier than normal onset or increased frequency of an age-related attribute or disease. Importantly, no genetic disorder exhibits acceleration of all signs of human aging. For this reason, these diseases are known as *segmental progeroid syndromes*, meaning each partially mimics an accelerated aging phenotype. Also, each disorder has a variable age of onset and rate of development of its distinct set of accelerated aging characteristics. Despite this variability, these syndromes provide valuable insight into the mechanisms involved in accelerated aging, and, by extrapolation, in normal human aging as well.

Progeroid syndromes as models of aging

Detractors argue that segmental progeroid syndromes do not reflect normal aging, usually pointing out symptoms unrelated to aging or the lack of specific normal aging characteristics.

Moreover, some accelerated aging symptoms described in progeroid syndromes may have subtle physiological differences that distinguish them from similar features of normal aging. This would suggest that the defect that underlies such an accelerated aging characteristic is distinct from defects that occur during normal aging. Clearly, normal aging is a genetically complex process that cannot be fully explained by comparison to several diseases involving a very small set of genes.

However, these weaknesses of progeroid syndromes as models of normal aging also highlight their strengths. The specific genetic defects that cause progeroid syndromes facilitate examination of biochemical deficiencies associated with certain accelerated aging characteristics. By contrast, the contributions of the many genes that impinge on normal aging are almost impossible to evaluate. It is likely that there are multiple underlying causes for all of the features of normal aging. Thus, the acceleration of specific aging characteristics that occur in progeroid syndromes may provide insight into specific pathways that fail and underlying mechanisms that operate, albeit at a slower pace, during the later development of similar characteristics during normal aging. Moreover, identification of defective genes that result in accelerated aging allows discovery of beneficial disadvantageous alleles of those genes (and other functionally related genes) that might delay or modestly hasten, respectively, the onset of normal aging characteristics. Below are brief descriptions of five genetic diseases that are regarded as the best models of accelerated aging.

Down syndrome

Down syndrome occurs about once in seven hundred births and is characterized by delayed and incomplete development as well as degeneration of many organ systems. Down syndrome exhibits an early onset of many aging characteristics, including graying and loss of hair, hearing loss, cataracts, increased tissue lipofuscin, and degenerative vascular disease, as well as increased frequency of autoimmunity and cancer, particularly childhood leukemia. Multiple neurological abnormalities, including early onset of senile dementia similar to that associated with Alzheimer's disease, may result from both decreased proliferation and increased apoptosis of neurons. Individuals with Down syndrome usually die by the age of forty.

Down syndrome is caused by having three (instead of two) copies of part or all of human chromosome 21, making it genetically much more complex than other segmental progeroid syndromes. Hypothetically, the extra chromosome alters gene expression levels that, in turn, cause metabolic defects that result in both the developmental problems and degenerative effects of Down syndrome. Chromosome 21 harbors the gene for the amyloid precursor protein. Increased production of this protein could be a factor in amyloid plaque development, which is diagnostic for senile dementia associated with Down syndrome and Alzheimer's disease. This chromosome also contains the Cu/Zn (copper/zinc) superoxide dismutase gene that is involved in the metabolism of reactive oxygen species. Imbalances in oxidative metabolism could lead to increased cellular damage, a scenario consistent with both the increased lipofuscin and oxidative DNA damage observed in Down syndrome and the proposed relationship between accumulation of oxidative damage and aging characteristics. However, the contribution of any particular gene on chromosome 21 to specific premature aging characteristics associated with Down syndrome remains unclear.

Adult progeria (Werner syndrome)

Werner syndrome is known as adult progeria because affected individuals appear relatively normal until adolescence and develop aging characteristics thereafter. It is an autosomal recessive disorder that afflicts fewer than ten out of a million persons, with the highest incidences in Japan and Sardinia. Werner syndrome patients have accelerated development of many aging characteristics (including graying and loss of hair, wrinkling and ulceration of skin, cataracts, atherosclerosis, and osteoporosis) and increased incidence of certain age-related diseases (such as cancer, diabetes, and hypertension). They do not have increased neurodegenerative problems such as Alzheimer's, Parkinson's, or Huntington's disease, although some dementia has been reported. Werner syndrome patients invariably die before age fifty, usually from cancer or complications due to severe atherosclerosis.

Amazingly, all of the characteristics of Werner syndrome result from mutations in one gene, known as *WRN*. Biochemical study of the WRN protein demonstrated its DNA unwinding (helicase) and DNA degradation (exonuclease) activities. Although the exact function of WRN remains unknown, its catalytic activities and reported interactions with proteins involved in DNA metabolism point to possible roles in DNA replication, repair, or recombination. The loss of WRN function in Werner syndrome causes DNA metabolic errors that result in elevated deletions, insertions, and translocations of chromosomal DNA. Cells lacking WRN also shorten their telomeres (the protective DNA sequences at each chromosome end) much faster than normal cells, suggesting a direct role for WRN in telomere maintenance. In somatic cells, telomere shortening occurs during each round of replication, and thus is a biomarker of cellular aging. Critically short telomeres prevent cell division, suggesting a relationship between cellular senescence and aging of organisms. Cells from individuals with Werner syndrome undergo rapid cellular senescence, probably caused by accelerated telomere loss, supporting the proposed relationship between short telomeres, cellular senescence, and certain aging characteristics. In general, the Werner syndrome phenotype points to a connection between the accumulation of genetic changes, cellular senescence, and aging.

Progeria (Hutchinson-Gilford syndrome)

In contrast to Werner syndrome, the symptoms of Hutchinson-Gilford syndrome (progeria) appear in infancy. Premature aging characteristics associated with progeria are loss of hair, reduction in subcutaneous fat, wrinkling of the skin, skeletal abnormalities (including osteoporosis), and severe atherosclerosis. Growth retardation and other features not associated with aging are also observed, but mental development appears normal. Progeria patients usually succumb by their early teens due to complications from atherosclerosis.

Progeria is extremely rare, striking about one in ten million individuals. The lack of an inheritance pattern implicates sporadic dominant mutations as the underlying cause. The most prevalent physiological abnormality associated with progeria is elevated hyaluronic acid in the urine. Notably, hyaluronic acid levels in the urine normally increase with age, although not approaching the levels observed in progeria. Hyaluronic acid is involved in maintenance of the skeletal, muscular, cutaneous, and vascular systems of the body, and is thought to block angio-genesis (vascularization). A potential defect in hyaluronic acid metabolism may thus disrupt many developmental pathways. Cells from Hutchinson-Gilford patients appear to have diminished replicative capacity, but not nearly as short a life span as cells from Werner patients. Nevertheless, the genetic and biochemical causes of progeria remain unknown.

Cockayne syndrome

Cockayne syndrome is an autosomal recessive disease that also appears early in childhood, although the age of onset and severity of symptoms are variable. Individuals with this disorder have growth retardation and multiple degenerative problems, including central nervous system degeneration that often results in deafness, vision deficits, and motor problems. Other age-related features are premature arteriosclerosis, progressive joint deformities, and loss of subcutaneous fat. Sun sensitivity is associated with Cockayne syndrome, although increased malignancy (including UV-related skin cancer) is not. Death usually occurs by early adolescence as a result of progressive neurodegeneration.

Cockayne syndrome is the result of mutations in one of five genes. Most affected individuals have defective *CSA* or *CSB* genes, although specific *XPB, XPD,* or *XPG* gene mutations result in Cockayne syndrome combined with another disease, xeroderma pigmentosum. This genetic complexity indicates that these five gene products impinge on a common pathway that is faulty in Cockayne syndrome. Extensive research has demonstrated that the problem lies in the complex coordination of transcription with DNA repair. In normal cells, certain types of DNA damage are removed faster from the template strand of transcribed genes than from the remainder of the genome. Individuals with Cockayne syndrome are deficient in this highly efficient repair of the transcribed strand of active genes and, consequently, have difficulty in resuming transcription following DNA damage. Persistent damage in the transcribed strand may sequester RNA polymerase, and the concomitant transcription deficits may explain many Cockayne syndrome abnormalities. Another hypothesis is that transcription blockage induces programmed cell death (apoptosis), and sufficient cell loss elicits aging signs and other characteristics of Cockayne syndrome. Inhibition of transcription or induction of apoptosis in neurons that contain increased endogenous oxidative DNA damage could explain the profound neurodegeneration associated with this disease. Ultimately, a failure in DNA metabolism is responsible for Cockayne syndrome.

Ataxia telangiectasia

Ataxia telangiectasia is an autosomal recessive disease that occurs in about one in forty thousand to three hundred thousand individuals. Characteristics of this disease appear during infancy and develop during childhood. There is a striking increase in cancer frequency, immunodeficiency, and acute neurodegeneration (particularly of the cerebellum) leading to multiple motor difficulties. Individuals with ataxia telangiectasia die prematurely of cancer or pulmonary disease (probably due to immunodeficiency).

Ataxia telangiectasia is caused by mutations in a large gene (designated *ATM*) that codes for a protein with phosphorylation (kinase) activity. Cells lacking ATM function are profoundly sensitive to ionizing radiation, have chromosomal instability (including increased telomere shortening), and premature replicative senescence. Research has demonstrated that ATM kinase is involved in regulating cell cycle progression in response to DNA damage by phosphorylating protein targets, particularly the tumor suppressor protein p53 that, in turn, either delays cell cycle progression or initiates programmed cell death. Thus, loss of ATM function results in survival of cells with damaged DNA and/or increased chromosomal breaks following replication of damaged DNA. These outcomes certainly contribute to increased tumorigenesis in ataxia telangiectasia. Notably, individuals with one mutated *ATM* allele (approximately 1 percent of the population) have a slightly elevated cancer risk, although without the overt phenotype of ataxia telangiectasia.

Unifying concepts

If segmental progeroid syndromes are informative with respect to normal aging, what have they revealed thus far? These diseases support the view that aging results from the accumulation of damage to cellular components caused by biochemical errors and/or deleterious agents over a lifetime—and they undermine the idea of a genetic program for aging. By this reasoning,

the rare occurrence of metabolic errors and the appropriate cellular maintenance processes in normal individuals cause damage to accumulate slowly, but this damage eventually causes enough harm to result in multiple aging characteristics. Specific types of errors are amplified in progeroid syndromes, resulting in increased cellular damage and certain premature aging characteristics. Interestingly, several progeroid syndromes show genetic instability (chromosomal aberrations and/or telomere shortening), suggesting connections between DNA damage and aging characteristics. Clearly, genetic damage accumulates even during normal life span and is directly related to increased cancer frequency with age. Although the relationship between DNA damage and other signs of normal aging is unclear, accumulation of oxidative damage to DNA, proteins, and membranes has been strongly implicated in many features of normal aging. Even if the biochemical defects in segmental progeroid syndromes do not directly imitate the types of mistakes made during normal aging, the cellular outcomes are probably similar—loss of cell cycle control (cancer), decrease in cell function, cellular senescence, and cell death (apoptosis). In turn, the accumulation of these cellular effects manifests itself in the physiological degeneration that we recognize as human aging.

DAVID K. ORREN

See also CELLULAR AGING; DNA DAMAGE AND REPAIR; GENETICS; LONGEVITY: SELECTION; MOLECULAR BIOLOGY OF AGING; PHYSIOLOGICAL CHANGES.

BIBLIOGRAPHY

ARKING, R. "Genetic Determinants of Longevity." In *Biology of Aging*, 2d ed. Edited by R. Arking. Sunderland, Mass.: Sinauer Associates, 1998. Pages 251–309.

BLACKBURN, E. H. "Telomere States and Cell Fates." *Nature* 408 (2000): 53–56.

CAPONE, G. T. "Down Syndrome: Advances in Molecular Biology and the Neurosciences." *Developmental and Behavioral Pediatrics* 22, no. 1 (2001): 40–59.

DYER, C. A. E., and SINCLAIR, A. J. "The Premature Aging Syndromes: Insights into the Ageing Process." *Age and Ageing* 27 (1998): 73–80.

FINKEL, T., and HOLBROOK, N. J. "Oxidants, Oxidative Stress, and the Biology of Aging." *Nature* 408 (2000): 239–247.

GOTO, M. "Hierarchical Deterioration of Body Systems in Werner's Syndrome: Implications for Normal Aging." *Mechanisms of Ageing and Development* 98 (1997): 239–254.

HANAWALT, P. C. "The Bases for Cockayne Syndrome." *Nature* 405 (2000): 415–416.

MARTIN, G. M. "Genetic Syndromes in Man with Potential Relevance to the Pathobiology of Aging." In *Genetic Effects on Aging.* Edited by D. Bergsma and D. E. Harrison. New York: Alan R. Liss, 1978. Pages 5–39.

MARTIN, G. M., and OSHIMA, J. "Lessons from Human Progeroid Syndromes." *Nature* 408 (2000): 263–266.

OSHIMA, J. "The Werner Syndrome Protein: An Update." *Bioessays* 22, no. 10 (2000): 894–901.

RAPIN, I.; LINDENBAUM, Y.; DICKSON, D. W.; KRAEMER, K. H.; and ROBINS, J. H. "Cockayne Syndrome and Xeroderma Pigmentosum." *Neurology* 55 (2000): 1442–1449.

REEVES, R. H.; BAXTER, L. L.; and RICHTSMEIER, J. T. "Too Much of a Good Thing: Mechanisms of Gene Action in Down Syndrome." *Trends in Genetics* 17, no. 2 (2001): 83–88.

SARKAR, P. K., and SHINTON, R. A. "Hutchinson-Guilford Progeria Syndrome." *Postgraduate Medical Journal* 77 (2001): 312–317.

SHILOH, Y. "Ataxia-Telangiectasia and the Nijmegen Breakage Syndrome: Related Disorders but Genes Apart." *Annual Review of Genetics* 31 (1997): 635–662.

VAN GOOL, A. J.; VAN DER HORST, G. T. J.; CITTERIO, E.; and HOEIJMAKERS, J. H. J. "Cockayne Syndrome: Defective Repair or Transcription." *The EMBO Journal* 16, no. 14 (1997): 4155–4162.

YU, C.; OSHIMA, J.; FU, Y.; WIJSMAN, E. M.; HISAMA, F.; ALISCH, R.; MATTHEWS, S.; NAKURA, J.; MIKI, T.; OUAIS, S.; MARTIN, G. M.; MULLIGAN, J.; and SCHELLENBERG, G. D. "Positional Cloning of the Werner's Syndrome Gene." *Science* 272 (1996): 258–262.

ACTIVITIES OF DAILY LIVING

See FUNCTIONAL ABILITY

ADMININISTRATION ON AGING

The Administration on Aging (AoA) is the U.S. federal agency charged with administering the Older Americans Act (OAA), the principal federal legislation promoting client advocacy, system building, and the delivery of social services for America's elderly population. AoA was created by Title II of the OAA, and is currently directed by the assistant secretary for aging within the office of the secretary of the Department of Health and Human Services (DHHS).

History and development of AoA

With some minor modifications, AoA has had two principal responsibilities since enactment of the OAA in 1965. First, AoA is the federal agency designated to administer all but one of the titles of the Older Americans Act. The largest of the grant programs is Title III, State and Community Programs, through which AoA works closely with a network of 9 federal regional offices, 57 state units on aging, 661 substate area agencies on aging, 228 Native American, Alaskan, and Hawaiian tribal organizations, and some 27,000 providers of services to elderly people. Through the considerably smaller Title IV program, AoA oversees the awarding of discretionary funds to public and private agencies and universities for building knowledge, developing innovative model programs, and training personnel for service in the field of aging. Under the Title VI program, AoA awards grants to provide supportive and nutrition services to older Native Americans, Alaskan Natives, and Native Hawaiians. Title VII, the Vulnerable Elder Rights Protection, addresses the needs of especially disadvantaged older people and brings together four separate programs: the long-term-care ombudsman program; programs for the prevention of abuse, neglect, and exploitation; state elder rights and legal assistance programs; and insurance/benefits outreach and counseling program (Administration on Aging, http://www.aoa.gov). (Title V, the Senior Community Service Employment program, is administered by the Department of Labor.)

AoA's second mission is broader, involving promoting awareness of the needs of the aging beyond grant administration, oversight, and evaluation. The wide-ranging charge to AoA is revealed in several of the duties and functions of the assistant secretary for aging, who heads AoA:

- To serve as the effective and visible advocate for older individuals within the Department of Health and Human Services and across the federal government more broadly
- To collect and disseminate information related to problems of the aged and aging
- To gather statistics in the field of aging that other federal agencies are not collecting

- To stimulate more effective use of existing resources and available services for the aged and aging, and to coordinate federal programs and activities to that effect
- To carry on a continuing evaluation of the programs and activities related to the objectives of the OAA, with particular attention to the impact of Medicare, Medicaid, the Age Discrimination in Employment Act, and the National Housing Act relating to standards for licensing nursing homes and other facilities providing care for vulnerable individuals
- To provide information and assistance to private organizations for the establishment and operation by them of programs and activities related to the OAA
- To strengthen the involvement of the Administration on Aging in the development of policy alternatives in long-term care by participating in all departmental and interdepartmental activities concerning development of long-term-care health services, review all departmental regulations regarding community-based long-term care, and provide a leadership role for AoA, state, and area agencies in development and implementation of community-based long-term care.

In short, AoA is the "federal focal point and advocacy agency for older people" (Koff and Park). As such, it is charged with providing leadership within the aging network of state and area agencies and of service providers for the elderly, and with coordinating activities of other federal agencies involved with aging. It is a very encompassing mandate and has been a challenging one for AoA to carry out over the years.

Organizational challenges to AoA

While attempting to carry out this encompassing mandate, AoA has had only limited organizational resources.

Funding. The monetary resources at the disposal of AoA are severely limited, given the breadth of its responsibilities. First, appropriations under the Older Americans Act are relatively small—$933 million in 2000 (excluding Title V)—especially given that the formal mandate of both AoA and the OAA includes addressing the needs of all 43 million Americans over the age of sixty. Thus, there is not quite $22 in OAA funding theoretically available to each older Ameri-

can. This is not, however, to say that the federal government overall does not devote enormous resources to older people, but rather that they are largely administered outside of AoA: expenditures for Social Security ($420 billion) and Medicare ($273 billion) benefits total $693 billion. However, these programs are administered by the Social Security Administration and the Health Care Financing Administration, respectively. With respect to funding, the situation described by Binstock at the time of AoA's origin remains largely unchanged today: AoA is given a somewhat vague responsibility to coordinate all activities of the federal government related to aging but is not given the resources to do so.

Organizational standing. Since AOA's founding in 1965, a major issue has been where it should be placed within the federal government. The struggle has largely been an institutional one, with advocates for the elderly in Congress generally wanting AoA to have high status and visibility, and officials within the executive branch wishing to keep AoA closely tied to other agencies within what is now the Department of Health and Human Services. Thus, in 1965 the secretary of the Department of Health, Education and Welfare (DHEW) succeeded in putting AoA in the Welfare Administration, against the strenuous objections of advocates of the aging who did not want AoA, the OAA, or older people themselves associated with "welfare." In 1967, advocates succeeded in having AoA placed in a new unit within DHEW, the Social and Rehabilitation Service, which advocates found preferable to the previous placement but not as high or as autonomous as they would have liked. In 1973, AoA was moved to the new Office of Human Development Services (OHDS), which also included agencies serving children, families, and the developmentally disabled. AoA remained there for many years, with a minor elevation in the late 1980s (reporting "to the secretary," not to "the Office of the Secretary"). Finally, in 1991 AoA was elevated out of OHDS and became a line organization within DHHS with the same formal standing as the Social Security Administration, the Health Care Financing Administration, and the Public Health Service, all much larger agencies than AoA (Koff and Park). The most recent change was the elevation of the commissioner on aging to assistant secretary for aging within DHHS, in order to facilitate the head of AoA's being able to deal more effectively with other federal agencies (Gelfand).

Because AoA has always been a small agency, this jockeying for organizational position has been more about status and symbols than about actual influence within the DHHS (Hudson, 1973). Nonetheless, symbols are important, and AoA's being at the same organizational level as much larger agencies and headed by an assistant secretary say a good deal about the positive view of older Americans that members of Congress wish to promote.

Personnel. After having long been a small agency within DHHS, AoA became even smaller during the 1980s. Between 1981 and 1989, AoA's staff declined from 252 to 162, a 36 percent decrease. A number of senior-level positions were left vacant for periods and then, often, filled with temporary appointments. Travel budgets were cut as well, the principal consequence being that AoA officials in the nine regional offices were unable to travel to their states to provide technical assistance and oversight to the agencies operating programs under the OAA (USGAO, 1991). Successive amendments to the OAA have brought additional responsibilities to AoA over the years, making these personnel cuts even more pressing (USGAO, 1992).

AoA in the twenty-first century

Despite the enormity of its charge and the relative paucity of its resources, the Administration on Aging has overseen many developments since its creation in 1965. As the agency principally responsible for implementation of the OAA, it helped bring into existence and nurture today's network for the aging. This is no small accomplishment; indeed, advocates for children have argued that there should be a "children's network" analogous to the one that AoA has created for the aging (Grayson and Guyer). Social services funded at a level of nearly $1 billion are delivered through these auspices every year; federal and state agencies in health and mental health care, long-term care, nutrition, and transportation have been made more responsive to elderly persons' concerns because of network activity that AoA helped bring about.

There have been many relatively minor changes in AoA's programmatic emphasis, but program administration and client advocacy remain the principal foci. The balance between these two has, however, changed over the years. The network agencies at the state and substate regional levels are well established and are able to operate quite well on their own, relatively independent of AoA. This reality should be understood as a compliment to AoA, not a critique of it. The founding spirit of the OAA was for these agencies to become self-sustaining and, in turn, influence other agencies and organizations serving the elderly at the state level. The success of AoA and of the agencies in attaining this status has allowed AoA to place relatively greater emphasis on its activities at the federal level and on promoting the needs of older people that extend well beyond the social services boundaries of the OAA delivery structure. Of the six goals set forth by AoA in its most recent strategic plan, most call on AoA to promote new ideas and awareness—"gerontologize America," "promote cross-cutting initiatives," "build a partnership between the aging and disability communities," and "address the diversity and special needs of the aged."

AoA remains a relatively small federal agency, and the national network it helped create no longer requires the levels of support and advice from AoA that it once did. That frees the assistant secretary for aging and agency staff to promote the needs of elderly people at the federal level and through activities that extend beyond the service programs of the network for the aging. Because resources available to AoA remain scarce, major changes in these arenas will be difficult to bring about. But the role is an important one, and AoA can devote relatively more energy to it than has been historically the case.

ROBERT B. HUDSON

See also AREA AGENCIES ON AGING; FEDERAL AGENCIES AND AGING; OLDER AMERICANS ACT.

BIBLIOGRAPHY

BINSTOCK, R. B. "Interest Group Liberalism and the Politics of Aging." *Gerontologist* 12 (1972): 265–280.

GELFAND, D. *The Aging Network*, 5th ed. New York: Springer, 1999.

GRAYSON, H., and GUYER, B. "Rethinking the Organization of Children's Programs: Lessons from the Elderly." *Milbank Quarterly* 73, no. 4 (1995): 565–598.

HUDSON, R. B. "Client Politics and Federalism: The Case of the Older Americans Act" Paper presented at the Annual Meeting of the American Political Science Association, New Orleans, 1973.

KOFF, T., and PARK, R. *Aging and Public Policy: Bonding the Generations*. Amityville, N.Y.: Baywood (USGAO). 1999.

U.S. General Accounting Office (USGAO). *Administration on Aging: More Federal Action Needed to Promote Service Coordination for the Elderly*. GAO/HRD 91-45. Washington, D.C.: U.S. Government Printing Office, 1991.

U.S. General Accounting Office (USGAO). *Administration on Aging: Harmonizing Growing Demands and Shrinking Resources*. GAO/PEMD 92-7. Washington, D.C.: U.S. Government Printing Office, 1992

ADULT DAY CARE

The National Adult Day Services Association (NADSA) defines an adult day center in its *Standards and Guidelines for Adult Day Services* (revised 1997) thus:

An adult day center is a community-based group program designed to meet the needs of adults with functional impairments through an individual plan of care. This is a structured, comprehensive program that provides a variety of health, social and related support services in a protective setting during any part of a day, but less than 24-hour care.

Individuals participating in adult day centers attend on a planned basis during specified hours. Adult day centers assist. . .participants to remain in the community, and this enables families and other caregivers to continue caring at home for a family member with an impairment.

This community-based program meets the needs of participants and their caregivers in a congregate setting. Participants generally provide their own transportation, though many adult day care centers provide or arrange for transportation.

Though each adult day center is staffed according to the needs of its participants, most programs operate with an interdisciplinary team that consists of activity staff, usually an activity director and assistants; program assistants who aid with personal care; a social worker; a registered nurse or licensed practical nurse; and a center director. In small programs the center director often functions as both the director and the social worker or the director and the nurse. Centers that serve a large number of participants may also employ a driver, secretary, and accountant. The average adult day center has a daily census of twenty-five to thirty participants. NADSA recommends a minimum staff-to-participant ratio of one to six. This ratio can be even smaller, depending upon the level of participant impairment. For example, if a program serves a large proportion of participants with dementia, the ratio of staff to participants should be closer to one to four.

The typical adult day center operates for eight to twelve hours each day. Because of the changing needs of caregivers, many centers are open five to seven days per week. Participants experience a structured day that includes meals, activities, exercise, and opportunities for informal socialization, as well as assistance with personal care when needed.

Benefits of the center setting

Adult day centers offer a variety of health and social services for one-third to one-half the cost of home health or nursing home care. Home health care agencies and nursing homes nationwide are facing shortages in the paraprofessional work force. Adult day centers are able to provide services with adequate staffing because their staffs, by and large, are not required to work evening and weekend shifts. Desirable hours and the congregate setting contribute to the efficacy and cost-effectiveness of adult day programs.

Adult day services are commonly referred to as "the best kept secret in long-term care." This community-based group program offers participants and their caregivers a viable alternative to nursing home care. Experts agree that despite the efficacy and cost-effectiveness of adult day services, they remain underutilized due to consumers' lack of awareness and inadequate reimbursement.

The facility

Adult day programs are offered in a variety of settings: in a freestanding building; on the campus of a hospital, nursing home, or assisted living facility; or in conjunction with another program, such as a home health agency. Participants can expect centers to offer services in a building that is handicapped accessible. Every center, regardless of the setting, must have bathrooms (one toilet for every ten participants at minimum, according to NADSA), staff offices, and activity space. Additional space may include therapy rooms or offices, a bathtub and/or shower room, laundry area with washer and dryer, nursing clinic, large and small activity spaces, and a kitchen area (for snack preparation). NADSA recommends a minimum of sixty square feet of space per participant. This figure excludes staff offices, corridors, bathrooms, closets, and similar space that is not solely for participants' activities.

Goals of the adult day program

The adult day center setting offers stimulation and growth for participants with impairments while providing respite for families and caregivers. Based on these premises, the NADSA *Standards* (revised 1997) establish the following goals for adult day centers:

- Promote the individual's maximum level of independence.
- Maintain the individual's present level of functioning as long as possible, preventing or delaying further deterioration.
- Restore and rehabilitate the individual to the highest possible level of functioning.
- Provide support, respite, and education for families and other caregivers.
- Foster socialization and peer interaction.
- Serve as an integral part of the community service network and the long-term care continuum.

These overall goals are coupled with each participant's individual plan of care to maintain an optimal level of physical and mental health.

Care models

Adult day services are delivered, most generally, in one of two program types: the social model or the medical model. The primary focus of the social model is opportunities for socialization and recreation. Such programs typically offer limited health care and rehabilitative services. Participants who attend social model programs usually enjoy fair physical health, but would otherwise lack opportunities to socialize with peers. If participants require medication during their time at the center, it is usually self-administered.

The medical model program has intensive nursing and rehabilitative services as the primary focus. Participants who attend such programs usually have multiple chronic conditions that require monitoring and/or a nursing intervention, and medication administration at least once during the day.

Approximately thirty-five states license or accredit adult day programs. For example, a center may be licensed as a social and/or a medical model. Each program determines which level of licensure is most appropriate.

Services offered

The types of services offered in an adult day care center vary according to whether the program is medical or social. Medical model programs offer nursing care provided by a registered nurse or a licensed practical nurse under a registered nurse's supervision. The nursing care can include medication administration, wound dressing changes, injections, and overall health monitoring. Medical programs also provide or arrange for physical, speech, and occupational therapy. Social model programs tend to be more limited in their scope of services. They emphasize opportunities for socialization, activities, and outings. Medical model programs offer similar social programming in addition to nursing care. Additional services that are offered in both types of programs are therapeutic activities; meals and snacks with special dietary accommodations (for example, diabetic or renal diet); door-to-door transportation; social services provided by a licensed social worker; shower or bath; toileting assistance; grooming; and caregiver support.

Participant profile

Each center's organizational leadership determines what level of participant impairment it can accommodate. This decision is based on the center's design, staffing complement, community demand, and, in some cases, available reimbursement. According to the NADSA, the average age of adult day participants is seventy-four years. Although the adult day center population is largely comprised of older adults, many centers across the country have developed programs to meet the needs of young, disabled adults. The majority of adult day participants are women. Common participant diagnoses include Alzheimer's disease or a related dementia, diabetes, stroke, Parkinson's disease, and cardiovascular disease. The primary reasons for attending an adult day center are the need for socialization, the need for caregiver respite, and the need for supervision or assistance with activities of daily living. Individuals attend adult day centers an average of three to four days per week.

Operating costs of adult day centers

The major costs of operating an adult day center are staffing, rent/mortgage, transportation (vehicle purchase, lease, or fee for service), food, and supplies (medical, activities, office). These costs help center directors determine the daily fee for participants. Though there are wide regional variations in the costs of operating an adult day program, the cost of hiring and maintaining a well-trained staff is frequently the single largest organizational expense.

Funding sources

Adult day services is one of the few industries that lacks uniform reimbursement. Every state has a different reimbursement mix, and within a state, funding can vary widely from county to county. Medicare does not reimburse for the cost of adult day services. Medicaid does reimburse the cost of such services, but not in every state. The states that have Medicaid reimbursement offer it through Medicaid waivers by reallocating funds that had previously been used for institutional long-term care to pay for community-based programs, such as adult day services, intended to help adults remain independent in their own homes and communities.

Long-term care insurance policies that are purchased by individuals sometimes cover the costs associated with adult day but because policies differ greatly, individual policies must be inspected to determine if adult day care reimbursement is a benefit, and if it is, at what level.

The Veterans Administration funds adult day services with money that previously was earmarked solely for nursing home care. Veterans with a service-connected disability may qualify for funding. The local or regional veterans hospital determines the level of available funding, and should be contacted for further information regarding adult day funding.

Selecting an adult day center

According to the NADSA's publication *Your Guide to Selecting an Adult Day Services Center*, the first step in selecting a high-quality adult day center is to determine the needs of the program participant and the caregiver. The program participant may have the following needs: a safe, secure environment; social activities; assistance with eating, walking, toileting, and medicines; physical, speech, or occupational therapy; health monitoring; accommodations for special dietary requirements; personal care; and exercise. A caregiver's needs may differ considerably. The caregiver may require reliable coverage in order to work outside of the home; occasional respite; assistance with transportation; support and education; or assistance in planning for care. After the most critical needs are identified, the local Area Agency on Aging is an excellent resource in locating programs in the community that meet those needs.

Potential program participants or caregivers should telephone several adult day centers and inquire about eligibility criteria and application procedures, and request printed information about the program, such as newsletters, brochures, and activity calendars. The program materials should contain information regarding ownership, years of operation, license or certification, hours and days of operation; availability of transportation; fees; conditions accepted, such as memory impairment, limited mobility, or incontinence; staff credentials and training; staffing ratios; health services and activities provided; and menus.

A visit to the adult day center is one of the most reliable means to judge a program's level of quality. According to the NADSA, the following questions are important: Do visitors feel welcome at the center? Do staff members spend time finding out what a prospective participant wants and needs? Do staff members clearly explain the center's activities and services? Do staff members give information about staffing ratios and qualifications, program procedures, costs, and caregiver expectations? Is the center clean, pleasant, and odor-free? Is the center wheelchair accessible? Is the furniture sturdy, clean, and comfortable? Do staff, volunteers, and participants appear cheerful? Are participants encouraged to help plan activities or make suggestions for program improvement? Current and past caregivers and participants may provide valuable information regarding a center's level of quality.

Adult day centers are an integral part of the long-term care continuum. Caregivers and participants benefit from the health and social services that are provided in a group setting for costs that are significantly lower than those typical in nursing home and home health care. And perhaps most important to caregivers and participants, adult day participants are able to continue living in the community while delaying or preventing inappropriate institutionalization.

DAYNA MCCRARY

See also DAY HOSPITALS; HOME CARE AND HOME SERVICES; LONG-TERM CARE; SOCIAL SERVICES.

BIBLIOGRAPHY

NATIONAL ADULT DAY SERVICES ASSOCIATION. *Your Guide to Selecting an Adult Day Services Center.* Washington, D.C.: NADSA, 1995.
NATIONAL ADULT DAY SERVICES ASSOCIATION. *Standards and Guidelines for Adult Day Services.* Washington, D.C.: NADSA, 1997.

ADULT PROTECTIVE SERVICES

Adult protective services represents the constellation of interventions used to promote safety and well-being for older persons (or other vulnerable adults) whose health or circumstances subject them to harm or threat of harm. Protective services have evolved since their origins, with current focus on elder abuse broadly defined. Most of the work, however, is directed at the needs of older persons suffering from self-neglect or neglect by a caregiver.

All states have laws mandating the protection of vulnerable older persons. Law implementation is handled by public departments of social services or state units on aging. These agencies function in four major ways to provide adult protective services: (1) receive and investigate reports or referrals; (2) assess client status and service needs; (3) arrange and coordinate or offer services to prevent or treat harm; and (4) seek legal intervention in the form of surrogate decision-making authority for the incapacitated older person or criminal penalty for the abuser, if indicated.

History

The evolution of adult protective services is both long and complicated. The original protection of adults was narrowly confined to legal intervention. It grew out of concern for the property of mentally incapacitated persons.

Adult protection began with the Law of Twelve Tables, established nearly twenty-five hundred years ago in Rome under the reign of Cicero. This law provided family surrogates with the right to manage the property of adults with severe mental illness. Fourteenth-century English common law gave the king responsibility for handling the property of those without the capacity to reason. Three hundred years later, colonial America adopted a policy of a protective nature.

Prior to the twentieth century the primary means of protecting older Americans was through institutional placement or guardianship appointment. Public benefits expanded in the 1950s enabling more older persons to reside in the community. As the numbers of older persons who lived outside of institutions grew, often without nearby family members, it became apparent that many were unable to provide for their own care or protection without assistance.

Discussions on the need for adult protective services began occurring nationally among such organizations as the Social Security Administration, Veterans Administration, and American Public Welfare Association. Emerging from these discussions were two important forums: the 1960 Arden House Conference on Aging and the 1963 National Council on the Aging's National Seminar on Protective Services for Older People. The latter led to the first definitive book on the subject, *Guardianship and Protective Services for Older People* by Gertrude Hall and Geneva Mathiasen.

The conferences served to define protective services and stimulate communities to develop related programs. In addition, during the late 1960s, seven research and demonstration projects in adult protective services were conducted in such places as Cleveland, Chicago, and San Diego. Their results suggested: (1) protective clients are those adults with reduced mental or physical capabilities who could not protect themselves or their interests; (2) between 7 and 20 percent of older persons are in need of protective services; (3) the concept of protective services must include access to a wide range of services and potential use of legal authority; and (4) protective services should be provided through a single auspice with a generous and flexible budget as well as the availability of multiple professional disciplines, with social work assuming the leadership role in case consultation.

Evaluation of the demonstration projects made adult protective services a subject of national concern. The findings suggested that few cases were closed because of successful intervention. Moreover, those findings from the Cleveland project at the Benjamin Rose Institute indicated that protective services increased the likelihood of institutionalization and the possible risk of death.

Nevertheless, the conferences and demonstration projects provided a momentum for adult protective services expansion during the early 1970s. This momentum was fueled by passage of Title XX of the Social Security Act in 1974, which provided funding for states to create and enlarge adult protective services as one of only two universal public welfare programs.

The discontent arising out of the demonstration projects grew stronger during the mid-to-late 1970s as a result of three factors: (1) the civil rights movement's concern that protective services abridged individual liberties; (2) the voices of various scholars, including law professor John Regan, on ethical dilemmas associated with protective intervention; and (3) the preference of social workers in public agencies to work with children rather than adults.

It may seem curious that adult protective services spread in light of negative program evaluation results and ethical concerns arising from the demonstration projects. There are at least two likely explanations for this. First, the spread of adult protective services occurred within the public sector while many of the demonstration projects took place within the voluntary sector. Because of differences between the two sectors, it was possible to infer that negative evaluation findings from one did not necessarily reflect upon the other. Second, a few states, such as Wisconsin and the Carolinas, were early leaders in adult protective services. They either obtained federal demonstration project grants or secured local public funding to run their own adult protective services programs. As a result, they helped to interest other states in adult protective services. However, most other states developed "protective services to qualify for Federal funds under title XX" (U.S. Senate Special Committee on Aging, pp. 10–11).

There were few publications on adult protective services during the late 1970s. John Regan and Georgia Singer presented Congress with a working paper on the topic, which included proposed model legislation. By 1980, twenty-five states had adopted some type of adult protective services law. Moreover, about as many had legislation pending or in draft.

It was at this time that the evolution of adult protective services detoured slightly, embracing elder abuse as the focus for intervention. The effect of the departure reestablished direction and offered legitimacy to protective services once again.

Characteristics on the part of adult protective services made elder abuse an easy problem area to embrace. First, the history of protective intervention always included concern for abuse, neglect, and exploitation. In addition, protective services has shown an ability to expand its targeted population when called upon to do so. Finally, the legal authority interest of protective services is mirrored in the potential needs of abused elders.

Elder abuse emerged as a subject of scholarly concern in the late 1970s and as a publicly recognized problem affecting older Americans during the 1980s. Although it has no universally accepted definition, generally elder abuse is regarded as a broad concept that has three basic categories: domestic elder abuse, institutional elder abuse, and self-neglect or self-abuse. Domestic elder abuse is inflicted by someone who has a special relationship with the older person, such as a family member. Institutional elder abuse occurs in residential facilities, like nursing homes. The various forms of elder abuse include physical abuse, sexual abuse, emotional abuse, neglect, and financial exploitation.

Current status

Adult protective services begins the new millennium reflecting both its historic base and recent influences. Without a federally enforced model, states developed their own laws, regulations, and service delivery systems. As a result, protective services vary across the country. This diversity is particularly evident in problem definition, program scope, services provided, state funding appropriated, and staff credentials. Nonetheless, nationwide adult protective services show notable consistency in their general approach and philosophical underpinnings.

Typically adult protective services are provided by public service agencies. Occasionally the responsibility is shared with private nonprofit organizations as well, usually through contract or formal agreement. Social work remains the dominant discipline involved in protective services. However, interdisciplinary and interagency coordination is routine, especially with health care, law enforcement, and since the early 1990s, domestic violence programming. Seventy percent of adult protective services laws give a single agency authority for investigating abuse and neglect reports of victims in both domestic and institutional settings. Sometimes the investigation is done in cooperation with long-term care ombudsman or other public agencies.

Ninety percent of states provide protective services to adults under age sixty, but 70 percent of adult protective services cases involve older persons as victims. Although the definitions for problems targeted by protective services differ by state law, everywhere the intent is to address forms of elder abuse, with the following forms covered by 85 percent or more states: physical abuse, financial exploitation, physical neglect, sexual abuse, self-neglect, and emotional abuse. Nearly 60 percent of reports received by protective services involve self-neglect or neglect by a caregiver. Twenty-four percent concern abuse, and just 12 percent represent exploitation.

Funding for adult protective services comes from various sources, including the Social Services Block Grant (descendant of Title XX), Older Americans Act, and state and local revenues. States differ in the scope of protective services, but certain activities are standard, including: report receipt, investigation, and substantiation; risk assessment and client evaluation; care planning, case management, service monitoring, and client advocacy; referral or provision of emergency, supportive, rehabilitative, or preventative services; possible use of legal intervention; and removal of the victim or perpetrator from the home, if needed. In addition, all protective services agencies have staff and professional training, public awareness, and data collection functions.

The principles of adult protective services emphasize individual autonomy above all else. This means that when intervening with adults freedom is more important than safety. Autonomy is never compromised simply because older adults live under circumstances of risk or danger. Unless determined incompetent or incapacitated, or infringing on the rights of others, they are supported in their choice of lifestyle. This perspective is in fundamental contrast with protective services during the 1960s and early 1970s, which was more paternalistic in nature. Other important principles of adult protective services

include: self-determination, participation of the adult in decision making, use of least restrictive service alternatives, primacy of the adult in care planning, ensuring confidentiality, and avoidance of causing harm or placing blame.

Issues and trends

Adult protective services have a long history of controversy and periods of unpopularity with the public. This pattern is no less true in the twenty-first century. Moreover, its sources remain the same as those delineated by Mildred Barry in her remarks at the 1963 Arden House Seminar on Protective Services for Older People: "One of our major problems in this field of protective care has been that our goals have not been clear, nor generally acceptable; nor the problem clearly defined, nor its extent and complexity known; nor have there been norms or standards upon which to base program objectives" (Barry, 1963, p. 1).

At the start of the new millennium adult protective services still suffer from vagueness of problem definition as evident both in law and through research. There is no consensus on the meaning of elder abuse as the target for protective intervention. Consequently, state laws and research studies differ in the definitions they use, making generalizations across jurisdictions or study findings very difficult. Also, without national prevalence data, it remains impossible to know the scope of the problem it addresses. Although national forums, including workshops held by the National Institute on Aging and National Center on Elder Abuse, have prioritized initiatives in these areas, they have yet to occur. Moreover, public skepticism regarding protective services continues to rest on questions surrounding its effectiveness along with ethical dilemmas that accompany its implementation, such as the appropriateness of mandatory reporting or the use of costly interventions for older persons whose situations represent repeated abuse or neglect.

Evaluative research on adult protective services since the 1970s is rare. Reason for case closure remains the primary outcome measure, although some states are employing risk assessment instruments to standardize it. An analysis of Illinois protective services clients indicated significant movement to low-risk status at case closure for the majority of cases. Among high-risk clients, the reasons usually given for case closure were institutionalization, death, service refusal, or relocation to another community (not unlike findings from the Benjamin Rose Institute in the early 1970s). The Three Models Project on Elder Abuse evaluated various interventions and found public protective services the least effective, in part because they lacked the resources to go beyond simple report receipt and investigation. In fact, adult protective services in most states are inadequately funded, particularly due to cuts and shifting in federal Social Services Block Grant revenues beginning in the 1980s.

A growing older population and increasing reports of elder abuse in both domestic and institutional settings have led to adult protective services becoming an established part of public welfare systems nationwide in spite of the controversy and skepticism that continue to plague them. Since the late 1980s there also has been a growth in professionalism among protective services workers, largely because of training opportunities and credentialing in some locales. Furthermore, networking through such organizations as the National Association of Adult Protective Services Administrators has helped decrease the historic isolation of protective services workers, improve protective standards, and enhance the knowledge base of the field.

GEORGIA J. ANETZBERGER

See also AUTONOMY; ELDER ABUSE AND NEGLECT; GUARDIANSHIP; SOCIAL SERVICES.

BIBLIOGRAPHY

ANETZBERGER, G. J. "Protective Services and Long-Term Care." In *Matching People with Services in Long-Term Care.* Edited by Z. Harel and R. E. Dunkle. New York: Springer, 1995. Pages 261–281.

BARRY, M. C. "Responsibility of the Social Welfare Profession in Providing Guardianship and Protecting Services." Paper presented at the Arden House Seminar on Protective Services for Older People, Harriman, New York, 10–15 March 1963.

BERGERON, L. R. "Decision-Making and Adult Protective Services Workers: Identifying Critical Factors." *Journal of Elder Abuse & Neglect* 10, nos. 3/4 (1999): 87–113.

BLENKNER, M.; BLOOM, M.; WASSER, E.; and NIELSON, M. "Protective Services for Older People: Findings from the Benjamin Rose Institute Study." *Social Casework* 52, no. 8 (1971): 483–522.

BURR, J. J. *Protective Services for Adults: A Guide to Exemplary Practice in States Providing Protective Services to Adults in OHDS Programs.* Washington, D.C.: U.S. Department of Health and Human Services, Office of Human Development Services, 1982.

BYERS, B., and HENDRICKS, J. E., eds. *Adult Protective Services: Research and Practice.* Springfield, Ill.: Charles C. Thomas, 1993.

CALLENDER, W. D., JR. *Improving Protective Services for Older Americans: A National Guide Series.* Portland, Me.: University of Southern Maine, Center for Research and Advanced Study, 1982.

FERGUSON, E. J. *Protecting the Vulnerable Adult: A Perspective on Policy and Program Issues in Adult Protective Services.* Ann Arbor, Mich.: The University of Michigan–Wayne State University, The Institute of Gerontology, 1978.

GOODRICH, C. S. "Results of a National Survey of State Protective Services Programs: Assessing Risk and Defining Victim Outcomes." *Journal of Elder Abuse & Neglect* 9, no. 1 (1997): 69–86.

MIXSON, P. M. "An Adult Protective Services Perspective." *Journal of Elder Abuse & Neglect* 7, nos. 2/3 (1995): 69–87.

OTTO, J. M. "The Role of Adult Protective Services in Addressing Abuse." *Generations* 24, no. 11 (2000): 33–38.

REYNOLDS, S. L. "Shedding New Light on Old Dilemmas: A Critical Approach to Protective Interventions." *Journal of Ethics, Law, and Aging* 1, no. 2 (1995): 107–119.

TATARA, T. *An Analysis of State Laws Addressing Elder Abuse, Neglect, and Exploitation.* Washington, D.C.: National Center on Elder Abuse, 1995.

TATARA, T. *Elder Abuse: Questions and Answers,* 6th ed. Washington, D.C.: National Center on Elder Abuse, 1996.

U.S. Senate Special Committee on Aging. *Protective Services for the Elderly: A Working Paper.* Washington, D.C.: U.S. Government Printing Office, 1977.

WOLF, R. S. "Major Findings from Three Model Projects on Elderly Abuse." In *Elder Abuse: Conflict in the Family.* Edited by K. A. Pillemer and R. S. Wolf. Dover, Mass.: Auburn House, 1986. Pages 218–238.

ZBOROWSKY, E. "Developments in Protective Services: A Challenge for Social Workers." *Journal of Gerontological Social Work* 8, nos. 3/4 (1985): 71–83.

ADVANCE DIRECTIVES FOR HEALTH CARE

Since the mid-1970s, much attention has been focused on the topic of advance or prospective health care planning. This activity has been promoted as a way for individuals to maintain some control over their future medical treatment even if they become physically and/or mentally unable to make and convey important decisions regarding issues of care. Advocates of advance health care planning also claim that it may help older persons and their families avoid court involvement in medical treatment decisions, conserve limited financial resources in a way that is consistent with patient autonomy or self-determination, and reduce the emotional or psychological burdens on families and friends in difficult crisis situations.

There are two main legal mechanisms available for use in prospective (i.e., before-the-fact) health care planning. One is the proxy directive, ordinarily in the form of a *durable power of attorney* (DPOA). This legal instrument names a proxy or agent who is authorized to make future medical decisions on behalf of the individual delegating the authority (namely, the principal or maker) in the event that the principal/maker later is unable to make decisions personally. The second legal device presently available for advance health care planning is the instruction directive, usually referred to as a *living will*, health care declaration, or natural death declaration.

In the United States, these legal mechanisms have their basis in various statutes enacted by state legislatures. In some other countries (e.g., England), advance directives have been recognized by the courts even though they have not been codified in the form of statutes.

Proxy directives

The standard power of attorney (POA) is a written agreement authorizing a person (named an agent or attorney-in-fact) to sign documents and conduct transactions on behalf of the principal or maker who has delegated away that authority. The principal can delegate as much (e.g., a general delegation) or as little (e.g., specifically delineating what types of choices the agent may and may not make) power as desired. The principal may end or revoke the arrangement at any time, as long as the principal remains mentally competent to do so.

The POA in its traditional form does not work well as a method for dealing with medical decision-making authority for older persons on a voluntary, prospective basis. The ordinary POA ends automatically when the principal who created it dies or becomes mentally incompetent. The theory underlying this is that, because a deceased or incompetent person no longer has the ability to revoke the POA, the law should exercise that right immediately for the principal. Thus, an older person who establishes a standard POA to help in managing medical affairs would be cut off from such assistance at exactly the time when assistance is needed the most.

In an effort to get around this problem, every state legislature has enacted legislation authorizing citizens to create (or execute) a durable power of attorney (DPOA). In contrast to the ordinary POA, the effect of a DPOA may endure or continue beyond the principal's later incapacity as long as that is what the principal intended in executing the DPOA.

To remove any ambiguity about the applicability of the DPOA concept to the area of medical decision making (including choices about life-sustaining medical treatments such as mechanical ventilators, dialysis, antibiotics, and cardiopulmonary resuscitation), almost every state has passed legislation that explicitly authorizes the use of the DPOA in the medical context. Some statutes use terminology such as *health care representative, health care agent,* or *health care proxy.* In addition, a number of states use a comprehensive advance directive statute to expressly authorize competent adults to execute both proxy and instruction directives; other states have separate statutes for each type of advance directive. Under most state laws, the health care providers for the principal who has executed a DPOA are disqualified from serving as agents under the DPOA. That statutory disqualification is intended to help avoid even the appearance, let alone the reality, of a conflict of interest when decisions have to be made about medical treatment for an incompetent patient.

Proxy directives provide the advantage, for both patients and their health care providers, of legally empowering a living, breathing advocate for the patient who can engage in discussions and decisions regarding medical treatment based on the most current information and other considerations. The proxy directive is irrelevant, however, for older adults who do not have available someone else whom they can trust to make future medical decisions for them.

Instruction directives

All but a few states have enacted legislation regarding instruction directives. Such statutes are often termed *natural death legislation*. Specific provisions vary from state to state. However, the common theme of natural death legislation is support of a patient's right, while the patient is still competent, to sign a written directive concerning the patient's wishes about the use of life-saving or life-sustaining medical treatments in the event of later serious illness and an incapacity to make decisions. Such a directive, often called a living will, protects or *immunizes* involved health care professionals and treatment facilities against possible civil or criminal liability for withholding or withdrawing medical treatments under the conditions specified in the directives.

Ordinarily, the principal is presumed to have the mental capacity to execute a health care directive and to revoke it, absent substantial evidence to the contrary. Just as is true for the DPOA, the legal force of an instruction directive goes into effect only when the patient, after signing the document, later becomes incapable of making medical decisions. In most cases, it is left to the individual's personal physician to determine when that person has become incapable of making decisions and, therefore, when the advance directive becomes effective.

Most advance directive statutes and forms use the approach of either check-off options for particular forms of treatment (e.g., "I do/do not want to be given antibiotics if I have a life-threatening infection") or extremely general standardized language to express preferences regarding particular forms of medical treatment (e.g., "If I am terminally ill, do not use any extraordinary or heroic medical measures to keep me alive."). However, a few states have taken the legislative approach of providing a more open-ended format for giving health care instructions. This creates an opportunity for individuals to write directives that express their values, beliefs, and preferences in their own words by responding to questions such as, "What would be your most important goal if you were critically ill, to stay alive as long as possible or to be made as comfortable and pain-free as possible?"

Restrictive advance directive statutes

In their advance directive statutes, many state legislatures have attempted to draw distinctions between artificial sustenance (i.e., feeding and hydration tubes inserted either surgically in the patient's stomach or manually through the patient's nose and throat), on the one hand, and other forms of life-sustaining medical treatment (e.g., ventilators, antibiotics) on the other. Specifically, many statutes try to make it more difficult procedurally for families or other proxy decision makers for incompetent patients to refuse or withdraw feeding and hydration tubes than to refuse or withdraw other forms of life-sustaining medical treatment. Advocates for these legal provisions sincerely believe they are necessary to protect especially vulnerable patients from unfair undertreatment; nonetheless, advance directive statutes that discriminate on the basis of the type of medical treatment being refused by the patient or surrogate are probably unconstitutional.

The courts and legislatures have consistently made it clear that state advance directive statutes are not intended to be the only means by which patients may exercise their right to make future decisions about medical treatment. For example, a patient might express wishes regarding future medical treatment orally to the physician during a medical appointment, with the physician recording the patient's words in the medical chart. When that patient later becomes incapable of making medical decisions, the patient's oral instructions are just as valid legally as would be a written document executed in compliance with all the statutory formalities found in the state's advance directive statute.

Enforcing advance directives

Presumably, most patients who express their wishes regarding future medical treatment by executing advance directives do so because they want and expect those wishes to be respected and followed. There is a substantial body of data, though, indicating that very often the stated wishes of patients regarding life-sustaining medical treatment are not respected and implemented. In actuality, critically ill patients frequently receive more aggressive medical treatment than they previously had said they would want.

State advance directive statutes all excuse a health care provider who chooses, for reasons of personal conscience, not to implement a patient's (or proxy's) expressly stated preferences regarding life-sustaining medical treatment, as long as that provider does not interfere with the patient being transferred to a different provider if that is what the patient or proxy wish. In the same vein, courts have refused to hold health care providers legally liable for failing to follow a patient's or proxy's instructions to withdraw or withhold particular forms of treatment, on the grounds that providing life-prolonging intervention can never cause the kind of injury or harm for which the legal system is designed to provide financial compensation.

Institutional policies and procedures

Congress enacted the Patient Self-Determination Act (PSDA) in 1990, codified at 42 United States Code §§ 1395cc(a)(1) and 1396a(a). This federal law applies to all hospitals, nursing homes, hospices, home health agencies, health maintenance organizations (HMOs), and preferred provider organizations (PPOs) that participate in the Medicare and Medicaid programs. Among other things, the PSDA requires each covered health care provider to adopt a formal policy, consistent with relevant state law, regarding how it will handle advance directives. The provider must make a copy of its policy available to each new patient at or before the time of admission or enrollment. In addition, the PSDA requires the health care provider to ask at admission or enrollment whether the patient has executed an advance directive. If the answer is no, the provider must offer the patient the chance to execute an advance directive then (if the patient is still mentally capable of doing so).

Do not orders

Many acute and long-term care providers have developed and implemented written protocols regarding physician orders to withhold particular kinds of medical treatments under specified circumstances taking place at some time in the future. Such orders are a variety of advance directive, and ordinarily are written by the physician with the agreement of the competent patient or the incompetent patient's proxy. Much attention has focused on Do Not Resuscitate (DNR) orders to withhold cardiopulmonary resuscitation (CPR) in the event of a patient's cardiac or respiratory arrest. Other forms of prospective physician instructions to withhold or limit life-sustaining medical treatments, such as Do Not Hospitalize or Do Not Intubate orders, also may be entered in the patient's medical record. The PSDA requires covered health care providers to adopt DNR policies.

In many places, policies and procedures for withholding potential life-sustaining medical treatments, such as CPR, from dying home-care patients have also been developed. Over half the states have passed statutes that explicitly authorize DNR, or No Code, orders to be applied in situations of cardiac or respiratory arrest taking place outside of a health care institution. Such orders, written in advance by the physician in consultation with the patient or proxy, would allow emergency medical personnel who are called to a dying patient's home to refrain from making an attempt to resuscitate the patient.

MARSHALL B. KAPP

See also AUTONOMY; COMPETENCY; GERIATRIC MEDICINE; REFUSING AND WITHDRAWING MEDICAL TREATMENTS.

BIBLIOGRAPHY

American Medical Association Council on Ethical and Judicial Affairs. "Optimal Use of Orders Not to Intervene and Advance Directives." *Psychology, Public Policy, and Law* 4 (1998): 668–675.

CANTOR, N. L. "Making Advance Directives Meaningful." *Psychology, Public Policy, and Law* 4 (1998): 629–652.

KING, N. M. P. *Making Sense of Advance Directives*, rev. ed. Washington, D.C.: Georgetown University Press, 1996.

LIANG, B. A. *Health Law & Policy*. Boston: Butterworth-Heinemann, 2000.

LYNN, J., and HARROLD, J. *Handbook for Mortals: Guidance for People Facing Serious Illness*. New York: Oxford University Press, 1999.

MEISEL, A. *The Right to Die*. 2d ed. New York: Wiley Law Publications, 1995.

RICH, B. A. "Personhood, Patienthood, and Clinical Practice: Reassessing Advance Directives." *Psychology, Public Policy, and Law* 4 (1998): 610–628.

ULRICH, L. P. *The Patient Self-Determination Act: Meeting the Challenges in Patient Care*. Washington, D.C.: Georgetown University Press, 1999.

INTERNET RESOURCES

Partnership for Caring. www.partnershipforcaring.org A national organization dedicated to public education and advocacy regarding the quality of care provided to individuals who are approaching the end of life.

AGE

It is difficult to imagine a world without age. Children would not grow up and then grow old. Humans would not have lives. Age is so central to the experience of living, that we have little reason to question the phenomenon. In the scientific study of aging, we scrutinize the ways we conceptualize the targets of our investigations (Schroots and Birren). In the English language age has two meanings. The first connotes time. Simply put, this is the time a person has existed since birth. The second meaning refers to specific stages of life, especially adulthood and old age. This will (1) examine the temporal meanings of age; (2) consider how age organizes human lives; and (3) reflect on age as a variable.

Age as time

Age—as an indication of the passage of time and the length of time something has been in existence or has endured—appears to be culturally neutral. Time is a physical aspect of our universe. Time and light are properties of our habitats. Humans use culture to interpret what happens in time. Although this is true, time is not culturally neutral. Time is a subject of cultural interpretation.

If time is relative and cultural, then how do we comprehend it? For time to be measured and understood, we need to recognize three issues. First, no human or any other organism has a specialized sense to measure time. Time is not directly perceptible by the senses through which we perceive the world. Secondly, because we cannot directly sense time, we must recognize time passage indirectly through events that happen in the world we can experience. Finally, continuities and discontinuities in these events enable us to recognize time. Continuity provides the experience of duration. Discontinuity interrupts stretches of stability with change and periodicity. Without continuity and discontinuities, time would be impossible to tell.

Time is calibrated through experiences of continuity and discontinuities. Age is the ordering and measuring of the time of life. Chronological age is the most common way of conceptualizing age. The ability to record and document a date of birth and then to ascertain the temporal duration from a present date is not all that obvious. Chronological age is a cultural invention. Only in the last half of the twentieth century did chronological age come to be used on a global basis. Yet, even in the twenty-first century there are still people who do not know their age. This ability to know one's age is the result of an incredible multicultural effort to measure time. The crown jewel of this effort is the Gregorian calendar (Duncan).

The Gregorian calendar is a device that measures and objectifies time. The invention of chronological age rests on three elements anchored in the Gregorian calendar. First, time is seen as extra-societal. Second, the sequence of days is not in the hands of religious specialists or rulers. Third, the time line is anchored in a specific temporal point. Although maintained and nurtured by the church throughout the Middle Ages, increased secularization stripped the calendar of its sacred significance. Priests and kings no longer manage calendrics. Days, months, and years are no longer a temporal march of saints' days. The workings of the year are understood by nearly everyone and are accessible to most with published calendars. The Gregorian calendar also employs the remarkable invention of a fixed point to begin the numbering of years. In the sixth century a little known monk, Dionysis Exiguus (Little Dennis), modified the Christian calendar to begin with the birth of Christ. Previously, the yearly count began with the installation of the current ruler. For instance, the year 2001 in the Gregorian count would be the first year of the rule of President George W. Bush in the United States and the forty-second year of the rule of Queen Elizabeth II in the United Kingdom. With the fixed point of a year one (zero had not been invented in the sixth century) the Christian world counts forward the years classed as A.D. (*anno Domini*, in the year of the Lord) and backward the years labeled as B.C. (before Christ).

With this long time line, which is extrasocietal but not extracultural, the calculation of chronological age is quite simple. All that is needed is knowledge of the present year number and subtraction of the birth year number. However, knowledge of one's birth year also requires considerable cultural data. Without written records, the past becomes imprecise and blurred. Certainly, in Europe, the earliest records were church recordings of baptisms, weddings, and deaths. Later, primarily in the nineteenth century, vital statistics (birth and death certificates along with marriage licenses) were routinely gathered, along with national census data. For these societies, chronological age had become one of the important items of information a state needed about its population. Likewise, individuals needed to know their age because age defined the rights of citizenship (working, voting, marriage, and entitlement to pensions and social security).

From the perspective of the twenty-first century, it is difficult to imagine a world without years and without chronological age. Yet humans survived for millennia without precision in temporal measurement. Calendars and chronological age are inventions of large-scale societies that appeared as early as five thousand years ago. Small-scale societies are not bureaucratically organized and work instead within a domestic framework. In these simpler societies, individuals have extensive personal knowledge about nearly everyone with whom they interact.

Age as a chronological number is irrelevant in small-scale societies. Instead age is a combination of biological and social maturity plus seniority. Kinship is the language of age with generational differences demarcating any division or age class. Generations are notably imprecise as indicators of time. With long periods of reproduction, children can be born more than twenty chronological years apart. Sometimes uncles can be chronologically younger than their generationally junior nieces and nephews. Generations simply define a line of descent with birth orders indicating relative age (senior and junior).

Age as numbered years is an index. Although useful for some purposes, indexes can be limited in meaning, that is, in years lived. Consequently, age also refers to stages of life. When one "comes of age," one enters adulthood, a life stage of full legal rights. Most commonly age refers to the last part of a normal life, or "old age."

Age organization and life courses

Aging embraces far more than old age. Aging is the entirety of life from conception to death. Lives as lived are also far more than a cycle of days, months, and an accumulation of years. Age as a measurement of time is only a chronometer measuring temporal duration similar to the way an odometer gauges distance traveled. When we examine lives through time, it becomes apparent that lots of things are happening in the same temporal interval. The life course is a perspective that takes as its unit human lives to comprehend situational complexity and what meanings and expectations societies have about the course of life.

Age organization has been a challenge to researchers, especially when they encountered societies where chronological age was not in use, but where age is important in social life. To clarify potential confusion a distinction between "age grades" and "age sets" was coined (Radcliffe-Brown). Age grades are divisions of life from infancy to old age. An age grade is a category of people in the same part of the life course. Age sets or age classes are not to be confused with age grades. Age classes are corporate, bounded groups of individuals, almost always men, who are of the same age grade. Once initiated, a man will pass through adulthood in an explicitly age-stratified system. When his age class makes its transition to the next life stage, he will advance with his peers. All societies have a classification of age grades, only a few have age classes. Age grading categorizes individuals by similarity of age-linked criteria and in so doing the life course is partitioned into stages defined by age norms. How this is done and for what purposes results in different life courses.

Comparative research indicates that there are at least three kinds of life courses (Fry). These are (1) staged life courses, (2) generational life courses, and (3) age-classed life courses. These differ by the way age is measured and used (chronological or generational), and by the type of society (large scale and industrialized or a small-scale, domestic organization).

1. *Staged life courses*. The staged life course is the accepted definition of a life course and is usually referred to as the institutionalized life courses. It assumes that age grades are life stages with which people plan their lives. The "age" in the age norms defining the stages are anchored in a social clock calibrated by chronological age. The institutions, legal norms, and state enforcement delimit these norms. Age grades divide this life course into three distinct segments: childhood/adolescence, adulthood, and old age. Life plans in this life course are ones of preparing and then launching oneself into adulthood. Adult status is a long period of

working, nurturing children, and launching them, in turn, into their adulthood. Old age is a period of withdrawal from the world of work and of benefiting from state-supported entitlement and the accumulation of one's prior resources (financial and otherwise).

2. *Generational life courses.* A generational life course is not as widely recognized, simply because a life course in small-scale societies has not received as much attention. A notable exception is the study of kinship. Generational life courses are defined in the web and language of kinship. Here, the social clock is calibrated by physical abilities that come with maturation (not chronology). Age grades are not sharply defined as we have seen generational calibration usually result in ambiguity of boundaries. A life plan in this life course is to mature into adulthood, have a family, work in subsistence, and live.

3. *Age-classed life courses.* As we noted above, life courses based on age classes attracted the attention of comparative researchers. Ethnographically, these have been well documented (Bernardi), but are not recognized as a decidedly different life course. For the few societies where age is formalized into classes, it is very difficult to argue that it is age per se that defines the classes. Again it is kinship. Age-classed life courses are a variant of generational life courses. In spite of variability, a minimal rule governing class membership is that father and son must belong to a different class. Hence, the generational calibration determines membership. Unlike informal age grades, age classes have sharp boundaries through the recruitment of membership and the closed corporate structure of the class. A life plan in one of these life courses (for example among the Massai) is for a male to enjoy the initial sets by fighting and attracting the attention of women; then to settle into being a householder, herding cattle and raising a family; then to ascent into eldership, and influence. Then one moves closer to and finally joins one's ancestors in death.

Although it is always possible to divide life into stages, it is unclear if people actually do and to what extent this impacts their lives. Of the three kinds of life courses, it is only the age-classed life courses that have explicit stages. We have little knowledge of those based on generational differences. The tripartite division of staged life courses is an artifact of assumptions that the state and social policy make about what citizens should be doing. Laws that use age as a criterion to define adulthood are norms that deny privileges to adolescents. Most obvious are those regulating work, marriage, driving, voting, and the consumption of alcohol. Adolescents should be completing their education. At the threshold to old age are laws defining entitlements that encourage exits from the labor force. Beyond these three divisions, people can and do make further refinements. For adulthood and old age, these range from two to eleven divisions with most ranging between three and five divisions in the nations studied, United States, Ireland, Hong Kong, and Botswana (Keith et al.). These are informal, variable, and are not institutionalized.

Age as a variable

Although age is central for research on aging and old age, researchers are ambivalent about chronological age as a variable. The simplicity of age as measured in years is very attractive. Because nearly all participants in such research know their birth years, it is subject to comparatively few measurement errors. At the same time, we may not know what the number of years lived really means. Age has been challenged as an "empty" variable because it is one-dimensional, a number indicative of duration, and has little relationship with events in a social world. Additionally, objections are raised against chronological age because of the way it is used in industrialized societies to regiment life and to unevenly distribute resources and privileges by age. This especially applies to education, work, and leisure. Education is for youth, work is a responsibility of adults, and leisure is a reward for older people.

Age will be an empty variable unless we acknowledge the cultural basis and reasons for knowing about it and use this knowledge to construct theories of aging. Numbers make for robust variables because numbers are relational (Crump). In addition to being numeric, chronological age is also linguistic. What is encoded in language is meaning. Age has the double meaning of disability and time. It is the temporal meaning of age that has the greatest potential as a variable. The continuities and discontinuities constituting time are nearly infinite. For human lives, the sidereal time calibrating chronological age is uninteresting. However, why humans use it and what meanings are assigned to years lived is interesting. Also, the multitude of events that happen to and within humans simultaneously in this time is precisely what we want to know about human aging. We identify these phenomena as different kinds of time. Organisms and genetic codes have biological clocks. Psyches have developmental schedules, especially in childhood. Societies have social clocks. The latter are rooted in the institutional structure of the social world in which people live. Life courses are made up of the intersections of the diverse parts of a social clock. Family cycles, work schedules, career trajectories, education, leisure, and even health all are calibrated by temporal norms. Norms are not just rules individuals follow. Norms are used to negotiate a complex world and other humans. Norms are knowledge of what should happen and as such are a form of currency used to understand, transact, and change the circumstances that comprise experience. It is the plurality of norms, of historical circumstances, of cultural context, that makes age such a powerful variable. With an expanded view of age and the cultural meanings of time, we create a full as compared to an empty variable.

CHRISTINE L. FRY

See also: AGE NORMS; AGING; AGE-PERIOD-COHORT MODEL; COHORT CHANGE; GERONTOCRACY; LIFE COURSE; STATUS OF OLDER PEOPLE: ANCIENT AND BIBLICAL WORLD.

BIBLIOGRAPHY

BERNARDI, B. *Age Class Systems: Social Institutions and Polities Based on Age.* Translated by David I. Kertzer. Cambridge, U.K.: Cambridge University Press, 1985.
CRUMP, T. "The Experience of Time." In *The Anthropology of Numbers.* Cambridge, U.K.: Cambridge University Press, 1990. Pages 81–91.
DUNCAN, D. E. *Calendar: Humanity's Epic Struggle to Determine a True and Accurate Year.* New York: Avon, 1998.
FRY, C. L. "Anthropological Theories of Age and Aging." In *Handbook of Theories of Aging.* Edited by V. L. Bengtson and K. W. Schaie. New York: Springer Publishing Company, 1999. Pages 271–286.
KEITH, J.; FRY, C. L.; GLASCOCK, A. P.; IKELS, C.; DICKERSON-PUTMAN, J.; DRAPER, P.; and HARPENDING, H. *The Aging Experience: Diversity and Commonality Across Cultures.* Thousand Oaks, Calif.: Sage, 1994.
RADCLIFFE-BROWN, A. R. "Age Organization Terminology." *Man* 21 (1929).
SCHROOTS, J., and BIRREN, J. E. "Concepts of Time and Aging in Science." In *Handbook of the Psychology of Aging.* Edited by J. E. Birren and K. W. Schaie. San Diego, Calif.: Academic Press, 1990. Pages 41–64.

AGE-BASED RATIONING OF HEALTH CARE

The idea of old-age–based rationing of health care in the United States began to emerge publicly in the 1980s and has been hotly debated ever since. In a 1983 speech to the Health Insurance Association of America, the economist Alan Greenspan pointedly wondered "whether it is worth it" to spend nearly one-third of Medicare, a federal program that provides national health insurance for virtually all people age sixty-five and older, on just 5 to 6 percent of Medicare insurees who die within the year (Schulte). In 1984 Richard Lamm, then governor of Colorado, was widely quoted as stating that older persons "have a duty to die and get out of the way" (Slater). Although Lamm subsequently said that he had been misquoted on this specific statement, he has continued to promulgate his view in a somewhat more delicate fashion to this day.

In the years following, discussion of this issue spread to a number of forums. Ethicists and philosophers began generating principles of equity to govern "justice between age groups" in the provision of health care, rather than, for instance, justice between rich and poor, or justice among ethnic and racial groups (e.g., Daniels; Menzel). Conferences and books explicitly addressed the subject with titles such as *Should Medical Care Be Rationed by Age?* (Smeeding).

The most prominent exponent of old-age–based rationing has been the biomedical ethicist Daniel Callahan, whose 1987 book *Setting Limits: Medical Goals in an Aging Society* received substantial popular attention. He depicted the elderly population as "a new social threat" and a "demographic, economic, and medical avalanche . . . one that could ultimately (and perhaps already) do [*sic*] great harm" (Callahan, 1987, p. 20). Callahan's remedy for this threat was to use "age as a specific criterion for the allocation and limitation of health care" by denying life-extending health care—as a matter of public policy—to persons who are aged in their "late 70s or early 80s"

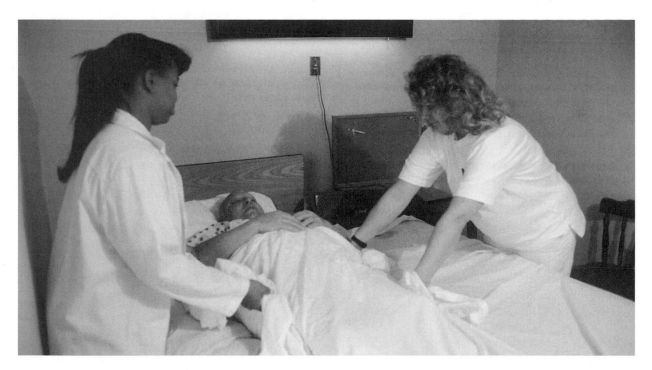

Nurses at a health care facility change the sheets, working around the elderly patient so that he does not have to get out of bed. (Photo Researchers, Inc.)

and/or have "lived out a natural life span" (p. 171). Specifically, he proposed that the Medicare program not pay for such care. Although Callahan described "the natural life span" as a matter of biography rather than biology, he used chronological age as an arbitrary marker to designate when, from a biographical standpoint, the individual should have reached the end of a natural life.

Setting Limits provoked widespread and continuing discussion in the media and directly inspired a number of books (e.g., Barry and Bradley; Binstock and Post; Homer and Holstein) and scores of articles published in academic journals and magazines. Many of these books and articles strongly criticized the idea of old-age–based rationing. Nonetheless, the notion of limiting the health care of older people through rationing is still frequently discussed. Callahan continues to publish his view in both academic journals and more popular forums (e.g., Callahan, 1994, 2000).

The most important feature of this debate, from a societal point of view, is that it has introduced the idea that the power of government might be used to limit the health care of older persons through explicit public policy. Many ob-

servers of medical care in the United States have long acknowledged that physicians have informally rationed the health care of older persons through day-to-day, case-by-case decisions in various types of circumstances. Moreover, informal old-age–based rationing has been extensive for many years in the publicly funded British National Health Service, which operates within a fixed budget provided by the government. British primary care physicians serve as "gatekeepers," determining whether their patients will be referred to specialists or will receive various medical procedures. It has been well documented that because of budgetary constraints, older persons are systematically excluded from certain types of referrals that are made for younger patients (see, e.g., Aaron and Schwartz). But these practices are not official policy.

Why ration?

Proponents of old-age–based rationing have set forth both economic and philosophical rationales for their views. Their economic argument is essentially that the costs of health care for older people will become an unsustainable economic burden for the United States during the next few decades because of population aging, thereby posing grave problems for the economy and making it very difficult for government to spend funds on other worthy social causes.

The number of older Americans will grow sharply during the first half of the twenty-first century as the baby boom—a cohort of seventy-six million persons born between 1946 and 1964—reaches old age. At the turn of the century, persons age sixty-five and older were about 13 percent of the U.S. population and accounted for one-third of the nation's public and private health care expenditures (about $400 billion out of a total $1.2 trillion in 2000). Per capita spending on persons in this age range is four times greater than on younger persons, largely because older people are far more likely to need health care than younger ones. The total number of older Americans, which was thirty-six million in 2000, will be seventy-six million by 2030 and will constitute 20 percent of the population. Consequently, the aggregate health care needs of the older population will be even greater in the future than they are now. For example, the proportion of national wealth (gross domestic product) spent on Medicare in 1998 was 2.5 percent; it is projected to more than double, to 5.3 percent, in 2025.

Moreover, the number of persons of advanced old age—in their late seventies and older—will increase markedly, and in this older age range the rates of illnesses and disabilities requiring health care are much higher than among the rest of the population. Even if important advances are made in treatments, illness prevention, and health promotion, they are unlikely to have a major impact in terms of eliminating the overall extent of illnesses and disabilities in advanced old age, and on the costs of caring for older persons in the next several decades. Indeed, the implementation of such advances will probably lead to more intensive use of medical care.

The philosophical arguments for old-age–based rationing are more varied than the economic arguments. The philosopher Norman Daniels (1988), for instance, poses an abstract problem of justice by depicting a society in which each individual has available a fixed sum of money for his or her lifelong health care. Without our knowing our particular individual positions in such a society, Daniels asks: How would we allocate, in advance, the availability of funds for care at various stages of life? His answer is that we would choose to make sure that we had enough for health care in our early and middle years, and allocate very little for our old age.

In contrast, Callahan propounds a communalist philosophy. He argues that it is inappropriate for older people to pursue their individualistic needs and aspirations. As he sees it, the meaning and significance of life for the elderly is best founded on a sense of limits to health care, and recognition that life cannot go on for long and death is on the way. This meaning of aging envisioned by Callahan requires older persons to adhere to a value of serving the young through politics, and more directly in one-on-one relationships. As he sees it, limiting lifesaving care for older persons would affirmatively promote the welfare of the elderly and of younger generations.

Critique of rationing proposals

The economic argument for old-age–based rationing has several major weaknesses. First, empirical evidence contradicts the assumption that population aging leads to unsustainable health care spending. Retrospective studies in the United States and elsewhere indicate that population aging, in itself, has contributed very little to increases in health care expenditures; among the major contributors have been new medical technologies and their intensive application. Moreover, cross-national studies (e.g., Binstock) provide no evidence that substantial and/or rapid population aging causes high levels of national economic burden from expenditures on health care. Health care costs are far from "out of control" or even "high" in nations that have comparatively large proportions of older persons or have experienced rapid rates of population aging. The public and private structural features of health care systems—and the behavioral responses to them by citizens and health care providers—are far more important determinants of a nation's health care expenditures than population aging.

Even if one were to accept the notion that greater and official health care rationing is essential for the future of the U.S. economy, it is not at all clear that old-age–based rationing of the kind that Callahan and others propose would yield sufficient savings to make a substantial difference in national health care expenditures. Although the proponents of rationing have not identified the magnitude of savings to be achieved through their schemes, it is possible to construct an example. Each year about 3.5 percent of Medicare is spent on high-cost, high-tech medical interventions for persons age sixty-five and older who die within the year. Suppose it were possible (although it rarely is) for physicians to know in advance that these high-cost efforts to save lives would be futile, and that it would be ethically and morally palatable for them to implement a policy that denied treatment to such patients, thereby eliminating "wasteful" health care. The dollars saved by rationing such care for persons age sixty-five and older (an age cutoff about fifteen years younger than proposed by Callahan) would be insignificant. In 1999, when Medicare expenditures were $217 billion, only $7.6 billion would have been saved through such a policy that, in any event, would be very difficult to implement practically, ethically, and morally. Viewed in isolation this is a substantial amount of money. But it would have only a negligible effect on the overall budgetary situation in the short or long run.

Economics aside, there are social and moral costs involved in policies that would ration health care on the basis of old age. One possible consequence of denying health care to aged persons is what it might do to the quality of life for all of us as we approach entry into the "too old for health care" category. Societal recognition of the notion that elderly people are unworthy of having their lives saved could markedly shape our general outlook on the meaning and value of our lives in old age. At the least it might engender the unnecessarily gloomy prospect that old age should be anticipated and experienced as a stage in which the quality of life is low. The specter of morbidity and decline could be pervasive and overwhelming.

Another cost lies in the potential contributions that will be lost to all of us. Many older persons who benefit from lifesaving interventions will live for a decade or more, and perhaps will make their greatest contributions to society, their communities, and their families and friends during this "extra" time. Human beings often are at their best as they face mortality, investing themselves in the completion of artistic, cultural, communal, familial, and personal expressions that will carry forward the meaning of their lives for generations to come. The great cultures of the world have viewed elderly persons as sources of wisdom, insight, and generativity (creativity; causing to be), as if in the process of bodily decline the exceptional qualities of the sage emerge. Generativity does not correlate with youth. Erik Erikson (1964) and others have argued that some forms of generativity may be more likely when one has completed a great measure of the developmental challenges that the life course presents.

Perhaps the foremost potential cost of any old-age–based rationing policy would be that it could start society down a moral "slippery slope." If elderly persons can be denied access to health care categorically, officially designated as unworthy of lifesaving care, then what group of us could not? Members of a particular race, religion, or ethnic group, or those who are disabled? Any of us is vulnerable to social constructions that portray us as unworthy. Rationing health care on the basis of old age could destroy the fragile moral barriers against placing any group of human beings in a category apart from humanity in general.

ROBERT H. BINSTOCK

See also ADVANCE DIRECTIVES FOR HEALTH CARE; AGE DISCRIMINATION; AGEISM; FUNCTIONAL ABILITY; INTERGENERATIONAL JUSTICE; STATUS OF OLDER PEOPLE; WISDOM.

BIBLIOGRAPHY

AARON, H. J., and SCHWARTZ, W. B. *The Painful Prescription: Rationing Hospital Care.* Washington, D.C.: Brookings Institution, 1984.

BARRY, R. L., and BRADLEY, G. V., eds. *Set No Limits: A Rebuttal to Daniel Callahan's Proposal to Limit Health Care for the Elderly.* Urbana: University of Illinois Press, 1991.

BINSTOCK, R. H. "Healthcare Costs Around the World: Is Aging a Fiscal 'Black Hole'?" *Generations* 27, no. 4 (1993): 37–42.

BINSTOCK, R. H., and POST, S. G., eds. *Too Old for Health Care: Controversies in Medicine, Law, Economics, and Ethics.* Baltimore: Johns Hopkins University Press, 1991.

CALLAHAN, D. *Setting Limits: Medical Goals in an Aging Society.* New York: Simon and Schuster, 1987.

CALLAHAN, D. "Setting Limits: A Response." *The Gerontologist* 34 (1994): 393–398.

CALLAHAN, D. "On Turning 70: Will I Practice What I Preach?" *Commonweal*, September 8, 2000, pp. 10–11.

DANIELS, N. *Am I My Parents' Keeper?* New York: Oxford University Press, 1988.

Former Woolworth employee Katherine Zajac, 84, appears at a news conference in New York on an age discrimination lawsuit filed by the U.S. Equal Employment Opportunity Commission against her former employer. The suit alleged that, during a two-year span, older employees were laid off and replaced by younger workers. (AP photo by Ed Bailey.)

Erikson, E. H. *Insight and Responsibility: Lectures on the Ethical Implications of Psychoanalytic Insight.* New York: Norton, 1964.

Homer, P., and Holstein, M., eds. *A Good Age: The Paradox of Setting Limits.* New York: Simon and Schuster, 1990.

Menzel, P. T. *Strong Medicine: The Ethical Rationing of Health Care.* New York: Oxford University Press, 1990.

Schulte, J. "Terminal Patients Deplete Medicare, Greenspan Says." *Dallas Morning News,* April 26, 1983, p. 1.

Slater, W. "Latest Lamm Remark Angers the Elderly." *Arizona Daily Star* (Tucson), March 29, 1984, p. 1.

Smeeding, T. M., ed. *Should Medical Care Be Rationed by Age?* Totowa, N.J.: Rowman & Littlefield, 1987.

AGE DISCRIMINATION

Age discrimination occurs when individuals are treated differently because of their chronological age. Children and youth are routinely treated differently than adults. They are required by law to attend school and denied the legal right to vote, drink alcohol, and work. This type of age discrimination is justified because of children's immaturity. Although people debate the chronological age that should be used to define adult status, few question the desirability of treating children differently than adults. Chronological age also is used to discriminate in favor of older people. Old age often entitles people to reduced taxes and discounts on drugs, admission fees, or bus and airline tickets. Medicare provides older people with national health insurance and Supplemental Social Security provides a guaranteed minimum income for older people. Discussions of age discrimination, however, seldom focus on the restrictions of children's rights or special privileges for older people. Rather, the primary concern of age discrimination involves situations where older people are treated in unfair and negative ways because of their advanced age. The following discussion focuses on the two most widely recognized areas of discrimination against the old—in employment and health care—but also addresses discrimination in driving laws and interpersonal interactions.

Employment and the ADEA

In 1967, three years after it enacted the Civil Rights Act prohibiting workplace discrimination on the basis of race, color, national origin, religion, or sex, the U.S. Congress passed the Age Discrimination in Employment Act (ADEA). This law and its amendments made it unlawful for employers of more than twenty workers to discriminate against a person past age forty because of his/her age. The ADEA of 1967 protected employees between ages forty and sixty-five against workplace discrimination in such areas as hiring, firing, promotion, layoff, compensation, benefits, job assignments, and training. The Department of Labor initially enforced the law, but in 1978 enforcement authority was transferred to the Equal Employment Opportunities Commission (EEOC), the agency responsible for overseeing other federal laws against discrimination in the workplace. The 1978 ADEA amendment prohibited mandatory retirement or other forms of age discrimination before age seventy (instead of sixty-five). The rather obvious illogic of allowing discrimination at chronological age seventy but not at sixty-nine was corrected in 1986 when ADEA was extended to cover all ages past forty.

Several occupation-specific exceptions to the ADEA protection are permitted, so that commercial airline pilots, air-traffic controllers, and public safety officers may be required to retire at set ages (fifty-five or sixty). Despite a court challenge by pilots, the Supreme Court in 1998 left intact the Federal Aviation Administration regulation requiring retirement at age sixty. In 1990, Congress again amended the ADEA with passage of The Older Workers Benefit Protection Act (OWBPA). This legislation addressed concerns that businesses were subtly practicing age discrimination by offering early retirement incentive programs (ERIPs) to entice older, high salary workers to leave voluntarily. The OWBPA set conditions that ERIPs must meet to avoid being challenged as age discriminatory and established minimum standards that employers must meet to request that employees voluntarily agree to waive their rights or claims under the ADEA.

The ADEA legislation responded to employers' rampant and blatant discrimination against older people. Before this legislation it was common for employers to include age restrictions in help wanted advertising (e.g., soliciting applicants under thirty-five) and to require workers to retire at a fixed chronological age (e.g., sixty-five). Passage of a law forbidding discrimination on the basis of age, however, has not eliminated age discrimination. To be sure, age discrimination now tends to be less overt than it was before the ADEA. Nevertheless, throughout the 1990s an average of more than fifteen thousand charges of age discrimination were filed annually with the EEOC. The actual number of instances of age discrimination, however, is estimated to be many times larger. Although employers routinely favor hiring younger applicants over older ones (past age forty), formal charges of this type of discrimination are uncommon. Furthermore, approximately 90 percent of all age discrimination charges are settled before official complaints are filed.

The starting point for an individual who believes that his or her employment rights have been violated is to file a charge of discrimination with the EEOC (or with a state fair employment practices agency if a state age discrimination law exists). Until a charge has been filed with the EEOC, a private lawsuit charging violation of rights granted by the ADEA cannot be filed in court. Once filed, the EEOC can handle age discrimination charges in a number of ways: it can provide mediation, seek to settle the charges if both parties agree, investigate a charge and dismiss it, or investigate and establish that discrimination did occur. When it establishes that discrimination occurred, the EEOC will attempt conciliation with the employer to remedy the situation. If unable to conciliate the case successfully, the EEOC has the option of bringing suit in federal court or of closing the case and giving the charging party the option of filing a lawsuit on his or her own behalf.

Because enforcement of the ADEA raises many complicated issues, a number of court decisions have tried to define its reach. A complete history of legal battles cannot be given here, but two Supreme Court rulings illustrate the types of issues that arise. First, the Supreme Court decision in January 2000 in *Kimel v. Florida Board of Regents* dealt with the constitutional issue of whether or not the federal legislation applied to state governments. Kimel had charged that Florida State University violated the ADEA by discriminating against older workers in making pay adjustments. The Supreme Court ruled that the ADEA did not apply to state government employees, so Kimel could not sue the state in federal court. A few months later, in June 2000, the Supreme Court decision in *Roger Reeves v. Sanderson Plumbing Products, Inc.* established that direct evidence of intention to discriminate was not required to convict an employer of age discrimination. The Court held that it is adequate to establish that the employer's stated reason for the action was untrue and that prima facie evidence, such as managers' ageist comments, suggest discrimination. The first ruling restricted the reach of the ADEA, but the second one made it easier for employees to win discrimination cases against their employers.

The occurrence of age discrimination in the workplace depends both on the demand for labor in the marketplace and employers' perceptions of older people's competence. A tight labor market, for example, discourages employers from practicing age discrimination. Several studies have examined management attitudes toward older workers. An AARP-funded survey interviewed senior human resource executives in four hundred companies in 1989, and Louis Harris and Associates interviewed over four hundred senior human resource managers in a 1992 survey. Both of these studies, as well as earlier ones, found that despite generally positive attitudes expressed toward older workers by the "gatekeepers" of employment, two areas of concern were widespread. First, there was a pervasive perception that older workers were more costly because of health care, pensions, and other fringe benefits. The perceived and real costs of providing benefits can serve as an economic incentive to discriminate against older workers. Second, there was a widespread perception of older workers as less flexible, less technically competent, and less suitable for training. Studies of older workers tend to refute the stereotypical view that they are less productive than younger workers. Although some physical and mental capacities decline with age (e.g., speed and reaction time), these changes tend to be small until advanced ages and may be compensated for by greater experience. At every age there is wide diversity of abilities and learning potential, so basing employment decisions on job-related criteria rather than arbitrary and misconceived notions about age is a fairer and more efficient use of people's skills.

Since the 1960s much effort has gone into protecting older workers' rights. Despite the failure of this legislation and litigation to end all unfair treatment of older people in the workplace, this issue has received far more attention in the United States than in Japan and most European countries where blatant age discrimination in employment is still accepted.

Older patients in the health care system

In the world of medicine, older people are routinely treated differently than younger people. Older patients tend to receive less aggressive medical treatment than younger patients with the same symptoms. A 1996 study, for example, found that older women are less likely to receive radiation and chemotherapy after breast cancer surgery, even though they are more likely than younger women to die from the disease. In 1997 the U.S. General Accounting Office reported to Congress that most of the Medicare beneficiaries diagnosed with diabetes are not receiving the recommended blood tests, physical exams, and other screening services to monitor the disease. Although anticlotting therapy has been shown to reduce the risk of death among heart attack patients, older patients are less likely than younger patients to receive this treatment. Patients over age seventy-five are more likely than younger patients with the same severity of illness to have do-not-resuscitate orders in intensive care units.

Older patients are also undertreated for mental health services, preventive care, rehabilitative services, and primary care.

Several factors contribute to the discrimination older people face in the health care system. First, many health professionals adhere to the traditional view of aging as a continual process of decline. Unaware of the distinction between processes of normal aging and disease, they frequently dismiss older patients' complaints and symptoms. Physicians, for example, may write off older adults' symptoms of depression as part of the normal aging process and therefore fail to refer them for psychiatric assessments. Furthermore, doctors often prefer using their skills to cure acute illnesses rather than managing chronic diseases and rehabilitation. Because chronic conditions are much more common among the old than the young, physicians trained to focus on discrete causes of diseases and their cures may ignore the opportunity to intervene and improve older patients' quality of life.

Robert Butler has criticized the medical profession for not investing more research into the chronic diseases of older persons. Chronic conditions that slowly and permanently reduce older people's physical functioning may be less spectacular than acute conditions, but they are more far-reaching than the diseases that have been more intensively researched. Older adults have been poorly represented in other medical research and funding priorities as well. Few research studies, for example, definitively show that specific treatments are beneficial to older patients. Without the empirical evidence of treatments' effectiveness on older adults, physicians may not prescribe certain interventions.

Poor communication between patient and doctor is another contributor to the undertreatment of older adults. Research has shown that doctors are more responsive, egalitarian, patient, respectful, and optimistic with younger patients than with older patients. Communication problems also arise because older patients are more likely to be passive and accept their physicians' diagnoses without question.

Finally, educational institutions contribute to biases against older people in the health care system. Although treating the elderly, especially the very old, can be remarkably different from treating younger patients, medical students are rarely trained to handle the multiple and complex medical problems of older adults. One study, for example, found that the average physician's knowledge of aging was equivalent to that of college undergraduates (West and Levy). As a result, there is a critical shortage of geriatricians, or doctors specially trained to deal with older adults' unique health problems. Further, textbooks that focus almost exclusively on problems of aging and underreport successes expose students to narrow views of the aging process.

The aging of the population will likely compound these problems in the coming decades as the numbers of people needing acute and long-term care increase dramatically. Older Americans comprise less than 13 percent of the U.S. population but account for about one-third of health care expenditures every year. One of the central questions facing the United States is how the health care system will handle a growing elderly population. One proposal addressing this challenge would limit health care provided to people above a certain age. Philosopher Daniel Callahan, for example, argued in his controversial 1987 book *Setting Limits* that the very old should not receive expensive health care services. Former Colorado governor Richard Lamm went even further in his oft-quoted statement that older persons "have a duty to die and get out of the way." Although few Americans would withhold health care to someone solely on the basis of age, there are many supporters of preferentially allocating medical services to younger patients. They view health care as a limited resource that must be allocated to achieve the greatest good for the greatest number of people. Proponents of age-based rationing argue that chronological age is an ethical, objective, and cost-effective criterion for allocating health care because older people have already enjoyed life and have less life to enjoy. The greatest challenge to age-based rationing of health care, however, is that there is no necessary correlation between age and physical health. Everyone does not age at the same rate, making age-based rationing of health care a prime example of discrimination against older adults.

Older drivers

Age discrimination is also evident in attempts to restrict older adults' driving. Although most older people are safe drivers, elderly persons are involved in more fatal crashes per miles driven than all but the youngest, most inexperienced drivers. Drivers eighty-five or over are more than ten times as likely to die in a crash than are drivers between the age of forty to forty-nine. Over the next several decades the number of older drivers is expected to double and the number of elderly traffic fatalities is predicted to triple. Concern that older drivers pose a risk to themselves and others leads some politicians to propose ending driving privileges at a set age, such as seventy-five or eighty-five. More common, however, are proposals to treat the licensing of older drivers differently. At least twelve states and the District of Columbia already do this, requiring older drivers to have more frequent vision tests and license renewals. A 1999 Missouri law uses ability rather than age to identify those who are at high risk of being involved in accidents. This law has drawn wide support because it acknowledges that using chronological age to restrict people's options ignores the diversity of older people's individual capabilities.

Interpersonal interactions and social segregation

Many older adults experience subtle forms of age discrimination when they interact with others. Older people in American culture are often devalued, avoided, and excluded from everyday activities. They may be segregated from children and younger adults and overlooked as candidates for useful work, either paid or unpaid. The role losses that typically accompany old age reduce older adults' social contacts and recognition. Older persons, for example, are sometimes excluded from family conversations or addressed in a patronizing manner. Religious institutions worried about attracting young people often neglect older members' needs. Churches and synagogues rarely structure their programs, budgets, and services to permit all age groups to participate equally. Older adults are also spatially segregated from other age groups in nursing homes and retirement communities. Even organizations that attempt to counter older adults' social rejection further serve to isolate them in seniors' centers and clubs. Thus, age discrimination functions not only blatantly in employment, health care, and driving laws, but also subtly in interpersonal relationships.

Conclusion

Prejudice and stereotyping lead to age discrimination that can affect everyone. It disadvantages older workers, resulting in an ineffective use of human resources. Ageist beliefs influence health care providers' professional training and service delivery, which in turn negatively affect older patients' treatment and health outcomes. Narrow views of aging lead people to ignore substantial differences among older adults' driving abilities and to underappreciate their social needs. Ongoing education is needed to inform those in power that age is a poor predictor of performance and ability and should not be a basis of discrimination.

PETER UHLENBURG

JENIFER HAMIL-LUKER

See also AGE-BASED RATIONING OF HEALTH CARE; AGE-ISM; AGE INTEGRATION AND AGE SEGREGATION; DRIVING ABILITY; JOB PERFORMANCE.

BIBLIOGRAPHY

Administration on Aging. *Mobility and Independence: Changes and Challenges for Older Drivers.* Available on the Internet, www.aoa.dhhs.gov

American Association for Retired Persons. *Business and Older Workers: Current Perceptions and New Directions for the 1990's.* Washington, D.C.: AARP, 1989.

BUTLER, R. "Dispelling Ageism: The Cross-Cutting Intervention." *Annals of the American Academy of Political and Social Sciences* 503 (1989): 138–147.

CALLAHAN, D. *Setting Limits: Medical Goals in an Aging Society.* New York: Simon and Schuster, 1986.

CROWN, W. H., ed. *Handbook on Employment and the Elderly.* Westport, Conn.: Greenwood Press, 1996.

Equal Employment Opportunities Commission (EEOC). *Facts About Age Discrimination.* Available on the Internet, www.eeoc.gov

FALK, U. A., and FALK, G. *Ageism, the Aged and Aging in America.* Springfield, Ill.: Charles C. Thomas Publisher, Ltd., 1997.

GOLDBERG, B. *Age Works: What Corporate America Must Do to Survive the Graying of the Workforce.* New York: The Free Press, 2000.

GRAVES, J. "Age Discrimination: Developments and Trends." *Trial* 35 (February 1999): 58–63.

MASSIE, D.; CAMPBELL, K.; and WILLIAMS, A. "Traffic Accident Involvement Rates by Driver Age and Gender." *Accident Analysis and Prevention* 27 (1995): 73–87.

MIRVIS, P. H. *Building the Competitive Workforce.* New York: John Wiley and Sons, 1993.

RUBENSTEIN, L.; MARMOR, T.; STONE, R.; MOON, M.; and HAROOTYAN, L. "Medicare: Challenges and Future Directions in a Changing Health Care Environment." *The Gerontologist* 35 (1994): 620–627.

SHAW, A. B. "In Defense of Ageism." *Journal of Medical Ethics* 20 (1994): 188–191.

WEST, H. L., and LEVY, W. J. "Knowledge of Aging in the Medical Profession." *Gerontology and Geriatric Education* 4 (1985): 97–105.

ZWEIBEL, N. R.; CASSEL, C. K.; and KARRISON, T. "Public Attitudes About the Use of Chronological Age as a Criterion for Allocating Health Care Resources." *The Gerontologist* (1993): 74–80.

AGE INTEGRATION AND AGE SEGREGATION

There are two distinct but related meanings of "age integration." First, it means breaking down age barriers; people's ages are not used to dictate what positions or roles they can hold or must give up. The second meaning of age integration is "cross-age interaction": people of different ages doing something together, such as working, learning, or having fun. These two aspects of age integration are related because more of either type is likely to be accompanied by the other. For example, when a work organization welcomes people of many different ages, it is likely to have a mix of ages working together. Still, these are distinct meanings of age integration, because an organization or society with one type of age integration would not necessarily have the other type. For instance, people can choose to be friends with people their own age even in a company that has broken down formal age barriers.

Matilda White Riley and John W. Riley, pioneers in the study of age integration, have developed a chart that depicts the life course in both an age-segregated society and an age-integrated society. It depicts ideal types, or extremes, which do not actually exist, but it is useful for thinking about age integration. The left-hand side of the chart depicts three life roles that are reserved for people of particular ages. Young people get education, middle aged people devote themselves to work, and leisure is reserved for older people. In the age-integrated model at the right-hand side of the chart, activities are no longer dictated by age. People may move in and out of education, work, and leisure over the course of their lives. When there are no longer rigid age norms to say what people can do at certain ages, people of different ages engage in the same activities.

Age integration is a concept that can be applied to all levels of society. At any given point in time, some societies are more age integrated than others, and the amount of age integration in a particular society will probably change over time. Institutions, organizations, groups, and individual lives can also be discussed in terms of age integration. At the institutional level, we might discuss higher education, and conclude that U.S. colleges and universities are far more age integrated than in the past. At the organizational level, many high-technology and dot.com companies hire mostly young people, whereas other kinds of companies are more age integrated. At the group level, the family is where people of different ages typically interact on a daily basis. At the individual level, some people live highly age-integrated lives as they move in and out of particular roles—such as work—over the course of their lives.

Historical changes in the level of age integration

The United States used to be a society in which people of different ages mingled throughout the day and across organizations and groups. The family farm and the one-room schoolhouse are historical examples of age integration. Until the 1970s most people did not retire to leisure. Retirement was primarily a safety net for older workers faced with ill health or unemployment (Henretta).

Then there was a long period of increasing age segregation. More and more parts of people's lives involved being with others of their own age. Industrialization brought increased specialization of all kinds, and age was an important category used to sort people. Society expected teachers to be experts on a particular age group, family members to specialize in different kinds of work, and people to move through major life roles in a fixed pattern. The labor force participation of older women and men declined, and was replaced by leisure retirement. Martin Kohli argues that over the course of the twentieth century, age was increasingly used to assign people to or prohibit them from particular activities. The result was a tendency toward a rigidly fixed life course. According to Riley and Riley, this tendency toward age-segregated structures began to approximate the age-differentiated "ideal type" structure in which people gain their education when young, work in middle-age, and enjoy their well-earned leisure time when they are old. Age-based grades, teams, jobs, and leisure activities seemed normal; people were expected to spend major portions of their days and lives with people of their own age.

One major problem with the age segregation of roles is that the gender division of labor that was the foundation of the industrial era and the age-segregated life course is almost extinct as the twenty-first century begins. Women have become permanent participants in paid work, which means that for most people, the middle years are now taken up with both paid work and family work. This has led to distress, conflict, and exhaustion as people try to juggle family and paid work responsibilities. At the same time, many older people don't have enough to do. In fact, retirement has been called a "roleless role." Many of the oldest members of society give up important activities such as paid work, caregiving, and community involvement.

The social problems caused by age segregation could be solved by a trend back toward age integration, though in a way that fits the realities of twenty-first-century life. Riley and Riley contend that there are already trends toward greater age integration as the third millennium begins. First, more and more people are living longer and longer. Researchers expect this trend to continue. When people live longer, it brings more chance for diversity over the course of their lives. There are more opportunities to take on new roles at various life stages and a greater chance that this will mean interacting with people of different ages. It also means that there are more cohorts of people born in different historical periods alive at the same time. Because growing up in particular historical periods shapes ideas, skills, and attitudes, there is more age-related diversity in a given year. In the year 2000, cohorts of people who are now old have lived through the Great Depression, World War II, the calm of the 1950s, and the struggle for racial and gender equality in the 1960s. Cohorts of people who are now young are growing up with sophisticated computer technology, less community involvement, relatively little agitation for major social change, and more serious crime. There are many cohorts in between who have been variously shaped by the major events of their childhoods, adolescences, early adulthoods, and beyond.

Second, there have been major changes in the work careers that typically anchored the middle stages of adult life. It used to be that the average worker "signed on" to a particular career in a given organization, and that was how he or she spent the middle period of his or her life. But the single work career is quickly becoming a relic of an earlier era. People cannot count on having their work life set for the middle years. Fast-paced technological change and globalization of the economy have resulted in a turbulent labor market. According to Robert Kuttner, employers now buy labor only for as long as they need it. Thus more and more people face periods of unemployment during the traditional work years.

This increasing age diversity has brought changes in the ages at which people enter different roles or phases of their lives. Matilda White Riley points out that we can no longer think of the course of people's lives as having clear-cut phases. Some people are having children late in life and some are retiring really early. In the United States, higher education is no longer reserved for adolescents, and continuous learning has become the norm.

Advantages and disadvantages of age integration

When age barriers that keep older people from productive activity are removed, both society and old people benefit. Social life is enriched by elders' talents, wisdom, and expertise. In turn, elders enjoy the esteem and well-being that come from contributing to society. There are demonstrated health benefits of active participation in social life.

Both older and younger age groups can benefit from reciprocal socialization and learning. In the year 2000, there is every indication that technology will continue to develop, and more and more aspects of life will require use of computerized systems. Young people know this new technology through both formal instruction and play. Many older people have had little experience with computers. The young can teach their elders this new skill. They can also expose older people to new ways of thinking, or get them interested again in an issue that they once cared about passionately. Peter Uhlenberg notes that society benefits when its young learn the importance of giving to others, and service to elders would be an important way to accomplish this. The elders, of course, can pass on the benefit of their life experience. Current examples include retired businesspeople who provide expert assis-

tance to small businesses, organization-based groups of retirees who take on particular community service projects, and mentoring programs that pair "grandparents" with youngsters. As older people pass on their wisdom and become known as individuals to younger people, ageist stereotypes are apt to lessen. When biases against older people are diminished, it will free them to make many more important contributions to society.

As people of different ages work, learn, and enjoy themselves side by side, this fosters solidarity across the generations, which can be important for policy making. As the baby boom cohort ages, it is clear that they will be a tremendous burden on younger people unless age integration gives elders the chance to help minimize that burden (Riley and Riley, 2000).

If age integration means that we no longer have to have our activities defined by age, then older people can participate more fully in all aspects of life and people can cut back on paid work whenever their family demands are greatest. A more age-integrated life course could address work-family conflict across the socioeconomic spectrum. For example, if people were no longer expected to get all or most of their education when they were young, then poor teenage mothers (and their children) might not be fated to forever trying to "catch up" (Loscocco).

Yet there are also disadvantages to a more age-integrated model of social life. One obstacle is the amount of change that such a trend brings with it. Many people resist change, feeling more comfortable leaving things the way they are. Some would surely be upset by changes that seemed to force them into or out of particular life roles. Those who have the most to gain from an age-graded life course might put up barriers to further movement toward an age-integrated society.

Diversity of any kind often brings tensions. People of different ages have been reared differently, and have lived through different historical forces and fads that have shaped them. People often hold tightly to age-based values, passions, and ideals. They may not be especially interested in learning about new perspectives or ways of doing things. Thus bringing age groups with differing perspectives together may cause conflicts that are absent in same-age structures and groups.

Nor are different generations apt to readily share resources or to modify the current generational contract in which those in the middle years support older cohorts with the promise that younger generations will support them. The economist Lester Thurow warns that age may supplant class as a basis of conflict in U.S. society in the third millennium. It may cost younger age groups too much to pay for programs that benefit the oldest members of society. This problem will be greatest during the years when the baby boom generation reaches its latest years. Still, as of the year 2000, the "age wars" that were predicted by some economists have not materialized (Foner). Young and middle-aged people have not challenged policies that appear to benefit the growing numbers of older people at the expense of other age groups. Foner contends that this is partly because there are demonstrated economic benefits to younger family members when their elders are protected or enriched by public policy. Also, aging is inevitable, so people are reluctant to challenge a program that they know they will need someday.

Serious age integration would require a fundamental shift in standard of living and social values. In the United States, for example, a premium is placed on productivity and material rewards. Economic institutions dominate all others. People would have to be willing to make do with less and companies would have to restructure reward systems. These appear to be daunting obstacles. Yet there is evidence in the year 2000 that many people want more simplicity and greater balance in their lives (see Loscocco for citations). Similarly, many more companies are beginning to accommodate people who do not conform to traditional work patterns that require employees to place work time above all else.

Prospects for the future

As Matilda White Riley argues, age integration is already under way in U.S. society at the dawn of the third millennium. Many retirement communities have sprung up near or on university campuses, with the express purpose of bringing people from different age groups together. Numerous community-based and national programs attempt to bring older people and children together (see Newman et al.). Most such programs are aimed at using the wisdom and experience of older people to benefit the young.

This can be especially advantageous in poor communities where the parents may be unable to give their children the attention, teaching, and emotional support that they need. But there are benefits to the older people, too, as discussed earlier.

The early retirement trend had abated as of the mid-1990s (Quinn). Improved health among older people and the tremendous hole that will be left as the baby boom cohort enters retirement age suggest this trend will continue for the first few decades of the twenty-first century at least. Cohort improvements in health and longevity may lead to a rethinking of age categories—with people in their seventies being considered middle-aged rather than "old," for example. People's expectations of themselves and those of potential employers may change accordingly.

However, it is impossible to predict what will happen in the future on the basis of past or current trends. The trend toward increased longevity could be slowed by the cumulative effects of increased pollution or new and more resistant diseases. Widespread economic and technological changes could fundamentally alter the way societies organize work. If age integration becomes much more widespread, it is possible that it will fuel conflict between age groups. For these reasons, greater age integration cannot be prescribed as a sure antidote to future social ills. Still, as age barriers are lifted and the benefits are realized, it is unlikely that society would return to age discrimination. At the turn of the third millennium, age integration offers considerable promise.

KARYN LOSCOCCO

See also AGE DISCRIMINATION; AGE NORMS; LIFE COURSE.

BIBLIOGRAPHY

BENGSTON, V. L., and ACHENBAUM, W. A., eds. *The Changing Contract Across Generations*. New York: Aldine DeGruyter, 1993.

FONER, A. "Age Integration or Age Conflict as Society Ages?" *The Gerontologist* 40 (2000): 272–275.

HENRETTA, J. C. "Recent Trends in Retirement." *Reviews in Clinical Gerontology* 4 (1994): 71–81.

KOHLI, M. "The World We Forgot: A Historical Review of the Life Course." In *Later Life: The Social Psychology of Ageing*. Edited by V. W. Marshall. Beverly Hills, Calif.: Sage, 1986. Pp. 271–303.

KUTTNER, R. *Everything for Sale: The Virtues and Limits of Markets.* New York: Alfred A. Knopf, 1997.

LOSCOCCO, K. A. "Age Integration as a Solution to Work-Family Conflict." *The Gerontologist* 40 (2000): 292–299.

NEWMAN, S.; WARD, C. R.; SMITH, J. O. W.; and McCREA, J. O. *Intergenerational Programs: Past, Present and Future.* London: Taylor and Francis, 1997.

QUINN, J. F. "Retirement Trends and Patterns in the 1990s: The End of an Era?" *Public Policy and Aging Report* 8 (1997): 10–15.

RILEY, M. W. "Aging and Society: Past, Present and Future" *The Gerontologist* 34 (1994): 436–446.

RILEY, M. W.; KAHN, R. L.; and FONER, A., eds. *Age and Structural Lag: Society's Failure to Provide Meaningful Opportunities in Work, Family and Leisure.* New York: Wiley, 1994.

RILEY, M. W., and RILEY, J. W. "Age Integration and the Lives of Older People." *The Gerontologist* 34 (1994): 110–115.

RILEY, M. W., and RILEY, J. W. "Age Integration: Conceptual and Historical Background." *The Gerontologist* 40 (2000): 266–270.

THUROW, L. C. "The Birth of a Revolutionary Class." *New York Times Magazine*, 19 May 1996, pp. 46–47.

UHLENBERG, P. "The Burden of Aging: A Theoretical Framework for Understanding the Shifting Balance of Caregiving and Care Receiving as Cohorts Age." *The Gerontologist* 36 (1996): 761–767.

AGEISM

The term *ageism* refers to a deep and profound prejudice against the elderly (Butler). In simple terms, ageism occurs when people stereotype others based on old age. Ageism occurs throughout society in varying degrees, in television, advertising, movies, stores, hospitals, and jobs.

Ageism is a process of stereotyping and discriminating against people because they are old. From a definitional perspective, ageism is like racism or sexism in that it treats people differently based on stereotypes about a group. While most people have a general knowledge or understanding of the history of racism or sexism, their understanding of "ageism" is likely to be limited to jokes about aging, greeting cards, or senior discounts that provide benefits for reaching a certain age.

Ageism as a term and as a process to be studied is relatively new, an ironic twist for the study of how society views getting old. Most studies of ageist attitudes tend to focus on its negative aspects. However, ageism can also have a positive perspective, such as when the attributes of age are deemed advantageous. For example, a positive view perceives an association between aging and greater wisdom, patience, and an enhanced appreciation of life's benefits.

Ageism can be intentional, meaning a deliberate process of thought and action to stereotype based on age. More commonly, it is inadvertent, when people unconsciously attribute certain characteristics to a person because of his or her age. In daily social interactions, ageism typically occurs without much notice or concern.

To understand ageism, one must understand the process of stereotyping. A stereotype is a well-learned set of associations that link a set of characteristics with a group. Stereotypes differ from personal beliefs, which are propositions that are endorsed and accepted as true. While all individuals learn about cultural stereotypes through socialization, only a subset of people endorse the stereotype and believe it to be true.

People respond to each other almost automatically using stereotypes based on race, age, and gender. Perceptions and judgments about others are made instantaneously, without conscious thought or effort, which is why stereotypes remain insidious. Stereotypes typically exaggerate certain characteristics of some members of a group and attribute the negative characteristic to aging. They do not recognize that individual characteristics vary greatly and also change over time.

Stereotypes about age and older persons

Ageism appears in many forms. A few examples illustrate how the behavior of an older person is described in an ageist manner, where the same behavior by a younger person is explained without stereotypes. When older people forget someone's name, they are viewed as senile. When a younger person fails to recall a name, we usually say he or she has a faulty memory. When an older person complains about life or a particular incident, they are called cranky and difficult, while a younger person may just be seen as being critical. If an older person has trouble hearing, she is dismissed as "getting old," rather than having difficulty with her hearing. Children also can hold negative stereotypes about older people. Some young children equate aging with being sick, unfulfilled, unhappy, or dying.

Older people also face stereotypes on the job. The most common stereotypes about older workers are that older workers are less productive, more expensive, less adaptable, and more rigid than younger workers.

As with stereotypes about other groups, the facts refute the stereotypes. While studies show that interest, motivation, and skill do not decline with age, some employers continue to perceive older workers as resistant to change, slow to learn new skills, and uncomfortable with new technologies. Studies consistently demonstrate that there is no correlation between age and job performance, despite the common stereotype that productivity declines with age. Indeed, research reveals that some intellectual functions may even improve with age. While the cost of certain employee benefits such as health and life insurance may increase with age, the data is lacking to support the stereotype that older workers cost more to employ than younger workers. Differences in salary costs are typically due to tenure rather than age.

Why ageism exists in American culture

A number of reasons contribute to ageism in American culture. Youth, beauty, and vitality are highly valued by Americans. The aging process is viewed as counter to these highly valued attributes. Good health is also touted by Americans. One of the most common stereotypes about aging is that it brings the loss of good health, which makes many fear the aging process. Of course, the real fear is that aging leads to death. Putting distance between oneself and aging thus alleviates the fear of dying.

While elders are still esteemed in many countries, American culture seems to have lost this perspective. Ageism has become ingrained in American culture as it is passed on to children from parents who hold ageist stereotypes. The same ageist myths and misconceptions that are held by adults are also held by teens and children. Americans make jokes and comments about growing old that perpetuate negative stereotypes about aging and older persons. The lexicon is replete with ageist terms that portray older people in a negative light, such as "old fogey," "old fart," "geezer," and "old goat."

Institutions and systems, as well as individuals, may unintentionally perpetuate ageism through their pursuit of independent objectives. For example, the greeting card industry plays on American's infatuation with youth by selling merchandise focused on the desire to be young and to fight aging. Greeting cards sell when they arouse certain emotions, such as making people laugh at jokes about getting old and exaggerated portrayals of old, decrepit people.

The mass media plays a powerful institutional role in shaping American attitudes as it similarly fixates on youth, beauty, and sex appeal. The media's portrayal of aging and older people can vary depending on its objective. For example, when the media focuses on older people as a potent block of voters or consumers for specialized products, older people may be portrayed as affluent, self-interested, and politically potent. When the focus shifts to general television programming or movies for the general public, the pictures of older people change dramatically. On television, seniors rarely appear in prime-time shows. On television or in movies, they are typically cast in minor roles, and are depicted as helpless victims or crotchety troublemakers.

The labor market is another system that perpetuates ageism. Employers, both private and public, engage in age discrimination when they fire older workers or refuse to hire or promote them because of ageist stereotypes. While the federal Age Discrimination in Employment Act (ADEA) prohibits age discrimination against most job applicants and employees age forty and older, the federal law contains exceptions that permit mandatory retirement of police, firefighters, highly paid executives, and state judges.

Governmental programs and policies that use age to categorize people to determine their eligibility for retirement or health benefits unintentionally fuel negative stereotypes, even though the purposes of such programs are to provide benefits or services to older persons and the elderly. By providing a retirement benefit at age sixty-two or age sixty-five, Social Security reinforces the perception that people should stop working and retire at those ages. While many Americans retire in their early sixties, many continue working full- or part-time and have no desire to retire. On the contrary, their desire is to be productive workers, despite the common view that older individuals are not "productive" members of society.

The health care system can also perpetuate ageist attitudes in dealing with older patients and the elderly. For example, a doctor treating an older person may dismiss his or her complaints as relating to a degenerative aging process, rather than addressing the potential medical cause of the problem. In other words, age is used as a determinative criterion for settling a question of treatment, in lieu of the more difficult search for the actual cause of the affliction.

The role of the media in supporting ageism

Mass media, particularly television and movies, define social roles in contemporary culture by presenting a steady and repetitive portrayal of images and a system of messages. Studies reveal the common perception in the media that youth sells and youth buy. This view causes television shows, movies, and advertisements to feature young characters to bring in large audiences and revenues. The media emphasize youth and beauty, fast-paced action and lives, and overly simplistic portrayals of individuals. This emphasis exacerbates the negative image of aging and the elderly in American culture, because the stereotypes of aging are the antithesis of the attributes upon which television and movies thrive.

The image of aging depicted in the media has generally been one of negative stereotyping, a portrayal that seems to be more negative than any other social group. In American culture, the aged are not depicted as experienced "elders." Rather, older people are tolerated and respected to the extent they can act like younger people and work, exercise, and have healthy relationships.

Research from the 1970s, 1980s, and 1990s, shows a continuing negative portrayal of older persons and the elderly by the media, manifested mostly through comments referring to decline and deterioration in old age.

The media also tend to exclude or severely underrepresent the elderly in the images presented on television compared to the proportion of elderly in the U.S. population. While the population age sixty-five and older represents almost 13 percent of the U.S. population, only about 8 percent of the roles in television commercials in the 1990s were of older persons (Tupper). Older women are almost invisible in prime-time television shows and movies.

Similarly, television advertising, which has a profound effect on influencing and shaping attitudes, repeatedly conveys negative stereotypes by representing older persons as feeble, forgetful, stubborn, and helpless. Repeated exposure to negative stereotypes about aging and the elderly in commercial advertising can lead to a devaluing of the elderly.

Advertisers clearly focus their marketing on younger women who are primarily responsible for household purchases. The common perception among advertising agencies is that younger age groups spend more than older age groups. Recent studies show that while sixty-five to seventy-four-year-old consumers outspend their counterparts in the thirty-five to forty-four-year-old category, ad agency staff ignored older audiences and underappreciated their potential and power as consumers.

Newspapers and magazines generally present neutral images of aging and do not create or support negative images of the elderly in their coverage of stories or in advertisements.

The evolution of ageism

In the workplace, there has been substantial progress in eliminating ageist policies and practices as a result of the federal ADEA. No longer can employers advertise for jobs limited to those "age thirty-five and younger," or mandatorily retire employees at age sixty-five. Training and promotion opportunities must be provided to employees without regard to age. Multi-million-dollar cases against companies who discriminated against older employees have made employers more vigilant in educating their employees about ageism and in instituting procedures and policies to prevent age discrimination. Publicity about large age discrimination cases against major U.S. corporations has brought a greater awareness among the public about ageism in the workplace.

Yet ageist attitudes, which may be hidden or subtle, persist in the workplace. For example, employers who do not want to hire older workers are likely to tell the older applicant that he is overqualified rather than too old. Similarly, older employees are often denied promotions because they lack potential or drive, which can be concealing ageist views that older workers are set in their ways. Supervisors and coworkers still make ageist comments about the ages or aging of older employees.

Attitudes about aging in the media have also improved over time. The vast population of aging baby boomers has led some commercial advertisers to target this growing consumer market with positive messages about middle age. By the 1990s the portrayal of older people in television shows had improved somewhat over the 1970s and 1980s. In the 1990s, prime time drama television shows, daytime serials, and commercial advertising featuring older persons presented a more neutral image or even an improved overall image of the aged by featuring older characters who appeared powerful, affluent, healthy, active, admired, and sexy.

Ways to reduce ageism

To reduce ageism, Americans first need to recognize the ageist stereotypes they hold and work to overcome those stereotypes by treating each person as an individual. Just as racism and sexism have been reduced to a certain degree in American society through education and training, the same techniques and strategies could help reduce ageism. Many employers and communities provide diversity training and lessons about ageism, and age discrimination should be included in these diversity programs.

Education about identifying and preventing ageist attitudes and practices should also be incorporated into the diversity programs in the schools, as well as in the workplace. For example, during African American History Month or Women's History Month, students learn to understand and appreciate the efforts and benefits against racism and sexism and to admire the successes of people of different races and genders. Similarly, literature and teaching within the classroom could show the diversity of aging to reduce and eliminate stereotypes. Case studies and lessons about age discrimination can be included in management school courses and textbooks to teach future supervisors and business leaders about the harmful consequences of ageism.

More positive images of older persons and of aging in the media would significantly reduce ageism in American culture. Featuring active, healthy, productive, and successful older persons in television shows, movies, and commercial advertising would counteract the negative perceptions many people have about aging and the elderly.

To reach this end, the advertising industry, which understandably focuses on income revenue, will have to recognize and appreciate the vast consumer potential of older people. Studies showing that older consumers are a significant market may provide the advertising industry with the impetus to target older audiences with more positive portrayals of aging.

The more young, old and middle-aged people see and relate to each other in ways that refute ageist stereotypes, the more likely the negative stereotypes will change toward more positive views about aging.

CATHY VENTRELL MONSEES

See also AGE DISCRIMINATION; IMAGES OF AGING; LANGUAGE ABOUT AGING; SOCIAL COGNITION.

BIBLIOGRAPHY

ACHENBAUM, W. A., and KUSNERZ, P. A. *Images of Old Age in America.* Ann Arbor, Mich.: Institute of Gerontology, 1978.

American Association of Retired Persons. *Business and Older Workers: Current Perceptions and New Directions for the 1990s.* Washington, D.C.: AARP, 1989.

BAILEY, W. T.; HARRELL, D. R.; and ANDERSON, L. E. "The Image of Middle-Aged and Older Women in Magazine Advertisements." *Educational Gerontology* 19 (1993): 97–103.

BELL, J. "In Search of a Discourse on Aging: The Elderly on Television." *The Gerontologist* 32 (1992): 305–311.

BRAMLETT-SOLOMON, S., and WILSON, V. "Images of the Elderly in Life and *Ebony*, 1978–1987." *Journalism Quarterly* 66 (1989): 185–188.

BUCHHOLZ, M., and BYNUM, J. E. "Newspaper Presentation of America's Aged: A Content Analysis of Image and Role." *The Gerontologist* 22, no. 1 (1982): 83–87.

DAIL, P. W. "Prime-Time Television Portrayals of Older Adults in the Context of Family Life." *The Gerontologist* 28, no. 5 (1988): 700–706.

DEMOS, V., and JACHE, A. "When You Care Enough: An Analysis of Attitudes Toward Aging in Humorous Birthday Cards." *The Gerontologist* 21, no. 2 (1981): 209–215.

DEVINE, P. G. "Stereotypes and Prejudice: Their Automatic and Controlled Components." *Journal of Personality and Social Psychology* 56 (1989): 5–18.

ELLIOT, J. "The Daytime Television Drama Portrayal of Older Adults." *The Gerontologist* 24 (1984): 628–633.

ENGLAND, P.; KUHN, A.; and GARDNER, T. "The Ages of Men and Women in Magazine Advertisements." *Journalism Quarterly* 58 (1981): 468–471.

MCEVOY, G., and CASCIO, W. "Cumulative Evidence of the Relationship Between Employee Age and Job Performance." *Journal of Applied Psychology* 74, no. 1 (1989): 11–17.

MEYROWITZ, J. *No Sense of Place: The Impact of Electronic Media on Social Behavior.* New York: Oxford University Press, 1985.

PLATT, L. S., and VENTRELL-MONSEES, C. *Age Discrimination Litigation.* Costa Mesa, Calif.: James Publishing, 2000.

ROBINSON, P. K. "Age, Health, and Job Performance." In *Age, Health, and Employment.* Englewood Cliffs, N.J.: Prentice-Hall, 1986. Pages 63–77.

STANGOR, C.; LYNCH, L.; DUAN, C.; and GLASS, B. "Categorization of Individuals on the Basis of Multiple Social Features." *Journal of Personality and Social Psychology* 207 (1992): 207.

STAUDINGER, V. M.; CORNELIUS, S. W.; and BLATES, P. B. "The Aging of Intelligence: Potential and Limits" *The Annals* 503 (1989): 43–45.

SWAYNE, L. E., and GRECO, A. J. "The Portrayal of Older Americans in Television Commercials." *Journal of Advertising* 16, no. 1 (1987): 47–54.

TUPPER, M. "The Representation of Elderly Persons in Prime Time Television Advertising." Masters Thesis, University of South Florida, 1995.

URSIC, A. C.; URSIC, M. L.; and URSIC, V. L. "A Longitudinal Study of the Use of the Elderly in Magazine Advertising." *Journal of Communication Research* 13 (1986): 131–133.

VASIL, L., and WASS, H. "Portrayal of the Elderly in the Media: A Literature Review and Implications for Educational Gerontologists." *Educational Gerontology* 19, no. 1 (1993): 71–85.

WALDMAN, D. A., and AVOLIO, B. J. "A Meta-Analysis of Age Differences vs. Job Performance." *Journal of Applied Psychology* 71, no. 1 (1986): 33–38.

WASS, H.; HAWKINS, L. V.; KELLY, E. B.; MAGNERS, C. R.; and MCMORROW, A. M. "The Elderly in the Sunday Newspapers: 1963 and 1983." *Educational Gerontology* 11, no. 1 (1985): 29–39.

AGE NORMS

Hopkins (CEO of large American broadcasting company): "...you're at an important stage of your career. How old are you?"

Rath (Hopkins's assistant): "Thirty-three."
Hopkins: "That's an important age. In the next six or seven years, you should really be on your way." (Wilson, p. 224)

Hopkins, a fictional character from Sloan Wilson's 1955 novel, *The Man in the Grey Flannel Suit*, believes age is a benchmark with which to gauge someone's career progress. Besides career progress, people may perceive appropriate ages or age ranges for numerous behaviors and life events. Social scientists studying aging take such perceptions as indicative of age norms, a focal concept in apprehending how age organizes social life. This review of age norms has several objectives: first, define age norms and distinguish between their formal and informal types; second, provide examples of age norms drawn from education, work, and family domains with an aim toward illustrating both their historical and contemporary variation; third, discuss the behavioral effects of age norms, including what it means to be on- or off-time and whether or not sanctions are brought to bear against those violating age-related rules; and finally, highlight some persistent controversies and limitations in age norm research.

What are age norms?

Age norms are a variety of social norms, which are rules for behavior and have three defining characteristics: they are shared, obligatory (i.e., contain a *should* or *ought* element), and backed by positive or negative sanctions (for classic treatments of social norms, see Blake and Davis). Age norms are commonly defined as social rules for age-appropriate behavior, including everyday actions and/or the timing and sequencing of major life events (e.g., marriage, parenthood, retirement; in sociological parlance, life events are typically role transitions). Thus, they constitute a *social clock* or temporal script potentially influencing attitudes and behavior (e.g., Hopkins's thinking in the dialogue above).

Formal and informal age norms

Age norms are woven into the fabric of many social institutions in both formal and informal ways. Formal age norms are codified in diverse laws and rules (Blake and Davis). They organize society by age in at least two interrelated ways: partitioning the population into general age-strata, each comprised of people assumed to possess similar capacities (e.g., using age to legally separate adulthood from pre-adulthood on the basis of presumed responsibility); and, second, using age to regulate individuals' access to assorted rights and responsibilities ranging from private to public domains (e.g., age of consent laws, obtaining a driver's license; see Cain, especially, pp. 345–352, for historical examples of these efforts).

The sociologist Bernice Neugarten and colleagues pioneered inquiry into informal age norms, which are unwritten and implicit, but there is scholarly disagreement over their precise definition and measurement. "Expectations regarding age-appropriate behavior" (Neugarten, Moore, and Lowe, p. 711), the "ages at which particular transitions ought to occur" (Settersten and Hagestad, 1996a, p. 179), or the "ages viewed as standard or typical for a given role or status by the modal group of members of a social system" (Lawrence, 1996, p. 211) are three common meanings. Age norms have been variously measured in surveys by asking about *ideal*, *best*, *appropriate*, or even *typical* ages associated with a variety of role transitions and/or everyday behaviors.

Variation in age norms

Differences in definition and measurement notwithstanding, selected age norms are presented to document their historical and subcultural variation since age norms are properties of social systems, and the latter are not constant across time and social space. Examples include formal norms from education, work, family, and domains.

Historical work suggest the United States grew increasingly age-conscious and regimented in both public and public and private domains beginning in the late 1800s and continuing well into the 1900s. For example, witness the transition from early school's age-heterogeneous classrooms to the strongly age-segregated nature of U.S. schools that gathered momentum at the turn of the nineteenth century as elementary and junior- and senior-high schools became institutionalized (Chudacoff). At work, people's labor force participation was circumscribed on one end of the life cycle by child labor laws (passed chiefly in the second half of the nineteenth century) and retirement and pension eligibility age prescriptions on the other (policies passed in the mid-1930s).

Age norms for family-related transitions have also changed over time. An 1889 advice manual written for women set the ideal age range for marriage between eighteen and twenty-six, based on the manual's author having consulted some distinguished physicians about what they deemed to be the proper timing of marriage (Chudacoff, p. 50). Attitudinal data from the 1940s through the 1980s through the 1980s show that the perceived ideal age for marriage dropped in the aftermath of World War II (early to mid-twenties) compared to previously (Modell), but has risen more recently. In the late 1980s, a majority of respondents thought that the appropriate age was the mid- to late-twenties (Settersten and Hagestad, 1996a).

Importantly, age norms not only change over time, but other research documents contemporaneous subcultural variation. For example, the above studies on marital timing revealed that expectations for women's marital timing remained consistently two to three years younger than that of men's throughout this time period. Besides gender, age norms also vary by age cohorts, education, occupation, and race/ethnicity (Settersten and Hagestad, 1996a).

Age norms and behavior

Despite plenty of evidence of both formal and informal age norms, we know less about their influence on people's actual behavior. One early statement suggested that age norms operate as a system of "prods and breaks. . .in some instances hastening an event, in others delaying it" (Neugarten et al., p. 711). While intuitively plausible, several critical issues warrant consideration. Life course researchers often investigate large-scale patterns in age-related attitudes and transitions through surveys of a general population. Shared attitudes are not equivalent to shared behavior, however (Newcomb, p. 268). Nor can we assume that age norms are responsible even when we observe regularities in timing and sequencing of transitions (Marini).

To best capture the behavioral effects of age norms, we should consider smaller groups like families, peer groups, or even an organization. Indeed, studies of these concrete settings, which organize our day-to-day experience, reveal age norms' effects as the following examples attest: the age-graded nature of schools affected kids' lunchroom seating patterns (Thorne, p. 42); family "kin-scripts," in some low-income, minority communities, "expect[ed] that designated adolescent females become 'early childbearers' since grandmothers often reared these children (Stack and Burton, p. 159); and organizational employees, like Hopkins at the beginning of this entry, used shared perceptions of typical age-related career progress to gauge their own and others' progress (including supervisors whose ratings of employees were influenced by such age judgements) (Lawrence, 1988).

Consequences of being off-time

Individuals whose behaviors/transitions meet expectations are said to be *on-time* while those who violate them are labeled *off-time*, whether early or late. Violating age deadlines may result in punishing sanctions, but evidence of this is mixed and actually mirrors the previous discussion on normative influences on behavior. While attitudinal evidence from surveys of the general public revealed that many respondents perceived few consequences to being off-time in work- and family-related transitions (e.g., Settersten and Hagestad, 1996a; 1996b), other studies of smaller groups indicated that age norm violation may be met with sanctions as ordinary as a disparaging mark to someone who is not adhering to a "kinscript" (Stack and Burton) or a poor performance evaluation for someone whose career progress lags behind the timetable (Lawrence). The latter finding suggests that age norms can actually promote ageism if age-appropriate expectations lead to stereotyping.

Being off-time may have other consequences as well, one of which is individual stress. Most difficult are those transitions which are unanticipated (e.g., widowhood at a young age) since there may be a vague script for guidance and minimal support from others. Even planned transitions, however, when off-time, may result in little social support if an individual assumes a status when others in his/her social circle do not (e.g., having children much earlier or later than one's friends). Moreover, since transitions are never accomplished in isolation from other roles, being off-time can result in role overload (e.g., early parenthood may interfere with finishing school).

Continuing controversies

Several controversies still surround the study of age norms despite their continuing significance to aging (see the useful, brief summaries of some of these issues in Dannefer, 1996). First, conceptualization and measurement difficulties continue. For example, if sanctions are a critical dimension of norms, then they ought to be measured (Marini; for an alternative view, see Lawrence). Yet few researchers have captured this essential component. Second, age norms' status in explaining behavior needs greater scrutiny. While role transitions have received the bulk of attention, age norms might be most visible in their obligatory sense (and backed by sanctions) in people's daily interactions and behavior (e.g., being admonished to "act your age"). Such data might also inform another debate over how strongly society is currently organized by age norms (and age more generally). Many scholars agree that American society became increasingly age graded and age conscious through the last half of the nineteenth and well into the twentieth century, but some argue that late-twentieth-century America became more *age irrelevant*, that is, transitions and behavior are less age defined than previously (e.g., Neugarten and Neugarten). If the latter is the case, then we would expect greater diversity in aging outcomes, yet it is precisely this diversity that the age norm tradition often historically missed given its conceptual emphasis on consensus and resulting methodological search for modal patterns (Dannefer). Historical and subcultural variation is critical for reminding us that particular age expectations do not reflect natural or universal aging outcomes (e.g., adolescents are rebellious), but rather are both cause and effect of particular societal arrangements. Undoubtedly, further exploration into these dynamics of age norms will continue to bear fruit in our study of aging.

JEFF LASHBROOK

See also AGE; AGEISM; LIFE COURSE.

BIBLIOGRAPHY

BLAKE, J., and DAVIS, K. "Norms, Values, and Sanctions." In *Handbook of Modern Sociology*. Edited by R. E. L. Fairs. Chicago: Rand McNally, 1964. Pages 456–484.

CAIN, L. "Aging and the Law." Edited by R. H. Binstock and E. Shanas. *In Handbook of Aging and the Social Sciences*. New York: Van Nostrand Reinhold, 1976. Pages 342–368.

CHUDACOFF, H. P. *How Old Are You? Age Consciousness in American Culture*. Princeton, N.J.: Princeton University Press, 1989.

DANNEFER, D. "The Social Organization of Diversity, and the Normative Organization of Age." *The Gerontologist* 36, no. 2 (1996): 174–177.

LAWRENCE, B. "New Wrinkles in the Theory of Age: Demography, Norms and Performance Ratings." *Academy of Management Journal* 31 (1998): 309–337.

LAWRENCE, B. "Organizational Age Norms: Why Is it So Hard to Know One When You See One?" *Gerontologist* 36, no. 2 (1996): 209–220.

MARINI, M. M. "Age and Sequencing Norms in the Transition to Adulthood." *Social Forces* 63 (1984): 229–244.

MODELL, J. "Normative Aspect of American Marriage Timing Since World War II." *Journal of Family History* 5 (Winter 1980): 210–234.

NEUGARTEN, B. L.; MOORE, J. W.; and LOWE, J. C. "Age Norms, Age Constraints, and Adult Socialization." *American Journal of Sociology* 70 (May 1965): 710–717.

NEUGARTEN, B. L., and NEUGARTEN, D. A. "Age in the Aging Society." *Daedalus* (Winter 1986): 31–49.

NEWCOMB, T. M. *Social Psychology.* New York: Holt, Rinehart, and Winston, 1950.

SETTERSTEN, R. A., JR. and HAGESTAD, G. O. "What's The Latest?: Cultural Age Deadline for Family Transitions." *The Gerontologist* 36, no. 2 (1996a): 178–188.

SETTERSTEN, R. A., JR. and HAGESTAD, G. O. "What's the Latest? II: Cultural Age Deadline for Educational and Work Transitions." *The Gerontologist* 36, no. 5 (1996b): 602–613.

STACK, C. B., and BURTON, L. M. "Kinscripts." *Journal of Comparative Family Studies* 54, no. 2 (1993): 157–170.

THORNE, B. *Gender Play: Girls and Boys in School.* New Brunswick, N.J.: Rutgers University Press, 1993.

WILSON, S. *The Man in the Grey Flannel Suit.* New York: Simon & Schuster, 1955.

AGE-PERIOD-COHORT MODEL

The *age-period-cohort model* is a theoretical model that aims to explain how society changes. In this model, variation over time is thought to occur because of the simultaneous operation of three factors: individual aging, period influences, and generational (or cohort) turnover.

Popular theories of social change rest on the idea that culture, social norms, and social behavior change through two main mechanisms: (1) through changes undergone by individuals, and (2) through the succession of generations (or cohorts). Thus, there is a linkage between individuals and social change. Several things connected to the lives of individuals have a bearing on how society changes. The goal of the age-period-cohort model is to understand the contribution of the effects of aging, time periods, and cohorts to any phenomenon that changes in the aggregate at the society level.

Changes to individuals that influence social change are normally thought to happen because of factors associated with two different phenomena. The first of these is *aging.* Simply put, people change as they get older. Aging is usually identified with differences among individuals that are linked to their getting older, becoming more mature as a function of having lived more of life, or because of physical or cognitive impairment. For example, the older people get, the more medications they take. America, as a whole, may be taking more medications because the population is getting older—an *age effect.* The second source of individual change comes about through people's responses to historical events and processes—sometimes called *period effects.* When the entire society gets caught up in and is affected by a set of historical events, such as a war, an economic depression, or a social movement, the widespread changes that occur are called period effects. The Civil Rights movement, for example, may have changed ideas about race for all ages of Americans, not just those birth cohorts growing up in the 1960s (if it affected primarily the young it would be called a cohort effect—see below). Similarly, not only were the youngest cohorts of women and men affected by the Feminist movement of the 1960s and 1970s, but the movement may have influenced the views of almost everyone living in the society at that time. In fact, it is impossible for most members of society to remain unaffected by some changes—such as the influence of computers on society.

The third source of change in society is *cohort succession,* which is the gradual replacement of earlier born cohorts by later ones. The terms "generation" and "cohort" are often used synonymously, and while in some cases this may be appropriate, we should clarify their meaning. The word *generation* is normally used in one of two different ways: first, as a kinship term, meaning a single stage in the succession of natural descent, referring to relationships between individuals who have a common ancestor; or second, as a group of people born at about the same time and therefore living in the same period of history who share an identity. Thus, within a given family, generations (in the first sense) are very clearly defined, and while generational replacement is a biological inevitability *within families*, the replacement of generations in this sense does not correspond in any neat manner to the historical process at the macro-social level because the temporal gap between generations is variable across families. For this reason researchers often prefer the term *cohort* for this second meaning of generation. A cohort is a group of people who have shared a critical experience at the same time. For example, people who enter college in a given year are referred to as an "entering college cohort" and those who graduate in the same year would be called a "graduating cohort." In each case, there is an event or experience in common that defines the cohort. When people talk about a group of people who share the same historical frame of reference during their youth, they often are using *year of birth* as the defining event (Ryder). Thus, the term "cohort" is often used as shorthand for "birth cohort," and is thought to index the unique historical period in which a group's common experiences are embedded. It is often correctly suggested that the term generation should *not* be used when we mean birth cohort (Kertzer). At the same time, we can tolerate use of the term generation in both ways, but reserve the term (in the second sense mentioned earlier) when the focus is on groups of people who share a distinctive culture and/or a self-conscious identity by virtue of their having experienced the same historical events at roughly the same time in their lives (Mannheim). In this sense generation is not the same as cohort—it implies much more. Thus, cohort differences (i.e. differences tied to year of birth) may be suggestive of generational differences. However, cohort differences may be necessary, but are not sufficient to say that generations truly exist in the sense of having a shared identity.

Earlier-born cohorts die off and are replaced by those born more recently. When the effects of historic events tied to particular eras mainly affect the young, the result is a cohort (or generation) effect. For example, it is sometimes suggested that civic engagement has declined in America overall, even though individual Americans have not necessarily become less civic minded. This may be because older, more publicly engaged citizens are dying off and being replaced by younger, more alienated Americans

who are less tied to institutions such as a church, lodge, political party, or bowling league. As a cohort effect, this refers simply to the effects attributable to having been born in a particular historical period, but as a generation effect (in the sense of Mannheim) it would also imply a status that is recognized both from outside and from within the group. When, for example, people say there is a *Depression generation* that is particularly self-consciously thrifty, they imply that the experience of growing up under privation permanently changed this set of cohorts' economic style of life and their identities due to their formative years. As these members of society die off, they may leave behind a somewhat less frugal set of cohorts.

Cohort replacement explanations of social change make several critical assumptions: (1) that youth is an impressionable period of life in which individuals are maximally open to the socialization influences of the social environment; (2) that people acquire their world views (values, beliefs, and attitudes) during these impressionable years and largely maintain those views over most of their lives; (3) that unique cohort experiences are formed due to the distinctive influences of historical events and experiences, and that there are clear differences across birth cohorts in typical beliefs and attitudes, i.e. there are cohort effects; and (4) that public opinion and social norms change gradually in the direction of the more recent cohorts. If the cohort differences become ingrained in the identities of social actors who take them into account in their behavior, then it may be appropriate to refer to this as "generational" replacement.

One of the major questions in research on social change is: Do the unique formative experiences of different cohorts become distinctively imprinted onto their world views making them distinct "generations," or do people nevertheless adapt to change, remaining adaptable in their dispositions, identities, and beliefs throughout their lives? Unique events that happen during youth are no doubt powerful. Certainly, some eras and social movements (e.g., the women's movement, or the Civil Rights era) or some new ideologies (e.g. Roosevelt's New Deal), provide distinctive experiences for youth during particular times. As Ryder put it: "the potential for change is concentrated in the cohorts of young adults who are old enough to participate directly in the movements impelled by change, but not old enough to have become committed to an occupation, a residence, a family of procreation or a way of life" (Ryder, p.848)

How do age, period, and cohort factors combine to shape social change, and how can their influences be studied using empirical data? The age-period-cohort model recognizes that these are all important causal factors. Unfortunately the individual parts of this model—namely the effects of aging, cohorts, and time periods—are not easy to understand in isolation from one another, and there are serious problems with uniquely identifying their separate effects. It is thus sometimes difficult to place any one interpretation on observed data. Generally speaking, it is necessary to concede that social change could be due to the operation of all three of these factors at once.

The best research designs for the study of aging are longitudinal studies of the same people over time. Often such designs control for cohort differences, but while it is possible to study how individuals change using such designs, it is usually more difficult to understand why they change as they do. Often, the best designs for studying cohort effects are repeated cross-sectional surveys, which do not study the same people but the same cohorts. Such survey designs can study the same cohorts over time, and while less useful for studying how individuals change, they can provide estimates of cohort replacement. There are many potential pitfalls that await the age-period-cohort analyst, and many precautions must be taken to guard against potential fallacies and errors of inference.

DUANE FRANCIS ALWIN

See also AGING; COHORT CHANGE; DEVELOPMENTAL PSYCHOLOGY; PANEL STUDY.

BIBLIOGRAPHY

KERTZER, D. I. "Generation as a Sociological Problem.&rdquo In *Annual Review of Sociology.* Edited by R.H. Turner and J.F. Short, Jr., Palo Alto, Calif: Annual Reviews Inc., (1983). Pages 125–149.

MANNHEIM, K. "The Problem of Generations." In *Essays on the Sociology of Knowledge.* Edited by Paul Kecskemeti, London: Routledge and Kegan Paul, (1952). Pages 276–320.

RYDER, N. B. "The Cohort as a Concept in the Study of Social Change." *American Sociological Review* 30 (1965): 843–861.

AGING

We tend to think of aging in terms of human beings living in time, and, in particular, as the chronology of human experience in later life. But human aging is set in a much wider context, encompassing the biological, geological, and cosmological spheres. Aging is the elegant and continuous means by which the forces of nature, from the microscopic to the universal, create the conditions for regeneration. Many scholars consider aging to be a great equalizer, because it submits all forms of matter, including biological life, to a common set of principles. In human life, there are forms of aging not tied to the individual life course, but to human creations and even whole societies. Buildings become beautiful through weathering; furniture gains a fine patina and great value as it ages; and wines and cheeses are deliberately aged through intricate processes of fermenting, ripening, curing, and storing to enhance their flavor. As for societies across time, they take on the status of "civilizations" if they trace their ancestry and lasting achievements across an extensive span, such as "Old World" European or Asian societies as compared to "New World" countries such as Canada or the United States. The concept of aging, grounded in the realities of both the biological and nonliving material worlds, has thus inspired the human artistic and cultural imagination for millennia.

Rates of aging

Everything that exists in time ages, but rates of aging within living and nonliving realms vary greatly. Geologists and paleontologists who study the earth's history use terms of reference in the hundreds of millions of years. Evidence for the earth's aging is sought in the erosion of mountain ranges or the effects of plate tectonics on the making of continents, and sedimented fossils of extinct plant and animal species mark out a precise record of the earth's aging. These, and related phenomena, beyond the human experience to discern, are subject to the restless vicissitudes of what scientists call the earth's *deep time*. Physicists, meanwhile, indicate the decay of subatomic particles in units of time so brief as to be unintelligible to the ordinary human mind. Living organisms also vary greatly, but within time spans ranging from minutes to millennia, rather than microseconds to millions or billions of years. From the days or weeks of unicellular organisms to the months of rodents or decades of primates, animal aging appears tied in part to size and complexity. Many plants, however, do not appear to have a "natural" lifespan: There are trees living up to three thousand years, such as the giant California sequoias (the General Sherman Tree in California's Sequoia National Park is estimated to be between three and four thousand years old). Among vertebrates, certain families of species seem to live longer than others: parrots among birds, tortoises among reptiles, and elephants and primates among mammals. What is biologically important is the tempo at which such creatures live their lives rather than the actual length of time they live. In turn, a species' or a creature's tempo is determined by laws of size, environmental niches, reproductive cycles, and metabolic rates. As Stephen Jay Gould notes, a rat may live at a faster rate than an elephant, but this does not mean that it lives any less than an elephant (Gould, 1977).

Among primates, Homo sapiens fully evince the paradox of aging posed by the higher primates. On the one hand, humans live the longest and take the longest time to mature. On the other hand, humans are the most "youthful" primate, because their lengthy *neotenic*, postnatal development ensures an extended retention of youthful mammalian features (such as a large brain relative to body size and a playful curiosity). Neoteny also means that humans, born relatively helpless and unformed, develop traits and characteristics outside the womb that most primates develop soon after birth, and with which most other mammals are born. Thus nature's experimentation with increased primate intelligence, carried to a high point in humans, has produced a course of life where more areas of behavior are shaped by societal and family learning than by instinct. The special product of this unique evolutionary experiment is human intelligence and the creation of culture and history as key forces in the species' development.

It is a cosmic irony, therefore, that this intelligence allows us to be aware of our own aging. As the only animal conscious of its own mortality, we have invented many different ways to deal with this knowledge across cultures and over the course of history. In Europe, Medieval and Renaissance thinkers saw aging and dying as part of the universal order, represented by the elements of the earth, the cycle of the seasons, and the movement of the planets. The modern biological and social sciences have developed theories of aging based on cellular, neurological, genetic, physiological, psychological, social, and demographic factors. Whereas cytogerontologists, such as Leonard Hayflick, locate the secrets of aging in cellular biology, those in the humanities, such as philosopher Ronald H. Manheimer, seek it in human wisdom and social relationships. Social and psychological gerontologists connect research on individual health, longevity, and cognitive abilities to wider issues of social inequality, gender, race, housing, and lifestyle. Broader still are demographic and global studies that profile the aging characteristics of whole populations. Thus, human aging, from the cell to the population, is a multifarious process that requires study using a multidisciplinary approach.

Measuring human aging

Despite their different backgrounds, researchers who study aging are challenged by the problem of how to measure it. While geological deep time is measured in large-scale epochs and eras, biological aging is calculated in maturational stages within specific life spans. *Life spans* represent longevity limits that are rarely achieved. The scientific community has set the human life span at 120 years. *Life expectancy* is the statistical figure based on the average person's length of life. In developed countries, medical advances and improved diet have allowed people to live longer and in greater numbers. Gerontologist Bernice Neugarten has divided the aging population itself into *young-old* and *old-old* categories to indicate this development. As the age curve lengthens, however, so do the possible number of diseases and incapacities suffered in later life. At the same time, in developing countries, poverty and the consequences of global inequality continue to undermine healthy populational aging.

Social aging is often measured in terms of *ages* or *stages* of life. For example, many African societies use complex and ritualized age-grade systems to identify the passages of life. Medieval European scholars mapped out seven ages of life according to a planetary model, beginning at birth with the moon and ending in old age with Saturn. Shakespeare's character Jaques, in *As You Like It*, articulated a memorable version of this model, making each age into a theatrical role: the infant, schoolboy, lover, soldier, justice, middle age, and old age—the "last scene of all . . . second childishness and mere oblivion, sans teeth, sans eyes, sans taste, sans everything." (act 2, scene 7)

Ages-of-life models became superseded in the nineteenth and twentieth centuries by the sciences of aging, particularly developmental psychology, geriatrics, and gerontology. These sciences increasingly associated aging with the second half of life, or *later life*, which follows early-life processes of maturation and socialization. In psychology, G. Stanley Hall pioneered aging studies of both early and later life with his two influential books, *Adolescence* (1904), and *Senescence* (1922). Erik H. Erikson, a more contemporary developmental psychologist, theorized eight stages of development across the life cycle. He marked each stage by psychosocial modes of growth, crises, and resolutions centered around identity. For instance, in young adulthood (stage 6), the antithesis between generativity and self-absorption creates care. In old age (stage 8), the antithesis between integrity and despair creates wisdom (Erikson 1982). However, the work of Erikson and others in developmental psychology has been criticized by cross-cultural and feminist psychologists for its individualistic, ethnocentric, and masculinist models of the life cycle.

Geriatrics and gerontology emerged as fields of study in the early twentieth century by borrowing the expertise generated in psychology, biology, and medicine. Geriatrics and gerontology introduced two lasting contributions to the measurement of aging. First, aging and old age have their own physical, emotional, and psychological dynamics distinct from other stages of life. Second, aging and old age are best understood if disease pathologies and normal senile conditions are separated. Early clinicians such as Jean-Martin Charcot, Ignatz L. Nascher, Elie Metchnikoff, and Edmund V. Cowdry attributed the problems of aging to specific degenerative processes in the cells, tissues, and organs of the body. Gerontology grew apart from geriatrics in the later twentieth century to include sociological, demographic, and policy studies. Gerontologists also attacked traditionally ageist notions of decline with new, positive measurements of creativity, wisdom, and the benefits of aging. Gerontological research on positive measurements of successful aging has continued with criticism of the negation of aging stemming from modern culture's adulation of youthfulness.

Structuring the life course

Researchers have come to understand more of the complexities of aging throughout the life course; an idea that connects aging to social, gender, family, generational, and environmental contexts. On an individual, or micro, scale, the life course is a lived embodiment of time from which people distill a rich and versatile archive of meaning, memory, narrative, and identity. On a structural, or macro, scale, the life course is an aggregation of knowledges, technologies, institutions, and lifestyles through which aging is socially and temporally organized. Whether people "act their age" or resist it; whether they reckon their time through linear calendars or cyclical anniversaries—they do so through the norms and roles made possible by particular life courses. In Western societies, since the nineteenth century, the modern life course has been structured according to various institutional, industrial, and commercial standards. For example, early life is age graded according to schooling criteria, while later life is age graded according to retirement criteria (usually 65 and over). The modern life course, in turn, evolved in the twentieth century to become an elaborate framework within which people coordinate family, cohort, and intergenerational relations.

Profound shifts in labor, retirement, demographic patterns, and social programs in the late twentieth and early twenty-first centuries have led cultural gerontologists to posit the rise of a *postmodern life course* (see Featherstone and Hepworth, 1991). The postmodern life course blurs or loosens the chronological and generational boundaries that have set apart childhood, middle age, and old age throughout the modern era. On the one hand, this has motivated marketing, cosmetic, and leisure industries to target *seniors*, *Third Agers*, or *boomers* (usually those 55 and over), and to recast later life as an active, youthful, consumer experience, one often associated with Hollywood film stars who exemplify the postmodern dream of growing older without aging. On the other hand, the postmodern life course creates new avenues of choice, mobility, well-being, and self-definition in later life, thus empowering senior citizens to innovate resourceful roles and ways of life both for themselves and those who will follow.

Metaphors of aging

Aside from scientific measurements of human aging and the social structuring of the life course, people understand what it means to age and grow older by producing their own metaphoric and symbolic images. The world's religious and literary traditions are a rich source of images about the aging process, while secular examples portray life as a *wheel*, a *journey*, a *race*, a *procession*, a *clock*, a *hill*, over which one climbs, or a return to *second childhood*. Metaphorical innovations in language can also shake up traditional conventions about aging. Terms such as *male menopause* or *midlife crisis* raise the issue of how individual and social aging are intertwined. The term *late midlife astonishment* (Pearlman, 1993) is a timely metaphorical antidote to centuries of negative images about middle-aged menopausal women. The *mommy track* is a creative metaphor about women's career path in the workplace, indicating that women must cope with combining careers and parenthood. Whatever their source, metaphors of aging serve to remind us that the human spirit renews itself, in large part, by confronting the paradoxes of living and dying in time.

STEPHEN KATZ

See also AGE; GERIATRICS; GERONTOLOGY; LIFE COURSE; PROLONGEVITY.

BIBLIOGRAPHY

ACHENBAUM, W. A. *Crossing Frontiers: Gerontology Emerges as a Science*. New York: Cambridge University Press, 1995.

BAUMAN, Z. *Mortality, Immortality and Other Life Strategies*. Oxford: Polity Press, 1992.

BINSTOCK, R. H., and GEORGE, L. K., eds. *Handbook of Aging and the Social Sciences*. San Diego: Academic Press, 1996.

BURROW, J. A. *The Ages of Man: A Study in Medieval Writing and Thought*. Oxford: Clarendon Press, 1986.

CHUDACOFF, H. P. *How Old Are You? Age Consciousness in American Culture*. Princeton, N.J.: Princeton University Press, 1989.

COLE, T. R. *The Journey of Life: A Cultural History of Aging in America*. Cambridge, U.K.: Cambridge University Press, 1992.

DANNEFER, D. "The Race is to the Swift: Images of Collective Aging." In *Metaphors of Aging in Science and The Humanities*. Edited by Gary M. Kenyon, James E. Birren, and Johannes J. F. Schroots. New York: Springer, 1991. Pages 155–172.

DANNEFER, D. "Neoteny, Naturalization, and Other Constituents of Human Development." In *The Self and Society in Aging Processes*. Edited

by Carol D. Ryff and Victor W. Marshall. New York: Springer, 1999. Pages 67–93.

ERIKSON, E. H. *The Life Cycle Completed: A Review*. New York: W. W. Norton, 1982.

FEATHERSTONE, M., and HEPWORTH, M. "The Mask of Ageing and the Postmodern Life Course." In *The Body: Social Process and Cultural Theory*. Edited by Mike Featherstone, Mike Hepworth, and Bryan S. Turner. London: Sage Publications, 1991. Pages 371–389.

FEATHERSTONE, M., and WERNICK, A., eds. *Images of Aging: Cultural Representations of Later Life*. London: Routledge, 1995.

FINCH, C. E., and KIRKWOOD, T. *Chance, Development, and Aging*. New York: Oxford University Press, 2000.

GILLIS, J. R. *A World of Their Own Making: Myth, Ritual, and The Quest for Family Values*. Cambridge, Mass.: Harvard University Press, 1996.

GOULD, S. J. "The Child a Man's Real Father." In *Ever Since Darwin*. Edited by S. J. Gould. New York: W. W. Norton and Co., 1977. Pages 63–69.

HALL, G. S. *Senescence: The Last Half of Life*. New York: D. Appleton, 1922.

HAYFLICK, L. "The Cellular Basis for Biological Aging." In *Handbook of the Biology of Aging*. Edited by Caleb E. Finch. New York: Van Nostrand Reinhold, 1977. Pages 159–186.

HOCKEY, J., and JAMES, A. *Growing Up and Growing Old: Ageing and Dependency in the Life Course*. London: Sage Publications, 1993.

KATZ, S. *Disciplining Old Age: The Formation of Gerontological Knowledge*. Charlottesville, Va.: The University Press of Virginia, 1996.

KENYON, G. M.; BIRREN, J. E.; and SCHROOTS, J. J. F., eds. *Metaphors of Aging in Science and The Humanities*. New York: Springer, 1991.

MANHEIMER, R. J. *A Map to the End of Time: Wayfarings with Friends and Philosophers*. New York: W. W. Norton and Co., 1999.

MONTAGU, A. *Growing Young*, 2d. ed. Granby, Mass.: Bergin and Harvey, 1989.

MOSTAFAVI, M., and LEATHERBARROW, D. *On Weathering: The Life of Buildings in Time*. Cambridge, Mass.: The MIT Press, 1993.

NEUGARTEN, B. L., and NEUGARTEN, D. A. "Changing Meanings of Age in the Aging Society." In *Our Aging Society: Paradox and Promise*. Edited by Alan Pifer and D. Lydia Bronte. New York: W. W. Norton and Co., 1986. Pages 33–51.

PEARLMAN, S. F. "Late Mid-Life Astonishment: Disruptions to Identity and Self-Esteem." In *Faces of Women and Aging*. Edited by Nancy D. Davis, Ellen Cole, and Esther D. Rothblum.

New York: Harrington Park, 1993. Pages 1–12.

RASMUSSEN, S. J. *The Poetics and Politics of Tuareg Aging: Life Course and Personal Destiny in Niger.* DeKalb, Ill.: Northern Illinois University Press, 1997.

SOKOLOVSKY, J., ed. *The Cultural Context of Aging: Worldwide Perspectives.* Westport, Conn.: Bergin and Garvey, 1997.

INTERNET RESOURCES

American Association of Retired Persons (AARP) (www.aarp.org).

Administration on Aging (www.aoa.dhhs.gov).

GeroWeb (www.iog.wayne.edu/GeroWeb).

The Gerontological Society of America (www. geron.org).

The National Aging Information Center (www. ageinfo.org).

AGING IN PLACE

Older people overwhelmingly prefer to age in place—to stay in their homes or apartments as they age, rather than move to new settings. Most of them do so: fewer than 10 percent live in nursing homes, assisted living or adult foster care facilities, or continuing-care retirement communities. In fact, during the 1990s, the number of people living in nursing homes in the United States declined although the number of people over age seventy-five rose. About 6 million older people who need assistance, including many with complex medical conditions, get help at home. Laws, regulations, and court decisions increasingly ensure the rights of people with disabilities to live in noninstitutional environments, with maximum control over the services they use.

Older people move less frequently than do people in any other age group. A long-time residence is more than just a building; it is the site of memories and a place to welcome friends and family. It represents familiarity—with people and community resources, the location of the light switches, and the local shortcuts—as well as privacy, control, and stability amid life changes such as widowhood or declining health. The longer one lives in a particular place, the harder it may be to leave, despite problems such as hard-to-climb stairs or unmanageable repairs. Moving requires considerable energy. Older homeowners—more than 75 percent of people over sixty-five own their homes free and clear—may find it especially hard to leave a place that not only em-

bodies status and autonomy but also is often their main economic asset. Sometimes the attachment to home is so strong that it "transcends any rational calculation of benefit" (Fogel, p. 20).

Especially as the proportion of people over sixty-five rises, aging in place presents both challenges and opportunities for older individuals and communities. The risk of illness and disability, and associated needs for assistance, rise with age; yet family assistance is increasingly limited due to smaller and more mobile families, a greater number of women in the workforce, and higher divorce rates. Professional assistance, such as nurses or home health aides, may be expensive, unavailable, or of low quality. Factors such as inaccessible housing and transportation add to the challenges. Too often the results are preventable illnesses, disability, and isolation, especially for those who live alone. The expense of aging in place can be daunting, running tens of thousands of dollars a year if round-the-clock care or extensive housing adaptations are needed. Public funding cuts in the 1990s reduced the amount of home care covered by Medicaid and Medicare. Long-term care insurance helps some people, but much of the cost must be paid out of pocket.

At the same time, the "increase in the elderly population will provide new and important economic and social resources to communities that are positioned to attract them" (Retirement Research Foundation 2000, p. 3). Older residents' needs and wants may stimulate new businesses and services. Construction of new elder-oriented housing frees up single-family homes, which are usually older and therefore more affordable for younger families. New construction and the renovations associated with real estate turnover create jobs and prompt spending. Older residents also have some distinct advantages over younger residents:

When retirees move out [and] families with children move in. . .it means more children swelling enrollment at local schools, more garbage to pick up, more cars on the road, more services generally. . . ."If you are not able to retain [seniors], you end up without the values they represent, and with services that are much more expensive than if they stayed." (Peterson, p. S14)

Accordingly, some communities are reducing taxes and enticing retirees with amenities such as free or low-cost transportation, free health screening, reduced tuition for college and adult education courses, and more and bigger senior centers.

The notion of "elder-friendly communities" captures community characteristics that address the challenges and capitalize on the opportunities presented by an aging population. Elder-friendly communities have a range of reasonably priced, high-quality health, social, and supportive services, such as transportation, housekeeping, and meals; affordable and accessible housing and businesses; and opportunities for older people to continue participating meaningfully in community life through volunteer, cultural, and recreational activities. For example,

In Blue Island, Illinois, Metropolitan Family Services has been using an asset-based approach to creating a more caring community for its older residents. . . . The effort began by identifying ways in which the elderly can use their talents to benefit the community and setting up a number of intergenerational service projects. The newly created Blue Island Commission on Successful Aging may bring public transportation and affordable housing options to this community for the first time. (Retirement Research Foundation, p. 4)

Although any urban, suburban, or rural setting can offer the advantage of familiarity or the disadvantage of isolation—an older person with impaired mobility may be as isolated in an urban high-rise as on a remote farm—types of locations differ in their support for aging in place:

- In urban areas, older people are more likely to be able to walk to stores and services, use public transportation, and access organized health and supportive services. Because of economies of scale, agencies, organizations, and businesses may offer cheaper or more convenient services, more choices, and isolation-fighting activities such as companion programs. On the other hand, the fast pace and rapid rate of neighborhood change and crime (or the fear of crime) can challenge an older person's ability to age in place well.
- Suburban areas have lower crime rates and lower population density; but because health and other services are more dispersed and public transportation is often in short supply, they are more expensive to deliver and harder to get to.
- In rural areas, quality-of-life advantages such as a strong sense of community and history may be outweighed by even more dispersed and expensive health, social, and transportation services than in the suburbs, and the lack of a trained labor pool. Rural housing and economic conditions are also worse, on average, than those of suburban or urban areas.

Because desire to age in place may center on the community as much as on the dwelling, some older people would consider moving to a different residence if their community had affordable supportive housing that promoted independence and balanced privacy with social interaction. Formal models include congregate housing, continuing-care retirement communities, and assisted-living and adult foster care facilities. However, supportive housing can also be found or developed in publicly subsidized or private apartments; housing cooperatives (which allow older people to retain their home equity while living in more supportive housing); and even neighborhoods. (Buildings or neighborhoods with a disproportionate number of older people, sometimes called naturally occurring retirement communities, offer many of the advantages of planned senior housing.) When enough older people live near each other, economies of scale or "clustering" services can reduce the costs, improve the efficiency, and enhance the flexibility of services. On-site service or resource coordinators often pull these elements together. They help residents to obtain services they need and want while contributing to creating the accessible environments, healthy communities, and choices that promote safe and dignified aging in place.

In addition to familiar supportive services such as housekeeping, meals, and transportation, a widening array of other services fosters aging in place: creative "low-tech" services (grocery and pharmacy deliveries, errand assistance, house calls by professionals such as podiatrists and hairdressers, assistance with paying bills and balancing checkbooks, and help with arranging multiple services); "high-tech" services (emergency response systems or interactive medication or pacemaker monitoring); assistance with housing adaptations (installing ramps and grab bars, eliminating thresholds, or installing an elevator); adult day care centers (offering meals, medical care, physical and occupational therapy, and social interaction); and community support for caregivers.

Confronting the challenges and capitalizing on the opportunities presented by aging in place will not be easy. Hope exists, however, in the variety and creativity evident in some states and localities.

SUSAN LANSPERY

See also ADULT DAY CARE; ASSISTED LIVING; CONGREGATE HOUSING; CONTINUING CARE RETIREMENT COMMUNITIES; HOME ADAPTATION AND EQUIPMENT; HOUSING: ALTERNATIVE OPTIONS; SOCIAL SERVICES.

BIBLIOGRAPHY

FOGEL, B. S. "Psychological Aspects of Staying at Home." In *Aging in Place.* Edited by James J. Callahan, Jr. Amityville, N.Y.: Baywood, 1992. Pages 19–28.
Grantmakers in Aging. *Elder-Friendly Communities: Opportunities for Grantmaking.* Annual conference proceedings, 2000. Dayton, Ohio. www.giaging.org
PETERSON, I. "As Taxes Rise, Suburbs Work to Keep Elderly." *New York Times,* February 27, 2001, p. S14.
Retirement Research Foundation. *Creating Caring Communities.* Retirement Research Foundation 1999–2000 report. Chicago, www.rrf.org

ALCOHOLISM

Alcoholism is an illness that is a common form of chemical dependence, and is often referred to as a substance abuse disorder. As with any behavioral disorder, some people are predisposed to it, but there are also strong cultural and environmental influences. Alcoholism is associated with many poor health outcomes.

Alcoholism can be tricky to define, in part due to cultural variability in what is acceptable, both behaviorally and in the attribution of illness. Most definitions of alcoholism, as in the formulation of the fourth edition of the American Psychiatric Association's *Diagnostic and Statistical Manual,* propose (1) that alcohol is taken more (in greater amounts or at more frequent intervals) than is personally or socially intended; (2) that seeking to use, using, and recovering from the effects of using take needed time from the fulfillment of personal, employment, or social obligations; and (3) that use persists despite advice to stop using. Such symptoms should occur repeatedly in order to meet most definitions of alcoholism. Definitions with a more medical ori-

entation include features such as experiencing a physiological alcohol withdrawal syndrome (e.g., nervousness; agitation; increased heart rate, blood pressure, and sweating) when alcohol consumption ceases; requiring other medications (e.g., benzodiazepines such as diazepam or chlordiazepoxide); or marked tolerance to the effects of alcohol. Later, as liver function becomes compromised, older adults with alcoholism can show decreased tolerance (i.e., noticeable effects following comparatively little alcohol intake).

Alcoholism is not rare among older adults: most estimates range between 2 and 10 percent of that population. Understanding exactly how commonly it occurs can be difficult, because there are estimated to be many hidden drinkers, especially among those who are socially isolated. There is also some evidence that estimates might not be stable over longer periods, due to cohort effects; that is, attitudes toward alcohol, learned earlier, may change as young generations become older. When calculating how commonly alcoholism occurs among older adults, it is usual to distinguish two groups: alcoholics who have grown older and those in whom alcohol abuse emerges for the first time in old age. Among the latter, alcoholism can result from a combination of difficulty coping with losses (either feared or actual) and sometimes new social isolation.

Given that alcoholism is not uncommon among older adults and that it can be difficult to define without the presence of medical complications, strategies to recognize alcoholism have been proposed. A popular one is the so-called CAGE questionnaire: Have you felt the need to *c*ut down on your drinking? Have you been *a*nnoyed by others' comments on your drinking? Have you felt *g*uilty about drinking? Have you needed an "*e*ye-opener"? Answering one of these positively suggests the need for further evaluation. A more detailed assessment is the twenty-five-item Michigan Inventory Questionnaire.

Another approach to identifying alcoholism is to screen for abnormalities that are detectable with standard blood tests, such as the red cell volume, the level of triglycerides or uric acid, and problems in the liver and biliary tree. Such an approach relies on a sympathetic physician who can introduce the fact that the constellation of such abnormalities is seen in people who have alcohol problems.

The medical consequences of alcoholism are legion, but a few are of special interest. Alcoholism often coexists with depression, and each exacerbates the other. Alcoholism is associated with memory impairment and even dementia. These cognitive effects can respond to cessation of alcohol consumption, and there is some evidence of amelioration with simple vitamin treatment. Alcoholism can be a cause of delirium in elderly people, especially when medical illness results in abrupt cessation of alcohol intake. Alcoholism is also implicated in falls and mobility impairment. Chronic alcohol use is well known to be associated with cirrhosis of the liver, which among its many complications includes inadequate metabolism of drugs processed by the liver or drugs bound to proteins. Drug interactions are also important. Social complications include (further) isolation, poverty, and legal difficulties.

Definitive treatment of alcoholism consists of the cessation of alcohol use. This is not commonly achieved without intense psychosocial support, such as is provided through Alcoholics Anonymous. Whether decreasing alcohol use to some minimal level can avert or militate the problems of alcoholism is a very controversial question. Supportive and nonjudgmental medical care can be a valuable aspect of the treatment of alcoholism. Physicians can judiciously prescribe medications for the treatment of anxiety and withdrawal. Access to treatment can be difficult for older alcoholics, however, especially those who are disabled or socially isolated. While the prognosis of untreated alcoholism in older adults is poor, treatment can potentially lead to amelioration. However, this is an area in need of further study.

Understood as a complex illness requiring medical and psychosocial support, and occurring often in a disadvantaged and isolated population, alcoholism in elderly people shares many features with other pervasive illnesses, such as dementia. Though treatment has proved difficult, the lessons learned from comprehensive care are likely to have resonance across a range of conditions that face an aging society. They suggest that systemic programs, individualized to accommodate varying needs and including intense psychological support, are needed to achieve effective outcomes in older adults.

KENNETH ROCKWOOD

See also DELIRIUM; DEMENTIA; DEPRESSION; DRUGS AND AGING.

BIBLIOGRAPHY

American Psychiatric Association. "Substance Abuse Disorders." In *Diagnostic and Statistical Manual*, 4th ed. Washington, D.C.: APA, 1994.

COOGLE, C. L.; OSGOOD, N. J.; and PARHAM, I. A. "Follow-up to the Statewide Model Detection and Prevention Program for Geriatric Alcoholism and Alcohol Abuse." *Community Mental Health Journal* 37, no. 5 (2001): 381–391.

SATRE, D. D., and KNIGHT, B. G. "Alcohol Expectancies and Their Relationship to Alcohol Use: Age and Sex Differences." *Aging and Mental Health* 5, no. 1 (2001): 73–83.

THOMAS, V. S., and ROCKWOOD, K. "Alcohol Abuse, Cognitive Impairment, and Mortality Among Older People." *Journal of the American Geriatrics Society* 49 (2001): 415–420.

ALTERNATIVE THERAPY

See HERBAL THERAPY

ALZHEIMER'S DISEASE

Alzheimer's disease (AD) is the most common cause of dementia worldwide. Because its incidence and prevalence increase with age, more and more people are expected to be affected by this common condition with the increasing longevity of populations and the large cohort of baby boomers coming to maturity. Fortunately there has been a rapid increase in understanding of the clinical presentation, natural history, and pathophysiology of AD. Furthermore, there are encouraging results in symptomatic therapy and there is hope for long-term stabilization and preventive treatment.

Clinical presentation

In 1982 Professor Barry Reisberg proposed a Global Deterioration Scale that summarizes seven steps in the progression of AD and serves as an excellent means to describe its natural history (see Table 1).

The symptoms of AD are thus a combination of progressive decline in intellectual abilities and functional autonomy, very often with psychiatric features such as anxiety and depression (mostly in stages 3 and 4), followed by delusions, hallucinations, and wandering (mostly in stages 5 and 6). The latter symptoms cause a severe burden for the families and lead to nursing home place-

Table 1
Natural history of Alzheimer's Disease, modified from the Global Deterioration Scale

Stages	Clinical phase	Clinical characteristics
1	Normal	
2	Forgetfulness	Subjective forgetfulness but normal examination
3	Early confusion	Difficulties performing at work or with complex hobbies, finding words, travelling in unfamiliar areas; detectable by family with subtle memory deficits on examination
4	Late confusion	Decreased ability to travel, to count, to remember current events
5	Early dementia	Assistance needed in choosing clothes, disorientation to time and place, decreased recall of names of grandchildren
6	Middle dementia	Supervision for eating, toileting, disorientation to time, place and persons; incontinence
7	Late dementia	Severe loss of speech, incontinence and motor stiffness

SOURCE: Author

ment in most countries. In the final stage of AD (stage 7), there are changes in motor tone and walking ability similar to those in Parkinson's disease. Death occurs within six to eight years after diagnosis, usually from pneumonia.

There is currently a great interest in the very early symptoms of AD, since early treatment with agents that modify the disease process can significantly delay progression from normal (stage 1) to minimal symptoms (stages 2 and 3), or from minimal symptoms to diagnosable AD (stage 4 and beyond). It appears that late onset depression with loss of interest, energy, or concentration; a long postoperative delirium; or subjective memory complaints with changes in abilities to handle finances, medication, phone, or transportation suggests the possibility of incipient AD.

Diagnosis

Most commonly family members initiate the diagnostic process by bringing the affected person to the attention of the family doctor. The progressive loss of memory for current or recent events is highlighted, with examples of missed appointments, bills paid late, and repeating stories on the phone. A decreased initiative and planning ability is often quite striking, with reduced participation in conversation. The diagnosis of AD is done primarily by a structured history with the patient and a knowledgeable informant. In addition to memory decline, the diagnosis of dementia requires a change in one other intellectual domain (such as language, recognizing objects and people, using tools, planning and adjusting to circumstances) that interferes with daily life and represents a decline from a previous level of functioning. The typical progression of AD as described in the previous section and a normal neurologic examination strongly support the diagnosis of probable AD (90 percent probability if a microscopic examination of the brain is made from a biopsy or autopsy, in which case the diagnosis can be definite). Other features can be found through history and physical examination that suggest alternative diagnosis: history of strokes or high blood pressure with asymmetric reflexes (vascular dementia or mixed AD and vascular dementia), visual hallucinations and gait instability early in the course (dementia with Lewy bodies), social disinhibition and loss of speech early in the course (fronto-temporal dementia). A concomitant disorder, such as depression, malnutrition, or hypothyroidism, would change the diagnosis of AD to "possible."

A mental status assessment is required when AD is suspected, and can range from the simple but short and reliable Mini Mental State Examination of Martial, Folstein, et al. to a structured and complete neuropsychological examination performed by a psychometrician. This may be required in highly educated individuals suspected of early stage AD, for whom the diagnosis is of some urgency because of occupational or social responsibility. Most often these tests need to be repeated within six to twelve months in order to conclusively demonstrate a decline in two cognitive domains.

The laboratory assessment of AD is currently done to support the clinical impression based on a careful history and physical examination. A minimum workup includes blood count of red and white cells; markers of thyroid, liver, and renal function; and blood sugar levels. In some countries routine additional tests include markers of nutritional deficiencies (B12, folic acid) and of previous infection with syphilis. Brain imaging using computer tomography or magnetic resonance imaging without infusion is most often performed in order to demonstrate brain atrophy and rule out tumors, blood clots, and strokes large or small. It is unusual for a brain scan to change the clinical diagnosis or management.

A number of putative biological markers of AD are under study as adjuncts to the clinical diagnosis. The best known are the blood apolipoprotein E genotype and spinal fluid levels of beta-amyloid fragments and tau. None of these markers has the specificity and sensitivity required for routine use, but this research is important for the day when individuals at risk of AD who are in presymptomatic stages will seek advice for preventive therapy.

Pathophysiology

The core pathology of AD was described by Alois Alzheimer early in 1907: extracellular senile or neuritic plaques made up of an amyloid core, surrounded by cell debris, and intracellular neurofibrillary tangles. More recently Robert Terry has emphasized the importance of neuronal cell loss, and Patrick McGeer has documented a strikingly enhanced cellular immune response in the brain of persons with AD. Peter Whitehouse has demonstrated a relatively selective loss of cholinergic neurons in basal forebrain structures, particularly the nucleus basalis of Meynert. This observation, coupled with the reduction in levels of the acetylcholine-synthesizing enzyme choline acetyltransferase, suggested a neurotransmitter deficiency amenable to pharmacotherapy, similar to dopamine deficiency in Parkinson's disease.

Genetic factors clearly play a major role in AD. Presenilin genes carried on chromosomes 1 and 14, and genes on chromosome 21 modifying beta-amyloid metabolism, cause AD at relatively young ages in a Mendelian dominant pattern. Other genes, such as apolipoprotein E on chromosome 19, increase the risk of AD but do not cause it. Many other genes related to late-onset

Table 2

Risk factors toward Alzheimer's Disease

Age
Apolipoprotein E4 genotype
Declining cognitive performance on serial assessments
Depression (men)
Family history of AD (first degree relatives)
Female gender
Lower education
Marital status (male, single)
Social isolation
Systolic arterial hypertension

SOURCE: Author

AD (the most common type) remain to be identified.

Acquired factors over a lifetime can positively or negatively modify the genetic risks. Epidemiological studies have confirmed and found risk factors (see Table 2) and protective factors for AD (see Table 3). Caution should be exerted, since the relative importance of such factors varies between studies. For instance, smoking was considered alternatively a risk and a protective factor; it is now considered neutral as far as AD (but a major risk factor for many other health conditions). High aluminum water content and closed head trauma have been considered risk factors, but the current consensus is that this is not the case. There is currently uncertainty as to the preventive value of hormone replacement therapy (HRT) in postmenopausal women.

Some of these factors clearly make biological sense: systolic hypertension increases the risk of strokes, an additional burden to the aging brain with plaques and tangles; apolipoprotein E4 carriers have a reduced ability to maintain synaptic plasticity (or repair) abilities; NSAIDs suppress the chronic brain inflammatory response associated with neuronal loss; higher education increases the density of synaptic connections; red wine contains a natural antioxidant. Some of these factors interact: higher education and longer HRT (if confirmed to be of value in ongoing randomized studies) will lead to a reduction in the risk of AD associated with female gender. It is hypothesized that a careful weighing of these risk and protective factors for individuals could lead to a preventive strategy in which advice would be proportional to the risk. For example,

Table 3
Protective factors toward Alzheimer's Disease

Fish consumption
Higher education
Large social network and active life style
Long term use of non-steroidal anti-inflammatory drugs
    (NSAIDS)
Marital status (married)
Red wine consumption

SOURCE: Author

a person carrying a double apolipoprotein E4 mutation (from both parents) and a positive family history of AD may want to take NSAIDs chronically. Other risk factors can be modified for all individuals, such as systolic hypertension. This strategy needs to be validated in prospective studies but offers hope of delaying onset of symptoms of AD by five to ten years for the population as a whole, thus significantly reducing the prevalence of AD within one generation.

Treatments

The global management of AD includes a number of steps (see Table 4). In most countries the family practitioner handles them all, in consultation with a variety of health professionals and other community resources throughout the course of AD. For instance, an atypical presentation or pattern of progression may suggest a diagnosis of dementia other than AD, and an expert diagnostic opinion may be needed. Depression or cognitive or behavioral symptoms unresponsive to standard pharmacotherapy may require a trial of another class of drug, with input from experienced clinicians.

Many patients in early stages of AD require treatment with an antidepressant, preferably of the selective serotonin reuptake inhibitor class, for six to twelve months. Most will want to try a cholinesterase inhibitor (CI) in an attempt to increase brain acetylcholine levels and improve symptoms. Randomized clinical trials and clinical experience have shown that in mild to moderately severe stages of AD (stages 3 to 6), therapeutic doses of CI cause an initial improvement, variable between individuals. After nine to twelve months the improvement above the starting point is followed by a slower decline in cognition

Table 4
Global management of Alzheimer's disease

Accurate diagnosis
Patient and caregiver education
Treatment of concomitant disorders such as depression
Elimination of non-essential drugs that could interfere with
    cognition
Advice on will-making, legal guardianship, and advance
    directives
Monitoring of driving ability and safety in use of household
    appliances
Referal to local Alzheimer Association for information and
    support groups
Discussion on use of current symptomatic drugs for AD
Helping caregivers to optimize the preserved functions of the
    patient
Monitoring for and treat neuropsychiatric symptoms as they
    emerge
Arranging support through local health services
Monitoring health and well-being of the caregiver
Planning with caregiver for a smooth transition to a nursing
    home
Making end-of-life decisions respecting advance directives

SOURCE: Author

and functional autonomy relative to patients not on CI, for periods lasting up to three years. It is likely but not yet fully established that CI delays the emergence of neuropsychiatric symptoms seen in stages 5 and 6. There has been some disappointment at the modest size of improvement, the relatively short duration of benefit, and the lack of predictability of who will improve. A more realistic expectation is a delay in progression of symptoms until drugs (currently in various phases of experimental testing) acting on the pathophysiology of AD are proven safe and effective, leading to a combination of symptomatic and stabilization therapy.

A number of possible treatments to delay progression of AD, based on data generated from large-scale epidemiological studies, human brain banks, and the transgenic animal models of AD (see Table 6), are available for evaluation. Large-scale randomized studies are required to test these, some as long as five years, depending on the therapeutic target (for instance, delaying emergence of cognitive symptoms in healthy elderly persons, or conversion from mild cognitive impairment to diagnosable AD).

Table 5
Cholinesterase inhibitors in use for the symptomatic treatment of Alzheimer's disease

Tacrine (Cognex)
Donepezil (Aricept)
Rivastigmine (Exelon)
Galantamine (Reminyl)

SOURCE: Author

Table 6
Testable hypothesis to delay onset or progression of Alzheimer's disease

Amyloid secretase inhibitors
Amyoid 'vaccine'
Anti-inflammatory drugs (NSAIDS or COX-2 selective)
Anti-oxidants
Induction of apolipoprotein E levels
Neurotrophic factors enhancers

SOURCE: Author

Conclusion

Although the human and societal cost of AD is staggering, there is hope that earlier and better diagnosis, increased knowledge of its natural history with support of the patient and family throughout the discase stages, effective symptomatic drugs, and potentially effective disease modification strategies will have a dramatic impact on the number of persons affected in the future, and the quality of life of persons currently affected. The fast pace of research and development in AD is unique in neurological history, and should lead to a better future for aging populations.

SERGE GAUTHIER

See also BRAIN; DEMENTIA; DEMENTIA, ETHICAL ISSUES; DEMENTIA WITH LEWY BODIES; ESTROGEN; FRONTO-TEMPORAL DEMENTIA; MEMORY; MEMORY DYSFUNCTION, DRUG TREATMENT; RETROGENESIS; VASCULAR DEMENTIA.

BIBLIOGRAPHY

BREINTNER, J. C. S. "The End of Alzheimer's Disease?" *International Journal of Geriatric Psychiatry* 14 (1999): 577–586.

GAUTHIER, S. *Alzheimer's Disease in Primary Care*, 2d ed. Martin Dunitz, 1999.

GAUTHIER, S. "Managing Expectations in the Long-Term Treatment of Alzheimer's Disease." *Gerontology* 45 (1999): 33–38.

MAYEUX, R., and SANO, M. "Treatment of Alzheimer's Disease." *New England Journal of Medicine* 341 (1999): 1670–1679.

MCKHANN, G.; DRACHMAN, D.; FOLSTEIN, M.; KATZMAN, R.; PRICE, D.; and STADLAN, E. M. "Clinical Diagnosis of Alzheimer's Disease: Report of the NINCDS-ADRDA Work Group Under the Auspices of Department of Health and Human Services Task Force on Alzheimer's Disease." *Neurology* 24 (1984): 939–944.

MEGEER, P.; SCHULZER, M.; and MCGEER, E. "Arthritis and Anti-Inflammatory Agents As Possible Protective Factors for Alzheimer's Disease: A Review of 17 Epidemiological Studies." *Neurology* 47 (1996): 425–432.

REISBERG, B.; FERRIS, S. H.; DE LEON, M. J.; and CROOK, T. "The Global Deterioration Scale for Assessment of Primary Degenerative Dementia." *American Journal of Psychiatry* 139 (1982): 1136–1139.

ROSENBERG, R. N. "The Molecular and Genetic Basis of AD: The End of the Beginning." *Neurology* 54 (2000): 2045–2054.

TERRY, R. D.; MASLIAH, E. E.; SALMON, D. P.; BUTTERS, N.; DETERESA, R.; HILL, R.; HANSEN, L. A.; and KATZMAN, R. "Physical Basis of Cognitive Alterations in Alzheimer's Disease: Synapse Loss is the Major Correlate of Cognitive Impairment." *Annals of Neurology* 30 (1991): 572–580.

THAL, L. "Potential Prevention Strategies for Alzheimer's Disease." *Alzheimer Disease and Associated Disorders* 10, suppl. 1 (1996): 6–8.

WHITEHOUSE, P.; PRICE, D. L.; CLARK, A. W.; COYLE, J. T.; and DELONG, M. R. "Alzheimer Disease: Evidence for Selective Loss of Cholinergic Neurons in the Nucleus Basalis." *Annals of Neurology* 10 (1981): 122–126.

AMERICANS WITH DISABILITIES ACT

Many older persons fall within the protections of the Americans with Disabilities Act (ADA), which was enacted by Congress as Public Law no. 101-336 on 26 July 1990 and signed by President George Bush, becoming effective in 1992. This legislation was intended primarily to expand to almost the entire public and private sectors the requirements regarding rights to employment, services, and public accommodations for disabled individuals which previously were imposed by section 504 of the Rehabilitation Act of 1973 only on federal contractors. Specifically, Congress in 1990 stated the purpose of the ADA as follows:

(1) to provide a clear and comprehensive national mandate for the elimination of discrimination against individuals with disabilities;
(2) to provide clear, strong, consistent, enforceable standards addressing discrimination against individuals with disabilities;
(3) to ensure that the federal government plays a central role in enforcing the standards established in this Act on behalf of individuals with disabilities.

The ADA is enforced by the U.S. Equal Employment Opportunity Commission (EEOC), the U.S. Departments of Justice and Transportation, and civil lawsuits brought by individuals who have suffered unlawful discrimination. The court costs and attorneys' fees of prevailing plaintiffs must be paid by defendants found guilty of discrimination. No entity may retaliate against an individual for filing a claim under the ADA. In addition, most states have adopted a state counterpart to the federal ADA, enforceable through state agencies and in state courts.

Aging certainly does not automatically equal disability, and vice versa. Indeed, age by itself cannot qualify as a disability under the ADA. Nonetheless, more adults than ever before are either developing disabilities in their later years or aging through life with disabilities. The likelihood of disability demonstrably increases with age.

Employment discrimination

Title I of the ADA prohibits private (both for-profit and not-for-profit) and public (i.e., government) employers with twenty-five or more employees from discriminating "against a qualified individual with a disability because of the disability of such individual in regard to job application procedures, the hiring, advancement, or discharge of employees, employee compensation, job training, and other terms, conditions, and privileges of employment."

Unlike the Age Discrimination in Employment Act (ADEA), passed by Congress in 1967, which only requires equal treatment for older workers (defined as persons at least forty years old), the ADA imposes affirmative obligations on employers regarding employment of the disabled. Specifically, the ADA defines unlawful discrimination to include the following:

(A) not making reasonable accommodations to the known physical or mental limitations of an otherwise qualified individual with a disability who is an applicant or employee, unless [the employer] can demonstrate that the accommodation would impose an undue hardship on the operation of the business of [the employer]; or
(B) denying employment opportunities to a job applicant or employee who is an otherwise qualified individual with a disability, if such denial is based on the need [of the employer] to make reasonable accommodation to the physical or mental impairments of the employer or applicant.

The ADA protects persons with a disability, which means, with respect to an individual:

(A) a physical or mental impairment that substantially limits one or more of the major life activities of such individual;
(B) a record [i.e., a history] of such an impairment; or
(C) being regarded [by others] as having such an impairment.

Many older persons ought to qualify as persons with a disability so defined.

Discrimination in public services and accommodations

Older individuals who qualify as persons with disabilities are also protected by Titles II and III of the ADA. These titles relate, respectively, to discrimination by public and private entities.

Title II. Title II provides that "[N]o qualified individual with a disability shall, by reason of such disability, be excluded from participation in or be denied the benefits of the services, programs, or activities of a public entity [defined as any department or agency of a state or local government], or be subjected to discrimination by any such entity." Banned discrimination might take the form of formal or informal barriers in the application process to obtain benefits (e.g., Medicare, Medicaid, Social Security), including unnecessarily complex application forms, inaccessible application sites, and long waiting times for appointments; reductions in public benefits and services; and undue intrusions into the disabled person's choices about services. "Qualified individual with a disability" is defined as "an individual with a disability who, with or without reasonable modifications to rules, policies, or practices, the removal of architectural, communication, or transportation barriers, or the provision of auxiliary aids and services, meets the essential eligibility requirements for the receipt of services or the participation in programs or activities provided by a public entity."

A major U.S. Supreme Court decision interpreted Title II of the ADA in 1999. In the case of *Olmstead* v. *L.C.* (119 S.Ct. 2176), the state of Georgia was sued by two women whose disabilities included mental retardation and mental illness. Both women lived in state-owned and -operated institutions, despite the fact that the professionals who were treating them had determined that they could be appropriately served in a community setting. The plaintiffs claimed that their continued institutionalization was a violation of their right under the ADA, to live "in the most integrated setting appropriate to the needs of qualified individuals with disabilities." The Supreme Court found that "unjustified isolation . . . is properly regarded as discrimination based on disability." The Court majority opinion observed that "institutional placement of persons who can handle and benefit from community settings perpetuates unwarranted assumptions that persons so isolated are incapable and unworthy of participating in community life," and "confinement in an institution severely diminishes the everyday life activities of individuals, including family relations, social contacts, work options, economic independence, educational advancement, and cultural enrichment."

Under *Olmstead*, states are now required to provide community-based services for persons with disabilities who would otherwise be entitled to institutional services when (1) the state's treatment professionals reasonably determine that community placement is appropriate; (2) the affected persons do not oppose community placement; and (3) community placement can be reasonably accommodated, taking into account the resources available to the state and the needs of others who are receiving state-supported disability services. The Court firmly cautioned, however, that nothing in the ADA condones termination of institutional settings (such as nursing homes or state mental institutions) for persons unable to handle or benefit from community service services.

Moreover, the state's responsibility, once it provides community-based services to qualified persons with disabilities, is not unlimited. Under the ADA, states are obligated to "make reasonable modifications in policies, practices, or procedures when the modifications are necessary to avoid discrimination on the basis of disability, unless the public entity can demonstrate that making the modifications would fundamentally alter the nature of the service, program, or activity." The Supreme Court indicated that the test as to whether a modification entails "fundamental alteration" of a program takes into account three factors: (1) the cost of providing services to the individual in the most integrated setting appropriate; (2) the resources available to the state; and (3) how the provision of services affects the state's ability to meet the needs of others with disabilities. According to the Court, a state can establish compliance with Title II of the ADA if it demonstrates that it has (1) a comprehensive, effectively working plan for placing qualified persons with disabilities in less restrictive settings and (2) a waiting list that moves at a reasonable pace not controlled by the state's endeavors to keep its institutions fully populated.

Title III. Title III of the ADA prohibits discrimination by public accommodations: "(a) No individual shall be discriminated against on the basis of disability in the full and equal enjoyment of the goods, services, facilities, privileges, advantages, or accommodations of any place of public accommodation by any person who owns, leases (or leases to), or operates a place of public accommodation."

The following private entities (both for-profit and not-for-profit) are considered public accommodations: places of lodging; establishments serving food or drink (e.g., restaurants); places of exhibition or entertainment; places of public gathering; sales or rental establishments; service establishments (including professional offices of attorneys and health care providers, as well as health care institutions); stations used for public transportation; places of public display or collection; places of education; social service center establishments; and places of exercise or recreation. Moreover, "No individual shall be discriminated against on the basis of disability in the full and equal enjoyment of specified public transportation services provided by a private entity that is primarily engaged in the business of transporting people. . ."

Title III imposes affirmative obligations on private entities. It requires places of public accommodation to do the following:

(ii) make reasonable modifications in policies, practices, or procedures, when such modifications are necessary to afford [covered] goods, services, facilities, privileges, advantages, or accommodations to individuals with disabilities, unless such entity can demonstrate that making such modifications would fundamentally alter the nature of such goods, services, facilities, privileges, advantages, or accommodations;

(iii) take such steps as may be necessary to ensure that no individual with a disability is excluded, denied services, segregated otherwise . . . treated differently than other individuals because of the absence of auxiliary aids and services, unless the entity can demonstrate that taking such steps would fundamentally alter the nature of the good, service, facility, privilege, advantage, or accommodation being offered or would result in an undue burden;

(iv) remove architectural barriers, and communication barriers that are structural in nature, in existing facilities, and transportation barriers in existing vehicles and rail passenger cars used by an establishment for transporting individuals. . .[New construction and alterations in public accommodations are also covered.];

(v) where an entity can demonstrate that the removal of a barrier under clause (iv) is not readily achievable, [the entity must] make such goods, services, facilities, privileges, advantages, or accommodations available through alternative methods if such methods are readily achievable.

One important limitation on the reach of Title III is that religious organizations are specifically excluded from coverage. Thus, there is no federal requirement that religious and social activities associated with places of worship be accessible to persons with disabilities.

Conclusion

Many questions relating to the eventual impact of the ADA on older persons, both individually and as a group, remain and await clarification through further regulatory and judicial interpretation in particular cases. It is certain, though, that the ADA provides broad, needed civil rights protections for older Americans with mental and physical disabilities in respect to programs sponsored or funded by state and local governments and to public accommodations provided by private enterprises.

MARSHALL B. KAPP

See also DISABILITY.

BIBLIOGRAPHY

American Bar Association, Commission on Mental and Physical Disability Law. *Mental Disabilities and the Americans with Disabilities Act*, 2d ed. Washington, D.C.: ABA, 1997.

ANSELLO, E. F., and EUSTIS, N. N., guest eds. "Aging and Disabilities: Seeking Common Ground." *Generations* 16 (1992): 3–99.

COLKER, R., and TUCKER, B. P. *The Law of Disability Discrimination*, 2d ed. Cincinnati, Ohio: Anderson, 1998.

GOSTIN, L. O., and BEYER, H. A. *Implementing the Americans with Disabilities Act: Rights and Responsibilities of All Americans*. Baltimore: Brookes, 1993.

GOTTLICH, V. "Protection for Nursing Facility Residents Under the ADA." *Generations* 18 (1994): 43–47

ROTHSTEIN, L. F. *Disabilities and the Law*, 2d ed. St. Paul, Minn.: West Group, 1997.

TUCKER, B. P. *Federal Disability Law*, 2d ed. St. Paul, Minn.: West Group, 1998.

WEST, J., ed. *The Americans with Disabilities Act: From Policy to Practice*. New York: Milbank Memorial Fund, 1991.

ANDROGENS

See ANDROPAUSE; MENOPAUSE

ANDROPAUSE

In men and women many physiological and psychological symptoms and biochemical changes attributed to an aging-related decline in gonadal hormones. Menopause in women is based on the end of the reproductive cycle associated with ovarian failure, and is characterized by the relatively abrupt onset of well-recognized symptoms. In contrast, the term "andropause" has been used to describe the slow, steady decline of testosterone in men as they age. This process is not universal in men, is more insidious in its onset, and its clinical presentation is more subtle and varied. For these reasons it has been suggested that androgen decline in the aging male (ADAM) is a more appropriate designation for this syndrome (Morales et al.).

Changes in the aging male

The andropause syndrome is difficult to detect clinically because the symptoms are often attributed to a more general aging process in the absence of specific disease. The characteristic symptoms include weakness, depression, fatigue, and changes in body hair and skin. In addition there is loss of libido, lean body mass, and bone mass, as well as decreased intellectual activity and spatial orientation ability. The severity and frequency of each symptom are variable.

Erectile function. Male aging is associated with a decline in sexual interest and activity and an increase in erectile dysfunction. In men between the ages of forty and seventy, 52 percent reported some degree of impotence (Gooren). This aging-related impaired sexual function is multifactorial with testosterone likely playing only a minor, if any, role. Testosterone appears more important in maintaining desire and nocturnal erections (Gooren). For most men with erectile dysfunction, therapies such as sildenafil (Viagra©), penile injections, vacuum-suction devices, and penile prostheses are more effective than testosterone.

Mood and cognition. Testosterone replacement often improves men's sense of overall well-being (Vermeulen). Improvements in libido, energy, and mood; a decline in anxiety; and increased aggressiveness in business transactions have all been described in hypogonadal (having low levels of testosterone) men receiving testosterone (Tenover 1992, 1994; Wang et al.), but how these findings translate to normal aging men is not clear.

Body composition. A decrease in both muscle tissue mass and some aspects of muscle strength have been associated with male aging (Tenover 1994). An increase in percent body fat has been reported in hypogonadal men compared to eugonadal men (Katznelson et al.). A role for testosterone in these changes is supported by the fact that testosterone replacement in young, healthy, hypogonadal men increases fat-free mass, muscle size, and strength, and decreases percent body fat (Bhasin et al.; Katznelson et al.; Tenover 1992). Several studies have reported an increase in grip strength with testosterone replacement (Morley et al.; Sih et al.), but the effect on more clinically relevant measures of strength is not known.

Bone density. Osteoporosis is a significant but underrecognized cause of morbidity and mortality in elderly men. As in women, bone density decreases and osteoporotic fractures increase with male aging (Abu et al.; Swerdloff and Wang). Hypogonadism is associated with a significant decrease in bone density (Katznelson et al.) and increased risk of fractures. Testosterone replacement significantly improves bone mineral density in hypogonadal men (Behre et al.; Katznelson et al.), but a reduction in fractures following normalization of bone mineral density has not been established.

Androgen levels. Only 1-2 percent of the testosterone in the circulation is free; the remainder is bound, either tightly to sex-hormone-binding-globulin (SHBG; 60 percent), or weakly to albumin (40 percent). Bioavailable testosterone includes only the free and albumin bound components. SHBG-bound testosterone is not available for tissue uptake (Gray et al.).

Bioavailable testosterone declines, and SHBG-bound testosterone increases, with increasing age. The implication of this is that hypogonadal men may have normal or only slightly reduced total serum testosterone levels. For this reason identification of these men is best accomplished by measurement of bioavailable testosterone (Gray et al.).

The clinical significance of the age-related decline in testosterone is unclear. There is considerable variation in serum testosterone among men of all ages, such that many healthy elderly men have levels within the normal range (Vermeulen). Total testosterone levels below the normal reference level are reported in 7 percent of men age forty to sixty, 20 percent of men age sixty to eighty, and 35 percent of men over eighty (Vermeulen and Kaufman).

Complications of testosterone replacement

Prostate growth, whether malignant or benign, is highly dependent on steroid hormones. A major concern is that testosterone replacement will stimulate the onset or hasten the development of prostatic carcinoma. The inhibitory effect of removing androgens on clinically diagnosed prostate cancer is well known. Whether replacing testosterone in hypogonadal men promotes development of de novo malignancies or progression of sub-clinical carcinomas is not known. To date, the small and short-term studies have not demonstrated an increased risk (Morales et al.). However, the level of experience at this time is insufficient to conclusively rule out a causal relationship (Morales et al.). For this reason, careful monitoring of these patients with serum prostate-specific antigen (PSA) and digital rectal exams are recommended.

The effect of testosterone on benign prostatic enlargement has also been a concern. The most recent data from placebo-controlled trials of testosterone replacement in hypogonadal men suggests that the changes in PSA, prostate volume, and lower urinary tract symptoms are clinically insignificant (Tenover, 1998). Current recommendations suggest serum PSA and digital rectal exam before instituting testosterone replacement, then yearly thereafter.

The effects of hypogonadism and testosterone replacement on lipid profiles and risk of cardiovascular disease are unclear. Interestingly, low serum testosterone levels appear to be associated with increased triglycerides and decreased levels of high-density lipoprotein (HDL) cholesterol; testosterone replacement appears to restore these to more favorable levels (Zmuda et al.). Several recent studies have suggested that hypogonadism may be a risk factor for coronary artery disease, although this remains to be fully explained (Philips et al.; Uyanik et al.). The impact of testosterone therapy on cardiovascular risk is not entirely clear, however; most current data suggest it does not induce an atherogenic profile (Vermeulen and Kaufman). Careful lipid monitoring should be provided for patients on testosterone replacement, particularly those with risk factors for coronary artery disease.

Current injectable, oral, and transdermal testosterone preparations (available in the United States only) without methyltestosterone are believed not to cause the liver toxicity described with previously used methylated forms of testosterone (Morales et al.).

Testosterone stimulates erythropoiesis (production of red blood cells) through an unclear mechanism and can result in increased hematocrit, increased hemoglobin, and hypercoagulability in as many as 24 percent of patients (Jockenhovel et al.; Winkler). For this reason hematocrit assessment on a three-month basis has been recommended for men on testosterone replacement.

Types of replacement therapy

Options for replacement include oral tablets and capsules, transdermal patches (scrotal and nonscrotal), and intramuscular injections. Older methyltestosterone oral formulations are undesirable because of their significant first-pass metabolism in the liver and significant liver toxicity. Testosterone undecenoate is absorbed through the lymphatic system and is thought to be free of liver toxicity (Nieschlag). Oral doses two or three times a day can reduce serum testosterone fluctuations, and may have a lower incidence of increased red cell mass in the blood and increased hematocrit.

Injectable testosterone is generally administered as a slow-release, oil-based preparation (testosterone enanthate or cypionate) that achieves supraphysiologic concentration approximately seventy-two hours after injection, then slowly declines over ten to fourteen days to a hypogonadal range. The wide fluctuation in levels during the dosing interval can produce enlarged breasts, breast tenderness, significant mood swings, and changes in libido and sexual function.

Transdermal patches have become available that provide a more physiologic approach to testosterone replacement by mimicking the normal diurnal variation in testosterone levels. The original patches were scrotal; more recently nonscrotal patches have become available (neither is currently available in Canada). Patches are applied at bedtime so that peak testosterone levels occur in the morning, then decline during the day (Nieschlag; Schow et al.). These patches appear to have most of the benefits of injected testosterone replacement. In addition there appears to be less aggressiveness, although these effects have not been studied in long-term trials (Morales et al.). Local dermatitis and higher costs have prevented their widespread use.

Conclusions

Current evidence supports the existence of progressive hypogonadism affecting many older men which has been labeled andropause or the ADAM syndrome. The diagnostic criteria for this syndrome, however, are imprecise because many of its symptoms, such as mood and energy level, are difficult to measure and separate from "normal" aging. In addition, possible changes in the androgen receptors with aging lead to uncertainty about the exact level of androgen required for optimum health. Also, many other hormone changes and disease states affect the aging man.

Nonetheless, testosterone appears to be a prominent hormone involved in this syndrome, and testosterone replacement in this population is used with increasing frequency. Androgen replacement should be instituted on the basis of the combination of low bone density or patient symptoms and low testosterone levels, and in the absence of other causes. A DRE (digital rectal examination) and PSA (prostate-specific androgen measurment) should be performed on all men prior to instituting testosterone replacement. Patients with known prostate or breast cancer (due to conversion to estrogen), abnormal DRE or elevated PSA or severe lower urinary tract symptoms are not suitable for testosterone replacement. Others will require careful follow-up to minimize the potential for long-term complications.

TROY SITLAND
JOHN GRANTMYRE

See also HAIR; MENOPAUSE; PROSTATE; SARCOPENIA; SEXUALITY.

BIBIOGRAPHY

ABU, E.; HORNER, A.; KUSEC, V. et al. "The Localization of Androgen Receptors in Human Bone." *Journal of Clinical Endocrinology and Metabolism* 82 (1997): 3493–3495.

BEHRE, H.; KLIESCH, S.; LIEFKE, E.; LINK, T. ; and NIESCHLAG, E.. "Long-term Effect of Testosterone Therapy on Bone Mineral Density in Hypogonadal Men." *Journal of Clinical Endocrinology and Metabolism* 82 (1997): 2386–2390.

BHASIN, S.; STORER, T.; BERMAN, N. et al. "A Replacement Dose of Testosterone Increases Fat-free Mass and Muscle Size in Hypogonadal Men." *Journal of Clinical Endocrinology and Metabolism* 82 (1997): 407–413.

GOOREN, L. "The Age Related Decline in Androgen Levels in Men: Clinically Significant." *British Journal of Urology* 78 (1996): 763–768.

GRAY, A.; FELDHAM, H.; and MCKINLAY, J. "Age, Disease and Changing Sex Hormone Levels in Middle-aged Men: Results of the Massachusetts Male Aging Study." *Journal of Clinical Endocrinology and Metabolism* 73 (1991): 1016–1025.

JOCKENHOVEL, F.; VOGEL, E.; REINHARDT, W. et al. "Effects of Various Modes of Androgen Substitution Therapy on Erythropoiesis." *European Journal of Medical Research* 2 (1997): 293–297.

KATZNELSON, L.; FINKELSTEIN, J.; SCHOENFELD, D.; ROSENTHAL, D.; ANDERSON, E.; and KLIBANSKI, A. "Increase in Bone Density and Lean Body Mass During Testosterone Administration in Men with Acquired Hypogonadism." *Journal of Clinical Endocrinology and Metabolism* 81 (1996): 4358–4365.

MORALES, A.; HEATON, J.; and CARSON, C. "Andropause: A Misnomer for a True Clinical Entity." *Journal of Urology* 163 (2000): 705–712.

MORLEY, J.; PERRY, M.; KAISER, F. et al. "Effects of Testosterone Replacement Therapy in Old Hypogonadal Males: A Preliminary Study." *Journal of American Gerontological Society* (1993): 41.

NIESCHLAG, E. "Testosterone Replacement Therapy: Something Old, Something New." *Clinical Endocrinology* 45 (1996): 261–262.

PHILIPS, G.; PINKERNELL, B.; and JING, T. "The Association of Hypotestosteronemia with Coronary Artery Disease in Men." *Arteriosclerosis and Thrombosis* 14 (1994): 701–704.

SCHOW, D.; REDMON, B.; and PRYOR, J. "Male Menopause: How to Define It, How to Treat It." *Postgraduate Medicine* 101 (1997): 62–79.

SIH, R.; MORLEY, J.; KAISER, F. et al. "Testosterone Replacement in Older Hypogonadal Men: A 12-Month Randomized Controlled Trial." *Journal of Clinical Endocrinology and Metabolism* 82 (1997): 1661–1667.

SWERDLOFF, R. and WANG, C. "Androgen Deficiency and Aging in Men." *Western Journal of Medicine* 159 (1993): 579–585.

TENOVER, J. "Effects of Androgen Supplementation in the Aging Male." *Journal of Clinical Endocrinology and Metabolism* 75 (1992): 1092–1098.

TENOVER, J. "Androgen Administration to Aging Men." *Endocrinology and Metabolism Clinic of North America* 23 (1994): 877–892.

TENOVER, J. "Androgen Deficiency in the Aging Male." *Aging Male* 1 (supp. 1998): 16.

UYANIK, B.; ARI, Z.; GUMUS, B. et al. "Beneficial Effects of Testosterone Undercenoate on the Lipoprotein profiles in Healthy Elderly men,

A Placebo Controlled Study." *Japanese Heart Journal* 38 (1997): 73–78.

VERMEULEN, A. "The Male Climacterium." *Annals of Medicine* 25 (1993): 531–534.

VERMEULEN, A. and KAUFMAN, J. "Ageing of the Hypothalamus-Pituitary-Testicular Axis in Men." *Hormone Research* 43 (1995): 25–28.

WANG, C.; ALEXANDER, G.; BERMAN, N. et al. "Testosterone Replacement Therapy Improves Mood in Hypogonadal Men—A Clinical Research Center Study." *Journal of Clinical Endocrinology and Metabolism* 81 (1996): 3578–3583.

WINKLER, U. "Effects of Androgens on Hemostasis." *Maturitas* 24 (1996): 147.

ZMUDA, J.; CAULEY, J.; KRISKA, A. et al. "Longitudinal Relation Between Endogenous Testosterone and Cardiovascular Disease Risk Factors in Middle-Aged Men. A 13-Year Follow-Up of Former Multiple Risk Factor Intervention Trial Participants." *American Journal of Epidemiolofy* 146 (1997): 609–613.

ANESTHESIA

"My diseases are an asthma and a dropsy and, what is less curable, seventy-five."

—Samuel Johnson.

Over 40 percent of all surgical procedures in the United States are performed on patients over age sixty-five, a remarkable statistic given that those over sixty-five comprise only 13 percent of the U.S. population. Elderly patients are more likely than their younger counterparts to suffer serious medical complications such as a heart attack, pneumonia, or kidney failure during or after an operation, further compounding the impact that caring for elderly patients has on the medical system.

Basics of anesthesia

There are three broad categories of anesthesia: local anesthesia, regional anesthesia, and general anesthesia. Local and regional anesthesia involve the injection of a drug, such as lidocaine or bupivacaine, that soaks into the nerves and blocks the electrical signals from traveling down the nerves. With local anesthesia the drug is injected under the skin in the area of the surgery where the nerves are diffusely spread about in the tissue, whereas in regional anesthesia the drug is injected next to large, discrete nerves traveling to the surgical area. For example, when injected at the right location in the armpit, the arm can be made completely numb, allowing surgery to proceed without the patient feeling any pain. A spinal anesthetic involves placing the needle between the vertebrae into the spinal sac. The drug then reaches the nerves that go to the lower half of the body, making the patient numb from approximately the upper abdomen down. An epidural anesthetic is similar to a spinal, only the needle is placed outside the spinal sac, and, typically, a catheter is inserted (and the needle removed). An advantage of the catheter is it is easier to give subsequent injections.

A general anesthetic renders the patient unconscious during surgery. Most often, unconsciousness is rapidly achieved by injecting a large dose of a sedative, such as pentothal or propofol. Since the drug wears off quickly, it is immediately followed by a gas anesthetic to keep the patient asleep. During surgery, narcotic painkillers may be used to reduce the amount of gas being used, and to get a head start on the pain control that may be required after surgery. Sometimes drugs that paralyze the muscles must also be used to facilitate the operation.

During the use of any anesthetic, the patient's vital signs are watched carefully and continuously. The electrical activity of the heart (electrocardiogram) is displayed on a monitor (see Figure 1); blood pressure is measured every few minutes with an automated machine; and the oxygen level in the arterial blood is measured via a device that clips to a finger. During a general anesthetic a machine will measure the concentration of the gas anesthetic, as well as the level of carbon dioxide coming from the lungs. Careful monitoring is important because all anesthetics can lower blood pressure, depress breathing, and impair many of the body's defense mechanisms. The amount of anesthetic given the patient must therefore be continuously adjusted to match the conditions present during surgery.

The unique challenge of the elderly patient

Aging decreases the ability of every organ system in the body to withstand stress, including those associated with surgery and anesthesia. Stress begins in surgery with the combined effects of the anesthetic and surgical trauma. After surgery, the patient faces a potentially long period of recovery from that trauma, as well as the stress of pain. Chronic diseases such as stroke,

Figure 1
When a person is under anesthesia, monitoring equipment is used to oversee the patient's vital signs.

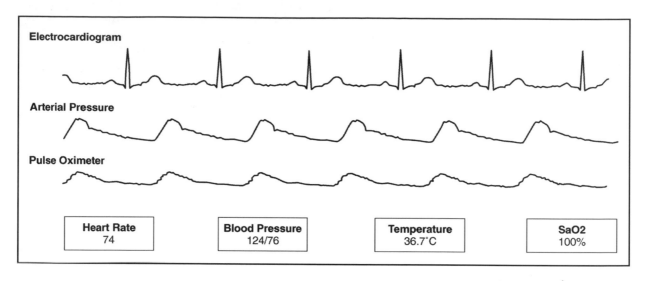

Electrocardiogram

Arterial Pressure

Pulse Oximeter

Heart Rate	Blood Pressure	Temperature	SaO2
74	124/76	36.7°C	100%

SOURCE: Author

heart disease, diabetes, or high blood pressure also compromise the body's ability to withstand stress and make the patient more vulnerable to complications such as a heart attack, pneumonia, kidney failure, or even death. Aging has its greatest adverse impact on older patients who also have medical illness. Among healthy people, the risk of complications from anesthesia and surgery increases only slightly with age. Among people with multiple chronic medical conditions, however, risk dramatically increases with age. The challenge to the care of elderly patients lies in tailoring the anesthetic to the patient's medical illnesses as well as taking into account the effect of age on the responses to the anesthetic. In all phases of anesthetic care, everything is done with an eye to reducing the likelihood that complications will occur.

Preoperative assessment

Before a patient has surgery, it must be determined that the expected benefits of the surgery outweigh the risks. With a healthy patient, this decision is usually straightforward; but this determination is more difficult for an elderly patient with multiple medical problems contemplating a high-risk surgery. Sometimes it is useful to get other specialists involved in order to perform more sophisticated tests that will better define the extent of the disease. Such testing may lead to therapy aimed at improving the medical status of the patient in order to decrease the risk of the surgery. For example, a patient with poorly controlled asthma might benefit from a few days of steroids to bring the asthma under control. With the current trend of performing as many surgeries as possible on an outpatient basis, many patients now go to preoperative clinics where their medical history and current condition can be assessed and further evaluation or treatment initiated well in advance of the scheduled surgery.

Intraoperative management

Virtually all anesthetic drugs have more pronounced effects on elderly patients. Drug effects typically last longer in older adults because metabolism (elimination of the drug from the body) slows with age. A given dose of a drug usually has a greater effect on older patients because higher initial blood levels are achieved than in young patients, thereby permitting more drug to enter the brain. In some cases the older brain is also more sensitive to the drug. In consequence, elderly patients usually receive small doses, and whenever possible drugs are used that possess a short duration of action.

Maintenance of a stable blood pressure is also more difficult with older patients. Blood pressure is the product of cardiac output (the amount of blood the heart pumps to the body per minute) and vascular resistance (how hard it is for blood to flow through the blood vessels). Vascular resistance is partly controlled by the brain. Aging is associated with increasing stimulation of the blood vessels by the brain and therefore vascular resistance increases with age. During anesthesia that stimulation is lost. Consequently, the vascular resistance decreases more than in a young adult and takes the blood pressure down with it. Furthermore, aging decreases the body's ability to resist changes in blood pressure, making changes in blood pressure due to external forces such as blood loss during surgery less opposed, and therefore more dramatic. Fortunately, modest swings in blood pressure, whether up or down, are usually well tolerated by almost every patient. Nevertheless, the control of blood pressure generally requires more direct manipulation by the anesthesiologist when caring for elderly patients.

The lungs are another area of great concern. Aging diminishes the transfer of oxygen to the blood, and anesthesia worsens this problem. Elderly patients are therefore likely to need extra oxygen for a longer period of time after surgery to prevent the risk of having periods of low blood-oxygen levels. Aging also increases the likelihood that portions of the lungs will compress and make the lungs more prone to pneumonia. The reflexes in the mouth and upper windpipe protect against regurgitated stomach contents from entering the trachea and damaging the lungs. These protective reflexes also diminish with age, again making the older patient at higher risk of low blood-oxygen levels or pneumonia. Deep breathing and coughing out secretions that accumulate in the lungs are important maneuvers done by the patient to help prevent low blood oxygen or pneumonia.

Although it is a controversial area, there is suspicion that surgery somehow causes blood to clot more easily. This tendency might be a good thing at the site of the surgery, but it may also lead to clots forming at diseased areas of the arteries that supply blood to the heart or brain. If so, such clots could lead to a heart attack or to a stroke. Prevention of such complications is a major area of current research.

Postoperative care

Surgery, especially operations where the chest or abdomen is opened, creates a significant stress to the patient that continues for at least several days after the surgery. Besides problems such as pneumonia or a heart attack, older patients are particularly prone to becoming confused within a day or two of surgery. Although the confusion almost always goes away, the condition may leave the patient in a more debilitated state for a long time thereafter, and thus requiring longer hospitalization and perhaps even nursing home care on discharge from the hospital. Patients may also suffer a potentially permanent decline in mental abilities in association with surgery. Prevention of these phenomena is an important area of current research.

Anesthesiologists have been particularly involved with preventing complications by helping to provide better pain control after surgery. A popular method of pain control is the administration of morphine via a pump controlled by the patient. Within certain safety limits, a small dose of morphine is given each time the patient pushes a button. Narcotics such as morphine have side effects, however, such as itching, nausea, and sedation. In part to avoid these problems, non-narcotic drugs have been gaining popularity. For surgery on the arms or legs, the use of long-lasting local anesthetics can safely extend the anesthetic for up to a day after surgery. Through mechanisms not yet fully understood, this technique may reduce the amount of pain experienced even after the local anesthetic has worn off.

Another option for pain relief after surgery is provided by the epidural catheter described previously. By administering a low concentration of both a local anesthetic and a narcotic through the catheter, excellent pain control can be achieved without affecting the patient's brain, allowing the patient to breathe more deeply and cough more easily, thereby helping to prevent pneumonia. Good pain control may also diminish the risk of other problems, such as a heart attack. The exact role of pain control with epidural catheters is still unclear, but it appears that complications can be reduced in high-risk (often elderly) patients.

Conclusion

The anesthetic care of the elderly patient is complex and demanding because of the effects of aging on organ function, plus the greater likelihood of chronic disease with increased age. Greater attention must be afforded such patients, beginning with the evaluation and optimization of the patient's medical status. The anesthetic requires close attention to detail, and, in selected patients, special techniques may be useful in lowering the risk of complications.

G. ALEC ROOKE

See also PAIN MANAGEMENT; REVASCULARIZATION: BYPASS SURGERY AND ANGIOPLASTY; SURGERY IN ELDERLY PEOPLE.

BIBLIOGRAPHY

LIU, S.; CARPENTER, R. L.; and NEAL, J. M. "Epidural Anesthesia and Analgesia—Their Role in Postoperative Outcome." *Anesthesiology* 85 (1995): 1474–1506.

MCLESKEY, C. H., ed. *Geriatric Anesthesia.* Baltimore, Md.: Williams & Wilkins, 1997.

MOLLER, J. T.; CLUITMANS, P.; RASMUSSEN, L. S.; et al. "Long-Term Postoperative Cognitive Dysfunction in the Elderly: ISPOCD1 Study." *Lancet* 351 (1998): 857–861.

MORGAN, G. E., and MIKHAIL, M. S. *Clinical Anesthesia,* 2d ed. New York: Lange Medical Books/McGraw-Hill, 1996.

MURAVCHICK, S. *Geroanesthesia.* St. Louis, Mo.: Mosby, 1997.

ROOKE, G. A. "Autonomic and Cardiovascular Function in the Geriatric Patient." *Anesth Clin NA* 18 (2000): 31–46.

TIRET, L.; DESMONTS, J. M.; HATTON, F.; and VOURC'H, G. "Complications Associated with Anesthesia—A Prospective Survey in France." *Canadian Anaesthetists' Society Journal* 33 (1986): 336–344.

ANEURYSM, ABDOMINAL AORTIC

See VASCULAR DISEASE

ANNUAL CHECK-UP

See PERIODIC HEALTH EXAMINATION

ANNUITIES

When planning for retirement, many Americans forget to plan for one of the most important risks—the risk of "living too long" and running out of money. Increases in life expectancy have resulted in people often spending twenty to thirty years (or more) in retirement. Women especially are in danger of experiencing this gap between length of life and retirement resources because, statistically speaking, they live longer than men. There is one investment product that is designed to protect against this risk—an annuity.

What is an annuity?

An annuity is a contract sold by a life insurance company that guarantees a stream of payments to the buyer (the *annuitant*) that begin at a specified time, often at retirement. With an annuity, the annuitant is literally buying a future income. There are different types of annuities. *Deferred annuities* are purchased either with a single payment or by regular premiums during the annuitant's working life with the specification that the funds are to be used at some future date. *Immediate life annuities* are bought at the time of retirement—the purchaser makes a single payment to an insurance company, which invests the money and begins to send the annuitant regular payments immediately.

Annuities provide a regular income that cannot be outlived. Monthly, semiannual, or annual payments are made until the annuitant dies. Therefore, an annuity provides a form of security that investments in stocks or bonds can't. Some annuities also name another person, such as a spouse, to continue getting income payments after the annuitant dies.

An annuity can be either *fixed* or *variable*. A fixed annuity has payments that are specified in the contract and usually remain the same, while a variable annuity has payments that go up and down based on underlying investments in the stock market or other securities.

There are also special kinds of annuities that are sold by charitable organizations that let an annuitant withdraw money in a lump sum. These annuities pay income only for a limited time.

Unfortunately, there is no magic formula for determining how much income is needed after retirement. Most financial planners agree that to maintain the same standard of living after retirement as before, an individual will need an annual income that is roughly 70 percent of his or her gross income before taxes while working. But this is only a rough estimate. Each person needs to refine it for his or her own situation.

Table 1
Purchasing power of a fixed $10,000 income.

When the Inflation Rate Is	At retire- ment you have	After 10 years its worth	After 20 years its worth	After 30 years its worth
3%	$10,000	$7,441	$5,537	$4,120
5%	10,000	6,139	3,769	2,314
7%	10,000	5,083	2,584	1,314

SOURCE: Actuarial Foundation, 2000

Table 2
Average annual investment returns, 1926–1998.

	Cash Investments	Bonds	Stocks
Total return	3.9%	5.7%	11.2%
Average rate of inflation	-3.1	-3.1	-3.1
Net return after inflation	0.8	2.6	8.1

SOURCE: Actuarial Foundation, 2000

Nor is it possible to know how long a person will need a retirement income. Life expectancy figures exist, but while they are useful for calculating what will happen with large numbers of people, they don't help in calculating how long an individual will live. Actuaries say longevity is a "moving target." For example, an actuarial table might indicate that people 65 years old can expect to live another twenty years, or to age 85. However, of that group, those who live to 75 can then expect to live to age 87.5; and those who live to 85 can expect to live to 91.5. And, since women tend to live longer than men, 65-year-old women are 8 percent more likely than 65-year-old men to reach age 80, and 81 percent more likely to reach age 90. Because this is true, married women usually survive their spouses, often with much less income than before.

How does inflation affect retirees?

The price of almost everything will probably go up every year. This is the effect of inflation, a major risk that nobody can predict. In the 1990s, annual inflation was about 3 percent—down from the 1980s, when inflation was about 5 percent, and the 1970s, when it was about 7 percent. Inflation can make a big difference in what a worker will be able to buy after retiring. Table 1 provides examples of how inflation can diminish purchasing power.

Most private pensions are not adjusted every year to provide enough money to counteract the effect of inflation. Many large public employers, such as the U.S. government and some state and local governments, do adjust the amounts of their employees' pensions every year for inflation, and Social Security automatically makes cost-of-living adjustments (COLAs). If most of an individual's retirement income will not be automatically adjusted for inflation, the effect of inflation should be considered a serious financial risk and taken into consideration when planning for retirement.

Many people believe they should take no risks with investing their retirement funds, so they keep their money in Treasury bills, certificates of deposit, or money market funds, which they regard as safe. These choices may not be the best alternatives in the long run, however, because such conservative "cash" investments produce the smallest net return after inflation. Historically, stocks offer the highest potential to keep ahead of inflation, as shown in Table 2.

While past results do not guarantee future performance, stocks can play an important long-term role in an investment strategy (unless the future is totally unlike the past). Other ways to fight inflation include annuities or pensions with automatic annual cost-of-living increases or variable annuities invested in a stock market portfolio. Variable annuities require very careful shopping, however, because they can have high costs and fees.

Why buy an annuity?

An annuity allows conversion of all or part of the annuitant's retirement savings to a guaranteed stream of lifetime income. Annuities are not for everyone, but they can be very helpful in securing retirement income by letting an insurance company bear the risk that the annuitant will live many more years after retirement. No matter how long the annuitant lives, the insurance company will send payments every month, quarter, half-year, or year. There is a price for this security, however. Once the annuity contract is signed, the annuitant cannot take assets out of the insurance company in a lump sum. The amount of income an annuitant will receive is based on a number of factors, including age, sex, the income option selected, and interest rates at the time of purchase. The income payments can stay level or gradually increase to offset inflation.

Alternatives to annuities

Though alternative investments are less dependable than annuities, they allow the retiree more control over his or her money. Rather than buy an annuity, a retiree could make systematic withdrawals from savings and investment income. To do that, a retiree must estimate how much he or she can afford to spend each year over a lifetime. But since nobody knows how long they will live, how well their investments will do, or how much inflation will fluctuate, they must rely on educated guesses. Even if a person's economic assumptions hold up over the long run, investment returns may fluctuate greatly from year to year. And, currently, after age seventy and one-half, withdrawals from funds invested in a 401(k) or traditional IRA must also satisfy complex IRS rules for minimum annual withdrawals. An immediate annuity automatically satisfies such rules.

It is important to remember that an annuity is a product sold by an insurance company, and part of the purchase price goes to cover insurance company expenses. These expenses, called *loadings*, cover the insurer's marketing and administrative costs.

Insurers use conservative assumptions for longevity. They recognize that only the healthiest people tend to buy an immediate annuity, and they use assumptions for investment returns that are based on investment in fixed-income securities such as bonds and mortgages. Buying an annuity also means giving up flexibility, since the buyer transfers some or all of his money to an insurance company. That money can't be used to invest in equities, for major expenses, or for health-related expenses should the buyer's health suddenly deteriorate.

Annuities are a form of insurance, just like homeowners or life insurance. As such, they are intended to cover the financial loss of rare but costly occurrences, the way homeowners insurance insures against a house burning down or life insurance insures against a young, healthy person dying. Insurance is generally not intended to cover predictable, affordable expenses. Thus, high deductibles may make sense in some situations. After all, why pay an insurance company to cover costs that can be predicted and are affordable? Accordingly, knowing that most people live at least ten to fifteen years after retirement, retirees may find it desirable to manage their own money over those years, pay for expenses until age seventy themselves, and later use an annuity as insurance against living to a very old age. In fact, younger retirees may find that an annuity does not provide much more income than fixed-income securities like CDs or Treasury securities.

Another issue to consider is the complexity and effort of managing one's own money. Often, people find managing their investments easy at age sixty-five, but more than they can handle at eighty-five. An annuity lets an insurance company do this work.

The picture also changes as retirees get older and find that an annuity pays substantially more current income than other fixed-income investments. Research in this area, though not complete, supports the concept that an insured annuity is more useful at older ages. Waiting until age seventy or eighty to buy an annuity is often a good strategy, as older retirees may be more concerned about outliving assets and less concerned about future inflation. Also, buying an annuity by age seventy and one-half avoids any violation of IRS rules for minimum required distributions.

Choosing a strategy

Table 3 compares two strategies for retirement: keeping all of one's savings invested while taking money out systematically over a lifetime, or using part of savings to purchase an immediate annuity. A third strategy is to wait until at least age seventy to buy an annuity.

Make systematic withdrawals. This means spending money at a rate conservatively estimated to last the rest of one's life and investing the balance until it is needed. This strategy allows a person to tap into his or her savings to pay for expenses. One may decide to withdraw a set amount or percentage from retirement savings each year. This method provides freedom to invest one's money however one desires, as well as the flexibility to respond to needs or opportunities that may arise. For example, many of today's

Table 3
Comparing two strategies for managing retirement nest eggs.

	Systematic Withdrawals	Immediate Annuity
How is income spread over the length of your life?	· Make withdrawals whenever you wish · May run out of money · May not live at a level you can afford · Lets you leave money to heirs if your investements do well or if you only live a few years after retiring	· Pays regularly no matter how long you live · If you convert all your assets, you will have nothing left over to leave to your heirs · Insurer's costs are part of the price you pay
Protection from inflation?	· Potentially	· Fixed annuities, no · Variable annuities, potentially
Is it flexible enough?	· You have complete control · You can always buy an annuity	· Terms of an annuity contract cannot be changed once issued
How are investing, bookkeeping, taxes, handled?	· You manage your investments · You must understand and comply with tax law regarding minimum required distribution	· Insurance company invests for you · Taxes are simple and predictable · Automatically satisfies IRS rules on minimum distributions
Who may not be happy with this method?	· Those who are uncomfortable handling their own	· People in poor health · Younger retirees

SOURCE: Actuarial Foundation, 2000

popular investment ideas, such as index funds, international funds, certificates of deposit, and money market funds, were unknown only a few decades ago, and other new concepts and products are likely to become available in the years ahead. A person can also easily change this strategy if purchasing an annuity begins to look attractive.

Using this approach, it is important not to withdraw too much money in any one year—especially early in retirement. Too much money withdrawn at any one time will deplete one's retirement savings. It is also prudent to be conservative and update the plan every four years.

Use some assets to purchase an immediate income annuity. To eliminate some of the un-certainty, one can apply part of one's funds to buy an immediate income annuity, or use a company pension to supplement one's monthly income. An income annuity will convert part of retirement savings into a stream of monthly income that lasts for the rest of one's life. No matter how long a person lives, immediate income annuities can be another building block of income that can't be outlived, and they can be added to other sources of income that are typically considered the foundation of a retirement income, such as personal savings, Social Security, and pension proceeds.

Wait to buy an annuity until at least age seventy. Instead of purchasing an annuity from an insurer at the time of retirement, a person may want to manage his or her own money until a certain age, and then buy an annuity. This strategy preserves more flexibility to deal with changes that may occur, and it recognizes that an insured annuity provides more valuable longevity insurance at advanced ages. In other words, a person could choose to self-insure the longevity risk until age seventy or beyond, then buy an annuity if he or she remains in good health.

How much retirement income should come from an annuity?

This is also a question with no single answer. One should first establish a base level of retirement income according to one's present level of spending and lifestyle. Several approaches are possible:

- No frills. The poverty level in 2000 was $8,350 for individuals and $11,250 for couples. If feasible, income should be at least 150 percent of the poverty level. In U.S. dollars in 2000, this would be $12,525 for individuals and $16,875 for couples.
- Refocus. One should establish a budget that takes into account anticipated retirement expenses. For example, many retirees move to smaller, less expensive homes.
- Aim high. Some people may be unwilling to retire with a reduced standard of living. It is a good idea to start with 70 percent of one's present income before taxes, and draw up a budget to pay for annual household expenses. Long-term costs like a new car and home maintenance need to be included.

It is also important to add up the guaranteed income that will be available to cover basic needs.

Determine what income is expected from Social Security, which will cover part of one's base guaranteed income, then determine what income you can expect from pension plans. Annuity income from pension plans often is a better deal than an annuity bought in the open market. This is especially true for women because of unisex rates that pension plans must use.

If a pension and Social Security don't provide enough income, some people may wish to buy an annuity to get more guaranteed retirement income. If they do provide enough, it is a good idea to reevaluate at least every three years.

Retirement plans should take into account the possibility of the following major risks:

- Inflation
- Decline in value of savings and investments
- Loss of ability to care for oneself or to make complex decisions
- Being outlived by one's spouse or other dependents
- Unexpected medical needs
- Caring for parents or adult children

An annuity can pay for long-term care or life insurance, with annuity payments going directly to an insurance company to pay premiums for such coverage. However, premiums on long-term care policies are often not locked in permanently at one rate. They can be raised after a policy is purchased. Some insurers now offer a combined annuity and long-term care insurance policy. This can be a better deal than buying two products separately, but requires very careful shopping.

Tax considerations

It is important that individual taxpayers, especially those with high incomes, consult a qualified tax advisor for information on their own situations. However, some general guidelines include:

- Annuity benefits are fully taxable if the annuity is purchased entirely with before-tax dollars, which are funds on which no tax has been paid, such as amounts held in tax deferred programs like IRAs or qualified pension plans.
- If the annuity is purchased with after-tax dollars (funds on which all income taxes have been paid), benefits are tax-free until life ex-

pectancy has been reached (an age calculated on IRS actuarial tables). Once reaching that age, benefits are fully taxable.
- Depending on the state, a person may pay little or no state income tax on retirement income. For retirees with high income, the state of residence can make a big difference.

How to shop for and purchase an annuity

A person should not put all his or her money into an annuity, because annuities don't allow withdrawals for unexpected expenses once the annuity income begins. Also, an annuity pays both principal and earnings, so while the annuitant gets a high guaranteed cash flow, heirs may receive considerably less.

An immediate annuity can be purchased with the funds available from a 401(k) plan, an individual retirement account (IRA), a savings account, a life insurance policy, an inheritance, or the money from selling a house. The following points should all be considered when shopping for an annuity.

Health status. One's health must be considered. After all, the reason to buy an annuity is the risk of outliving one's assets. For a person in good health, an annuity makes sense, but for someone in poor health, it's less likely to be a good buy unless an annuity with survivor benefits for the use of a spouse or heir is purchased. Some companies offer *impaired life* annuities to purchasers with medical conditions likely to shorten their lives, such as diabetes or heart disease.

Use a strong insurer. Check the financial rating of the insurance company to make certain that the company is going to be there for many years.

Find good rates. Compare rates among different insurers using a trusted insurance agent, accountant, actuary, tax professional, the Internet, or a personal contact. Comparing contracts for fixed annuities requires no physical work or paperwork. Comparing rates for variable annuities is a little more complex, and one should not be in a hurry to lock in interest rates. Money can be put in other investments until one is ready to buy an annuity.

Seek other help. A state insurance department won't recommend a company, but it can help if there are problems with a company or representative. Check to see how the annuity would be covered in the event that a company ever becomes unable to pay benefits. Some states won't guarantee any more than $100,000 worth of annuity value.

ANNA M. RAPPAPORT

See also ASSETS AND WEALTH; BEQUESTS AND INHERITANCES; CONSUMER PRICE INDEX AND COLAS; ESTATE PLANNING; LIFE EXPECTANCY; PENSIONS, PLAN TYPES AND POLICY APPROACHES; RETIREMENT PLANNING.

ANTI-AGING

See BIOMARKERS OF AGING; LIFE-SPAN EXTENSION

ANTI-AGING RESEARCH: ETHICAL AND RELIGIOUS PERSPECTIVES

The Spanish explorer Ponce de Leon was looking for the Fountain of Youth when he sailed across the Atlantic to the New World, and antiaging researchers continue the perennial quest (Van Tassel). It is also a quest that has attracted numerous venture capitalists and is the focus of a myriad of biotechnology companies. A definitional distinction is necessary here. The *life expectancy* of any species is the average length of life for all members of the species taken together. Human life expectancy in modern industrialized countries is close to eighty. The *life span* of any species is the longest period that any single member of that species has lived. Thus, the human life span is thought to be 120 to 125.

Antiaging researchers challenge the notion of a so-called natural life span as they learn more about the genetic mechanisms of cell aging and eventually intervene (Banks and Fossel; Fossel, 1998). Some argue that the human life span might be radically extended in the future, perhaps to several centuries. Yet other scientists, especially Leonard Hayflick, are skeptical of the empirical possibility of radical life extension. The claims of antiaging researchers have been overstated, he argues. Survival to the age of reproductive success is the law of evolution, after which cellular and physiological disorder accelerate. Hayflick set the absolute maximum of the human life span at about 120 years, and predicts modest increase in life expectancy (perhaps to

eighty-two years by the year 2050.) Aging, Hayflick contends, is not a disease and cannot be overcome. Debate over the possibility of radical life span extension continues.

Cautious ethical optimism

The more optimistic ethical view is that there is no reason to be especially critical of the idea of extended lives, so long as a number of conditions can be met regarding health, including intact memory and cognition. There is in principle no religious or philosophical ethical proscription against extension of the human life span consistent with reasonable health. But a coherent first goal might be the extension of human life into the late eighties without the current plague of Alzheimer's disease, which afflicts an estimated 40 percent of those age eighty-five. Few people would welcome the protraction of such terrible morbidity in our efforts to extend life (Post). If science makes major progress against the progressive, irreversible, and chronic debilitating diseases of old age—especially diseases of neurodegeneration—then further developments in life extension might be welcomed by some.

Would it not be interesting to have Albert Einstein still available to students at 150 years of age? Would it not be of value to have a person of lucid mind who could tell historians directly about life in colonial America? If a person loves life and will be happy if it can be extended, then there is really no obvious reason for ethical criticism, or so the argument goes.

Rabbi Neil Gillman presents one Jewish perspective that is surely provocative, yet also quite coherent. Gillman argues that according to Judaism, there is nothing redemptive in death, which really is the enemy of life. Embodied life is inherently good and precious in God's eyes. Death is a chaotic force, argues Gillman, and Judaism affirms efforts to immortalize our bodily lives. Other rabbis, however, take a less sanguine view of radical life extension, pointing out the degree of wisdom in the natural intergenerational flow of life within society.

There has been a place for antiaging research and the goal of radical life extension in the history of science from the late 1890s. J. B. S. Haldane, the great Oxford University biologist, affirmed radical life extension in the 1930s with the publication of *Possible Worlds*, realizing that the implications of the then nascent biological revolution were immense as the species learns of the malleability of nature and of human nature. Yet this was precisely the future against which the Oxford theologian C. S. Lewis wrote in 1944. Thus, it is valuable to turn now to those who are most articulate and thoughtful in their warnings about the brave new world of antiaging and radical life extension, should it be a real possibility.

The goodness of natural limits

Are critics unnecessarily importing "moral" concerns (i.e., "moralizing") into the antiaging field? Where are ethical and theological proscriptions legitimate, if at all?

The bioethical critics of antiaging research and radical life extension lament the fact that "we" are unable to accept death, that we rage against it to the point of wishing to overcome it with emergent technological sophistication. Bioethicist Daniel Callahan argues that we must learn to accept the idea of a "natural life span," one that might reach its conclusion sometime around age eighty, for then surely we have more or less had adequate time to enjoy our creative capacities, raise children, and experience what life has to offer. Leon Kass, with great eloquence and depth, highlights the importance of life-span limits in making room for new generations who deserve to take their rightful place in the world. Theologians speak meaningfully about aging and death as natural solutions to the human problem of solipsism—that is, our human tendency to see ourselves as the center of the universe and to value others only as they contribute to our own agendas "in orbit around ourselves." Aging and death encourage within us an "ontological humility." After all, the argument concludes, it is a blessing to die because life becomes a dreary business, and its brevity allows us to value the time that we have.

Conclusions

So, is the problem with our culture that we are unable to infuse decay, dependency, and death with moral and spiritual value? Or should we strive against morbidity, decline, and death with scientific, theological, and ethical vigor?

With regard to western Christianity, Thomas Aquinas (*Summa Theologica* I, question 97, article 1) asked "Whether in the State of Innocence Man Would Have Been Immortal?" He responded by citing St. Paul (Romans 5:12, "By sin death came into the world.") and asserted that before sin the body was "incorruptable," that is, immortal.

It should come as no surprise that the great Renaissance Christian humanists extolled the advent of the scientific assault on aging and mortality, providing the original mandate of modern antiaging science. It therefore seems that the Christian tradition, like Judaism, is complex and ambivalent in its attitude toward so-called acceptable dying.

Thus, we must be careful not to overstate the religious and ethical arguments either for or against continued human life-span extension, nor prematurely reach uninformed or unimaginative closure on the issue. The future will be different from the present, but by how much? And how much will biological power over longevity lead us away from the wisdom of nature and human nature toward a dystopian vision of "fabricated man" in which the species is divided into those to whom the technology of radical life extension is available and those of a lower class to whom such technology is unavailable? How will intergenerational relations and justice between the generations be affected? What sort of character would one expect to find in people who grasp at radical life extension, rather than accepting the naturalness of dying within the current life span?

No issue of human "enhancement" is more pointed both ethically and religiously than the potential application of radical antiaging technologies. The issue is only further complicated by the libertarian and entrepreneurial interests that would make such enhancement available according to one's ability to pay, by the potential for disturbing class division, and by the potential protraction of morbidity and even of severe dysfunction. The issue of human cloning appears relatively minor in comparison.

STEPHEN G. POST

See also CELLULAR AGING; GENETICS; LIFE SPAN EXTENSION; THEORIES OF BIOLOGICAL AGING: DNA DAMAGE; THEORIES OF BIOLOGICAL AGING: ERROR CATASTROPHE.

BIBLIOGRAPHY

BANKS, D. A., and FOSSEL, M. "Telomeres, Cancer, and Aging." *Journal of the American Medical Association* 278 (1997): 1345–1348.
CALLAHAN, D. *Setting Limits: Medical Goals in an Aging Society.* New York: Simon & Schuster, 1987.

FOSSEL, M. "Telomerase and the Aging Cell." *Journal of the American Medical Association* 279 (1998): 1732–1735.

GILLMAN, N. "Theological Perspective." Unpublished paper from the conference "Extended Life, Eternal Life: Biotechnological 'Immortalization'—Its Scientific Basis, Future Prospects, and Ethical and Theological Significance." (University of Pennsylvania, 5–6 March 2000).

HALDANE, J. B. S. *Possible Worlds.* Reprint. New York: Transactions Publications, 2000.

HAYFLICK, L. *How and Why We Age.* New York: Ballantine Books, 1994.

KASS, L. *Toward a More Natural Science: Biology and Human Affairs.* New York: Free Press, 1985.

LEWIS, C. S. *The Abolition of Man.* Reprint. New York: Simon & Schuster, 1996.

POST, S. G. *The Moral Challenge of Alzheimer Disease: Ethical Issues from Diagnosis to Dying.* Baltimore, Md.: The Johns Hopkins University Press, 2000.

VAN TASSEL, D. D., ed. *Aging and the Completion of Being.* Philadelphia, Pa.: The University of Pennsylvania Press, 1979.

ANTIDEPRESSANTS

Depression in older adults is now being recognized as a severe and widespread health problem. Despite the availability of newer and safer antidepressants, depression is often unrecognized and undertreated in this population. Currently, there are several classes of antidepressants available for treatment of depression. They could be classified as monoamine oxidase inhibitors (MAOIs), tricyclic antidepressants (TCAs), selective serotonin reuptake inhibitors (SSRIs), and the miscellaneous group.

Monoamine oxidase inhibitors (MAOIs)

Monoamine oxidase inhibitors (MAOIs) were the original antidepressants. MAOIs are very potent but more risky to use, particularly in older patients. MAOIs work by blocking the enzyme monoamine oxidase either reversibly or irreversibly. MAOIs that block the enzyme irreversibly are Iproniazid, Phenelzine, and Tranylcypromine. While taking these medications, patients have to avoid certain food products such as cheese (which contain higher levels of tyramine) as well as many over-the-counter cold medications. In combination with MAOIs these drug-food and drug-drug interactions may cause alarming increases in blood pressure and could be lethal. Since safer antidepressants are available now, these medications are seldom used.

Reversible inhibitors of monoamine oxidase, such as moclobemide and selegiline (only at lower doses) were introduced with the claim that they may not have the dangerous interactions like the irreversible MAOIs. Nonetheless, recent reports suggest that they should also be used very cautiously.

Tricyclic antidepressants (TCAs)

Tricyclic antidepressants (TCAs) work by increasing the availability of the neurotransmitters norephinephrine and serotonin in the synaptic space between nerve cells in the brain. Until recently this group of antidepressants was the "gold standard" in the treatment of late-life depression and is still used as a standard to compare newer antidepressants. This group includes medication such as amitriptyline, amoxapine, clomipramine, desipramine, doxepin, imipramine, maprotyline, nortriptyline, protriptyline, and trimipramine. Medications in this group have been shown to slow conduction of electrical impulses in the heart and could be lethal if a patient were to overdose with them. The TCAs also have anticholinergic side effects (dry mouth, blurred vision, constipation, urinary retention, etc.) to which older patients are very sensitive and thus are not currently used as first-line medication for late-life depression. Despite this, nortriptyline is the best studied antidepressant for acute and continuation treatment of depression in older patients. If nortriptyline is used, it is essential that plasma concentrations be monitored, since there is a proven blood level range at which it is effective and safe. It is also recommended that the electrocardiogram (ECG) be assessed prior to starting and during treatment.

Common side effects of the TCAs include dry mouth, urinary retention, confusion, constipation, blurred vision, dizziness (may lead to falls and fractures), and sedation.

Selective serotonin reuptake inhibitors (SSRIs)

Selective serotonin reuptake inhibitors (SSRIs) act by increasing the concentration of serotonin available to nerve cells. Currently the most prescribed antidepressants in the world, this group includes of citalopram, fluoxetine, fluvoxamine, paroxetine, and sertraline. The SSRIs are safer and better tolerated than MAOIs and TCAs. There is still some lingering controversy as to whether they are as potent as the older antidepressants for very severe depression. The SSRIs are generally not lethal in overdose, which is a significant benefit in the elderly depressed patients who are at the highest risk for suicide. The common side effects of SSRIs include nausea, vomiting, diarrhea, headaches, anxiety, sexual problems, and sleeplessness. Usually the side effects are temporary in nature. In elderly people, fluoxetine has been reported to cause some weight loss, agitation, and also stays in the body for a long time. Also, it should be noted that fluvoxamine is not approved by the FDA (Food and Drug Administration) for the treatment of depression. Medications in this group are also known to interact with other drugs often causing a reduced metabolic breakdown. Of the available SSRIs, citalopram and sertraline have relatively lesser drug interactions and are well tolerated in older people. These medications are also associated with some unusual side effects predominantly in elderly people. One such side effect is the decrease in sodium in the blood (hyponatremia). The other is the report of higher incidence of Parkinson's disease–like movement problems in elderly people. There have been some recent reports of falls in elderly patients even with the use of SSRIs (which were previously thought not to increase the risk of falls in the elderly when compared to TCAs).

Miscellaneous

There are other antidepressants that do not belong to the previous categories mentioned and are grouped together here.

There is some data showing that the antidepressant buproprion is effective in late-life depression. It is thought to work by increasing the amount of dopamine available to the brain nerve cells and hence may be an attractive alternative medication. It has few interactions with other medications and fewer sexual side effects compared to the SSRIs but there is some concern for seizures at higher doses.

Nefazodone works somewhat like the SSRIs, but also has some other specific pathways through which it acts. Limited information is available at this time about the effectiveness of this medication in late-life depression. It can cause some very serious drug interactions.

Venlafaxine works by increasing both norepinephrine and serotonin, as do the TCAs. However, it is much more selective than the TCAs in affecting other nerve systems, which contribute to side effects. Nonetheless increases in blood pressure and nausea may be significant problems for some patients when using this medication.

Mirtazapine works at multiple sites in the brain to induce its antidepressant effect. There is information that it may help older patients, particularly those at risk of significant weight loss. Mirtazapine does increase appetite and also causes sedation, which may actually be helpful for some older people.

Methylphenidate is not considered an antidepressant but is sometimes used for older depressed people who are significantly withdrawn and lack motivation. Therefore it may be particularly useful in older depressed people undergoing rehabilitation. Limited data is available for its effect in depression.

St. John's Wort, a popular herbal remedy for mild to moderate depression, has not yet been thoroughly evaluated in older adults. However, St. John's Wort has recently been found to cause important drug interactions for many medications commonly used in the elderly, such as digoxin.

LALITHKUMAR K. SOLAI
BRUCE G. POLLOCK

See also DEPRESSION; ELECTROCONVULSIVE THERAPY; INTERPERSONAL THERAPY; PROBLEM SOLVING THERAPY.

BIBLIOGRAPHY

DUNNER, D. L. "Therapeutic Consideration in Treating Depression in the Elderly." *Journal of Clinical Psychiatry* 55 (1994): 48–57.
GEORGOTAS, A.; MCCUE, R. E.; HAPWORTH, W.; FRIEDMAN, E.; KIM, M.; WELKOWITZ, J.; CHANG, I.; and COOPER, T. B. "Comparative Efficacy and Safety of MAOIs Versus TCAs in Treating Depression in the Elderly." *Biological Psychiatry* 21 (1986): 1155–1166.
GLASSMAN, A. H., and ROOSE, S. P. "Risks of Antidepressants in the Elderly: Tricyclic Antidepressants and Arrhythmia-Revising Risks." *Gerontology* 40 (1994): 15–20.
LEBOWITZ, B. D.; PEARSON, J. L.; SCHNEIDER, L. S.; REYNOLDS III, C. F.; ALEXOPOULOS, G. S.; BRUCE, M. L.; CONWELL, Y.; KATZ, I. R.; MEYERS, B. S.; MORRISON, M. F.; MOSSEY, J.;

NIEDEREHE, G.; and PARMELEE, P. "Diagnosis and Treatment of Depression in Late Life: Consensus Statement Update." *Journal of the American Medical Association* 278 (1997): 1186–1190.

LEO, R. J. "Movement Disorders Associated with the Serotonin Selective Reuptake Inhibitors." *Journal of Clinical Psychiatry* 57 (1996): 449–454.

NEWHOUSE, P. A. "Use of Selective Serotonin Reuptake Inhibitors in Geriatric Depression." *Journal of Clinical Psychiatry* 57 (1996): 12–22.

REYNOLDS III, C. F.; FRANK, E.; PEREL, J. M.; MAZUMDAR, S.; and KUPFER, D. J. "Maintenance Therapies for Late-Life Recurrent Major Depression: Research and Review Circa." *International Psychogeriatrics* 7 (1995): 27–39.

RICHELSON, E. "Synaptic Effects of Antidepressants." *Journal of Clinical Psychopharmacology* 16 (1996): 1–9.

SCHNEIDER, L. S. "Pharmacological Considerations in the Treatment of Late-Life Depression." *American Journal of Geriatric Psychiatry* 4 (1996): 51–65.

SOLAI, L. K.; MULSANT, B. H.; and POLLOCK, B. G. "Update on the Treatment of Late-Life Depression." In *The Psychiatric Clinics of North America—Annual of Drug Therapy*. Edited by David L. Dunner and J. F. Rosenbaum. Philadelphia: W. B. Saunders Co., 1999: Pages 73–92.

THAPA, P. B.; GIDEON, P.; COST, T. W.; MILAM, A. B.; and RAY, W. A. "Antidepressants and the Risk of Falls among Nursing Home Residents." *New England Journal of Medicine* 339 (1998): 875–882.

ANXIETY

Anxiety is a normal part of life, and it occurs over the entire life span. In particular, the experience of anxiety continues into later life. Just as younger people worry about things important to their stage of life, such as school, job, finances, and family, so too do older adults worry about health, family, finances, and their mortality. Elderly persons are as likely to react with fear or panic when danger is imminent as are their younger counterparts. Anxiety is a normal response to certain situations, and it can be useful in helping people to cope with problems and to manage threatening situations. Anxiety alerts us to threats and provides the physiological readiness needed for action. It may be very intense in certain situations yet still be considered normal.

Figure 1

Important risk factors for anxiety disorders in elders and younger adults

Risk factor	Important in Elders	Important in Young Adults
Gender (increased in female)	Yes	Yes
Chronic medical illness	Yes	No
Physical limitations/disability	Yes	No
Recent losses/grief	Yes	No
Family History	Yes/No	Yes
External locus of control*	Yes	Yes
Negative childhood life event (e.g., trauma, loss of parent)	No	Yes
Depression	Yes	Yes
Smaller social network	Yes	No
Cognitive decline	Yes/No**	No

* A personality marker defined as the extent to which an individual views himself of herself to be in control of life, rather than being a victim of fate; individuals with this trait are at increased risk for mood and anxiety disorders.

** Some reports show increased anxiety disorders in cognitively impaired elderly, others show no increase or a decrease.

SOURCE: Author

However, if it occurs when there is no threat, or if its intensity is far higher than the situation warrants, it is likely to be a symptom of an *anxiety disorder*. Excess anxiety that occurs repeatedly and leads to distress and disablement is usually caused by an anxiety disorder.

Elders are susceptible to many of the same treatable anxiety disorders that are seen in younger people. Sometimes this is because the disorder has been a lifelong condition. In other cases, its onset is in late life, and then risk factors are somewhat different than in younger people (see Figure 1). However, anxiety disorders seem to be more difficult to diagnose in the elderly population, and the treatments that have proven efficacy in younger populations are largely untested in elderly persons. The following three case examples exemplify the presentation of common anxiety disorders in older adults, and also illustrate the difficulties of diagnosing and treating these disorders.

Case one: generalized anxiety disorder

Ethel, age seventy-one, has always been a nervous woman. When interviewed by a psychiatrist, she describes feeling worried about future events that might happen. She explains she has had these worries "for as long as I can remember." At times, she has bouts with fatigue, headaches, and muscle aches. She says that what bothers her most is her chronic insomnia, and she has taken many different medications for sleep throughout her life. "I take my sleeping pills and I do just fine," she says. However, her family doesn't agree. Her daughter is distressed by Ethel's constant need for reassurance: "When mom's really worried about something, she'll phone me ten to twenty times in a day. Sometimes she seems paralyzed by her worries." When asked about this, Ethel reveals that she does have difficulty controlling her worries and that she takes an extra sleeping pill in the daytime for "nerves."

Ethel has classic signs of *generalized anxiety disorder,* a condition marked by constant distressing worries that the person finds difficult to control. Up to 2 percent of elderly people are afflicted by this condition at any time, which tends to be chronic (either constant throughout life, as in Ethel's case, or waxing and waning). Few people with this condition ever seek treatment for it. It is typical for older adults with generalized anxiety disorder to have many physical symptoms, such as Ethel's fatigue and headaches, so they often seek care from primary-care and specialty doctors for these physical symptoms, receiving unnecessary medical workups and medications without ever realizing the psychological basis for their problems.

When underlying anxiety is recognized by a doctor, it is often treated with a medication in the class called *benzodiazepines.* Valium (diazepam) is a well-known example of this type of medication. Unfortunately, this is not necessarily the best treatment, as benzodiazepines have side effects such as memory impairment, slowed reaction time (for example, when driving), and impaired balance, compounding problems an elderly person might have already. If so, these side effects are potentially of serious concern. Other treatments known to be efficacious for generalized anxiety disorder in younger adults, such as certain types of antidepressant medications and psychotherapies such as *cognitive-behavior therapy* may be better choices. However, these treat-

ments have not yet been proven efficacious in the elderly population, though there are many reports of them alleviating this condition. In Ethel's case, her primary-care physician eventually convinced her of the underlying anxiety basis behind her symptoms and the need for a different type of medication. She was willing to try this because she trusted him, and within weeks both she and her daughter were feeling much better. She understood that this treatment would probably be needed long-term.

Case two: agoraphobia

Jim, age sixty-seven, never had any "nerve problems" in his life, according to his family. However, after suffering from a stroke, in which he lost movement on the left side of his body and fell, hurting his face and arm, he developed debilitating fears. After hospitalization, Jim received physical rehabilitation to help him regain his functioning. Nevertheless, he remains a "prisoner in his own home," as his son describes it: "Dad was fiercely independent before the stroke and did everything himself; now, he seems afraid to do anything alone." Jim says that because of his stroke-related weakness he can longer do many of the things outside the house that he used to do; he feels his walking is too unsteady. Jim's physical therapist is surprised at the degree of restriction. The therapist says that Jim does have enough strength; he simply becomes very fearful walking when someone is not nearby. When pressed, Jim agrees he has a great fear of falling: "Of course I'm scared; I could fall at any time and break my hip." Oddly, he is not reassured either by his physical therapist telling him that he is very unlikely to fall, nor by descriptions of other stroke sufferers who regained their independence. Jim cannot shake the anxiety that overcomes him when he thinks of going for a walk. As a result, Jim is considering moving from his home to a personal care home.

Jim's case is one of *agoraphobia,* literally "fear of the marketplace." This condition is characterized by fear of being trapped and unable to escape, or being alone and unable to get help in the event of having a physical problem. Agoraphobia is a common disorder in older individuals; it is estimated that it affects up to 8 percent of elderly persons. In younger individuals, agoraphobia usually develops after someone has experienced one or more panic attacks. In the elderly, however, agoraphobia often occurs for other reasons.

Older adults can develop agoraphobia after medical events such as stroke, or traumatic events such as falls. The disorder can be difficult to detect, partly because the very nature of the disorder is to avoid going places, and this inhibits the person from seeking treatment. Jim's case exemplifies another diagnostic difficulty in the elderly: they often tend to normalize anxious behavior by either denying it exists or attributing it to realistic medical-related concerns.

Unfortunately, Jim's case illustrates a very common problem—that of anxiety disorders compounding or amplifying a disability caused by medical events. In Jim's case, a stroke that might only lead to minor changes in function is instead a severely disabling event when combined with agoraphobia. Another issue in this case is the need to rule out a *depressive disorder*. Depression is very common in elderly persons who have suffered medical events such as stroke, and it is frequently seen in those who suffer from an anxiety disorder. In Jim's case, his amplified disability might be not only from agoraphobia, but from depression as well. The optimal treatment of agoraphobia in younger adults is *exposure therapy*, by which the individual is repeatedly exposed to the feared situation while receiving professional advice from a therapist. As with other treatments for anxiety disorders, the efficacy of exposure therapy in older adults is unproven but promising. Some medications also help relieve agoraphobic symptoms, but these are also unproven in elderly persons.

Case three: obsessive-compulsive disorder

Susan, who is seventy, agrees that she is a very "clean" person. She spends much of each day cleaning and ordering her house. She describes having this behavior ever since childhood, when she avoided getting muddy and dirty. She says that her husband doesn't mind: "He says I'm a good housekeeper." Susan seems happy, too; proud of her clean house. However, more probing with questions reveals the extent of her problem: she explains that, all her life, she has felt very anxious about dirt, germs, and disorder. Earlier in her life she spent essentially all of each day cleaning, sometimes confining herself to one small square of a room, "so I could really get it clean." This behavior led to the loss of her only job (ironically, as a cleaning woman) and, for a time, estrangement from her husband and children. Her anxiety disorder was complicated by depression in her thirties and forties.

For the last several years, Susan has been taking a medication similar to Prozac (fluoxetine). She is doing much better: "Now I only spend three hours per day cleaning, and I can eat in a restaurant without bringing my disinfectant." But she still acknowledges significant distress at times, and while her relationship with her family is improved, there is still significant strain when her children bring their children over. "I just have to clench my teeth and bear it when they spill something."

Obsessive-compulsive disorder (OCD) is a combination of obsessions—repetitive, intrusive, unwanted thoughts, images, or impulses—and compulsions—repetitive acts done to ward off obsessions and/or to reduce anxiety. OCD occurs in about 1 percent of the elderly population and, since it is chronic, it will probably increase as individuals with this disorder enter the ranks of the aged. Susan's case exemplifies the chronic nature of OCD: she has suffered with it for sixty-plus years! Her case also illustrates an unfortunate complication of anxiety disorders: depression. The disability, in terms of job difficulties and strained relationships, is also typical of chronic anxiety disorders at any age. Susan's response to medications known as *serotonin reuptake inhibitors* is typical: helpful but incomplete. In younger adults, a type of psychotherapy known as behavior therapy can be effective; however its efficacy is unknown in elderly persons.

Other disorders

A *panic attack* is defined as a sudden intense feeling of fear associated with physical symptoms such as chest pain, shortness of breath, dizziness, shaking, feeling hot or cold, sweating, and nausea—in short, the symptoms caused by adrenaline release in a *fight-or-flight* response. A typical panic attack lasts about ten minutes. *Panic disorder* is diagnosed in people who have recurrent unexpected panic attacks along with persistent fear of these attacks or fear of what they mean or what they might cause. While this disorder is believed to be relatively rare in the elderly population, it may be that the disorder is difficult to diagnose because elderly individuals and their doctors attribute such physical symptoms to cardiac, respiratory, or other medical conditions. This misattribution has been illustrated earlier in this entry with other types of anxiety disorders as well.

Social phobia, also called *social anxiety disorder*, is a common disorder that typically begins early in life and usually lasts in some form throughout the life span; not surprisingly, it is seen in elderly persons, with about 1 percent suffering from the disorder. Its main feature is a fear of being criticized or humiliated while being observed or scrutinized by others. Its most common form is *stage fright,* or public-speaking phobia, but in the more severe cases, fear of eating, talking, or even being seen in public can paralyze individuals. Typically, elderly persons will have lived with this disorder for their entire lifetime and have *adapted;* that is, they have avoided feared situations (such as speaking in public) for so long that they view their lives as unaffected.

Specific phobias are the most common anxiety disorders: they are an intense, irrational fear of some situation. Common examples are *acrophobia:* fear of high places; and *claustrophobia:* fear of enclosed places. While considered less severe than other disorders, they can sometimes be quite disabling (e.g., the acrophobic who quits his job in a high-rise building). Similar to social phobia, elderly persons with specific phobias will probably have had these conditions for their entire life and have changed their lifestyle to avoid the feared situation or object.

Post-traumatic stress disorder (PTSD) is a type of response to an event that threatens or causes serious physical harm or even death, while also causing feelings of horror and/or helplessness. For example, being mugged or raped, or being shot at in battle can cause PTSD. It is diagnosed if the individual reexperiences the trauma in the form of nightmares, visions, or flashbacks, and if he or she exhibits chronic avoidance behavior and hyperarousability. The prevalence of this disorder is unknown in older adults. While it is common in such groups as combat veterans, it can also occur after serious medical events such as stroke and heart attack. In younger adults, PTSD tends to be chronic, lasting decades, and it is typically only partly responsive to medication (serotonin reuptake inhibitors). The course and response to treatment of this disorder in elderly persons is unknown, but as the combat veterans from the Korean and Vietnam wars grow older, much more will need to be known about this disorder as it presents in older adults.

Many older adults have problems with anxiety at some point in their life but do not have symptoms that meet the criteria for one (or more) of the above-described disorders. This is partly because the disorders described above were validated in younger age groups; thus, they may not describe the underlying disorder of many elderly persons suffering from symptomatic anxiety. As research in the field of geriatric psychiatry increases, anxiety disorders unique to older adults may be discovered. In any event, an older adult who suffers from anxiety should not be dismissed simply because their symptoms do not share features with the disorders described above.

The case examples presented here show some typical features of anxiety disorders as they present in older adults: they are common, though less so than younger adults, and they are not simply a "normal" reaction to aging or medical events. Further, they tend to be chronic and lead to much distress and disability, especially in combination with disabling chronic medical conditions such as stroke.

The problems with recognition and treatment of anxiety disorders in later life are twofold. First, there is the difficulty recognizing the disorder in an individual who may have lived with anxiety their entire life and view it as normal, or who may misattribute anxiety symptoms to medical problems common in this age group. Second, treatment options are for the most part unproven in older populations, due to the lack of controlled clinical trials for elderly persons with anxiety disorders. On the other hand, it is known that elderly people with depression respond to medication and psychotherapy just like their younger counterparts, and it is likely that this will be true for anxiety disorders as well. In the future, understanding of the presentation and treatment of anxiety disorders in the elderly will improve if there is better education of the public about these disorders and more treatment research to assure that potential treatments can find their place with elderly populations, just as in younger adults.

ERIC LENZE
M. KATHERINE SHEAR

See also DEATH ANXIETY; DEPRESSION; GERIATRIC PSYCHIATRY.

BIBLIOGRAPHY

American Psychiatric Association. *Diagnostic and Statistical Manual of Mental Disorders,* 4th ed. Washington, D.C.: APA, 1994.
BEEKMAN, A. T. F.; DE BEURS, E.; VAN BALKOM, A. J. L. M.; DEEG, D. J. H.; VAN DYCK, R.; and VAN

TILBURG, W. "Anxiety and Depression in Later Life. Co-occurrence and Communality of Risk Factors." *American Journal of Psychiatry* 157 (2000): 89–95.

FLINT, A. J. "Epidemiology and Comorbidity of Anxiety Disorders in the Elderly." *American Journal of Psychiatry* 151 (1994): 640–649.

FLINT, A. J. "Management of Anxiety in Late Life." *Journal of Geriatric Psychiatry* 11 (1998): 194–200.

KRASUCKI, C.; HOWARD, R.; and MANN, A. "Anxiety and Its Treatment in the Elderly." *International Psychogeriatrics* 11 (1999): 25–45.

APHASIA

See LANGUAGE DISORDERS

AREA AGENCIES ON AGING

In 1965, when the Older Americans Act (OAA) was passed, all aging program allocations went from the State Unit on Aging (SUA) in each state directly to service providers. During the late 1960s and early 1970s, social movements precipitated a move towards community-based planning for government-funded programs. The result of this shift was that local decision-making occurred at the regional, rather than state or national, level. Thus, in 1973, the OAA was reauthorized, creating the Area Agencies on Aging (AAA). An Area Agency on Aging is a public or private agency designated by a state to address the needs and concerns of all older Americans at the local level. This regional approach provides everyone with an opportunity to participate in the planning of services for older adults in their community.

The OAA also established the Native American Aging Programs, known as Title VI. Through these programs, funds are provided to a tribal organization, which serves the same function for the American Indians, Aleuts, Eskimos, and Hawaiians as the AAA provides to the states.

Creating an AAA

The OAA gives the SUAs the authority to divide a state into planning and service areas. Since 1973, these areas have been synonymous with AAAs. In creating a planning service area and designating an AAA, the OAA mandates that the states must consider, ". . .the geographical distributions of older individuals in the state, the incidence of need for supportive services, nutrition services, multipurpose senior centers, and legal assistance, the distribution of older individuals who have the greatest economic need (with particular attention to low-income minority individuals) residing in such areas, the distribution of older individuals who are Indians residing in such areas, the distribution of resources available to provide such services or centers, the boundaries of existing areas within the state which were drawn for the planning or administration of supportive service programs, the location of units of general purpose local government within the state, and other relevant factors" (Older Americans Act, Section 3025).

At the national and regional level, the aging network includes:

- The Administration on Aging and its ten regional offices, which are part of the Department of Health and Human Services
- Fifty-seven state offices on aging at the state and territorial level
- 655 Area Agencies on Aging
- 230 Native American Title VI aging programs.

An integral part of every AAA is its advisory board. The purpose of the advisory board is to provide input into the development and implementation of the planning document for the AAA. This advisory board also functions as the eyes and ears of the community, ensuring constant feedback to the AAA on its initiatives.

An AAA can be either a public or a nonprofit agency designated by the SUA to address the needs and concerns of all older adults at a designated local level. If the AAA is a public agency, it is usually located within an umbrella organization, such as a county or city government or a regional planning council. The name *Area Agency on Aging* is a generic name; specific names may vary by location. Regardless of what name is utilized, every AAA must be listed in the yellow pages of phone books under the title *Area Agency on Aging*, thus ensuring that anyone in the country can easily access their local AAA.

Function and responsibility of an AAA

The main function of an AAA is to be the community focal point in administering OAA program objectives. The main objective for an AAA is to create aging programs in the local community that will foster, assist, and encourage independence in older adults. To meet these objectives, agencies assume the following responsibilities:

- Assessing the needs of older persons in the community
- Identifying service gaps in the community, and finding solutions to meet the needs of the community and fill the service gaps
- Developing a comprehensive and coordinated service plan, called an Area Plan, which is submitted to the State Unit on Aging for approval
- Funding services with available resources, based on need
- Monitoring service providers and evaluating the effectiveness of service
- Serving as a visible and effective advocate for all older adults in the planning service area

Not all AAAs perform the same function in every community, but they all serve as a conduit to services for older adults. Nationally, all AAAs are responsible for administering OAA funds. In addition, many states designate the AAA to administer other funds, including Medicaid Waiver funds, state general fund revenues for older adult programs, Title XX funds, and even some local tax-generated service dollars. Area Agencies on Aging administer these funds largely through contracts with local service providers. Technically, AAAs may only provide information, referral, outreach, and case management services; a waiver from the state is required to provide other direct services. In order to provide other services, an AAA must demonstrate that no other provider is available, or that an adequate supply of services for older adults does not exist.

The planning process

Part of the responsibility of each AAA is the development a four-year Area Plan, which is a strategic plan on aging. The SUA then incorporates these plans into its master plan, which in turn is submitted to the Administration on Aging (AoA). The planning process for the Area Plan is carefully orchestrated. It must include input from the community, older adults, service providers, and any other interested parties. This ensures that the local community is both informed about aging issues and has an opportunity to shape the services provided. In addition, the community has an opportunity to be educated

about trends in the aging population, limitations in funding, needs, gaps, and funding shortfalls. Using all the information captured in the public forum process, the AAA creates a draft, which is open for public comment. After community input is gathered, the advisory council and staff make the necessary adjustments to the Area Plan, and it is submitted to the SUA for approval.

It should be noted that the OAA has had insufficient funds for programs since its inception. The shortage was especially apparent from 1980 through 2000. During this period, there was little growth in funding, while inflation and the growth of the over-sixty population actually decreased the per capita dollars available to serve older adults. The lack of funding caused many AAAs to seek new sources of financial support. In 2000, however, with the reauthorization of the OAA, Congress supported the largest increase ever for the OAA and funded $125 million for an Adult Caregivers Program.

The other important component of the AAA is coordination. Even though the OAA does not fund all aging programs, AAAs have the responsibility to coordinate other available sources of revenue to avoid duplication, enhance services, and create a comprehensive service network. For example, if a local United Way concentrates its funding on medical transportation, the AAA can then direct its resources to another priority service.

Accessing services

The AAA and Title VI agency in each community provide information and assist individuals in accessing services that fall into five broad categories: information and access services, community-based services, in-home services, housing, and elder rights.

Information and access services consist of the following: *Information and referral assistance,* which provides assistance with locating services available in the community; *health insurance counseling,* which helps older adults understand their rights under Medicare, Medicaid, and managed care, and provides information about Medigap and other long-term care insurance policies; *client assessment,* which consists of a home visit by a trained professional to assess needs and service eligibility; *care management,* which is a plan of care developed in consultation with the client and family to ensure maximum independence and autonomy for the client; *transportation* for older adults to medical appointments, shopping, and meal sites; *caregiver support,* which provides education, counseling, and resources to caregivers while they are providing care to a spouse, older family member, or friend; and *retirement planning and education* to help older adults nearing retirement to focus on issues such as pension, health concerns, legal issues, and work and leisure options.

Community-based services comprise *employment services* to assist older adults in finding meaningful employment through the use of skill assessment, job counseling, and job placement; *senior centers* to provide social, educational, recreational, and physical activities for older adults, as well as a meal site; *congregate meals,* which are served to older adults in a senior center or group setting for the purpose of providing a nutritious meal in a highly social environment; *adult day services,* which provide community-based care for functionally impaired older adults, usually during the day hours, providing a respite for caregivers; and *volunteer opportunities.*

In-home services include *home delivered meals,* usually a midday or evening nutritious meal delivered to an older adult who is unable to prepare a meal. Meal delivery also provides a social contact for the meal recipient, which may be the homebound older adult's only live contact with the outside world. *Homemaker* assistance provides help with light housekeeping, laundry, cooking and shopping for the individual who just needs a little help living in the community, while *chore services* include major housecleaning, pest control, snow removal, and yard work. *Telephone reassurance* provides a regular daily call to an older adult. This service can reduce the feeling of isolation, and it provides a check on the older person's well-being. *Friendly visiting* provides a friendly visit to a homebound older adult; and *emergency assistance and weatherization* provides assistance paying fuel bills. The *emergency response system* provides older adults with an electronic device that can be activated to call for help. *Home health services* include visiting nursing, medication dispensing, health monitoring, various therapies, and instruction for individuals and family members, while *personal care services* provide assistance in bathing, grooming, feeding, mobility and other activities. *Respite care* provides a needed short-term break for caretakers by providing care for an older person.

Housing services include *senior housing,* which provides alternatives designed to meet the needs of older adults who wish to remain in an independent living environment, and *alternative community-based living facilities,* which includes a range of housing options that bridge the gap between independent living and nursing homes. This includes assisted living and adult foster care.

Elder rights provide legal and social help to older adults. *Legal assistance* provides legal advice and counsel for older persons and families who have legal and financial concerns; *elder abuse prevention programs* are designed to alleviate situations of abuse, neglect, or self-neglect—these programs include adult protection, guardianship, and conservatorship; and *ombudsmen services* are available to investigate and resolve complaints that involve older persons living in long-term care facilities.

Having to cope with the failing health of a spouse, family member, or friend can be emotionally draining, and finding the right help can be difficult and frustrating. However, through the AAA system, even relatives who live out of town can access necessary services, as a local AAA can provide information about the agencies in other localities. In this way AAAs serve as gatekeepers of information—they can provide answers about aging services in their community, as well as access to a nationwide network of AAAs. They provide security for the family that must live away from parents, and provide needed support to the older citizen trying to live at home with honor and dignity.

ROBERT LOGAN

See also ADMINISTRATION ON AGING; CONGREGATE AND HOME-DELIVERED MEALS; HOME CARE AND HOME SERVICES; HOUSING; OLDER AMERICANS ACT; SENIOR CENTERS; SOCIAL SERVICES.

INTERNET RESOURCES

Administration on Aging. The AoA website provides information on the Older Americans Act. www.aoa.gov

National Association of Area Agencies on Aging. The N4A website is a good source of information on AAAs. www.n4a.org

ARTHRITIS

Background

The prevalence of arthritis (chronic damage of the joints) increases with age because the most common form, osteoarthritis, is age related, and also because chronic arthritis, particularly rheumatoid arthritis, persists into old age even when starting in early adult life (Silman and Hochberg). Osteoarthritis and rheumatoid arthritis are common, and represent two distinct but related mechanisms of joint disease in old age: respectively, "wear and tear" and inflammation.

The clinical features of arthritis. Pain is the predominant symptom. Most pronounced on movement, it also occurs at rest, after exercise, and at night. The other main complaint is stiffness, occurring in the morning and after exercise, when it is termed "gelling." In inflammatory arthritis, morning stiffness exceeds thirty minutes. Joint swelling is common, due to synovitis (inflammation of the joint lining), synovial effusions (swelling due to fluid in the joint cavity), and bony swelling around joints. Crepitus, grating when joints are moved, characterizes osteoarthritis. Arthritis causes muscle weakness that may be profound. Finally, there may be loss of movement due to joint swelling, muscle weakness, and deformities when joints are damaged.

The effects of arthritis. Arthritis causes disability and impairs quality of life due to the direct effect of inflammation of the synovium (synovitis). The pain, inflammation, and joint destruction of synovitis are compounded by muscle weakness and decreased sense of joint (proprioception) (British League Against Rheumatism).

Osteoarthritis

Osteoarthritis is common and, at older ages, becomes virtually universal. It is an active process, not just wearing out of joints or "degenerative joint disease" (Joint Working Group of the British Society for Rheumalology and, Research Unit of the Royal College of Physicians).

Causes and disease mechanisms. There are progressive changes in osteoarthritic cartilage. Initially the collagen (the material that provides important lining of bones) framework is damaged by changes in structural complex sugars (proteoglycans), in the cartilage matrix, and in

water content. Attempted repair increases the number and activity of cartilage cells (chondrocytes). This leads to the production of degradative enzymes. Subsequent fissuring, cartilage ulceration and matrix loss makes damage irreversible. There is variable accompanying inflammation of the synovium that lines the joints, as well as changes in adjacent bone. Predisposing factors for osteoarthritis include age, female sex, family history (indicating genetic predisposition), obesity, previous trauma, repetitive occupational stress, and previous inflammation, such as rheumatoid arthritis. Osteoarthritis increases with age. By sixty-five years most people have X-ray evidence of osteoarthritis, though under 30 percent have symptoms.

Clinical features. Pain is the dominant symptom. It is usually activity related, varies in severity, and has periods of remission. Associated symptoms include morning stiffness (usually under thirty minutes), postexercise gelling, bony swelling, limited movement, and muscle weakness. Examination shows bony swelling, tenderness, and crepitus. Effusions, usually in the knees, are common.

Osteoarthritis can involve one or many joints. Generalized osteoarthritis involves the small joints of the fingers, especially those at the knuckles closest to the ends, as well as the wrists, knees, and hips.

Investigations. Blood tests are usually normal, although some elevation of tests for inflammation can be seen. Tests for the protein known as rheumatoid factor are negative. X-rays show joint space loss, and increased bone underneath and at the edges of joints, called subchondral sclerosis and marginal bony outcroppings (osteophytes), respectively. In late disease, joints can be totally destroyed. Isotope bone scanning (scintigraphy) shows increased activity of the joints in early disease.

Rheumatoid arthritis

Rheumatoid arthritis, the most common type of inflammatory arthritis, is characterized by persisting inflammatory synovitis resulting in joint damage and systemic reactions, although it can vary in its severity and general effects (Scott et al.; Sewell).

Causes and disease mechanisms. The cause of rheumatoid arthritis is unknown, but is variously attributed to autoimmunity, bacterial infec-

Figure 1
How joints are affected by arthritis.

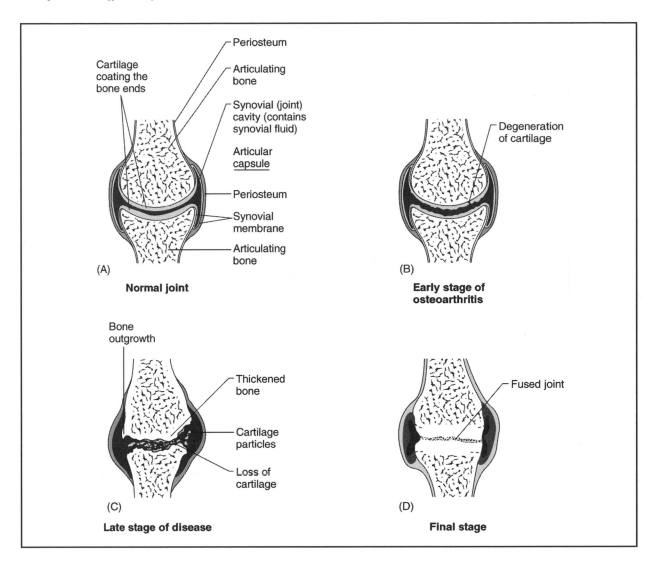

SOURCE: Drawing by Hans and Cassidy for the Gale Group.

tion, or viral infection. The synovium is infiltrated with white blood cells called lymphocytes, which are seen where inflammation is chronic. Synovial cells proliferate and blood vessels increase markedly. Synovial fluid contains many white blood cells known as polymorphonuclear leukocytes. There are accompanying destructive changes in joint cartilage and bone.

Rheumatoid arthritis is associated with rheumatoid factor production. Several different immunoglobulin classes can be involved, especially IgM and IgA. A minority of cases remain seronegative. Rheumatoid arthritis has a genetic com-

ponent. It involves three times more women than men, its prevalence increases with age, and it involves 0.25–1 percent of adults and 3–5 percent of elderly women.

Clinical features. The onset of rheumatoid arthritis is usually insidious over several months, though some cases have an acute onset. Characteristic features are joint pain, swelling, and morning stiffness lasting several hours. Typically it involves small joints of the hands and wrists in a symmetrical distribution. Large joint involvement indicates severe disease. In early disease the findings are subtle, while in late disease there

Figure 2
The normal knee joint

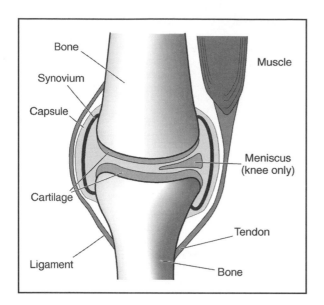

SOURCE: Author

are obvious changes, such as the self-descriptive swan-neck and "boutonnière" deformities in the fingers. Large joint damage causes immobility and disability.

Features apart from joint inflammation (extra-articular features) are common. Rheumatoid nodules at sites like the elbow indicate severe, rheumatoid factor–positive disease. Other extra-articular features include dry eyes and dry mouth (Sjögren's syndrome), leg ulcers, nerve damage, lung disease, and inflammation of the pericardium, sclera, and blood vessels.

Investigations.   Blood tests are usually abnormal. Rheumatoid factors are antibodies produced by the individual against constituent proteins (auto-antibodies). They bind to one end of normal immunoglobulin, the Fc portion. They occur in about two-thirds of cases, as well as in other disorders with persisting immune inflammation and in many healthy individuals. Other abnormalities reflect the systemic inflammatory response. The erythrocyte sedimentation rate is elevated. Specific measures of acute inflammation, such as C-reactive protein, are also elevated. By contrast hemoglobin levels can be low.

Juxta-articular erosions, a key diagnostic finding, are next to the joint on X-rays of the hands and feet. Other changes are osteoporosis around the joints and loss of joint space. In late disease there is destruction and ankylosis (fusion of the joint due to bone growth). Scintigraphy shows increased blood flow around involved joints in early disease, though such findings are not specific.

Seronegative arthropathies

Seronegative arthropathies usually involve only a few joints, are less severe than rheumatoid arthritis, and tests for rheumatoid factor are negative, (hence the term "seronegative"). Psoriatic athritis, the most important type in elderly people, is a specific type of arthritis seen in association with psoriasis. Other disorders include reactive arthritis, colitic arthritis in inflammatory bowel disease, and the peripheral arthritis of anklyosing spondylitis, a disorder characterized by involvement of the spine.

Classification and causes.   Unifying themes are the presence of an infective trigger and the genetic risk associated with HLA-B27, one of the genes found in normal human white blood cells. This is found 95 percent of cases of ankylosing spondylitis and less often in the other disorders.

Ankylosing spondylitis, colitic arthritis, and reactive arthritis usually begin in early adult life; in the elderly the predominant clinical concern is their late consequences, mainly due to joint failure. Psoriatic arthritis may present de novo in the elderly.

Clinical features.   There are a number of clinical patterns of psoriatic arthritis, including oligoarthritis (arthritis that involves only a few joints); a symmetrical polyarthritis, often indistinguishable from rheumatoid arthritis; distal arthritis of the distal interphalangeal joints; and arthritis mutilans, a rare cause of severe joint damage. Other forms of seronegative arthritis predominantly involve oligoarthritis.

Investigations.   There are no specific laboratory tests. Acute-phase reactants like the ESR and C-reactive protein may be elevated. Rheumatoid factor is usually negative. X-rays may show marginal erosions. Isolated destruction of individual joints with pencil and cup deformities suggests psoriatic arthritis. Axial disease with sacroilitis and spinal fusion characterize ankylosing spondylitis.

Gout

Causes and disease mechanisms.   Gout is a form of inflammatory arthritis that results from the deposition of urate crystals in the synovium (Van Doornum and Ryan). Uric acid, the end product of metabolism of some important proteins, results from endogenous purine metabolism with an important, though minor dietary contribution. In other words, while diet has some impact on gout, the idea of gout as chiefly the result of too much rich food and drink (the "patrician malady") is untrue. Hyperuricemia is seen prior to episodes of arthritis and progesses to gout when large increases in body stores of uric acid make it impossible for the body to adapt. Synovial urate crystals activate inflammatory pathways either directly or after coating by proteins such as immunoglobulins.

Hyperuricemia (high uric acid levels in the blood) is common, with a male predominance; it involves 5 percent of men. Risk factors include obesity, renal disease, high alcohol intake, and diuretic use. It is also seen as part of "syndrome X," which consists of abdominal obesity and high blood pressure, and is a potent risk for arthroscelerosis and heart disease. Gout is less common, involving 0.2–0.5 percent of men.

Clinical features. Gout may be precipitated in patients with hyperuricemic gout by excess alcohol, metabolic disturbances due to surgery or trauma, or diuretic therapy. Classical gout involves the big toe (podagra), making it exquisitely painful, red, swollen, and tender. The onset may involve multiple joints, particularly those of the lower limbs. It is unusual for both lower limbs to be affected at the same time. Initial attacks often resolve after a few days and can be followed by recurrent episodes. These can progress to chronic arthritis. Some cases with established gout have subcutaenous urate crystals deposits (known as tophi) in the pinnae of the ears, fingers, and elbows.

Investigations. If joint fluid from an affected joint is aspired (which is often very difficult to do), detecting intracellular uric acid crystals under the microscope is diagnostic. Most patients have elevated serum uric acid levels, though only a minority of patients with hyperuricemia have gout. Acute attacks result in an elevated ESR and high white cell count. In established gout X-rays show punched-out erosions with sclerotic margins, often distant from the joint margins.

Figure 3
Heberden's and Bouchard's nodes

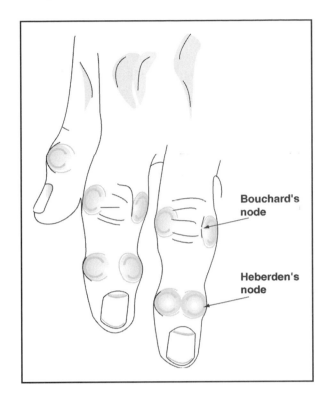

SOURCE: Author

Calcium pyrophosphate deposition disease

Some patients have a disorder similar to gout without synovial fluid uric acid crystals (Fam). Instead they have intracellular calcium pyrophosphate dihydrate crystals, a condition known as pseudogout. Such crystals also occur in osteoarthritis and a range of arthropathies, so that they are an important cause of arthritis in older people.

Causes and disease mechanisms. Calcium pyrophosphate is widely distributed in the body, and it is unclear why it sometimes forms crystals that induce inflammation. These crystals are often associated with metabolic disturbances such as parathyroid disease and a blood disorder known as hemochromatosis. Pathologically the crystals trigger a cascade of inflammatory pathways that mirrors gout.

Pyrophosphate crystals account for up 50 percent of acute attacks of crystal arthritis. Similar crystals are seen in the cartilage of many elderly people, a condition termed chondrocalcinosis. Seen in a minority of seventy year olds but the majority of ninety year olds, its pathological significance is often uncertain.

Clinical features. As is suggested by the name, acute pseudogout is similar to classical gout and can be precipitated by metabolic disturbances such as trauma. The arthritis develops suddenly, with one or several inflamed, painful, swollen, and tender joints. It typically involves knees, shoulders, and wrists. Many patients have recurrent episodes. Some cases have chronic arthritis, often with some joint inflammation occurring over and above osteoarthritis.

Investigations. Intracellular pyrophosphate crystals are visible on polarizing light microscopy of aspirated synovial fluid. X-rays may show chondrocalcinosis, indicating crystal deposition in joint cartilage. Blood tests either are normal or show evidence of mild inflammation with a raised ESR.

Other arthropathies. Other forms of arthritis important in the elderly include septic arthritis and arthritis linked to polymyalgia rheumatica and malignancy. Septic arthritis often complicates pre-existing chronic arthritis, particularly rheumatoid arthritis, and results in an acute exacerbation of joint problems and systemic involvement. Unless there is a high threshold of diagnostic suspicion, it can be difficult to diagnose until the joint sepsis is advanced. Arthritis in polymyalgia rheumatica and malignancy is mild, polyarticular, nonerosive, and seronegative for rheumatoid factor.

Management

General principles. Management aims are controlling pain, minimizing disability, reducing progressive joint damage, and limiting functional and social handicaps. Most arthropathies can be managed by family physicians with a minority of cases needing specialist referral; the exception is rheumatoid arthritis, which invariably needs specialist input. General management principles for most forms of arthritis comprise patient education, lifestyle advice, treating pain with analgesics, and treating pain and inflammation with non-steroidal anti-inflammatory drugs (NSAIDs).

Nondrug treatments. Advice, education, and support that benefit patients or their care givers can be provided by medical and a variety of support staff (Puppione). Self-efficacy, maintaining general health and fitness, and avoiding obesity all need emphasis. Aids and appliances, such as walking sticks and footwear, have modest benefits, though not all elderly patients are willing or able to use them.

Exercise program that improve general fitness and muscle strength are effective. They involve lifestyle changes such as regular walking and specific muscle-strengthening program like quadriceps exercises. There is good evidence that they are effective in osteoarthritis, but evidence for rheumatoid arthritis and other arthropathies is less convincing.

Analgesics and NSAIDs. Simple analgesics like acetaminophen are effective and safe in all forms of arthritis in the elderly (American College of Rheumatology). One disadvantage is that patients are reluctant to take enough acetaminophen (e.g., 1 gram four times daily). Other analgesics,such as tramadol and dihydrocodeine, are effective in relieving arthritic pain, though constipation with dihydrocodeine and disorientation with both drugs limit their use. Compound analgesics, especially coproxamol (dextropropoxyphene and acetaminophen) are widely used, though there is limited evidence that they are better than acetaminophen.

Nonsteroid anti-inflammatory drugs (NSAIDs) are widely used to treat pain and inflammation. Short courses of NSAIDs reduce pain and joint swelling over several days or weeks, and maintain these benefits for several months. There is limited evidence for longer-term benefits. The drawback with NSAIDs is their frequent adverse reactions. The most important are gastrointestinal reactions, which range from mild indigestion to severe gastrointestinal ulcers, hemorrhages, and perforations. Other reactions include rashes and renal and liver impairment. There are variations in the prevalence of severe gastrointestinal reactions with different NSAIDs. Older drugs like indomethacin cause more problems than newer drugs like nabumetone. Recently introduced coxibs like rofecoxib and celecoxib, which selectively inhibit COX-2 enzymes, have greater gastrointestinal safety (Jackson and Hawkey). Gastrointestinal risks are also reduced by co-prescribing prostaglandin analogues like misoprostol, proton-pump inhibitors like omeprazole, or H-2 antagonists like randitine.

Disease modifying antirheumatic drugs (DMARDs). These chemically diverse drugs control synovitis in rheumatoid arthritis and seronegative arthritis by modulating the immune response (Simon and Yocm). They reduce synovitis, decrease erosive damage, and improve long-term function. They are given in addition to analgesics and NSAIDs. DMARDs include methotrexate, sulfasalazine, leflunomide, azathioprine, cyclosporin, gold injections, and antimalarials (chloroquine and hydroxychloroquine). All except the antimalarials require regular monitoring for blood and liver toxicity.

DMARDs should be started soon after the diagnosis of rheumatoid arthritis has been established. Combinations of two or more DMARDs are often used, for example, triple therapy with methotrexate, sulfasalazine, and hydroxychloroquine. A recent development has been the introduction of antitumor necrosis factor (TNF) alpha immunotherapy, usually combined with methotrexate, to supplement DMARD therapy in severe disease.

Steroids. Local steroid injections benefit active inflammatory arthritis involving a single joint, irrespective of the cause, provided there is no sepsis. They can be repeated several times but should not be used excessively.

Systemic steroids, given intramuscularly or orally, are effective in acute active inflammatory arthritis, whatever the cause. They have a rapid onset of action, but their benefits may not be sustained. Their long-term use is limited by osteoporosis, thinning of the skin, increased sepsis, and other adverse reactions. It is imperative to prevent osteoporosis by giving calcium and vitamin D, with additional preventive therapy such as biphosphonates, in elderly patients on long-term systemic steroids therapy.

Other local treatments. Intra-articular artificial synovial fluid injections benefit osteoarthritis and reduce pain for up to six months. Local NSAIDs applied topically as creams or gels offer small benefits for osteoarthritis with limited adverse effects. There are similar benefits with local capsaicin, also applied topically as a cream.

Other medical treatments. Gout is treated by allopurinol, which inhibits uric acid formation. It has no value in acute gout and, because it may precipitate acute attacks, requires initial NSAID coprescription. Colchicine is an alternative approach in gout, but its efficacy is limited by diarrhea. Septic arthritis requires antibiotics; the choice depends upon the organisms involved.

Surgical treatment. The most important surgical treatment for osteoarthritis and joint failure is replacement. Many different joints can be replaced, but knees and hips are most important. Replacment reduces pain and improves function with few perioperative and postoperative complications. Most prostheses last many years. Indications for surgery include persistent pain, poor function, and anatomical evidence of joint destruction. Contra-indications include obesity, poor general health, and relative youth (as prostheses do not last indefinitely). Outcomes are better with single joint replacements, but many patients do well with multiple joint replacements. Other surgical interventions, including attempts to salvage existing joints by surface replacement, have fewer beneficial effects.

DAVID SCOTT

See also PAIN MANAGEMENT.

BIBLIOGRAPHY

American College of Rheumatology, Subcommittee on Osteoarthritis Guidelines. "Recommendations for the Medical Management of Osteoarthritis of the Hip and Knee. 2000 Update." *Arthritis and Rheumatism* 43, no. 9 (2000): 1905–1915.
British League Against Rheumatism. *Disability and Arthritis*. London: The League, 1994.
FAM, A. G. "What Is New About Crystals Other Than Monosodium Urate?" *Current Opinions in Rheumatology* 12, no. 3 (2000): 228–234.
KIRWAN, J. R.; CURREY, H. L.; FREEMAN, M. A.; SNOW, S.; AND YOUNG, P. J. "Overall Long-term Impact of Total Hip and Knee Joint Replacement Surgery in Patients with Osteoarthritis and Rheumatoid Arthritis." *British Journal of Rheumatology* 33 (1994): 357–360.
JACKSON, L. M.; AND HAWKEY, C. J. "COX-2 Selective Nonsteroidal Anti-inflammatory Drugs: Do They Really Offer Advantages?" *Drugs* 59, no. 6 (2000): 1207–1216.
Joint Working Group of the British Society for Rheumatology and Research Unit of the Royal College of Physicians "Guidelines for the Diagnosis, Investigation and Management of Osteorthritis of the Hip and Knee." *Journal of the Royal College of Physicians* (London) 27 (1993): 391–396.
PUPPIONE, A. A. "Management Strategies for Older Adults with Osteoarthritis: How to Promote and Maintain Function." *Journal of the American Academy of Nurse Practitioners* 167–171.
SCOTT, D. L.; SHIPLEY, M.; DAWSON, A.; EDWARDS, S.; SYMMONS, D. P.; AND WOOLF, A. D. "The

Clinical Management of Rheumatoid Arthritis and Osteorthritis: Strategies for Improving Clinical Effectiveness." *British Journal of Rheumatology* 37, no. 5 (1998): 546–554.

SEWELL, K. L. "Rheumatoid Arthritis in Older Adults." *Clinics in Geritaric Medicine* 14, no. 3 (1998): 475–494.

SILMAN, A. J.; AND HOCHBERG, M. C. *Epidemiology of the Rheumatic Diseases*. Oxford: Oxford University Press, 1994.

SIMON, L. S.; AND YOCM, D. "New and Future Drug Therapies for Rheumatoid Arthritis." *Rheumatology* (Oxford) 39, supp. 1 (2000): 36–42.

VAN DOORNUM, S.; AND RYAN, P. F. "Clinical Manifestations of Gout and Their Management." *Med J* 172, no. 10 (2000): 493–497.

ASSESSMENT

Comprehensive Geriatric Assessment (CGA) is the term most commonly used to refer to the specialized process by which the health of some elderly people is assessed. CGA has four characteristics:

1. It is multi-factorial, encompassing items traditionally regarded both as "medical" and "social."
2. Its emphasis is on the functional ability of the person being assessed.
3. It includes an inventory of both assets and deficits.
4. It is action oriented, that is, it provides the basis for the subsequent management plan for the patient who is being assessed.

To consider this process in more detail, we can examine each of the items identified in the opening sentence: Some people, are assessed, by a specialized process. CGA is not meant for all elderly people, only some. Two features identify those individuals who might benefit from CGA: the person should have compromised function; and, they should have more than one thing wrong. Compromised function is key: people who are engaged in all activities in which they would like to be engaged, at a level that is fully satisfying for them, normally do not require CGA, even if they might have one or more medical illnesses, such as high blood pressure or osteoarthritis. But when elderly people find that they can no longer can perform certain activities necessary for them to remain independent, including things like looking after their household

or getting dressed, then they become potential candidates for CGA. The other criterion for a person to become a candidate for CGA is to have more than one active medical problem that in some way is gives rise to, or appears to give rise to, the problem with function. To say that an elderly person has compromised function and multiple medical problems is another way of saying that that person is frail.

People with multiple problems require *assessment* of those problems. This assessment is in contrast to the usual medical approach, which begins with a diagnosis of the medical problem. Diagnosis is the process whereby clues from talking to (called taking the history) and examining the patient yield a pattern that is recognizable as having a single cause. Although more than one problem can be active at once, the traditional emphasis in medical diagnosis is on distilling many symptoms (what the patient tells the physician) and signs (what the physician finds on the examination) into a single cause, called the diagnosis.

The first practitioners of geriatric medicine recognized that this approach, while essential in sorting out the medical problems of frail elderly people, was inadequate in meeting their health needs. For example, many frail elderly people who are medically ill also are *deconditioned*—that is, they are weaker, especially in the shoulders and hips, more prone to fall, and more prone to abnormalities of fluid balance—but deconditioning is not a traditional medical diagnosis. Knowing how intensively to rehabilitate someone who is deconditioned in a hospital requires some understanding of their home circumstances: Will they have to climb stairs at home? Is there someone readily available to help? Is that person able and willing to help? Such practical methods fall outside the traditional domains of medical diagnoses, and their systematic inventory is what underlies the "assessment" process. Many authors believe that the term "assessment" has too narrow a focus, and that a proper assessment should not only give rise to a plan for addressing the problems thus identified, but should also include the management of the problems themselves, at least after they are stabilized. As a consequence, the term *geriatric evaluation and management* is sometimes preferred to describe what traditionally has been known as CGA.

Methods of CGA

The specialized nature of CGA lies in the systematic approach to a patient's problems. Although variation exists among practices, most methods of CGA include, in addition to an evaluation of the patient's medical diagnosis, an assessment of the following domains:

1. *Cognitive function.* Problems that give rise to impairment of thinking, language, memory, and other aspects of cognition include syndromes such as dementia, delirium, and depression. Typically, cognition is screened using a brief instrument such as the Mini-Mental State Examination (MMSE). The MMSE tests several aspects of cognition, including memory, attention, concentration, orientation, language, and visual-spatial function. If this screening test detects an abnormality, then a more detailed evaluation is required.

2. *Emotion.* The domain of emotion includes a screening of mood, to look for signs of depression, as well as an evaluation of common problems such as anxiety, or disorders of the mental state such as delusions or hallucinations. In addition, health attitudes are assessed, including the level of motivation, which is particularly important for patients who are being screened for participation in a rehabilitation program.

3. *Communication.* Communication assessment typically includes a screening of vision, hearing, speech, and language.

4. *Mobility.* The assessment of *mobility* that is, the ability to move about in bed, transfer in and or of bed, and walk is particularly important, as it is necessary for independence. In addition, because so many older people have atypical presentations of their illness, careful evaluation of their mobility as it first declines and then gets better allows clinicians to readily determine whether their patients are improving or getting worse. Given that many frail elderly people do not demonstrate the usual signs of sickness as they become ill (for example, they may not show an elevated temperature or white cell count when they have an infection), having a ready means to track illness progression and recovery is of great practical benefit, and careful assessment of mobility and balance allows this to be done.

5. *Balance.* The assessment of balance is distinct from the assessment of mobility. Again, its importance lies both in its intrinsic value in relation to independence and in its value of improving or worsening health in the setting of acute illness.

6. *Bowel function.* Bowel function is typically assessed by inquiring about the patient's bowel habit and by physical assessment, which should include a rectal examination.

7. *Bladder function.* It is important to understand whether an older person is having difficulty with urination. In men, this often reflects disease of prostate. In either sex, the presence of urinary incontinence is of particular importance. As with problems in mobility and balance, the significance lies not just in the incontinence per se, but in incontinence as a sign of illness, within the genitourinary system and elsewhere.

8. *Nutrition.* Interestingly, nutrition is often neglected in the traditional medical examination. It is important to assess the patient's weight and to note the presence of weight loss, and the time over which this weight loss has occurred. Routine laboratory investigations also offer some insight into an elderly person's nutritional status.

9. *Daily activities.* In some ways this is at the heart of the assessment. It is extremely important to know whether older people are capable of fully caring for themselves in their particular setting. These activities traditionally are divided into "instrumental" activities of daily living, such as using a telephone, or doing shopping, caring for finances, and administering medications, and "personal" activities of daily living, such as bathing, dressing, or eating. Understanding where problems exist and how they presently are dealt with is essential to knowing how an illness impacts on an older person.

10. *Social situation.* In addition to inquiring about the usual living circumstances, and whether there is a caregiver, the part of the assessment concerning social situation is the most distinct from the traditional medical examination. While it is clear that the patient enjoys primacy in the physician-patient relationship, it is also the case that the needs of the caregiver cannot be ignored. Indeed, where an older person is dependent in essential activities of daily living, the caregiver becomes the most important asset to the maintenance of independence. It is therefore essential to understand how caregivers feel about their caring role, and whether, and under what circumstances, they can see themselves continuing in it.

The efficacy of CGA has been formally tested in a number of randomized, controlled trials, so that it now forms part of evidence-based medicine. These trials have shown that, compared with usual care, elderly people—especially those who are frail—achieve many important health outcomes when provided with CGA-based care. For example, they are more likely to be discharged from the hospital without delay, more likely to be functional when discharged and up to a year later, less likely to go to a nursing home, and less likely to die within two years of follow-up.

A thorough CGA, including the standard history and physical examination, typically takes between an hour and an hour and a half to complete, and it can take even longer. This is more than twice the length of many initial consultations with a clinician, and so a CGA requires special effort and commitment on everyone's part. Nevertheless, it represents a reasonable way to come to grips with the needs particularly of frail older people, and in consequence to set appropriate and achievable goals to maintain independence, or to otherwise intervene for the benefit of the patient.

KENNETH ROCKWOOD

See also BALANCE AND MOBILITY; DAY HOSPITALS; FRAILTY; FUNCTIONAL ABILITY; GERIATRIC MEDICINE; MULTIDISCIPLINERY TEAM; SURGERY IN ELDERLY PEOPLE.

BIBLIOGRAPHY

PHILIP, I., ed. *Assessing Elderly People in Hospital and Community Care* London: Farrand Press, 1994.
ROCKWOOD, K.; SILVIUS, J.; AND FOX, R. "Comprehensive Geriatric Assessment: Helping Your Elderly Patients Maintain Functional Well-being." *Postgraduate Medicine* 103 (1998): 247–264.
ROCKWOOD, K.; STADNYK, K.; CARVER, D.; MACPHERSON, K.; BEANLANDS, H. E.; POWELL, C.; STOLEE, P.; THOMAS, V. S.; AND TONKS, R. S. "A Clinimetric Evaluation of Specialized Geriatric Care for Frail Elderly People." *Journal of the American Geriatric Society* 48 (9) 2000: 1080–1085.

ASSETS AND WEALTH

This entry deals with the wealth holdings of older Americans and also addresses a number of interrelated issues, such as how much wealth the typical older household owns and in what form they decide to hold their wealth. The more difficult question of why some older American households have accumulated so much wealth while many others have almost nothing at all is also discussed. Finally, this entry explores what the future plans of the elderly might be about the disposition of this wealth.

Data sources

Until the last decades of the twentieth century, little was known about the wealth of older adults. This was unfortunate since household wealth is an important complementary measure of command over economic resources. While we knew a good deal about income differences, little was known about how much personal wealth older people had and how and why that wealth got distributed. The principal reason was the absence of high quality data on the wealth holdings of older people. Fortunately, this problem was remedied during the 1990s by the availability of an important new data resource—the Asset and Health Dynamics of the Oldest Old (AHEAD).

AHEAD has fundamentally changed our knowledge about wealth holdings of older Americans. In addition to containing sufficient sample sizes for the elderly population, AHEAD is unique in its integration of high-quality economic modules alongside in-depth information about respondents' health, family structure, and cognition. During its baseline in 1993, AHEAD included 6,052 households (8,222 individuals) with a least one individual born in 1923 or earlier. In terms of substantive content, AHEAD focuses on the key concerns in this age group—the relationship of life-cycle changes in physical and cognitive health in old age to dissavings and asset decline. Individual respondents are followed up at two year intervals.

A distinct advantage of AHEAD compared to other surveys of older populations is that a very comprehensive and detailed set of questions were asked to measure household wealth. Besides housing equity, household assets were separated into the following eleven categories: other real estate; vehicles; business equity; IRA or Keogh; stocks or mutual funds; checking, savings or money market funds; CDs, government savings bonds, or treasury bills; other bonds; other assets; and other debt. The wealth data in AHEAD has been shown to be of generally high

Table 1

Mean Net Worth by Race and Ethnicity (Households age 70 and over, July 2000, in dollars)

	All	White	Black	His-panics
Total Net Worth	213,405	234,279	62,449	72,674
Home Equity	87,185	93,277	40,608	50,069
Financial Assets	82,573	92,853	10,024	10,464
Real Assets	43,647	48,150	11,817	12,140

SOURCE: Author

quality (Juster and Smith). This improvement in quality appears to be largely the result of dedicated survey administrators and staff and the use of some new innovative survey methods that enhance the quality of wealth measurement in social science surveys.

The principal new technique that has enhanced data quality on household wealth is the use of what has been termed *unfolding brackets*. A persistent problem in household surveys that requested information about the values of assets involves very high levels of item nonresponse. Originally, this was thought to indicate a great reluctance to reveal sensitive information about a household's financial status, but it is now believed simply to reflect uncertainty about precise values. Unfolding brackets helped deal with that uncertainty by asking respondents who answered wealth questions with a "do not know" or "refuse" a series of sequential questions requesting that they place the values of their assets within certain prespecified limits. For example, unfolding brackets converted a 45 percent full item nonresponse in stock value in AHEAD to only 8 percent of cases with no information on value. The use of unfolding brackets also produced significantly higher estimates of wealth holdings among the elderly. For example, Juster and Smith show that mean nonhousing wealth is 9 percent larger due to the use of unfolding brackets in AHEAD.

The distribution of wealth among older Americans

To document patterns of wealth disparities among older Americans, Table 1 presents esti-

mates of mean net worth by race and ethnicity obtained from the baseline 1993 AHEAD survey. This table also separates total household wealth into its principal component parts—housing equity, financial assets, and tangible assets (cars, business, real estate other than the main home). Expressed in July 2000 dollars, mean wealth of 1993 American households that contained a person over age sixty-nine was $213,405. Using means as the yardstick, home equity ranks first closely followed by total financial assets with combined tangible assets a distant third. While it is often believed that the elderly have few economic resources at their disposal, this is certainly not the case when their average wealth levels are compared to those of younger households. For example, in 1994, median household wealth of those over age sixty-five was 7.5 times that of those twenty-five to thirty-four years old.

Race and ethnic disparities in wealth are quite large. For every dollar of wealth an older white household has, black households have twenty-seven cents and Hispanic households have almost one-third as much wealth as their white counterparts. Whites have more assets in all major subcategories, but their advantage is smallest in home equity and largest in financial assets. Stunningly low levels of financial assets among older minority households are revealed here. While minority households have about half as much home equity as whites do, white financial assets exceed those held in minority households by a factor of nine to one. These more liquid financial assets may be a better index of the resources a household has on hand to meet emergencies.

Table 2 highlights the extent of wealth inequality among the elderly by listing net worth at selected percentiles of the wealth distribution. In contrast to a mean wealth of $213,405, the average or median household (at the fiftieth percentile) has $105,198, a reflection of a severely skewed wealth distribution. The top 1 percent of the population in this age group possesses about 10 percent of the wealth, and the top 5 percent possess 27 percent. While there are many older households with little wealth to tap into during difficult times, these data remind us that there coexist many other older households who are among the most affluent households in the country. Furthermore, the enormous wealth inequality in America clearly has little to do with race or ethnic issues. Even among whites, wealth disparities are large. White households at the ninetieth

Table 2
Percentile Distribution of Total Net Worth and
Financial Assets (July 2000, in dollars)

Total Net Worth

Percentile	All	White	Black	His-panics
10	650	2,364	0	0
20	13,593	25,058	0	0
30	43,734	56,736	1,241	0
50	105,198	118,673	30,968	23,640
70	199,167	219,691	60,578	70,149
90	488,166	529,536	160,988	182,619
95	751,752	803,760	245,856	244,674

Financial Assets

Percentile	All	White	Black	His-panics
10	0	0	-709	-307
20	0	296	0	0
30	1,182	2,600	0	0
50	11,820	17,730	0	0
70	53,190	62,646	1,182	591
90	210,396	236,400	23,640	23,876
95	366,420	392,007	54,372	53,190

SOURCE: Author

percentile have 224 times more wealth than white households at the tenth percentile.

Inequality is even more pronounced when the focus is limited to financial wealth holdings where half of this population group holds only about 1 percent of all financial wealth. Neither the average older black nor the average older Hispanic household has any financial wealth at all. Even the bottom third of older white families has less than $3,000 in liquid assets at their disposal, and one in five has less than $300.

These then are the basic facts about wealth among older American households. They are characterized by modest wealth holdings for the typical older household, large inequalities in wealth, large racial and ethnic differences in wealth, and very little evidence of any prior savings behavior by poor or even middle-class older households.

The first question is to what extent income differences across older households account for these large wealth disparities. Household income and wealth are strongly positively related, albeit in a highly nonlinear way. Financial assets and total net worth all increase at a more rapid rate

than income as we move from lower income to higher income older households. Above the median income there are very large increases in household wealth as income rises; in contrast below the median household income, there is little difference in wealth across income groups. It turns out that this simple nonlinear relationship between wealth and income goes a long way toward explaining the large racial and ethnic wealth differences among older households documented in Tables 1 and 2. In contrast to whites, black and Hispanic households are concentrated below median incomes while white households are much more likely to be situated above the median where wealth increases much faster than household income does.

Income differences alone, however, are unable to account for the vast inequality in wealth holdings among older households. While less commented upon, the diversity in wealth holdings even among households with similar incomes is enormous. Among median income households over age seventy, total net worth varies from $390,060 among those in the top 5 percent to only $3,546 among the bottom 10 percent. Similarly, variation in financial assets for median income households runs from $178,177 (the top 5 percent) among the lowest 20 percent of such median income households. The within-income diversity of wealth holdings holds true even among households in the lowest income decile. About one in ten such households have more then $41,000 in financial wealth while more than half of them have only $400 or less. At the other end of the spectrum, one in every five households in the top decile of average household income have accumulated less than $6,000 in financial assets over their lifetimes.

Net worth also varies significantly across marital categories. Not surprisingly, wealth is highest among married respondents. By far the largest discrepancy takes place among those who had separated or divorced. Median net worth of those households is only one-fifth the wealth of married households. In all cases, married couples' net worth is far more than twice that in other household configurations, indicating that something more than simply combining two individuals' assets into one married household is going on. The analysis in Lupton and Smith suggests that married couples apparently save significantly more than other households, an effect not solely related to their higher incomes nor to the simple aggregation of two individuals' wealth.

Theory

What are the primary motives for wealth accumulation and savings that produce such large diversity in wealth holdings among older households? The most widely known model is the *life-cycle model,* which emphasizes savings (and dissavings) to deal with timing issues surrounding noncoincidence in income and consumption (see Browning and Lusardi). In this theory, individuals will tend to want to "smooth" consumption so that they will save when income is high and dissave when income is low. Since income is relatively low during the postretirement years, households should accumulate assets during working lives after which older adults should run down their assets at the end of life.

The evidence about whether households will eventually dissave during the postretirement period has been in dispute in part due to very small samples available for older American households. Table 3 lists mean and median household wealth by age of the respondent. Within this AHEAD sample, both mean and median household wealth decline sharply with age. However, one cannot deduce from this pattern alone a pure life-cycle reduction in assets during old age. Other contaminating factors including across-cohort increases in wealth, which will tilt the cross-sectional age-wealth profiles downward, and differential mortality by wealth have made it difficult to test this hypothesis. Since cross-sectional data cannot control for these contaminating factors, the panel nature of surveys such as AHEAD must be used. At this time, there are too few waves of this panel to answer this question conclusively.

Another motive for saving involves bequests (Hurd). Three motives are thought to be important: altruistic, strategic, and accidental. As the label implies, "altruistic" bequests exist because individuals care about future generations, particularly their children and grandchildren (Becker). Altruistic bequests should rise with the income of the donors and fall with the income of recipients so that altruism implies that the largest bequests should go to the least well-off children.

The strategic motive sees bequests as the outcome of an implicit contract between the generations. For example, parents may use the prospect of future bequests to induce their children to provide assistance to them when they are old. If such services are not rendered, the implicit threat is to reduce or even eliminate the future

Table 3
Mean Net Worth by Age (Households age 70 and over, July 2000, in dollars)

Age	70-75	76-80	81-85	86+
Mean Net Worth	251,561	215,294	168,401	121,525
Median Net Worth	130,020	100,825	77,066	41,370

SOURCE: Author

bequest. The sharp distinction between altruistic and strategic motives comes from for whom the bequest recipients are likely to be (Cox; Bernheim, Shleifer, and Summers), with the altruistic model implying that the least well off children should be the recipients.

One difficulty in testing for the importance of bequest motives relates to the distinct possibility that some considerable amounts of bequests are "accidents" (Yaari). Since they cannot foresee with certainty the time of their deaths, individuals may run the risk of dying too late, having run out of resources to finance their consumption. They will accumulate wealth to guard against this uncertain date of death—those who die early will leave bequests even though they do not have any bequest motive per se. As a practical empirical matter, it has proven difficult to distinguish between altruistic and accidental bequests.

One test of the bequest motive involves variation in rate of wealth decumulation at older ages as a function of variables that should be correlated with the strength of a bequest motive. A strong bequest motive should diminish rates of wealth decumulation. An obvious test involves comparisons of rates of wealth decline at old age among those households with children and those without children. A consistent finding is that there appears to be little difference in rates of wealth decline across these types of families (Hurd).

Another test of the bequest motive as well as the life-cycle hypothesis can be derived from questions asked about the intended bequests individuals plans to make when they die. Hurd and Smith report that current wealth holdings of older households significantly exceed their average desired bequest. Since they plan to leave bequests much less than their current wealth, the strong implication is that individuals must on average anticipate significant dissaving before they die.

A related aspect of bequests involves the extent to which past inheritances can explain the diversity in current wealth holdings by households. It turns out that financial inheritances represent but a fraction of total net worth so that levels and distributions of wealth would be largely the same even if the maximum contribution of financial inheritances are taken into account. For example, very few of the households in the AHEAD sample received any significant financial inheritances (Smith, 1997).

Besides household income, life-cycle factors, and bequests, why is there so much diversity in wealth holdings among older Americans? This question is on the frontier of current research, and a full consensus on which explanations rank highest in importance has not been reached. The reasons lie in very different savings rates across households as well as different ex post rates of return on those savings. Differences in realized rates of return will produce wide differences in wealth holdings over time as households increasingly differentiate themselves based on their good fortune.

Wealth and savings differences across older households also result from substantial taste differences operating through time and risk preferences, the onset of bad health shocks, high old age income replacement rates through social insurance and pension programs, more extensive family support networks, and asset tests in means-tested social insurance programs that discourage asset possession.

Poor health is a pervasive risk that may limit the ability of older households to hold onto their previously accumulated wealth. In middle and at older ages, there are pronounced effects of new health events on household income and wealth (Smith, 1999). While additional medical expenses are part of the reason for this depletion in economic resources, they by no means accounts for the bulk of it. In middle age, reductions in household income associated with health effects on labor supply are equally important. At both middle and older ages, new health shocks appear to reduce individuals' expectations about their life expectancy and their desire or ability to leave bequests to their heirs.

Another factor that may affect wealth accumulation of older people involves the high retirement income replacement rates from pensions and Social Security that exist for some older households. These replacement rates represent the fraction of household income that will be replaced by pensions and Social Security at the time these households are expected to retire. On an after-tax basis, for example, most households in the lower quarter of the income distribution currently appear to enjoy almost full income replacement when they retire. At least for retirement purposes, the incentive to save for these low income households is almost nil.

The importance of pension and social security annuities also argues that household wealth as conventionally measured above ignores critical components of wealth that can loom large, especially for households nearing and in retirement. Virtually all households anticipate a flow of Social Security benefits when they retire. More than half of them are also counting on the income from their pensions. When discounted to the present, these expected income flows translate into considerable amounts of wealth. For example, combined Social Security and pension wealth are as important as household wealth for the average family in their fifties. This distortion caused by the conventional wealth concept is much larger among low income and minority families. Among black and Hispanic households, conventional household wealth is less than one-third of their total wealth. For these minority households, social security wealth is especially critical and represents by far the largest part of their wealth. Wealth is an important but complex economic resource and new methods have been developed to obtain better measurement. We should anticipate that our knowledge about how wealth is distributed among older Americans will be increasing quite rapidly in the next few decades.

JAMES P. SMITH

See also BEQUESTS AND INHERITANCES; ECONOMIC WELL-BEING; ESTATE PLANNING; LIFE CYCLE THEORIES OF SAVINGS AND CONSUMPTION; PENSIONS, PLAN TYPES AND POLICY APPROACHES; POVERTY.

BIBLIOGRAPHY

BECKER, G. S. *A Treatise on the Family.* Cambridge, Mass.: Harvard University Press, 1981.

BERNHEIM, B. D.; SHLEIFER, A.; and SUMMERS, L. H. "The Strategic Bequest Motive." *Journal of Political Economy* 93, no. 6 (1985): 1045–1076.

BROWNING, M., and LUSARDI, A. "Household Saving: Micro Theories and Micro Facts." *Journal of Economic Literature* 34 (December 1996): 1797–1855.

COX, D. "Motives for Private Income Transfers." *Journal of Political Economy* 95 (1987): 508–546.

HURD, M. D. "Savings of the Elderly and Desired Bequests." *American Economic Review* 77 (1987): 298–311.

HURD, M. D., and SMITH, J. P. "Anticipated and Actual Bequests." In *The Economics of Aging.* Edited by David Wise. Chicago, University of Chicago Press, 2001.

JUSTER, F. T., and SMITH, J. P. "Improving the Quality of Economic Data: Lessons from HRS and AHEAD." *Journal of the American Statistical Association* 92, no. 440 (1997): 1268–1278.

LUPTON, J. , and SMITH, J. P. "Marriage, Assets, and Savings." In *Marriage and the Economy.* Edited by Shoshana Grossbard-Shecht. Cambridge University Press, 2000.

SMITH, J. P. "Wealth Inequality among Older Americans." *Journal of Gerontology* 52B (May 1997): 74–81.

SMITH, J. P. "Healthy Bodies and Thick Wallets." *Journal of Economic Perspectives* 13, no. 2 (Spring 1999).

SMITH, J. P. "Inheritances and Bequests." In *Wealth, Work, and Health: Innovations in Measurement in the Social Sciences.* Edited by James P. Smith and Robert Willis. Ann Arbor: University of Michigan Press, 1999.

YAARI, M. E. "Uncertain Lifetime, Life Insurance, and the Theory of the Consumer." *Review of Economic Studies* 32 (1965): 137–150.

ASSISTED LIVING

Assisted living has emerged as a significant option for older adults seeking long-term care services. Yet a standard, national definition of assisted living has proven elusive. It is defined, in part, by companies and owners through their marketing efforts. It is also defined by state regulations governing the licensing of facilities, and there are wide variations among states in how assisted living is defined and licensed.

Assisted-living philosophy

While the definition of assisted living varies widely across states, there are several core terms that appear in state definitions. Assisted living is generally viewed as home-like and offers residential units and the availability of supportive and health-related services available to meet scheduled and unscheduled needs, twenty-four hours a day. Assisted living is viewed as the consumer's home, and as such includes the amenities that people generally expect in a residence, including a door that locks, a private bathroom, temperature control, a food preparation area, and the freedom to make choices about the types of services that are available. In addition, twenty-eight states have included a philosophy of assisted living (up from twenty-two states in 1998 and fifteen in 1996). These statements describe assisted living as a model that promotes the independence, dignity, privacy, decision-making, and autonomy of residents, and supports aging in place.

Regulations specifically governing assisted living have grown rapidly. By 2000, twenty-nine states and the District of Columbia had a licensing category or statute using the term *assisted living*, and four other states were in the process of developing such regulations. By contrast, only twenty-two states had such regulations in 1998. However, assisted-living facilities are regulated in the other states under rules that may use other terms, such as *residential care facilities* or *personal care homes*.

In 2000, states reported a total of 32,886 licensed facilities with 795,391 units or beds, a 30 percent increase over 1998. However, information was not reported by all states. Assisted living has developed primarily as a private pay market. However, by mid-2000, thirty-eight states covered services in residential settings—under either assisted-living or board-and-care licensing categories—through Medicaid, and coverage was being planned in three other states plus the District of Columbia. While the number of states covering services in residential settings has grown, the number of beneficiaries served remains limited with about 60,000 people served, a 50 percent increase in two years. Over 36 percent of the units (or beds) are located in three states: California (136,719), Florida (77,292), and Pennsylvania (73,075). Since 1998, the number of licensed facilities has soared in Delaware (by 214 percent), Iowa (144 percent), New Jersey (139 percent), and Wisconsin (119 percent). Ten states reported growth in licensed facilities of between 40 percent and 100 percent in the past two years: Alaska, Arizona, Kansas, Indiana, Massa-

J. Willard Marriot Jr. (left) jokes with Brighton Gardens assisted living resident Mike Goldman at the senior citizen facility in Saddle Creek, New Jersey, in 1998. Marriott International, best-known for its hotels, has built or purchased more than 100 assisted living facilities, which it views as an expanding market. (AP photo by Mike Derer.)

chusetts, Minnesota, Nebraska, New York, South Dakota, and Texas.

Within the industry and among state officials, there is often a debate about where assisted living lies on a social-medical continuum. Hawes et al. found that some operators view assisted living as a nonmedical model (without RN staffing) that provides high privacy and low service. Others view it as a high-privacy/high-service model that offers a wide range of services, aging in place, and private units. Over half of all the facilities were considered low-privacy/low-service models that offered shared units and limited health services. The study also pointed out that many in the industry question whether privacy and service level were accurate variables to use in describing assisted living. The report concludes that there is no agreement at the operational level on what constitutes assisted living.

The Hawes report also examined whether facilities support aging in place, the ability to receive additional services as needs change. Fifty-four percent would not retain residents needing transfer assistance, 68 percent would not serve residents needing nursing care, and 55 percent would not retain people with severe cognitive impairment. Twenty-four percent of assisted-living residents received help with three or more activities of daily living (ADLs), compared to 84 percent of nursing-home residents. The authors note that these findings suggest that assisted living may not serve as a substitute for nursing-home care. However, in the absence of assisted living, it is likely that many residents with fewer ADL impairments would seek nursing home placement. The differences in impairment levels between residents of assisted-living facilities and nursing homes may in fact be due to the availability of assisted-living facilities to serve residents with relatively low needs.

Findings from Hawes et al. contrast with those from Mollica which indicate that 87 percent of state licensing agencies feel that assisted-living facilities are providing as high a level of care as allowed by regulation. Anecdotally, licensing-agency staff indicate that some facilities may be serving people longer than they should (based on their staff capacity and training), even though the level of need is consistent with what is allowed by regulation.

The 1999 U.S. General Accounting Office (GAO) study of assisted living in four states (California, Florida, Ohio, and Oregon) concluded that these facilities support aging in place. Seventy-five percent of facilities included in the report said that they admitted residents who have mild to moderate memory or judgment problems, are incontinent but can manage on their own or with some help, have a short-term need for nursing care, or need oxygen supplementation. However, this level of care may be limited since it implies that people with severe memory loss who need more than occasional assistance with incontinence or who need nursing services for longer periods would not be served.

Privacy and living units

The size, layout, and shared nature of living units is an issue that often creates conflict in policy development. Older board-and-care rules allow shared rooms, toilets, and bathing facilities. Existing facilities that want to be licensed for assisted living often oppose rules requiring apartment-style units and single occupancy. Some states have grandfathered existing buildings or maintain separate board-and-care categories that allow shared rooms.

Single occupancy apartments or rooms dominate the private market. A 1996 survey of non-profit facilities conducted by the Association of Homes and Services for the Aging found that 76 percent of the units in free-standing facilities and 89 percent of units in multilevel facilities were private (studio, one-, or two-bedroom units). A similar survey by the Assisted Living Federation of America in 2000 found that 87.4 percent of units in ALFA member facilities were studio, one-, or two-bedroom units and 12.6 percent were semiprivate. Hawes et al. found that 73 percent of the units were private and meet the privacy aspect of the philosophy of assisted living, but only 27 percent of the facilities had all private units.

A 1998 survey of assisted-living facilities by the National Investment Conference (NIC) found that cooking appliances were more likely to be available in geographic areas where there was greater competition among facilities. The inclusion of stoves in living units is declining, however, and facilities are more likely to include microwave or toaster ovens in units. The survey also found that 17 percent of residents shared a unit. Fifty-two percent said that they shared their unit for economic reasons, 30.4 percent for companionship, and 14.9 percent because a private unit was not available. Just under 65 percent of those who shared a unit were satisfied with the arrangement, while 35.7 percent would prefer a single unit.

Nationally, consumer demand and competition are more likely than regulatory policy to determine whether studio or apartment-style living units are available. Licensing rules in eleven states and Medicaid-contracting specifications in four states require apartment-style units.

States seeking to facilitate aging in place and to offer consumers more long-term care options allow more extensive services. These states view assisted-living facilities as a person's home. In a single-family home or apartment in an elderly housing complex, older people can receive a high level of care from home health agencies and in-home service programs. Several states extend that level of care to assisted-living facilities.

The extent and intensity of services generally follow state criteria. Services can be provided or arranged that allow residents to remain in a setting. Mutually exclusive resident policies, which prohibit anyone needing a nursing-home level of services from being served in board-and-care facilities, have been replaced by aging-in-place provisions. However, drawing the line has been controversial in many states. In many states, some nursing home operators see assisted living as competition for their patients and oppose rules which allow skilled nursing services to be delivered outside the home or nursing-home setting.

Most states require an assessment and the development of a plan of care that determines what services will be provided, by whom, and when. Residents often have a prominent role in determining what services they will receive and what tasks they will do for themselves. A key factor in assisted-living policies is the extent of skilled nursing services that are allowed.

Hawes et al. found that nearly all facilities (94 percent) provided or arranged for assistance with self-medication; 97 percent assisted with bathing; and 94 percent offered help with dressing. Although nearly all states allow central storage of medications, 88 percent of the facilities provided or arranged this service. Arizona, for example, has three service levels that allow supervisory care services, personal-care services, and directed-care services. Residents in facilities with a supervisory care license may receive health services from home-health agencies. Facilities with a personal-care services license can provide intermittent nursing services and can administer medications. Other health services may be provided by outside agencies. Directed-care service facilities provide supervision to ensure personal safety, cognitive stimulation, and other services for residents who are unable to direct their own care.

Negotiated risk

One of the innovations of assisted living is the focus on consumer control and decision-making. At times, residents express preferences that raise concerns among facility staff. To mediate these differences, eighteen states use a negotiated-risk process to involve residents in care planning and to respect resident preferences that may pose a risk to the resident or other residents. Residents, family members, and staff meet to review issues about which there is disagreement. During this process, the parties define the services that will be provided to the resident with consideration for their preferences. The resulting agreement lists needs and preferences for a range of services and specific areas of activity under each service. To many regulators, negotiated service agreements are part of a philosophy that stresses consumer choice, autonomy, and independence, as opposed to a facility-determined regimen that includes fixed schedules of activities and tasks, which might be more convenient for staff and management. Placing the residents' needs and preferences ahead of the staff and administrators helps turn a "facility" into a home.

Selecting an assisted-living facility

Choosing a facility can be time-consuming and confusing. The Assisted Living Federation of America and the American Association of Homes and Services for the Aging have consumer checklists that can be used to frame information people might want about a facility. Other resources exist within each state. The agency responsible for licensing facilities may also have a checklist. In narrowing down the list of potential facilities, consumers should ask the licensing agency about any problems with compliance with state regulations. The state department on aging may also have information about assisted-living facilities.

Perhaps the key area is understanding what one is buying—the living unit, services, and activities—and how much this will cost. When reviewing the resident agreement or contract, one should make sure it is consistent with the marketing materials. It is also important to read the agreement to see the circumstances under which the facility may ask a resident to move. Understanding what services will be available if a resident gets sick or needs more assistance than when he or she moved in is one of the most important aspects of entering an assisted-living facility. Another important issue is what happens if a resident spends all of his or her resources and no longer has enough monthly income to pay the fee. As the supply of facilities expands, operators may be joining the growing number of facilities that contract with Medicaid to serve residents who qualify. It is important to ask if the facility participates in the Medicaid program.

Assisted living is a welcome addition to the array of long-term care services. Yet the nature and level of services vary, and it is important for potential residents to do their homework. It is better to seek the information before there is an emergency requiring a quick decision.

ROBERT MOLLICA

See also BOARD AND CARE HOMES; FINANCIAL PLANNING FOR LONG-TERM-CARE.

BIBLIOGRAPHY

Assisted Living Federation of America, Coopers and Lybrand. *2000 Overview of the Assisted Living Industry*. Washington, D.C.: ALFA, 2000.

GULYAS, R. *The Not-for-Profit Assisted Living Industry: 1997 Profile*. Washington, D.C.: American Association of Homes and Services for the Aging, 1997.

HAWES, C.; ROSE, M.; and PHILIPS, C. D. *A National Study of Assisted Living for the Frail Elderly. Results of a National Survey of Facilities*. Myers Research Institute, 1999.

MOLLICA, R. *State Assisted Living Policy: 2000*. Portland, Maine: National Academy for State Health Policy, 2000.

National Investment Conference and the Assisted Living Federation of America. *National Survey of Assisted Living Residents: Who Is the Customer?* Washington, D.C.: ALFA, 1998.

U.S. General Accounting Office. *Assisted Living: Quality of Care and Consumer Protection Issues in Four States*. Washington, D.C.: GAO, 1999.

ATHEROSCLEROSIS

See VASCULAR DISEASE

AUTOBIOGRAPHY

See LIFE REVIEW; NARRATIVE

AUTONOMY

Autonomy expresses the idea that persons should direct their own actions and be free from coercion or undue influences by others on their actions and deliberations. The concept of autonomy has touched all areas of social life and has had a pronounced effect on medical ethics and medical practice. Patient autonomy emerged in the 1960s and 1970s in the great social movement that created a diverse range of civil rights, some constitutionally protected, including expanded individual rights in health care, such as access to abortion, end-of-life decision making, and privacy. The clearest expression of autonomy in medicine is the doctrine of *informed consent.*

Informed consent defines a set of patient rights and reciprocal obligations for health professionals. Informed consent means that patients have a right to make autonomous choices about their medical care. To do so, they must be given information about their medical condition, treatment alternatives, and the burdens and benefits associated with the recommended treatment and its alternatives. Since this information is largely in the hands of physicians, the doctrine of informed consent creates the obligation that physicians disclose information to patients and allow patients to make their own medical decisions. An implication of informed consent is that patients can refuse treatment.

The right to refuse treatment, including life-saving or life-sustaining treatments, has come to be firmly established in law. Recognizing that patients sometimes lack the ability to make their own medical decisions, legislatures created *advance directives.* Advance directives empower patients to direct their future medical care even when they have lost the ability to make their own medical decisions. These ideas have radically transformed late twentieth-century medicine. In a similar vein, the concept of autonomy has affected our understanding of aging and being old as well.

On the positive side, autonomy has supported criticisms of ageism and other social attitudes and practices that limited the freedom of elders or that relegated elders to a secondary social status. Autonomy has also supported the elimination or modification of age-based discrimination, such as a mandatory retirement age or the proscription of the use of age in employment decisions. Autonomy is also at work in the idea that elders in retirement should remain active and engaged. Their social function is to enjoy an earned leisure and to maintain independence from the responsibilities characteristic of their preretirement lives. The principle of autonomy has thus introduced into gerontology a focus on the individual who is regarded independent of other individuals or social structures like the family. It has highlighted a certain understanding of the autonomous individual as one who has the capacities for self-directed and independent action, deliberation, and decision-making, and it has made these values preeminent. These assumptions demarcate a standard view of autonomy that has important implications for aging.

Key features

Four features of this view of autonomy are particularly significant for aging. First, the autonomous person is regarded outside a developmental framework and is assumed to fully possess all autonomy-related faculties. Thus, the standard view of autonomy has no ready way to accommodate incapacity. Second, autonomy implies independence and self-direction. States of dependence are regarded as problematic for true autonomy. Third, autonomy focuses on the individual in abstraction from social structures like the family, so the aged individual is seen as possessing value, purpose, and rights separate from the social and personal relationships that provide everyday support and assistance. Fourth, the standard view of autonomy incorporates a simplifying assumption that freedom of choice or decision-making expresses the most important dimension of being autonomous. Each of these features of autonomy creates a range of problems in the context of aging.

Standard treatments of autonomy focus on individual action and choice without regard for the medical, psychological, or social context of the individual whose autonomy is at issue. This creates special problems for thinking about those processes of aging that create dependencies or compromise the capacities of the elder. In these situations, autonomy and its corollary of rights cannot fundamentally aid elders whose struggle is not against oppression, but to maintain a personal sense of worth and dignity in the face of loss. In stressing the robust exercise of freedom, autonomy can distort the complex phenomenology of aging by vastly oversimplifying what being autonomous involves as one grows old.

Actual expressions of autonomy throughout the life span are always subject to a wide range of circumstances and conditions. For example, metabolic states can induce confusion and alter one's ability to think clearly or to carry out intended choices. Psychological states can distort one's ability to perceive reality accurately and can affect decision-making. Social factors also influence the ways in which one experiences the world and the choices that one practically envisions.

A society that prizes an idealized view of individual action and choice and that values independence, self-direction, and self-control understandably tends to disvalue conditions that compromise action or involve decisional impairments or states of dependence. The paradox of autonomy in aging is that the ideal of autonomy expressed in the robust independent decision maker is incongruent with some of the realities of loss that are associated with growing old. This raises the question: How can the ideals of autonomy be reconciled with the realities of aging?

Implications for aging

Frail elders who have experienced medically related incapacity often receive medical care in home with assistance from family members, neighbors, or friends. They sometimes rely on others for assistance in securing health care, filling prescriptions, or in complying with recommended medical regimens. Respecting the actual autonomy of such an elder entails more than respecting the right of informed consent or confidentiality. Respecting the actual autonomy of the elder requires that health professionals carefully examine the ways that the standard delivery of health care services can compromise an already impaired autonomy. For example, if elders require assistance in receiving health care services because they have hearing or visual impairments, assistive hearing devices or large-type patient information material or prescription medicine instructions can minimize or eliminate the direct reliance of some elders on others for the most basic elements of medical care.

Emphasizing informed consent can be problematic whenever elders are inclined to defer to authority figures. Such elders are more inclined to accept physician advice than are people in their middle years. For these elders, the right to informed consent is less meaningful than is the opportunity to receive authoritative advice from a physician. Because these elders would prefer to be told what to do rather than being provided with an array of choices, the challenge for physicians involves identifying the basic values or beliefs of patients and incorporating them into a treatment plan.

When physical infirmity associated with aging reduces a person's ability to act independently, it may not alter the person's decisional capacity. Focusing on independence of action may obscure the fact that actual expressions of autonomy always involve two distinct elements, a decisional and an executional element. A person may be autonomous in the sense of being able to make his or her own decisions, but may not be able to carry them out. Hence, autonomy is not lost when a person is unable to carry out a decision because of frailty or physical infirmity. To respect such a person's autonomy requires more than simply allowing them to make choices. It creates the obligation to assist them in carrying out their choices. Thus, respecting actual autonomy in the domain of choice entails that we assist elders in realizing their choices. This can be a formidable challenge in some instances, but in other circumstances minor accommodations are all that is needed.

Assistive devices ranging from hearing aids or wheelchairs to direct assistance in carrying out activities of daily living can serve to sustain the reality of autonomy in a frail elder. Autonomous choice in abstraction from the existential setting of choice is meaningless if the conditions required for its execution cannot be fulfilled. Autonomy that is impaired somewhat by executional inabilities can become a significant problem if the material means for providing executional assistance are not available. For this reason, poverty directly impairs one's autonomy, yet is a condition that is seldom regarded as infringing freedom. Although limitations in executional abilities occur throughout life, they are more significant as one ages and suffers the disabilities associated with growing old. Analogously, decisional impairments associated with dementia or Alzheimer's disease does not obliterate autonomy, but does create challenges for how autonomy of such persons is to be respected.

Because a person can no longer make autonomous choices, it does not mean that their autonomy cannot be respected. All autonomous choices are based on the person's preferences or values that are developed, often over a lifetime. The beliefs and values that guide a person's life is thus the key to respecting their autonomy whenever one's decisional capacity is impaired. In the absence of formal advance directives, these beliefs and values can provide a basis for respecting an elder's autonomy. To do so, however, one needs to know who the elder is. This requirement creates resource demands on caregivers and on a system of care that focuses on respecting patients' choices without regard for the background values or reasons that guide the choice.

Loss of independence is often regarded as the most serious impairment of autonomy. This view creates unrealistic expectations in the context of growing old. In America, ownership or occupancy of one's own home is a cultural value epitomized in the phrase that one's home is one's castle. It is no wonder, then, that living independently at home has become the last stand for elders struggling to maintain their self-respect and sense of dignity. Unfortunately, the requirements for assistance in daily living can become so great that elders cannot provide for themselves in the home. Hence, a struggle ensues between protecting the welfare of the elder and maintaining the elder's sense of identity and independence. Ironically, this struggle exists because we have not taken the demands of autonomy seriously enough.

Social considerations

As a society, we have ignored the material and social conditions that are required for autonomy to flourish. We have allowed autonomy-thwarting institutions to dominate the care of the infirm and sick old. Rather than building autonomy-sustaining institutions, long-term care of elders has accepted a medical paradigm of the delivery of services rather than a paradigm of providing an environment suitable for sustaining a compromised autonomy.

The nursing home in America has become the icon of the loss of independence. The nursing home often is a setting in which the individual is subject to impersonal institutional rules rather than self-control. Even when elders do not require skilled care, the medical model that dominates nursing homes creates a hierarchical and professionally dominated setting that forces residents to live under significant restrictions. In this context, it is understandable that reformers have used the concept of autonomy as a watchword for reform, but reforms that feature increased choices or rights cannot address the personal loss of dignity that elders experience.

Autonomy has traditionally supported liberation. In the nursing home, a patient rights' movement has developed that insists that residents of nursing homes be accorded basic rights, including degrees of self-governance and, most importantly, preservation of the rights that they possessed outside the nursing home. Liberating elders from an oppressive system, however, is not feasible if the elders truly need the supportive services that the nursing home provides.

While autonomy is an important value, respect for autonomy is a remarkably abstract formula for expressing the complex range of ethical obligations associated with respecting elderly persons. Persons deserve respect not only because they are capable of self-determination, but also because they are persons. In actuality, persons exhibit varying degrees and kinds of autonomy. Unfortunately, emphasizing the ideals of independence and unfettered decision-making that dominates most treatments of autonomy cannot be developmentally sustained throughout the life span. In contrast, respect for actual autonomy means that society must address the concrete actuality of the persons in question.

To respect autonomy thus requires that we develop policies and procedures that move beyond a focus on individual choice or decision-making to take into account developed personality and the limitations that actually define people as they age. The challenge of autonomy in aging is the challenge of respecting elders' actual expressions of autonomy in the face of compromised capacities without losing the protections afforded by the rights associated with traditional readings of the principle of autonomy.

GEORGE J. AGICH

See also ADVANCE DIRECTIVES FOR HEALTH CARE; AGE DISCRIMINATION; LIFE SPAN THEORY OF CONTROL; REFUSING AND WITHDRAWING MEDICAL ATTENTION.

BIBLIOGRAPHY

AGICH, G. J. *Autonomy in Long-Term Care*. New York: Oxford University Press, 1990.

GAMROTH, L. M.; SEMRADEK, J.; and TORNQUIST, E. M., eds. *Enhancing Autonomy in Long Term Care: Concepts and Strategies*. New York: Springer Publishing Company, 1995.

MCCULLOUGH, L. B., and WILSON, N. L., eds. *Long-Term Care Decisions: Ethical and Conceptual Dimensions*. Baltimore and London: John Hopkins University Press, 1995.

MOODY, H. R. *Aging: Concepts and Controversies*. Baltimore and London: John Hopkins University Press, 1998.

SCHNEEWIND, J. B. *The Invention of Autonomy: A History of Modern Moral Philosophy*. Cambridge: Cambridge University Press, 1997.

B

BABY BOOMERS

Baby boomers are all those born in the United States between 1946 and 1964. As illustrated in Figure 1, in the post–World War II period the General Fertility Rate (GFR) in the United States rose from what had been an all-time low in 1936 of 75.8 children per 1,000 women of childbearing age to a high of 122.7 in 1957—and then fell to a new all-time low of 65.0 in 1976. All races, religions, and ethnic groups participated in the boom. Total births per year during that period grew from 2.3 million to 4.3 million and then fell to 3.2 million. The baby boom is defined as having occurred during the peak years of this roller coaster ride: its legacy was a population bulge destined to leave its imprint on each phase of the life cycle. That imprint included the creation of an "echo boom" of births during the 1980s and 1990s.

Because the baby boom lasted nearly twenty years, many have objected to treating the baby boomers as a single cohort, associating younger baby boomers more with "Generation X" than with older baby boomers—but the original appellation has held through the years, and tends still to refer to the entire population bulge produced during the boom.

Similar baby booms occurred during the same period in many other western industrialized nations, with peak fertility rates in Canada, New Zealand, and Iceland even higher than those in the United States. However, the term "baby boomer" has tended to be used most commonly in reference to those born in the United States—and they are the focus of this entry. Figure 2 compares the baby booms in the United States, Canada, Australia, New Zealand, Ireland, and Iceland, nations that experienced the most pronounced and prolonged booms.

There are approximately seventy-nine million baby boomers in the United States at the beginning of the twenty-first century: about 29 percent of the total population. (The population estimates and medium projections are taken from the 2000 U.S. Census.) Following the boom in 1965, 38 percent of the total population were baby boomers, but by 2050 their share is projected to drop to only 5 percent, with eighteen million surviving at age eighty-five or older in that year. As they retire their numbers will grow relative to the size of the working-age population, until in 2030 there will be three retired baby boomers for every ten workers (and about four retirees in total for every ten workers—a ratio projected to remain fairly constant thereafter). Nevertheless, despite their declining share in total population, they do and will remain a characteristic bulge in the age structure throughout their lifetime.

What caused the baby boom?

There is no consensus regarding the cause of the baby boom: social scientists suggest a complex mixture of economic, social, and psychological factors. The majority of it occurred not through an increase in family size but rather through a sharp decline in the proportion of women choosing to remain childless (Westoff). For many older women these were births postponed during the Depression and World War II. They account for most of the immediate 1946–1947 "spike" in births associated with returning

Figure 1

A comparison of the historic U.S. birth rate and numbers of births in the United States. (Total Fertility Rate [TFR] is the number of births a woman would experience throughout her childbearing years, at current age-specific rates.)

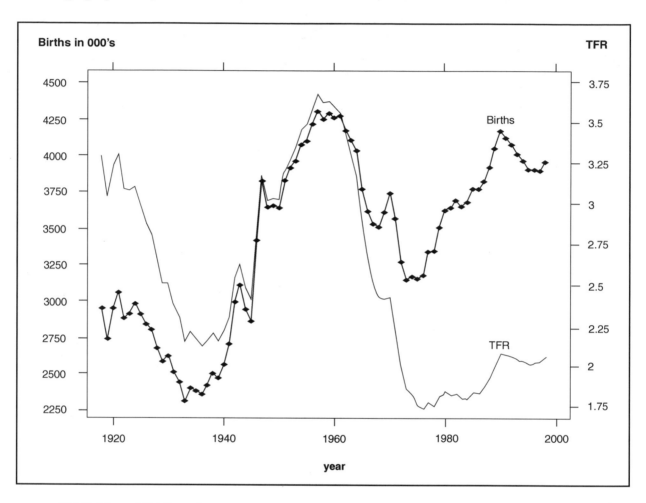

SOURCE: *Vital Statistics* and *Natality*, various years.

troops at the end of the war. But in addition younger women departed from a historic upward trend in female labor force participation in order to stay home and start families—a departure that lasted for nearly twenty years. Exhilaration and optimism after the war seemed to combine with a general feeling of affluence in a booming postwar economy, and generous provisions for returning GIs, to make young couples feel able and willing to support children (Bean; Jones).

But this apparently positive relationship between income and fertility fails to explain why fertility rates then suddenly plummeted in the early 1960s, causing the "baby bust." There was

a tendency at the time to attribute the decline to the introduction of the birth control pill in 1963—but it is generally acknowledged now that the pill merely facilitated a trend that originated several years earlier, in the late 1950s. Economists have attempted to develop a "unified theory" to explain both the boom and bust. Their focus has been primarily on three factors: male income, the female wage, and material aspirations (desired standard of living). They assume that fertility will tend to rise as male income rises, but fall when material aspirations increase and when female wages rise. The female wage is assumed to represent the value of time foregone in the labor market in favor of childbearing: the "opportunity cost" or "price" of women's time

Figure 2

A comparison of baby booms in several western nations using the Total Fertility Rate (TFR, which equals the number of births a woman would experience throughout her childbearing years, at current age-specific rates). The "official" baby boom years are indicated (1946–1964), and the dashed line marks a TFR of 2.1, which is replacement-level fertility.

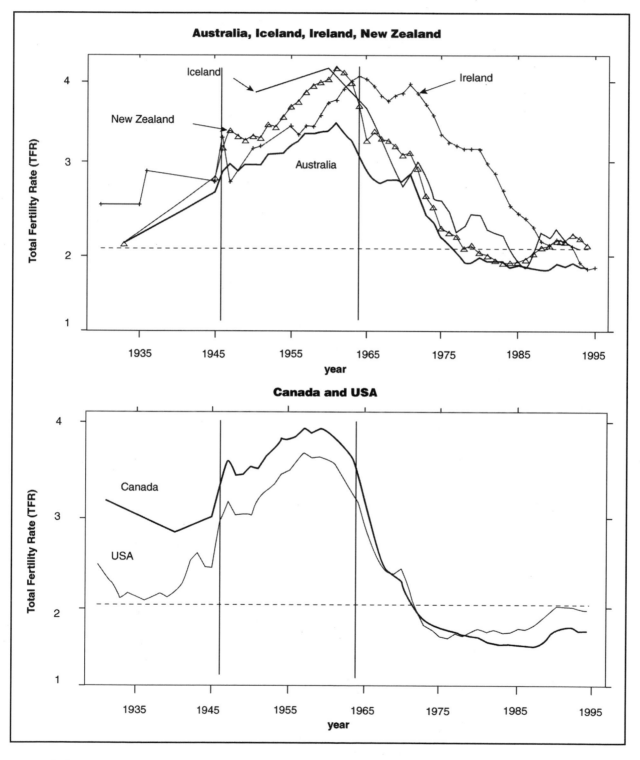

SOURCE: Author

spent in caring for children and hence a significant element in the cost of raising children.

One school of economic thought suggests that the baby boom in the 1950s was caused by rising male incomes and falling women's wages (as women were displaced from wartime jobs), while in the later decades falling male income and rising female wages generated the baby bust (Butz and Ward). Unfortunately data needed to test this hypothesis fully are not available for the complete boom—and bust—period although the data that are available suggest that these two factors account for only a portion of the baby boom (and bust).

However, adding the third factor—material aspirations—provides a more complete explanation for the phenomenon. This third factor has been the focus of another school of thought among economists, which assumes that shifts over time in the desired standard of living temper young adults' responses to intergenerational changes in income. That is, it is assumed that young adults will feel affluent only if their income—regardless of its absolute level—allows them to meet or exceed their material aspirations, which are assumed to be in large part a function of the standard of living they experienced while growing up (Easterlin). And a couple's ability to achieve a given standard of living is affected by the size of their birth cohort relative to that of their parents. An excess supply of younger, less-experienced workers depresses their wages relative to older workers, and excess demand produces the opposite result (Welch; Macunovich, 1999). Since those older workers are the parents of the young adults, and are assumed to affect their children's desired standard of living, it is assumed that large cohorts will have a difficult time achieving their material aspirations—and conversely small cohorts will be favored.

This economic approach assumes that the fertility cycle experienced between 1936 and 1976 was one of the demographic adjustments young adults made in response to "relative cohort size"–induced changes in "relative income." It suggests that the small cohorts born during the Depression entered the labor market in the 1950s with relatively low material aspirations and found themselves favored not only by the strong economy but also by their small relative cohort size. Their high relative income generated the baby boom, but when the boomers themselves entered the labor market in the 1970s and 1980s their experience was diametrically opposed to that of their parents: high material aspirations coming out of their parents' homes, but low earnings relative to those expectations thanks to their large cohort size. The boomers' fertility rates plummeted as they scrambled to maintain their desired standard of living (Macunovich, 1998).

The boomer lifestyle

Low fertility is not the only characteristic that differentiates the baby boomers from their parents' cohort. Female labor force participation soared among the boomers, and young women began moving into previously male-dominated professions, while marriage rates declined precipitously and cohabitation and divorce rates increased dramatically. Age-specific crime rates and drug use among young males soared as baby boomers passed through the fifteen to twenty-four age group. Some social scientists believe that these changes were demographic adjustments made primarily in response to low relative income. And although average male earnings fell for baby boomers—especially in relative terms—the term *yuppie* (young urban professional) was coined to describe the high-consumption, low-savings lifestyle of many boomers.

The baby boomers were the first generation of children and teenagers with significant spending power, and that, combined with their numbers, fueled the growth of massive marketing campaigns and the introduction of new products—and new terminology, such as "pop group" and "hippie"—targeted at the boomers' current stage in the life cycle. Fashion followed the boomers' needs—from the mini-skirt and bellbottoms to "relaxed fit" jeans. Even fringe commercial enterprises benefitted, as, for example, the nation began wearing army surplus clothing, and drug use spread, some say as a result of the boomers' heavy participation in the Vietnam War. (At the war's peak during the 1968–1970 period, 31 percent of boomer males twenty to twenty-one years old were serving in the military.)

Overcrowded schools introduced "porta-cabin" classrooms and half-day sessions when the boomers were young, and later the day-care industry emerged to accommodate boomers who chose to combine career and parenthood. The country's identity seemed shaped by the boomers, from the "youth culture" in the 1960s and 1970s to the "greying of America" in the early twenty-first century. The evolution of the automobile provides a prime example of the boomers' life-cycle impact. Station wagons became the vogue in the 1950s in response to the needs of boomers' parents. Those vehicles mutated into minivans to accommodate "yuppie" boomers in their thirties and forties and then into sport utility vehicles for boomers who had become so-called empty nesters, many going through "midlife crisis." The next stage in this progression is a car/van that accommodates devices for the disabled, in anticipation of baby boomers in old age.

Boomers in retirement

But despite the tendency for the entire culture to take on the boomers' current persona as it evolves through the life cycle, the boomers are in reality an extremely diverse group. Income inequality is high among the baby boomers: one study suggests that inequality among the boomers is nearly 15 percent greater than it was among their parents at the same age (Easterlin et al.). In the mid-1990s median income in white boomer families was nearly twice that of black boomer families, while the poverty rate among black and Hispanic boomers was more than double that of whites (Levy). "Leading edge" boomers (those born during the first half of the boom) have fared better economically than their younger counterparts. Boomers who served in Vietnam have never been able to close the wage gap with their more fortunate counterparts who stayed at home (Angrist). Half of full-time private wage and salary workers among the baby boomers were not covered by private pensions and nearly half of baby boomers did not own homes as they progressed through middle age (Kingston).

Approximately eighteen million baby boomers are members of racial minorities. As a result, the Census Bureau projects that while 87 percent of the elderly population in 1990 were white non-Hispanic, this proportion will drop to 76 percent in 2030 and to 70 percent in 2050. Some suggest that because members of minority groups work disproportionately in "physically arduous and partially disabling working conditions," they may be disproportionately affected by increases in the early retirement age (Kingston; Lee and Skinner).

Over one-tenth of baby boomers are high school dropouts, including 4 percent with less than a ninth-grade education. Baby boomers' median household income at the start of the 1990s, after adjusting for inflation, was less than that of a similar household in their parents' generation. Similarly, the proportion of baby boomers heading single-parent households has tripled relative to their parents at the same age. Ninety percent of those households were reported to have less wealth than income, and income levels only one-third the size of that for married couples with children (Kingston).

Those thought to be at the greatest risk with regard to retirement prospects are singles— especially single mothers, and more than one-tenth of female baby boomers head their own households— and those with lower levels of education, those with nonstable employment patterns, non-homeowners, and the youngest of the baby boomers.

In general, analysts tend to agree that boomers will on average exceed their parents' standard of living in retirement—and will do so by a substantial margin—although some suggest that replacement rates (the ratio of retirement to pre-retirement income) may fall (Easterlin; Congressional Budget Office; Employment Benefit and Research Institute; House Ways and Means Committee). They have, on average, exceeded their parents' standard of living at all points in the life cycle to date by 50 to 60 percent and more on a per capita basis. However, there is some disagreement on this topic, based on analyses that focus solely on male earnings and family or household income, rather than on per capita income (Levy and Michel).

In addition, some have emphasized the effects of the demographic adjustments made by the boomers to raise per capita incomes (delayed/ foregone marriage, reduced fertility, and increased divorce). It is suggested that the boomers in retirement are less likely than their parents to be living with a spouse, and are likely to have fewer adult children. As a result, although economic well-being may be relatively high for the average baby boomer in retirement, total well-being may suffer (Easterlin et al.).

Analysts disagree about the adequacy of boomers' savings for retirement. Some project that 50 percent more retired boomers than non-boomers will receive income from private pensions, with nearly three-quarters of boomers receiving some pension money and the average boomer receiving nearly two-fifths of retirement income from pensions—some 60 percent more than is received by non-boomers (Andrews and Chollet). However, many have voiced concern about the boomers' savings; and in this case the younger boomers seem to be doing better than the older boomers. The median ratio of wealth to income for younger boomers has risen about two-thirds relative to that of their parents, but for older boomers the ratio has remained relatively constant. And while their parents' savings benefitted from windfall gains later in life, it has been suggested that the boomer ratio of wealth to income will fall as retirees age, because of lack of protection against inflation in private pension plans. In addition, some feel that many baby boomers' plans are subject to high levels of risk, and that many baby boomers are underestimating their longevity in saving for their retirement (House Ways and Means Committee).

It has been projected, based on the current system, that Social Security will provide 60 to 70 percent of retirement income for boomers in the bottom half of the income distribution in 2019. For most baby boomers, retirement incomes will be well above those of today's retirees (50 to 60 percent higher), and will be more than adequate, but the projections indicate that the proportion of elderly baby boomers who will be poor or near-poor may reach almost 20 percent, with the majority of these being singles, and especially single women (House Ways and Means Committee).

However, some have questioned the reliability of the more optimistic forecasts, due to what they see as significant effects of the baby boom on the economy itself—in areas such as the housing market and stock market, interest rates, savings, and inflation rates (Fair and Dominguez). Based on these historic effects some suggest a potential "asset meltdown" when retiring baby boomers cash in their holdings, a view that remains highly controversial.

DIANE J. MACUNOVICH

See also COHORT CHANGE; POPULATION AGING.

BIBLIOGRAPHY

ANDREWS, E. S., and CHOLLET, D. "Future Sources of Retirement Income: Whither the Baby Boom." In *Social Security and Private Pensions*. Edited by Susan M. Wachter. Lexington, Mass.: Lexington Books, 1988.

ANGRIST, J. D. "Lifetime Earnings and the Vietnam Era Draft Lottery: Evidence from Social Security Administrative Records." *The American Economic Review* 80, no. 3 (1990): 313.

BEAN, F. "The Baby Boom and Its Explanations." *The Sociological Quarterly* 24 (Summer 1983): 353–365.

BUTZ, W. P., and WARD, M. P. "The Emergence of Countercyclical U.S. Fertility." *American Economic Review* 69, no. 3 (1979): 318–328.

COLEMAN, D. Zip files of total and age-specific fertility rates. Available as part of the *Oxford Population Project* at 1999.

Congressional Budget Office. "Baby Boomers in Retirement: An Early Perspective." Washington, D.C.: Congressional Budget Office, September, 1993.

EASTERLIN, R. A. *Birth and Fortune*. 2d ed. Chicago: University of Chicago Press, 1987.

EASTERLIN, R. A.; SCHAEFFER, C. M.; and MACUNOVICH, D. J. "Will the Baby Boomers be Less Well Off than their Parents? Income, Wealth and Family Circumstances Over the Life Cycle in the United States." *Population and Development Review* 19, no. 3 (1993): 497–522.

Employment Benefit Research Institute. "Baby Boomers in Retirement: What Are Their Prospects?" EBRI Special Report SR-23. Washington D.C.: Employment Benefit Research Institute (July 1994).

FAIR, R. C., and DOMINGUEZ, K. M. "Effects of Changing U.S. Age Distribution on Macroeconomic Equations." *American Economic Review* 81, no. 5 (1991): 1276–1294.

House Ways and Means Committee. "Retirement Income for an Aging Population." U.S. House of Representatives, Ways and Means Committee Paper No. 100-22 (27 August 1987).

JONES, L. Y. *Great Expectations: America and the Baby Boom Generation*. New York: Ballantine Books, 1981.

KINGSON, E. "The Diversity of the Baby Boom Generation: Implications for the Retirement Years." Prepared for Forecasting and Environmental Scanning Department, American Association of Retired Persons, April 1992.

LEE, R. D., and SKINNER, J. "Assessing Forecasts of Mortality, Health Status, and Health Costs During Baby Boomers' Retirement." Presented at a conference on Retirement Income Modeling, September 1994. Washington D.C.: National Academy of Science, 1994.

Levy, F. *The New Dollars and Dreams: American Incomes and Economic Change*. New York: Russell Sage Foundation, 1998.

Levy, F., and Michel, R. C. *The Economic Future of American Families*. Washington, D.C.: The Urban Institute Press, 1991.

Macunovich, D. J. "Fertility and the Easterlin Hypothesis: An Assessment of the Literature." *Journal of Population Economics* 11 (1998): 53–111.

Macunovich, D. J. "The Fortunes of One's Birth: Relative Cohort Size and the Youth Labor Market in the U.S." *Journal of Population Economics* 12, no. 2 (1999): 215–272.

Macunovich, D. J. "Baby Booms and Busts in the Twentieth Century." In *International Encyclopedia of the Social and Behavioral Sciences*. Edited by Neil J. Smelser and Paul B. Baltes. Oxford: Pergamon Press. Forthcoming, 2002a.

Macunovich, D. J. *Birth Quake: The Baby Boom and Its Aftershocks*. Chicago: University of Chicago Press. Forthcoming, 2002b.

Pampel, F. C., and Peters, E. H. "The Easterlin Effect." *Annual Review of Sociology* 21 (1995): 163.

Schieber, S. J., and Shoven, J. B. "The Consequences of Population Aging on Private Pension Fund Saving and Asset Markets." Working Paper No. 4665. National Bureau of Economic Research, Cambridge, Mass.: (March 1994).

U.S. Census Bureau. "Population Estimates by Single Year of Age." For the year 2000 Census. Available on the Internet at www.census.gov

U.S. Census Bureau. "Population Projections by Single Year of Age." For the year 2000 Census. Available on the Internet at www.census.gov

Welch, F. "Effects of Cohort Size on Earnings: The Baby Boom Babies' Financial Bust." *Journal of Political Economy* 87 (1979): S65–S97.

Westoff, C. F. "Some Speculations on the Future of Marriage and Fertility." *Family Planning Perspectives* 10, no. 2 (1978): 80.

BALANCE AND MOBILITY

The ability to stand and walk, often taken for granted, is necessary for full independence in daily activities and integration in society. Balance and mobility often decline with aging, and specific diseases also lead to deficits. The contracted living space, need for care, falls, and injuries that result from this decline are important sources of illness in older persons, are costly to society, and are important determinants of caregiver burden and even the need for nursing home placement.

Normal walking involves propelling one's body forward as one's feet catch up and prevent a fall. Walking is, therefore, inherently unstable. A foot strikes heel-first, then rocks forward, with the toe the last part to leave the ground. Gait is divided into a stance phase, when both feet are on the ground, and a swing phase, when one foot is off the ground. Stride length is the distance from the heel strike of a particular foot to the next heel strike of that foot.

Investigation of aging-related changes in mobility was largely initiated in the late 1960s by Dr. Patricia Murray, a kinesiologist at the Medical School of Wisconsin. She found that older adults had slower walking speeds, shorter stride lengths, longer stance phases, and less foot clearance off the ground. Older adults also have less arm swing and a trunk that is bent slightly forward. Figure 1 displays these differences. Some investigators have found that older adults have an irregular cadence (step frequency).

Balance requires contributions from several systems: motor, sensory, and cognitive. Muscles, typically lower limb or hip, contract to maintain balance. Older adults may have weaker muscles, delayed reaction times, coactivation (so that muscles with opposite actions contract together, thereby stiffening a joint), and disorganized muscle contraction (so that muscle groups are not working together). The sensory system is also important. Vision, the vestibular system of the inner ear, and proprioceptive nerves (those which detect the position of joints and muscles) are all important in balance, and can all become less functional with age. Cognition also contributes, because attention, which can decline with age, is important in maintaining balance. The balance system is redundant, in that deficits in one system can be compensated for by the other systems. The changes mentioned above can occur with aging and also with specific diseases.

Transfers must also be considered. "Transferring" is the term used for moving from one condition to another, such as out of a bathtub, chair, or car, or getting into bed. The ability to transfer depends on many factors, including strength, balance, vision, and flexibility. The characteristics of the transfer surface and the presence or absence of adaptive aids can have an impact on transfer ability.

Figure 1

Limb position differences between older (left) and younger (right) men at the moment of heel strike.

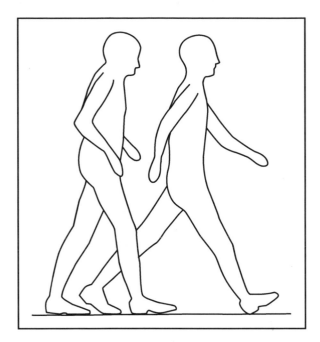

SOURCE: Murray et al. *Journal of Gerontology.* (1969): 176

These changes with aging are averages, and not all older adults age at the same rate. A group of eighty-year-olds will have a much wider range of abilities than a group of twenty-year-olds. Some of the eighty-year-olds will have abilities that are indistinguishable from those of the average twenty-year-old, while others will be totally dependent. Heterogeneity of abilities is a characteristic of older age.

Mobility also requires energy, and so blood circulation and oxygenation must be adequate to meet the body's needs. Any impairment in heart, lung, or blood vessel function will impair mobility.

The effects of mobility deficits associated with aging or disease can often be minimized through the use of walking aids, such as canes or walkers. These aids are just that—tools that help older adults maintain their independence—though many seniors view them as restrictive signs of aging and are reluctant to use them. Similarly, a wheelchair can provide freedom and independence to someone who might otherwise be bedbound or housebound.

The role of the environment in mobility should not be forgotten. For example, it is more difficult to get out of a very low chair or one without arms. A very soft bed makes it harder to roll over. Given the multiple components of balance, a darkened room will have a negative impact.

The clinical assessment of mobility

During the clinical assessment of balance and mobility it is crucial to actually observe an individual's mobility, to watch him or her get up and walk. Mary Tinetti, a Yale geriatrician, demonstrated that a standard neurological examination—of power, reflexes, sensation, and tone—less effectively identified impaired balance and mobility when compared with examination of actual standing and walking performance.

The assessment of balance and mobility can be facilitated by use of the principle of hierarchy. Someone who can perform a difficult task, such as climbing stairs, can be assumed to be able to safely perform simple tasks, such as getting out of a chair. Of course, an individual's abilities do not always strictly follow the hierarchy, but the principle holds in most situations.

A typical assessment of balance and mobility starts with the person in bed. He or she is watched rolling over, sitting up, getting out of bed, walking, and sitting down in a chair—and sometimes also watched turning, standing still, standing still under more challenging conditions (with eyes closed, withstanding a nudge, reaching forward), and climbing stairs. Use of the usual walking aid is permitted. Using the principle of hierarchy, an individual who is known to be able to perform at a high level, for example, walking, is observed performing only more challenging tasks, such as climbing stairs, not simple tasks like rolling over in bed. Formal balance and mobility tests are sometimes used; these are described in the review by MacKnight and Rockwood (1995a).

The balance and mobility assessment has implications for a patient's treatment and care needs. Any deficits in balance or mobility will have an important impact on an older adult's daily life. All of the basic and instrumental activities of daily living depend, to some extent, on independence in balance and mobility. For example, a patient who cannot roll over in bed will need to be turned every few hours to prevent pressure sores; one who can transfer and walk, but not stand safely for any length of time, will need to have the home modified so that tasks such as cleaning oneself and cooking can be done seated. Physiotherapy, occupational therapy, and other interventions can be directed to specific deficits.

A number of common patterns of gait abnormalities are seen in older adults:

1. Nonspecific gait abnormality of aging; also sometimes disparagingly called the senile gait. People who exhibit this gait have some features of parkinsonism, with flexion at the hip and knees, forward trunk flexion, decreased arm swing, narrow stance, tendency to shuffle, and decreased gait velocity. Many older adults exhibit some features of this gait.

2. Deconditioned gait, which is caused by disuse. Patients with this gait have most of the features of the nonspecific gait abnormality of aging. They also have weak muscles, particularly hip flexors (the muscles used to bend the hip). Scissoring is often present during walking, with one foot straying into the path of the other, leading to decreased walking balance. Step length, path, and frequency are very irregular. The deconditioned gait may also be related to sarcopenia, a significant loss of muscle mass that may be associated with aging.

3. Hemiplegic gait is caused by a stroke. A stroke leads to weakness and spasticity (increased tone, particularly when the muscles are stretched). The classic hemiplegic gait involves an arm flexed at the elbow and held close to the body, with the leg on the same side held in a straight, stiff position and moved forward in a circular pattern (circumduction). Depending on the severity and extent of the stroke, these arm and leg conditions may or may not be present to varying degrees.

4. Antalgic, or painful, gait is the limping gait. In older adults it is often due to osteoarthritis of the knee or hip. Treatment involves using a walking aid to shift the body's weight off the affected limb, pain control, weight loss, exercise to strengthen surrounding muscle, and sometimes replacing the affected joint with an artificial one.

5. Parkinsonian gait is most commonly caused by Parkinson's disease, although other conditions, such as late Alzheimer's disease or side effects of drugs such as antipsychotics, can sometimes cause this gait abnormality. It is characterized by a narrow stance with short shuffling steps, the body stooped forward with knees and hips bent slightly, and a tremor in both hands, which are held at the sides. It is often difficult for the patient to start walking and, once started, it is often difficult to stop. This is known as festination. Some patients need to run into a wall or other obstacle in order to stop.

6. Gait apraxia is the inability to carry out the previously learned motor activity of walking, despite normal strength, sensation, and joints. These patients often have difficulty initiating gait, taking broad-based, irregular steps. Gait apraxia is often due to cerebrovascular disease in the deep white matter of the brain.

7. Fear of falling, although not strictly a gait disorder, is experienced by many patients who have had an important fall or other fright, such as getting stuck in the bathtub. They develop a significant fear of falling that then limits their mobility (and can lead to deconditioning). These patients often stay close to furniture and walls, take short, tentative steps, and prefer to walk with the support of another.

Frailty and atypical illness presentations

Falls are common in older adults; approximately 50 percent of community-dwelling seniors fall each year, and 10 percent of these suffer an important injury, such as a fracture, bleeding around the brain (subdural hematoma), or skin laceration. Falls and immobility are rarely caused by a single deficit, but rather the interaction of multiple acute and chronic abnormalities. A common mistake in the care of older adults is to search for *the* cause of a fall, rather than addressing the multiple deficits. The presence of a stroke, orthostatic hypotension (one's blood pressure falls when one stands up), or weakness of a particular muscle group, for example, would be an unusual cause of a fall without other predisposing factors.

Falls and immobility in older adults are generally manifestations of frailty. Frailty can be thought of as the interaction among many strengths and weaknesses of an individual, giving rise to current abilities and vulnerability to further loss. Many of these weaknesses may not be detrimental by themselves, and not readily apparent—what Dr. Linda Fried calls "subclinical disability"—but when they are mixed together, they are important. For example, mild and individually unimportant impairments in vision, strength, proprioception, and reaction time can combine together to produce frequent falls.

If such an individual develops a urinary tract infection, which is relatively harmless in healthy adults, he or she may find the mobility deficit greatly exacerbated. This phenomenon of atypical illness presentations leads to the common illness behavior in older adults of "taking to bed." A senior who exhibits a change in mobility most certainly has a new illness, though not necessarily one involving the neuromuscular system. These atypical illness presentations involve symptoms and signs not expected on the basis of the underlying disease. For example, a patient with pneumonia would be expected to present with cough, fever, and shortness of breath, and to have abnormal findings on examination of the lungs. A frail older adult will commonly present with delirium, functional decline, falls, or other atypical presentations, without necessarily having symptoms or signs associated with the lungs. The atypical illness presentations are also known as "Geriatric Giants," a term coined by the British geriatrician Bernard Isaacs.

The treatment of immobility and falls involves addressing both the new problem (if one is present) and the frailty. This requires a multifactorial approach. M. E. Tinetti demonstrated that a multidisciplinary team—a nurse addressing potentially harmful medications and orthostatic hypotension, a physiotherapist supervising exercise, and an occupational therapist making the home safer—reduced the incidence of falls in community-dwelling seniors. An approach aimed at a single component of the problem, such as weakness only, will likely prove unsuccessful.

CHRIS MACKNIGHT

See also ARTHRITIS; BALANCE, SENSE OF; DISEASE PRESENTATION; DIZZINESS; FRAILTY; HIP FRACTURE; PARKINSONISM; STROKE; WALKING AIDS.

BIBLIOGRAPHY

BRONSTEIN, A. M.; BRANDT, T.; and WOOLLACOTT, M. *Clinical Disorders of Balance, Posture, and Gait.* London: Arnold, 1996.
FRIED, L. P.; HERDMAN, S. J.; KUHN, K. E.; RUBIN, G.; and TURANO, K. "Preclinical Disability: Hypotheses About the Bottom of the Iceberg." *Journal of Aging and Health* 3 (1991): 285–300.
GURALNIK, J. M.; FERRUCCI, L.; SIMONSICK, E. M.; SALIVE, M. E.; and WALLACE, R. B. "Lower-Extremity Function in Persons Over the Age of 70 Years as a Predictor of Subsequent Disability." *New England Journal of Medicine* 332 (1995): 556–561.
MACKNIGHT, C., and ROCKWOOD, K. "Assessing Mobility in Elderly People. A Review of Performance-Based Measures of Balance, Gait and Mobility for Bedside Use." *Reviews in Clinical Gerontology* 5 (1995a): 464–486.
MACKNIGHT, C., and ROCKWOOD, K. "A Hierarchical Assessment of Balance and Mobility." *Age and Ageing* 24 (1995b): 126–130.
TINETTI, M. E., and GINTER, S. F. "Identifying Mobility Dysfunctions in Elderly Patients: Standard Neuromuscular Examination or Direct Assessment?" *Journal of the American Medical Association* 259 (1988): 1190–1193.
TINETTI, M. E.; BAKER, D. I.; MCAVAY, G.; CLAUS, E. B.; GARRETT, P.; GOTTSCHALK, M.; KOCH, M. L.; TRAINOR, K.; and HORWITZ, R. I. "A Multifactorial Intervention to Reduce the Risk of Falling Among Elderly People Living in the Community." *New England Journal of Medicine* 331 (1994): 821–827.
TINETTI, M. E.; INOUYE, S. K.; GILL, T. H.; and DOUCETTE, J. T. "Shared Risk Factors for Falls, Incontinence, and Functional Dependence: Unifying the Approach to Geriatric Syndromes." *Journal of the American Medical Association* 273 (1995): 1348–1353.

BALANCE, SENSE OF

In the 1990s specific factors contributing to falls in older adults were identified, including reduced postural or balance control. Age-related reductions in balance control may be due to impairments in the musculoskeletal system and/or the different nervous subsystems, including the neuromuscular, sensory, and higher-level adaptive systems.

Musculoskeletal system

Research has indicated that lower extremity muscle strength is reduced by as much as 40 percent between the ages of thirty and eighty, and is even further reduced in nursing home residents with a history of falls. This is accompanied by an age-related loss of muscle fibers, with type II (fast twitch) fibers being lost at a faster rate than type I (slow twitch). As a result, maximum isometric force development decreases, the muscles fatigue more rapidly, and the rate of tension development in muscles is slower. There is also an age-related decrease in range of motion and spinal flexibility, leading to a characteristic flexed or stooped posture in many older adults.

Neuromuscular systems

The first studies examining age-related changes in balance control during quiet stance were performed in the 1960s and showed that sway begins to increase at about fifty years of age. A study in the 1990s found a significant increase in sway in healthy older adults, with the greatest amount of sway found in older adults with a history of falls.

Though clinical examination of quiet stance may tell us something about age-related changes in balance, it is in dynamic conditions, where balance is threatened, that most falls occur. Thus research has addressed this question by using a moving platform to provide an external threat to balance. Measures of balance control have included postural muscle response characteristics (electromyograms or EMG), kinematics (body motion), and kinetics (muscle forces such as center of pressure, or COP, used to recover balance).

Studies examining age-related changes in postural muscle response characteristics elicited when balance was threatened showed that the muscle response organization of older adults and younger adults was similar, with responses being activated first in the stretched ankle muscle and radiating upward to the muscles of the thigh. However, clear differences between the two groups are also seen. These include: (1) slower onsets and smaller amplitudes for ankle muscle responses (resulting in a longer time to stabilize sway after a balance threat); (2) occasional disruption in muscle response organization; and (3) co-activation of the antagonist muscles along with the agonist muscles at a given joint (a strategy that stiffens the joints, possibly to compensate for other limitations in balance control). Figure 1 shows the research paradigm used to study reactive balance control in older adults and the difference in the center of pressure path of a young, healthy, and balance-impaired older adult when recovering balance. Note that the path is much longer for the balance-impaired older adult than the healthy and young adults.

When responding to a balance threat one can use one of three types of response strategies: sway primarily about the ankle joints, hip movement, or a step. Several labs have found that older adults use a strategy involving hip movements or stepping rather than ankle movements significantly more often than young adults. Use of a hip strategy for balance control in older adults may be related to pathological conditions such as ankle muscle weakness or loss of peripheral sensory function. Clinical tests show that scores for muscle strength and proprioceptive sensation (i.e., joint and muscle sensation, which contributes to a sense of where our limbs are located with respect to the rest of the body) are lower for unstable older adults than for young and stable older adults for most muscles tested.

Sensory systems

Many of the changes in balance function in older adults may be due to deterioration in the different sensory systems contributing to balance, including the somatosensory (cutaneous and proprioceptive), visual, and vestibular (inner ear) systems. Tactile sensitivity decreases with age. Research examining reactive balance control in patients with peripheral neuropathy has found delays in muscle onset latencies in response to platform perturbations.

Age-related changes in the influence of vision on balance control can be tested by creating the illusion of postural sway through visual flow generated by an experimental moving room. Normally, young adults show small amounts of sway in response to visual flow, since their proprioceptive systems indicate no sway. However, healthy older adults respond to visual flow with increased sway, and balance-impaired older adults show the most visually induced sway of the three groups. This may be due to decreased somatosensory information available for balance in older adults, due to peripheral neuropathy.

Research on age-related reduction in the function of the vestibular system indicates a loss of 40 percent of the vestibular hair and nerve cells by seventy years of age. The vestibular system contributes to the amplitude of postural responses to balance threats, and thus, older adults with vestibular loss would show inappropriately small responses to balance threats. The vestibular system serves as an absolute reference system to which the other systems (visual and somatosensory) may be compared and calibrated, and is thus critical for optimal balance function.

Figure 1
Balance statistice for a young adult; a stable older adult; and an unstable older adult.

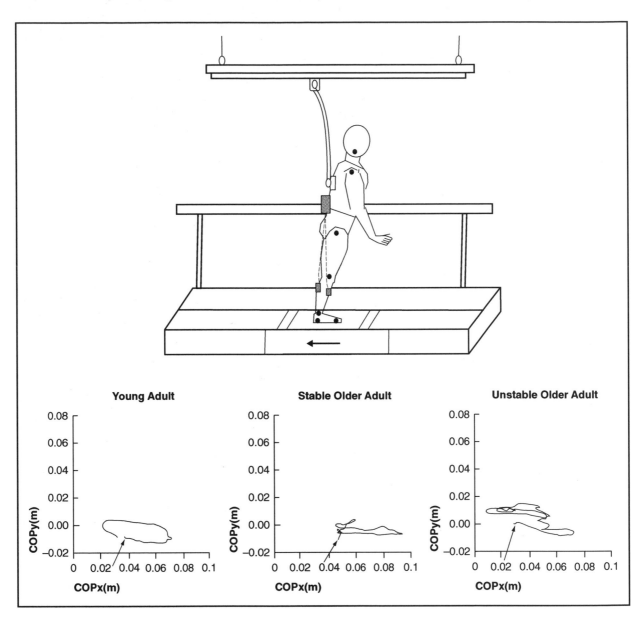

SOURCE: Author

Higher-level adaptive and cognitive systems

Higher-level systems, such as the cerebellum, are responsible for integrating information from the three sensory systems, and then adapting postural responses to meet the demands of changing sensory conditions. In the 1980s and 1990s a number of laboratories examined the ability of healthy and balance-impaired older adults to adapt senses to changing conditions during quiet stance using posturography testing. Results showed that healthy active older adults were not significantly different from young adults in amount of body sway except in conditions where both ankle joint inputs and visual inputs were reduced or absent. In these conditions, half of the older adults lost balance on the first trial for these conditions, requiring the help of an assistant. However, most of the healthy older adults maintained balance on the second trial within these two conditions. This suggests that they are capable of adapting postural responses to meet changing sensory conditions, but only with practice in the condition. Balance-impaired older adults had a larger percentage of falls in any condition with misleading somatosensory cues. Thus, a problem contributing to balance-impairment in many older adults is the inability to adapt responses to changing sensory conditions.

Studies in the 1990s began to determine if attentional requirements of postural control increase in older adults, by using a dual task paradigm in which older adults are asked to balance while performing a second cognitive task (e.g., a math task). Results indicate that balance is more attentionally demanding in older than younger adults and is highest in balance-impaired older adults. Attentional demands increase as the complexity of the balance task increases (e.g., responding to a slip).

Balance retraining

To determine if balance function can be improved with training, in the 1990s research labs began to design and test different balance training programs. High-resistance muscle strength training studies have found that age-related declines in muscle strength are partially reversible, especially in frail older adults, such as nursing home residents. Dynamic balance training involving Tai Chi (an ancient Chinese discipline of meditative movements) also has been shown to reduce the risk of falls in healthy older adults. Studies focusing on sensory retraining, in which older adults practiced standing under changing sensory conditions (e.g., standing on foam, eyes open versus closed, head tilted) showed significant reductions in sway over ten days of training. Multidimensional exercise programs, including combinations of lower extremity strength and flexibility exercises, static and dynamic balance exercises, and participation in an aerobic activity (usually walking) have also improved balance and mobility function and reduced the likelihood of falls among older adults with a history of falling.

MARJORIE H. WOOLLACOTT

See also BALANCE AND MOBILITY; VISION AND PERCEPTION.

BIBLIOGRAPHY

ANIANSSON, A.; HEDBERG, M.; HENNING, G.; et al. "Muscle Morphology, Enzymatic Activity and Muscle Strength in Elderly Men: A Follow Up Study." *Muscle Nerve* 9 (1986): 585–591.

FIATARONE, M. A.; MARKS, E. C.; RYAN, N. D.; MEREDITH, C. N.; LIPSITZ, L. A.; and EVANS, W. J. "High-Intensity Strength Training in Nonagenarians: Effects on Skeletal Muscle." *Journal of the American Medical Association* 263 (1990): 3029–3034.

INGLIS, J. T.; HORAK, F. B.; SHUPERT, C. L.; and RYCEWICZ, C. "The Importance of Somatosensory Information in Triggering and Scaling Automatic Postural Responses in Humans." *Experimental Brain Research* 101 (1994): 159–164.

LIN, S-I. "Adapting to Dynamically Changing Balance Threats: Differentiating Young, Healthy Older Adults and Unstable Older Adults." Ph.D. diss., University of Oregon, 1997.

LIPSITZ, L. A.; JONSSON, P. V.; KELLEY, M. M.; and KOESTNER, J. S. "Causes and Correlates of Recurrent Falls in Ambulatory Frail Elderly." *Journal of Gerontology* 46 (1991): M114–122.

SHELDON, J. H. "The Effect of Age on the Control of Sway." *Gerontology Clinics* 5 (1963): 129–138.

SHUMWAY-COOK, A.; WOOLLACOTT, M.; BALDWIN, M.; and KERNS, K. "The Effects of Cognitive Demands on Postural Control in Elderly Fallers and Non-fallers." *Journal of Gerontology* 52 (1997): M232–240.

WOLF, S. L.; BARNHART, H. X.; KUTNER, N. G.; et al. and the Atlantic FICSIT Group. "Reducing Frailty and Falls in Older Persons: An Investigation of Tai Chi and Computerized Balance Training." *Journal of the American Geriatric Society* 44 (1996): 489–497.

WOOLLACOTT, M. H.; SHUMWAY-COOK, A.; and NASHNER, L. M. "Aging and Posture Control: Changes in Sensory Organization and Muscular Coordination." *International Journal of Aging and Human Development* 23 (1986): 97–114.

BEDSORES

See PRESSURE ULCERS

BEHAVIOR MANAGEMENT

Behavior management refers to a class of therapeutic techniques for altering behavior by changing one or more aspects of an individual's environment. The aspects that are changed are those believed to contribute most significantly to the occurrence or maintenance of behaviors that are problematic for the individual himself/herself or for other individuals in the environment. Environmental changes are also made for the purpose of increasing positive behaviors that are considered desirable or adaptive. Behavior management techniques have been used most often with older adults to decrease problem behaviors that result from dementing illnesses, such as Alzheimer's disease (AD). Behavior problems associated with dementia are very common and place a great deal of stress and burden on the people who care for these elders. Behavior problems associated with dementia include disruptive vocalization (e.g., repetitive questions, cursing, chronic screaming), physical aggression (e.g., hitting, pinching, biting), and motor restlessness (e.g., wandering, inappropriate disrobing). Techniques that focus on environmental change are used with older adults who have dementia because their cognitive limitations (e.g., problems with memory and abstract reasoning) often prohibit the use of other therapeutic techniques, such as cognitive-behavioral or insight-oriented therapy, that rely on more complex cognitive abilities for success.

Behavior management techniques are derived from Albert Bandura's social learning theory, which asserts that observable behaviors emerge from an interaction between the person and environmental events. Antecedent events precede a behavior in time and can elicit the behavior or decrease the probability that a behavior will occur. For example, approaching a dementia patient from behind (antecedent) can startle the patient and elicit physical aggression (problematic behavior). Conversely, if a patient appears anxious, using calming speech and soothing touch (antecedent) can prevent physical aggression (problematic behavior) from occurring. Environmental events that follow a behavior in time (i.e., consequent events) can similarly increase or decrease the probability that the behavior will continue once it occurs or that it will reoccur in the future. For example, if the therapeutic goal is to increase an isolated nursing home resident's social interactions with other residents, staff provision of positive attention (consequent) when the resident interacts socially can serve to reinforce or increase the probability of the resident's interaction (desirable behavior). Conversely, if a resident becomes agitated during a social situa-

tion, relocating the resident to his/her bedroom (consequent) can serve to suppress the agitation, or decrease the probability that it will reoccur during similar social situations (desirable behavior).

Thus, behavior management techniques can be classified into two categories: (1) antecedent strategies, which are used before a behavior occurs in an effort to prevent or elicit a behavior, and (2) consequent strategies, which are used after a behavior occurs in an effort to prevent the continuation and recurrence of a behavior or to reinforce a behavior. Although both can be effective, antecedent techniques are used more often than consequent strategies with older adults because they are easier to apply, require less caregiver time, and are generally considered less manipulative, and therefore more acceptable, by caregivers and professionals.

Antecedent strategies

Several variations of antecedent strategies have been used in nursing homes and community settings. Strategies that have been researched include altering the general physical and/or social environment of elders, teaching communication skills to caregivers, and providing auditory stimulation for elders.

Early work in this area emphasized altering the physical environment in nursing homes to reduce disorientation, provide sensory stimulus variation, and increase social interaction. Disorientation, understimulation, and infrequent social interaction contribute to problem behaviors such as repetitive questions and wandering, as well as to psychopathologies such as depression and anxiety. Procedures for altering the physical environment include creating a more homelike environment and constructing environments that reduce unnecessary environmental stimuli while providing adequate variation of sensory stimuli. Planned environments consisting of a very large central area with bedrooms on the periphery (to reduce disorientation), individualized personal areas, and soothing colors have been used effectively for increasing interest in the environment and increasing the frequency of pleasurable activities, such as reading. With the specific goal of increasing social interaction, other effective antecedent strategies include rearranging furniture; adding plants, pictures, and other decorations; providing conversational partners such as peers, children, or pets; and offering group activities. Another antecedent strategy to promote social interaction is the use of communication books. These handheld books contain pictures of relatives and friends, along with descriptions of the pictures, and are designed to promote and enhance the conversations of nursing home residents with other individuals in their environment. In the community, similar strategies have been used effectively to address the common and stressful problem of repetitive questions and statements. The use of environmental cues, such as signs, labels, color codes, and calendars that help the individual interact with the environment, without asking repetitive questions, has been particularly useful.

The effects of teaching nursing home staff and family caregivers about effective communication skills has also been researched. The verbal interactions of nursing staff and family caregivers can strongly influence the occurrence of behavioral problems among individuals with dementia. Caregivers can be taught to announce care activities (e.g., bathing) to reduce disorientation and anxiety, and thus also reduce the likelihood of physical aggression by the individual with dementia during a care activity.

Auditory stimulation strategies have been used effectively to decrease disruptive vocalization, the most common form of agitation in the nursing home. These strategies include the use of relaxing music and comforting sounds or voices. Specifically, environmental sounds (e.g., gentle ocean, country stream) and relaxation audiotapes have been used, as well as audiotapes that contain conversations about cherished memories, anecdotes about family, and other treasured experiences of the resident's life.

Consequent strategies

Although providing consequences, such as relocating a resident to his/her bedroom after agitation occurs, has been used successfully, most consequent strategies involve the use of verbal praise or *planned ignoring*, and are integrated into a treatment plan that focuses on antecedent techniques. Planned ignoring involves terminating caregiver attention when it is believed that attention is reinforcing the problem behavior. For example, caregivers are taught never to argue with a dementia patient because, although arguing may appear aversive, this response can actually reinforce a patient's contentious behavior (e.g., insisting that this is not her home). Planned ig-

noring of the patient's statements, combined with getting him/her onto another topic (an antecedent strategy), is often effective in diverting an unpleasant verbal interaction.

Another example of consequent strategies combined with antecedents is the use of prompted voiding for urinary incontinence. In prompted voiding, patients with dementia are verbally prompted (i.e., reminded) to use the bathroom every one or two hours. Verbal prompting is an antecedent to using the bathroom. However, an important component of prompted voiding is the provision of verbal praise after the patient uses the toilet appropriately (reinforcing consequence).

Behavior management techniques are considered by many to be the most effective form of treatment for the unique problems and psychopathologies associated with dementia. Other forms of behavioral therapy, including problem-solving skills training and cognitive-behavioral therapy are used commonly among older adult populations without dementia-related impairments.

Louis D. Burgio
Susan E. Fisher

See also ALZHEIMER'S DISEASE; ANXIETY; CONGNITIVE-BEHAVORIAL THERAPY; DEMENTIA; DEPRESSION.

BIBLIOGRAPHY

ALLEN-BURGE, R. S.; STEVENS, A. B.; and BURGIO, L. D. "Effective Behavioral Interventions for Decreasing Dementia-Related Challenging Behavior in Nursing Homes." *International Journal of Geriatric Psychiatry* 14 (1999): 213–232.

BANDURA, A. *Social Foundations of Thought and Action: A Social Cognitive Theory.* Englewood Cliffs, N.J.: Prentice-Hall, 1986.

BURGIO, L. D., and FISHER, S. E.. "Application of Psychosocial Interventions for Treating Behavioral and Psychological Symptoms of Dementia." *International Psychogeriatrics* 12 (2000): 351–358.

BURGIO, L. D., and STEVENS, A. B. "Behavioral Interventions and Motivational Systems in the Nursing Home." In *Annual Review of Gerontology and Geriatrics.* Edited by R. Schulz, G. Maddox, and M. P. Lawton. New York: Springer, 1998.

KENNET, J.; BURGIO, L. D.; and SCHULZ, R. "Interventions for In-Home Caregivers: A Review of Research 1990 to Present." In *Handbook of Dementia Caregiving: Evidence-Based Interventions for Family Caregivers*. Edited by R. Shultz. New York: Oxford University Press, 2000. Pages 69–98.

LAWTON, M. P. "Environmental Approaches to Research and Treatment of Alzheimer's Disease." In *Alzheimer's Disease, Treatment, and Family Stress*. Edited by E. Light and B. Lebowitz. Rockville, Md.: National Institute of Mental Health, 1989. Pages 340–362.

BEQUESTS AND INHERITANCES

Approximately 2.4 million adults died in the United States in 1999, leaving estates valued at over $196 billion to their families, charities, federal and state governments (via estate taxes), and others. Easily the largest share of estates goes to spouses. Children and charities also receive sizable amounts. Wealth transfers of this magnitude can have significant effects, yet researchers are still working to understand why people leave bequests. Several theories exist, but none fully explains the patterns of bequest distribution observed. The existence of estate taxes likely influences financial choices later in life, and perhaps the distribution of bequests as well. In 1999 the U.S. government collected $22.9 billion in estate and gift taxes—1.25 percent of all revenues collected. State governments collected over $6.1 billion in additional taxes.

Distribution of estates

One problem facing researchers is a lack of detailed information on why people accumulate wealth and how they distribute it at death. This is hardly surprising, given that most families consider death and the ensuing distribution of the decedent's possessions to be a fairly private matter. Since 1916, the federal government has taxed estates. The documentation of these estates that accompanies estate tax returns provides some insights into how people distribute their wealth at death. In 1999, only estates in excess of $650,000—just over 4 percent of all decedents—were required to file tax returns. Since these data focus on higher-income individuals they may not be representative of all decedents, but they do include the vast majority of wealth held by older individuals.

Table 1

Distribution of Estates from Returns Filed in 1999

	(dollar values in millions)	Percent of Gross Estate
To Spouse	$55,662	28.3
Federal Estate Taxes	$22,920	11.7
To Charities	$14,575	7.4
Debts and Mortgages	$6,504	3.3
State Estate Taxes	$6,125	3.1
Funeral and Other Expenses	$4,505	2.3
Bequests to Children	$22,443	11.4
Bequests to Other Relatives	$12,261	6.2
Bequests to Non-Relatives	$1,588	0.8
Other	$49,853	25.4
Total	$196,436	100.0

SOURCE: Author

First, how do elderly individuals keep their wealth? One way to answer this is to look at wealth holdings at death. For estate tax returns filed in 1999, $79.4 billion of the wealth was in stocks—by far the largest category at 40 percent of wealth holdings. The next largest category was bonds, which include state and local bonds ($20.2 billion), federal savings bonds ($0.9 billion), other federal bonds ($6.0 billion), corporate and foreign bonds ($2.5 billion), and bond funds ($0.8 billion). Over 11 percent ($22.5 billion) of decedent wealth was held in cash or in cash management accounts. Another 10.7 percent ($21.0 billion) was held in real estate other than personal residences.

Table 1 shows how people distribute their wealth at death. The largest share, almost $55.7 billion, went to the surviving spouse. This is even more significant in light of the fact that only 42 percent of these decedents were survived by a spouse. Nearly 12 percent of decedent wealth went to the federal government for estate taxes, and another $6.1 billion was paid to state governments. Over $14.5 billion went to charities, $6.5 billion went to pay off existing debts and mortgages, and $4.5 billion went to pay funeral and other estate expenses. Bequests to children and others were estimated from 1989 data. The "Other" category includes many trusts that could not be connected to individuals. The data also suggests that daughters tend to receive slightly more in bequests than do sons.

Table 2
Average Bequests by Married and Unmarried Decedents, by Beneficiary AGI (all values in thousands of dollars; 1989 data)

Beneficiary AGI Before Death	AVERAGE BEQUESTS GIVEN BY MARRIED DECEDENTS			AVERAGE BEQUESTS GIVEN BY UNMARRIED DECEDENTS		
	To Children	To Grandchildren	To Other Relatives	To Children	To Grandchildren	To Other Relatives
Less than $0 to $50,000	$217	$94	$98	$372	$136	$404
$50,000 to $100,000	$279	$302	$67	$471	$374	$205
$100,000 to $250,000	$388	$512	$110	$630	$414	$241
$250,000 and above	$1,061	$2,551	$102	$1,534	$1,069	$476

SOURCE: Author

Table 2 shows the average bequest amounts given by 1989 decedents, with the recipients divided by prebequest adjusted gross income (AGI). Clearly higher-income individuals receive significantly larger bequests on average than do lower-income individuals. Comparing the left-hand side of Table 2 with the righthand side indicates that unmarried decedents give more, and larger, bequests to relatives than do decedents survived by a spouse. This makes sense because spousal bequests are untaxed. Most likely the first member of a couple to die leaves most of his or her wealth to the spouse. This ensures that the surviving spouse has sufficient funds to live and allows the survivor to collect additional information about potential heirs before the estate is finally disbursed.

Reasons for leaving bequests

For years researchers have sought to understand why people leave bequests. The sheer quantity of wealth involved makes this an important question. Several broad categories of possible reasons for bequests exist, but none successfully explains all observed patterns. The most likely explanations of intergenerational bequests are intergenerational altruism and some form of exchange. Altruism or some type of "joy of giving" probably motivates bequests to charitable organizations. Most likely different people experience different bequest motives. This section describes them.

First one must wonder whether bequests to descendents are intentional or accidental; that is, simply the result of life ending before spending all the money. In a 1991 study, B. Douglas Bernheim examined the types of wealth held by retirement-age individuals. He concluded that the evidence strongly suggests bequests are indeed intentional. If people were interested only in ensuring that they had enough money for their own expenses, one would expect more people to purchase annuities. Annuities provide income for the rest of a person's lifetime, regardless of how long he or she may live. Their purchase relieves the concerns many may have about running out of money, but generally they cannot be passed to others at death. (Couples can purchase annuities that provide income until both of them die, and some annuities can be passed to non-spouses at death, but generally the benefits are substantially reduced.) Instead, elderly people hold their wealth in stocks, bonds, and other bequeathable forms. This suggests that people intend to leave their wealth to others after they die, and are not simply making sure their money lasts as long as they do.

Intergenerational altruism. Children, grandchildren, and other different-generation relatives receive more total bequests than do charitable organizations. A leading theory of intergenerational bequests suggests that people give such bequests because they are altruistic; that is, they care about the well-being of their children and grandchildren. An altruistic parent experiences a benefit from his or her children's happiness. One way a parent can influence a child's happiness is to give some of his or her wealth to the child. In a 1988 survey of older individuals, John Laitner and F. Thomas Juster (1996) found that 45 percent of respondents with children considered leaving an estate or inheritance to be very or quite important. During life, a parent may be reluctant to part with much of his or her wealth because of uncertainty about how long he or she will live and future financial needs. At death, the parent no longer has these concerns, and his or her wealth can be freely distributed to descendents.

To test this theory, researchers first assume that parents feel equally altruistic about all of their children. If this is true, then it would follow that parents distribute bequests in a manner that equalizes their children's after-bequest income and wealth. This theory is tested by examining how bequests are distributed among children to see if poorer children receive larger bequests and wealthier children receive smaller bequests. The data show that roughly two-thirds of all decedents distribute bequests almost equally to all children. Those who do not distribute bequests equally do indeed show some tendency to give larger bequests to poorer children, but the tendency is not as strong as expected.

Exchange-motivated bequests. The failure to confirm intergenerational altruism as a major bequest motive leads researchers to suspect that many bequests are motivated by some form of intergenerational exchange. B. Douglas Bernheim, Andrei Shleifer, and Lawrence Summers (1985) studied a large number of older people and the types and frequency of contact they had with their children. They also examined the types of wealth held by survey participants. The types of contact studied were phone calls and visits by the children to their parents. The researchers found that the more bequeathable wealth parents had, the more children contacted their parents. The hypothesis here is that the parents' wealth induces the children to make more frequent contact. Children may even compete for larger shares of the estate. In families with only one child, the child tended to contact the parents less frequently than did children in larger families. With no one to compete against, only children had less financial incentive to contact their parents frequently.

Other researchers have sought evidence that bequests are part of an intergenerational exchange. Some have examined bequest data for signs that parents give larger bequests to richer children, the theory being that richer children are more likely to have the financial resources required for frequent long-distance calls and visits. Unfortunately, these tests also fail to conclusively explain why people leave bequests to particular beneficiaries.

Developing accurate tests of the reasons people leave bequests is extremely difficult. One problem facing researchers is a lack of quality data. Estate tax data provide some insights into the bequests of wealthy individuals, but lack information on 96 percent of the population. They contain no data on child-to-parent contact and lack direct information on children's wealth. Other data sets contain information about wealth holdings of a broader set of parents and children, but since they survey living individuals, they have no information on bequests. Also, the initial assumption that parents care equally about all of their children is unlikely to be true.

The bottom line here is that one may never know the exact cause(s) of intergenerational bequests. Most likely each of these motives operates to different degrees for different individuals. Some are altruistic, and others are not; some reward children who call and visit, and others do not. The future challenge may be to further understand how much of the population acts from each of these motives.

Charitable bequests. Charitable bequests comprise roughly 14 percent of nonspousal bequests. These bequests are not divided evenly among different types of charities. Of the $10 billion left to charitable organizations in 1995, $3.2 billion (31.6 percent) went to educational, medical, or scientific organizations, and $3.1 billion went to private foundations. Only $970 million went to religious organizations and $273 million went to the arts and humanities. The remainder went to charities in a number of smaller categories.

Charitable bequests are most often the result of a sincere desire to help others. Some people are motivated to replace reductions in government-funded social services. Others may feel they have worked hard for their money and would rather put it to good use than have their children spend it. Occasionally, decedents seek to perpetuate the family name with a building or establishment of a scholarship, but these instances are clearly in the minority. Also, the

Table 3
Estate Tax Liability by Size of Gross Estate
(1999 Returns)

Size of Gross Estate	Number of Returns Filed	Gross Estate (millions)	Tax Liability (millions)
$600,000 to $1 million	49,898	$38,959	$804
$1 million to $2.5 million	40,779	$60,547	$5,330
$2.5 million to $5 million	8,626	$29,164	$4,572
$5 million to $10 million	3,050	$20,757	$3,893
$10 million to $20 million	1,063	$14,495	$2,854
$20 million and up	577	$32,515	$5,467
Total	103,993	$196,436	$22,920

SOURCE: Author

structure of the estate tax (see below) clearly encourages charitable bequests.

Estate taxes

Enacted in 1916, the federal estate tax has gone through many changes over the years. Marginal tax rates have ranged from 1 percent to as high as 77 percent. There have been limits on how much can be transferred to spouses and others, and there have been changes in the ways estates are valued. This section briefly describes the major components of the federal estate tax as it existed through most of the twentieth century. Note that the Economic Growth and Tax Relief Reconciliation Act of 2001 includes gradual reductions in the estate tax, with complete elimination in 2010.

Table 3 shows the amount of tax collected from estates of different sizes. The progressive nature of the estate tax is quite evident here. Nearly half of the estates had a value of less than $1 million, and these estates paid 3.5 percent of the tax due that year. At the other extreme, a small portion (approximately 0.5 percent) of estates had a value above $20 million, and paid 23.8 percent of the total tax.

The federal estate tax has several objectives, the foremost being to raise revenue for the federal government. While the portion of federal revenues derived from the estate tax has generally been fairly small (typically less than 2 percent), it did exceed 5 percent in several Depression era years and approached 10 percent in 1936. Opponents of the estate tax have argued that this small contribution to federal revenues is not sufficient to prevent its elimination.

A second objective of the estate tax is to complement the income tax system to ensure all income is taxed. Much wealth is held in capital gains, which are not considered income until realized (i.e., when the underlying asset is sold). When a person holding an asset that has appreciated dies, no income taxes are paid on the appreciation. When the asset is transferred to another individual, the basis on which capital gains taxes will have to be paid becomes the then current value of the asset—usually much higher than the price paid by the original owner. The new owner will have to pay capital gains taxes only on the increase in value that occurs after he or she receives the asset. By collecting estate taxes on the value of the transferred asset, the estate tax complements the income tax and ensures that all capital gains are taxed. Without the estate tax, owners of capital assets would have to keep track of the original purchase price, regardless of who made the purchase and how long ago the purchase occurred.

A third objective is to reduce concentrations of wealth. Some view large inheritances as contrary to a major value of American society: equal opportunity for all. They see estate taxation as a way of "leveling the playing field." The values in Table 2 suggest that estate taxes do little to reduce familial wealth concentrations. However, it is possible that the difference between bequests received by lower- and higher-income individuals would be even greater in the absence of the estate tax.

A fourth objective is to reduce competition between states for wealthy individuals. Some states could seek to encourage wealthy people to move there by advertising their low (or nonexistent) estate tax rates. The federal estate tax ensures that decedents' estates will be taxed similarly regardless of their state of residence. While some differences between state estate tax laws exist, almost all of them are smoothed out by the structure of the federal estate tax. (See "Tax Credits," below.)

Determining estate taxes.   To figure the tax due on an estate, one must first calculate the value of the estate. This includes the value of real estate holdings, stocks, bonds, pensions, businesses, cash, and proceeds from life insurance policies owned by the decedent. Often decedents have transferred assets to others prior to death. Some assets must be included in the calculation of a decedent's estate if they were transferred to others within three years preceding death.

Assets can be valued at the date of death or six months after death. This allowance recognizes that it can take a considerable amount of time to settle an estate and the value of the estate may decrease in that time. There is also a method of valuing property used in a closely held farm or business. Such property sometimes would have a greater value under a different use than under its current use. For example, a five-hundred-acre farm may have a certain value as farmland, but a much higher market value if sold for residential property. Rather than forcing the estate to consider the value of the land as residential, it can be valued as farmland. Certain restrictions apply to using this "special use" valuation, and there is a maximum as to how much of the market value can be excluded from the estate. In 1995, 456 estates used the "special use" valuation, for a reduction of $171 million in gross estate value.

Once the gross estate value has been determined, a number of deductions are allowed. The largest of these is bequests to the spouse. Initially this deduction was limited to a fraction of the gross estate, but this limit was removed in 1982. Recognition that estate taxes would be paid at the death of the surviving spouse made limiting the spousal deduction unnecessary. Other allowable deductions include charitable bequests, debts of the decedent (e.g., mortgages and medical debts), and expenses incurred by the estate (e.g., funeral expenses and attorney's fees). Table 1 gives 1999 values for these deductions.

Tax credits.   Initially, the first $50,000 of an estate was exempt from taxation—similar to the standard deduction allowed for personal income taxes. The exemption amount was increased periodically (and decreased in 1932) until 1977, when it was repealed and replaced with a credit. This credit, called the "unified credit," is by far the largest credit provided for in the estate tax, reducing estate tax liability by roughly $18.5 billion in 1999. Since this credit eliminates all estate tax liability for most estates, it is often more convenient to speak in terms of the amount of an es-

tate it effectively exempts from taxation. For example, in 1999 the unified credit amount was $211,300. An estate valued at exactly $650,000 (after deductions) would have had an initial liability tax of exactly $211,300. Applying the unified credit (i.e., reducing tax liability by the amount of the credit) leaves a final liability of $0. The initial tax liability on estates smaller than $650,000 is less than $211,000, so the unified credit eliminates all tax liability for these estates. For larger estates the unified credit effectively eliminates the tax that would be due on the first $650,000 of the estate. Under the Economic Growth and Tax Relief Reconciliation Act of 2001, the effective exemption rises to $3.5 million in 2009. This credit gets its name from the fact that it unifies the exemptions for the estate, gift, and generation-skipping transfers taxes.

The state death tax credit is the other major credit allowed under the estate tax. This credit provides a one dollar reduction in federal estate taxes due for each dollar of state estate taxes paid. The credit is capped at an amount that varies with the size of the taxable estate. Most states simply charge estate taxes equal to the maximum allowable federal credit amount. In fact, there is little incentive for states to do otherwise. States that charge a smaller amount do not save their constituents any money; they only allow them a smaller credit against their federal estate taxes—in effect letting the federal government collect tax revenues the state could have collected. States that charge a larger amount are providing a disincentive for wealthy people to live in their state. In 1999, the state death tax credit reduced federal estate taxes by approximately $6.0 billion.

Behaviorial effects

The estate tax can influence the behavior of wealthy older individuals, even if it simply causes them to consult a professional estate planner in order to minimize estate tax liability. Other behavioral effects may include increased work effort and savings, increased charitable bequests, and decreased capital gains realizations.

First, since estate taxes directly reduce the amount of a parent's wealth actually received by an heir, they can lead to increased work effort and savings. A parent intending an heir to receive a specific dollar amount would have to save more (and perhaps work more) than if there were no estate taxes. Other parents could decide estate taxes are so high that it is impractical to leave any sizable bequests. This could lead to decreased savings and work effort among older individuals. It is extremely difficult to determine how significant either of these behavioral effects may be in practice.

Second, by exempting charitable bequests from taxation, the estate tax directly encourages such bequests. A simple example will illustrate why this is so. Suppose Susan is deciding how to allocate her estate, knowing it will face a marginal tax rate of 55 percent. She has allocated all of her estate except for $10,000, which could be given either to charity or to a cousin. If it is given to the cousin, the government will collect its share, leaving the cousin with only $4,500. If it is given to a charity, the charity will receive the entire $10,000. Many people choose the charity when confronted with this actual choice of giving $4,500 to an heir or $10,000 to charity. Several studies of this issue produced similar results. For example, Gerald Auten and David Joulfaian (1996) concluded that charitable gifts could be as much as 12 percent lower in a world without estate taxes.

Third, the fact that the appreciated value of capital assets (e.g., stocks and bonds) in an estate is not subject to capital gains or income taxes encourages older individuals not to sell such assets. The wealth associated with these assets will be subjected to the estate tax whether or not the asset is sold before death. But if an individual sells an asset before death, he or she will be liable for capital gains taxes on the appreciated value. The individual will then have less to bequeath. In contrast, an individual who does not sell an asset before death can bequeath the entire value of the asset. Economists continue to debate whether or not estate taxes actually encourage older individuals to hold capital assets longer than they should.

Finally, the behavioral effects of bequests themselves should be considered. Studies show that the larger the inheritance received by a person, the more likely he or she is to reduce the work effort, and perhaps even to retire. The effect, however, is relatively small. Joulfaian (1998) reported that among 1995 beneficiaries, only 9 percent of unmarried bequest recipients had quit work three years later. Of couples with both spouses working when they received an inheritance, 98.5 percent still had at least one spouse working three years later. This result likely understates the effect of bequests because it cannot indicate whether retirement was accelerated but did not occur within the three-year study period.

ROBERT P. REBELEIN

See also ASSETS AND WEALTH; ESTATE PLANNING; FINANCIAL PLANNING; INTERGENERATIONAL EXCHANGES; PENSION; TAXATION.

BIBLIOGRAPHY

AUTEN, G., and JOULFAIAN, D. "Charitable Contributions and Intergenerational Transfers." *Journal of Public Economics* 59 (1996): 55–68.

BERNHEIM, B. D. "How Strong Are Bequest Motives? Evidence Based on Estimates of the Demand for Life Insurance and Annuities." *Journal of Political Economy* 99 (1991): 899–927.

BERNHEIM, B. D.; SHLEIFER, A.; and SUMMERS, L. H. "The Strategic Bequest Motive." *Journal of Political Economy* 93 (1985): 1045–1076.

JOHNSON, B. W., and ELLER, M. B. "Federal Taxation of Inheritance and Wealth Transfers" In *Inheritance and Wealth in America*. Edited by R. K. Miller and S. J. McNamee. New York: Plenum Press, 1998. Pages 61–90.

JOHNSON, B. W., and MIKOW, J. M. "Federal Estate Tax Returns, 1995–1997." In *Statistics of Income Bulletin*. Washington D.C.: Statistics of Income Division, Internal Revenue Service, 1999. Pages 69–130.

JOULFAIAN, D. *The Federal Estate and Gift Tax: Description, Profile of Taxpayers, and Economic Consequences*. Office of Tax Analysis Working Paper no. 80. Washington D.C.: U.S. Department of the Treasury, 1998.

JOULFAIAN, D., and WILHELM, M. O. "Inheritance and Labor Supply." *Journal of Human Resources* 43 (1994): 1205–1234.

LAITNER, J., and JUSTER, T. F. "New Evidence on Altruism: A Study of TIAA-CREF Retirees." *American Economic Review* 86 (1996): 893–908.

SEATER, J. J. "Ricardian Equivalence." *Journal of Economic Literature* 31 (1993): 142–190.

BEREAVEMENT

For older Americans, the loss of a loved one is a relatively common occurrence, yet it is often severely distressing and can have dire implications for mental and physical health. Over two million people die in the United States each year. Each of those deaths leaves behind a wake of grief that ripples through a web of surviving fam-

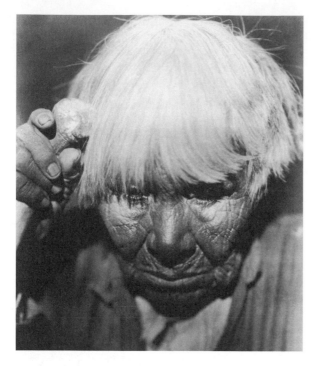

Photographer Edward S. Curtis called this 1924 photograph "Old Woman in Mourning—Yuki;" it shows a bereaved elderly woman from the Yuki Indian tribe in California holding a bone against her right temple as she conducts an elaborate mourning ritual. (Library of Congress)

ily members and friends. Older people are especially likely to experience such losses. Of the nearly one million people who are widowed each year, about 70 percent are over age sixty-five. For older people this highly prevalent occurrence is also one of the most painful. In a study of widowed people over age fifty, Dale Lund and colleagues found that 72 percent of participants reported that the death of their spouse was the most stressful event they ever experienced. Other studies of older adults have found that bereavement magnifies the risk of psychological disturbances, such as increased symptoms of anxiety, depressive symptoms, and major depressive episodes, as well as new or worsened physical illnesses, greater use of medication, and poorer self-rated health. These health complications, in turn, may result in more frequent use of health care services, such as visiting a doctor or receiving care in a hospital, thus making the issue of bereavement important in discussions of controlling health care costs. In addition, researchers have found that suicide and death in general are more likely to occur in the period following a significant loss.

This entry begins by addressing the concept of the "normal" grieving process and the various dimensions of which it may be composed. It then examines what are considered pathological reactions to loss, how these are related to and differentiated from the dimensions of normal grief, the rates at which they occur, and the extent to which these disorders overlap. Next is a discussion of the factors that have been found to influence whether a person will suffer a pathological bereavement response. Last is a review of the current pharmacological and psychotherapeutic treatments found to be effective in ameliorating bereavement-related distress.

Components of normal grief

What is a normal, or uncomplicated, response to losing a loved one? Due to the stressful nature of the event and the broad spectrum of grief manifestations that can result, there is no single, simple answer to this question. As outlined by Selby Jacobs, the array of common symptoms includes yearning for the lost person, preoccupation with the deceased, sighing, crying, dreams or illusions involving the deceased, searching for the lost loved one, anger, protesting the death, anxiety, sadness, despair, insomnia, fatigue, lethargy, loss of interest in previously enjoyable activities, loss of a sense of meaning, emotional numbness, nightmares, and being unable to accept the loss. Normal grief generally involves some subset of these features, with symptom intensities varying widely between individuals and over time.

In the form of a simple list, this collection of symptoms is somewhat bewildering. How are these emotional and behavioral responses related to one another? Are there sets of associated symptoms that tend to be exhibited as groups? Theorists have attempted to construct frameworks that draw connections between these manifestations in order to deepen understanding of the grieving process.

Stephen Shuchter and Sidney Zisook postulated that normal grief generally follows three stages. First, according to their model, there is a period of shock and disbelief, during which the bereaved person cannot accept that the loss has occurred. This gives way to an intermediate stage of acute mourning in which the individual is forced to confront the reality of the loss, resulting in increasing physical and emotional discomfort and social withdrawal. Ultimately, the person is able to assimilate the loss into the greater context of his or her life, and gradually returns to normal levels of functioning.

While this model is appealing for its simplicity, it is somewhat restrictive. By invoking uniform, sequential stages of grief progression, this framework cannot accurately describe a large percentage of the varied bereavement responses. Another approach, taken by Jacobs, is to look at the bereavement process as made up of multiple dimensions, or sets of symptoms, each of which can be present simultaneously, to varying degrees. As time passes, one dimension may replace another as the predominant grief manifestation, thus creating the appearance of stages but maintaining greater flexibility in the overall model.

Separation anxiety. Taking this approach, the question becomes What are the primary dimensions of grief? One of the most fundamental components seems to be a group of symptoms that have been labeled "separation distress" or "separation anxiety." This includes what Erich Lindemann has called the pang of grief—episodes of intense longing and yearning for the deceased, characterized by preoccupation with thoughts of the lost person, sighing, crying, and, in some cases, dreams, illusions, or even hallucinations involving the deceased. Behaviorally, this is manifested as searching for the lost person by seeking out places and things identified with that person, as if hoping to bring the deceased back to life. This searching behavior, often done unconsciously, ultimately meets with frustration, commonly resulting in another pang of grief.

The reason for such a reaction becomes more clear when we consider the concept of separation anxiety in the framework of attachment theory, which was initially developed by John Bowlby to explain how and why babies and children form bonds with their parents. Bowlby observed that young children exhibit pronounced "attachment behaviors," such as crying, touching, following, and calling, that serve to keep them in close contact with their parents or other protective individuals, known as "attachment objects." Bowlby hypothesized that these attachment behaviors came about, and were perpetuated in humans through evolution, because of the selective advantage such behaviors confer. Children who maintain relationships with parents and membership in social groups will be provided protection from predators, easier access to food, and improved ability to contend with competitors, all of which improve their chances of surviving to the age of reproduction. Thus, ingrained through evolutionary processes, attachment behavior is thought to be a "primary drive," hardwired into the neural circuits of the brain.

With this perspective, it becomes understandable why isolation from an attachment figure is a threatening situation that results in feelings of alarm, anxiety, anger, loneliness, and insecurity. This separation distress, which is defined as the reaction to the danger of losing an attachment object, is readily observable in infants and young children upon separation from a parent. While adults do not usually exhibit this behavior as frequently and explicitly as children do, the loss of a close relationship does result in the separation distress that makes up a component of normal grief, and in excessive reactions, or dysfunctional grief (described later).

Traumatic distress. Mardi Horowitz outlined two components of a traumatic stress response. The first involves intrusive symptoms aroused by a fear that the event will recur: frightening perceptions (such as illusions, nightmares), hypervigilance (always being "on the lookout"), startle reactions, feelings of helplessness, and insecurity. The second component, partly in reaction to the intrusive symptoms, consists of strategies for psychologically avoiding thoughts of the traumatic event: denial that the death occurred, dissociation (becoming detached from one's environment), emotional numbing, and avoidance of any place or thing that would result in painful memories of the event. Often, bereavement occurs in conjunction with an objectively traumatic event (e.g., natural disaster, war, accident). In such cases, the bereaved person may be traumatized by the event as well as by the impact of losing a loved one(s).

Depressive symptoms. It is generally acknowledged that some depressive symptoms are common in normal grief (e.g., sadness, despair, loss of interest in activities, significant weight loss or gain without dieting, insomnia, and fatigue). Full depressive episodes also occur secondary to a major interpersonal loss.

Pathological grief

It is clear from the above discussion that the manifestations of grief are manifold. Yet, if all of these variations can be seen as normal reactions to the loss of an intimate, then how is the pathological differentiated from the normal? First, this is done on the basis of the severity of the symptoms (their intensity and/or frequency). Second, duration is a factor. In normal grief there is a gradual reduction in symptoms, acceptance of the death, and reinvestment in new activities and relationships; when this process is prolonged, there is reason for concern. Third, to be considered a disorder, the symptoms must cause a clinically significant disruption in the bereaved individual's social, occupational, or other important domains of functioning. Finally, some symptoms are more rare and are found predominantly in pathologic forms of grief. The most common bereavement-related psychiatric disorders are considered below.

Major depression. When persistent and intense, the depressive symptoms present in normal grief can lead to a diagnosis of major depressive disorder. In addition to these symptoms, Jacobs and Paula Clayton have found that those suffering from major depressive disorder following a loss may experience hopelessness, worthlessness, low self-esteem, guilt, a slowing of movement, and thoughts of suicide. Since these symptoms are uncommon in bereaved people who are not clinically depressed, they seem to be key markers of depression following a significant loss. Studies have found that between 12 and 32 percent of widowed people are depressed in the first six months following the loss. A study by Carolyn Turvey and others found the rate of syndromal depression in the recently widowed to be nine times higher than that in married individuals. Furthermore, two years after the loss, the bereaved subjects were still more likely to be depressed than those who were married. Other studies have found that between 5 and 10 percent of widowed people are continuously or "chronically" depressed for at least two years following the loss.

Post-traumatic stress disorder, anxiety disorders. A death that is perceived as particularly violent or unexpected may result in clinically significant levels of what has been described as "traumatic distress." Those experiencing these symptoms (e.g., reexperiencing the traumatic event with intrusive thoughts; avoidance and numbness in reaction to the trauma; hypervigilance or hyperarousal at cues related to the exposure) at high intensities and frequencies generally meet diagnostic criteria for post-

traumatic stress disorder (PTSD) and/or other anxiety disorders. More research is needed to determine whether the likelihood of developing PTSD following loss depends on the nature of the death (e.g., whether it occurred in a violent or unexpected manner) because available evidence on this is mixed. PTSD is less common than depression in the context of bereavement.

In addition to PTSD, other anxiety disorders are related to some symptoms of traumatic distress. Studies have found that up to one in four recently bereaved people may meet criteria for some anxiety disorder within two months of the loss. However, Paul Surtees found that these anxiety disorders rarely appear without concurrent depression, and resolve more quickly over time.

Traumatic grief. Until recently, there had been no diagnostic classification for people suffering from bereavement-specific symptoms, such as those associated with extreme separation anxiety (e.g., yearning and searching for the lost person). Motivated by the apparent need for such a diagnosis, a group of experts in the areas of bereavement and trauma convened in 1997 to examine this issue. The workshop reviewed a series of studies of independent samples of bereaved people and found that elements of separation distress and traumatic distress form a single cluster, and that this cluster is distinct from depressive and anxiety symptom clusters. This means that people who experience severe symptoms of separation distress also tend to suffer from certain symptoms of traumatic distress. In addition, this single cluster of traumatic and separation distress symptoms was found to persist for months or years in a significant minority of bereaved subjects.

Furthermore, these symptoms, unlike depressive symptoms, did not respond to interpersonal psychotherapy, either alone or in combination with the tricyclic antidepressant nortriptyline. Finally, these symptoms predicted substantial morbidity (e.g., suicidal thoughts, hypertension, increased smoking) over and above the level predicted by depressive symptoms. The evidence reviewed indicated that aspects of separation distress and traumatic distress seem to constitute a single, distinct disorder that merits its own set of diagnostic criteria. The panel participants discussed the symptoms that should be included in a diagnosis and, ultimately, proposed a consensus set of criteria for the disorder, which they called traumatic grief (see Table 1).

Table 1
Diagnostic Criteria for Traumatic Grief

Criterion A:
1. Person has experienced the death of a significant other.
2. The response involves intrusive, distressing preoccupation with the deceased person (e.g., yearning, longing, or searching).

Criterion B:
In response to the death, the following symptoms are marked and persistent:
1. Frequent efforts to avoid reminders of the deceased (e.g., thoughts, feelings, activities, people, places).
2. Purposelessness or feelings of futility about the future.
3. Subjective sense of numbness, detachment, or absence of emotional responsiveness.
4. Feeling stunned, dazed, or shocked.
5. Difficulty acknowledging the death (e.g., disbelief).
6. Feeling that life is empty or meaningless.
7. Difficulty imagining a fulfilling life without the deceased.
8. Feeling that part of oneself has died.
9. Shattered world view (e.g., lost sense of security, trust, or control).
10. Assumes symptoms or harmful behaviors of, or related to, the deceased person.
11. Excessive irritability, bitterness, or anger related to the death.

Criterion C:
The duration of disturbance (symptoms listed) is at least six months.

Criterion D:
The disturbance causes clinically significant impairment in social, occupational, or other important areas of functioning.

SOURCE: Author

A diagnosis of traumatic grief requires meeting both criterion A (separation distress) and criterion B (bereavement-specific traumatization occurring as a result of the loss). Preliminary studies indicate that people experiencing a majority of criterion B symptoms to a marked and persistent degree can be said to meet this criterion. A 1999 study in the *British Journal of Psychiatry* found that four out of the eight criterion B symptoms tested were required for a highly specific (excluding those without the disorder) and sensitive (including those with the disorder) diagnosis of traumatic grief. Criterion C, specifying a minimum duration of two months, and criterion D, requiring clinically significant impairment, may serve to further differentiate the disorder from a normal, or uncomplicated, grief response. However, additional research is necessary to determine the optimal mix of symptoms, duration, and impairment required for a diagnosis. Studies have found that between 10 and 20 percent of widowed people who have lost their spouse within six months meet criteria for traumatic grief.

Comorbidity. Psychiatric comorbidity (i.e., the presence of multiple disorders) is common following bereavement. In a study by Gabriel Silverman and colleagues (2000), traumatic grief, PTSD, and major depressive episode were found to overlap with each other to similar degrees. Of those with traumatic grief, 47 percent also received a diagnosis of major depressive episode, 33 percent met criteria for PTSD, and 40 percent had traumatic grief alone (these percentages sum to over 100 because 20 percent of those with traumatic grief received all three diagnoses).

Traumatic grief has also been found to predict lower energy levels; lower levels of social functioning; higher rates of hospitalization and physical health events, such as heart attack, cancer, and stroke; lower self-esteem; changes in sleeping and eating habits; and heightened levels of thoughts of suicide.

Risk factors for pathological grief

To some extent, the severity of the grief experienced by an individual can be predicted, given the presence or absence of identified risk factors for maladjustment to the loss. Current knowledge about such risk factors is reviewed below.

Demographic characteristics. Younger people have often been found to experience higher levels of grief. This may be understandable, in part, because they are more likely to be mourning a death that is considered untimely. However, Catherine Sanders found that though this was true initially for younger widows, two years following the death they had made significant improvements in their mental health, while older widows, who initially had lower levels of grief, now had more anxiety, loneliness, and feelings of helplessness, and also had declined in physical health. This difference over the long term may be explained, at least partially, by younger widowed people's greater resilience and tendency to feel less vulnerable following the loss of their spouse.

Though women tend to report more symptoms than men, Colin Murray Parkes and R. J. Brown found that between two and four years after the loss, widows were no more depressed than married women the same age, whereas widowers were still more depressed than married men. It is hypothesized that the reason for this is that during marriage, men may be more likely to depend on a spouse for emotional support and social contacts. When this resource is no longer available, these men, not in the habit of meeting new people, often isolate themselves or throw themselves into their work. Women, on the contrary, are more likely to cope with the loss by seeking out social support that might facilitate the bereavement process.

Low socioeconomic status has also been found to contribute to poor bereavement adjustment, worse health, reduced social participation, and greater loneliness. Unemployment is also a risk factor for depression following bereavement.

Nature of the death.   If the death is particularly sudden, unexpected, or violent, the bereaved person may be predisposed to a pathological reaction, particularly to elements of traumatic distress and PTSD. Similarly, experiencing multiple losses near each other in time, known as "bereavement overload," has been found to increase risk of psychopathology.

Nature of the relationship.   If the bereaved person was highly dependent (emotionally, physically, or otherwise) on the deceased person, or if their lives were largely intertwined with shared activities (an "enmeshed" relationship), the loss will result in major disruption in the survivor's daily life. Feelings of purposelessness, loss of meaning, and a shattered worldview are likely to be prominent and contribute to a diagnosis of traumatic grief. One study (*The Gerontologist*, 2000) by Holly Prigerson and colleagues found that, following the loss of their spouse, people who had harmonious marriages used a significantly greater number of health services than those whose marriages were discordant.

The nature of the relationship is partly dependent upon the personality and "attachment style" of the bereaved person. Attachment disturbances, such as excessive dependency or insecure or anxious attachment, are likely to result in severe separation distress following the loss. Such disturbances are often established during childhood, when the ability to form secure attachments is learned. A study by Gabriel Silverman and others (2000) found that adversities experienced during childhood (physical or sexual abuse, death of a parent) were significantly associated with traumatic grief, while adversities occurring in adulthood (nonbereavement traumatic events and death of a child) were associated with PTSD. This suggests that there is a vulnerability to traumatic grief explicitly rooted in childhood experiences.

Social support.   Lack of social support (i.e., friends or family who are available to provide emotional and practical help) has been widely cited as a risk factor for poor bereavement adjustment. However, Lund notes that simply having available family members is not enough, because such "support" can be negative (e.g., judgmental, inconsiderate, pushy, demanding, unreliable). Rather, only empathetic support, stable over time, appears to result in lower rates of depression and more positive ratings of coping, health, and life satisfaction.

Treatment

While there have been no randomized, controlled, clinical trials of treatment for traumatic grief, inferences can be made from studies done treating PTSD, separation anxiety disorder, and depression.

Pharmacotherapy.   Considering a review of this literature done by Jacobs, it seems that selective serotonin reuptake inhibitors might be more effective for the broad range of traumatic grief symptoms than tricyclic antidepressants. The latter tend to affect intrusive, anxious, and depressive symptoms alone, while the former reduce these symptoms as well as manifestations of avoidance, particularly avoidance stemming from distress over reminders of the loss.

Psychotherapy.   Though findings have been mixed, both psychodynamically oriented treatments and behavioral/cognitive treatments have, in some studies, demonstrated effectiveness in treating pathological grief. When addressing bereavement-related distress, it is important for the therapist to review the relationship to the deceased person and the circumstances of the death. In addition, the therapist should advise the patient on what to expect from the grieving process. Though as yet there is no treatment designed to specifically address the symptoms of traumatic grief, M. Katherine Shear and Ellen Frank are developing and testing one such therapy based on Edna Foa's treatment for PTSD. Continued strides in this direction are cause for optism in the search for efficacious treatments for traumatic grief and other bereavement-related disorders.

GABRIEL K. SILVERMAN
HOLLY G. PRIGERSON

See also ANTIDEPRESSANTS; ANXIETY; COGNITIVE-BEHAVIORAL THEORY; DEPRESSION; WIDOWHOOD.

BIBLIOGRAPHY

BOWLBY, J. *Attachment and Loss.* Vol. 3, *Loss, Sadness and Depression.* New York: Basic Books, 1980.

CHEN, J. H.; BIERHALS, A. J.; PRIGERSON, H. G.; KASL, S. V.; MAZURE, C.; SHEAR, M. K.; REYNOLDS, C. F.; DAY, N.; and JACOBS, S. "Gender Differences in Health Outcomes Resulting From Bereavement-Related Emotional Distress." *Psychological Medicine* 29 (1999): 367–380.

CLAYTON, P. J. "Bereavement." In *Handbook of Affective Disorders.* Edited by E. S. Paykel. London: Churchill Livingstone, 1982. Pages 403–415.

HOROWITZ, M. J. *Stress Response Syndromes: PTSD, Grief, and Adjustment Disorders.* Northvale, N.J.: Jason Aronson, 1997.

JACOBS, S. *Traumatic Grief: Diagnosis, Treatment, and Prevention.* Philadelphia: Brunner/Mazel, 1999.

LINDEMANN, E. "Symptomatology and Management of Acute Grief." *American Journal of Psychiatry* 101 (1944): 141–148.

LUND, D. A.; CASERTA, M. S.; and DIMOND, M. F. "The Course of Spousal Bereavement in Later Life." In *Handbook of Bereavement.* Edited by M. S. Stroebe, W. Stroebe, and R. O. Hansson. Cambridge: Cambridge University Press, 1993. Pages 240–254.

"Number of Deaths, Death Rates, and Age-Adjusted Death Rates for Ages 15 Years and Over, by Race, Sex, and Marital Status: United States, 1998." *National Vital Statistics Reports* 48, no. 11 (24 July 2000): 78–79, Table 22.

PARKES, C. M., and BROWN, R. J. "Health After Bereavement: A Controlled Study of Young Boston Widows and Widowers." *Psychosomatic Medicine* 34 (1972): 449–461.

PRIGERSON, H. G.; SHEAR, M. K.; JACOBS, S. C.; REYNOLDS, III, C. F.; MACIEJEWSKI, P. K.; DAVIDSON, J. R. T.; ROSENHECK, R.; PILKONIS, P. A.; WORTMAN, C. B.; WILLIAMS, J. B. W.; WIDIGER, T. A.; FRANK, E.; KUPFER, D. J.; and ZISOOK, S. "Consensus Criteria for Traumatic Grief: A Preliminary Test." *British Journal of Psychiatry* 174 (1999): 67–73.

PRIGERSON, H. G.; FRANK, E.; KASL, S. V.; REYNOLDS, III, C. F.; ANDERSON, B.; ZUBENKO, G. S.; HOUCK, P. R.; GEORGE, C. J.; and KUPFER, D. J. "Complicated Grief and Bereavement-related Depression as Distinct Disorders: Preliminary Empirical Validation in Elderly Bereaved Spouses." *American Journal of Psychiatry* 152 (1995): 22–30.

PRIGERSON, H. G.; BIERHALS, A. J.; KASL, S. V.; REYNOLDS, III, C. F.; SHEAR, M. K.; NEWSOM, J. T.; and JACOBS, S. "Complicated Grief as a Disorder Distinct From Bereavement-related Depression and Anxiety: A Replication Study." *American Journal of Psychiatry* 153 (1996): 1484–1486.

PRIGERSON, H. G.; BRIDGE, J.; MACIEJEWSKI, P. K.; BEERY, L. C.; ROSENHECK, R. A.; JACOBS, S. C.; BIERHALS, A. J.; KUPFER, D. J.; and BRENT, D. A. "Influence of Traumatic Grief on Suicidal Ideation Among Young Adults." *American Journal of Psychiatry* 156 (1999): 1994–1995.

PRIGERSON, H. G.; MACIEJEWSKI, P. K.; and ROSENHECK, R. "The Interactive Effects of Marital Harmony and Widowhood on Health, Health Service Utilization and Costs." *The Gerontologist* 40 (2000): 349–357.

PRIGERSON, H. G.; SHEAR, M. K.; FRANK, E.; BEERY, L. C.; SILBERMAN, R.; PRIGERSON, J.; and REYNOLDS, III, C. F. "Traumatic Grief: A Case of Loss-Induced Trauma." *American Journal of Psychiatry* 154 (1997): 1003–1009.

PRIGERSON, H. G.; BIERHALS, A. J.; KASL, S. V.; REYNOLDS, III, C. F.; SHEAR, M. K.; DAY, N.; BEERY, L. C.; NEWSOM, J. T.; and JACOBS, S. "Traumatic Grief as a Risk Factor for Mental and Physical Morbidity." *American Journal of Psychiatry* 154 (1997): 616–623.

RAPHAEL, B.; MIDDLETON, W.; MARTINEK, N.; and MISSO, V. "Counseling and Therapy of the Bereaved." In *Handbook of Bereavement.* Edited by M. S. Stroebe, W. Stroebe, and R. O. Hansson. Cambridge: Cambridge University Press, 1993. Pages 427–453.

REYNOLDS, C. F.; MILLER, M. D.; PASTERNAK, R. E.; FRANK, E.; PEREL, J. M.; CORNES, C.; HOUCK, P. R.; MAZUMDAR, S.; DEW, M. A.; and KUPFER, D. J. "Treatment of Bereavement-Related Major Depressive Episodes in Later Life: A Controlled Study of Acute and Continuation Treatment with Nortriptyline and Interpersonal Psychotherapy." *American Journal of Psychiatry* 152 (1999): 202–208.

SANDERS, C. M. "Risk Factors in Bereavement Outcome." In *Handbook of Bereavement.* Edited by M. S. Stroebe, W. Stroebe, and R. O. Hansson Cambridge: Cambridge University Press, 1993. Pages 255–267.

SHUCHTER, S. R., and ZISOOK, S. "The Course of Normal Grief." In *Handbook of Bereavement.* Edited by M. S. Stroebe, W. Stroebe, and R. O. Hansson. Cambridge: Cambridge University Press, 1993. Pages 23–43.

SILVERMAN, G. K.; JACOBS, S. C.; KASL, S. V.; SHEAR, M. K.; MACIEJEWSKI, P. K.; NOAGHIUL, F. S.; and PRIGERSON, H. G. "Quality of Life Impairments Associated with a Diagnosis of Traumatic Grief." *Psychological Medicine* 30 (2000): 857–862.

SILVERMAN, G. K.; JOHNSON, J. G.; and PRIGERSON, H. G. "Preliminary Explorations of the Effects of Prior Trauma and Loss on Risk for Psychiatric Disorders in Recently Widowed People." *Israel Journal of Psychiatry* (in press).

SURTEES, P. G. "In the Shadow of Adversity: The Evolution and Resolution of Anxiety and Depressive Disorder." *British Journal of Psychiatry* 166 (1995): 583–594.

SUTHERLAND, S., and DAVIDSON, J. "Pharmacotherapy for Post-Traumatic Stress Disorder." *Psychiatric Clinics of North America* 17 (1994): 409–423.

TURVEY, C. L.; CARNEY, C.; ARNDT, S.; WALLACE, R. B.; and HERZOG, R. "Conjugal Loss and Syndromal Depression in a Sample of Elders Aged 70 Years or Older." *American Journal of Psychiatry* 156 (1999): 1596–1601.

BIOGRAPHY

See NARRATIVE

BIOLOGY OF AGING

The phenomenon of aging means quite different things to different people. Most gerontologists would agree that aging is a process, or set of processes, of gradual development and then decline that characterize the life span of an organism. Beyond that, there is very little agreement, and indeed there are many who would argue with this description. In part this lack of agreement is the result of the fact that aging is a very complex phenomenon involving biological, behavioral, and social factors. These various and very varied realms interact to produce the life span trajectory of each single organism on the planet. Adding to this complexity are the cultural, political, and economic assumptions about aging that shape the ways individuals and their institutions think about the "problems of aging."

Biogerontology

The study of the biology of aging, or *biogerontology,* has as its primary objective understanding the basic processes that underlie aging and age-related disease. For some this means increasing human life span, for others it means increasing human health-span. In either case, the ultimate objective is to reduce human suffering. Whether one wishes to extend human life span or alleviate age-related disease, understanding the underlying processes of aging is essential. Aging is not simply the result of the passage of time. Think of the life spans of guppies, dogs, horses, and humans. All age at a regular rate, but the rate of aging is vastly different from one species to another. Is aging different in each species, or does the same set of processes run at different speeds in different species? What do we actually mean by aging? The simplest definition is the loss of *homeostatic ability* with the passage of time. Homeostatic ability is the ability to maintain internal stability. That is, the ability of an organism to maintain a stable internal environment in the face of environmental challenges such as changes in temperature, humidity, air quality, and so on. At the most basic level, the loss of this ability is the primary deficit of aging.

What most of us think of as aging, however, is the loss of teeth, hair, muscle strength, memory, and reproductive ability, as well as the accumulation of wrinkles, joint pain, and what are commonly called the infirmities of old age. These changes are age related, but are not aging itself. They are not the inevitable consequence of aging, but rather the often-observed accompaniments of aging. The concept of "normal aging" is used to try to distinguish between aging as a process or set of processes, from aging as the result of the accumulation of damage from environmental insult, the ravages of disease, and the wear and tear of living. Normal aging is assumed to mean the age changes that result from basic biological processes. Whether normal aging actually can be studied is a matter of some controversy, although most gerontologists believe that the concept is meaningful.

The details of normal versus disease-related (or pathological) aging are the grist for biological theories of aging. These theories are attempts to explain the data we observe as we study aging organisms of many species and to construct frameworks that relate these explanations to a basic understanding of what aging means. Some of these theories assume that aging processes are not the same as wear and tear or the consequence of disease, while others assume that aging is essentially the result of these factors. The major biological theories of aging are described in a separate entry on theories.

Other approaches to the study of aging look at age-related diseases directly (geriatric medicine), at the aging of populations and incidence of age-related diseases in these populations (demography and epidemiology), and at the social and behavioral changes that characterize aging (social gerontology and gerontological psychology).

Research approaches

The areas of interest that fall within the purview of the biology of aging mirror the fascinating areas of biology today. Aging as a process, or set of processes, affects virtually all of our bodily organs and systems. At the most basic level, some portions of our aging patterns are set in our genes. The reliable differences in the life spans of various species are clear evidence of genetic "programs" that set the general boundaries of species life span. The environment modifies these boundaries, but guppies do not live eighty years, and humans often do. Genes are important in the differences in longevity between individual members of a single species (e.g., long- and short-lived humans), but environmental factors play a major role in these differences. Living in a toxic environment or making deleterious lifestyle choices can have a significant effect on individual longevity.

Genetic analyses

A major area of investigation in the biology of aging is the search for genes that influence life span and an understanding of how these genes exert their influence. Studies in lower organisms such as yeasts and fungi show that there are genes, called *longevity assurance genes*, that assure that cells function long enough for the organism to live out its normal life span. Cancer occurs when these longevity assurance functions go awry. Understanding the mechanisms by which a delicate balance between longevity assurance and disease are maintained is one of the very promising areas of biogerontology.

Knowing that a particular gene or set of genes have an effect on an aging parameter does not in and of itself tell us anything about how the genes produce that effect. Molecular biology and molecular genetics are the research areas devoted to seeking such explanations. These research programs look at molecular function in aging organisms from plants and small worms (*Caenorhabditis elegans*) to fruit flies (*Drosophila melanogaster*) to mammals and humans. Understanding the mechanisms by which genes turn molecular and cellular functions on and off at various times in the life span of organisms will eventually lead to the ability to modify those processes. This is the promise of molecular and genetic therapies, tailored to an individual's very specific genetic makeup, that is causing great excitement at the beginning of the twenty-first century.

Model systems

A basic assumption that underlies a great deal of this research is that the use of models for research on human aging is valid and informative. Models for research include a wide variety of organisms, including yeast, worms, rodents, and nonhuman primates. Many genes are common to the genomes of all of these organisms. Humans share genes even with yeasts. Thus it is assumed that phenomena observed in these model organisms provide relevant information about how aging occurs in the human species.

Cell senescence

Cellular functions are basic life processes throughout the life span of any organism. In most tissues in the body, cells must reproduce themselves (replicate) on a regular basis in order for the tissue, and thus the organism, to survive. The study of *cell replication,* and the changes that occur with aging (*cell senescence*), is an important branch of biogerontology.

The seminal observations of Leonard Hayflick on the senescence of cells in culture are at the core of this research. Hayflick showed that cells in culture appear to senesce (grow old) and cease dividing after about fifty population doublings. When one cell splits into two, that is one population doubling. When those two cells become four that is the next doubling, and so on. This observation, made in 1965, puzzled gerontologists for decades as no mechanism could be found to explain how cells in culture could count the number of times they divided. Research on telomeres and the phenomenon of telomere shortening has provided at least one workable mechanism. Telomeres are chains of DNA at the ends of each chromosome that get shorter at each cell division in most tissues. The role of telomeres and the enzyme telomerase (telomerase controls telomere shortening) in aging and in cancer is a very promising and exciting area of research.

Hormonal changes

The endocrine system controls the production and distribution of hormones throughout the body. Many hormones decline with advancing age. Decline in the levels of reproductive hormones (e.g., testosterone and estrogen) could contribute to loss of function in older individuals. The degree to which such decline is responsible for loss of function, and what can safely be done about it, are important research questions.

Replacing reproductive hormones, or their precursors, could be dangerous since these hormones also play a role in the development of cancers of the reproductive organs. Hormone replacement therapy for postmenopausal women is often desirable, but its desirability depends upon a number of factors, such as family history, personal history, lifestyle, and risk tolerance. Hormone replacement therapy for male reproductive hormones and for growth hormones in both genders is much more controversial. The ready availability of hormone precursors in the form of dietary supplements poses a significant public health problem. Large numbers of people are taking substances that might cause harm without an understanding of the risks.

Nutrition

Nutrition is another area of biogerontologic research that intersects with the dietary and diet supplement industry. The study of the nutritional requirements of older people includes understanding their eating habits, their ability to absorb nutrients, their ability to metabolize those nutrients, and the role of over or under nutrition on health and longevity. A particularly interesting branch of this research is the study of the effects of restricting calorie intake. Caloric restriction, with adequate nutrition, is the only experimental manipulation currently known to extend life span. Understanding how caloric restriction produces extended longevity could pro-

vide valuable clues to basic aging processes as well as suggest new therapies for age-related diseases.

Life span alteration

The study of life span extension includes genetic, hormonal, and nutritional components that are part of the subject matter of biogerontology. The impact of success in achieving life span extension is of great interest to social and psychological gerontology, to practitioners of geriatric medicine, and to policy makers in virtually every nation in the world.

The other side of the life span coin is exemplified by the diseases that mimic accelerated aging. Research on these *human progeroid syndromes* such as progeria and Werner's Syndrome, is being conducted in order to try to cure or prevent the diseases. Understanding how the genes responsible for these diseases produce their life-shortening effects is another approach to finding the key aging processes needed to ensure "normal" life spans.

Neural aging

Research on the aging of the brain, nervous system, and neuroendocrine systems constitutes a major portion of biogerontology. Brain cells do not usually replicate and thus must last for most of the life span of the organism. Neurodegenerative diseases that destroy the functionality of neurons and other neuronal tissues, such as in Alzheimer's disease, are a major source of disability in the last third of human life span. Here again, understanding what goes wrong may provide valuable information about normal function as well as lead to effective therapies to combat these terrible diseases.

From this brief summary of the subject matter of the biology of aging it is obvious that aging affects virtually every aspect of our lives. The tremendous strides in this understanding that have resulted from the application of molecular techniques to aging research are described, and the promise that ongoing research holds for better understanding and even better therapies provides positive examples of the benefits of biological research for all of us.

RICHARD L. SPROTT

See also AGING; EPIDEMIOLOGY; GERIATRIC MEDICINE; PHYSIOLOGICAL CHANGES; THEORIES OF BIOLOGICAL AGING.

BIBLIOGRAPHY

AUSTAD, S. N. *Why We Age.* New York: John Wiley & Sons, 1997.

KIRKWOOD, T. *Time of Our Lives.* New York: Oxford University Press, 1999.

SCHNEIDER, E. L., and ROWE, J. W., eds. *Handbook of the Biology of Aging.* New York: Academic Press, 1996.

SPROTT, R. L., and PEREIRA-SMITH, O., eds. *The Genetics of Aging. Generations* 24 no. 1 (2000): 1–85.

BIOMARKERS OF AGING

The process (processes) of aging is a complex phenomenon. Aging in the biological sense is the loss of the ability to maintain *homeostasis,* that is, the loss of the ability to meet challenges from the environment, such as heat or cold or infection, by overcoming the challenge and restoring normal function. Loss of homeostatic ability can occur at the level of the whole organism or in one or more of its parts. Organisms of different species age at different rates. Fruit flies live about two months, mice three to four years, chimpanzees perhaps seventy-five years, and humans as long as 120 years. Despite these very big differences in maximum life span, all of these organisms age in the sense described above. A very few, such as bristlecone pines, turtles, and some fish species age very little. Within a species, individuals age at similar but not identical rates.

Given all the variability in rate of aging observed between and within species, how can we compare the aging status of one organism with that of another. Is a two-month-old fruit fly comparable to an eighty-year-old human? Clearly their chronological ages (age in days or years) are vastly different. Their biological ages are perhaps the same! How can we tell? To understand the concept of biological age as something different from chronological age, let us examine the following example. Suppose that after years of slaving away in the laboratory a gerontologist believes he has discovered the magic elixir that will double life span. How could he test this substance to determine that it actually works? If he gives it to a forty-year-old human subject with a life expectancy of eighty-five years, he will have to wait at least 130 years to be sure his elixir doubles life

span. Obviously this is not possible, much less practical. What this scientist needs is a measure, or set of measures, that can determine the *rate* at which an organism is aging in less than the full life span of the organism. He could then measure the rate of aging of his test subject before and after giving the elixir to see if the rate of aging changes in response to this treatment. Such a measure would be called a biomarker of aging.

Biomarkers of aging, then, are measures of the rate at which organisms, or organ systems within an organism, are aging. The assumptions that underlie the concept of biomarkers of aging are that organisms age at different rates and thus chronological age is not a good predictor of remaining life expectancy, that different tissues, organs, and organ systems within an organism may age at different rates, that these differences can be measured and predicted, and finally that it may be possible to alter the rate of aging of any or all of the components of organisms.

From both a theoretical and a practical point of view, it is also assumed that no single biological measure is likely to ever be found that can accurately assess the rate of aging of a complex organism like a human being. It is therefore assumed that panels of biomarkers made up of a variety of measures will have to be constructed in order to assess the rate of aging of such an organism. These panels of biomarkers will likely be made up of measures that assess all or many of the organ systems within the individual, such as the cardiovascular system, the brain, the liver, bones, memory, and so on. Individual biomarkers might decline with age, like fine motor skills, rise, like the number of rings in a tree trunk, or even rise at one point in the life span and fall at another, like hormone levels.

The interrelationships between individual biomarkers within a panel of biomarkers may be important clues to the interactions of various organs and organ systems in determining the life span of individuals. These interactions will very likely be extraordinarily complex and certainly different from one individual to another. Each individual inherits a different set of genes, and these genes encounter different environments due to experiences and lifestyle differences among individuals. Biomarkers that have the greatest generality across individuals will signal important processes for that species. Biomarkers with great generality across species will signal very important processes for all living things. A primary motivation for biomarker research is to find such general characteristics.

While some potential biomarkers might be theoretically very accurate, it may be impossible or unethical to obtain them. Accurately counting the number of remaining functional brain cells, for example, would result in the death of the individual being assessed. Measuring the ability of the individual to recover from some extreme stress like pain or cold would be unethical.

In order for a biomarker of aging to be useful, certain criteria need to be met. These criteria include the following:

1. The rate at which the biomarker itself changes should reflect some measurable parameter that can be predicted at a later chronological age. For example, if the biomarker were rate of change in memory ability, it should be tied to a particular memory phenomenon that can be predicted at a known interval (e.g., one year) and can be measured (e.g., numbers recalled from a list after a few minutes of intervening activity).
2. The biomarker should reflect some basic biological process (e.g., heart rate).
3. The biomarker should not reflect disease (e.g., Alzheimer's disease).
4. The biomarker should be widely reproducible across similar species (e.g., all mammals).
5. The biomarker should not cause harm to the individual being assessed.
6. The biomarker should be reproducible and should be measurable in a relatively short time interval compared to the life span of the organism being assessed (e.g., days for fruit flies and months for humans).

A major problem in biomarker research is determining the validity of the biomarker. Validity of a biomarker means that it measures what it purports to measure, that is, rate of aging. Finding that a particular measure goes down in some predictable fashion as the organism ages does not mean that the measure reflects biological age. For example, skin wrinkles with advancing age, but skin wrinkling is almost entirely the result of exposure to sunlight and is exacerbated by smoking. Thus, skin wrinkling is a measure of exposure to environmental damage. Some individuals show little or no wrinkling because of lifestyle choices. Similarly, hair turns gray with advancing age. Some individuals are fully gray by their thirties while others show little gray at

very advanced ages. While we all see graying hair as a symbol of age, graying hair is not a good predictor of remaining life. It is therefore not a good biomarker. Still other measures, like rings in the trunk of a tree, may be good chronometers (measures of the passage of time) but still not be good biomarkers (a ten-year-old tree of a short-lived species will have as many rings as a ten-year-old tree of a long-lived species).

A biomarker of aging may be valid even if it does not have *face validity*. The concept of face validity refers to the apparent relationship between a measure and what it is supposed to be a measure of. For example, gray hair, if it were actually a good biomarker, would have face validity, as we all believe that there is a relationship between gray hair and aging. But how about a measure of rate of fingernail growth? Is there any reason to suppose that fingernails grow faster or slower as a result of advancing age? Most of us would assume not, yet some investigators have proposed this measure as a biomarker. Such a measure may lack face validity and yet be a valid biomarker.

Still another important aspect of a good biomarker is its reliability. A reliable measure produces the same result (score) each time it is used (assuming that the thing being measured has not changed). This reliability should be demonstrable across different observers and across different subjects.

Another problem in finding good biomarkers of aging is that so many measures are indicators of disease rather than measures of "normal" function. Indeed, some gerontologists believe that aging is not a process or set of processes, but rather is the cumulative effect of damage caused by wear and tear and disease. Still others believe that aging is itself a disease. Searching for biomarkers of aging only makes sense if there really are underlying biological processes to be measured.

Since finding good biomarkers is apparently so difficult, why bother? One of the major reasons for searching for biomarkers is that their discovery might provide useful information about the underlying processes. If, for example, some measure of immune function were found that accurately predicted the survival of the individual or that individual's immune system, then it would follow that the measure is in some way tied closely to an important aspect of immune aging. Then a search could begin to understand how the immune measure is related to aging and why it changes with age. This in turn could lead to biological insight about aging and to new therapies to "repair" aged immune function.

By far the most common motivation for searching for biomarkers of aging outside of the laboratories of basic scientists is the search for a "cure" for aging and its debilitating diseases. The term *antiaging medicine* has been coined to describe this search. The search for a cure for aging is ancient and appears eternally attractive. A great deal of what is being presented to an avid populace at the beginning of the twenty-first century as valid antiaging medicine rests upon the assumption that valid, reliable biomarkers of aging have been identified and can be administered in the clinic or even in health food stores. Despite common assertions to the contrary, most reputable scientists do not believe that science has yet reached the point where the rate of aging of individuals can be measured in any meaningful fashion. This is a controversial area, and a great deal of money can be made selling "cures" in the form of dietary supplements, hormone replacement regimens, and even books about how to slow down aging.

The antiaging movement has investigators who run the gamut from solid, careful, and thoughtful to outright quacks. Certainly great caution should be exercised before following any so-called recommended antiaging regimen. Many are costly and useless, and some are very probably dangerous. No dietary supplement strategy or course of hormone therapy should be undertaken without first obtaining a physical examination by a physician.

In addition to the unethical abuse of the concept of biomarkers of aging by unscrupulous purveyors of "cures" for aging, the successful development of biomarkers would raise new ethical issues. If we were actually able to assess the rate of aging of an individual, and therefore predict remaining life span or even "healthspan," would our society put such information only to beneficent uses? Could we prevent discrimination in the workplace or in health care systems based on longevity potential? Would persons with shorter life expectancies be able to buy life insurance? Could we prevent the exploitation of such individuals by a new breed of charlatan pandering to the fears of "short-lifers"?

Finally, the development of biomarkers of aging as part of a strategy to find ways to length-

en life assumes that success in this endeavor would be a good thing. Not all theorists would necessarily agree. Other theorists are not worried as they do not believe that it is possible to develop biomarkers of individual rates of aging. Their view is that while it may be possible to develop measures that predict the average rate of aging for a large number of individuals in a population, it is not possible to assess the aging rate of each individual and predict his or her remaining life span.

The only known intervention at the beginning of the twenty-first century that reliably increases life span is caloric restriction. Calorically restricted animals (mostly rats and mice) are widely used for biomarker research and a great deal is known about the ways in which they age. Yet even after decades of intensive research, it is not possible to predict just which animal will live longest and which will die early. Human beings are more complex than rats and mice in many ways. Assertions by antiaging clinics and spas that they have valid biomarkers of aging and can use them to provide remedies and cures for aging should be viewed with the greatest of skepticism. The search for biomarkers of aging can provide humankind with potentially great rewards of greater health and a life of independence if pursued with compassion and integrity. Reputable scientists are working hard to produce such an outcome. Consumers need to be vigilant as well.

RICHARD L. SPROTT

See also LIFE SPAN EXTENSION; NUTRITION; PHYSIOLOGICAL CHANGES; THEORIES OF BIOLOGICAL AGING.

BIBLIOGRAPHY

BAKER, G. T. and SPROTT, R. L., eds. "Biomarkers of Aging." *Experimental Gerontology* 23, no. 4/5 (1998): 223–438.
WACHTER, K. W., and FINCH, C. E., eds. *Between Zeus and the Salmon: The Biodemography of Longevity.* Washington, D.C.: National Academy Press, 1997.

BLOOD

The blood is a complex organ composed of cells of diverse form that perform diverse functions. Red blood cells or *erythrocytes* deliver oxygen to the tissues of the body. *Platelets* govern primary hemostasis, plugging damaged blood vessels after trauma to stop bleeding. The white blood cells (*neutrophils*, *macrophages*, *eosinophils*, *basophils*, and *B- and T-lymphocytes*) are all involved in different aspects of immunity from infection. Although most aspects of blood physiology do not change throughout adult life, some disorders of the blood, particularly anemia and neoplastic diseases, do occur more frequently with increasing age.

Aging and blood cell production

In mammals, the cells of the blood are produced in the bone marrow. Blood cell production depends upon a small population of cells known as hematopoietic stem cells (HSCs). In the bone marrow milieu, these cells can differentiate to give rise to mature cells of any of the eight blood cell lineages. This process, the development of these eight highly specialized cell types from the pluripotent HSC, is called hematopoiesis.

Most mature blood cells are rather short-lived. For example, red blood cells (erythrocytes) survive for three to four months after they are released into the blood from the bone marrow; neutrophils last only about a week. To maintain appropriate numbers of blood cells the bone marrow continuously produces new blood cells—normally about 1 percent of the red blood cells and 10 percent of the granulocytes of the body are replaced each day. Thus, unlike most adult body tissues, which may lose the capacity to undergo cell division (e.g., nerve tissue) or divide only in response to stress (e.g., liver and kidney), the cells of the bone marrow divide actively throughout life; this may have implications for blood homeostasis in aging humans. In the early 1960s, Leonard Hayflick observed that human diploid cells grown in the laboratory could divide only a finite number of times even under optimal conditions. This phenomenon, known as the "Hayflick Limit," is caused in part by erosion of tandem repeat DNA sequences at the telomeres of chromosomes. These sequences are added to the ends of chromosomes by a specific enzyme, telomerase, which is not active in adult cells. Every time a cell divides there is loss of part of the telomeric repeat array, resulting in progressive loss of these sequences and eventually in impairment of essential cell functions. It has been suggested that the requirement for continuous cell division in the bone marrow may therefore result, in older adults, in "exhaustion" of HSCs.

Some observations in humans and in laboratory animals lend support to the notion of HSC exhaustion. The cellularity of the human bone marrow diminishes with increasing age. At birth, 80–100 percent of the marrow is made up of hematopoietic cells, with the balance occupied by fat, whereas in adults younger than sixty-five years the marrow cellularity is approximately 50 percent, further declining to 30 percent by age seventy-five. Furthermore, hemoglobin levels, which indicate the number of circulating red blood cells, are lower, on average, in older adults (see below). In human and mouse bone marrow, hematopoietic progenitor cells from older individuals exhibit reduced capacity to proliferate in vitro. A more physiologic assessment of HSC function may be obtained from transplantation studies. In mice, bone marrow cells from older donors work as well as those from young mice in restoring hematopoiesis in irradiated recipients, while in humans, bone marrow transplants are successfully performed from donors in their seventies. Old HSCs appear, therefore, to be of equal quality to younger ones, insofar as this can be estimated, but to be fewer in number with age. Overall, theoretical considerations combined with the laboratory and clinical data suggest that aging does reduce the proliferative capacity of HSCs. This reduction is too small to be clinically significant under normal circumstances, although it may result in a reduction in the reserve capacity of the marrow, and could account for an increased susceptibility to anemia in older adults.

Aging and anemia

The chief function of red blood cells is to deliver oxygen to the metabolizing tissues of the body. To ensure adequate performance of this essential function, the quantity of circulating red blood cells or red cell mass (as reflected by the blood hemoglobin level) is tightly regulated. If the red cell mass falls then the amount of oxygen delivered to body tissues is reduced. The peritubular cells of the kidney are particularly sensitive to reductions in oxygen delivery. Under such conditions, these cells are stimulated to release the hormone erythropoietin, which in turn acts upon the bone marrow to increase the production of red blood cells. This leads to improvement in oxygen delivery to body tissues, including the kidney, and thus secretion of erythropoietin is suppressed and the rate of red blood cell production reduced. In this way, red cell production may increase as much as tenfold in times of need, and the red cell mass is usually maintained in a very narrow range.

When these regulatory mechanisms fail, and the red cell mass falls to an abnormally low level, *anemia* results. Anemia may be caused by an increased rate of red cell loss or from a decreased rate of red cell production. Blood loss may be caused by bleeding or by a shortening of the red blood cell life span (known as *hemolysis*). Red cell production may be suppressed by exposure to various toxins (e.g., certain drugs or radiation), by nutritional deficiencies (e.g., of iron, folic acid, or vitamin B12), by bacterial or viral infections, or by involvement of the marrow by primary or metastatic cancer.

It has been shown in numerous population studies that older adults have, on average, lower hemoglobin levels than do younger adults. These observations have led some investigators to conclude that a decline in red cell mass is inherent to the aging process, and that age-specific normal ranges ought to be employed in diagnosing anemia in older people. This issue is complicated, however, by the fact that disorders associated with anemia occur more frequently with increasing age. When only healthy subjects are studied, however, the difference in mean hemoglobin between older and younger adults largely disappears. Therefore anemia in an elderly person cannot be ascribed simply to "old age"; an underlying cause should be sought.

Neoplastic diseases of the blood

With the exception of acute lymphoblastic leukemia, which has its peak incidence in childhood, cancer of the blood is a disease of older adults. While the "cause" of cancer is not entirely understood, great advances in our understanding of the nature of this disease were made in the last two decades of the twentieth century. It is now apparent that in most, and likely in all, cancers, genetic mutations lead to alterations in the normal cellular programs of differentiation, proliferation, and programmed cell death (*apoptosis*). Many of these discoveries have come from research on the cancers of the blood.

Myelodysplasia

The synonymous terms *myelodysplasia* and *preleukemia* refer to acquired abnormalities of the bone marrow that precede the onset of acute leukemia. These conditions are characterized by chronic anemia, often in combination with reduced white blood cell and platelet counts. Accordingly, patients with myelodysplasia experience symptoms of fatigue, recurrent infections, and easy bruising or bleeding. Paradoxically, despite the reduced numbers of mature blood cells in the peripheral blood, the bone marrow in myelodysplasia shows increased proliferation of developing blood cells. The development of these blood cells is abnormal, however, and their fate is to be destroyed before they can leave the marrow and enter the blood. Myelodysplasia is rarely diagnosed in patients younger than fifty years, and the peak incidence of this disease is seen in the age range eighty to eighty-four years. No cure for myelodysplasia is known, but the symptoms of this condition can be alleviated by transfusions of red cells and platelets and in some cases by injections of the hormone erythropoietin, which stimulates red cell production. These therapies do not alter the natural progression of myelodysplasia to acute leukemia, which may occur over the course of months or years, and which is heralded by the accumulation of cells called *blasts* in the marrow. These cells are the hallmark of acute leukemia.

Acute leukemia

The term *leukemia* comes from the Greek, meaning "white blood," and refers to a set of diseases in which neoplastic white blood cells (blasts) accumulate in the blood and bone marrow. These cells fail to differentiate into mature, functional cells of the eight normal lineages, and furthermore suppress the growth of normal blood cells. The symptoms of acute leukemia are a consequence of a lack of normal red blood cells (anemia), white blood cells (*leukopenia*), and platelets (*thrombocytopenia*), deficiencies that result, respectively, in fatigue, susceptibility to infection, and bruising or bleeding. This disease progresses rapidly, and without treatment is invariably fatal, usually within weeks or months. The treatment of acute leukemia is based upon the use of chemotherapy and radiation therapy, sometimes with the addition of bone marrow transplantation. The goal of these treatments is to destroy all of the leukemic blasts, and to allow the residual normal HSCs to repopulate the bone marrow and restore normal blood production. The first aim of treatment is to eradicate all detectable leukemic blasts in a patient—if this is achieved, the disease is said to be in *remission*. Remission is not, however, tantamount to cure; almost invariably a small number of leukemic cells survive the therapy and eventually the leukemia returns or *relapses*. Acute leukemia may develop from preexisting myelodysplasia, or it may arise de novo. Like myelodysplasia, acute leukemia is more common in older adults than in younger adults; approximately 60 percent of cases are diagnosed in patients older than sixty years. Numerous clinical studies have shown, however, that older adults with acute leukemia are significantly less likely to achieve remission or cure than are younger patients. Currently, even with the best available therapy, few people older than sixty years diagnosed with acute leukemia survive longer than three years. There are likely two reasons for this poorer prognosis. First, the therapies for acute leukemia are themselves toxic and harsh. Older patients are more likely to have other significant health problems, and are therefore more susceptible to the adverse effects of therapy and are less likely to receive as high a dose. Second, the biology of acute leukemia appears to be different in older adults, perhaps because of accumulation of additional genetic mutations in HSCs over time. In older adults, acute leukemia is more likely to follow a period of myelodysplasia (see above), or to occur after previous exposure to chemotherapy for another malignancy. Leukemia in older patients is also more likely to exhibit certain characteristic chromosomal abnormalities in the leukemic clone. These features are associated with a poorer response to therapy, whether in younger or older patients.

Chronic leukemia

In contrast to acute leukemia, the chronic leukemias are slowly developing conditions and may be present for years while causing minimal symptoms. The two main forms of chronic leukemia seen in adults are chronic myeloid leukemia (CML) and chronic lymphocytic leukemia (CLL).

Chronic myeloid leukemia is characterized by the accumulation of an abnormal clone of cells of the neutrophil lineage (a type of white blood cell), in various stages of differentiation, in the bone marrow, the peripheral blood, and the spleen, which typically becomes massively enlarged. In the *chronic phase* of CML there are few symptoms, but this phase inevitably gives way, after a period of two to five years, to an *acute phase* or *blast crisis*, which resembles acute leukemia and carries a grave prognosis. CML cells invariably carry a chromosomal translocation affecting chromosomes 9 and 22, which is known as the Philadelphia chromosome; this translocation results in the fusion of two genes, BCR and ABL. The presence of the BCR-ABL fusion appears to be necessary and sufficient for the development of CML. Currently, the mainstays of therapy for CML are *interferon alpha*, a natural substance that can induce long-term remissions in this disease, and allogeneic bone marrow transplantation. A recently developed drug that specifically inhibits the action of BCR-ABL shows tremendous promise as a CML treatment.

In chronic lymphocytic leukemia, there is accumulation of a clone of abnormal lymphocytes. This initially causes no symptoms, but over time there is progressive accumulation of the malignant cells in the lymph nodes, bone marrow, and spleen. Anemia and thrombocytopenia result, with symptoms of fatigue and bruising or bleeding. Normal lymphocytes are suppressed, and susceptibility to infections is increased. CLL runs an indolent course, and often no treatment is needed for several years following diagnosis. No cure for CLL is currently available, and treatment comprises supportive measures, such as red cell transfusion, and chemotherapy with oral or intravenous agents to control bulky disease in lymph nodes and spleen.

Cancers of the lymphatic system

Lymphoma is cancer of the lymphocytes and arises outside the bone marrow, in the lymph nodes, the spleen, or the lymphatic tissue of the gut. This disease typically causes enlargement of the lymph nodes and constitutional symptoms such as fever, sweats, and weight loss. Frequently, lymphoma invades the bone marrow, causing anemia, thrombocytopenia, and leukopenia. There exists a great number of subtypes of lymphoma that differ substantially in their clinical behavior, ranging from indolent or "low grade" lymphomas that may cause minimal symptoms to aggressive "high grade" lymphomas that run a stormy course and require urgent treatment. Lymphoma is treated with chemotherapy, sometimes combined with radiation therapy. Although some cases of lymphoma can be cured, these remain in the minority.

Multiple myeloma is a neoplastic disease affecting the antibody-producing cells, or plasma cells. Like other malignancies of the blood, the incidence of this condition increases with age; 98

percent of cases occur in patients older than forty years. In myeloma, malignant plasma cells accumulate in the bone marrow. These malignant cells produce great quantities of an antibody, known as a *monoclonal paraprotein*. This antibody is not produced in response to infection and is useless to the body. Indeed, the paraprotein may injure the kidney, and as malignant plasma cells accumulate, normal plasma cells, and other bone marrow cells, are suppressed and the production of normal antibodies is severely impaired. Anemia is also frequently present. In addition, the malignant cells secrete chemicals, known as cytokines, which cause the bones to lose calcium and weaken. Hence, patients with myeloma may experience fatigue, frequent infections, pain and fractures of bone, and kidney failure. No cure for multiple myeloma is known, although treatment with chemotherapy may temporarily reduce the burden of malignant cells and alleviate symptoms. Drugs that stimulate the bones to retain calcium have been proven effective in reducing bone loss and its complications.

The presence of a paraprotein is not sufficient to establish the diagnosis of myeloma. Indeed, monoclonal paraproteins are common in older adults, but usually occur in the absence of the accumulation of malignant plasma cells, anemia, bone destruction, and kidney damage characteristic of myeloma. These cases are referred to as "monoclonal gammopathy of unknown significance" (MGUS). Some cases of MGUS probably represent early myeloma, or a pre-malignant condition that leads to myeloma. In most cases, however, this condition remains entirely benign.

RICHARD A. WELLS

See also CANCER, BIOLOGY; CANCER, DIAGNOSIS AND MANAGEMENT; CELLULAR AGING.

BIBLIOGRAPHY

BALDWIN, J. G. "Hematopoietic Function in the Elderly." *Archives of Internal Medicine* 148 (1988): 2544–2546.
COHEN, H. J. "Disorders of the Blood." In *Oxford Textbook of Geriatric Medicine*. Edited by J. G. Evans and T. F. Williams. Oxford, U.K.: Oxford University Press, 1992. Pages 435–441.
LATAGLIATA, R.; PETTI, M. C.; and MANDELLI, F. "Acute Myeloid Leukemia in the Elderly: 'per aspera ad astra'?" *Leukemia Research* 23 (1999): 603–613.
NILSSON-EHLE, H.; JAGENBURG, R.; LANDHAL, S.; SVANBORG, A.; and WESTIN, J. "Decline of Blood Haemoglobin in the Aged: A Longitudinal Study of an Urban Swedish Population from Age 70 to 81." *British Journal of Haematology* 71 (1989): 437–442.
TIMIRAS, M. L., and BROWNSTEIN, H. "Prevalence of Anemia and Correlation of Hemoglobin with Age in a Geriatric Screening Population." *Journal of the American Geriatrics Society* 35 (1987): 639–643.
WHITTAKER, J. A., and HOLMES J. A., eds. *Leukaemia and Related Disorders*, 3d ed. Oxford, U.K.: Blackwell Science Ltd., 1998.
WILLIAMS, W. J. "Hematology in the Aged." In *Hematology*, 5th ed. Edited by E. Beutler, M. A. Lichtman, B. S. Collier, and T. J. Kipps. New York: McGraw-Hill Inc., 1995. Pages 72–77.
ZAUBER, N. P., and ZAUBER, A. G. "Hematologic Data of Healthy Very Old People." *Journal of the American Medical Association* 257 (1987): 2181–2184.

BOARD AND CARE HOMES

Board and care homes are a community-based residential option for older adults requiring care and services. As part of the continuum of care from home to nursing home, they assist primarily those not needing nursing or medical care but unable to live independently due to physical or cognitive impairments. Homes range in size and in extent to which the environment is institutional, from very small, family-style, residential settings in communities of single-family homes to larger, multiroom, more "institutional" facilities (Morgan et al., 1995). Regardless of size, board and care facilities offer residents shelter (room), meals (board), twenty-four-hour supervision, and a range of services, often for a minimal cost.

Defining board and care

The legal definition of what constitutes a board and care home depends on local, state, and national statutes, and is related to the health and welfare agencies that monitor homes. Nomenclature varies widely. As noted by Robert Rubinstein, the middle range of care settings includes such alternatives as sheltered housing, domiciliary care, adult foster care, small congregate homes, and assisted living. The same name may be used for different types of settings in different states, making it hard to distinguish board and care facilities (McCoy and Conley). However, the term "board and care" is often used to describe the range of non-nursing home care arrangements, including many of those listed above.

Distinctions between board and care and "assisted living" are blurred. Assisted living is the name given to a consumer-focused residential model emphasizing privacy, independence, decision making, and autonomy. Moreover, the label "assisted living" has been used to differentiate this type of housing from conventional board and care housing and the negative connotations that some people associate with it (GAO, 1992; Kane et al.). In many states considerable overlap exists between board and care and assisted living, and the terms may be used interchangeably (Mollica).

Size is often a distinguishing feature in board and care settings. In particular, small board and care homes are often distinguished from larger, multiunit, purpose-built facilities. Both size and coresidence of the operator differentiate small, family-type homes from larger, more institutional, staffed homes. Studies of small board and care homes have found them to be much like extended family settings in single-family homes. The majority of small home operators are middle-aged women, many of whom have limited education (Morgan et al., 1995). Living spaces and meals are often shared in these small homes, which are believed to serve a more vulnerable adult population who are poor, have inadequate kin and other support, and suffer from long-term disabilities, mental illness, mental retardation, and chronic physical conditions (Eckert and Lyon).

Estimated numbers of beds

The number of board and care facilities is difficult to establish, since there is no generally accepted definition of what constitutes such a facility or any systematic way to count them. With the emergence of purpose-built facilities offering assisted living services during the 1990s, the numbers of older adults being served in non-medical care settings has increased substantially. Prior to the boom in assisted living, a 1987 industry survey identified about 563,000 board and care beds in 41,000 licensed homes nationally. A 1992 GAO study found some 75,000 licensed and unlicensed homes serving a million people, including half a million disabled older adults. A 1999 GAO report on assisted living that includes board and care facilities, estimates the number of beds in the United States at between 800,000 and 1.5 million. The report notes that consumer demand is expected to grow significantly as the projected number of elderly Americans in need of long-term care doubles between 2000 and 2020.

Resident characteristics

Studies of home residents find that most of them are older, frequently widowed, and lacking proximate kin (Morgan et al., 1995). Some homes accept younger physically or mentally disabled adults as well as elderly residents. In the mid-1980s it was estimated that older people constitute 40 to 60 percent of the board and care population, with the largest category of residents being older, functionally impaired women (Dobkin).

Most home residents have multiple health problems or cognitive problems that make it risky or impractical to live independently (Dittmar and Smith; Morgan et al., 1995). In many cases the number of limitations in Activities of Daily Living among residents in board and care homes approaches that found among nursing home residents (Morgan et al., 1995; Morgan et al., 2001).

In small homes, a high percentage of residents are economically disadvantaged, receiving support from Supplemental Security Income or state programs to provide for their care (Morgan et al., 1995). Fees that residents pay for care and housing come from state-funded programs, personal savings, Social Security or other retirement benefits, family contributions, or private insurance. Since fees range from a few hundred dollars to several thousand dollars per month, board and care has met a need to provide an alternative for low-income elderly persons, who would be unable to afford the newer assisted-living facilities on meager private resources.

Services

The goal of board and care facilities is to provide housing and supportive services to individuals who are sufficiently impaired to require regular assistance with or supervision of daily tasks but are not in need of medical intervention (i.e., nursing care) on a regular basis. As with many older adults, needs at these midlevel facilities are for assistance with personal care, mobility, and supportive services, such as meals, laundry, medication management, and housekeeping.

The services provided in board and care homes, while variable across facilities, focus on helping with the daily tasks and personal care needs of residents, rather than with health care services. The range of services provided to residents is quite broad, responding both to their diverse needs (driven by both physical and cognitive impairments) and to variations among the facilities in terms of size, willingness to deal with more difficult or advanced care needs, and the fees paid for care (Morgan et al., 1995). Some homes offer a substantial range of services, while others provide a limited set at lower cost. In general, however, basic services to residents include meals, room, twenty-four-hour oversight, assistance in personal care (bathing, dressing, etc.), homemaking services, and assistance with mobility and with taking medications (Morgan et al., 1995). In addition, recreation, transportation, beautician/barber, and laundry services may be included. To the extent that homes attempt to keep residents from relocating to nursing homes, more advanced care may also be arranged, including assistance with feeding, toileting, mobility, and orientation, and even some nursing services. These services, enabling homes to keep residents and permit them to "age in place" as health declines, may be provided outside the home or by outside service providers delivering care within the board and care home.

Funding and regulation

The topics of funding and regulation are typically discussed together, since they are related. For much of its history, board and care has operated as a "grassroots" option, out of view of public funding and regulation (Morgan et al., 1993; Nolin and Mollica, 2001). While public sources of funding have been unavailable throughout most of this history, board and care homes have also, until recently, been largely unregulated, especially if they are small (Morgan et al., 1995). Given that public funding has focused on medical needs of older adults via Medicare, and nursing homes via Medicaid, the nonmedical housing and support provided by board and care homes has been privately paid by most residents or their families. In some cases, state programs have provided support to the poorest elders living in board and care homes (Dobkin, 1989).

That situation has been changed by the utilization of Medicaid waiver monies and funds to support community-based care, thus providing public monies to support the care of older adults residing in board and care homes in some states. This change has been motivated by the generally lower costs for board and care than for nursing homes, with the expectation that public costs overall would remain lower for individuals able to remain in board and care facilities rather than nursing homes (Nolin and Mollica, 2001).

At the same time that funding is beginning to flow from federal sources, states are moving rapidly in the direction of regulating smaller, non-nursing home facilities, driven both by the boom in assisted living and by the earlier reports of poor care in board and care homes (GAO, 1992). State regulations include size requirements, staffing, services, whether units may be shared, transfer policy, and resident rights (see Mollica, 2001). It is unclear whether board and care will flourish, change, or disappear under the dual thrusts of state regulation and the growth in private-pay assisted living facilities.

J. Kevin Eckert
Leslie A. Morgan

See also Assisted Living; Housing; Long-Term Care.

BIBLIOGRAPHY

Dittmar, N., and Smith, G. P. *Evaluation of Board and Care Homes: Summary of Survey Procedures and Findings*. Denver, Colo.: Denver Research Institute, 1983.

Dobkin, L. *The Board and Care System: A Regulatory Jungle*. Washington, D.C.: American Association of Retired Persons, 1989.

Eckert, J. K., and Lyon, S. "Regulation of Board and Care Homes: Research to Guide Public Policy." *Journal of Aging and Social Policy* 3, no. 3/4 (1991): 147–162.

General Accounting Office (GAO). *Board and Care Homes: Elderly at Risk from Mishandled Medications*. House Select Committee on Aging, HRD 92-45. Washington D.C.: U.S. Government Printing Office, 1992.

General Accounting Office (GAO). *Assisted Living: Quality-of-Care and Consumer Protection Issues in Four States*. GAO/HEHS-99-27. Washington, D.C.: U.S. Government Printing Office, 1999.

Kane, R.; Wilson, K. B.; and Clemmer, E. *Assisted Living in the United States: A New Paradigm for Residential Care for Frail Older Persons*. Washington, D.C.: American Association of Retired Persons, 1993.

McCoy, J., and Conley, R. "Surveying Board and Care Homes: Issues and Data Collection

Problems." *The Gerontologist* 30 (1990): 147–153.

MOLLICA, R. L. "State Policy and Regulations." In *Assisted Living: Residential Care in Transition.* Edited by Sheryl I. Zimmerman, Philip D. Sloane, and J. Kevin Eckert. Baltimore: Johns Hopkins University Press, 2001.

MORGAN, L. A.; ECKERT, J. K.; and LYON, S. M. "Social Marginality: The Case of Small Board and Care Homes." *Journal of Aging Studies* 7, no. 4 (1993): 383–394.

MORGAN, L. A.; ECKERT, K. J.; and LYON, S. M. *Small Board-and-Care Homes: Residential Care in Transition.* Baltimore: Johns Hopkins University Press, 1995.

MORGAN, L. A.; GRUBER-BALDINI, A. L.; and MAGAZINER, J. "Resident Characteristics." In *Assisted Living: Residential Care in Transition.* Edited by Sheryl I. Zimmerman, Philip D. Sloane, and J. Kevin Eckert. Baltimore: Johns Hopkins University Press, 2001.

NOLIN, M., and MOLLICA, R. In *Assisted Living: Residential Care in Transition.* Edited by Sheryl I. Zimmerman, Philip D. Sloan, and J. Kevin Eckert. Baltimore: Johns Hopkins University Press, In press.

NOLIN, M. A., and MOLLICA, R. L. "Residential Care/Assisted Living in the Changing Health Care Environment." In *Assisted Living: Needs, Policies in Residential Care for the Elderly.* Edited by Sheryl Zimmerman, Philip D. Sloane, and J. Kevin Ekert. Baltimore: John Hopkins University Press, 2001.

RUBINSTEIN, R. L. "Long Term Care in Special Community Settings." In *Long Term Care.* Edited by Z. Harel and R. Dunkle. New York: Springer, 1995.

BRAIN

Humans and other vertebrates possess a central nervous system (CNS)—the brain and spinal cord—containing specialized cells called neurons. The nervous system is essential for virtually every aspect of life and, along with the body's other systems (muscular-skeletal, endocrine, etc.), performs the following seven basic, interrelated tasks:

1. Maintenance of vital functions, including control of the cardiovascular system and homeostasis (regulation of temperature, weight, internal milieu in general).
2. Obtaining information via the sensory systems (auditory, visual, somatosensory, olfactory, etc.) and processing that information. Information about ourselves and the world is provided by the sensory portions of the nervous system.
3. Storage and retrieval of information by the processes of learning and memory. Changes occur in the brain every time something new is learned, and the changes often last in the form of memories. Moreover, the brain must be adept at retrieving that information from storage when needed.
4. Production of behavior, including movement, locomotion, autonomic responses, and communicative behavior such as language. The brain's motor systems operate skeletal muscles that move the limbs, facial muscles, mouth, vocal cords, and so on.
5. Integration of information and output: tying things together to make "decisions" ranging from simple reflexes to complex social and cognitive processes (intelligence, language, spatial orientation, etc.).
6. Modulation of the overall activity levels of the brain and body associated with emotion, arousal, and sleep.
7. Carrying out the genetic mandate to pass on one's genes to the next generation, especially with respect to sex, reproductive behavior, parenting, and aggression.

It is evident from our everyday observations that any or all of the seven functions may operate at sub-par levels as people get older. For example, maintaining body temperature may become more difficult under extreme conditions; the eyes, ears, and other senses may not pick up as much as they used to; it can become harder to remember names; athletic skills decline; "intelligence" for new technological concepts seems poorer compared to that of young people; a good night's sleep is often harder to get; and the frequency of sexual activity may change. Because all seven functions are beholden to the nervous system, it follows that age-related changes in the system's components are part and parcel of these problems.

Understanding how the nervous system and its components fare as individuals age, how age-related neural changes are manifested behaviorally, and how this knowledge may be used to improve the quality of life is an immensely daunting task because, irrespective of aging, the nervous system is bafflingly complex.

Figure 1

Midsagittal view of the human brain, which would be visible if the brain was separated into two halves and viewed from the (inside) cut surface.

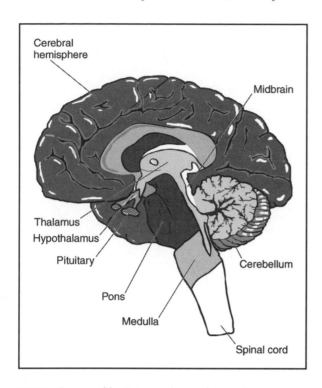

SOURCE: Suggested by Rosenzweig, Mark R.; Leiman, A. L.; Breedlove, S. M. *Biological Psychology.* Sunderland, Mass.: Sinauer Associates, 1999.

The nervous system and its complexity

The number of neurons in the human brain is vast—many billions (although glial cells, which provide various support functions, are even more numerous). A thread-like axon (nerve fiber) extends from the neuron, often branching repeatedly, to provide functional connections to other neurons located at its endings (terminals), sometimes at remote locations within the nervous system. Electrical impulses (action potentials) are generated in or near a neuron's cell body and travel outward along the axons, much as telegraph impulses are sent from an operator, traversing wires to receiving destinations (other neurons). A unique feature of neurons that greatly increases the number of axon terminals that can contact them are dendrites—elaborate tree-like arrays emanating from the cell body. The evolution of extensive dendritic trees, coupled with branching axons, has led to the development of neural "wiring diagrams" of enormous complexity. The situation is further complicated by the properties of synapses, the sites where dendrites and axon terminals "communicate." For the most part, the communication between neurons uses chemical neurotransmitters that are typically stored in the axon terminals. Packets of neurotransmitter molecules are released by mechanisms associated with the arrival of nerve impulses generated by the axons' parent neuron. The neurotransmitter quickly diffuses across the narrow synaptic cleft to reach a dendrite or cell body of the target neuron. The neurotransmitter molecules find their way to synaptic receptors, specialized sites in or on the receiving neuron that react with the neurotransmitter. The reaction between neurotransmitter and synaptic receptors alters some physiological properties of the receiving neuron, changing its activity and output. This neuron is, of course, connected to other neurons via the synapses made by its own axon terminals, which are in turn affected. And so on.

A number of different types of neurotransmitters are used by the nervous system, such as acetylcholine, dopamine, serotonin, and many others. Moreover, for a particular neurotransmitter there can be a variety of receptor types on one receiving neuron or another, so that the same neurotransmitter can produce different effects. The large number of possible permutations of neurotransmitter and receptors confer yet another layer of complexity upon the brain.

All of these highly varied, interacting aspects of neural circuits somehow work together in a manner that miraculously allows the nervous system to accomplish its basic functions. By the same token, they provide many "targets" for deleterious age-related changes. Reviewing some basics of the nervous system structure and function and their neurogerontological implications will help impart a sense of the mischief that aging can visit upon the nervous system. Then, after addressing a few of the basic functions, some possible ways by which age-related changes in the nervous system might be modified for the better will be outlined.

Organization of neurons into a nervous system and basic neuroanatomy

For meaningful behavior to occur, information from the body and environment must get into the brain, and instructions from the brain must be delivered to the muscles and glands so

Figure 2
Basic features of neurons.

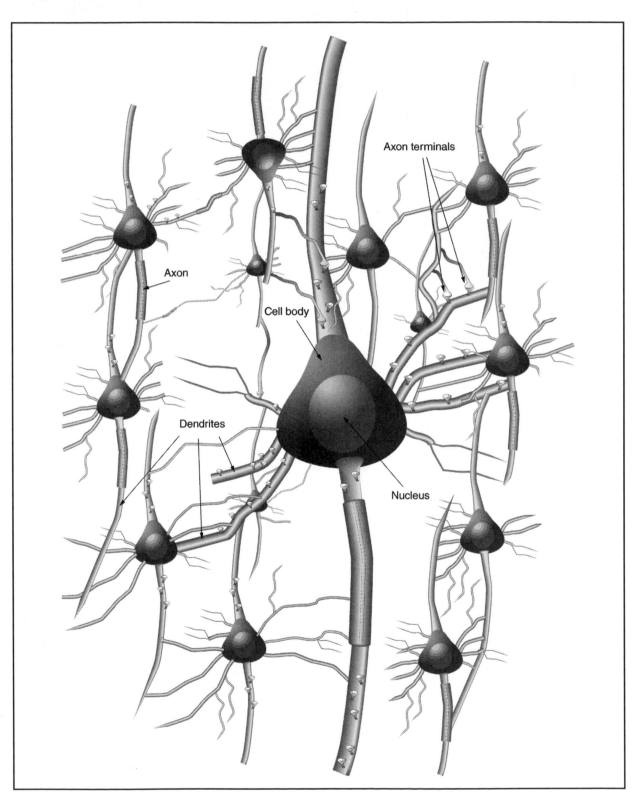

SOURCE: Suggested by Rosenzweig, Mark R.; Leiman, A. L.; Breedlove, S. M. *Biological Psychology* Sunderland, Mass.: Sinauer Associates, 1999.

that the body can perform. The portion of the nervous system that provides this interface is called the peripheral nervous system. It has two basic subsystems: the somatic system and the autonomic system. The somatic system brings information into the brain via axons originating in the sensory organs and sends messages outward through axons to skeletal muscles causing them to contract. The autonomic system is linked to our emotions and arousal states, and activates glands (e.g., sweat glands), smooth muscles (e.g., controlling the pupils of the eye, blood vessels, etc.), and heart. The autonomic system contains two subsystems: the sympathetic system readies us for action (increases heart rate, dilates pupils), whereas the parasympathetic system has the opposite effect, restoring us toward a resting level when warranted. Some age-related changes often occur in the peripheral systems, such as loss or thinning of nerve fibers or changes in the "target organs" (muscles and glands), and these may result in poorer performance.

In the central nervous system (CNS), the spinal cord extends below the brain, encased by the vertebral bones of the neck and back. The spinal cord relays incoming sensory messages from the periphery to the brain and outgoing instructions from the brain to spinal cord neurons whose axons leave the CNS to activate muscles. However, in addition to being a relay to and from the brain, the spinal cord itself contains impressive assemblies of neuronal circuitry that perform a number of sensory-motor behaviors, such as withdrawal from a painful stimulus or rhythmic movements associated with locomotion. Changes in the spinal cord can occur in older people that make it less efficient at relaying the information up and down.

Merging with the spinal cord is the brainstem, the lowest region of the brain. Its basic subdivisions (moving upwards) are the medulla, pons, and midbrain. At the top of the brainstem is the thalamus. The neural traffic between the brain and spinal cord travels along axons that traverse the brainstem. In addition, sensory information (coded in trains of action potentials) enters the brainstem from the head and the special sense organs (ears, eyes, etc.), while other messages leave the brainstem to control the face, mouth, eyes, and so on. The brainstem controls a number of activities without a necessary contribution from higher levels of the brain. For example, comparison of acoustic input from the two ears to compute the location of sounds in space is a function of brainstem circuits. Some regions of the brainstem are especially vulnerable to age-related changes that can affect a variety of behaviors.

Behind the brainstem, near the base of the skull, is the cerebellum. It plays key roles in coordinating movements, balance, and even some types of learning. The cerebellum has numerous axons communicating with the brainstem that, in turn, communicate with the higher regions of the brain and the spinal cord below. The cerebellum is required for balance, posture, gait, and the adjustment and coordination of movements. Age-related changes observed in neurons of the cerebellum include loss of dendrites and spines and changes in neurotransmitter systems, and these are likely to affect movements.

The bulk of the brain lies above and around the thalamus. The basal ganglia are prominent parts of the interior brain adjacent to the thalamus, and deal with movement (they play important roles in cognition, as well). To the side, but folded over so as to sit deep in the middle of the brain, is the hippocampus, a structure that is essential for certain types of learning and memory as well as spatial behaviors. The amygdala, along with the hypothalamus and other parts of the limbic system, comprise the "emotional brain." At the base of the brain is the hypothalamus, a collection of small subdivisions that regulate a number of essential functions such as eating and drinking, body temperature, biological rhythms, and reproductive behavior. The hypothalamus produces hormones that influence the release of other hormones by the neighboring pituitary gland. At least some of these hormone systems become less responsive with age because of reduced production by hypothalamic neurons, changes in receptor sensitivity for the hormones, and/or changes in the endocrine glands. The fact that relatively small hypothalamic subdivisions control important biological functions has suggested that subtle changes might contribute to aging in a fundamental way.

If one looks at a human brain, it is dominated by two large, folded cerebral hemispheres. On the surface of the hemispheres (and folded into the creases or sulci) are several layers of neurons that comprise the cerebral cortex. The cerebral cortex, working in concert with the rest of the brain, is capable of incredible feats, most notably in humans, in which its size and complexity far exceeds that of other species. Language, complex thoughts, logic, and many other "higher" functions are beholden to a highly advanced cerebral cortex. The left and right hemispheres communicate with one another with millions of axons, most of which are contained in a huge band of axons called the corpus callosum. Studies have found evidence that the transfer of information between cerebral hemispheres across the corpus callosum can be slowed or diminished with age.

Neurobiology and aging

In order to understand how the "slings and arrows" of aging can affect the brain, some basics of neurobiology must be appreciated.

Neurons lack the capacity to regenerate. With a few exceptions, new neurons are not produced once the maximum number is established early in life, and the ability of CNS neurons to be repaired when damaged is quite limited. We can lose neurons as we age, but we cannot grow new ones. The exact number of neurons lost by the human brain during aging has been elusive, plagued by methodological issues that include technical difficulty in counting neurons, post-mortem changes that can occur in human brains from autopsy, differences in the pre-mortem condition of young and old people who are autopsied (for example, older people are more likely to have died from chronic illnesses that could have resulted in brain pathology), and the unwitting inclusion of patients with undetected dementia. Even when nonhuman animals are studied, inconsistencies arise, stemming from species differences, variability among genetic strains within the same species, and the fact that different parts of the brain often show different age changes. All of this suggests that no general pattern of neuron loss occurs in aging nervous systems. However, there is a growing consensus that some older studies probably overestimated the degree to which neurons die as people age. The current view is more optimistic: at least in the neocortex, many (perhaps most) healthy older people exhibit a minimal loss of neurons, although other brain regions may be more vulnerable.

Neurons require a disproportionate share of the blood supply. Neurons have a ravenous appetite for the blood's precious cargo of glucose and oxygen, and the percentage of the body's blood and oxygen consumption in the brain at any time is far out of proportion with the rest of the body. It has to be this way because reducing the supply of blood/oxygen to neurons results in impairment, damage, or destruction depending on the severity and duration. Thus, conditions that reduce the brain's blood supply, such as atherosclerosis, diabetes, and, of course, stroke are cause for concern. Each of these conditions becomes more prevalent with age, as do other changes in the vascular system serving the brain, even in the absence of diseases.

Neurons are at risk from various toxins. Over a lifetime, neurons, like other cells, are exposed to toxins. These can be environmental or endogenous—produced by the brain itself. For example, glutamate is the major neurotransmitter used by neurons to synaptically activate (excite) other neurons. Under certain conditions, such as hypoxia or tissue damage, the effects of glutamate can become exaggerated, resulting in excessive entry of calcium into the neurons, and such excitotoxic events prove to be damaging to neurons. If aging were associated with weakening of the defenses against excitotoxicity, negative age effects could accrue. Indeed, this process appears to be involved in certain types of dementia and neurodegenerative conditions that can accompany aging.

The neuron's nucleus regulates many functions. The synthesis of proteins is coded by DNA, the genetic material found in the nucleus of neurons and other cells. Many varieties of protein are produced for use as structural components of neurons (e.g., the microtubules and microfilaments in axons that transport molecules used for neurotransmitters and provide structural support), enzymes that control the numerous biochemical reactions necessary for cellular activities, synaptic receptors, and many other uses. Damage to DNA that can accrue in cells with age has the potential to alter many facets of neuronal physiology.

Dendritic branches and spines are at risk with aging. The size, shape, orientation, and complexity of the neuron's dendritic tree have a great deal to do with the number of functioning contacts that can be made with other neurons. Dendritic spines are small extensions that provide many additional sites for synapses. One of the best documented age-related changes in neurons is a reduction in the number of dendritic branches and spines. Even if neurons do not die off, a loss of synaptic contacts is likely to reduce the information-processing capacity of neural circuits, negatively affecting brain function.

Parts of the brain are differentially vulnerable to aging.   Age effects vary greatly among different components of the nervous system. Various behavioral and cognitive functions are affected to different extents, depending on how each brain region fares. For example, the hippocampus is very important for storing memories. Research has shown that portions of the hippocampus are often damaged during aging, and this may be responsible for learning and memory deficits.

The speed of information processing slows with age.   Behavior and cognition tend to become slower with age. Indeed, behavioral/cognitive slowing has been proposed as a marker of aging (i.e., a measure that can differentiate chronological age from functional age). There is a good deal of research indicating a general slowing of brain processes, with cognitive slowing likely to reflect the sluggishness of smaller components (sensory, motor, and interconnected central circuits). Possible causes of slowing might include slower conduction of action potentials because of changes in the axons; slower synaptic transmission because of structural and/or chemical changes; diminished intracellular metabolism (e.g., associated with damage to energy-producing mitochondria); reduced production of neurotransmitters or other critical products; impaired gene expression (e.g., associated with DNA damage); and many other potential changes that would interfere with optimal neural performance. Changes in the peripheral sensory and motor systems (e.g., loss or thinning of axons) probably make only small contributions to slowing. More salient are the central neural circuits that intervene between stimuli and responses.

Aging and the basic functions of the nervous system

Only a few examples of how aging affects the seven functions of the nervous system are presented, but they show the types of age effects that have been observed.

Obtaining information with the sensory systems.   The neural means by which sensory stimuli are experienced involve multistage processes requiring high-quality representation of stimuli by the peripheral sensory apparatus, undistorted neural messages carried by action potentials into the brain, and accurate processing of the information by the central sensory systems. Disruption of any of these processes with age would have the potential to cause problems in the sensory domain. The sad truth is that our sensory abilities almost inevitably decline with age. The rate and severity of the decline may vary considerably among individuals and across sensory modalities within individuals, but few, if any, octogenarians possess the same sensory capacities they started out with. All the sensory modalities suffer with age, including hearing and the auditory system.

The term "presbycusis" or "presbyacusis" is typically used to describe the changes in hearing associated with aging. Whereas the most commonly mentioned manifestation of presbycusis is a loss of sensitivity for high frequency sounds, the types of hearing problems confronting older listeners extend to speech perception, hearing in noisy backgrounds, distorted loudness of sounds, and tinnitus ("ringing in the ears"). Presbycusis typically involves progressive damage to the inner ear: the cochlea (where acoustic events are ultimately translated to neural events) and the cochlear neurons (where sounds are coded as trains of action potentials and sent, via the auditory nerve, to the brain for processing). Damage to any part of the cochlea diminishes the amount and quality of auditory input to the brain, with deleterious effects on hearing.

It is in the CNS where the action potential–coded sensory information originating in the inner ear is somehow transformed into auditory perception and experience. The central components of the auditory system are threatened by two adverse correlates of aging. First, changes in the structure or function of the brain's neurons occur in the context of biological aging discussed above. Second, an otherwise "healthy" central auditory system may be secondarily affected by damage to the cochlea. It has been shown that, when certain central neurons are deprived of their normal synaptic input, physiological and anatomical changes are induced. The effects can produce additional hearing deficits. Because the altered neurons provide input to other neurons, the effects could spread. Because the central sensory systems of older individuals might be affected in two rather different ways, it is useful to differentiate two types of age-related central changes. The term *central effects of biological aging* (CEBA) refers to sensory changes stemming from age-related changes in neurons, metabolism, support systems, and so on. The term *central effects of peripheral pathology* (CEPP) also refers to sensory changes associated with modifications of neurons and neural circuits in the brain. However, these are secondary to the removal or alteration of peripheral sensory input. It would be expected that CEBA and CEPP often occur in combination, since many older people have some loss of receptor function as well as various CNS deficits.

Whether CEBA, CEPP, or both are at work, the changes that occur in the auditory CNS are multifaceted. Some neurons die off or come to perform less efficiently, becoming "sluggish" in their responses to sound. By contrast, other neurons come to respond more vigorously, probably because aging is accompanied by deficits in inhibitory neurotransmitters, which normally dampen the responses of neurons and prevent hyperactivity. A combination of these and other types of central changes are likely to contribute to difficulties that many older people have in understanding speech, even when it is loud enough for them to hear.

The storage of information (learning and memory). Research indicates that, to varying extents (according to individual differences, genotype, species, etc.), circuits and neurotransmitter systems relevant for learning and memory often exhibit deleterious changes with age; deficiencies in any of these can cause some sort of learning/memory deficit. Learning and memory involve modifications (plasticity) of synapses in neural circuits. For example, one type of synaptic change associated with learning is *long-term potentiation* (LTP): lasting changes in neural responses induced by situations similar to those involved with learning. Experiments have shown changes in LTP in hippocampus neurons of old rats that have learning deficits. Thus, in addition to the general types of changes that occur in aging nervous systems, processes specific to learning may be affected as well.

Production of behavior (movement, etc.). Whereas some of the age-related declines in motor skill are associated with a decrease in muscle mass and a loss of strength, the most important and interesting stories are found in the workings of the nervous system. A large portion of the nervous system is devoted to movement—deciding what to do, planning how to do it, and carrying it out. Each has been demonstrated to exhibit some degree of age-related change that might result in less effective movement. For example, the primary motor cortex is the major

source of descending axons to the motor neurons of the spinal cord that control the muscles. Several studies have described abnormalities in the large neurons of the primary motor cortex of older brains, including a loss of dendrites and dendritic spines. In addition to the motor cortex, the basal ganglia (the next lower set of structures controlling movement) are involved in self-initiated, complex movements, the control of postural adjustments, and other aspects of motor behavior. The effects of damage to the basal ganglia are evident in the motor symptoms of Parkinson's and Huntington's diseases, disorders affecting these structures. Some of the mild motor disturbances that occur in healthy older people could be a consequence of less severe basal ganglia damage that has been observed during normal aging.

Modulation of behavior (emotion, arousal, stress). Our behavior varies constantly—up and down, this way and that way—in accordance with emotions, arousal, and biological clocks. One powerful modulator of behavior is stress: Various stimuli, events, or situations that are actually or potentially threatening (stressors) elicit activation of the sympathetic nervous system and a sequence of hormonal reactions, including the release of glucocorticoid hormones from the adrenal gland. Whereas the stress response is adaptive (e.g., it increases the probability of surviving dangerous situations), too much stress is generally considered to be a bad thing. Indeed, high blood pressure, suppression of the immune system, and exacerbation of diseases are known concomitants of stress. Thus, the relationship between stress and aging is potentially important. Moreover, there is evidence that, over time, glucocorticoids can actually damage the hippocampus, contributing to negative changes in the aging brain.

Modifying changes in the aging nervous system

Neural plasticity is a term that describes the ability of synapses, dendrites, axons, and other aspects of neurons to change—usually in an adaptive fashion. Plasticity is very potent in developing organisms, and it is now established that older brains retain much capacity for change as well. Research has shown that new synapses can form in older brains in response to injury or environmental manipulations, and that dendrites continue to be modifiable. However, the process generally takes longer and may not reach the magnitude typical of younger brains. The ability of the adult nervous system to engage mechanisms of synaptic plasticity has at least two important implications. First, degenerative tendencies may be counteracted by replacement of damaged synapses and repair of neural circuits. Second, the nervous system can continue to manifest the normal, adaptive types of synaptic plasticity exhibited by young individuals.

The dynamic properties of the older nervous system provide potential opportunities for the development of strategies aimed at modulating the direction or severity of negative age-related changes. A number of approaches are being investigated by researchers. In one way or another, most approaches attempt to enhance neural functioning by promoting the activity of various neurotransmitters or other physiologically important substances that protect neurons from age-related damage or improve neural functioning per se. For example, diets that promote the general health of cardiovascular and other systems are also good for the nervous system.

Neurotrophic factors such as *nerve growth factor* (NGF) are essential for the maintenance, growth, and survival of neurons both during development and in adults. Administration of neurotrophic factors has been shown to retard or prevent neural degeneration in experimental animals, and infusion of NGF may be able to prevent shrinkage of neurons typically observed with age. It appears that neurotrophic factors may have a variety of potentially beneficial effects on the aging nervous system. Some of these may be harnessed for clinical use.

Calorically restricted diets can extend longevity of rodents, slow certain age-related physiological declines, and decrease tumors and diseases. Although much of this research has focused on non-neural systems, there is ample evidence that dietary restriction modulates aging of the brain. Effects of dietary restriction on some of the general concomitants of neural aging, such as accumulation of lipofuscin ("age pigment") in neurons, the efficacy of glial cells, and loss of dendritic spines, have been reported.

Relatively simple environmental manipulations can have beneficial effects on the brain. Young and old rats living in an "enriched" environment (e.g., ten rats per cage, large space, toys) may exhibit a thicker cerebral cortex, compared to like-aged unenriched rats. Enhance-

ment of dendritic growth and complexity have also been demonstrated in studies of environmental enrichment. Some evidence has linked neurotrophic factors to environmental enrichment and improved cognitive performance. The expression of NGF has been found to increase under these conditions. It could be that enriched environments or behaviors are associated with increased neural activity, which results in an upregulation of nerve growth factors, which in turn leads to enhanced neuronal survival, growth, and plasticity.

Unfortunately, age-related damage to neurons can be too severe to be managed by neurotrophins or environmental manipulations. This is especially true of neurodegenerative diseases. In such cases, transplantation or grafting of new neurons into the damaged site might prove to be feasible approach. The main problems are survival of the graft and, more importantly, appropriate rewiring of circuitry with the host brain. There is a tendency of the grafted tissue to make contacts appropriate for their neurotransmitters and circuits, although this depends on brain region and other variables. The possibility of replacing brain tissue lost to aging—thereby restoring function—is intriguing. Although controversial and inconsistent, improvements have been obtained by grafting tissue from the adrenal gland or fetal substantia nigra into Parkinson's patients. Encouraging results have been obtained from animal research in other brain regions as well, and several studies have shown that fetal brain tissue can be successfully transplanted into the brains of aged rodents. A big issue is whether complex behaviors and cognitive processes of humans might ever benefit from neural grafting. It is one thing to enhance dopamine activity in Parkinson's patients and another to replace intricate neural circuitry underlying cognitive processes. The latter may never be attainable. For now, the utility of neural grafts is likely to be found in their capacity to generate growth factors and other beneficial substances, or boost the activity of certain circuits by replenishing neurotransmitters.

JAMES WILLOTT

See also ALZHEIMER'S DISEASE; BALANCE AND MOBILITY; CELLULAR AGING; DEMENTIA; EMOTION; HEARING; INTELLIGENCE; LANGUAGE DISORDERS; MEMORY; NEUROBIOLOGY; NEUROTRANSMITTERS; PARKINSONISM; STRESS AND COPING.

BIBLIOGRAPHY

ALBERT, M. L., and KNOEFEL, J. E., eds. *Clinical Neurology of Aging*, 2d ed. New York: Oxford University Press, 1994.

AMENTA, F. *Aging of the Autonomic Nervous System*. Boca Raton, Fla.: CRC Press, 1993.

CRAIK, F. I. M., and SALTHOUSE. T. A. *The Handbook of Aging and Cognition*. Hillsdale, N.J.: Erlbaum, 1992.

MANN, D. M. A. *Sense and Senility: The Neuropathology of the Aged Human Brain*. New York: Chapman and Hall, 1997.

MORLEY, J. E., and KORENMAN, STANLEY G. *Endocrinology and Metabolism in the Elderly*. Boston: Blackwell Scientific Publishers, 1992.

NUSSBAUM, P. D. *Handbook of Neuropsychology and Aging*. New York: Plenum, 1997.

SAPOLSKY, R. M. *Stress, the Aging Brain, and the Mechanisms of Neuron Death*. Cambridge: MIT Press, 1992.

SCHNEIDER, E. L., and ROWE, J. W. *Handbook of the Biology of Aging*, 3d ed. San Diego: Academic Press, 1990.

SCHNEIDER, E. L., and ROWE, J. W. *Handbook of the Biology of Aging*, 4th ed. San Diego: Academic Press, 1996.

WILLOTT, J. F. *Aging and the Auditory System: Anatomy, Physiology, and Psychophysics*. San Diego: Singular Press, 1991.

WILLOTT, J. F. *Neurogerontology: Aging and the Nervous System*. New York: Springer Publishing Co., 1999.

BREAST

Anatomy and physiology

The human breasts are paired organs lying on the anterior chest, extending from the second to the sixth ribs. The breasts in other animals are usually multiple and extend on to the abdomen, which explains the rare anomaly of multiple paired breasts that occasionally occurs in humans. The breasts are thought to be modified sweat glands, and therefore lie in the subcutaneous fat in front of the pectoral (chest) muscles. The breast has a central nipple through which the fifteen to twenty milk ducts exit; the nipple is usually protuberant, but can be inverted in some women.

The breast develops in young girls at around the age of ten or eleven due to the increasing release of pituitary hormones in puberty. The gland grows into the normal conical or rounded adult shape by around sixteen years of age, but swells considerably in pregnancy when milk production occurs. During the normal menstrual cycle, many women experience breast tenderness and swelling during the seven to ten days prior to menstruation.

Changes with aging

As a woman ages, the glandular component is replaced by fat, and the breast becomes softer and hangs lower as the suspensory ligaments inside the breast stretch. As the breast ages, the milk-producing sacs (lobules) may dilate with fluid and lead to the information of breast cysts, which sometimes enlarge sufficiently to be felt as lumps. The increase in fat content makes the older breast more lucent to X rays and easier to compress, so the clarity of a mammographic picture is greater in the older woman, making a small tumor more visible. This fact explains the greater accuracy of mammograms in older women and the adoption of population mammographic screening in women over forty-five years of age. As the breast ages, the skin gets thinner and the breast consists mainly of soft fat, making the breast more liable to bruising or trauma.

Estrogen replacement therapy (ERT), used to control hot flashes, tends to oppose the reduction of density that occurs with age and can produce tenderness, swelling, and lumpiness in the breast, manifestations normally seen in younger women. Thus, women on ERT may find their breast to be tender and fuller while on therapy. Surveys of ERT have shown a slight increase in breast cancer risk after more than fifteen years of estrogen use, but this problem is balanced by the improved quality of life on the therapy. Studies do not seem to indicate any major increase in the risk for breast cancer from ERT in women with a family history.

Breast diseases

As the breast ages, some diseases become more common. Breast cysts occur in about 7 percent of women and are usually seen between the ages of forty and sixty. These are easily treated by aspiration of the cyst fluid, which may be facilitated using ultrasound guidance. The breast gradually becomes less lumpy after menopause, as the fall in estrogen levels causes shrinkage of the gland tissue, with a relative increase in the fat content. Eventually, the breast becomes pendulous, a change that tends to be accelerated in heavier, fuller breasts. Oversize and pendulous breasts can be corrected by a surgical reduction mammoplasty, or by a simple "hitch up" operation if no tissue needs to be removed.

Breast cancer is the most common malignancy in females, and the lifetime risk is roughly one in ten. Breast cancer is strongly associated with age; it is uncommon below thirty years of age, but common after the age of forty-five. The cancer usually originates from faulty cell division in the breast lobules, and it may initially commence as a noninvading type of cancer whereby malignant cells line the ducts within the breast (intraductal noninvasive cancer—also know as ductal carcinoma in situ, or DCIS). Invasive cancer occurs when the malignant cells acquire the ability to break through the duct walls and invade into the surrounding breast tissue. Further spread can occur via the blood vessels or lymphatic channels, which can also become invaded by cancer cells. These cells can then travel via the bloodstream to the bones, brain, lungs, or liver. Lumps that may indicate breast cancer can be detected by self-examination, mammography, and ultrasound, and tumors as small as four or five millimeters can be seen by these techniques. Once detected by these methods, a needle can be used to obtain a biopsy of either cells or tissue to make a diagnosis. Current therapy may involve surgical removal of the lump (lumpectomy) or the breast (mastectomy), followed by chemotherapy, radiotherapy, and hormone therapy. Different combinations may be used, depending on the individual patient or tumor, but hormonal therapies are used more often in older women.

When tumors are found to be large on initial diagnosis, chemotherapy and/or radiation therapy may be given before surgery. The results of therapy have been improving, and mortality from breast cancer is falling in most developed countries due to better combinations of therapy, as well as a reduction in tumor size due to mammographic screening. Around 85 percent of women with a smaller cancer of less then one inch (2.5 cms) with no nodal spread can expect to survive ten years after modern therapy.

Despite these modern therapies, many women still die from breast cancer, and prevention of breast cancer may be the preferred way to reduce deaths. Studies in the United States have shown a substantial reduction in breast cancer in high-risk women taking the antiestrogen drug tamoxifen for two years. Current studies are exploring other hormone interventions in women at high risk of breast cancer.

R. E. MANSEL

C

CANADA

The 2001 census found that Canada has a population of 31 million people who are heavily concentrated in communities located within 100 miles of the Canada–United States border. There is further concentration of the population in cities and towns, as over 60 percent of all Canadians live in the twenty-five metropolitan areas that have populations of over 100,000, and 80 percent live in urban areas. Despite their vast landmass, the three northern territories (Yukon, Northwest Territory, and Nunavut) contain only about three-tenths of one percent of the total population. Like all other industrialized countries, Canada experienced significant aging of its population over the twentieth century. In 2001, 12.6 percent of the population was over age sixty-five (very similar to the United States, where 12.4 percent was over the age of sixty-five). As the size of the older population has increased, interest in aging and the place of older people in Canadian society has grown.

History of population aging

Data on the aging of Canada's population over the twentieth century are shown in Table 1. Although the population over age sixty-five increased 2.5 times between 1901 and 2001 (from 5.0 percent to 12.6 percent), the rate of change was not uniform over the century. During the first half of the century population aging progressed at a gradual pace, so that by midcentury 7.8 percent of all Canadians over sixty-five. This aging occurred primarily because of declining fertility, and would have been greater if there had not been large-scale immigration during the

first several decades. Because immigrants were concentrated in the young adult ages, their large flow temporarily reduced the proportion of the population that was old. Then, in response to the baby boom and revival of immigration after World War II, the proportion of elderly in the population actually declined slightly between 1951 and 1961 (from 7.8 percent to 7.6 percent). During the last third of the century, Canada experienced very low fertility and rapid population aging occurred. By the beginning of the twenty-first century, the proportion of the population over age sixty-five reached an all time high of 12.6 percent.

Data in Table 1 also show that the proportion in the oldest-old category (over eighty-five) more than tripled between 1951 and 2001. That population is of special interest because people at this stage of life are the heaviest users of health care services. Despite the rapid increase in the oldest-old category, it still constitutes less than 2 percent of the total population. An even more extreme age category is centenarians. The 1921 census found only 183 persons over age one hundred, but the number in this category grew to over three thousand by 2001 (a sixteen-fold increase).

Statistics Canada makes projections of the population by age and sex, and their projected age distributions for the years 2011 and 2026 are shown in Table 1. In the first decade of the twenty-first century, population aging is expected to continue at about the same pace it followed at the end of the previous century. But then starting in 2011, an unprecedented increase in the older population is anticipated. In just fifteen years, the percent of elderly will jump from 14.5 percent to 21.4 percent. The explanation for this

A Canadian senior citizen holds a kettle as she approaches a counter with additional pots and pans at the Boundary Waters Canoe area in the Quetico Provincial Park, Ontario. (Corbis photo by Michael S. Yamashita.)

dramatic development is, of course, the baby boom (1945 to 1963), and the subsequent baby bust. The first wave of the baby boom will reach age sixty-five around 2010, and then for nearly two decades successive cohorts of baby boomers will be crossing the threshold of old age. Canada, like other industrialized countries, will face a challenge of how to maintain its pension and health care benefits for older people in an era when the ratio of retired persons to workers is so much greater than it has ever been before.

Distribution of older people

Variations in the proportion of those over sixty-five across Canada are explained by differences in fertility and by past migration patterns. The territories in the north are characterized by very high fertility, and they have relatively few older people. Among the provinces, the oldest populations in 2001 were in Saskatchewan (14.6 percent over age sixty-five) and Manitoba (13.6 percent over age sixty-five). These prairie provinces have experienced slow growth for several decades, as many youth have moved out, leaving a disproportionate number of older people. In contrast, areas with significant growth due to in-migration tend to have younger populations. For example, Alberta and Ontario have both grown rapidly and have relatively fewer older people (9.9 percent and 12.4 percent over age sixty-five, respectively). The exception to this pattern is British Columbia, which was the fastest growing province in the 1990s, but does not have an especially young population (12.7 percent over age sixty-five). Indeed, Victoria, British Columbia, has the unofficial title "Canada's Senior Capital" because 18.2 percent of its population is over age sixty-five. (Statistics Canada, 1999).

In 1996, most (78 percent) older Canadians lived in urban areas, and one-third resided in the four metropolitan areas with populations exceeding one million (Toronto, Montreal, Vancouver, and Ottawa). However, about one-fifth of Canada's older population lives in rural areas. Given the vast landmass of Canada, many of these areas have exceedingly low population density, making the delivery of services to seniors particularly difficult. Many rural communities are trying to develop economic opportunities to retain their younger populations and thereby be able to provide more services for seniors. The success of these endeavours has varied within and across provinces, but is the basis of important policy and planning concerns in all provinces.

Table 1
Distribution of Canada's Population by Age, 1901–2026

Age	Year						
	1901	1931	1951	1981	2001	2011	2026
0–24	54.0	50.4	45.7	41.7	32.3	29.0	25.5
25–44	26.2	27.3	28.9	29.5	17.1	27.6	26.4
45–64	13.9	16.7	17.7	15.0	23.9	28.9	26.6
65–74	3.4	3.9	5.3	6.1	6.9	7.8	12.1
75–84	1.4	1.4	2.0	2.8	4.3	4.6	6.8
85+	0.3	0.2	0.4	0.8	1.4	2.1	2.8
	100.0	100.0	100.0	100.0	100.0	100.0	100.0
Total No.	5,371,315	10,376,786	14,009,429	24,343,180	31,081,887	33,361,700	36,190,600
65+	5.0	5.6	7.8	9.7	12.6	14.5	21.4
No. 65+	269,388	575,822	1,086,273	2,360,980	3,922,534	4,845,900	7,753,000

SOURCE: Adapted from Statistics Canada, Census of Canada 1901, 1931, 1951, and 1981. The Preliminary Population Estimate, *The Daily*, November 20, 2001, and "Population Projections for 2001, 2006, 2011, 2016, 2021 and 2026, July 1." in *CANSIM Matrix 6900*. Ottawa: Statistics Canada website, 2001.

Characteristics of the older population

Sex ratio. In Canada, as elsewhere, almost 3 percent more males than females are born each year. This surplus of males continues up to about age forty-five, after which females become an increasingly large majority. By the time one gets to old age, the number of females significantly exceeds the number of males. In 2001, women constituted 57 percent of all older Canadians, and 70 percent of those past age eighty-five. These ratios are expected to remain about the same until 2026 (Statistics Canada, 1999). The reason for the changing sex ratio with age is that females experience lower death rates than males at every age. By looking at sex differences in life expectancy at birth, one can see how much advantage females have over males in longevity. Life expectancy is the average number of years that one would live under age-specific death rates existing at a particular time. Death rates around 1920 resulted in women's life expectancy exceeding men's by two years (61 versus 59). By 1970 the gender gap in life expectancy had grown to seven years (76 versus 69). In recent decades the gender gap has declined a little, and in 1996 was below six (81.4 versus 75.7) (Statistics Canada, 1999). The imbalanced sex ratio in later life caused by differential mortality has implications for gender differences in aging.

Marital status. The excess number of older women compared to men means that chances of being married in old age differ by sex. While almost 75 percent of older men are married, only 41 percent of older women are married. Corre-spondingly, almost half of older women are widowed as compared to 13 percent of older men. This difference is even more dramatic among those age eighty-five and over, where just over half of men, but less than 10 percent of women, are married, and twice as many women as men are widowed (80 percent versus 39 percent). Given the sex differences in marital status, it is not surprising that more older women than men live alone (38 percent versus 16 percent). Among those aged eighty-five plus, the gap between women and men living alone is even greater (58 percent versus 29 percent) (Statistics Canada, 1999).

Living arrangements. Most older Canadians (93 percent) live in private households, but as cohorts age, an increasing proportion is cared for in institutions. The proportion living in institutions in 1996 increased from only 3 percent for those aged sixty-five to seventy-four to 34 percent of the population over age eighty-five. Within the oldest-old population, women, who are more likely to be widowed and have more functional limitations than men, are more likely than men to be institutionalized (38 percent versus 24 percent) (Statistics Canada, 1999). The disproportionate number of women among the older population and their greater likelihood of being institutionalized result in 70 percent of all long-term care residents being women.

Immigrant status. As a country that is largely the result of immigration, the ethnic and linguistic diversity in Canada is substantial. The original settlers were predominantly from England, Scotland, France, Ireland, and Wales, but were joined by immigrant families from Germany, Ukraine, Poland, Russia, and China in the nineteenth century. The heaviest immigration to Canada, relative to the nonimmigrant population, occurred between 1906 and 1915, and immigrants in this period tended to be young adult males. This pattern of immigration had important implications for the age and sex structure of the aging population during the latter part of the twentieth century. Even as recently as 1996, a remarkable 27 percent of all Canadians past age sixty-five were foreign born. Toward the end of the twentieth century, the largest number of immigrants came from Asia and Latin America (more than half of the immigrants since 1980 have come from Asia) (Statistics Canada, 1999). This new immigration pattern suggests that in the future there will be even greater ethnic variation in the older population than there is today. One result of the immigration history is that it creates an important difference between the languages and cultures of many seniors and those of the persons who are delivering services to seniors.

Labor force participation. Over the twentieth century the labor force participation rate declined continuously as retirement became institutionalized. This pattern continued in the late twentieth century as the proportion of those over age sixty-five still in the labor force declined from 11 percent in 1981 to 6 percent in 1998. Not surprisingly, a higher proportion of older men than women was in the labor force in 1998 (10 percent versus 3 percent). The distribution of employed older persons across occupational categories was fairly uniform: 21 percent employed in farming, 17 percent in professions, 15 percent in sales, 12 percent in both services and managerial occupations, and the remaining in clerical, manufacturing, construction, and transportation. Of course participation in the labor force is not the only way for older people to make productive contributions to Canadian society. About 23 percent of seniors participate in formal volunteer roles, and a majority (58 percent) report that they provide informal assistance to others outside their own homes. Slightly more women than men contribute in this way. As retirement has become nearly universal among people over age sixty-five, the most notable change in the labor force age structure since the mid-1970s has been the marked decrease in participation by those age fifty-five to sixty-four. Among men in what

was once considered a preretirement age category, labor force participation declined from 74 percent in 1976 to 56 percent in 1998. Over this same time period, women ages fifty-five to sixty-four slightly increased their level of involvement in the labor force (from 30 percent to 36 percent). It is noteworthy that 22 percent of women, but only 2 percent of men, over age sixty-five never participated in the paid labor force (Statistics Canada, 1999).

Poverty and economic status. The proportion of older people in Canada with incomes below what Statistics Canada labels the "low income" cutoff declined from 34 percent in 1980 to 20 percent in 1998. This is the same as the percent of children with low incomes, and slightly higher than the percent of nonold adults. Within the older population, women are twice as likely as men to have low incomes (27 percent v 13 percent), and more than half (53 percent) of unattached older women have low incomes. Provincial variations in average income are substantial, with territories and provinces in the Atlantic region having lowest average incomes, and seniors living in Ontario, Alberta, and British Columbia having average incomes about $5,000 above the Canadian average. The primary source of income for seniors is Old Age Security, which provides 29 percent of all income received by people over age sixty-five. Other sources are employment-based pensions (21 percent), Canada and Quebec Pension Plan benefits (21 percent), investments (17 percent), and employment (8 percent). There is a variety of programs in most provinces that supplement the incomes of seniors in need. Another indicator of economic well-being is home ownership. A majority of senior families (84 percent), and almost half of unattached seniors, own their own homes (Statistics Canada, 1999). Some provinces contribute to the rent of low-income seniors through a variety of programs, and some provide support services to enable older people to remain in their own homes after developing functional limitations.

Health status. Less than one-fourth of older Canadians report their general health is only "fair" or "poor", and 40 percent report that it is "excellent" or "very good." The remainder (38 percent) report good health. Nevertheless, 82 percent of those aged sixty-five and over reported having at least one long-term chronic condition. Regarding more serious conditions, 28 percent report being limited in at least some activities because of a chronic health conditions.

—Among seniors between ages sixty-five and seventy-four, slightly more men than women report some limitation (23 percent versus 21 percent), but past age eighty-five women are more likely than men to report limitations (54 percent versus 42 percent). By far the most commonly reported chronic condition among both men and women is arthritis, which increases with advancing age; 53 percent of those aged eighty-five and over have this problem. Heart disease also increases throughout the later years of life to a peak of 22 percent at age eighty-five, but high blood pressure peaks between ages seventy-five and eighty-four at 35 percent. Another significant chronic disease, diabetes, remains almost constant at about 11 percent through later life (Statistics Canada, 1999).

Health care.   The public health care insurance system in Canada contributes to the sense of well-being and financial security of all Canadians, especially of older Canadians. The national system includes all medically necessary treatment as legislated by the Canada Health Act. However, the degree to which long-term care (home care and facility care) is provided or covered varies substantially from province to province. While most provinces cover prescription drugs and vision care for seniors, the existence and amount of copayment vary across the provinces. All provinces have policies and service delivery programs to meet long-term care needs. The most comprehensive programs with lowest copayment requirements are in Manitoba and Quebec, and the least comprehensive and most costly to the consumer are in Alberta, Ontario, and Nova Scotia.

Summary

Canada is a large, diverse, and aging country. Some population projections indicate that one-fourth of the population may be over age sixty-five by 2041. The population is aging in a manner much like that of the United States, but the challenge of a low population density is not experienced to the same degree in the United States. The low population density in rural areas presents Canadians with the challenge of how to deliver health, social, and commercial services to older people throughout the country. Provinces are responding to this challenge in varying ways, consistent with their history, political, and philosophical orientations. The general, social, and health conditions are also similar in Canada and the United States, but the differences in health care delivery and insurance and in pensions contributes to a greater sense of well-being and security among Canadians, particularly among senior Canadians.

BETTY HAVENS

See also CANADA, HEALTH CARE COVERAGE FOR OLDER PEOPLE; CANDA, INCOME PROTECTION FOR RETIREES; POPULATION AGING.

BIBLIOGRAPHY

ANDERSON, G. F. and HUSSEY, P. S. "Population Aging: A Comparison among Industrialized Countries." *Health Affairs* 19 (2000):191–203.

BASAVARAJAPPA, K. G. and RAM, B. *Historical Statistics of Canada*. Ottawa: Statistics Canada, Catalogue Number 11-516-XIE, 2001.

Organisation for Economic Co-operation and Development. *Labour Force Statistics, 1979–1999*. Paris: OECD, 2000.

Statistics Canada. *Census of Canada, 1981, Volume 1*. Ottawa: Statistics Canada, Catalogue Number 82-901, 1982.

Statistics Canada. "Population Projections for 2001, 2006, 2011, 2016, 2021 and 2026, July 1." in *CANSIM Matrix 6900*. Ottawa: Statistics Canada website, www.statcan.ca

Statistics Canada. *A Portrait of Seniors in Canada, Third Edition*. Ottawa: Statistics Canada, Catalogue Number 89-519-XPE, 1999.

Statistics Canada. "Preliminary Population Estimate." *The Daily*. (November 20, 2001): 1.

Statistics Canada. *Statistics Canada's Low Income Cut-offs, 1992 Base*. Ottawa: Statistics Canada, Catalogue Number 13-207-XPB, 1998.

CANADA, HEALTH CARE COVERAGE FOR OLDER PEOPLE

Canada is a parliamentary democracy in which the division of powers between the federal and provincial governments determines how health and social support services are funded and administered. The division of powers between the federal and provincial governments for health and social services was originally prescribed in 1867 in the British North American Act (BNA Act). This distribution of authority remained unchanged after the Canadian constitution was repatriated from Britain in 1982. At this time the Constitution Act was proclaimed.

The Canadian federal government is responsible for:

tions continue to be physician fees and, in most provinces, diagnostic and pharmaceutical services.

Federal-provincial tensions

In 1995, four themes emerged from the National Forum on Health, which was convened to advise the federal government on innovative ways to improve the health care system. These themes were (1) focus on values, (2) strike a balance in resource allocation, (3) renew a focus on determinants of health, and (4) shift to a paradigm of evidence-based decision-making.

A national debate continues about the extent to which the federal government should be able to exercise authority over the way health services are provided within the current funding arrangements. In the provinces of Alberta and Ontario, initiatives to open the door to private provision of acute care services are being proposed and implemented. Meanwhile, although Canadians are concerned about waiting times for some services, a majority, when polled, continue to value Canada's universal health insurance system and to be against increased privatization of health services.

Organization and delivery of health services

All acute care services and physician-provided primary care services for older people in Canada are funded through the universal public insurance system at no charge to the individual. A majority of physician services have always been provided by physicians on a fee-for-service basis. Continuing and community care services have historically been provided by a combination of public, private, and voluntary (not-for-profit) service providers.

Continuing care services fall under the category of extended health services in the Canada Health Act and as such are not fully insured services. Extended health care services that are covered by the Canada Health Act include certain aspects of long-term residential care (nursing home intermediate care and adult residential care services) and the health aspects of home care and ambulatory care services. Continuing care services are distinct across provinces, and while many provinces can include the same elements there is no nation-wide continuing care system, as these services are a matter of provincial jurisdiction.

In Canada, most medical care for older people is provided by family physicians. Although training programs in geriatric medicine have increased and geriatricians are more widely available than in the past, acute geriatric services (those provided by specialists in geriatric medicine working in conjunction with an associated multidisciplinary team) continue to be poorly understood and improperly utilized or underutilized in conventional physician referral processes.

The term continuing care is now used to describe the full range of care services for older people and people with disabilities in six provinces (British Columbia, Alberta, Manitoba, Nova Scotia, Prince Edward Island, and Newfoundland) and in the Northwest Territories. Saskatchewan uses the term "supportive services" and the Yukon and Quebec do not use a single umbrella term to describe their full array of services. Continuing care services are offered in Canada by private (for-profit) providers, and the voluntary (not-for-profit) sector, as well as by publicly funded provider organizations. Whatever the ownership of a continuing care center, residents typically pay an accommodation charge.

The newer models of care, and some other programs for older people in Canada, incorporate the five best practices that have been identified as characteristics of the most efficient continuing care systems in the world. These practices are: (1) a system of single entry, (2) coordinated assessment and placement, (3) a coordinated case management system, (4) a client-care level classification system, and (5) administrative arrangements.

The newer models of care for older people are designed to promote client-centered care by offering more individualized choice of programs and services, with the option to choose and purchase services, a la carte, in a residential environment. While some programs of this nature are offered through the continuing care system, others are privately owned and operated as senior housing in which residents have the opportunity to purchase a "care package."

Home and community care

In most provinces, some home care (sometimes called community care) services are publicly funded up to a maximum capped amount. During the 1990s, the emphasis in home care programs shifted from that of supportive care for the chronically ill and disabled to substitution for acute care. This is particularly the case for home care programs in urban centers, where the pressure to offer "sub-acute" home care services intensified following hospital bed closures. Professional health services provided by registered nursesor rehabilitation disciplines continue to be subsidized; however, clients now pay out of pocket for services such as health supervision, personal care, and homemaking. Some programs no longer provide these services, leaving it up to clients and family members to locate and arrange for them.

The affordability and accessibility of home care remains problematic for people with chronic illness and disability in many parts of Canada. In at least one Canadian province it has been demonstrated that the impact of funding reductions in health and social programs affected older people disproportionately. Home care services have not traditionally operated around the clock and through the week, although this is beginning to change. Charges for supplies and medications, which would be covered by the universal health insurance plan if a person were in the hospital, must often be paid out of pocket once a person returns to the community. Such disincentives mitigate against the preferences and ability of older people to receive needed services in their homes.

Informal care

Family and friends provide a substantial portion of the care received by older people, whether they live in institutions or in their own homes. Informal care is based on normative or voluntary interpersonal association, while formal care arises from a client-agency relationship and is provided by specially trained persons. The major group of formal caregivers is employees of direct service organizations. In a 1998 study conducted within several continuing care environments, Keating, Douzeich, Fast, Dousman, and Eales observed that family members provided approximately forty hours per month of direct services to residents. It is to be expected that the amount of informal care provided in the home would significantly exceed this. Provision of informal care in Canada has followed what Keating et al. (1998) term as a *substitution model* (as opposed to a complementary model), in which informal care is seen to be a cost-effective means for substituting for formal care, which often takes place in an institution and is hence more costly to society.

During the 1990s, as the health system was restructured in Canada, opportunities for formal care of older people were limited, thus shifting much of the burden of care to informal caregivers. Such a shift in responsibility from facility-based to home-based care carries with it the need to provide support for informal caregivers. Increases in respite services and home care services, including options for weekend and night services, are slow in coming as various health service sectors, including acute care, compete for scarce health care funds. Direct remuneration or tax exemptions for informal caregivers have yet to be seriously considered as policy options in the Canadian context.

Coordination and integration of services

The need for improvements in the coordination and integration of services has been identified as an urgent priority at every level of government responsible for health and human services. Following consultation with health care policy makers and decision-makers, continuity of care was identified as a priority area for research funding by the Canadian Health Services Research Foundation (CHSRF). Although care (case) management models and processes are used to coordinate care within home care and certain other programs, case management is not a common feature within the Canadian health system, as is the case in other industrialized countries. Boundary-spanning case management roles remain relatively rare, and individuals cannot generally engage independent professional case managers to assist them in navigating through the complex web of community-based and formal health services. Ironically, case management is more evident in the disability management dimension of private health and disability insurance than in any other part of the Canadian health system.

Use of health services by older Canadians

Increases in the number of older people are often cited as the reason that costs are rising in the health care system. Total health expenditures for individuals ages seventy-five to eighty-four account for the largest health expenditures (16.7 percent), while those eighty-five years and older are the second largest (11.6 percent). The lowest health care expenditures (8 percent) were noted amongst the fifteen to twenty-four age group (Health Canada, 2001, p.19).

The assumption that a rise in the population of seniors is the cause of high health system costs has been termed as *demographic determinism* by (Gee and McDaniel as cited in Chappell, 2001, p. 82) For example, seniors may be labeled as bed blockers in acute care when there are no beds available in a long-term care setting or when resources are unavailable for community-based care. Increased support in the home, special care units, and transitional facilities may help to alleviate such pressures. A working paper by Oxley and Macfarlen points out that growth in health care spending attributable to aging is estimated at less than 5 percent, and that other cost drivers include the use of new technology, the cost of new drugs, changing consumer expectations, and new changing patterns of disease. They conclude that it is not the aging of the population per se that has an impact on health care costs, but rather the overall increase in the population.

A team of prominent Canadian health economists has challenged the dire predications of skyrocketing costs of health services for older people. Highlighting contradictory evidence, they question why this alarmist rhetoric is so prominent in health policy discourse. They conclude that it has a superficial plausibility or intuitive appeal, but also that it serves identifiable interests—particularly of those who wish to make the argument that the present Canadian health system is "unsustainable" and to provide an "objective" argument for increased privatization (Evans, et.al., p. 186-187).

It has been demonstrated that population-based health interventions can make dramatic improvements in the health of older people and reduce overall health system costs. The use of low-cost support services to assist seniors to remain independent in their homes is one such intervention. Proactive outreach designed to identify and monitor older people with known health risks is another. The Capital Health Authority, in Edmonton, Alberta, has been nationally recognized for its innovative program of immunizing older people and their care providers against influenza, resulting in reduced incidence, severity, and hospital utilization.

Sustainability Since about 1990, advocates of the increased privatization of health services have argued that the public system is stretched to the limit and that opening more private clinics and surgical facilities will decrease the burden on the public system. Proponents also emphasize that this would provide more choice for the consumer, who may not want to wait in the public queue. In some provinces in Canada, a few private clinics are now operating parallel to the public system. Proponents of a parallel private system cite economic arguments that indicate that care provided in these clinics is inexpensive or more efficient than care provided in the public system. While this may seem to be the case, many of the providers of private care take on the less complex cases, which is referred to as cream-skimming because the less complex cases are generally not as costly as those handled in the public system.

Critics of privatization also point out that the creation of a two-tiered system threatens the fundamental principles of an equitable and universal health care system that is accessible to all. Deber and Baranek note that ". . .proposals for allowing a parallel private insurance tier within a universal health care system are commonly challenged on the grounds of access and equity; analysts argue that priority for scarce health resources should be based on need and ability to benefit rather than on willingness and ability to pay for those resources." (pg. 5457)

It is often suggested that the introduction of private services will reduce waiting times, and there is a prevailing myth that the situation of waiting lists is unique to Canada. However, as Tuohy, Flood, and Stabile note, "There is no evidence that waiting lists in the public sector are reduced by allowing privately insured options such as those that exist in Britain, New Zealand and Australia. On the contrary, we find that public sector waiting lists for hospital services in these systems are similar to or longer than those in Canada. Long public waiting lists, that is, appear to fuel demand for private insurance; but private options do not reduce the length of public waiting lists or waiting time. . . ."

The issue of user fees has also been debated to address issues of cost within the system. Advocates believe that there is unnecessary use of the health system by some people because it is "free," and that if user fees are imposed people will use health services only when they really need them. This approach is criticized as having a negative and disproportional effect on those already disadvantaged, particularly people with low or fixed incomes who are likely to be in the poorest health to begin with and need to access services more often. This point of view continues to be generally supported by public opinion in Canada. A survey conducted by the Conference Board of Canada (see Kirby and LeBreton) revealed that only 23 percent of Canadians supported the introduction of user charges for physician services. Since 1995, there has been a decrease in the number of individuals who support an increase in private health care.

Health and human resources. In the last two decades, professional schools in Canada have made some progress in adding gerontological knowledge to their general curricula. However, more training opportunities and incentives are needed to attract and retain health professionals and specialists to work with the growing number of older people in Canada. Geriatric medicine is a young specialty in Canada, having been formally recognized by the Royal College of Physicians and Surgeons in 1981. After completing training in internal medicine, physicians wishing to become specialists in geriatric medicine undertake a further two years of training. In 2001, about 150 people held this specialist qualification in Canada. A small number of family physicians now obtain additional training in health care of elderly people in a program recognized by the Canadian College of Family Practice. While the number of physicians with training or specialization in geriatric medicine has increased, remuneration for these professionals is not sufficiently competitive to attract and retain the needed numbers.

The Gerontological Nursing Association, a specialist group constituted under the auspices of the Canadian Nurses Association, has encouraged the development and credentialing of gerontological nursing through a national certification process. Master of Nursing programs across the country currently provide advanced practice preparation in care of the elderly and chronically ill. Although wider use of advanced-practice nurses has been advocated for over twenty years as a proven means for delivering quality, cost-effective care to older people and their families, there are relatively few positions available in the health system for nurses with this level of preparation.

Multidisciplinary training opportunities are provided in gerontology centers at a number of Canadian universities. Other practitioners receive training in departments of physical education and recreation. Unfortunately, the expertise of social workers and psychologists is underutil-

ized in health programs for older people in Canada.

Infrastructure. As in other industrialized countries, Canada is dealing with issues of resource allocation that affect the availability of and access to health services. There are particular challenges in making health services accessible to rural aboriginal, and multicultural populations. Rural and urban dispartities in Canda are compounded by problems of climate and transportation. Education, employment, and housing are less readily available in some rural areas, particularly in some aboriginal communities. Relatively small populations in many rural areas make communication economies of scale and culturally sensitive care difficult to achieve.

The physical infrastructure of the existing health system is often inadequate to the needs of older people. In some parts of the country, rudimentary physical accessibility for people with disabilities remains problematic. Older continuing care centers were built to resemble hospitals, in the mistaken belief that this design would lead to greater efficiencies in providing care. Ironically, as the older population is increasing, funds for infrastructure have decreased, and many of these institutionally designed buildings remain in use. Community health centers have been advocated as a way of building low-cost infrastructure that would help to provide people, including seniors, with integrated health services that are delivered close to home.

Summary

Canada has a history of innovative and communitarian health policy, which has resulted in a highly accessible system of health care with relatively low administrative costs. The availability of universal health insurance for hospital and medical services protects all Canadians, including older people, from the catastrophic effects of illness. The community and continuing care services that people need as they grow older or develop chronic illness are delivered by public, voluntary, and private providers and are not fully insured.

The health status of older Canadians is generally good and has improved significantly in recent years. Although the aging of the Canadian population is often identified as a threat to the sustainability of the universal health insurance system provided under the Canada Health Act, this has been shown to be misleading. Population-oriented health interventions such as immunization of older people and their caregivers against influenza have been shown to make dramatic improvements in health and to reduce health demand and costs in the health system. Older people in Canada are generally satisfied with their own health status and the health system, and they contribute substantially to the health and well being of the communities in which they live through volunteer service.

DONNA L. SMITH
TARANJEET K. BIRD
JOHN W. CHURCH

BIBLIOGRAPHY

ADASKIN, E. "Organized Political Action: Lobbying by Nurses Associations." In *Canadian Nursing Faces the Future: Development and Change.* Edited by A. Baumgart and J. Larsen. Toronto: C. V. Mosby, 1988. Pages 474–487.

Alberta Health and Wellness. *Long Term Care Review, (LTC) Part I. Healthy Aging: New Directions for Care.* Final Report of the Policy Advisory Committee. Edmonton, Alberta: Alberta Health and Wellness, 1994.

Alberta Health and Wellness. *Long Term Care Review, Future Scenarios: Continuing Care Service Needs in Alberta.* Edmonton, Alberta: Alberta Health and Wellness, 1994.

BERGMAN, B. "Communities with Medical Schools; A Great Group Rising to the Challenge: The Edmonton Health Region Provides the Best Services in its Select Category." *Maclean's* 113 no. 23. (2000): 22–23.

BERGMAN, B. "Leader of the Pack: Edmonton Is No.1 in the First-Ever Ranking of Health Service in Canada's Major Centers." *Maclean's* 112 no. 23. (1999) pp. 28–30.

CHAPPELL, N. L., and PENNING, M. J. "Sociology of Aging in Canada: Issues for the Millennium." *Canadian Journal On Aging* 20, no. 1 2001 pp. 82–111.

CRICHTON, A.; ROBERTSON, A.; GORDON, C. AND FARRANT, W. "Development of Canada's Welfare State Programs." In *Health Care a Community Concern? Developments in the Organization of Canadian Health Services.* Calgary, Alberta University of Calgary Press, 1997. p. 27–35.

DEBER, R.; GILDNER, A.; and BARANEK, P. "Why Not Private Health Insurance? Actuarial Principles Meet Provider Dreams." *CMAJ* 161 no. 5 (1999): 5457.

DECTER, M. "Plan to End the Hospital Crisis There Are Three Main Causes of the Problems: The Flu Epidemic, a Squeeze on the System, and Lack of Alternatives to the Emergency Rooms." *Maclean's* 113 no. 3 (1999): 28–29.

DENNIS, G., ed. *The Emergence of Social Security in Canada—Major Themes.* 2d edition. Vancouver: University of British Columbia Press, 1991.

EVANS, R. G.; BARER, M. L.; and MARMOR, T. R. *Why Are Some People Healthy and Others Not?* Montreal: University of Montreal, 1996.

FLOOD, C. ed. "The Structure and Dynamics of Canada's Health Care System." In *Canadian Health Law and Policy.* Edited by J. Downie and T. Caulfield. Toronto: Butterworth Publishing, 1999.

GUEST, D., ed. *The Emergence of Social Security in Canada—Major Themes* revised 2d ed. British Columbia. University of British Columbia Press, 1994.

HARTMANN-STEIN, P. E. "Foreword." In *Innovative Behavioural Healthcare for Older Adults. A Guidebook for Changing Times.* Edited by P. E. Hartmann-Stein. San Francisco: Jossey-Bass Publishers, 1993. Pages ix–xi.

Health Canada. 2001. www.hcsc.gc.ca/

Health Canada. *Seniors Guide to Federal Programs and Services.* 2001. www.hc-sc.gc.ca/

HOLLANDER, M. *Innovations in Best Practice Models of Continuing Care for Seniors.* Report Prepared on Behalf of the Federal/Provincial/ Territorial Committee (Seniors) for the Ministers Responsible for Seniors. 2001. www.hc-sc.gc.ca/

HOLLANDER, M. J., and WALKER, E. R. *Report of Continuing Care Organization and Terminology.* Prepared on behalf of the Federal/ Provincial/ Territorial Committee of Officials (Seniors) for the Minister Responsible for Seniors. 2001. www.hc-gc.ca/

KANE, R. A., and KANE, R. L. "Long-Term Care for the Elderly in Canada." In *Caring For An Aging World. International Models for Long-Term Care Financing and Delivery.* Edited by T. Schwab. New York: McGraw Hill Information Services, 1989. Pages 193–211.

KEATING, N.; DOUZEICH, L.; FAST, J.; DOSMAN, D.; and EALES, J. *Partners in Caring: Services Provided by Formal and Informal Caregivers to Seniors in Residential Continuing Care.* EPICC Series, Evaluating Programs of Innovative Continuing Care. Edmonton, Alberta: University of Alberta, 1998. Pages 1–57.

KIRBY, M. J. L., and LEBRETON, M. *The Health of Canadians—The Federal Role.* Volume One. *The Story So Far.* Interim Report on the State of the Health Care System in Canada. The Standing

Senate Committee on Social Affairs, Science, and Technology, 2001.

LALONDE, M. *A New Perspective on the Health of Canadians: A Working Document.* Ottawa: Government of Canada, 1974.

LESEMANN, F., and NAHMIASH, D. "Home-Based Care in Canada and Quebec: Informal and Formal Services." In *Home-Based Care, the Elderly, the Family, and the Welfare State an International Comparison.* Edited by F. Lesemann and C. Martin. Ottawa: University of Ottawa Press, 1993. Pages 82–94.

LESEMANN, F., and ULYSSE, P. J. *Population Aging: An Overview of the Past Thirty Years.* 1997. www.hc-sc.gc.ca

National Advisory Council on Aging [NACA] *Report Card. Seniors in Canada.* Ottawa, Ontario: Minister of Public Works and Government Services Canada, 2001.

National Forum on Health *Changing the Health Care System—A Consumer Perspective: Summary Report.* Ottawa, Ontario: NFH, 1996.

National Union Research [NUR] *Defending Canada's Public Pension Plans.*

NORTHCOTT, H. C., and WILSON, D. M. *Dying and Death in Canada.* Aurora, Ontario: Garamond, 2001.

OXLEY, H., and MACFARLAN, M. *Health Care Reform: Controlling Spending and Increasing Efficiency,* Economic Department Working Papers No. 149 OECD: Paris, 1995.

PARISI, L. E. "Legal Framework for Health-Care Services." In *Nursing Management in Canada.* Edited by J. M. Hibberd, and D. L. Smith. Toronto: W.B. Saunders, 1999.

PRINGLE, D. *Aging and the Health Care System: Am I in the Right Queue?* National Advisory Council On Aging. 1998. www.hc-sc.gc.ca/

ROCKWOOD, K.; MACKNIGHT, C.; and POWELL, C. "Clinical Research on Older Adults in Canada: Summary of Recent Progress." *Canadian Journal on Aging* 20, no. 1 (2001): 1–17.

STORCH, J. L., and MEILICKE, C. A. "Political, Social, and Economic Forces Shaping the Health Care System." In *Nursing Management in Canada.* Edited by J. M. Hibberd, and D. L. Smith. Toronto: W.B. Saunders, 1999. Pages 3–21.

TRUEMAN, G., and TRUEMAN, C. "The Determinants of Health." In *The Canadian Health Care System.* Edited by D. M. Wilson. Alberta, Ontario: University of Alberta, 1995.

TUOHY, C. H.; FLOOD, C. M.; and STABILE, M. "How Does Private Finance Affect Public Health Care Systems? Marshalling the Evidence from OECD Nations." Ontario Medical Association. www.oma.org

WEST, M. "Ensuring Choices and the Best Possible Care." In *Seniority. In Search of the Best Nursing Homes and Alternative Care in Canada.* Toronto, Ontario: Addison-Wesley, 1991.

WILSON, D. Canadian Healthcare Association (Ed). In *Long Term Care in Canada.* Ottawa, Canada (in press).

WILSON, D. M. "Where Do We Go from Here? The 72 Billion Dollar Question." In *Efficiency vs. Equality. Health Reform in Canada.* Edited by M. Stingl and D. Wilson. Halifax, Nova Scotia: Fernwood, 1996. Pages 165–177.

WILSON, D. M. "My Kind of Death: End-of-Life Care Preferences of Canadian Senior Citizens with Caregiving Experience." *Journal of Advanced Nursing,* 31 no. 6, (2000): 1416–1421.

WILSON, D. M. "Public and Private Health-Care Systems: What the Literature Says." *Canadian Public Administration.* no. 2, (2001): 204–231.

WILSON, D. M., and ROSS KERR, J. C. "Alberta's Deficit-Elimination Agenda—How Have Seniors Fared?" *Canadian Journal on Aging* 17, no. 2, (1998): 197–211.

CANADA, INCOME PROTECTION FOR RETIREES

Means-tested and social insurance programs have evolved to provide income support to people who cannot, or are not expected to, support themselves. Thanks to old-age income protection schemes, typically referred to as *social security,* growing numbers of men and women around the world face an economically secure old age, free of work. Between 1940 and 1999, the number of countries with programs that provide cash benefits to older persons, the disabled, and survivors rose from thirty-three to at least 167.

Social security programs take a variety of forms. They may be noncontributory and paid for out of general revenues, or they may require contributions from workers and employers. They may be defined benefit plans, which use a formula to calculate benefits based on some combination of earnings and years of employment, or defined contribution plans, whose benefits depend on plan contributions. Some provide a flat-rate benefit to all residents of a country, subject to certain conditions; others are based on work histories and years of earnings. Programs may be targeted to individuals or families with income and/or assets below a certain level; others pay benefits to anyone who has met the contribution requirements. Mandatory savings programs, such as provident funds, are found in a number of countries, and in a few countries, mandatory private pensions add another layer of income protection in old age.

In the more developed countries of the world, social security coverage is nearly universal. The continued aging of the population of the more developed countries is prompting many of them to reassess their social security systems in light of rising old-age dependency ratios and concern that the public sector might not be able to maintain current levels of support without substantially higher taxes. In many countries, efforts to reduce the rate of growth of social security expenditures while ensuring adequate retirement income have resulted in the reform of old-age social insurance schemes along with the promotion of occupational pensions and individual saving for old age. This has been the case in Canada, whose approach to old-age support shares a number of features with that of the United States, while it also differs in fundamental ways.

Canada, like the United States, has a public, mandatory, contributory, earnings-related pension program covering almost all workers, which provides a portion of the income workers will need in retirement. Disability benefits are available in both Canada and the United States. Both countries also offer tax incentives to encourage employers to offer private pensions and residents to save for their own retirement. Canada, however, provides what is referred to as a *universal benefit*, although it is subject to recovery from higher income persons. Supplemental payments may be available to those with inadequate income. The United States lacks a universal benefit, but it, too, offers protection to very low-income elderly through a separate, means-tested program of income support, the Supplemental Security Income Program.

Public income support programs for older nonworkers

Two national programs help protect older Canadians from destitution in old age: (1) the Old Age Security program, which includes the Old Age Security pension (OAS), the Guaranteed Income Supplement (GIS), and the Allowance (including the Allowance for the Survivor); and (2) the Canada Pension Plan (CPP). Canadian law allows the provinces to opt out of the CPP if they offer a similar pension plan. The province

of Quebec has chosen this route and established the Quebec Pension Plan (QPP), which is very similar, but not identical, to the CPP.

The Old Age Security pension is a universal monthly benefit available to persons age sixty-five or older, regardless of employment history, who are either Canadian citizens or legal residents who have lived in Canada for at least ten years since turning eighteen. The full Old Age Security pension is paid to persons who have resided in Canada for at least forty years since turning eighteen; partial benefits are paid for shorter residency. Benefits, which are financed from general revenues, are paid monthly and, to protect purchasing power, adjusted quarterly based on increases in the Consumer Price Index. Pensioners with individual net income above a certain level must repay all or part of the OAS in what is known as a *clawback*.

The Guaranteed Income Supplement is an income-tested monthly benefit paid to recipients of the Old Age Security pension who have little other income—among whom, unmarried persons, especially women, predominate. The amount of the GIS depends on marital status as well as income; any money other than the Old Age Security pension is defined as income for the purpose of determining the GIS amount. GIS benefits decline as OAS benefits rise. The GIS is indexed quarterly to reflect increases in the Consumer Price Index. The government bears the whole cost of these benefits, which may be supplemented by income-tested benefits in the provinces. Over one-third of all Old Age Security pensioners receive full or partial GIS benefits, although this figure varies widely by province.

The Allowance may be paid to spouses, partners (including common-law and same-sex partners), and survivors. These benefits are based on need and limited to persons between the ages of sixty and sixty-four who have lived in Canada for at least ten years since turning eighteen. Benefits, which are indexed quarterly, are converted to an Old Age Security pension when a recipient turns sixty-five.

Older Canadians may also be eligible for provincial or territorial income supplements in addition to federal income security. Other benefits, such as tax relief, that assist low-income older persons are available as well.

The government-funded OAS, GIS, Allowances, and provincial and territorial supplements guarantee a minimum income for older Canadians that is not enough to lift all older persons above the poverty level. As is the case in the United States, poverty in old age is far more common among women and the unmarried, who are predominantly women. Nonetheless, as is also the case in the United States, without these programs the poverty rates would be substantially higher.

The Canada Pension Plan and the Quebec Pension Plan are earnings-related pension programs administered by the government, paying full retirement benefits at age sixty-five. Early reduced benefits may be paid starting at age sixty, and benefits are increased if receipt is delayed up to age seventy. Beneficiaries must have made at least one year of contributions to qualify for this pension. In the United States, eligibility for retired worker benefits under Social Security requires forty quarters, or ten years, of contributions. All workers in Canada, between the ages of eighteen and seventy, including the self-employed, must contribute to the Canada Pension Plan or the Quebec Pension Plan. As with the Old-Age and Survivors Insurance (OASI) program in the United States, contributions are paid only on earnings up to an annually adjusted maximum and not on investment or other sources of income. Unlike the United States, earnings below a minimum, set at C$3,500, are not subject to pension taxation in Canada. Benefits are indexed only at the beginning of the year.

In 2001, Canadian workers and their employers in both the CPP and QPP each paid 4.3 percent of the worker's earnings up to the maximum of C$38,300, which is indexed to average wage growth. The exempt first C$3,500 of earnings is not indexed. Self-employed workers contribute the employer's and the employee's share. The employer-employee contribution rate will rise to 4.95 percent of wages by 2003, where it is scheduled to remain.

Legislation enacted in 1998 introduced changes that move the Canada Pension Plan from pay-as-you-go financing, where contributions in any one year are largely paid out in benefits that year, to a system with greater funding. Designed to help pay future pension benefits in an aging Canada, the reserves are to be invested in a diversified portfolio of securities, rather than solely in provincial bonds, which was the practice until recently. In the United States, substantial reserves that will help pay for the baby boomers' retirement have been building in the Social Security Trust Funds, and proposals have been made to invest a portion of these reserves in equities.

The formula used to calculate benefits at the time of retirement in Canada adjusts previous earnings to make them comparable to average national earnings at the time a worker retires. The adjustment is based on the maximum pensionable earnings for the previous five years. Up to 15 percent of low-income years may be deducted from the pension calculation, as well as years when someone was caring for a child under the age of seven. In the United States, benefits are based on thirty-five years of earnings; only the five years of lowest earnings (out of forty) are deducted from the benefit calculation. For many women, these are years of zero earnings spent caring for young children. The resultant pensions in Canada, which are gender-neutral, are designed to replace about 25 percent of average earnings.

Spousal benefits are not paid under the Canada Pension Plan or the Quebec Pension Plan. However, survivors' benefits are payable to legally married and common-law survivors. These benefits amount to 60 percent of the spouse's retirement pension, up to a maximum, and are reduced for retirement below the age of sixty-five. In the United States, the spousal benefit, which amounts to a maximum of 50 percent of a Social Security beneficiary's retired worker benefit, remains an important feature of the Social Security program. Upon widowhood, survivors—99 percent of whom are women—become eligible for 100 percent of the decedent's Social Security benefit.

The Canada Pension Plan provides credit splitting upon divorce or separation. Based on the premise that marriage or a common-law relationship is an economic partnership, credit splitting acknowledges that both partners are entitled to share the pension credits earned by either partner during their marriage or cohabitation. Upon divorce or separation, pension credits earned during cohabitation are combined and divided equally between the partners, even if one spouse never contributed to the CPP. Such splitting generally works to the advantage of the lower earner in a partnership, typically the wife, and produces a higher retirement benefit than otherwise would have been received. Pension sharing, or assignment, enables spouses who are retired to split their combined CPP benefits equally if one of the spouses requests this.

Credit splitting and pension sharing remain rare in pension systems around the world. In the United States, a divorced spouse who has been married for at least ten years is also eligible for spousal benefit of up to 50 percent of the other spouse's retired worker benefit. A surviving spouse—whether a widow or divorcée who had been married ten or more years—will collect 100 percent of the former spouse's benefit if that is higher than her own benefit. Common law partners may also be eligible for spousal and survivor benefits in states that recognize these marriages. Earnings sharing, as it is called in the United States, has been proposed for Social Security; under these proposals, spouses would split equally the contributions, even zero contributions, made to Social Security during the years that they were married. Although extensively studied in the 1980s, earnings sharing has not advanced legislatively in the United States.

Canadian workers may be eligible for disability benefits if they have worked and contributed to the Canada Pension Plan or Quebec Pension Plan for a specified period. To qualify for disability benefits, a worker must have "severe and prolonged incapacity [physical or mental] for any gainful activity" (U.S. Social Security Administration, 1999, p. 65). Benefits consist of a basic flat-rate payment and a payment based on earnings. At age sixty-five, disability benefits are converted to a retirement pension. Access to health insurance is an important component of financial well-being in old age, and virtually all Canadians are eligible for publicly funded health care in Canada. In the United States, the Social Security Disability Insurance program helps workers who are unable to "engage in substantial gainful activity due to impairment expected to last at least one year or result in death" (U.S. Social Security Administration, 1999, p. 372). The programs of both countries require a *recency of work* test to qualify for disability benefits.

Private income support programs for older nonworkers

Canadians are encouraged to save for retirement through registered pension plans (RPPs) and registered retirement savings plans (RRSPs). Registered pension plans, which may be referred to as private or occupational pensions, are of two basic types: (1) a defined benefit plan and (2) a money purchase, or defined contribution plan. Most RPPs require employee contributions. Like their counterparts in the United States, defined benefit plans in Canada promise a specific benefit based on earnings and years of covered service; employers are required to fully fund these plans. A defined contribution plan merely defines the contribution level; payment at retirement depends on accumulated contributions and the return on the investment of those contributions.

While the CPP and QPP cover virtually all workers in the paid labor force, registered pension plans covered only about 40 percent of paid workers in 1997. Private pension plans in the United States cover approximately half of the workers in the paid labor force. In both countries, coverage is greater among employees in larger establishments than in small ones. Men and higher-wage workers are more likely to be covered than women and low-wage workers. In neither country are cost-of-living adjustments required.

A registered retirement savings plan is a tax-deductible savings plan that, up to certain limits, allows individuals to claim tax deductions for retirement contributions. Contributions accumulate tax free, as do individual retirement account (IRA) contributions in the United States. Funds are subject to taxation when they are received, unless used to purchase a retirement annuity or registered retirement income fund, in which case tax deferment continues until the funds are received as retirement income. As of 1999, Canadian tax filers who claimed retirement savings set aside over 11 percent of their income for retirement; 55 percent of that was in RRSPs, and 45 percent in RPPs.

Summary

There are three levels in Canada's retirement income system. The first level is the Old Age Security program, the second is the Canada Pension Plan, and the third is private savings, which includes individual savings and private or employer-sponsored pension plans. The U.S. retirement income system also has three components: Social Security, employer-provided pensions, and individual savings. Canada's Old Age Security program and the U.S.'s Social Security program are intended to provide a foundation of old-age support supplemented by income from the other levels of the system. In neither country is any one component of the system intended to serve as the sole source of retirement support, unlike a number of European countries, which have very generous replacement rates (retirement benefits as a percentage of pre-retirement earnings) in their public social security programs.

One of the most significant differences between the Canadian and the U.S. social security programs is that Canada offers a universal pension and the United States does not. A key similarity between the two systems is the mandatory, earnings-related component that covers workers in the two countries and that requires contributions from both workers and their employers. These earnings-related programs both provide relatively modest replacement rates that are adjusted to keep pace with inflation. There is a greater use of general revenues to support older persons in Canada than in the United States.

Neither the Canadian publicly financed retirement income system nor the one in the United States provides all of the financial support middle-income retirees are likely to need in old age. Both countries attempt to have these benefits supplemented by employer-provided pensions and individuals savings. Both countries make supplemental benefits available to the needy elderly, although the programs that do this are very different from one another.

Despite differences in the public retirement income systems of Canada and the United States, both contribute roughly the same amount to total retirement income, though less of the total comes from the earnings-related pension in Canada than in the United States. About 50 percent of the aggregate income of persons age sixty-five and older in Canada in 1997 came from the OAS (29 percent) or the CPP/QPP (21 percent), while about 46 percent of the aggregate income of the sixty-five-plus population in the United States in 1998 came from publicly funded pensions, mainly from Social Security. Canada's Guaranteed Income Supplement goes to a much higher proportion of older persons than does the U.S.'s SSI, although GIS is not, according to Turner (2001), a poverty program like the U.S.'s Supplemental Security Income program.

Another significant difference between the Canada Pension Plan and the U.S. Social Security program is the diversified investment of reserves currently permitted in the CPP but not in the U.S. Social Security program. Credit splitting

also distinguishes the publicly financed income retirement system in Canada from that in the United States.

Improvements in both systems over the years have resulted in sharp declines in the proportion of poor or low-income elderly. Though economic security continues to elude many retirees, especially women, the availability of indexed benefits guaranteed for life has gone a long way toward enhancing the economic security of older nonworkers in Canada and the United States. As a result, retirement in comfort and dignity is a reality for growing numbers of retirees in both countries.

Detailed information on income support for older nonworkers in Canada can be found at the web site of Human Resources Development Canada (www.hrdc-drhc.gc.ca). Information for U.S. programs can be found at www.ssa.gov.

SARA E. RIX

See also CANADA; CANADA, HEALTH CARE COVERAGE FOR OLDER PEOPLE; INCOME SUPPORT FOR NONWORKERS, NATIONAL APPROACHES; SOCIAL SECURITY, HISTORY AND OPERATIONS; SOCIAL SECURITY, LONG-TERM FINANCING AND REFORM; WELFARE STATE.

BIBLIOGRAPHY

Congress of the United States, Congressional Budget Office. *Earnings Sharing Options for the Social Security System.* Washington, D.C.: Congressional Budget Office, 1986.

FIERST, E. U., and CAMPBELL, N. D., eds. *Earnings Sharing in Social Security: A Model for Reform.* Washington, D.C.: Center for Women Policy Studies, 1988.

GUNDERSON, M.; HYATT, D.; and PESANDO, J. E. "Public Pension Plans in the United States and Canada." In *Employee Benefits and Labor Markets in Canada and the United States.* Edited by W. T. Alpert and S. A. Woodbury. Kalamazoo, Mich.: W. E. Upjohn Institute for Employment Research, 2000. Pages 381–411.

Human Resources Development Canada. "Did You Know? The Three Floors of the Retirement Income System." World Wide Web document, 2000. www.hrdc-drhc.gc.ca

Human Resources Development Canada. "Facts, Impact, and Context—Canada's Public Pensions." World Wide Web document, 2000. www.hrdc-drhc.gc.ca

International Social Security Association. *Social Security Worldwide, 2001—Edition 1.* Geneva:

International Social Security Association, 2001.

National Council of Welfare. *A Pension Primer.* Ottawa: National Council of Welfare. Available at www.ncwcnbes.net

Statistics Canada. "Proportion of Labour Force and Paid Workers Covered by a Registered Pension Plan (RPP) by Sex." Statistics Canada, 2001. Available at www.statcan.ca

Statistics Canada. "Retirement Savings Through RRSPs and RPPs." Statistics Canada. Available at www.statcan.ca

Turner, J. "Risk Sharing Through Social Security Retirement Income Systems." In *Pay at Risk: Risk Bearing by U.S. and Canadian Workers.* Edited by J. Turner. Kalamazoo, Mich.: Upjohn Institute for Employment Policy, 2001.

U.S. House of Representatives, Committee on Ways and Means, Subcommittee on Social Security. *Report on Earnings Sharing Implementation Study.* Washington, D.C.: U.S. Government Printing Office, 1985.

U.S. Social Security Administration. *Income of the Population 55 or Older.* Washington, D.C.: U.S. Government Printing Office, 2000.

U.S. Social Security Administration. *Social Security Programs Throughout the World—1999.* Washington, D.C.: U.S. Government Printing Office, 1999.

CANCER, BIOLOGY

Complex multicellular organisms contain two basic classes of cells: *mitotic* and *postmitotic.* Postmitotic cells cannot divide, although they may function throughout adult life. Examples of postmitotic cells include mature neurons, adipocytes (fat cells), and mature muscle cells. Mitotic cells, by contrast, retain the ability to divide throughout life. Mitotic cells may divide continually, or they may divide only when there is a need for cell replacement or tissue repair. Mitotic cells include the differentiated (specialized) cells of epithelial tissues, such as skin, liver, colon, lung, breast, and prostate. They also include certain cells of the immune system, such as T and B lymphocytes, and cells that support epithelial and postmitotic cells, such as fibroblasts and glia. Cancers never arise from postmitotic cells, but only from mitotic cells.

Cancers in children and young adults tend to be caused by defects in development or tissue maturation. Early-life cancers include certain cancers of the developing immune system (leukemias), retinoblastoma (cancer of the developing retina), and osteosarcoma (bone cancer). Early-life cancers tend to arise from precursors to postmitotic cells (i.e., a neuroblastoma tumor is composed of precursors to neurons), or mitotic cells that support epithelial or postmitotic cells (for example, fibrosarcoma or glioblastoma tumors are composed of fibroblasts and glial cells, respectively).

By contrast, most cancers that arise during middle and old age derive from epithelial cells and, to a lesser extent, the immune system. Epithelial tissues such as skin, stomach, and colon are composed of cells that are constantly sloughed off and replaced, and therefore contain cells that proliferate constantly throughout life. Other tissues show periodic or relatively slow proliferation. Examples include the breast, where epithelial cells proliferate with each estrus cycle, and the mature immune system, where cells proliferate in response to specific antigens. Tissues that show constant or periodic cell proliferation are particularly prone to developing tumors later in life. Tissues in which cells divide relatively infrequently are much less susceptible to developing into cancer with age. Examples include liver and kidney tissue, as well as cells that support and direct the functions of epithelial and postmitotic cells, such as fibroblasts and glia. However, chronic injury, toxicity, or infection can greatly increase tumor incidence in these tissues.

What is cancer?

Cancer is the proliferation (growth) of malignant cells—cells that grow inappropriately, disrupt normal tissue structure and function, and, frequently, can survive in the blood stream and proliferate at distal sites. Cancer, if unchecked, can kill the organism in which it exists.

Loss of growth control *per se* does not define a cell as malignant. Malignant cells have additional properties, specifically an ability to migrate and infiltrate the surrounding normal tissue (invasiveness) and induce a blood supply to feed the growing tumor (angiogenesis). Cancer cells invariably lose their differentiated properties (anaplasia), and they eventually acquire the ability to colonize and invade distal tissues (metastasis).

Loss of growth control. All cancers are characterized by abnormal cell growth (hyperproliferation, or *neoplasia*). Neoplasias may be benign (not invasive or metastatic) or malignant (invasive and frequently metastatic). Benign tumors are rarely fatal, because their growth, however abundant, is rarely unlimited (and, additionally, they are rarely invasive or metastatic). Malignant tumors, by contrast, tend to grow progressively, even if slowly.

Normal cell proliferation is controlled by an exquisite balance between processes that stimulate growth and those that inhibit growth. When this balance is upset, abnormal growth occurs. Abnormal growth is generally caused by an increase in growth-stimulatory processes, as well as a decrease in growth-inhibitory processes.

External signals.   Many growth stimulatory and inhibitory processes are triggered by signals that originate outside the cell (the cellular microenvironment). These external signals can be delivered by small diffusible molecules, such as growth factors, cytokines or circulating hormones, or by large molecules, such as components of the extracellular matrix or basement membrane. They can also be delivered by adjacent or nearby cells. For example, *fibroblasts*, which produce the collagen-rich matrix (stroma) that underlies most epithelial layers, signal and instruct the epithelial cells. External growth-regulatory molecules generally act by binding and altering transmembrane cell-surface receptors. The altered receptors then associate with or modify intracellular proteins at the underside of the cell-surface. These molecules, in turn, produce small diffusible chemical signals inside cells that, by interacting with or modifying yet other intracellular proteins, eventually send a signal to the cell nucleus. In the nucleus, specific genes that stimulate or inhibit progression through the cell cycle are then switched on or off.

Cellular senescence.   Cell proliferation can also be governed by signals that originate within cells. A prime example is cellular senescence, an intrinsic program that causes mitotic cells to irreversibly withdraw from the cell cycle.

Most cells from adult organisms cannot divide indefinitely, owing to a process termed *replicative senescence*. In humans (and certain other species), replicative senescence occurs because cells lose a small amount of DNA from the chromosome ends (the telomeres) after each round of DNA replication, and cells irreversibly arrest growth when they acquire one (or more) critically short telomere. Such cells are said to be replicatively senescent. Mitotic cells enter a state that closely resembles replicative senescence when

Figure 1
Human fetal fibroblasts, prior to replicative senescence (Presenescent panel, left), grow in culture until they form a single, ordered, continuous layer on the culture dish. After about fifty doublings, the cultures become senescent (Senescent panel, middle). The senescent cells are flattened and enlarged, and form a layer with many gaps. The right panel shows cells from a human fibrosarcoma, a tumor formed from fibroblasts. The tumor cells form a disorganized layer, and will eventually grow atop one another. All the cells in the panels were stained for the presence of the senescence-associated beta-galactosidase, an enzyme that is expressed by senescent cells. Cells that express this enzyme appear as darker areas in the panels.

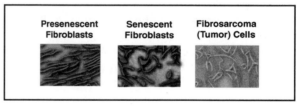

SOURCE: Author

they experience sublethal DNA damage, supraphysiological growth signals, or expression of certain oncogenes (genes that promote neoplastic growth). Replicative senescence, then, is a special example of a more general process termed *cellular senescence*. Short telomeres, DNA damage, over-exuberant growth signals, and oncogenes all have the potential to change a normal cell into a precancerous or cancer cell. Thus, cellular senescence, or the senescence response, suppresses tumorigenesis by preventing the growth of cells at risk for malignant transformation.

Cellular senescence appears to be a major barrier that cells must overcome in order to become malignant. Several lines of evidence support this idea. First, most, if not all, malignant tumors contain cells that have overcome cellular senescence. (Many tumor cells accomplish this by expressing telomerase, the enzyme that replenishes the telomeric DNA that is lost during DNA replication. Telomerase is expressed by the germ line and early embryonic cells, but is repressed in most adult cells.) Second, some oncogenes act by allowing cells to ignore senescence-inducing signals. Cells that express such oncogenes continue to proliferate despite short telomeres, DNA damage, or other potentially oncogenic conditions. Third, cellular senescence is controlled by the p53 and pRB tumor-suppressor proteins, the two most commonly mutated tumor suppressors in human cancers. Finally, mutant mice have been generated in which cells fail to respond to senescence signals. Such animals invariably die from cancer at an early age.

Cellular senescence is also thought to contribute to aging. At first glance, this idea may seem at odds with its tumor-suppressive function. It is consistent, however, with the theory of evolutionary antagonistic pleiotropy. This theory predicts that, because the force of natural selection declines with increasing age, some traits that were selected to optimize fitness during development or young adulthood can have unselected deleterious effects in aged organisms. In the case of cellular senescence, the irreversible growth arrest may be the selected trait that prevents the proliferation of cells at risk for malignant transformation. Other features of the senescent phenotype, such as resistance to programmed cell death and changes in cell function, may be unselected and deleterious.

Some senescent cells are resistant to programmed cell death (apoptosis), and all senescent cells display changes in cell function. The functional changes can be striking. For example, senescent fibroblasts secrete degradative enzymes, inflammatory cytokines (small molecules that attract macrophages or neutrophils), and growth factors. Thus, senescent fibroblasts can create a microenvironment that resembles chronic wounding, which can disrupt tissue structure and/or function as senescent cells accumulate. Senescent cells appear to be relatively rare in young tissues, but more common in old tissues. As discussed below, their ability to disrupt tissue structure may contribute to aging, as well as the rise in late-life cancers.

Apoptosis. Most tissues achieve and maintain proper size by a balance between cell proliferation and death. All cells are capable of an orderly suicide process, termed *programmed cell death* or *apoptosis*. Apoptosis is important during embryogenesis, where it can rid the fetus of excess or damaged cells, or cells that fail to receive signals needed for proper function. Apoptosis is also important in adults, where it helps maintain the size of cell populations or tissues. Equally important, apoptosis removes damaged cells from adult tissues, and thus is another tumor-suppressive mechanism.

Many tumor cells develop defects in the control of apoptosis. Consequently, many tumor cells survive under circumstances that would cause their normal counterparts to die. There is limited but compelling evidence that, in at least some tissues, apoptosis declines with increasing age. This decline may also contribute to the increase in age-related cancer.

Loss of differentiation. Another feature of cancer is abnormal differentiation, or *anaplasia*. All cells contain the same DNA, and hence the same genome (30,000 to 50,000 genes, in humans). However, each cell expresses (transcribes into RNA and translates into protein) only 10 to 20 percent of its genome. The selective expression of genes is termed *differentiation*, and it is responsible for the characteristics that distinguish different cell types from each other.

Differentiation begins early in embryogenesis. By adulthood, most tissues have matured and function much as they will throughout life. Nonetheless, differentiation is an ongoing process in tissues that rely on stem cells for renewal or repair. Stem cells are mitotic cells that, upon division, either produce another stem cell or produce a differentiated cell. In the skin, for example, stem cells renew themselves, but more frequently they give rise to basal keratinocytes. Basal keratinocytes, in turn, divide and differentiate into cells that form the upper layers of the epidermis. Throughout life, basal cells divide and progressively differentiate into upper keratinocytes, including the outermost postmitotic cells, which are eventually sloughed off. The stem cells divide relatively infrequently, but often enough to maintain the pool of basal cells. Differentiation not only determines which specialized proteins are made by a cell, but also whether cells are mitotic or postmitotic, whether a cell proliferates or dies, and whether and how a cell migrates or communicates with other cells.

Because differentiation integrates cell growth and death with function, it is not surprising that tumors invariably show signs of abnormal differentiation. Tumor cells are generally less differentiated than surrounding normal cells, and the most aggressive tumors tend to be the least differentiated. Some cancers may arise directly from the least differentiated cells in a tissue, or from the stem cells. In other cases, a cancer cell may acquire an abnormal pattern of gene expression, leading to a less differentiated state.

Childhood and young-adult cancers tend to be poorly differentiated, generally arising from precursor or stem cells. Cancers of old adults, by contrast, include both poorly differentiated and relatively well-differentiated tumors.

Angiogenesis, invasion, and metastasis. Malignant tumors acquire the ability to migrate and invade the surrounding normal tissue (invasiveness). They also stimulate the formation of blood vessels (angiogenesis), which provide the growing tumor with nutrients. The most malignant tumors acquire the ability to survive in the blood stream and colonize distal tissues (metastasis). These abilities are also characteristic of fetal cells. Hence, the anaplasia of tumor cells is often responsible for their invasive, metastatic, and angiogenic properties.

Cancer cells become invasive when they secrete enzymes that degrade the extracellular matrix and stroma, and they become angiogenic when they secrete cytokines that attract endothelial and other cells needed for blood vessel formation. Many tumor cells also secrete factors that cause stromal fibroblasts to secrete degradative enzymes and endothelial attractants. Although cancer incidence increases exponentially with age, tumors in very old individuals tend to be less aggressive than tumors in middle-aged adults. This age-dependent difference may reflect the response of the surrounding host cells. Indeed, some tumors are less vascularized in older hosts because their endothelial cells respond much less well to tumor-derived angiogenic factors.

Metastasis requires that solid tumor cells acquire the ability to survive in the hostile environments of the bloodstream and a foreign (ectopic) tissue. Most normal cells (and even most preneoplastic or benign tumor cells) undergo apoptosis when placed in a foreign environment. Metastatic tumor cells either fail to sense environmental cues that normally cause cell death, or they fail to execute the apoptotic program. In addition, metastatic tumor cells frequently express cell-surface proteins that allow them to adhere to and infiltrate an ectopic site.

Genomic instability. Another hallmark of malignant tumors is genomic instability. A prime cause of cancer is the accumulation of mutations. Most cancers develop from preneoplastic cells—cells that have acquired mutations (one, or a few) that confer a growth or survival advantage. Preneoplastic cells are not malignant, but are predisposed to malignant transformation upon acquiring additional mutations. During the 1980s and 1990s, cancers were thought to develop because cells successively acquired a discrete number of mutations, generally half a dozen or so, depending on the tissue. However, recent findings show that most tumors harbor many mutations, often exceeding several dozen.

Spontaneous mutation at any locus tends to occur once every hundred thousand or so cell divisions. How, then, do tumors acquire dozens of mutations during progression to malignancy? Most cancer cells eventually acquire a mutation in one or more genes that ensure genomic stability—the remarkable fidelity with which nuclear DNA and chromosome organization are maintained. These proteins, often referred to as *guardians of the genome,* include the p53 tumor suppressor, which halts the cell cycle when DNA is damaged. They also include proteins that regulate chromosome segregation during mitosis and participate in DNA repair. As discussed below, some of these genes can be considered longevity assurance genes—genes that, when lost or mutated, shorten life span and accelerate certain age-related pathologies.

Once a cell loses the activity of one or more guardians of the genome, the genome becomes unstable and mutations occur much more frequently. A high mutation rate allows cancer cells to evolve rapidly. Thus, the genomic instability of cancer cells allows rapid selection for cells that have ever more aggressive and malignant properties.

What causes cancer?

Cancer is caused by a combination of genetic and epigenetic factors. Genetic factors include mutations, both germ line and somatic, and polymorphisms. Mutations substantially change the expression levels, activities, or functions of encoded proteins. Many childhood cancers, and a minority of adult cancers, are caused by germ-line mutations—inherited mutations that are present in the DNA of every cell in the organism. By contrast, most adult cancers are caused by somatic (non-germ-line) mutations—mutations acquired by a somatic cell during development, maturation or, most commonly, adulthood. On the other hand, polymorphisms—minor sequence variations that only subtly change protein expression, activity, or function—rarely cause disease, but can predispose individuals to develop diseases, including cancer. Individuals within a species differ, despite a common genome, largely because most genes exist in multiple forms (polymorphisms) that differ by one or a few nucleotides. Perhaps the best known example is the ApoE4 variant of the ApoE gene, which predisposes individuals to Alzheimer's disease. Polymorphisms that are thought to predispose individuals to developing cancer occur in genes that control cell growth, differentiation, or apoptosis, or enzymes that metabolize carcinogens or anticarcinogens.

Epigenetic factors that cause cancer include reversible changes to DNA, such as DNA methylation or posttranslational modification of DNA-associated proteins, such as histones. Such changes generally alter the compaction of chromatin (DNA plus associated proteins), which can have profound effects on gene expression. In addition, the tissue structure and hormonal milieu in which a potential cancer cell exists can strongly influence whether, and to what extent, it progresses to form a malignant tumor. The influence of tissue structure may be particularly important for the development of late-life cancers.

Cancer-causing mutations. Cancer-causing mutations range from single base changes (point mutations) to gross rearrangements, losses, and/or amplifications of large regions of chromosomes. The latter mutations generally occur when cancer cells develop genomic instability. What are the targets of cancer-causing mutations? Given the features of cancer cells—abnormal growth, resistance to apoptosis, loss of differentiation, and genomic instability—there are many genes that, when mutated, can contribute to malignant transformation. In general, these genes fall into either of two categories: oncogenes and tumor suppressor genes.

Oncogenes. Oncogenes are mutant forms of normal cellular genes termed *proto-oncogenes*. Proto-oncogenes generally encode proteins (proto-oncoproteins) that stimulate cell proliferation, regulate apoptosis, or restrain differentiation. In normal cells, the activities of proto-oncoproteins are tightly regulated. Mutations that convert a proto-oncogene into an oncogene often render the encoded protein resistant to

normal regulatory constraints, or cause the protein to be overexpressed. Mutations that convert proto-oncogenes to oncogenes generally result in a *gain of function*; that is, the mutation confers new or supraphysiological properties to the protein. Such mutations are dominant because only one of the two gene copies need be mutant in order for the mutation to exert its effects.

Proto-oncoproteins include growth factors, growth-factor receptors and their signal transduction proteins, growth-stimulatory transcription factors, and antiapoptotic proteins. Activating mutations range from subtle point mutations to gross chromosome rearrangements that create novel chimeric proteins.

An example of a simple activating point mutation is illustrated by members of the RAS proto-oncogene family. RAS proteins bind GTP (guanosine triphosphate) in response to growth-factor receptor occupancy, whereupon they transduce a growth-stimulatory signal. Shortly thereafter, the intrinsic GTPase activity of the RAS proteins converts the bound GTP to GDP (guanosine diphosphate), thereby attenuating the growth signal. Oncogenic mutations in RAS tend to be point mutations that abolish GTPase activity, but not GTP binding, thereby causing a constitutively active growth signal. The other end of the spectrum is illustrated by the ABL proto-oncogene, which encodes a protein tyrosine kinase that promotes cell death in response to DNA damage. ABL is converted to an oncogene when a chromosome breakage and rejoining event translocates the *ABL* gene, which is located on chromosome 9, to the *BCR* gene on chromosome 22. This translocation produces a novel fusion protein, BCR-ABL, which is a highly active, unregulated protein kinase. In contrast to the normal ABL protein, the BCR-ABL protein inhibits apoptosis after DNA damage, thereby allowing damaged cells to survive and proliferate.

Oncogenic mutations can also simply increase proto-oncogene expression. Two examples are MYC and BCL2, which encode a transcription factor that stimulates cell-cycle progression and a protein that inhibits apoptosis, respectively. Occasionally, a translocation moves these proto-oncogenes to a chromosome region containing the immunoglobin genes. When this occurs in a pre-B lymphocyte, where the immunoglobin genes are highly transcribed, MYC and BCL2 are overexpressed. This, in turn, promotes uncontrolled cell proliferation in the case of MYC, or resistance to cell death in the case of BCL2.

Thus, some mutations cause activation or overexpression of proto-oncogenes, creating oncogenes with supraphysiological or new functions, which in turn promote cell growth or inhibit differentiation or cell death.

Tumor suppressor genes. Tumor suppressors inhibit cell growth, promote differentiation, or stimulate apoptosis. They also suppress genomic instability, allowing cells to sense or repair DNA damage. In contrast to the gain-of-function mutations that activate proto-oncogenes, oncogenic mutations in tumor suppressor genes generally delete or inactivate the gene (loss of function). In most cases, both gene copies must be inactivated before loss-of- function is obvious. Thus, oncogenic mutations in tumor suppressor genes tend to be recessive.

Tumor suppressors include growth inhibitors and their receptors and signal transducers, transcription factors, proapoptotic proteins, and proteins that sense or repair DNA damage. Inactivating mutations are often chromosome aberrations that delete large segments of DNA. However, more subtle mutations (for example, point mutations) can also inactivate tumor suppressors.

The most widely studied, and possibly most important, tumor suppressor genes are RB and TP53, which encode the pRB and p53 proteins. These proteins are at the heart of two major tumor-suppressor pathways, each comprised of many interacting proteins. They are critical for the control of cellular senescence and are mutated in over 80 percent of human cancers.

pRB is a nuclear protein that indirectly controls the transcription of many genes. pRB is phosphorylated by several protein kinases, most prominently cyclin-dependent kinases (CDKs). When underphosphorylated, as it is in nondividing cells, pRB prevents the initiation of DNA synthesis. pRB is progressively phosphorylated by CDKs as cells progress through G1 (the phase of the cell cycle that precedes the period of DNA synthesis (S phase)). Phosphorylated pRB is inactive and cannot prevent cell-cycle progression. Growth factors and inhibitors promote or prevent cell proliferation ultimately by controlling pRB phosphorylation. Many cancer cells have deletions or inactivating mutations in both copies of RB, and thus fail to arrest growth in response to growth-inhibitory signals. Some cancer cells lack pRB mutations, but harbor inactivating mutations in the p16 tumor suppressor or overexpress cyclins D or E; p16 inhibits the CDKs that phosphorylate pRB, while cyclins D and E stimulate these CDKs. Thus, most mammalian cancers harbor mutations in the pRB pathway such that pRB is either physically or functionally inactive.

Most mammalian cancers also harbor mutations in the p53 pathway, whose functions overlap and differ from those of the pRB pathway. p53 is a transcription factor that also halts cell-cycle progression—it is phosphorylated and stabilized in response to DNA damage, whereupon it induces genes that either halt progression into S phase and mitosis, stimulate repair, or induce apoptosis. Among the genes induced by p53 is the CDK inhibitor p21, providing an interaction between the p53 and pRB pathways. p53 plays a pivotal role in damage sensing and repair and is considered a guardian of the genome. Its function is abrogated by deletion (loss of function), but also by point mutations, which alter its properties as a transcription factor (gain of function). Many cancer cells harbor mutations in p53. Such cells fail to properly repair damaged DNA, but also fail to die. Consequently, they develop genomic instability, which accelerates mutation accumulation. Cancer cells that lack mutations in p53 generally have mutations in regulators of p53 expression or function.

Epigenetic factors and the cellular microenvironment.   Nonmutational (epigenetic) events can also play a critical role in the development of cancer. Within cells, physiological modification of DNA—such as methylation of cytosine—can strongly influence gene expression. Methylated DNA is generally transcriptionally silent, largely because it is packaged into chromatin that is very compact. Loss of normal methylation can cause inappropriate proto-oncogene expression; conversely, inappropriate methylation can silence tumor suppressor genes.

Chromatin compaction is regulated largely by the presence of, and modifications to, histones and other DNA-binding proteins. These proteins are stripped from the DNA (and must be faithfully replaced) each time a cell undergoes DNA replication or during repair. Errors in replacement, or changes in cell physiology that alter the expression or modification of chromatin-compaction proteins, can also result in inappropriate proto-oncogene expression or silencing of tumor suppressor genes.

Outside the cell, the surrounding milieu or microenvironment can be a critical determinant of whether and how a cell harboring oncogenic mutations expresses itself. It has been known for several decades that tumor cells may develop into a fully malignant tumor, slow-growing and relatively benign tumor, or no tumor at all, depending on the tissue into which it is transplanted. It is now also known that all cells sense their microenvironment through specific receptors, including cell-surface receptors. Some of these receptors bind soluble growth factors and inhibitors, whereas others (integrins) bind extracellular matrix components. In some tumors, these receptors are mutated. Most frequently, however, tumor cells express an altered pattern of receptors and integrins.

Experiments have shown that by manipulating the cellular microenvironment, particularly the extracellular matrix, some tumor cells can be induced to lose their malignant properties, including their ability to form tumors in animals. Conversely, chronic disruption of the cellular microenvironment—for example, by cells that ectopically express a protease that degrades the extracellular matrix—can promote the development of cancer. Even apparently normal tissue contains cells that harbor potentially oncogenic mutations. Such cells are prevented from progressing to more malignant phenotypes by the normal microenvironment, while disruption of the microenvironment allows such cells to express their oncogenic potential. Thus, the microenvironment within a tissue can be a powerful tumor-suppressive mechanism that, in many cases, is dominant over oncogenic mutations.

Cancer and aging

The largest single risk factor for developing cancer is age. The incidence of cancer increases exponentially with age, although death from cancer (cancer mortality) may decline at very old age. The inevitable age-dependent rise in cancer incidence is a feature of multicellular organisms that contain a substantial fraction of mitotic cells. Model organisms such as *Drosophila melanogaster* (flies) and *Caenorhabditis elegans* (worms) are composed primarily of postmitotic cells, and hence do not develop cancer. Mammals, on the other hand, contain tissues that have a large population of mitotic cells, many of which tend to develop cancers with increasing age. There are a number of known and suspected causes of age-dependent susceptibility to cancer.

Mutations increase with age. There is little doubt that mutations are a critical cause of cancer. Virtually all tumors harbor mutations. In fact, most tumors harbor dozens of mutations, many of which are detectable as large genomic amplifications or losses. The copious genomic changes that are characteristic of most tumor cells reflect an end stage in tumorigenesis—the point at which cells have presumably acquired genomic instability. Hence, mutations are rampant and have enabled the tumor cell to overcome the substantial intrinsic (e.g., cellular senescence) and extrinsic (e.g., cellular microenvironment) tumor-suppressive mechanisms. Prior to this stage, however, cells accumulate mutations, at least some of which are potentially oncogenic, in an age-dependent manner. Thus, mitotic (but, interestingly, not postmitotic) tissues have been shown to accumulate a variety of mutations with increasing age, as detected by a neutral mutation-reporter gene integrated into the genome of transgenic mice. Likewise, p53 mutations have been shown to accumulate in apparently normal tissue, particularly in skin exposed to ultraviolet radiation. Finally, apparently normal human tissue has been shown to accumulate mutations, particularly loss of heterozygosity, which predisposes cells to loss of tumor suppressor genes. Thus, potentially oncogenic mutations accumulate with increasing age.

Aging tissue and cellular microenvironments. Given that the tissue microenvironment can exert a powerful suppressive effect on oncogenically mutated genomes, mutation accumulation alone cannot explain the exponential rise in cancer incidence with age. Although this phenomena has been explained by the accumulation of four to eight critical mutations, tumors typically harbor dozens of mutations. Moreover, as noted above, cells with oncogenic mutations are present in normal tissue. Finally, the difference between a nonaggressive and relatively benign tumor and an aggressive metastatic tumor cannot be easily explained by the number of mutations alone.

One possible explanation for the age-dependent rise in cancer is that mutation accumulation synergizes with the cellular microenvironment provided by aged tissue. Many tissues show an age-dependent decline in tissue function and structure, the latter often obvious by simple histological inspection. The cause(s) of the changes in tissue structure are incompletely understood. One cause may be the accumulation of senescent cells, which, as discussed earlier, secrete enzymes and cytokines that disrupt normal tissue architecture. However, other factors—such as crosslinking of extracellular matrix molecules by nonenzymatic glycation, or changes in circulating hormone levels—may also contribute to age-dependent changes in tissue structure and the cellular microenvironment.

Results from cell culture and animal experiments support the idea that aged tissues are a more fertile environment than young tissues for the growth of cancer cells. There is also evidence that senescent cells can create a more favorable environment than presenescent cells for the growth of tumor cells. Thus, the functional and structural changes that occur in aging tissues are likely an epigenetic cause for the development of cancer.

Despite the increased incidence of cancer with age, cancer mortality tends to decline at very advanced ages. Some cancers tend to be more indolent (slower growing and less aggressive) when they develop in very old individuals, compared to middle-aged individuals. The reasons for this are not well understood. As discussed earlier, angiogenesis may be less efficient in very old individuals. In addition, the hormonal milieu in very old individuals may be less conducive than that of middle-aged individuals to tumor progression. Whatever the case, cancer poses a major limitation to the health and longevity of mammals, and it appears to result from an accumulation of mutations, as well as from age-dependent changes in tissue structure and function.

Tumor suppressor and longevity assurance genes. During the evolution of complex multicellular organisms, there was a need to evolve genes that would protect organisms from developing cancer, that is, tumor suppressor genes. As such, at least some tumor suppressor genes act as longevity assurance genes (LAGs)—genes that function to assure the health and fitness of organisms during their reproductive life span. Among mammals, cancer incidence begins to rise at about the midpoint of the maximum life span, or after reproductive fitness declines. Thus, tumor suppressors are effective LAGs, postponing cancer in young organisms during the peak of reproduction and declining in efficacy, or even acting with antagonistic pleiotropy, only after reproductive fitness has declined.

Tumor suppressor genes encode a variety of proteins, and many of them function during development as well as in adults (e.g., those that control fundamental features of the cell cycle, differentiation, or apoptosis). Such genes cannot be considered LAGs *per se* because their functions are also critical for normal development. However, other tumor suppressor genes, such as TP53, are classic LAGs because they are dispensable for normal development but critical for preventing cancer in young organisms.

At least among mammals, the rate of aging, the rate of cancer development, and maximum life span are very tightly linked. Thus, most mice live a maximum of roughly three years and develop cancer largely after a year and a half or so, whereas the human maximum life span is roughly 120 years—cancers develop largely after fifty years or so. Despite this remarkable species difference in the rates of cancer development and aging, the major tumor suppressor pathways—those controlled by p53 and pRB—are well conserved between mice and humans. That is, the mouse and human proteins that participate in the p53 and pRB pathways are very similar in their sequence and function. There are, however, many gaps in our knowledge about the molecular mechanisms that link cancer and aging.

JUDITH CAMPISI

See also BREAST; CANCER, DIAGNOSIS AND MANAGEMENT; CELLULAR AGING; CELLULAR AGING: CELL DEATH; CELLULAR AGING: TELOMERES; GENETICS, TUMOR SUPPRESSION.

BIBLIOGRAPHY

BACCHETTI, S., and WYNFORD-THOMAS, D. "Telomeres and Telomerase in Cancer." *European Journal of Cancer* 33 (1997): 703–792.

BALDUCCI, L., and BEGHE, C. "Cancer and Age in the USA." *Critical Reviews in Oncology/Hematology* 37 (2001): 137–145.

BISHOP, J. M. "Cancer: The Rise of the Genetic Paradigm" *Genes and Development* 9 (1995): 1309–1315.

CAHILL, D. P.; KINZLER, K. W.; VOGELSTEIN, B.; and LENGAUER, C. "Genetic Instability and Darwinian Selection in Tumours." *Trends in Cell Biology* 9 (1999): M57–M60.

CAMPISI, J. "Cancer, Aging and Cellular Senescence." *In Vivo* 14 (2000): 183–188.

DENG, G.; LU, Y.; ZLOTNIKOV, G.; THOR, A. D.; and SMITH, H. S. "Loss of Heterozygosity in

Normal Tissue Adjacent to Breast Carcinomas." *Science* 274 (1996): 2057–2059.

DEPINHO, R. A. "The Age of Cancer." *Nature* 408 (2000): 248–254.

DIMRI, G. P.; LEE, X.; BASILE, G.; ACOSTA, M.; SCOTT, G.; ROSKELLEY, C.; MEDRANO, E. E.; LINSKENS, M.; RUBELJ, I.; PEREIRA-SMITH, O.; PEACOCKE, M.; and CAMPISI, J. "A Biomarker that Identifies Senescent Human Cells in Culture and in Aging Skin In Vivo." *Proceedings of the National Academy of Sciences USA* 92 (1995): 9363–9367.

DOLLE, M. E. T.; SNYDER, W. K.; GOSSEN, J. A.; LOHMAN, P. H. M.; and VIJG, J. "Distinct Spectra of Somatic Mutations Accumulated with Age in Mouse Heart and Small Intestine." *Proceedings of the National Academy of Sciences USA* 97 (2000): 8403–8408.

GRAY, J. W., and COLLINS, C. "Genome Changes and Gene Expression in Human Solid Tumors." *Carcinogenesis* 21 (2000): 443–452.

HANAHAN, D., and WEINBERG, R. A. "The Hallmarks of Cancer." *Cell* 100 (2000): 57–70.

MCCULLOUGH, K. D.; COLEMAN, W. B.; SMITH, GARY J.; and GRISHAM, JOE W. "Age-Dependent Induction of Hepatic Tumor Regression by the Tissue Microenvironment after Transplantation of Neoplastically Transformed Rat Liver Epithelial Cells into the Liver." *Cancer Research* 57 (1997): 1807–1813.

MCLEOD, K. "Tumor Suppressor Genes." *Current Opinion in Genetics and Development* 10 (2000): 81–93.

MILLER, R. A. "Gerontology As Oncology: Research on Aging As a Key to the Understanding of Cancer." *Cancer* 68 (1991): 2496–2501.

PARK, C. C.; BISSELL, M. J.; and BARCELLOS-HOFF, M. H. "The Influence of the Microenvironment on the Malignant Phenotype." *Molecular Medicine Today* 8 (2000): 324–329.

REED, J. C. "Mechanisms of Apoptosis Avoidance in Cancer." *Current Opinion in Oncology* 11 (1999): 68–75.

SAGER, R. "Senescence As a Mode of Tumor Suppression." *Environmental Health Perspectives* 93 (1991): 59–62.

SHERR, C. J. "Cancer Cell Cycles." *Science* 274 (1996): 1672–1777.

WEINBERG, R. A. "How Cancer Arises." *Scientific American* 275 (1996): 62–70.

ZETTER, B. R. "Angiogenesis and Tumor Metastasis." *Annual Review of Medicine* 49 (1998): 407–424.

CANCER, DIAGNOSIS AND MANAGEMENT

While the group of Americans sixty-five years or older comprise about 13 percent of the population, 60 percent of all newly diagnosed cancers and 70 percent of all deaths from cancer occur in this age group, emphasizing the magnitude of this disease in older adults. All the major cancers primarily affect older adults, with the risk of developing cancer increasing as age increases. Of the most common cancers, 77 percent of prostate cancers, 74 percent of colon cancers, and 66 percent of lung cancers occur in elderly persons. Breast cancer, often thought to be a premenopausal disease, occurs 48 percent of the time in older women.

After heart disease, cancer is the second leading cause of death among older adults, with mortality rates increasing with advancing age. Thus not only does cancer occur at an increased rate in older adults, the possibility of dying from this disease increases as well. This phenomenon is not due to chronological age alone but is also related to the biologic characteristics of the tumor and the overall health and well-being of the older adult.

Cancer is a disease in which normal cells become abnormal with uncontrolled growth and the tendency to invade healthy tissue. Cells undergo this change, called malignant transformation, through the steps of initiation, promotion, and progression.

Initiation is the process in which the DNA of a cell is altered. External factors such as chemical carcinogens (e.g., tobacco smoke), physical carcinogens (e.g., radiation), or certain viruses and internal factors such as inherited mutations can trigger initiation. After initiation, the altered cell may exist for a long period of time without causing any problems. It is, however, susceptible to future alterations.

Promotion is the alteration of normal growth regulation. This may occur through the activation of cellular genes or oncogenes that stimulate growth, or by the deactivation of genes that normally keep growth in check, tumor suppressor genes.

Finally, during the progression step the tumor continues to grow and acquire additional DNA mutations. These abnormal cells develop the ability to invade healthy tissues, or metastasize. Metastatic potential requires additional cellular characteristics such as the ability to disrupt surrounding tissue and promote growth of new blood vessels.

In an attempt to explain the epidemiological relationship between cancer and aging, several hypotheses have been suggested. These include the possibility that aging may simply allow for the passage of sufficient time to accumulate cellular alterations. Some experiments suggest that aging cells may be more susceptible to carcinogens. Once damage occurs, it is compounded by a decreased ability to repair damaged DNA sequences.

Another area of research interest has been the role of telomeres, which are short stretches of DNA present at the ends of chromosomes. Telomeres act like anchors, protecting the stability of the rest of the DNA. As cells age, telomeres shorten, leading to genetic instability and possible mutation. Malignant cells activate a normally inactive enzyme, telomerase, a telomere-repairing enzyme, to preserve their telomere length.

The goal of diagnosis for cancer is to find and treat the disease in its early stages, yielding the best survival rates. However, in elderly persons, delays in diagnosis may occur. The person must recognize the abnormal symptoms and have knowledge of the warning signs of cancer. Some older adults may explain away their new symptoms as another change due to the aging process. Physicians may delay diagnostic tests by failing to recognize new signs and symptoms in a patient with multiple disease processes.

Some clinicians believe that cancers behave less aggressively in elderly persons but research findings have been inconclusive. Once a warning symptom is noticed, older adults do not delay any more than younger people in seeking medical help. However, such symptoms and signs may be less obvious in older people due to the presence of other chronic diseases and physiologic changes. Thus, the diagnosis of cancer in older people requires vigilant attention and high suspicion of symptoms by the older adult and the physician.

In general, treatment options for cancer consist of surgery, radiation, chemotherapy, or hormonal therapies. Although these treatment choices are similar to those provided to younger patients, the treatment decision process is more involved.

A person's level of function and well-being involves the interaction between physical, emotional, social, and cognitive states. Because of these relationships, any intervention in one area will influence the level of function in the other areas and vise versa, with the level of function in the other areas influencing the success of the intervention. These interactions become more evident and important in the older adult because aging leads to progressive reduction in the reserve capacity of these four areas. Thus, in the elderly person with cancer, successful treatment will be influenced not only by that person's biologic and physical status but also by the presence of other illnesses, depression, and level of social support.

Since aging is an individualized process and chronological age only partially reflects the decrease in functional reserve, a comprehensive geriatric assessment is recommended to evaluate the true functional capacity of the elderly person with cancer. A comprehensive geriatric assessment can provide information on treatment tolerance and the likelihood of therapeutic complications, unmask coexisting conditions, and reveal social impediments to cancer treatment. An important additional component to decision-making is the value of the older adult's own assessment of both the quantity and the quality of potential survival during and after the treatment for the cancer. In this way, judgments weighing the risks versus the benefits of diagnostic and therapeutic interventions can be made.

Surgery may be accomplished in elderly persons with mortality and morbidity rates that are similar to younger patients. Surgical success is influenced more by the presence of other illnesses and declines in physiologic functions than by chronological age. Older adults may actually prefer the acute and time-limited stress of surgery to the more chronic or protracted courses of chemotherapy or radiation therapy.

Unlike surgery, radiation therapy has no appreciable acute mortality and is generally not limited by associated medical conditions. Side effects are determined by dose and volume of tissue irradiated, and in elderly persons the radiation effect on normal tissues is enhanced approximately 10 to 15 percent.

Due to the decline in kidney function with age, aging affects the drug properties and elimination of chemotherapeutic agents. The degree of side effects and the potential response depend predominantly on the aggressiveness of the chemotherapy regimen. Thus, chemotherapy agents must be used in dosages that have acceptable response rates with acceptable levels of side effects. Hormonal therapy for breast and prostate cancer works at least as well in elderly patients as it does in younger persons.

Supportive care should always be a part of any therapy plan. Pain relief, nutritional support, the supportive role of nursing, and communication between physicians, patient, and family regarding decisions about care directives, terminal care, and utilization of hospice services help maximize the ability to tolerate the treatment as well as the disease.

Cancer occurs in the elderly with great frequency and further research is needed to reveal the interaction of the aging process with malignant transformation. The overall approach to the formulation of a diagnostic and treatment plan for the older adult involves systematic evaluation of their functional capacity and well-being.

PEARL H. SEO, M.D., M.P.H.
HARVEY JAY COHEN, M.D.

See also ASSESSMENT; BLOOD; BREAST; CANCER, BIOLOGY; CELLULAR AGING: TELOMERES; DNA DAMAGE AND REPAIR; PALLIATIVE CARE; PROSTATE; SURGERY IN ELDERLY PEOPLE.

BIBLIOGRAPHY

BALDUCCI, L., and EXTERMANN, M. "Cancer and Aging: An Evolving Panorama." *Hematology/Oncology Clinics of North America* 14 (2000): 1–16.
COHEN, H. J. "Oncology and Aging: General Principles of Cancer in the Elderly." In *Principles of Geriatric Medicine and Gerontology*, 4th ed. Edited by W. Hazzard. New York: McGraw-Hill, 1999. Pages 117–130.
HUNTER, C. P.; JOHNSON, K. A.; and MUSS, H. B., eds. *Cancer in the Elderly.* New York: Marcel Dekker, 2000.
YANCIK, R., and RIES, L. A. G. "Aging and Cancer in America: Demographic and Epidemiologic Perspectives." *Hematology/Oncology Clinics of North America* 14 (2000): 17–23.

CAREERS IN AGING

The rapid growth of the older population, especially the oldest old—those over eighty-five (Hobbs and Damon)—has resulted in a greater demand for a variety of services traditionally provided by the family. However, family structure has changed; in particular, women today are more likely to have commitments outside the home. Thus, professional service providers have started to offer assistance to older persons and careers in aging have come into being.

Early development of the field

At the same time that women began establishing careers outside the home, other conditions emerged which created a need for services to the elderly. Lower birthrates resulted in fewer adult children available to provide care; an increase in life expectancy led to more older persons with chronic diseases requiring many years of support; and the sheer numbers of the elderly increased dramatically. Almost simultaneously, specialized services were developed as professionals became aware of the unique needs to be met and the increased income available to pay for these services. Older people's needs are almost overwhelming; more than 40 percent of persons older than age seventy need help with one or more daily activities (National Academy on an Aging Society). Although this need continues to be met in large part by family members, at an estimated cost of $196 billion annually, every year there is an increase in professional services to augment or replace home care (National Academy on an Aging Society).

Professionals in care for the aging emerged from health and human service fields. They had been trained to work with all age groups, with an emphasis on child and family needs. As their senior clientele increased, experience with this group led some professionals with applicable skills to concentrate on the needs of the elderly. They demonstrated their interest in the older clientele by participation in age-related workshops and conferences, as well as membership in professional associations. As the professions developed a strong gerontology component, specialized services emerged within many fields, including medicine, rehabilitation, pharmacy, counseling, housing, and recreation. Networks were built among professions that began to specialize in service to the elderly, and the term "gerontologist" gained greater acceptance.

The first generation of professional gerontologists developed almost serendipitously, whereas the second cohort was greatly influenced by government-funded programs.

The Administration on Aging (AoA), a unit of the Department of Health and Human Services, had extensive influence on the creation of careers in the field of aging. AoA undertook several approaches to career development. Over $500 million was provided annually to establish and maintain service programs for older persons. These programs led to the employment of many people who had interest or experience in working with the elderly. The funding also included the creation and dissemination of training materials and consumer information, and coordination of the growing variety of age-related community projects. The latter resulted in the establishment of the National Association of Area Agencies on Aging and the National Association of State Units on Aging, which supported professionals interested in facilitating services to the elderly.

AoA's greatest impact on careers involved financial support to undergraduate and graduate students who wanted to gain knowledge and skills in gerontology. Its funding also facilitated internships and volunteer experiences leading to future employment of health and human service professionals. The funding was also used to create nearly two hundred instructional certificate or degree programs in community colleges, four-year schools, and universities between 1967 and 1990 (Peterson, Hickey, and Stillman). Although such financial support was allocated for only two or three years to each school, it provided sufficient seed money to launch ongoing programs that continued to graduate gerontological professionals ready for jobs within the network for the aging.

The AoA approach of funding degree and continuing education programs as well as community programs has been supplemented by foundations. However, the financial support of the latter has not been as large or as consistent as that of AoA. While aging is not the highest priority for many foundations, they are nevertheless supporters of innovative approaches to serving the aging and have continued to provide assistance to many agencies. Grantmakers in Aging is an organization that brings together the age-conscious foundations and facilitates joint projects (Peterson, Douglass, and Seymour).

The contribution of higher education

Encouraged by the availability of funding, faculty at American colleges and universities ex-panded their instructional offerings related to aging. Typically, at first noncredit workshops were conducted, but credit courses soon followed. The first national survey of gerontology courses offered, carried out in 1957, reported that only fifty-seven colleges and universities in the United States were offering credit courses in aging (Donahue). By 1992, 1,639 (54 percent of all colleges and universities in the United States) offered such courses (Peterson, Wendt, and Douglas). At the turn of the twenty-first century, it is speculated that nearly all major institutions of higher learning offer at least a few credit courses in gerontology. This availability created an awareness among students of the variety of such courses and the diversity of jobs existing under the umbrella of gerontology, and in turn encouraged some students to explore this career option. The publicity of courses on aging is a successful method of promoting gerontology careers.

Career opportunities

In 1987 the National Institute on Aging projected that the field of aging would grow dramatically, and that by 2000 many more professional gerontologists would be needed in a variety of fields (National Institute on Aging). Observations support these conclusions; however, it is widely accepted that instructional programs have not met the demand for trained professionals.

The recruitment of personnel for the field of aging, as with any profession, depends heavily on the innate attractiveness of the field, which usually includes such attributes as salary, job security, personal job satisfaction, and opportunity for advancement. Studies have found that the salaries of gerontology professionals are comparable to those of similar human service professionals (Peterson et al., 1995). Responses to surveys on job satisfaction indicate that 90 percent of respondents were satisfied with the education they received, and a similar percentage felt they had achieved reasonable career advancement. Job satisfaction was high, and led many persons to stay in the field of aging for many years (McLeran et al.).

Peterson, Wendt, and Douglas surveyed the career paths of gerontology professionals after they had completed a master's degree program in gerontology. They reported that when gerontology was a second career, advancement occurred 41 percent of the time.

It is widely believed that career opportunities are excellent in the field of aging. The book *100 Best Careers for the Year 2000* (Field) lists medicine as the best career, with gerontology the second most attractive. With the continuing increase in the size of the older population, there is a major undersupply of trained professionals, and persons with gerontology education will continue to be in demand. It is estimated that a total of over one million people work in all aspects of the field of aging (Kahl). However, fewer than ten thousand persons graduated annually with a gerontology degree, or even a course or two in gerontology (Peterson et al., 1982). The obvious conclusion is that most people who work in the field of aging have had little or no academic gerontology instruction. Gerontology education could enhance their understanding and effectiveness as skilled and knowledgeable professionals in aging. Participation in continuing education and in-service education programs, which are widely available, could meet this need.

At the turn of the twenty-first century, there is no precise definition of which jobs are included under the umbrella of occupations in aging. Some researchers would include all who come in contact with seniors regularly in the course of their work to be in the field of aging, while others would say that unless the work is primarily concerned with seniors and their age-related characteristics and concerns, it is not an aging occupation. The truth probably lies somewhere in between; a career in aging could be said to exist when a person's primary occupation is with or for persons over the age of sixty.

Some of the careers which are commonly accepted to fall within the scope of a career in aging include direct service jobs for the elderly, which can be found in counseling, housing, health care, recreation, retirement planning, and advocacy; program planning for seniors, which includes needs assessment, program design, and community planning; administration of senior-focused programs or organizations, which includes supervision of employees, financial management, and coordination of programs; education about or for seniors, which incorporates teaching college students, employed persons (through continuing education and in-service training), and the seniors themselves who seek practical and personal enrichment instruction; and research, incorporating the mental, physical, or social aspects of aging.

Job seekers have traditionally found these positions in mental and physical health facilities, such as hospitals and nursing homes; in rehabilitation clinics, including physical and occupational therapy departments; social service centers, including senior centers and day care centers; through corporations' departments focusing on product design, marketing, and personal services; housing for independent and assisted living; community agencies providing coordination, funding, and public information; and federal, state, and local government programs.

The bridge from college to career can begin with a positive internship experience. College gerontology programs usually require a field placement assignment, which frequently leads to employment in the agency or business where the student is placed. The cooperating community agency becomes better informed on how gerontology-trained persons can enhance its business, and the student gains practical experience (McCrea, Nichols, and Newman).

Entering the profession can be greatly facilitated by institutions of higher education that establish job placement programs for their graduates. Through their contacts with community agencies, providers of internships, graduates, and professional colleagues, it is possible to create an employment network. This can also apply to employees who have been part of in-service training or continuing education programs. The computer provides on-line job searches as well. However, as in any new field, helping the potential employer see the advantages of a gerontology-trained person may be a vital step in job placement. Gerontology programs need to offer guidance for entering the job market that includes securing and preparing for interviews; students need to learn how to promote the advantages their gerontology skills bring to a particular employer.

Future career opportunities

The oldest old, generally defined as those over the age of eighty-five, are the fastest-growing portion of the older population. In 1900 there were 122,000 people in this category in the United States. By 1990 the number had increased to three million. This group will not grow as rapidly during the years between 2000 and 2010, because of the smaller number of people born during the 1930s, but after that date, growth of this segment will be very rapid (Hobbs and Damon) and will result in social and economic pressures on their children, other caregivers, and society.

The interest in the oldest old results from their high level of difficulty in carrying out personal care tasks. These functional limitations must generally be compensated for with assistance from family members or hired professionals. Increasing levels of disability may require the more specialized caregiving that can be provided by trained professionals.

Persons over sixty-five will increase from 35 million in 2000 to 40 million in 2010 (Hobbs and Damon), but the impact may not be as strongly felt, or at least not felt in the same areas of professional service. With the many advances in medicine, an increasing percentage of these elderly persons will fall in the category "well old" (over sixty-five). Although they will not require the basic health services of the old old, they will demand service for their own needs and desires. This is where new careers in aging are already beginning to emerge. Professionals with gerontology training can meet the unique needs of this group in such areas as financial counseling, insurance, travel and recreation, housing, transportation, participation in cultural and artistic endeavors, education for second and third careers, special interest education, computer literacy, spiritual and social expression, and community activism.

The demographic data further suggest the challenges to be met by educational institutions that seek to prepare professionals to serve this growing clientele. More college-level educational gerontologists will be needed who can teach the unique principles of older adult education. The resulting graduates will be better able to create effective senior learning opportunities in the community.

Higher education also requires gerontologists who are both researchers and teachers. Gerontology-related research is an ever-broadening field because more information is needed in such areas as demographics, for planners in all fields; pharmacy, regarding drug interactions and the efficacy of alternative health programs; and sociology and psychology, for understanding the diversity of the aging as individuals and as groups. Careers in teaching gerontology are also expanding with the advent of distance learning courses for the professional as well as of enrichment courses for seniors.

Opportunities for careers in aging grew substantially during the last quarter of the twentieth century, and there are many indications for future growth. The rate of increase in professional gerontology is directly tied to how well certain professional challenges are met in the future.

- Even though this career field has grown significantly, there needs to be an increased awareness of the opportunities presented by, and the desirability of, this career choice. When compared with other professionals on the bases of academic preparation, salaries, and job satisfaction, a 1995 survey of gerontological personnel found salaries comparable with other professions, the educational preparation as relevant and useful, and the subsequent employment as fulfilling. Furthermore, 90 percent of survey respondents indicated they would recommend the program to others, and that they would enroll in the program again if given the opportunity (Peterson, Douglass, and Lobenstine).
- Potential employers who are not trained in gerontology are less likely to seek gerontologically trained employees. As increasing numbers of gerontology graduates rise to administrative positions and as community information becomes more widespread, this concern can be met.
- Potential senior clients who have accepted negative ageism stereotypes are reluctant to seek out gerontology specialists. The living examples of the well old and their stories of how they have maintained their vitality can help seniors take a more active role in their own future. The increasing educational level of tomorrow's seniors and the mass media's dissemination of information can have a positive effect.
- Negative societal attitudes about seniors inhibit support of senior services other than those for health and income needs. The well old may be the best advertisement and advocates for more positive attitudes.
- Professional standards need to be defined as they pertain to both the professionals and the institutions that train them. Professional certification is still not available through a gerontology program (Fairchild et al.). As long as people can enter the field without some measure of their knowledge beyond that of receiving a degree, careers in aging will remain underrecognized and insecure. A related concern is the lack of accreditation of

professional gerontology training programs. In the world of professions, accreditation has come to be a determination of quality. The Association for Gerontology in Higher Education has developed a quality review process for gerontology programs (AGHE Program of Merit). Professional gerontology associations will continue to keep these concerns under review.

- The lack of cultural diversity in the cadre of gerontology professionals inhibits services to the broad diversity of older persons. Intentional recruitment by colleges can help bridge this gap.
- The availability of financial assistance for gerontology students is a growing need as college costs rise (American Association of Retired Persons). Less government and philanthropic funding is available for scholarships and for new and innovative programs. Colleges, and gerontology departments in particular, can intensify their search for student support. Advocates for seniors, who may also include the seniors themselves, can work for community program support.

These challenges and more need to be met with creative solutions if career opportunities are to expand to meet the needs of a diverse older population. It will require determined, knowledgeable leadership from people employed in the field of aging. The national associations on aging are the most likely groups to lead the effort and coordinate the work of others. They can bring together educational institutions to advance training, seek foundations to fund education and programming, and promote community awareness and involvement. Ultimately, there must be an intergenerational effort uniting concerned persons of all ages to further advance the opportunities for careers in aging.

DAVID A. PETERSON

See also ADMINISTRATION ON AGING; GERONTOLOGY; NATIONAL INSTITUTE ON AGING.

BIBLIOGRAPHY

American Association of Retired Persons. *The 2000–2001 AARP Andrus Foundation Undergraduate Scholarship Program for Study of Aging and Finance.* Washington, D.C.: AARP, 2000.

Assocation for Gerontology in Higher Education. *AGHE Program of Merit.* Washington, D.C.: AGHE, 1999.

DONAHUE, W. T. "Training in Social Gerontology." *Geriatrics* 15 (1960): 501.

FAIRCHILD, T., et al. *Gerontological Education and Job Opportunities in Aging.* Washington, D.C.: Association for Gerontology in Higher Education, 1998.

FIELD, S. *100 Best Careers for the Year 2000.* New York: Prentice-Hall, 1992.

HOBBS, F., and DAMON, B. *65+ in the United States.* Washington, D.C.: U.S. Bureau of the Census, 1996.

KAHL, A. "Careers in the Field of Aging." *Occupational Outlook Quarterly* 32 (1988): 2–21.

MCCREA, J. M.; NICHOLS, A.; and NEWMAN, S. *Interorganizational Service-Learning in Gerontology.* Washington, D.C. : Association for Gerontology in Higher Education, 1998.

MCLERAN, H.; POPE, H.; LOGAN, H.; and JACOBSEN, J. *Career Pathways for Graduates of Midwestern Gerontology Programs.* Iowa City: University of Iowa, 1990.

National Academy on an Aging Society. *Caregiving: Helping the Elderly with Activity Limitations.* Washington, D.C.: NAAS, 2000.

National Institute on Aging. *Report on Education and Training in Geriatrics and Gerontology.* Washington, D.C.: National Institutes of Health, 1987.

PETERSON, D. A.; DOUGLASS, E.; and SEYMOUR, R. *Aging Education and Training: Priorities for Grantmaking Foundations.* Washington, D.C.: Association for Gerontology in Higher Education, 1997.

PETERSON, D. A.; DOUGLASS, E.; and LOBENSTINE, JOY. *Careers in Aging: Opportunities and Options.* Washington, D.C.: Association for Gerontology in Higher Education, 1996.

PETERSON, D. A.; WENDT, P.; and DOUGLASS, E. *Development of Gerontology, Geriatrics, and Aging Studies Programs in Institutions of Higher Education.* Washington, D.C.: Association for Gerontology in Higher Education, 1994.

PETERSON, D. A.; HICKEY, T.; and STILLMAN, P. *Gerontology Program Self-Study: Evaluating an Existing Program.* Washington, D.C.: Association for Gerontology in Higher Education, 1994.

PETERSON, D. A., et al. *A National Survey of Gerontology Instruction in American Institutions of Higher Education.* Washington, D.C.: Association for Gerontology in Higher Education, 1987.

PETERSON, D. A., et al. *Survey of Gerontology Education.* Washington, D.C.: Association for Gerontology in Higher Education, 1995.

CAREGIVING, INFORMAL

Although the majority of elderly people are able to manage independently in the community, a significant minority, particularly among those eighty-five and older, requires long-term assistance. Despite the popular association of frailty with nursing home placement, the majority of long-term care is provided in the community by family members, particularly spouses and adult children, with supplemental assistance from friends and neighbors. A 1997 study by the National Alliance for Caregiving and the American Association of Retired Persons estimated that 70 to 80 percent of all the in-home care for older people with chronic impairments is provided by families. According to the same study, nearly 25 percent of all households contain an adult who has provided care for an elderly person within the past year.

What is informal caregiving?

Caring for a frail elder can encompass a wide variety of tasks, from occasional help with heavy chores to daily assistance with personal care tasks. Family members provide instrumental assistance and financial management and, along with friends, offer emotional support. Relatives also mediate relationships between their elderly relatives and health care providers or social service agencies. Caregiving continues even if the elder relative enters a nursing home. Informal caregivers, particularly spouses and adult children, provide this complex mix of assistance for relatively long periods of time. One study estimated that caregiving for an elderly parent lasts an average of five to seven years, with caregivers helping the elderly care recipient between six and ten hours per week (Azarnoff and Scharlach). Another study estimated that American women will spend eighteen years caring for older family members, in comparison to only seventeen years for children (Stone, Cafferata, and Sangl).

As with many transitions in the life course of older families, the transition to the caregiver role is an unscheduled one. Sometimes the shift occurs suddenly, as when an older person suffers a stroke. More often, however, the transition begins almost imperceptibly, with caring for an older person at first entailing more a sense of responsibility than tangible assistance. A number of the adult daughters interviewed by Jane Lewis and Barbara Meredith felt they had "just drifted into caring" and were unable to identify the point at which they had assumed a caregiving role.

The types of assistance that gerontologists label as "caregiving" emerge gradually from the intergenerational exchanges that characterize family relationships. For most adult children, reciprocal exchanges of help with their parents are more common than one-way help, with the parental generation providing the bulk of the assistance. John Logan and Glenna Spitze report that elderly parents provide more assistance to their children than they receive in return at least until the parents are seventy-five years old. By that time, over half of elderly parents are receiving help from one or more children, although 30 percent of parents continue to provide assistance to at least one child. Their results do not argue against the importance of informal care to elderly parents encountering illness or disability. Informal caregiving is indeed the first line of defense against institutional placement in very old age. But Logan and Spitze's work reminds us of the importance of considering family care within a life course perspective.

Who are the family caregivers of frail elders?

The informal networks of older people are dominated by kin. For impaired elderly people who are married, the spouse is the first line of support. Spouses handle a broader range of tasks, provide more hours of assistance, and are more likely to provide personal care than are other caregivers. Husbands and wives are also more likely than other categories of caregivers to handle caregiving responsibilities on their own, without supplemental help from other informal caregivers or from formal services. The caregiver in an elderly couple is most likely the wife, since women generally live longer than men and are younger than their husbands. Most studies of spousal caregiving report that husbands experience lower levels of burden than wives. Husbands are also more likely than wives to receive supplemental assistance.

When a spouse is not present or when the level of support provided by the spouse is not sufficient, other family members—particularly adult children—step into the caregiving role. Research has demonstrated that children assist over shorter periods of time and provide less intensive assistance than do spouses, with the difference most pronounced among sons. Daughters are more likely than sons to assume the role of primary caregiver, even when the number and gender distribution of all siblings are considered. Daughters provide more hours and a broader range of tasks than do sons, who are less likely to provide daily assistance with routine household tasks or personal care. Daughters are more likely than sons to be monitors of care—assessing need, finding someone to provide the needed assistance, and making sure that tasks are performed correctly. The highest participation of sons in parental caregiving is found in families without daughters.

Elderly people without children living nearby compensate by developing close relationships with other kin and with friends or neighbors. Victor Cicirelli, who has studied sibling relationships in late life, reports that a small percentage of elderly persons rely on siblings for psychological support, for help with business dealings and homemaking, and as companions for social or recreational activities. Deborah Gold argues that elderly siblings serve as ready sources of support in times of crisis or as backups to regular caregivers. Consistent with gender differences in other relationships, sisters both give and receive more help than brothers.

Relationships with extended kin, including aunts, uncles, cousins, nieces, and nephews, vary in both emotional closeness and exchanges of assistance. The amount of assistance provided by extended kin ranges from moderate to low, with the level of help declining with the distance of the kinship relationship. Variation in the level of help also reflects differences in geographic proximity, norms embedded in ethnic culture, and individual family histories. Researchers report that extended kin occupy more pivotal roles in the helping networks of African-American elders than of white elders, a difference that persists when controlling for economic resources.

While older people, especially those without close kin, rely on friends or neighbors, these helpers provide a more limited range of assistance. Friends provide emotional support and, along with neighbors, offer assistance with occasional tasks like running errands or providing transportation. But friends or neighbors are rarely mentioned as a source of help with daily household chores or personal care in long-term illness. Older women are more likely than older men to have developed a network of close friendships that would foster the provision of informal care. The role of friends in providing informal care in late life also varies with ethnicity. For example, research indicates that African-American friendships exhibit greater exchange of both instrumental and emotional support than do white friendships. Friends also play a greater role in linking elders to formal services among ethnic minority elders.

The majority of the literature on caregiving for frail elders is consistent with the concept of a hierarchy of preferred caregivers. The hierarchical compensatory model, developed by Marjorie Cantor, posits that involvement of informal helpers reflects a normatively defined preference hierarchy based on the relationship between the care provider and the older care recipient (Cantor and Little). This notion of "preferred helpers" is used to explain the successive involvement of spouse, adult children, other family members, and friends and neighbors described in the empirical literature. The selection order becomes relevant when a previous category of helper is unavailable (a situation referred to as "substitution") or is unable to provide enough help to satisfy the older person's needs (a situation referred to as "supplementation"). This approach argues that the availability of helpers rather than the types of assistance needed by the older person explains the composition of informal networks (Miller and McFall).

The empirical research on informal caregiving is generally consistent with this preference hierarchy, but the hierarchical compensatory model does not explain which adult children or which other relatives will be recruited into the support networks of frail elders. Researchers studying the selection or recruitment of specific individuals as caregivers have identified characteristics of the elderly person, the potential caregiver, and their relationship as key predictors. Marital status of the care recipient is an importance factor, since spouses are the first-line caregivers. Gender is another factor. Most caregivers are women, but the gender of the elderly care recipient is also important. The predominance of adult daughters over adult sons can in part reflect the fact that most widowed parents are women, and older women may prefer to receive hands-on personal assistance from a daughter than from a son because of taboos involving intimate body contact (Lee). Geographic proximity is a prerequisite for routine, daily assistance, but emotional support and financial assistance can be accomplished over the miles.

Economic resources of both parents and adult children also mediate caregiving strategies. Affluent elderly families sometimes prefer to hire private-sector outside help with instrumental tasks. Hiring people to perform occasional chores allows older people to feel that they are still managing on their own, minimizing demands on their children and other informal helpers, and retaining control of the caregiving situation. Social class also influences the experience of providing family care, since affluent families have resources to hire supplementary assistance or purchase market alternatives for caregiving tasks.

There are also race and ethnic differences in regards to caregiving. For example, African-Americans are more likely to see informal caregiving as their familial responsibility. Cagney and Agree found that African-Americans were more likely to postpone the hiring of formal caregivers or the implementation of institutionalization than were white families.

Researchers have also focused on competing demands on the time and resources of informal caregivers, exploring the hypothesis that other family and employment responsibilities "pull" from caring for elderly relatives. Most of these studies focus on adult children caring for elderly parents. For example, some studies suggest that parental caregiving falls most heavily on unmarried adult children. Other studies explore employment as a constraint on the flexibility of adult children in responding to parental needs, but, with the exception of a slight decrease among adult sons, most studies report that employment has no impact on relationships between adult children and their elderly parents. Logan and Spitze tested the impact of particular configurations of roles on parental caregiving by adult children. They report that combinations of roles have no effect beyond the individual effect of specific roles. They conclude that stresses reported by caregivers who occupy multiple roles come not from the particular configuration of responsibilities but from the stressful responsibility of caring for a frail elderly parent.

The consequences of providing informal care

Informal caregivers often experience a number of negative outcomes, including emotional strain, financial losses, disruptions of plans and lifestyles, and health declines. Gerontologists distinguish between caregiver burden, which refers to management of tasks, and caregiver stress, which refers to the strain felt by the caregiver. Both burden and stress are highest within informal networks of Alzheimer's patients. There are a number of reasons why caring for a frail elderly person leads to more burden and stress than providing other types of informal assistance. First, the total task load can be greater, with caregiving obligations involving several generations and perhaps several households. As the range of assistance needs to expand, scheduling and supervising becomes more difficult. Lifting and assisting nonambulatory adults involves heavy physical labor, and helping people with personal care tasks violates norms of privacy.

Secondly, caregiving is often done alone, and caregivers who do not receive outside help often express feelings of isolation. Maintaining friendships becomes increasingly difficult, since caregiving disrupts social routines and restricts mobility. Neighbors and friends who had previously dropped in as part of a normal social routine withdraw as the caring tasks become more disruptive or distasteful. Informal helping networks often diminish as disability increases, until caring for the most severely impaired elderly usually falls on one person.

The strains of caregiving reverberate throughout families. Watching an older relative negotiate losses can initiate a process of anticipatory bereavement. Married couples struggle with the loss of time for each other when caring for an older parent or parent-in-law. Children can resent loss of their caregiving parents' attention, the disruption of their social life, more crowded households, and financial sacrifices when family resources are directed to caring for their grandparent. Siblings sometimes disagree over how to care for an elderly parent, and primary caregivers often complain that their sisters and brothers not only fail to carry their share of the burden but also fail to appreciate their efforts. Although the research literature emphasizes negative outcomes, many caregivers report satisfaction from fulfilling the needs of an older relative. These families report that sharing this last stage of life strengthens relationships and enhances self-esteem.

Caregivers who live with older care recipients usually report higher levels of stress than caregivers who maintain separate households. This result is not surprising, since limited financial resources and serious disability are the major impetus to shared living arrangements. Caregivers who live with the care recipient are always "on call," with a resulting loss of privacy, autonomy, and sleep. They may avoid the work of managing and traveling between two households, but they lose control over personal time and space.

Recent studies have explored the economic costs of caregiving. Arno, Levine, and Memmott estimate the economic value of informal caregiving at $196 billion in 1997. This figure exceeds the combined estimates of the cost of formal health care ($32 billion) and nursing home care ($83 billion). This amount is approximately 18 percent of the total national health care expenditures. As these figures indicate, the costs of community care cannot be estimated accurately with an exclusive focus on public expenditures. When elders are cared for in institutional settings, the costs of providing care include the wages paid to nursing home employees. When relatives or friends in the community provide the same care, the economic costs are overlooked because no money changes hands.

A key factor in assessing economic costs is the impact of caregiving on labor force participation and productivity. Caregivers who remain in the work force sometimes report that their work performance suffers. In one study, about one-third of employed caregivers reported being so tired that they could not work effectively. Some had to reject jobs requiring travel away from home, overtime, or irregular hours. Data from the National Long Term Care survey revealed that 40 percent of employed caregiving daughters had rearranged their work schedules, 23 percent cut back on hours, and 25 percent took time off without pay to balance the dual demands of paid work and family care (Quadagno).

The economic consequences are most severe for caregivers who limit their work time. Caregivers who undertake part-time work confront the disadvantages common to part-time workers, including low status, few opportunities for advancement, and limited fringe benefits. The visibility of women's caregiving obligations sometimes means that employers devalue their productivity and commitments to paid work (Williams). Caregivers who leave the labor market for substantial periods can have difficulty finding jobs at comparable wages. For many

older caregivers, leaving the work force amounts to early retirement, especially given the low probability of reemployment among older workers.

The future availability of informal caregivers

Increases in the proportion of elderly persons, particularly those over eighty-five years of age, have lead to forecasts of increasing demands on family members to provide informal long-term care in the future. Changes in medical care mean that older people spend less time in the hospital, often discharged with more intense needs for care.

Meanwhile, there is concern that the availability of family caregivers has declined. Changes in fertility have led to what family sociologists describe as a "beanpole family," with fewer adult children available to assume caregiving responsibilities. The prevalence of divorce and remarriage will be higher in future cohorts of elders. Some studies report a decrease in the exchange of support between divorced fathers and their children, although a similar decline has not been confirmed among divorced mothers and their children. A study by Merrill Silverstein and Vern Bengtson found that children of divorced parents express a lower sense of obligation to parents than do children from intact families. Labor force rates among women raise concerns about the ability of adult daughters to continue to provide the majority of home care for parents requiring personal care. In addition, divorce impacts the number of available caregivers, because daughters-in-law often provide care to their husbands' parents.

Women's multiple responsibilities for paid and unpaid labor raised concerns regarding what became known as "women in the middle" or "the sandwich generation." Women in the middle are middle-aged and occupy the middle position in multigenerational families. Responsible for homemaking and paid employment, these women were caught between demands of caring for young children and caring for their frail elderly parents. Despite the intensity of demands on women occupying these multiple roles, recent research indicates that the prevalence of the phenomena may be less widespread than initially believed. Occupying multiple roles of spouse, parent, adult child of an elderly parent, and employed worker is relatively common among people in their forties and fifties. But the parents of people with dependent children are likely to be relatively healthy. By the time most adult daughters face caregiving demands from their elderly parents, their own children are usually living independently, thus reducing the likelihood of experiencing simultaneous demands from both older and younger generations.

Logan and Spitze found little evidence to support fears that demographic trends such as the aging of the population, increased divorce rate, declines in family size, or increasing labor force participation rates among women are disrupting family networks and shifting elder care responsibilities to public institutions. Contrary to the myth that family resources disappear when public supports become available, research on informal caregiving indicates that local networks dominated by geographically proximate kin provide the vast majority of long-term care to frail elders and families, turning to supplemental formal assistance only when the elderly relative's needs exceed the resources of informal caregivers. Nevertheless, the availability of formal support services is crucial to the ability of families to care for frail elderly relatives within community settings.

Policy recommendations addressing informal caregiving

A growing body of literature calls for programs to alleviate stress and burden on caregivers, including support groups, day treatment centers, respite care, home health, and housekeeping assistance. Although these programs can extend the length of time in which informal networks can provide care, many gerontologists suggest that they are essentially palliative or band-aid approaches that fail to alter the structural arrangements that produce caregiver burden and stress.

Recognition of the long-term disruptive affects on employment has generated recommendations for caregiving leaves and greater job security. The U.S. Family and Medical Leave Act (FMLA) addresses employed caregivers' need for job protection, but other aspects of the legislation curtail its potential benefits, particularly for women. Small businesses employing fifty or fewer employees are exempt from the FMLA. Over half of all private sector employees, including a disproportionately large number of women, work for such firms. Furthermore, most workers cannot afford to take an unpaid leave from work.

Family-friendly workplace policies are advocated as another approach to alleviating strains of providing family care across the life course, including care for frail elderly relatives. But family-friendly policies are often sold to business as strategies for recruiting and retaining valued employees, strengthening company loyalty, reducing absenteeism, and enhancing work performance (Hochschild). Thus, these policies are designed to help employees find ways to cope with caregiving demands that interfere with job performance. They do nothing to change the features of the workplace that contributes to strain.

Public opinion surveys indicate that most Americans believe that the government has an obligation to finance care for elders who cannot afford to purchase care themselves. However, as Atchley claims, "economically pressured state and federal governments have an interest in shifting as much of this financial responsibility onto the family as possible" (p. 213). Development and provision of formal services reflects a context in which care of the frail elderly is defined as a private responsibility of families, with formal intervention most likely at crisis points or when informal resources are exhausted or unavailable (Hooyman and Gonyea).

ELEANOR PALO STOLLER
LISA MARTIN

See also FILIAL OBLIGATIONS; KIN; PARENT-CHILD RELATIONSHIP.

BIBLIOGRAPHY

ARNO, P.; LEVINE, C.; and MEMMOTT, M. "The Economic Value of Informal Caregiving." *Health Affairs.* Bethesda, Md.: Project HOPE, The People to People Health Foundation, Inc., 1999.

ATCHLEY, R. *Social Forces and Aging: An Introduction to Social Gerontology*, 9th ed. Belmont, Calif.: Wadsworth Publishing Co., 2000.

AZARNOFF, R., and SCHARLACH, A. "Can Employees Carry the Eldercare Burden?" *Personnel Journal* 67 (1988): 67–69.

CAGNEY, K., and AGREE, E. "Racial Differences in Skilled Nursing Care and Home Health Use: The Mediating Effects of Family Structure and Social Class." *Journals of Gerontology, Series B: Psychological and Social Sciences* 54 (1999): S223–S236.

CANTOR, M., and LITTLE, V. "Aging and Social Care." In *Handbook of Aging and the Social Sciences*. Edited by R. Binstock and E. Shanas. New York: Van Nostrand, 1985.

CICIRELLI, V. *Sibling Relationships across the Lifespan*. New York, N.Y.: Plenum Press, 1995.

GOLD, D. "Continuities and Discontinuities in Sibling Relationships Across the Life Span." In *Adulthood and Aging: Research on Continuities and Discontinuities*. Edited by Vern L. Bengtson. New York, N.Y.: Springer Publishing Company, 1996. Pages 228–245.

HOCHSCHILD, A. *The Time Bind: When Work Becomes Home and Home Becomes Work*. New York, N.Y.: Metropolitan Books, 1997.

HOOYMAN, N., and GONYEA, J. *Feminist Perspectives on Family Care: Policies for Gender Justice*. Thousand Oaks, Calif.: Sage Publications, 1995.

LEE, G. "Gender Differences in Family Caregiving: A Fact in Search of a Theory." In *Gender, Elders and Family Care*. Edited by J. Dwyer and R. Coward. Newbury Park, Calif.: Sage, 1995.

LEWIS, J., and MEREDITH, B. "Daughters Caring for Mothers: The Experience of Caring and its Implications for Professional Helpers." *Ageing and Society* 8 (1988): 1–21.

LOGAN, J., and SPITZE, G. *Family Ties: Enduring Relationships Between Parents and their Grown Children*. Philadelphia, Pa.: Temple University Press, 1996.

MILLER, B., and McFALL, S. "Stability and Change in the Informal Task Support Network of Frail Older Persons." *The Gerontologist* 31 (1991): 735–745.

National Alliance for Caregiving and the American Association of Retired Persons. *Family Caregiving in the U.S.: Findings from a National Survey*. Bethesda, Md.: National Alliance for Caregiving, 1997.

QUADAGNO, J. *Aging and the Life Course: An Introduction to Gerontology*. Boston: McGraw-Hill, 2000.

SILVERSTEIN, M., and BENGTSEN, V. "Intergenerational Solidarity and the Structure of Adult Child-Parent Relationships in American Families." *American Journal of Sociology* 103 (1997): 429–460.

STONE, R.; CAFFERATA, G.; and SANGL, J. "Caregivers for the Frail Elderly: A National Profile." *The Gerontologist* 20 (1987): 616–627.

WILLIAMS, J. *Unbending Gender: Why Family and Work Conflict and What To Do About It*. New York: Oxford University Press, 2000.

CASE MANAGEMENT

Case management in health and social service programs for older adults has evolved since the 1970s. This evolution reflects a changing public policy environment, a clearer appreciation of the challenges of living with chronic illness faced by older adults and their caregivers, and the development of a variety of approaches to financing and providing services across the full continuum of care, including primary, acute, in-home, community-based, and long-term services. As a result, case managers are located in hospitals, clinics, community agencies providing in-home services, Area Agencies on Aging, adult day care centers, and health maintenance organizations. Case managers may be employed in government programs, nonprofit community agencies, and for-profit service providers, or may be in private practice. They attempt to rationalize the system of care for older adults and their caregivers.

Definition

There has been considerable discussion about what is an appropriate name for case management. In some programs the case management function is called "care management," "care coordination," or "care planning." There is an ongoing concern that the term "case management," conveys an undesired sense of bureaucracy. Clients and caregivers have expressed their view that they "are not cases and do not want to be managed." Although widely used, the term "case management" remains unclear and confusing, describing benefit management, management of an acute event or of community-based interventions, or other types of client management across the continuum of care.

The overall goal of care or case managers is to facilitate collaborative and cost-efficient interactions among providers that effectively integrate medical, psychological, and social services in order to provide timely, appropriate, and beneficial service delivery to the client. Such integration can encompass clients and their families, health care providers, community agencies, legal and financial resources, third-party payers, and employers (Gross and Holt).

At the most general level, case management can be defined as a coordinating function that is designed to link clients with various services based on assessed need. Case management has evolved in recognition of the fact that the fragmented and complex systems of care create formidable obstacles for older, disabled individuals and their families. There is a need for coordination of care because caregivers and chronically ill older persons may require services from several providers. Although operationalized in various ways, case management has a common set of core components that includes outreach, screening, comprehensive assessment, care planning, service arrangement, monitoring, and reassessment (Applebaum and Austin; White).

Outreach activities are designed to identify persons likely to qualify for and need health and social support services as well as case management. Case-finding efforts help ensure that eligible individuals are served. Screening is a preliminary assessment of the client's circumstances and resources to determine presumptive eligibility. Potential clients are screened by means of standardized procedures to determine whether their status and situation meet the program's target population definition. Accurate screening is critical. Effective outreach and screening are necessary for efficient program operation and management.

Comprehensive assessment is a systematic and standardized process for collecting detailed information about a person's physical, mental, and psychological functioning and informal support system that facilitates the identification of the person's strengths and care needs (Schneider and Weiss; Gallo et al.). Typically, comprehensive assessment focuses on physical health, mental functioning, ability to perform activities of daily living, social supports, physical environment, and financial resources. Many programs have adopted rigorous standardized multidimensional instruments.

Information collected during the assessment process is used to develop a plan of care. Care planning requires clinical judgment, creativity, and sensitivity as well as knowledge of community resources. Case managers consider the willingness and availability of informal caregivers to provide care. Balance between formal and informal services is a major consideration in the care planning process. Clients and caregivers participate in the process. The care plan specifies services, providers, and frequency of delivery. Costs of the care plan are also determined. Care planning is a key resource allocation process and is a critical case management function. Service ar-

rangement involves contacting formal and informal providers to arrange services specified in the care plan. Case managers often must negotiate with providers for services when making referrals to other agencies. When they have the authority to purchase services on their clients' behalf, case managers order services directly from providers.

Case managers monitor changes in clients' situations and modify care plans to meet clients' needs. Ongoing monitoring combined with timely modification of care plans helps ensure that program expenditures reflect current client needs and are not based on outdated assessment data. Reassessment involves determining whether there have been changes in the client's situation since the last assessment. Systematic and regularly scheduled reassessment also helps in evaluating the extent to which progress has been made toward accomplishing outcomes specified in the care plan.

History

The nature of any case management service is defined and constrained by the program within which it is embedded (Beatrice; Applebaum and Austin). Therefore, many models of case management have been developed over time, reflecting changes in the goals of specific health and social service demonstration projects and programs designed to serve chronically ill older adults.

Case management in community-based long-term care programs developed in a series of demonstration projects between 1971 and 1985 (Kemper et al.; Applebaum and Austin; Cargano et al.). In 1971 no mechanism for funding in-home and community-based services was available, so it was necessary to identify funding to support the development of a community-based delivery system. Funds were made available through a waiver of the traditional restrictions imposed by the standard Medicare and Medicaid programs. This permitted the expenditure of funds for services provided outside of hospitals and nursing homes. These projects sought to demonstrate the development of a comprehensive and coordinated system of in-home and community-based services for older adults that would make available alternatives to premature or inappropriate nursing home placement. The projects also investigated whether community-based services would cost less than nursing home care for eligible clients. Although these demonstrations differed in a variety of ways, they all included case management and an expanded array of in-home and community-based services. In these projects, case managers were nurses and social workers. They were responsible only for coordinating care plans that included in-home and community-based services. They had limited involvement with, and no authority in, the traditional health care system that provides primary, acute care, and skilled in-home nursing services.

Integrating health care

A basic flaw in the community-based long-term care demonstration projects was absence of health care services. Case managers could only develop care plans and coordinate covered community-based and in-home services. Clearly this approach does not adequately address the health care needs of older adults, who are major utilizers of health care services. In order to effectively address this reality, it was necessary to develop delivery systems that integrate services across the continuum of care, with particular attention to involving primary care physicians.

The Program of All-inclusive Care of the Elderly (PACE) and the Social Health Care Maintenance Organization (S/HMO) were developed to completely integrate services and financing for both acute- and long-term care services. Both programs incorporate a capitated payment for each participant, blending Medicare and Medicaid funds. In capitated programs, providers agree to provide a comprehensive package of services for a predetermined cost. This funding method introduces strong incentives for providers to establish cost containment mechanisms and to carefully monitor participant service utilization patterns. Case managers play a key role in these settings where providers have assumed financial risk.

PACE is based on the ON LOK program, which has been in existence in San Francisco since 1971 (Ansak). It is built on the adult day care model, and participants regularly attend a center where they receive primary care, and nursing, recreational, personal care, day health, preventive, rehabilitative, and social services. Case management in PACE involves an interdisciplinary team located on-site. Contracted services, which include hospital, nursing home, and specialist care, are also managed by the team. A team capable of effectively and efficiently managing the complex and changing needs of a frail population is composed of members who are strong in their specific disciplines, and have skills and attitudes that facilitate collaboration. Case management, as practiced by PACE teams, is focused on providing integrated health and social services within specific fiscal limits. The PACE model has been disseminated widely and has been implemented in diverse settings (Chin Hansen). The Balanced Budget Act of 1997 made PACE a permanent provider under Medicare and a state option under Medicaid, and authorized further expansion of the program.

The Social Health Maintenance Organization (S/HMO), which was launched in 1985, enrolls a cross section of Medicare-eligible persons. The program receives a capitated Medicare and Medicaid blended payment for each enrollee and assumes financial risk. All enrollees receive Medicare benefits. Frail clients also receive a limited long-term care supplement that is controlled by a case management unit composed of nurses and social workers.

Case management has been prominent in every S/HMO site. Case managers assess chronic care needs, authorize services for enrollees, and assist enrollees in obtaining noncovered services and benefits. S/HMO case managers coordinate service delivery and are responsible for facilitating continuity of care across the delivery system at key transition points, including hospital admission, hospital discharge, starting home care services, and nursing home placement.

S/HMO experience provided significant insights regarding physician involvement and highlighted the need to create policies and processes to enhance physician involvement in postacute care. In the original sites, primary care physicians were not consistently involved with their patients who were receiving long-term care benefits. (Leutz; Finch et al.). In addition, the S/HMO focused attention on the need to streamline assessment and more closely coordinate Medicare skilled care with community care benefits. S/HMO programs have demonstrated that enrollees benefit from efforts of case managers to maximize their care options.

Case management in Medicare

Older adults needing case management are often identified and assessed in the health care system. While chronic illness generates the greatest health care costs, medical management programs continue to focus primarily on managing acute events. Medicare beneficiaries in need of case management fall into two groups: individuals recently discharged from the hospital who have difficulty leaving home to receive needed services, and individuals receiving Medicare home health services. Medicare beneficiaries receive care through either the original fee-for-service Medicare program or through Medicare HMOs (Cassel et al.).

In the original fee-for-service Medicare program, an individual beneficiary's care is not formally coordinated among practitioners and providers involved in a case at any given time. In reality, postacute Medicare coverage and reimbursement policies serve to separate providers. There is no patient-centered case management mechanism. There is also the potential for inappropriate coordination where conflict of interest may influence care plan decisions.

From 1993 to 1995 the Health Care Financing Administration tested three different case management approaches in the original Medicare program. Although findings were mixed, case management was identified as a potentially useful service. Several factors were identified that could strengthen the case management function: full physician involvement in the care management process, highly focused goals and interventions, trained and experienced case management staff, and incentives to reduce or control Medicare costs (Foley).

The way Medicare reimburses postacute care providers will affect care management. In a cost-based reimbursement system, case managers provide assessment and coordination, and can act as a check on excessive utilization and disorganized service delivery. In a prospective payment system (Medicare risk in HMOs), case managers could facilitate beneficiary access to covered services by documenting care needs, assure appropriate communication of medical orders to providers, and make referrals for non-Medicare services.

In 1997 the Robert Wood Johnson Foundation convened an HMO Work Group on Care Management, which identified geriatric case management as an essential component for HMOs. The group, which included representatives from major health insurance companies and nationally recognized geriatricians, identified case management programs that HMOs

should have in place to operate a successful Medicare risk program (Brummel-Smith). The group suggested the following components for the case management program: case selection (determining the need for intervention through information gathering), problem identification (assessing problems and potential interventions), planning (designing plans of care that reflect immediate, short-range, and ongoing needs and interventions), coordination (providing high-risk enrollees with appropriate and timely services), monitoring (periodic reassessment to determine necessary care plan modification), and evaluation (determining cost, quality of life, and quality of care outcomes). These are similar to the generic model of case management described earlier.

Whatever approach is adopted regarding case management in the original or Medicare risk programs, it will be necessary to address two basic considerations: the focus and scope of case management and the independence of case managers. These fundamental issues also apply to case management at any point on the continuum of care. While case managers may operate from a client/patient/beneficiary-centered approach, they will also be responsible for monitoring and controlling service utilization. They could also be responsible for making referrals and procuring both Medicare and non-Medicare services across the continuum of care from community resources. Medicare policy could also directly provide for and authorize access to case management itself.

Case managers' independence has two aspects, clinical and financial. There has been a continuing debate regarding the extent to which case management should be separated from the direct provision of services. A case manager who is not independent from a hospital, home health agency, nursing home, or community-based service provider may have a conflict of interest which affects his or her capacity to develop care plans that fully reflect the client's interests. Case managers face ethical dilemmas when their role creates conflict between advocating for clients and functioning as an agent for the delivery system that employs them (Browdie).

Consumer-directed care

An innovation in publicly funded community-based long-term care services for older adults is consumer-directed care. Choice and control are key elements in this approach. Consumer di-

rection ranges from the individual independently making all decisions and managing services
directly, to using a designated representative to
manage needed services. Although public long-
term care programs generally employ case managers to arrange and monitor supportive services
in the community, a number of programs provide significant opportunities for clients to direct
their services rather than relying on case managers to do so.

The Cash and Counseling Demonstration
(CCDE) is testing the direct cash payment approach to funding personal care assistance in the
community. In the demonstration, Medicaid-
eligible clients, having passed an initial screening, will be randomly assigned to the agency-
based case management group (control) or to the
cash option group (treatment). Persons assigned
to the cash option group develop a care plan describing how they will use the funds. An assigned
counselor approves the plan. If the care plan primarily involves hiring a personal care assistant,
the consumer is then responsible for screening,
hiring, scheduling, training, managing, and, if
necessary, firing the assistant. The CCDE (based
at the University of Maryland Center on Aging
and evaluated by Mathematica) will provide important information and insights regarding the
efficacy of agency-based, compared to consumer-
directed, case management of personal care assistance (Simon-Rosinowitz et al.).

Conclusion

Case management is a response to the complexity and fragmentation of health and social
service delivery systems. While there are common components, the practice of case management varies by setting. Although case managers
assist with locating and coordinating services, the
range of services they can coordinate and the options that are available will vary widely, depending on where on the care continuum the client is
assessed as needing case management assistance.
Any case management function reflects the program's financing and directly affects case manager's professional discipline, scope of client care,
and manner of blending advocacy and cost containment responsibilities.

CAROL D. AUSTIN
ROBERT W. MCCLELLAND

See also ADULT DAY CARE; CONSUMER DIRECTED CARE;
DAY HOSPITALS; HEALTH AND LONG-TERM CARE PRO-
GRAM INTEGRATION; HOME CARE; LONG-TERM CARE;
MEDICAID; MEDICARE; SOCIAL SERVICES.

BIBLIOGRAPHY

ANSAK, M. "The ON LOK Model: Consolidating
Care and Financing." *Generations* 14, no. 4
(1990): 73–74.

APPLEBAUM, R., and AUSTIN, C. *Long Term Care
Case Management: Design and Evaluation.* New
York: Springer, 1990.

The Balanced Budget Act of 1997. H.R. 2015. 105th
Cong., 1st sess. Washington, D.C.: U.S. Government Printing Office, 1997.

BEATRICE, D. "Case Management: A Policy Option for Long-Term Care." In *Reforming the
Long-Term Care System.* Edited by J. Callahan
and S. Wallack. Lexington, Mass.: D. C.
Health Lexington Books, 1981. Pp. 121–162.

BROWDIE, R. "Ethical Issues in Case Management from a Political and Systems Perspective." *Journal of Case Management* 1, no. 3
(1992): 87–89.

BRUMMEL-SMITH, K. "Special Series: Geriatrics in
Managed Care. Essential Components of Geriatric Care Provided Through Health Maintenance Organizations: The HMO Work Group
on Care Management." *Journal of the American
Geriatrics Society* 46, no. 2 (1998): 303–308.

CARGANO, G.; APPLEBAUM, R.; CHRISTIANSON, J.;
PHILLIPS, B.; THORTON, C.; and WILL, J. *The
Evaluation of the National Channeling Demonstra-
tion: Planning and Operation Experience of the
Channeling Projects.* Princeton, N.J.: Mathema-
tica Policy Research, 1986.

CASSEL. C.; BESDINE, R.; and SIEGEL, L. "Restructuring Medicare for the Next Century: What
Will Beneficiaries Really Need?" *Health Affairs*
18, no. 1 (1999): 16–24.

CHIN HANSEN, J. "Practical Lessons for Delivering Integrated Services in a Changing Environment: The PACE Model." *Generations* 23,
no. 2 (1999): 22–28.

FINCH, M., KANE, R., et al. *Design of the 2nd Generation S/HMO Demonstration: An Analysis of Multiple Incentives.* Minneapolis: University of
Minnesota Press, 1992.

FOLEY, L. *Care Management: Policy Considerations
for Original Medicare.* Washington, D.C.: Public
Policy Institute, American Association of Retired Persons, 1999.

GALLO, J.; REICHEL, W.; and ANDERSON, L. *Handbook of Geriatric Assessment,* 2d ed. Gaithers-
burg, Md.: Aspen, 1995.

GROSS, E., and HOLT, E. *Care and Case Management Summit Discussion Paper.* Chicago: Foundation for Rehabilitation Education Research

and National Association of Professional Geriatric Case Managers, 1998.

KEMPER, P.; APPLEBAUM, R.; and HARRIGAN, M. *A Systematic Comparison of Community-Care Demonstrations*. Madison: Institute for Research on Poverty, University of Wisconsin-Madison, 1987.

LEUTZ, W. "Five Laws of Integrating Medical and Social Services: Lessons from the United States and the United Kingdom." *Milbank Quarterly* 87, no. 1 (1999): 77–110.

SCHNEIDER, B., and WEISS, L. *The Channeling Case Management Manual*. Washington, D.C.: Assistant Secretary for Planning and Evaluation, Department of Health and Human Services, 1982.

SIMON-RUSINOWITZ, L.; MAHONEY, K.; and BENJAMIN, A. "Payments to Families Who Provide Care." *Generations* 22, no. 3 (1998): 69–75.

WHITE, M. "Case Management." In *The Encyclopedia of Aging*. Edited by G. Maddox. New York: Springer, 1995. Pp. 147–150.

CATARACTS

See EYE, AGING-RELATED DISEASES

CELLULAR AGING

When they are placed in a culture environment, human cells exhibit a finite proliferative capacity and are usually able to divide only forty to sixty times before reaching a senescent (nondividing) phase. The limited proliferative capacity of human cells in a culture environment is thought to result from multiple environmental and genetic mechanisms, and has been widely used as a model of human aging. The hallmark of senescence is the inability of cells to replicate their DNA following stimulation with the appropriate growth factors. Senescent cells are not dead, and in fact can be maintained for long periods with appropriate culture techniques; however, they no longer divide. The irreversible growth-arrested condition of senescent cultures is distinct from the G_0 (resting) phase that young cells enter when deprived of growth factors. In spite of their apparent inability to complete DNA replication following stimulation, the DNA synthetic machinery of old cultures remains intact, as is demonstrated by the fact that senescent cells can be forced to replicate their DNA by infection with simian virus 40.

Many factors are believed to contribute to the process of senescence. The appearance of growth inhibitors in late passage cells has been frequently reported. For example, poly A+ RNA, derived from senescent fibroblasts, inhibits entry into DNA synthesis when microinjected into proliferation-competent cells. It has also been observed that the expression of replication-dependent histones is repressed in senescent cells while a variant histone is uniquely expressed. The factors controlling senescence are dominant over those that control proliferation. Fusion of late passage cells with early passage normal cells and with immortal cells has been used to demonstrate that the nonproliferative phenotype of senescent cells is dominant over normal proliferative cells and immortalized cells (for review, see Cristofalo and Pignolo). Changes in cellular signaling pathways have been observed in senescent cells that may significantly alter the way in which cells respond to growth factors and other stimuli (Cristofalo et al.).

The shortening of chromosomal telomeres appears to be a major factor that limits proliferative life span. Telomeres protect chromosomes from degradation, rearrangements, end-to-end fusions, and chromosome loss. During replication, DNA polymerases require an RNA primer for initiation, but they are unable to replace the primer with DNA when they have completed synthesis. As a result, telomeres become slightly shorter each time DNA is replicated. Immortalized cells avoid this problem by expressing an enzyme that compensates for telomere loss by adding repetitive DNA units to the telomeres after mitosis. The importance of telomeres to senescence has been demonstrated by showing that senescence is delayed and possibly eliminated by overexpression of telomerase in normal cells (Bodnar et al., 1998). In summary, expression of growth inhibitory genes, changes in cellular signaling, and telomere loss are all factors that govern cellular senescence. However, the relationship of senescence, and the factors that cause it, to the aging of organisms remains a subject of much controversy.

VINCENT J. CRISTOFALO
R. G. ALLEN

See also CELLULAR AGING: BASIC PHENOMENA; CELLULAR AGING; TELOMERES; THEORIES OF BIOLOGICAL AGING.

Figure 1

Some internal structures found in a normal human cell. The cell depicted in this figure remains in the body and therefore exhibits no effects of senescence.

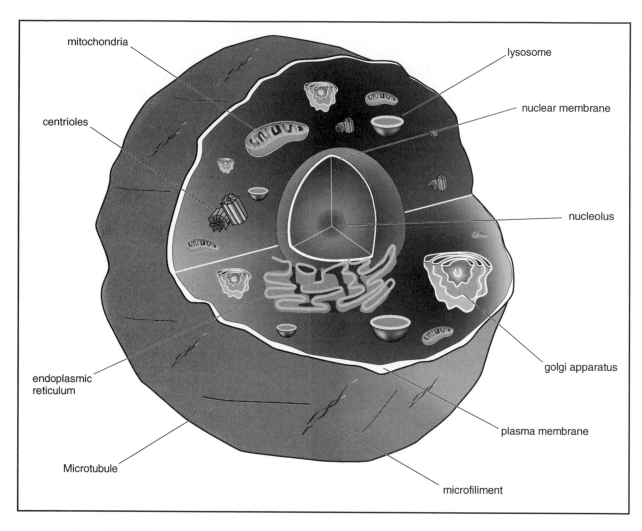

SOURCE: Author and GGS Inc.

BIBLIOGRAPHY

BODNAR, A. G.; OUELLETTE, M.; FROLKIS, M.; HOLT, S. E.; CHIU, C.-P.; MORIN, G. B.; HARLEY, C. B.; SHAY, J. W.; LICHTSTEINER, S.; and WRIGHT, W. E. "Extension of Life-span by Introduction of Telomerase into Normal Human Cells." *Science* 279 (1998): 349–352.

CRISTOFALO, V. J., and PIGNOLO, R. J. "Replicative Senescence of Human Fibroblast-like Cells in Culture." *Physiological Reviews* 73 (1993): 617–638.

CRISTOFALO, V. J.; VOLKER, C.; FRANCIS, M. K.; and TRESINI, M. "Age-Dependent Modifications of Gene Expression in Human Fibroblasts." *Critical Reviews in Eukaryotic Gene Expression* 8 (1998): 43–80.

CELLULAR AGING: BASIC PHENOMENA

Development proceeds through many steps that ultimately produce germ (reproductive cells) and somatic (nonreproductive) cell lineages. The germ cell lineage population is potentially immortal, because the genes it carries can be passed on indefinitely. The somatic cells will ultimately age and die. Early studies by Carrel and coworkers suggested that, when isolated from organisms, individual somatic cells were immortal. This view remained prominent for many years, though subsequent studies showed that it was actually untrue.

Figure 2

Stages of cell cycle and various stages of mitosis. Also depicted are senescence ($G_{senescent}$) and the escape from senescence to immortality that can occur after treatment with the SC-40 virus.

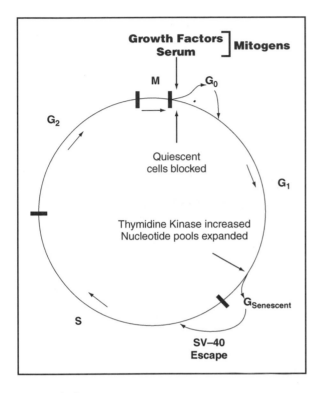

SOURCE: Author

Studies conducted in many laboratories have shown that after the migration of cells from tissue pieces into culture vessels there is a phase of rapid proliferation, followed by one of declining proliferative capacity, and ultimately a total loss of mitotic activity. Cultures that have entered this permanently quiescent state are termed "senescent." During this later nonmitotic phase, the cells change in size and morphology, become granular in appearance, and accumulate debris. The loss of proliferative capacity in human diploid cell culture populations is a well-regulated phenomenon. As populations of cells divide successive times, the generation time of the culture increases, and there is also failure of an increasing fraction of the population to replicate at all. There is strong evidence that substantial heterogeneity develops in populations of cells as they proliferate, with some members of the population exhibiting a high proliferative capacity while others are capable of only a small number of divisions.

Cellular senescence has been observed in a variety of cell types. Although the proliferative capacity differs between various types of cells, for any given cell type the proliferative capacity tends to be relatively constant. The inability of cell cultures to proliferate indefinitely is neither the result of technical difficulties nor of the depletion of essential metabolites. Hayflick and Moorhead (1961) concluded that the limited lifespan phenomenon observed in human diploid cells might be programmed, and/or that accumulation of genetic damage might limit proliferative capacity. They suggested that the limited proliferative lifespan of cell cultures was an expression of cellular aging *in vitro*.

Changes in cell morphology and contact

The steady loss of replicative potential is accompanied by a greater heterogeneity of cell sizes; cells near the end of their proliferative capacity tend to be much larger than those that have doubled a small number of times. A number of subcellular structures also change with age (see Figure 1). An increase in nuclear size, in nucleolar size, and in the number of multinucleated cells parallels the increase in cell size seen in slowly replicating or nonreplicating cells. Prominent Golgi apparati, evacuated endoplasmic reticula, increased numbers of cytoplasmic microfilaments, vacuolated cytoplasm, and large lysosomal bodies have been observed in senescent human fibroblasts.

Cultures near the end of their proliferative potential display a reduced harvest density and a lowered saturation density at the plateau phase of growth; that is, the number of cells per unit area is lower in near-senescent cultures that exhibit inhibition of growth due to contact with neighboring cells. At the end of their life span *in vitro*, substantial cell death occurs; however, a stable population emerges that can exist in a viable, nonproliferative state for many months. This stable population is capable of maintaining only an extremely low saturation density, equivalent to less than 5 percent of that reached by cultures that have doubled a small number of times. The observed decrease in saturation densities probably reflects an increased sensitivity to intercellular contact, rather than increased numbers of larger cells. Changes at the level of extracellular matrix (ECM; proteins secreted by the cell that remain attached to the cell), specific secretory proteins not connected with the ECM, and membrane-associated molecules occur in cells near the end of their proliferative life, but it is unclear whether they account for alterations in the nature of cell contact among these cells.

Senescence and cell-cycle progression

The growth arrest observed in senescent cultures is not random; senescent cells appear to stop dividing at a unique point in the cell cycle. Treatment of cells that have divided a relatively small number of times with growth stimulators (generically referred to as *mitogens*) is followed by a so-called gap phase (G_1), which is a period during which cells appear quiescent (see Figure 2). In fact, many biochemical changes occur during G_1, but these are not apparent from gross cell morphology. After G_1, cells enter a synthesis (S) phase in which chromosomes are replicated. A second pause or gap occurs after the S phase (G_2) and before mitosis (M). When essential growth factors are removed or decreased, young cells may enter a distinct quiescent phase called G_0. The cells in living tissues are generally thought to be in a G_0 state of growth. Much evidence supports the view that cultures of senescent cells are blocked in late G_1 near the G_1/S boundary in the cell cycle. It is clear, though, that the irreversibly arrested condition ultimately reached by senescent cells is distinct from the G_0 phase young cells enter or any other definable stage of the cell cycle. When senescent cultures are maintained with reduced levels of mitogens that induce a quiescent state (G_0) in early-passage cells, the pattern of gene expression exhibited by senescent cells is different from that of a functional G_0 state. Furthermore, chromatin condensation patterns are consistent with arrest in late G_1. The fact that cells near the end of their proliferative life can express some of the gene characteristics of the G_1/S boundary suggests an abortive attempt to initiate DNA synthesis and arrest that growth in a unique state.

The reason that senescent cells fail to enter the S phase is unclear. Both young and senescent cells appear to respond to fresh mitogens by carrying out some of the same cell-cycle processes in roughly the same time frame. However, the ability to complete the mitogen-initiated cascade of signal transduction pathways and to synthesize DNA is lost in senescent cells. In fact, the hallmark of senescence in culture is the inability of cells to replicate their DNA following stimulation with mitogens.

In general, the synthesis rate of macromolecules decreases as cells approach the end of their proliferative life span *in vitro*, while the cellular content of macromolecules (except DNA) increases. This observation seems to indicate that, in senescent cells, there is a general dysregulation of coordinated processes, which uncouples DNA synthesis from the synthesis of other macromolecules. The synthetic rates of DNA, RNA, and protein decrease in cultures nearing the end of their proliferative potential, which may be related to altered chromatin template activity in senescent cells. Gorman and coworkers tested the possibility that the replicative enzymes themselves and/or replication-associated processes such as control of DNA hierarchical structural orders, were reduced or altered during senescence. They observed that, when treated with simian virus 40 (SV40), senescent cells can initiate an additional round of semiconservative DNA synthesis in old cells, indicating that the proteins necessary for DNA synthesis can still function in senescent cells following at least some types of stimuli.

Growth signals and senescence

If the cellular machinery that replicates DNA is intact in senescent cells, then it is possible that the proteins that carry some of the signals that stimulate DNA replication are diminished in senescent cells. Human diploid cells, near the beginning of their *in vitro* replicative life span, vigorously respond to stimulation with serum or a combination of certain growth factors by initiating DNA synthesis and mitosis. As these cells approach the end of their proliferative potential in culture, they become increasingly resistant to mitogenic signals. The basis for this loss of responsiveness cannot be attributed to any dramatic reductions in the number of cell-surface growth-factor receptors, nor to changes in the binding affinities with which these receptors bind their ligands (the generic name given to substances that bind to receptors). Instead, the intracellular proteins that convey signals from receptors to the nucleus decrease in number or become inactive.

Cells respond to mitogens through the intracellular actions of secondary events, including phospholipid turner, protein kinase C activation, and calcium mobilization. Alterations in post-receptor transduction pathways have been documented for each of these pathways. Repression of c-fos transcription in senescent cells is evidence for an early block in one or more pathways potentially required for DNA synthesis. However, this alone does not account for the cessation of growth in senescent cells, since overexpression of c-fos fails to prevent senescence. Interestingly, in skin fibroblast cultures derived from individuals with Werner syndrome (a disease of precocious aging), c-fos expression in response to serum is equal in both young and senescent cultures. The expression of some late-acting cell-cycle-regulated genes, is also lower in senescent cells. Thus, it is the attrition of multiple signaling pathways associated with cell growth, rather than a decrease in any one pathway, that appears to govern the appearance of a senescent phenotype.

It is also known that the expression of certain genes that suppress growth, such as p53, p21, and p16, increases in senescent cells. These changes in expression may exert profound effects on the proliferative life of cultures. Treatment of normal cells with antisense p53 and retinoblastoma protein (pRB) extends the life span of senescent cells in a cooperative manner. Disruption of tumor/growth suppressor genes such as p21, a gene controlled by p53, can extend proliferative life span. Additionally, transfection of human tumor cells that lack p53 with the wild-type gene can induce a senescent phenotype; yet elimination of p53, and hence p21, fails to prevent senescence in human cells. Loss of p16, an inhibitor of cell cycle regulatory proteins, has also been reported to extend proliferative life span. Constitutive activation of the cellular-signaling protein MEK (a component of the MAP Kinase cascade) induces both p53 and p16 and results in permanent growth arrest in primary mouse fibroblasts. In contrast, overexpression of constitutively active MEK causes uncontrolled mitogenesis and transformation in cells lacking either p53 or p16. Although these changes might at first appear to suggest that signaling proteins decline while growth-inhibitory proteins increase—as part of a coordinated mechanism—this may not be the case. At least one of the growth inhibitory genes (p16) appears to increase, because the family of proteins (Id proteins) that block its transcription in young cells decline in senescent cells. Thus, the senescence-associated increase in p16 results partially from loss of an inhibitor, rather than from direct stimulation of transcription.

The Genetics of cellular senescence

Skin fibroblasts from pairs of monozygotic twins show no significant difference in replicative life span within each pair, but do show such differences among pairs. In heterokaryons, which are formed by the fusion of two different cells, the nonproliferative phenotype of senescent cells in culture is dominant over normal proliferative cells and over immortalized cells, but not over immortalized variants having high levels of DNA polymerase α (DNA pol α) or those transformed by DNA tumor viruses. There are numerous reports documenting the presence of inhibitors of DNA synthesis in senescent cells, although the nature of these inhibitors is poorly understood, and whether any of them plays a causal role in senescence is unclear. The idea that senescent cells actively make an inhibitor of DNA synthesis, however, is supported further by the observation that expressible RNA derived from senescent fibroblasts, when microinjected into proliferation-competent cells, can inhibit their entry into DNA synthesis.

Some of the most compelling evidence in support of a genetic component for cellular senescence has been the finding that introduction of particular chromosomes into immortalized cells causes them to acquire a senescent, or at least a nongrowing, phenotype. Evidence that the cessation of proliferation is a programmed phenomenon is seen in studies that used SV40 large T antigen to produce a reversible escape from cellular senescence. This evidence suggests that senescence confers at least two distinct mortality states.

Genetic influences over the process of cellular senescence would necessarily be reflected in reproducible changes in gene expression. The list of molecular markers of senescence in culture has dramatically increased as the result of examining genes isolated from selective libraries and monoclonal antibody pools. Remarkably, the number of genes isolated by these methods includes those involved with the ECM, secretory proteins involved in growth-factor-mediated function, differentiation and shock proteins, inhibitors of DNA synthesis, and genes of unknown function.

Cellular senescence and aging in organisms

Aging changes in organisms involve different kinds of cells and tissues and may result from multiple mechanisms. Thus, the aging of postmitotic cells, such as neurons, may proceed by a different set of mechanisms than that of proliferating tissues such as skin, the lining of the gut, or the blood-forming elements. Extracellular matrix macromolecules, such as collagen and elastin, also change with age, and presumably through mechanisms that are unique to them. There are also potentially profound effects resulting from interactions among these components during aging. Questions that have long been pondered by researchers studying proliferative senescence is whether the phenomenon occurs *in vivo* and whether it reflects changes that occur in organisms as they age. It is generally accepted that aging occurs at a cellular level. If this is true, then the mechanisms that control aging operate, and should be quantifiable, at a cellular level. But do the same mechanisms lead to cellular senescence? There is no simple answer to this question.

One of the strongest supports for the use of the cell-culture senescence model in studies of aging was the demonstration of a relationship between species' maximal life span and proliferative life span. There is also a donor-age-associated decline in mitotic activity and proliferation rates in a wide variety of human and rodent tissues *in vivo*. Both of these observations seem to suggest that the factors controlling the life span of intact organisms also control the growth characteristics and proliferative potential of cells in a culture environment. It has been observed that cells from patients with accelerated aging syndromes, such as Werner syndrome, have a reduced proliferative capacity compared with control cells from normal donors of the same ages. Additionally, this disease is associated with decreased mitotic activity, DNA synthesis, and cloning efficiency. Other types of diseases can also strongly modulate proliferative life expectancy. The effects of diabetes are particularly pronounced. All of these observations would appear to suggest that the physiological condition of the donor is reflected to some extent by the rate of cellular senescence observed *in vitro*.

On the other hand, studies by Robbins et al. (1970) were unable to identify any cells in the skin of older individuals with the phenotype that emerges *in vitro*. This raises the question of whether or not proliferative senescence actually occurs in the tissues of intact organisms? One of the strengths of the cell-culture model is that it has permitted the study of a single cell type; however, this can also be a limitation. Most studies of cell proliferation are unable to elucidate the relative contribution of intrinsic versus extrinsic factors. For example, do cells only senesce when separated from other types of cells and extracellular matrices, as in a culture environment? A group of studies bearing on this point involved the serial transplantation of normal somatic tissues to new, young, inbred hosts each time the recipient approached old age. In general, normal cells serially transplanted to inbred hosts exhibit a decline in proliferative capacity and probably cannot survive indefinitely. Additionally, it has been reported that proliferative capacity is diminished in spleen cells derived from old animals and transplanted into young irradiate hosts, and that mouse epidermis from old donors retain an age-associated increase in susceptibility to carcinogens regardless of whether they were transplanted into young or old recipients.

Donor age and proliferative life span

What has generally been accepted as the strongest evidence supporting the usefulness of the cell senescence model of aging has been reports from several laboratories of a negative correlation between donor age and proliferative life span *in vitro*. On the basis of these observations, it follows that the physiological effects of aging *in vivo* are reflected by the life span of cells maintained *in vitro*. Other laboratories report that the colony-forming capacity of individual cells also declines as a function of donor age. These observations, and the relationship between growth potential and maximal species life span is generally regarded as clear evidence of a direct relationship between aging *in vivo* and *in vitro*.

In spite of the fact that the relationship between donor age and proliferative lifespan became widely accepted, the correlations reported were always quite low. Furthermore, the studies were never standardized for biopsy site or culture conditions, which further added to individual variation and further decreased the correlation. Probably the most important problem with human studies was that so few of them actually assessed the health status of the donors from whom the cell lines were established. Many of the cell lines used were established from cadavers. It is known that diseases such as diabetes exert a profound affect on the proliferative potential of cell cultures. It is probable that other diseases can also affect *in vitro* proliferative capacity. The failure to screen for donor health probably skewed the results of many studies. These factors were seldom discussed when considering the correlations between donor age and proliferative lifespan. Instead, the relatively low correlations were seen as the result of individual variations in a highly outbred and otherwise uncontrolled population, and it was generally accepted that stronger correlations would be found in a longitudinal study where cell lines were established from a small group of individuals throughout their life. Due to the relatively large numbers of lines examined, the correlations reported found general acceptance, even though they were weak. Nevertheless, it remained difficult to assess whether the reported correlations between donor age and replicative life span indicated any compromise of physiology or proliferative homeostasis *in vivo*.

In order to address some of the problems with standardization and health status, 124 cell lines, established from 116 donors who participated in the Baltimore Longitudinal Study of Aging (BLSA), and 8 samples of fetal skin were examined by Cristofalo and coworkers (Cristofalo, et al., 1998). In this study, all of the donors were medically evaluated and determined to be healthy (by the criteria of the BLSA). None of the donors had diabetes when the cell lines were established. The results of this study showed that in healthy donors there was no relationship between donor age and proliferative life span. A longitudinal study was also performed to evaluate the effects of age on *in vitro* life span within individuals. Multiple cell lines established from the same individuals at time intervals spanning as long as fifteen years were compared. Surprisingly, this longitudinal study also failed to reveal any relationship between donor age and proliferative capacity in the five individuals studied. In fact, the proliferative potentials of cultures established when donors were older was found to be greater than that in lines established at younger donor ages in four of the five donors.

In spite of these findings, the fact that the colony-forming capacity of individual cells had also been reported to decline with donor age still seemed to support a relationship between donor age and proliferative potential in culture. However, the colony-forming assay is strongly influenced by variations in growth rates. Both the initial growth rates and the rate of thymidine incorporation into cells is dramatically higher in fetal fibroblast lines than in adult lines, which in-

dicates that cell lines established from fetal skin initially divided more frequently, even though the replicative life span of these cell lines do not exceed that observed in the postnatal cell lines. It would seem equally relevant that the rate of thymidine incorporation and initial growth rates of large groups of lines established from adults do not vary significantly with respect to age. In view of differences in initial growth rates and intraclonal variations in the proliferative potential of single cells, it seems probable that the clone-size distribution method of estimating proliferative life span and an actual determination of replicative life span measure different things.

It should be noted that studies supporting the inverse relationship between donor age and proliferative life span are not limited to human cells. Studies of rodent skin fibroblasts also appeared to support the existence of a small, though significant, inverse correlation between donor age and replicative life span. Furthermore, it was observed that treatment of hamster skin fibroblasts with growth promoters could extend the proliferative life of cultures established from young donors but had negligible effects on cultures established from older donors. However, even in rodents, the relationship between donor age and proliferative potential is not entirely clear. For example, an examination of hamster skin fibroblast cultures established from the same donors at different ages reveals no age-associated changes in proliferative potential in animals older than twelve months.

In vitro studies on aging have used two kinds of cell cultures. The predominant one has been fetal- or neonatal-derived cultures that show aging changes when subcultured at regular intervals; some of these alterations parallel aging changes *in vivo*. The other related paradigm is that of cells derived from donors of different ages and studied after only one, or a few, subcultivations. In either case, attempts to relate changes in these individual cells to changes occurring in organisms as they age forms one basis of the use of the *in vitro* model for studies of *in vivo* aging.

Biomarkers of cellular aging *in vitro* and *in vivo*

The failure to confirm the relationship between donor age and proliferative life span does not invalidate cell culture as a model for aging studies, because other significant alterations occur during senescence *in vitro* that also occur during aging *in vivo*. These changes include an increased number of copies of genetic material, increased cell size, decreased mitogenic response to growth signals, a decline in the expression of genes involved in growth control, increased expression of genes of the extracellular matrix, and various changes in cell morphology. In addition, a correlation between replicative capacity and initial telomere length of cells derived from donors up to ninety-three years of age has been reported.

However, not all changes that occur during senescence *in vitro* occur during the aging of organisms. For example, the induction of the *c-fos* gene following stimulation with serum is lost in senescent cells but is undiminished in old individuals. Even markers that have gained relatively widespread use have been found to detect different phenomena when they occur both *in vivo* and *in vitro*. One marker thought to be potentially universal was reported by Dimri et al. (1995), who observed increases in cytochemically detectable β-galactosidase activity (SA β-gal) at pH 6.0—both in cell cultures and in tissue sections obtained from old donors. They also observed that immortal cells exhibited no SA β-gal staining under identical culture conditions. Additionally, they interpreted their results as providing a link between replicative senescence and aging *in vivo*. These observations appear to be supported by studies in rhesus monkeys. This model has gained widespread use as a crude measure of senescence; however, a number of subsequent studies have shown that it is actually not as specific or universal as first claimed. For example, SA β-gal positive cells have been observed in quiescent cultures of mouse cells as well as some types of human cancer cells that were chemically stimulated to differentiate, even though none these cell types can be classified as senescent. Furthermore, one biochemical analysis demonstrated that β-gal activity was present at both pH 6.0 and pH 4.5 in a number of different tumor cells. Other studies failed to detect any correlation with donor age either in tissue sections or in skin fibroblast cultures established from donors of different ages. It was also observed that staining in skin sections occurred only in the lumen of sebaceous glands and shafts of hair follicles, which is consistent with detection of microbial invasion, rather than actual changes in the biochemistry of the human cells in tissue sections (Severino, et al., 2000). The source of these discrepancies cannot be entirely elucidated; however, it is clear that this type of staining cannot be used as a marker for all types of aging under all conditions.

An important biomarker that is linked to the cessation of mitotic activity associated with cellular senescence is the progressive loss of chromosomal telomeric repeats. The telomeres of human chromosomes are composed of several kilobases of simple repeats: (TTAGGG)n. Telomeres protect chromosomes from degradation, rearrangements, end-to-end fusions, and chromosome loss. During replication, DNA polymerases require an RNA primer for initiation. The terminal RNA primer required for DNA replication cannot be replaced with DNA, which results in a loss of telomeric sequences with each mitotic cycle of normal cells. The observation that telomere shortening correlates with senescence provides an attractive model for the way in which cells might "count" divisions. Telomere shortening has been observed in aging models both *in vitro* and *in vivo*.

An examination of some biomarkers of senescence lends at least some support to the hypothesis that the phenomenon occurs *in vivo*. For example, the messenger RNA (mRNA) for the angiogenesis inhibitor EPC-1 declines more than one-hundred-fold with proliferative aging in culture. Although the EPC-1 mRNA is readily detected in tissue sections from both young and old donors, the total amount of EPC-1 mRNA is also lower in older individuals. Furthermore, it is present in a mosaic pattern in the skin sections from older individuals. Thus, the decrease occurs only in some cells. Similarly, the average length of telomeres, which decreases progressively with increasing numbers of mitoses, exhibits large variations in multiple subclones established from one individual, again suggesting different telomere lengths are associated with different tissue regions *in vivo*. These observations suggest that loss of proliferative potential, *in vivo*, occurs in a mosaic pattern, and that both long- and short-lived cells may lie in close proximity in tissues. In a culture environment, the cells with the greatest growth capacity will ultimately become predominant in the culture. Hence, the selection during the procedure to establish cultures probably obscures differences in proliferative capacity that exist *in vivo*.

Senescence and differentiation

Although most of the studies of cellular senescence have focused on similarities to aging, some have considered homologies with developmental processes. A commonly held view is that cellular aging may follow a differentiation lineage model. In fact, it has been suggested that the finite life span of cells may represent a differentiation of cell types, and that the process of diploid cell growth may have an *in vivo* counterpart in hyperplastic processes (uncontrolled proliferation). Chronological time appears to be significantly less important than division events in the progression of the phenomenon. Although the state of differentiation may change in cells that senesce *in vitro*, there is, in fact, no evidence that the changes in gene expression observed in fetal cells as they senesce, *in vitro*, are tantamount to differentiation, *in vivo*. While analogous changes can be found, they are greatly outnumbered by the dissimilar features that characterize these two distinct phenomena. Hence, a comparison of senescence-associated changes and differences that exist between fetal and postnatal cells reveals little similarity.

At least some analogous similarities exist between senescence in fetal fibroblasts and developmental changes that occur *in vivo*. For example, it has been observed that addition of platelet-derived growth factor-BB (PDGF-BB) stimulates an increased mRNA abundance of the transcript encoding PDGF-A chain in fetal and newborns and a relatively small response in adult cells. Senescence *in vitro* of newborn fibroblasts appears to result in the acquisition of the adult phenotype by decreasing their response to PDGF-BB. On the other hand, there are a number of differences reported between cell lines established from fetal and adult tissues that are related to growth factor requirements for proliferation and migration that remain disparate, even as these cultures become senescent. For example, fetal dermal fibroblasts will proliferate in either plasma or serum, while adult dermal fibroblasts require serum. It is also noteworthy that the expression of some genes, such as SOD-2, increases during proliferative senescence but only in some types of fibroblasts; in other types of fibroblasts no change is observed (see Allen, et al., 1999). It might be expected that cells placed in culture will be deprived of those signals that direct the normal sequence of developmental pathways, and that differentiation, if it occurs, is to an aberrant state. Alternatively, fetal cell lines may arise from different precursor cells than adult fibroblasts, and thus merely differentiate to a different fibroblast type. What is apparent from studies of senescence is that similarities as well as discrepancies are observed when it is compared to either aging or development. As a result of this, the model is obviously less useful for predicting aging or development changes *in vivo* than it is for studying known changes in an isolated cell system.

VINCENT J. CRISTOFALO
R. G. ALLEN

See also CELLULAR AGING; CELLULAR AGING: CELL DEATH; CELLULAR AGING: TELOMERES; PHYSIOLOGICAL CHANGES, FIBROBLAST CELLS; PHYSIOLOGICAL CHANGES: STEM CELLS; THEORIES OF BIOLOGICAL AGING.

BIBLIOGRAPHY

ALLEN, R. G.; TRESINI, M.; KEOGH, B. P.; DOGGETT, D. L.; and CRISTOFALO, V. J. "Differences in Electron Transport Potential Antioxidant Defenses and Oxidant Generation in Young and Senescent Fetal Lung Fibroblasts (WI-38)." *Journal of Cellular Physiology* 180 (1999): 114–122.

BRUCE, S. A.; and DEAMOND, S. F. "Longitudinal Study of In Vivo Wound Repair and In Vitro Cellular Senescence of Dermal Fibroblasts." *Experimental Gerontology* 26 (1991): 17–27.

CARREL, A., and EBLING, A. H. "Age and Multiplication of Fibroblasts." *Journal of Experimental Medicine* 34 (1921): 599–523.

CRISTOFALO, V. J.; VOLKER, C.; FRANCIS, M. K.; and TRESINI, M. "Age-Dependent Modifications of Gene Expression in Human Fibroblasts." *Critical Reviews in Eukaryotic Gene Expression* 8 (1998): 43–80.

CRISTOFALO, V. J., and PIGNOLO, R. J. "Cell Culture As a Model." In *Handbook of Physiology: Aging.* Edited by E. J. Masoro. New York: Oxford University Press, 1984. Pages 53–82.

CRISTOFALO, V. J.; PIGNOLO, R. P.; CIANCIARULO, F. L.; DIPAOLO, B. R.; and ROTENBERG, M. O. "Changes in Gene Expression During Senescence in Culture." *Experimental Gerontology* 27 (1992): 429–432.

CRISTOFALO, V. J.; DOGGETT, D. L.; BROOKS-FREDERICH, K. M. and PHILLIPS, P. D. "Growth Factors as Probes of Cell Aging." *Experimental Gerontology* 24 (1989): 367–374.

CRISTOFALO, V. J.; ALLEN, R. G.; PIGNOLO, R. P.; MARTIN, B. M.; and BECK, J. C. "Relationship between Donor Age and the Replicative Life Spans of Human Cells in Culture: A Reevaluation." *Proceedings of the National Academy of Sciences of the United States of America* 95 (1998): 10614–10619.

CRISTOFALO, V. J.; VOLKER, C.; and ALLEN, R. G. "Use of the Fibroblast Model in the Study of Cellular Senescence." In *Aging Methods and Protocols.* Edited by Y. Barnett and C. R. Barnett. Totowa, N.J.: Humana Press, 1984.

DIMRI, G. P.; LEE, X.; BASILE, G.; ACOSTA, M.; SCOTT, G.; ROSKELLEY, C.; MEDRANO, E. E.; LINSKENS, M.; RUBELJ, I.; PEREIRA-SMITH, O.; PEACOCKE, M.; and CAMPISI, J. "A Biomarker that Identifies Senescent Human Cells in Culture and in Aging Skin In Vivo." *Proceedings of the National Academy of Sciences of the United States of America* 92 (1995): 9363–9367.

FENG, J.; FUNK, W. D.; WANG, S.-S.; WEINRICH, S. L.; AVILION, A. A.; CHIU, C.-C.; ADAMS, R. R.; CHANG, E.; ALLSOPP, R. C.; YU, J.; LE, S.; WEST, M. D.; HARLEY, C. B.; ANDREWS, W. H.; GREIDER, C. W.; and VILLEPONTEAU, B. "The RNA Component of Human Telomerase." *Science* 269 (1995): 1236–1241.

GORMAN, S. D., and CRISTOFALO, V. J. "Reinitiation of Cellular DNA Synthesis in BrdU-Selected Nondividing Senescent WI-38 Cells by Simian Virus 40 Infection." *Journal of Cellular Physiology* 125 (1985): 122–126.

HAYFLICK, L., and MOORHEAD, P. S. "The Serial Cultivation of Human Diploid Cell Strains." *Experimental Cell Research* 25 (1961): 585–621.

LIN, A. W.; BARRADAS, M.; STONE, J. C.; VAN AELST, L.; SERRANO, M.; and LOWE, S. W. "Premature Senescence Involving p53 and p16 Is Activated in Response to Constitutive MEK/MAPK Mitogenic Signaling." *Genes and Development* 12 (1998): 3008–3019.

LUMPKIN, C. K., JR.; McCLUNG, J. K.; PEREIRA-SMITH, O. M.; and SMITH, J. R. "Existence of High Abundance Antiproliferative mRNA's in Senescent Human Diploid Fibroblasts." *Science* 232 (1986): 393–395.

MEDCALF, A. S. C.; KLEIN-SZANTO, A. J. P.; and CRISTOFALO, V. J. "Expression of p21 Is Not Required for Senescence of Human Fibroblasts." *Cancer Research* 56 (1996): 4582–4585.

OHTANI, N.; ZEBEDEE, Z.; HUOT, T. J. G.; STINSON, J. A.; SUGIMOTO, M.; OHASHI, Y.; SHARROCKS, A. D.; PETERS, G.; and HARA, E. "Opposing Effects of Ets and Id Proteins on p16^{INK4a} Expression During Cellular Senescence." *Nature* 409 (2001): 1067–1070.

OSHIMA, J.; CAMPISI, J.; TANNOCK, C. A.; and MARTIN, G. M. "Regulation of c-fos Expression in Senescing Werner Syndrome Fibroblasts Differs from That Observed in Senescing Fibroblasts from Normal Donors." *Journal of Cellular Physiology* 162 (1995): 277–283.

PIGNOLO, R. J.; ROTENBERG, M. O.; and CRISTOFALO, V. J. "Alterations in Contact and Densi-ty-Dependent Arrest State in Senescent WI-38 Cells." *In Vitro Cellular and Developmental Biology* 30A (1994): 471–476.

ROBBINS, E.; LEVINE, E. M.; and EAGLE, H. "Morphologic Changes Accompanying Senescence of Cultured Human Diploid Cells." *Journal of Experimental Medicine* 131 (1970): 1211–1222.

RUBIN, H. "Cell Aging *In Vivo* and *In Vitro*." *Mechanisms of Ageing and Development* 98 (1997): 1–35.

SEVERINO, J.; ALLEN, R. G.; BALIN, S.; BALIN, A.; and CRISTOFALO, V. J. "Is β-Galactosidase Staining a Marker of Senescence In Vitro and In Vivo?" *Experimental Cell Research* 257 (2000): 162–171.

SHELTON, D. N.; CHANG, E.; WHITTIER, P. S.; CHOI, D.; and FUNK, W. D. "Microarray Analysis of Replicative Senescence." *Current Biology* 9 (1999): 939–945.

SMITH, J. R., and WHITNEY, R. G. "Intraclonal Variation in the Proliferative Potential of Human Diploid Fibroblasts: Stochastic Mechanisms for Cellular Aging." *Science* 207 (1980): 82–84.

CELLULAR AGING: CELL DEATH

Cell death during aging is an important issue, and it is important to understand what cell death is, and what it is not, as there are several phenomena that use similar terminologies. Perhaps the best known of these is cellular senescence.

Cellular senescence

First identified in the late 1960s by Leonard Hayflick and his collaborators, the term *cellular senescence* refers to the fact that normal, nonmalignant cells of vertebrates do not divide indefinitely in culture, but in time terminally differentiate and enter a prolonged postmitotic phase, eventually dying in the culture dish. Because the number of divisions that the cells can undergo is inversely related to the age at which they were explanted, cellular senescence has been associated with aging—though there is little evidence that, except in limited situations, individuals at the ends of their lives have "run out of cells." The mechanism for cell senescence is not completely understood. One explanation for the limitation in cell replication is based on the importance of the end-piece, or telomere, of a chromosome. The manner in which DNA is

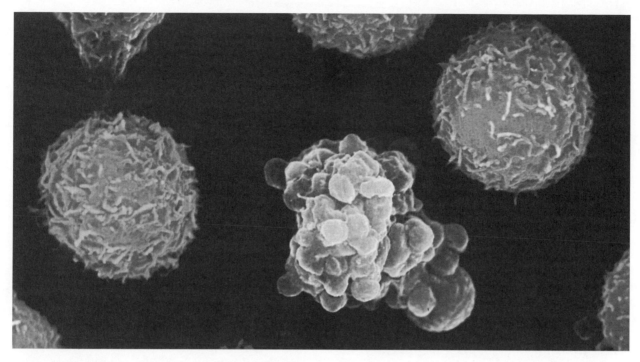

Scanning electron micrograph (SEM) image showing the death of a cell (apoptosis). (Phototake photo by Gopal Murti.)

replicated results in the loss of a small portion of DNA (an Okazaki fragment) from the end of the chromosome with each replication. This problem is addressed by the addition to the end of the DNA, during early embryonic life, of a stretch of meaningless, noncoding DNA called a telomere. Thus, at each division a piece of this expendable DNA is shed. Under culture conditions, or in conditions of excessive proliferation, such as chronic challenge to the immune system, the cells eventually use up their telomeres and cease proliferation. Cancerous cells reacquire the embryonic ability to reconstruct the telomere, and thus become immortal.

Cell death: programmed, apoptosis, and necrosis

Cell senescence is distinct from what is properly called *cell death.* Cells can, of course, encounter violent situations in which proteins precipitate, membranes are ruptured, or their access to energy sources is destroyed. In these situations, cells typically lose the ability to maintain their volumes against osmotic forces, and they swell and rupture (technically, lyse), spilling their contents and provoking an inflammatory response. This process is called either *necrosis* or *on-*

cosis, and is seen in acute situations such as infarct (a region of tissue suddenly deprived of blood flow, as when a clot lodges in a small artery or arteriole), severe chemical toxicity, and extreme thermal damage.

Necrotic cells, generated in an uncontrolled manner, create many problems for an organism because of inflammation and because of the leakage of potentially dangerous chemicals or enzymes. Also, cells lysing from infection may spew out viruses or other pathogens. As a protective mechanism, therefore, organisms can preempt such deaths by invoking a much more biological and controlled response, known as *apoptosis,* or *programmed cell death.* These forms of death are a sort of cell suicide, in which cells self-destruct in a controlled and contained manner. All cells carry within themselves the capacity to self-destruct, but are normally restrained from doing so. If this restraint is removed when a cell is challenged, it will default to the self-destruct mode and, assuming that the challenge is not so severe that the cell becomes necrotic, it will undergo this physiological form of death.

The term *programmed cell death* derived originally from developmental and embryonic observations, and it emphasizes the idea that specific genes regulate the death of cells. Many of these genes have now been recognized and are described below. In developmental situations, death frequently, if surprisingly, requires the synthesis of new proteins, perhaps including those involved in killing the cell. The morphology is more often than not apoptosis. However, apoptosis does not necessarily require protein synthesis and is usually not programmed (meaning that the sequence of death is coded in the genes) except in the generic sense that it was pre-programmed into the cell and simply required release or activation.

The apoptotic cell is recognized by several characteristics. It is a rounded, blebbing cell, with limited permeability of its cell membrane. In an active process, it has moved a component of the inner cell membrane, phosphatidyl serine (PS), to the external surface. The exposed PS will serve as a signal to the phagocytes that will consume it. The chromatin (the complex of protein, DNA, and RNA that can be strained, rendering the chromosome—Greek for colored body—visible) coalesces in the nucleus and frequently marginates, or condenses, along one side of the nuclear membrane. The DNA then fragments into pieces that are multiples of 180 base pairs (nucleosomal fragments), detectable by electrophoresis or by TUNEL (Terminal deoxyUridine Nucleotide End Labeling) *in situ*. There are, however, many gray areas, and some cells may display intermediate patterns.

There are many entry points into apoptosis, and there are several variants, depending on tissue type and history. Three of these variants may be summarized as follows:

Caspase-dependent apoptosis. A chief effector of apoptosis is caspase-3, a highly specific protease. Proteases are enzymes that digest proteins. They are divided into several categories, with one classification referring to an amino acid in the enzyme that is essential for its activity. Caspases contain an essential cysteine, contributing the "c" in the name of the enzyme. Also, most proteases recognize a specific amino acid sequence in the substrate and cut the substrate protein at that site. Caspases identify a sequence of four amino acids terminating in aspartic acid. Thus the name *caspase* is derived from *Cysteine ASPartyl protease*. Very few proteins have the appropriate sequences, but those that do, and are thus destroyed by caspase-3, include cytoskeletal components that maintain the shape of the cell,

enzymes necessary for synthesizing messenger RNA, and enzymes needed for repair of DNA damage. Caspase-3 exists in cells as an inactive proenzyme, with its activity blocked by extra amino acids added during its synthesis. This extra sequence begins with a site recognized by other caspases. Thus, other caspases remove this sequence and activate the enzyme. The active enzyme can also activate other pro-caspase-3 molecules (autoactivation). This process is well described by Earnshaw, Martins, and Kaufmann (1999).

Fas-dependent apoptosis. In many situations, particularly in the immune system, the number of cells is tightly regulated. Cell number has to be increased rapidly to fight an infection and reduced again after the infection subsides. Failure to precisely control numbers may result in autoimmune reactions, in which the body makes antibodies to its own proteins, generating life-threatening inflammations, or to the loss of too many cells, leading to increased susceptibility to infection or an inability to conquer an infection. Thus, mechanisms for cell death are very elaborate in the immune system, though the control mechanisms are used by other cells as well. Many of these cells carry on their surface one member of a family of closely related proteins. One of the most common proteins is called *Fas*, after an activity first recognized by immunologists. Fas can bind the protein *Fas Ligand*, which itself may either circulate in the blood or be attached to another cell. Fas bound to Fas Ligand can also attach to one or two similarly linked Fas molecules, forming *dimers* (two molecules linked) or *trimers* (three molecules). All of the Fas molecules stretch across the cell membrane to the intracellular side. The dimer or trimer forms interact with other proteins on the inside of the cell in a complex reaction that ultimately results in the freeing of pro-caspase-8 from an inactive bound form. This caspase-8 becomes activated and activates caspase-3, leading to apoptosis. Other receptors in the Fas Ligand family include those binding tumor-necrosis factor, and all members of the family contain similar amino acid sequences and structures, including a region important for the activation of caspases called the *death domain*.

Fas-independent apoptosis. Apoptosis may also be activated by mechanisms independent of the Fas-FasL pathway. For instance, any of a number of mechanisms may damage mitochondria, leading to the depolarization of the mitochondria, opening of a charge-dependent pore (the mitochondrial membrane permeability transition pore), and leakage of cytochrome c and other mitochondrial components into the cytoplasm. The cytochrome c displaces an inhibitor from pro-caspase-9, allowing its activation, whereupon it activates caspase-3.

Caspase-independent cell death.   Some cell deaths, most typically those of large, cytoplasm-rich cells or postmitotic cells, do not rely heavily on caspases. They therefore display a somewhat different morphology from that described below and exhibit rather an autophagic morphology. In autophagy—literally, self-eating—the bulk of the cytoplasm is destroyed in large lysosomal vesicles (autophagosomes) before the morphology becomes more classically apoptotic.

Cell death genes

Many genes are now thought to function primarily in apoptosis. Most consist of families of genes whose different functions reflect the nuances of regulation of cell death. For instance, Fas is a member of a large family of receptor proteins. Caspases, a family including at least eleven enzymes, have evolved from a single caspase in a nematode worm. (Important enzymes are conserved from animal to animal throughout evolution. However, many amino acids may change and animals may keep more than one variant, splitting an original single enzyme into two related enzymes.) Other than the products of the genes mentioned above, there are inhibitors of cell death, such as Bcl-2, which is likewise a member of a family of genes. Since Bcl-2 must form dimers to function, the complexes that it forms with other family members may lead to inhibition or activation of apoptosis. Thus, some family members, such as bax, are proapoptotic. The activity of several genes specifically increases or decreases in apoptosis, but their specific function in apoptosis is not known.

Cell death and aging

"Running out of cells" because of apoptosis does not cause aging. Nevertheless, apoptosis is considered to be an important gerontological issue for many reasons. Diseases that increase with aging include cardiovascular diseases, deterioration of the immune system, neurodegenerative diseases such as senile dementia/Alzheimer's type, and cancer. Apoptosis plays a major role in all of these diseases, as it is ably described by Huber Warner (Warner, Hodes, and Pocinki, 1997; Warner, 1999).

Many cancers, such as B-cell lymphoma, are diseases of cell death rather than cell proliferation; that is, the excess of cells arises from the failure of cells to die on schedule rather than from excess production. B-cell lymphoma arises from the inappropriate activation of Bcl-2 (the name of the gene derives from the disease), which protects the cells from death. For many other cancers, conversion to the most dangerous phase involves the loss of a surveillance mechanism, a protein called p53, that can detect abnormal DNA. This change (loss or alteration of p53) occurs in as many as 50 percent of some tumors. P53 can either block mitosis of a cell with abnormal DNA, or, if mitosis has already begun, force the cell into apoptosis. In the absence of p53, the abnormal cell survives. Therefore, mutation or loss of p53 is considered to be an ominous development in the progress of a cancer. For those cancer cells that do not appear to derive directly from abnormalities of apoptosis, there is some hope of eventually targeting signals to cancer cells to force them into apoptosis. (Cancer cells do not typically lose the ability to undergo apoptosis, but they become insensitive to the signals.)

Conversely, many of the problems of the immune system in the elderly stem from a failure to maintain high numbers of specific types of lymphocytes. Throughout life the number of immunocompetent cells is adjusted by a balance of proliferation and specifically induced apoptosis. For instance, loss of cells in AIDS is caused by suicide of cells that are not heavily infected with HIV, but are located near cells that are infected. Biomedical research aims to prevent these losses.

Autoimmune diseases, which also increase with aging, probably result from dysregulation of the controlled and normal down-regulation of the immune system. Indeed, the two best animal models of autoimmune diseases are mice in which Fas and Fas Ligand are mutated and ineffective. In many neurodegenerative diseases, most dramatically Alzheimer's disease, the cells that die have been under chronic stress before they succumb. Dead neurons cannot be replaced, but if the suicide of these stressed cells can be prevented, the disease can be alleviated or prevented. Even in an acute situation, such as an infarct (more frequent among the elderly), only those cells immediately affected by the infarct die by necrosis. Many cells on the periphery are injured, and only later undergo apoptosis. The delayed and apoptotic death of these cells indicates that there is a window in which these cells might be protected, thus lessening damage.

Future expectations

Apoptosis research was quite extensive at the end of the twentieth century, and it focused on several goals:

- Blockage of apoptosis by inhibition of caspases. Several inhibitors of caspases are now known. Although inhibition of caspase may not protect a cell limited for other reasons, it is likely to produce a "zombie" cell, which continues to exist but is incapable of performing a specific function such as conducting an impulse or contracting, and in acute situations such as a heart attack it may buy time.
- Maintenance of challenged systems. For instance, approaches used in addressing the loss of cells in AIDS include supportive therapies and administration of growth factors that are known to suppress apoptosis.
- Targeting of apoptosis. Attempts have been made to control apoptosis by attacking the machinery of apoptosis (such as caspases, particularly in acute emergencies such as stroke), but since most cells possess the machinery for apoptosis, regulation of apoptosis is more likely to focus on identifying the cells to be controlled and arranging a mechanism to specifically target these cells, using inhibitors or ligands to achieve the up- or down-regulation of the apoptosis machinery.

RICHARD A. LOCKSHIN
ZAHRA ZAKERI

See also CELLULAR AGING: TELOMERES; DNA DAMAGE AND REPAIR; THEORIES OF BIOLOGICAL AGING.

BIBLIOGRAPHY

EARNSHAW, W. C.; MARTINS, L. M.; and KAUFMAN, S. H. "Mammalian Caspases: Structure, Activation, Substrates, and Functions During Apoptosis." *Annual Review of Biochemistry* 68 (1999): 383–424.
HAYFLICK, L. "Human Cells and Aging." *Scientific American* 218, no. 3 (March 1968): 32–37.
KERR, J. F. R.; WYLLIE, A. H.; and CURRIE, A. R. "Apoptosis: A Basic Biological Phenomenon with Wide-Ranging Implications in Tissue Kinetics." *Journal of Cancer* 26 (1972): 239–257.
LOWE, S. W. "Cancer Therapy and p53." *Current Opinion in Oncology* 7, no. 6 (1995): 547–553.
WARNER, H. R. "Apoptosis: A Two-Edged Sword in Aging." *Annual of the New York Academy of Science* 887 (1999): 1–11.
WARNER, H. R.; HODES, R. J.; and POCINKI, K. "What Does Cell Death Have to Do with Aging?" *Journal of the American Geriatrics Society* 45, no. 9 (1997): 1140–1146.
ZAKERI, Z.; BURSCH, W.; TENNISWOOD, M.; and LOCKSHIN, R. A. "Cell Death: Programmed, Apoptosis, Necrosis, or Other?" *Cell Death and Differentiation* 2 (1995): 83–92.

CELLULAR AGING: DNA POLYMORPHISMS

Many, if not the majority, of genetic loci in individuals in outbred, or wild, populations (including human) can have alternative versions of the gene, called *alleles*, that may or may not specify different genetic information. The term *genetic polymorphism* is used to describe a Mendelian trait that is present in at least two phenotypes (the observable physical characteristics of an organism) that are specified by different alleles and are present at a frequency of greater than 1 to 2 percent in the population. In contrast to a polymorphism, a *rare* genetic variant is one that is present in the population at a frequency of less than 1 percent, and most commonly at very low frequencies. Most, but not all, of the mutations that cause genetic diseases are in this category. For example, the alleles associated with Werner syndrome, a genetic disorder displaying a number of features of accelerated aging, are rare variants (see below).

The ABO blood group was the first human genetic polymorphism to be described—a discovery of immense theoretical and practical importance. Demonstrating that multiple alleles can occur at a specific genetic locus, often at comparable frequencies in the population, ultimately led to an understanding of the genetic basis of phenotypic variation in animal populations. The practical significance of this pioneering discovery is that it led to the routine use of whole-blood transfusions in the practice of medicine. Since this seminal observation, many polymorphic traits have been described and, although the precise number is not known at this time, it is now believed that the majority of the genetic loci in human genome are polymorphic. The number of alleles at any polymorphic locus is extremely variable. At some loci, such as the human leukocyte antigen (HLA) genes in the major histocompatibility complex (MHC), literally dozens of alleles have been identified. Thus, with this degree of variation throughout the human genome, it is highly likely that every individual on earth, with the exception of identical twins, possesses a unique genotype.

DNA polymorphisms are defined as any alternative DNA sequence that is present in 1 to 2 percent or more of the population. The extent of genetic variation at the DNA level greatly exceeds that which is present in gene products (i.e., proteins). DNA polymorphisms are more frequent in sequences that are not involved in the regulation or specification of gene products. This part of the genome does not seem to affect the phenotype of the organism, and, therefore, mutations in these sequences are very likely to be selectively neutral and could accumulate more rapidly than in genetically active areas.

DNA polymorphic variants can be deletions, duplications, or inversions of segments of DNA. Two types of DNA sequences that are highly polymorphic are minisatellites that are composed of tandemly repeated 10 to 60 base-pair (bp) sequences and microsatellites that are segments composed of tandem repeats of 1 to 3 bp sequences. These sequences have proven to be very useful for gene mapping because: (1) they are distributed throughout the genome; (2) they are highly polymorphic in that the number of repeats is extremely variable; and (3) individual alleles can be identified by amplification of sequences by the polymerase chain reaction (PCR) and the size difference of these sequences determined by gel electrophoresis.

The most common type of DNA polymorphism, accounting for most genetic variation among human populations, is the single nucleotide change (single nucleotide polymorphism, or SNP). Since the completion of the first drafts of the human genome sequence, the identification and location of SNPs has progressed very rapidly. A working draft of the sequence assembled by the International Human Genome Sequencing Consortium is in a public database on the World Wide Web and can be easily accessed at http://genome.ucsc.edu. As of mid-2001, 1.42 million SNPs throughout the genome had been identified, with estimates that 60,000 SNPs are within

regions that are transcribed into RNA. SNPs in these sequences could cause an amino acid change in the protein product specified by the gene, which, in turn, could have biological consequences. Moreover, it is currently estimated that 85 percent of the coding regions (exons) in genes are within 5,000 bp of a SNP; thus, it is almost certain that polymorphisms air in the regulatory elements of some genes and could, therefore, have an affect on the level of activity of these loci. In addition, SNPs are of sufficient density throughout the genome to serve as markers for the identification and mapping of specific combinations of alleles (haplotypes) that are associated with specific phenotypes. To accomplish this, informative SNPs (in or near genetic loci) will have to be identified and their frequencies in various populations determined. This will require a huge number of SNPs to be identified in many thousands of individuals. This endeavor will require the development of very efficient assays to screen such large populations, and a number of laboratories are developing highly efficient screening for such studies.

A database designed to serve as a central repository for SNPs, and for short deletion and insertion polymorphisms, has been established by the National Center for Biotechnology Information (NCBI) in collaboration with the National Genome Research Institute (see its website at www.ncbi.nlm.nih.gov/SNP/index.html). This repository also contains data derived from other species, both mammalian and nonmammalian, and is linked to national databases that contain other biological information. This repository will contain a large amount of information; for example, the update of 1 July 2001 indicated that 2,985,822 SNPs had been submitted (but not all fully characterized) to this database. Other public databases of human SNPs that are accessible on the Web have been established. One is located at the University of Utah in Salt Lake City (www.genome.utah.edu/genesnps), and another has been established in Europe sponsored by a consortium of major institutions (http://hgbase.cgr.ki.se).

DNA polymorphisms and aging

The wide variation in the maximum life span, even among mammalian species, is well established and is related to the genetic endowment of each species. There are also qualitative and quantitative differences in the phenotype of aging among mammalian species. For example, the extensive atherosclerotic involvement of the arterial system associated with extensive morbidity (illness) and mortality with advancing age is virtually unique to humans. On the other hand, the extent to which genetic differences are responsible for the variation in longevity between individuals within a species is unknown. The variation of individual life spans is evident in populations of inbred organisms, indicating that environmental factors and, very likely, chance events contribute to this variability. However, the extent of the genetic contribution to this inter-individual variation in the manifestation of aging and maximum survivability remains to be established.

It is generally accepted that aging and life span are regulated by multiple genes. Although the precise number is not known, it has been speculated that relatively few genes may be directly involved in this process. The most direct approach to the identification of aging and longevity genes would be to search for quantitative trait loci (QTL). These loci contain genes that regulate traits, such as blood pressure, that can be defined in specific units of measurement (in the case of blood pressure, the units would be millimeters of mercury) and are, in most cases, regulated by multiple genes. Longevity, which can be measured in units of time (e.g., days or years), is another example of a quantitative trait. A QTL study of aging might, for example, involve strains of laboratory mice that exhibit significantly different maximum life spans. Genetic loci that effect the phenotype (in this case, longevity) and their relative contribution, can be identified by a sophisticated analysis of data derived from the segregation pattern of polymorphic markers in relation to the phenotype (longevity) of the offspring from crosses between the strains, and from back crosses.

This type of genetic analysis is not realistically feasible with human subjects. However, association studies, another experimental approach to the identification of "aging genes," can be carried out in human subjects. Such studies involve the search for linkage between a specific polymorphic allele(s) or DNA polymorphism(s) and a specific trait. For example, one could compare the frequency of polymorphic alleles of a gene in an exceptionally long-lived population (e.g., centenarians) and a well-defined control population. A number of studies have been carried out with the human leukocyte antigen (HLA) loci in the

major histocompatibility complex (MHC), one of the most polymorphic class of genes in the mammalian genome. These studies have yielded conflicting results, probably due to a number of methodological problems, including inaccurate identification of specific alleles in the pregenomic era. Similar studies designed to establish linkage between the incidence of a specific age-associated disease and specific alleles of a polymorphic locus have provided new information of considerable interest. For example, the association of the e4 allele of the apolipoprotein E gene, a gene that codes for a protein involved in lipid transport in the vascular system, with an elevated risk of developing Alzheimer's disease is now well established.

Clearly demonstrable associations, such as that between apolipoprotein B and Alzheimer's disease, are infrequent. More subtle associations are difficult to detect because of the relative paucity of genetic markers (e.g., SNPs) that, up to this time, have been identified in the human genome. Moreover, aging and the regulation of life span are multifactorial phenotypic traits, regulated by multiple genes interacting with the environment. Therefore, it is unlikely that polymorphic variants at a single locus will have a profound effect on the aging process or longevity; what is more likely is that combinations of alleles (haplotypes) will be associated with specific aging phenotypes. As indicated above, highly efficient methods to determine the frequency of SNPs in human populations are being developed, which will make the haplotyping of large numbers of individuals within a population feasible. The task may be simplified by the emerging observation that human genetic diversity is surprisingly limited. Theoretically there could be hundreds, even thousands, of variants at each locus, but in reality the number of alleles at most loci appears to be small, only two or three in many cases.

Aging at the cellular level

All DNA polymorphisms that affect the phenotype of the organism are expressed in some fashion at the cellular level, even if only in the secretion of an abnormal gene product that acts at a site distant from the secretory cell. Alleles of genes involved in basic cellular functions could affect the phenotype of multiple cell types, or in some cases all cell types. For example, polymorphisms in genes involved in DNA synthesis or cell division could alter the function of cells that are actively proliferating or are potentially capable of proliferation. On the other hand, a variant gene involved in an essential function such as aerobic respiration could potentially alter the phenotype of every cell in an organism.

The replication and repair of nuclear (genomic) DNA involves a variety of functions that are essential for cell survival. These metabolic processes are essential for the accurate transmission of genetic information from one generation of a cell or organism to the next, and for the maintenance of normal gene function. Diminished fidelity of DNA replication and/or repair will result in an increased mutation rate, which can lead to decrements of cell function, cell death and/or increased risk of transformation to a malignant (cancerous) cell type. There have been a number of experimental observations that suggest (but do not prove) that the accumulation of genomic mutations in somatic cells is a causal mechanism of aging both at the cellular and organismal levels. This hypothesis, generally attributed to Szilard, implies that the efficiency and fidelity of DNA replication and repair affect the rate of aging and maximum life span. Some of the observations that are consistent with this hypothesis are:

1. The efficiency and extent of the repair of DNA damage induced by ultraviolet light (UV) is directly related to the maximum life span of the species. This result correlates with the observation that lower levels of DNA damage and mutations are present in experimental animals that are on a diet that restricts caloric intake. Dietary restriction has been shown to extend maximal life span in multiple species and has been extensively exploited as an experimental model in aging research.

2. Normal human cells in tissue culture can divide only a limited number of times. This is often referred to as *replicative senescence* and is associated with changes in cell structure and gene activity. It now appears that one mechanism that determines the replicative potential of some cell types in cultures and in tissues is the extent of loss of specialized hexanucleotide repeat sequences of DNA (telomeres) at the ends of the chromosomes. Approximately fifty to one hundred bp are lost from this region with each cell division. This occurs because telomerase, the enzyme that synthesizes these repeat sequences, is

functionally inactive in most human somatic cells. It has been postulated that after a sufficient number of replications these structures become so short that the cells perceive them as damaged DNA and irreversibly cease cell division.

3. The Werner syndrome, a rare genetic disease that is associated with decreased longevity and many features (but not all) of premature aging, is caused by a mutation in a helicase gene. This class of genes catalyzes the unwinding of the double helix of DNA, which is necessary for a number of essential functions, such as DNA replication and repair and messenger RNA transcription. Cultured cells derived from individuals with Werner syndrome display numerous abnormalities in their chromosomes and complete fewer cell divisions before the onset of replicative senescence than cultures derived from normal (non-Werner) individuals.

4. Some investigators have recently reported that the frequency of gene mutations in cell populations in the body increases with age. These observations are consistent with a diminution of the fidelity of DNA replication and/or repair with advancing age. Alternatively, this age-associated increase of mutation frequency could merely reflect a steady accumulation through time. At the present time there is no definitive evidence for the existence of decrements in the efficiency and/or fidelity of DNA replication or repair with advancing age.

There are a large number of proteins involved in the replication and repair of DNA. At this time there are 125 genes known to be directly involved in DNA repair. The products of these genes perform many specific functions in the repair process, including: recognition of damaged sites (DNA binding proteins); excision of the damaged region (exonucleases and endonucleases); replication of a new strand following excision of the damaged area (polymerases); and ligation of the newly synthesized segment of the strand (ligases).

Following completion of the first draft of the human genome, the identification of polymorphic alleles in these loci has proceeded very rapidly. For example, as of July 2001, 252 SNPs had been identified in genes that are associated with DNA repair. Moreover, more genes that code for proteins that are involved in DNA repair are being discovered. Even allowing for some inaccuracies at this time in the current Utah database, the frequency of this class of DNA polymorphisms is such that the existence of alleles with differing functional activities is almost a certainty.

The identification of specific alleles or groups of alleles (haplotypes) that effect the aging phenotype and/or longevity will involve multiple experimental approaches, as described above. If specific allelic associations are shown to be associated with some aspect of aging or longevity, the next step will be to establish a causal relationship between the alleles and the aging process. These studies will include a biochemical characterization of each allele to identify functional alterations, such as increased enzymatic activity. Transgenic technology—the insertion or deletion of genes into the germ line of experimental animals—will certainly play a pivotal role in establishing a cause-and-effect relationship between specific alleles or haplotypes and the aging phenotype.

Potential significance

Whether studies of the effect of DNA polymorphisms in genes involved in the replication and repair of DNA lead to significant new insights into the causes of aging will not be known until such studies have been completed. The potential significance is high, however. A convincing demonstration that genes involved in DNA replication and repair effect the life span and the phenotype of aging would provide strong support for the hypothesis that mutations in somatic cells contribute to the aging process.

Will these studies be of importance in other areas of biomedical research? The answer to this question is most certainly "yes." All aspects of DNA metabolism are essential for the survival of virtually all organisms. The identification, mapping, and functional studies of polymorphic loci will provide important new information about the mechanisms of DNA replication and repair. At a more applied level, these studies will almost certainly increase our understanding of many diseases, including cancer. It is now generally accepted that this disease is caused by gene mutations in somatic cells, and studies of the nature and extent of variation in genes involved in DNA repair and replication will be a very important area of cancer research.

Whether studies of genetic variation in aging will have practical applications is, again, dependent on the outcome of research in this area. An obvious possibility is that information derived from these studies will permit the identification of individuals who are at increased risk for the development for specific age-related conditions and diseases. Such developments would raise some ethical concerns, mainly concerning the potential for discrimination. On the other hand, with the development of effective therapies and preventive programs, the ability to accurately predict the risk of developing specific diseases years, or even decades, in advance of their onset would be of immense practical value in the treatment of elderly patients.

THOMAS H. NORWOOD

See also ACCELERATED AGING: HUMAN PROGEROID SYNDROMES; ALZHEIMER'S DISEASE; CANCER, BIOLOGY; CELLULAR AGING: TELOMERES; DNA DAMAGE AND REPAIR; GENETICS: GENE EXPRESSIONS; GENETICS: GENE-ENVIRONMENT INTERACTION; STRESS.

BIBLIOGRAPHY

BAUMFORTH, K. R. N.; NELSON, P. N.; DIGBY, J. E.; O'NEIL, J. D.; and MURRAY, P. G. "The Polymerase Chain Reaction." *Journal of Clinical Pathology: Molecular Pathology* 52 (1999): 1–10.

BLACKER, D., and TANZI, R. E. "The Genetics of Alzheimer's Disease: Current Status and Future Prospects." *Archives of Neurology* 55, no. 3 (1998): 294–296.

CARUSO, C.; CANDORE, G.; ROMANO, G. C.; LIO, D.; BONAFE, M.; VALENSIN, S.; and FRANCESCHI, C. "Immunogenetics of Longevity. Is Major Histocompatibility Complex Polymorphism Relevant to the Control of Human Longevity? A Review of Literature Data." *Mechanisms of Ageing and Development* 122 (2001): 445–462.

FINCH, C., and KIRKWOOD, T. B. L. *Chance, Development, and Aging.* New York: Oxford University Press, 2000.

FLINT, J., and MOTT, R. "Finding the Molecular Basis of Quantitative Traits: Successes and Pitfalls." *Nature Reviews Genetics* 2, no. 6 (2001): 437–445.

International Human Genome Sequencing Consortium. "Initial Sequencing and Analysis of the Human Genome." *Nature* 409 (2001): 860–921.

The International SNP Working Group. "A Map of Human Genome Sequence Variation Containing 1.42 Million Single Nucleotide Polymorphisms." *Nature* 409 (2001): 928–933.

KENT, J. "Human Genome Browser." In *Human Genome Project Working Draft*. World Wide Web document. http://genome.ucsc.edu

LANDER, E. S. "The New Genomics: Global Views of Biology." *Science* 274 (2001): 536–546.

MARTIN, G. M. "Genetics and Pathobiology of Ageing." *Philosophical Transactions of the Royal Society London: Biological Sciences* 352 (1997): 1773–1780.

MARTIN, G. M.; OSHIMA, J.; GRAY, M. D.; and POOT, M. "What Geriatricians Should Know about the Werner Syndrome." *Journal of the American Geriatric Society* 47 (1999): 1136–1144.

RONEN, A., and GLICKMAN, B. W. "Human DNA Repair Genes." *Environmental and Molecular Mutagenesis* 37 (2001): 241–283.

SZILARD, L. "On the Nature of the Aging Process." Proceedings of the National Academy of Sciences (USA). 45 (1959): 30–45.

VIJG, J.; DOLLÉ M. E. T.; MARTUS, H.-J.; and BOERRIGTER, M. E. T. A. "Transgenic Mouse Models for Studying Mutations In Vivo: Applications in Aging Research." *Mechanisms of Ageing and Development* 98 (1997): 189–202.

VIJG, J. "Somatic Mutations and Aging: A Reevaluation." *Mutation Research* 447 (2000): 117–135.

VENTNER, J. C., et al. "The Sequence of the Human Genome." *Science* 291 (2001): 1304–1351.

VOGEL, F., and MOTULSKY, A. G. "Population Genetics: Description and Dynamics." In *Human Genetics. Problems and Approaches*, 3d ed. Edited by F. Vogel and A. G. Motulsky. New York: Springer, 1997. Pages 497–508.

WRIGHT, W. E., and SHAY, J. A. "Cellular Senescence as a Tumor-Protection Mechanism: The Essential Role of Counting." *Current Opinion in Genetic Development* 11 (2001): 98–103.

CELLULAR AGING: TELOMERES

Aging is a complex process that occurs on multiple levels. The end result of aging is that life span is limited in multicellular organisms. The cells that make up multicellular organisms also have limited life spans. The limitation on cellular life span is comprised of two parts: (1) cells become unable to continue dividing but remain metabolically active, and (2) at some future time cell death occurs. Many cells in the human body are continually undergoing cellular division. Cellular division is a normal condition of certain tissues; examples include hair growth, the sloughing off of skin every several days, and the complete turnover and replacement of the cells of the immune systems every few months. In some instances, cellular division occurs in order to heal damaged tissues. Thus, having a limited number of cellular divisions available could contribute to aging by slowing down processes such as wound healing, as well as affecting general tissue maintenance.

In the 1960s, Leonard Hayflick first noted that human cells undergo a limited number of divisions when placed in culture. Furthermore, he noted that the number of divisions cells undergo is related to the number of prior divisions undergone by the cells. This observation suggested the existence of an intracellular clock that marked the division history of each cell. In addition, it suggested that once a predetermined number of divisions has occurred, a signal (or signals) is generated that prevents the cell from undergoing further divisions. The timing mechanisms underlying and regulating this process remained elusive until the end of the twentieth century. The first of these clocks to be identified and characterized, the *telomere*, is active in several human cell types.

Telomeres are chromosome caps

Telomeres are specialized structures present at the end of liner chromosomes; they serve the essential function of protecting and stabilizing chromosome ends. The telomere was first defined in the 1930s following observations that naturally occurring chromosome ends behave differently than chromosome breaks induced by damaging agents such as ionizing radiation. Both structures are ends of double-stranded DNA molecules. However, chromosome ends are stable, allowing accurate transmission of chromosomes from generation to generation without loss of genetic material, whereas induced breaks are very unstable, reacting with other chromosomes in the cell to create rearrangements and chromosome fusions. In addition, broken ends of DNA trigger cellular protective responses. These responses act either to allow the DNA damage to be repaired, or to remove the cell from the population by cellular suicide, called *apoptosis*. Even though telomeres are the physical end of a DNA molecule, they do not trigger these protective responses. These observations indicated that there is something special about naturally occurring chromosome ends.

Telomere structure

Telomeres are made up of short tandem repeats of a simple DNA sequence and associated proteins. In humans, and all other vertebrates, the telomeric DNA sequence is 5'(TTAGGG)3', oriented towards the end of one DNA strand, with the complimentary sequence 5'(CCCTAA)3' oriented towards the interior of the chromosome. The duplexed telomeric repeats are arranged in tandem and are present in more than a thousand copies at the end of each human chromosome. At the very end of the chromosome there is a single-stranded protrusion of the G-rich strand that extends for twenty or more repeats.

The first protein components of the human telomeric complex were identified in the mid-1990s. These proteins bind to the double-stranded telomeric repeats and are instrumental not only in promoting stability through formation of specialized structures, but also in regulating other aspects of the telomere, such as the number of repeats present. Within five years of identifying the first telomeric protein, TRF1, the number of proteins known to be present at human telomeres had expanded greatly. These included not only those that bound directly to the telomeric repeats, such as TRF1, and a related protein, TRF2, but also interacting proteins that serve to modify telomeric proteins, such as *tankyrase,* which binds to TRFI and adds to the protein long chains of ADP-ribose (a molecule which affects protein function). Finally, proteins that were previously identified as being involved in DNA repair and recombination have also been localized to telomeres, although the role of these proteins at the telomere remains unclear.

Experiments carried out by the laboratories of Titia de Lange and Jack Griffith in 1999 identified the something special that allows telomeres to impart stability on chromosome ends. These researchers purified telomeres and associated proteins from human and mouse cells and used electron microscopy to directly visualize the structure of mammalian telomeres. Their results demonstrated that the telomere exists as a dosed circular structure, called the *telomere loop,* or *t-loop.* The single-stranded DNA protrusion at chromosome ends, in combination with telomeric binding proteins, is critical in promoting the formation of the t-loop. This structure sequesters the naturally occurring ends of the DNA molecule, the telomere, rendering the chromo-

Figure 1

Diagram of telomere structure in cells that allow telomeres to cap and stabilize the ends of chomosomes. The single-stranded protrusion invades the double-stranded telomere to create the telomere loop, or t-loop, sequestering the end of the DNA molecule and preventing it from activating the DNA damage-sensing machinery. This process is likely aided by the action of telomeric proteins.

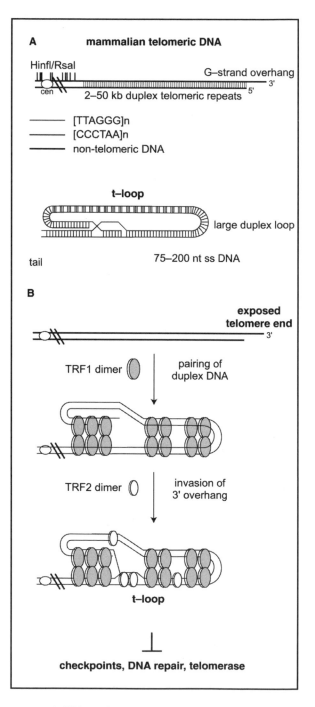

SOURCE: Griffith, Jack D. "Mammalian Telomeres End in a Large Duplex Loop." *Cell* 97 (1999): 503–514.

some end unreactive and invisible to the DNA damage-sensing machinery.

Telomeres and replication

In order for a cell to divide and create two equal daughter cells, the chromosomes must be replicated. Telomeres represent a unique challenge to the cell with respect to replication. Eukaryotic DNA replication occurs unidirectionally on each template strand. The enzymes that synthesize DNA, *polymerases*, require short RNA molecules to act as primers for new strand synthesis, and synthesis occurs in one direction only. Following extension, the primer is removed and the resulting gap filled in. This works well for most of the chromosome, but a problem arises at the very end of the chromosome. Upon removal of the final primer from the daughter strand, a gap remains that can not be replicated. This, in turn, would result in gradual loss of DNA from the chromosome ends each time the chromosome is replicated, and thus at each cell division. The inability of conventional cellular machinery to replicate the ends of DNA molecules came to be known as the *end-replication problem*. However, it was apparent that a mechanism for replicating chromosome ends existed, because chromosomes are faithfully transmitted to progeny.

Elizabeth Blackburn and Carol Greider first identified the enzyme responsible for telomere replication in a unicellular protozoan, *Tetrahymena thermophila*. This enzyme, called *telomerase*, is minimally composed of an RNA molecule and a protein subunit. The RNA molecule, in humans called hTER—for *h*uman *te*lomerase *R*NA, acts as a template to allow the addition of nucleotides to the end of the chromosome. The extension reaction is catalyzed by the protein component, in humans called hTERT—for *h*uman *te*lomerase *r*everse *t*ranscriptase. Thus, loss of telomeric DNA due to the end-replication problem may be balanced by an addition of telomeric repeats by telomerase. Telomerase is active in the germ line (the egg and sperm), where it acts to polish off the replication of chromosome ends so that each generation begins life with chromosomes similar to their parents. However, telomerase is not active in most cells of the body, with the result that DNA is gradually lost from the ends of our chromosomes each time a cell divides.

Telomeres and replicative senescence

As discussed above, cells have a finite division potential, often called the *Hayflick limit*. Interestingly, the number of divisions a cell is capable of undergoing in culture is inversely proportional to the age of the donor. That is, cells derived from younger individuals will undergo mote divisions than those from older individuals. Thus, the limitation on division potential is hypothesized to play a role in aspects of human aging. Cells that have reached their division limit undergo a process called *replicative senescence*, which is accompanied by morphological changes and changes in gene expression patterns. Interestingly, the Hayflick limit is ordained by the total number of divisions experienced by a cell and not by elapsed time. Senescent cells are alive (metabolically active), but can no longer be induced to divide. For many human cell types, the onset of replicative senescence has been linked to the length of the telomere.

The first clue that telomeres might play a role in capping the total number of divisions any given cell may undergo came from observations in the late 1980s made by Howard Cooke and co-workers. These investigators noted that telomeres in the germ line were longer than telomeres present in somatic tissue (i.e., blood) from the same individual. Over the next several years, a number of laboratories demonstrated that telomeres are shorter in older individuals than in younger individuals and that telomeres become shorter with increased numbers of cell divisions in culture. In addition, it was noted that chromosome instability of a type that would be predicted to accompany loss of telomere function, such as fusion of chromosome ends, is increased in older individuals. This was also observed in cultured cells as they approached senescence. There are two essential points to these observations. First, telomeres only shorten if cells divide. Metabolically active cells that are quiescent (those that do not divide) do not lose telomeric DNA. Secondly, telomeric DNA is only lost in somatic (body) cells, which do not, as a rule, contain telomerase activity. Based on these observations, it was proposed that the telomere might act as the elusive intracellular clock that triggered senescence. This became known as the *telomere hypothesis* of cellular aging. This hypothesis suggests that attrition of telomeric DNA eventually compromises telomere function. This would result in a signal being generated that causes the cell to undergo replicative senescence

Figure 2

Conventional DNA synthesis requires RNA primers to initiate replication. The primers are then removed and the gaps filled in. Upon removal of the most terminal primer, a region of unreplicated DNA remains. This results in loss of DNA from the end of the chromosome each time the cell divides.

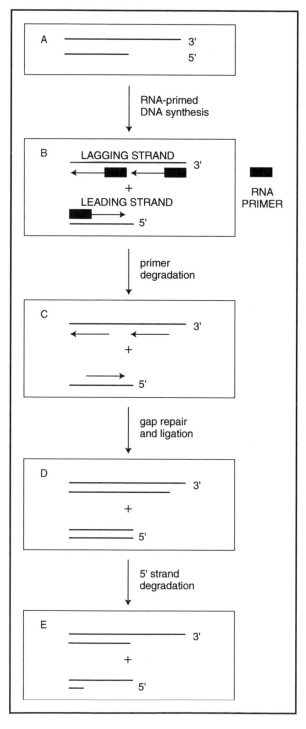

SOURCE: Reddel, R. (see Bibliography).

and cease dividing. Although these observations were suggestive of a causal relationship between functioning telomeres and the ability to divide, the link between telomere loss and replicative senescence remained correlative.

Following the identification and cloning of the RNA and catalytic components of telomerase, it became possible to force expression of this enzyme in primary human cell cultures. Primary human cell cultures have a finite division capacity and do not contain telomerase activity. In the late 1990s it was finally directly demonstrated that, for specific cell types, expression of telomerase and the concomitant extension of telomeric DNA is sufficient to impart cellular immortality—the potential for an infinite number of divisions. The inverse is true as well. Thus, inhibition of telomerase activity in immortal cells, such as tumor-derived cell lines, results in telomere loss and culture senescence. These experiments directly demonstrated a causal link between maintenance of telomeric DNA and a cells ability to divide. In a series of experiments, de Lange and coworkers demonstrated that disruption of telomeric structure by removing the telomeric protein TRF2 resulted in loss of protective function and a senescent-like growth arrest. These experiments identified the first type of signal that might emanate from telomeres to elicit cellular responses. According to the t-loop model described above, loss of TRF2 would open the end of the chromosome by disrupting the t-loop. This, in turn, alarms the cell because the telomere now resembles a broken DNA molecule and results in activation of the ATM-dependent and p53-dependent DNA damage response pathway. Activation of p53 has been linked to both senescence and apoptosis. Thus, cells that are unable to sequester chromosome ends through maintenance of the t-loop structure, either because the telomere is too short or due to absence of essential proteins, are prevented from dividing further by activating the senescence or apoptotic pathways. The question of whether complete loss of function is required to evoke senescence, or whether the cell has some means of identifying a short but still functional telomere, has yet to be answered.

Telomeres and premature aging syndromes

There are several human syndromes that manifest as premature aging, including Hutchinson-Gilford progeria and Werner syndrome.

Figure 3

Telomerase contains, at the minimum, an RNA molecule and a catalytic subunit. The catalytic subunit of the enzyme, hTERT, uses a region of the RNA moiety, hTER, as a template for the addition of telomeric DNA on the chromosome ends. In this way, net telomere gain can offset the DNA lost due to the end-replication problem.

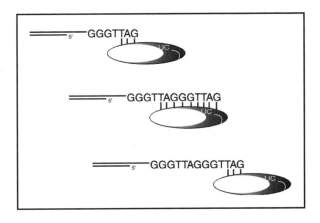

SOURCE: Reddel, Roger R. "The Role of Senescence and Immortalization in Carcinogenesis." *Carcinogenesis* 21 (2000): 477–484.

Cell lines derived from individuals with progeria are capable of attaining fewer divisions before becoming senescent than are cells from age-matched unaffected individuals. In addition, telomeres in cells derived from individuals with Hutchinson-Gilford progeria are shorter than age-matched unaffected individuals, again linking telomere length with cell division capacity and, indirectly, with aging. Interestingly, experiments have demonstrated that cells derived from individuals with Werner syndrome not only undergo senescence after fewer divisions, but also that this occurs when the telomeres in these cells are, on average, longer than those in parallel cultures not containing the Werner mutation. This observation suggested that the premature senescence in cells derived from individuals with Werner syndrome might be disconnected from telomere length, and instead result from other factors, such as accumulated DNA damage. However, David Kipling and coworkers demonstrated that forced expression of telomerase in Werner syndrome cells conferred immortality, indicating that the telomere-length-based clock is active in this genetic background.

The link between telomere shortening, replicative senescence, and aging at the organism level is supported by a series of studies carried out by the laboratories of Ronald DePinho and Carol Greider. These investigators generated a mouse that was deficient for telomerase. Mice usually have extremely long telomeres, but in the telomerase-deficient mice the telomeres became shorter with each generation, and the later generations of these mice exhibited characteristics consistent with premature aging. For example, these animals have a compromised ability to heal wounds, exhibit premature graying, and have a shortened lifespan. These studies linked short telomeres with some characteristics observed in older adults, suggesting that telomere-length-dependent effects on cellular division might also play a role in aging at the level of the organism. The strength of the contribution of telomere-length-based replicative senescence to the aging process as a whole remains to be determined, however.

Telomeres as tumor suppressors

The observations discussed above clearly linked telomeres to the ability of cells to divide and proliferate. Simultaneously with these studies, and key to the development of the telomere hypothesis of cellular aging, the link between telomere stabilization and tumorigenesis was becoming clear. One feature of tumor cells is their unlimited cell-division potential, or immortality. It was first reported in 1990 that telomeres were shorter in tumors than in adjacent healthy tissue from the same individual. These observations prompted the suggestion that the cell divisions leading to tumor formation resulted in telomere loss. However, telomere length in tumor-derived cell lines remain stable over time in culture, despite continuing cell division. This observation indicated that cells that have transformed and become tumors have some means of overcoming the end-replication problem. The obvious candidate for achieving stabilization of telomeric DNA was telomerase. Studies in the early 1990s did, in fact, suggest that this enzyme was active in some tumors and immortal cell Lines. However, these studies were hampered by the lack of sensitivity of the assay used to detect telomerase.

A highly sensitive assay to detect telomerase activity was developed in 1994, and shortly thereafter, surveys of cell lines and tumors were begun to determine if telomerase activity was a common feature. The unambiguous results were that the majority (80–90 percent) of all human tumors, as well as the majority of immortal transformed cell lines, contain telomerase activity. One implication is that telomerase activation would stabilize telomere length and allow the cell to circumvent cellular senescence. However, the timing of telomerase activation during tumorigenesis is unclear, and some discussions suggest that this may occur after at least a transient abolition of telomere function (see below). These observations, together with the links between telomeres and cellular senescence, have provoked the suggestion that telomere length might act as a tumor suppressor mechanism by limiting the number of divisions any given cell might undergo.

Telomeres, genome stability, and cancer

The hallmark of telomeres is their ability to confer stability on chromosome ends and prevent chromosome ends from activating the cellular surveillance mechanisms protecting cells from the deleterious effects of DNA breaks. Chromosomes with critically short telomeres become compromised in chromosome-end stability, and, because telomeres are generally shorter in tumors than in adjacent healthy tissue, it was suggested that telomere dysfunction could contribute to tumorigenesis by increasing genomic instability. In the short term, this genomic instability might promote tumor formation by allowing growth-advantageous mutations (i.e., mutations that permit cells to remain viable under conditions when, normally, the cells would die) to accumulate rapidly. However, this scenario requires that the cellular mechanism(s) that normally monitor telomere length and prevent cells with critically short telomeres from dividing be blocked. Under these conditions, cells with critically short telomeres would continue dividing. These cells would enter a period of extreme chromosomal instability. Eventually, however, such rampant genome instability might prove deleterious to tumor survival by generating mutations in genes that are essential for cellular survival. Thus, stabilization of the genome, perhaps through activation of telomerase, would have a selective advantage. Experiments carried out by the DePinho and Greider groups utilizing telomerase-deficient mice support the idea that transient telomere malfunction may promote tumorigenesis.

Figure 4

Summary of the link between telomere length, replicative senescence, and tumorigenesis. In the germ line, telomerase is active and telomere length is stable. In somatic cells, telomerase is not active. As a result, telomeres become shorter with each division until a critical length is reached and the cells undergo replicative senescence. If this process is bypassed through mutation of regulating proteins, the cells will continue to divide until telomere function is lost. This results in a period of genome instability, which possibly promotes tumorigenesis through hypermutation. Reactivation of telomorase permits maintenance of telomeric DNA conferring immortality and genome stabilization.

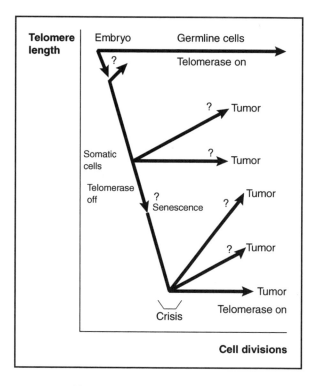

SOURCE: Greider, Carol. "Mammalian Telomere Dynamics: Healing, Fragmentation, Shortening, and Stabilization." *Current Opinion in Genetics and Development* 4 (1994): 203–211.

Telomeres, aging, and cancer

The experiments described here link telomeres to two sides of a single coin: cellular mortality and immortality—or aging and cancer. The salient points with respect to cellular aging, given the assumption that replicative senescence as observed in cultured cells contributes at some level to aging, are: (1) telomeres are shorter in somatic (body) cells than in the germ line (egg and sperm), (2) telomeres are shorter in older individuals than in younger individuals, and (3) telomeres get shorter with increased number of cellular divisions undergone in culture. On the flip side of the coin, most tumors have bypassed the telomere-length-dependent limitation on cellular proliferation, usually through the activation of telomerase. Finally, stabilization of telomere length by forced expression of telomerase is sufficient to confer an unlimited division potential, or cellular immorality, while inhibition of telomerase with concomitant telomere shortening causes growth arrest in immortal cells.

There is, however, an important caveat to the arguments discussed here. As noted above, telomere length acts as a type of clock in many human cell types. However, there are cell types that utilize some other clock mechanism to limit the number of divisions they undergo, including thyroid epithelial cells and breast epithelial cells. These cells enter replicative senescence while still having telomeres of sufficient length for many more divisions. Furthermore, simple expression of telomerase is not sufficient to confer immortality on these cell types. It is believed that even these cells, given circumvention of their primary clock, eventually become dependent on telomere length for continued division. The observation that most human tumors, including thyroid and breast tumors, have telomerase activity and stable telomeres would support this idea. Thus, the cumulative data indicate a key role for telomeres in the processes of cellular senescence and tumorigenesis.

DOMINIQUE BROCCOLI

See also CANCER BIOLOGY; DNA DAMAGE AND REPAIR; GENETICS: LONGEVITY ASSURANCE; THEORIES OF BIOLOGICAL AGING.

BIBLIOGRAPHY

ARTANDI, S. H., and DEPINHO, R. A. "A Critical Role for Telomeres in Suppressing and Facilitating Carcinogenesis." *Current Opinion in Genetics and Development* 10 (2000): 39–46.

BLACKBURN, E. H. "Switching and Signaling at the Telomere." *Cell* 106 (2001): 661–673.

COLLINS, K. "Mammalian Telomeres and Telomerase." *Current Opinion in Cell Biology* 12 (2000): 378–383.

COOKE, H. J., and SMITH, B. A. "Variability at the Telomeres of the Human X/Y Pseudoautoso-mal Region." *Quantitative Biology* 51 (1986): 213–219.

DE LANGE, T. "Telomere Dynamics and Genome Instability in Human Cancer." In *Telomeres*. Edited by E. H. Blackburn and C. W. Greider. Cold Spring Harbor, N.Y.: Cold Spring Harbor Laboratory Press, 1995.

GREIDER, C. W., and BLACKBURN, E. H. "Identification of a Specific Telomere Terminal Transferase Activity in Tetrahymena Extracts." *Cell* 43 (1985): 405–413.

GRIFFITH, J. D.; COMEAU, L.; ROSENFIELD, S.; STANSEL, R. M.; BIANCHI, A.; MOSS, H.; and DE LANGE, T. "Mammalian Telomeres End in a Large Duplex Loop." *Cell* 97 (1999): 503–514.

HAHN, W. C.; STEWART, S. A.; BROOKS, M. W.; YORK, S. G.; EATON, E.; KURACHI, A.; BEIJERS-BERGEN, R. L.; KNOLL, J. H. M.; MEYERSON, M.; and WEINBERG, R. A. "Inhibition of Telomerase Limits the Growth of Human Cancer Cells." *Nature Medicine* 5 (1999): 1164–1170.

HARLEY, C. B. "Telomeres and Aging." In *Telomeres*. Edited by E. H. Blackburn and C. W. Greider. Cold Spring Harbor, N.Y.: Cold Spring Harbor Laboratory Press, 1995. Pages 247–263.

HARLEY, C. B.; VAZIRI, H.; COUNTER, C. M. and ALLSOPP, R. C. "The Telomere Hypothesis of Cellular Aging." *Experimental Gerontology* 27 (1992): 375–382.

HASTIE, N. D.; DEMPSTER, M.; DUNLOP, M. G.; THOMPSON, A. M.; GREEN, D. K.; and ALLSHIRE, R. C. "Telomere Reduction in Human Colorectal Carcinoma and with Ageing." *Nature* 346 (1990): 866–868.

HAYFLICK, L. "The Limited In Vitro Lifespan of Human Diploid Cell Strains." *Experimental Cell Research* 25 (1965): 614–636.

REDDEL, R. R. "The Role of Senescence and Immortalization in Carcinogenesis." *Carcinogenesis* 21 (2000): 477–484.

RUDOLPH, K. L.; CHANG, S.; LEE, H. W.; BLASCO, M.; GOTTLIEB, G. J.; GREIDER, C.; and DEPINHO, R. A. "Longevity, Stress Response, and Cancer in Aging Telomerase-Deficient Mice." *Cell* 96 (1999): 701–712.

SHAY, J. W., and BACCHETTI, S. "A Survey of Telomerase Activity in Human Cancer." *European Journal of Cancer* 33 (1997): 787–791.

VAN STEENSEL, B.; SMOGORZEWSKA, A.; and DE LANGE, T. "TRF2 Protects Human Telomeres from End-to-End Fusions." *Cell* 92 (1998): 401–413.

VAZIRI, H., and BENCHIMOL, S. "Reconstitution of Telomerase Activity in Normal Human Cells Leads to Elongation of Telomeres and

Jeanne Calment of France receives flowers from five-year-old Thomas nine days before her 122nd birthday in 1997. Before her death later that year, Calment was the oldest known living human in the world. (AP photo Florian Launette.)

Extended Replicative Life Span." *Current Biology* 8 (1998): 279–282.

WYLLIE, F. S.; JONES, C. J.; SKINNER, J. W.; HAUGHTON, M. F.; WALLIS, C. ; WYNFORD-THOMAS, D.; FARAGHER, R. G. A. and KIPLING, D. "Telomerase Prevents the Accelerated Ageing of Werner Syndrome Fibroblasts." *Nature Genetics* 24 (2000): 16–17.

CENTENARIANS

Old age is often viewed as a time of disability and loss. Shakespeare captured it in Act II, Scene 7 of *As You Like It*: "Last scene of all,/ That ends this strange eventful history,/ Is second childishness and mere oblivion,/ Sans teeth, sans eyes, sans taste, sans everything." Centenarians often prove these dismal lines wrong, and demonstrate that the compression of morbidity hypothesis (that it is possible for most of us to live a long, healthy life) may be true.

The word "centenarian" is derived from the Latin for "of a hundred," and refers to someone who has lived to be one hundred years of age or older. The term "supercentenarian" refers to people 105 years and older. The number of cen-tenarians in developed countries has doubled every decade since the 1960s. This is related to the dramatic decline in mortality rates seen in developed countries worldwide.

Age verification

Whenever centenarians are studied, there must be a process in place to verify their reported age. In the 1960s and 1970s there were many reports of extremely long-lived populations in a number of places, including Georgia in the Caucasus and Vilcabamba, Ecuador. Some individuals claimed to be up to 180 years old. When these claims were investigated in further detail, proof of age was not available. Detailed life histories, with discussion of historical events in relationship to what age the person was at that time, were inconsistent. Dr. Thomas Perls, a geriatrician at Harvard University, and colleagues developed a rigorous age verification protocol for use in the New England Centenarian Study. They prefer a birth or baptismal certificate, or if these are not available, a passport or military certificate issued many years before. Other records, such as a family Bible, are also acceptable. Multiple supporting documents are preferred over a single document.

The longest proven life span for a human is 122 years, for Jeanne Calment, a woman who died in Arles, France, in 1997. Her age was carefully validated. She was a model of health most of her life, and lived alone until the age of 110. The longest verified life span for a male was that of Christian Mortensen, a Danish man who emigrated to the United States; he died in 1998 at the age of 115.

Epidemiology of centenarianism

Several research teams have attempted to estimate the prevalence of centenarianism, that is, the proportion of the population who are one hundred years and older. Since the number of centenarians is growing much faster than the total population, the prevalence of centenarianism will likely increase in the coming decades. Among the population-based studies with rigorous age verification conducted in the 1990s, the prevalence ranged from 38 per million total population (in Sweden) to 135 per million (in Sardinia). Census-based studies give larger prevalences, but there are concerns that, at these extreme ages, the census data may not be accurate.

These data are all from Western nations. The limited population-based data from other countries suggest that centenarian prevalence is much lower in non-Western nations. This will likely change as these countries experience the demographic shift that has already occurred in the West, the transition from predominantly young to predominantly older populations.

Mortality rates increase exponentially with age; that is, one's chance of dying is higher in each successive year of one's life, and the rate of increase also rises each year. This is known as the Gompertz Law of Mortality. Centenarians, however, do not comply with this law. At around age ninety the rate of increase seems to slow, and at age 110 mortality rates actually decline. Figure 1 illustrates this. Note that the y-axis is logarithmic. The black line is the exponential increase predicted by the Gompertz Law. The red line is the actual observed data, from Japan and western Europe. The blue line is the equation that best fits the mortality data at all ages; the green line provides the best fit for those 105 and older.

Figure 1
Age trajectories of death rates.

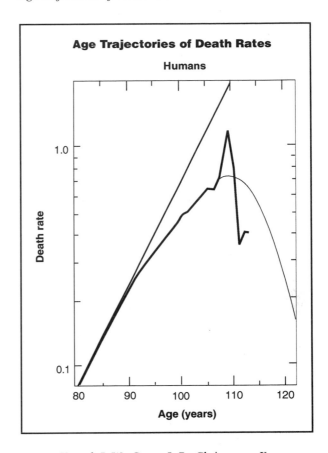

SOURCE: Vaupel, J. W.; Carey, J. R.; Christensen, K.; Johnson, T. E.; Yashin, A. I.; Holm, N. V.; Iachine, I. A.; Kannisto, V.; Khazaeli, A. A.; Liedo, P.; Longo, V. D.; Zeng, Y.; Manton, K. G.; and Curtsinger, J. W. "Biodemographic Trajectories of Longevity." *Science* 280 (1998): 857.

Characteristics of centenarians

The bulk of centenarians are women. At any age women have a greater life expectancy than men, and by the time one reaches one hundred, the sex ratio is four women to one man. The one place where this does not seem to be the case is the island of Sardinia, where the ratio is two women to one man. This finding is not yet explained, though the fact that Sardinia has had a relatively closed gene pool for thousands of years raises the possibility that Sardinians carry a sex-specific gene that promotes longevity. Among supercentenarians the sex ratio is five women to one man.

Figure 2

Percentage of centenarians functioning independently over the course of the previous 10 years in their lives.

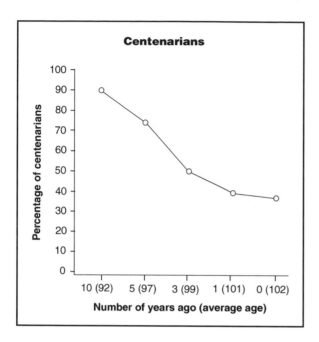

SOURCE: Hitt, R.; Young-Xu, Y.; Silver, M.; Perls, T. "Centenarians: The Older You Get, The Healthier You Have Been." *Lancet* 354 (1999): 652.

Many centenarians continue to function independently. In the New England Centenarian Study, 40 percent of centenarians were completely independent, and close to 90 percent had been independent ten years earlier, at an average age of ninety-two (see figure 2). In the Italian Centenarian Studies, with close to four hundred subjects, about 25 percent were in perfect health. Another 30 percent were in relatively good health. Interestingly, males who live this long do very well compared to females, making up 30 percent of those in perfect health but only 15 percent of those in poor health.

Centenarians escape many of the common diseases associated with aging. Cancer, heart disease, and diabetes are all less common in centenarians than in seventy- or eighty-year-olds. One important aging-related disease is dementia. The incidence and prevalence of dementia increase exponentially with aging but, as with other diseases, many centenarians do not suffer from dementia. Between 40 percent and 60 percent of subjects in studies from Europe, the United States, and Japan were diagnosed with dementia. The others were cognitively normal. When brain tissue from centenarians without dementia is examined, it often does not show any of the changes typically associated with Alzheimer's disease or stroke. These data show that common aging-related diseases are not inevitable, and it is possible to live into very late life and remain well. Serenity may be a personality characteristic of centenarians. Several of the studies found that many of their subjects were easygoing and relaxed.

The metabolic state of centenarians is paradoxical. Several groups have found that healthy, functional centenarians have metabolic characteristics that are commonly associated with disease, such as unfavorable cholesterol profiles, with high concentrations of harmful substances such as triglycerides and low-density lipoprotein cholesterol (LDL-C) and low concentrations of the beneficial high-density lipoprotein cholesterol (HDL-C). They also have high levels of proinflammatory cytokines such as interleukin-6, and high levels of prothrombotic substances. Several theories try to explain these paradoxical findings. Among them is Claudio Franceschi and colleagues' Inflamm-Aging. Inflamm-Aging hypothesizes that aging is due to environmental stresses, particularly inflammatory ones, and that people who live very long, healthy lives may have one, or both, of two characteristics. Either they avoid these stresses, which is unlikely, or, more likely, they have a particular mix of genes (their genotype) that is robust and can minimize the negative effects of the inflammation. A similar theory is François Schächter's Compensatory Adaptation, which suggests that centenarians have a genotype which allows them to better resist internal or external stresses that would cause disease in an individual with a less favorable genotype.

Why some people live to be one hundred

The characteristics of healthy centenarians suggest that they are not examples of delayed or slow aging. Rather, healthy centenarians have experienced an aging process different from that of the general population. James Vaupel's heterogeneity of frailty hypothesis supports this, showing that very long-lived groups follow different trajectories of aging, compared to short- or average-lived populations. Genetics are likely an important factor in becoming a healthy centenarian. T. T. Perls's group in Boston, among others, has shown that centenarianism clusters in families. Unfortunately, when the association between specific human genes and longevity has been investigated, the results have often been inconsistent. The best candidates are mitochondrial genes; the gene for tyrosine hydroxylase, an enzyme involved in cellular respiration; and possibly the apolipoprotein E, a protein involved in cholesterol metabolism and function. Studies in the fruit fly *Drosophila melanogaster* and the nematode *Caenorhabditis elegans* demonstrate that genes involved in the insulin signaling pathway exert an important effect on longevity.

This may be one of the mechanisms through which caloric restriction promotes longevity. No such effects of the insulin signaling pathway have yet been identified in humans, however. What is shared by these candidate genes is an involvement in gene-environment interactions, allowing an individual to suffer less harm from environmental stressors than others without one of these beneficial genotypes, in keeping with the Inflamm-Aging and Compensatory Adaptation theories. These genes do not seem to slow an aging clock, if such a clock exists in humans. Other investigators wonder if extreme longevity is caused by the absence of genotypes that promote disease; evidence for this is lacking as of 2001.

Women with fewer children seem to live longer. Observational data from humans support this, and studies with nematodes and insects also demonstrate that less fertile individuals live longer. This may be an example of one theory of aging at work, George Williams's Antagonistic Pleiotropy. Antagonistic pleiotropy holds that some genes which may be beneficial (in this case, genes that cause one to be reproductively successful) are harmful later in life, leading to disease or accelerated aging. Conversely, genes that are detrimental early in life (and so make one less successful at reproduction) may be beneficial in late life, promoting longevity. The data from insects support the latter explanation more so than the former.

Good genes are not likely the only reason explaining the achievement of long, healthy lives. A number of childhood factors, including parental literacy, a stable home life, and good childhood health promote longevity. Higher educational achievement and socioeconomic status are beneficial. Not smoking and maintaining a healthy weight are also important.

What centenarians can tell us

Although centenarians, who have lived through changes most people can only imagine, can teach us much about the past, history is not the only thing that can be learned from them. The study of centenarians can provide new perspectives on several unsolved puzzles of humans and human biology. For example, why do people age, and how do they age? What can be done to help more people live longer, healthier lives? What will the future look like, when there is a much larger proportion of very old, possibly very frail, people in the population? What adaptations will families, society, and public policy need to undergo to deal effectively with this aging population?

CHRIS MACKNIGHT

See also COMPRESSION OF MORBIDITY; GENETICS, LONGEVITY ASSURANCE; GENETICS, PARENTAL INFLUENCE; LIFE EXPECTANCY; LIFE SPAN EXTENSION; LONGEVITY, SELECTION; OLDEST OLD.

BIBLIOGRAPHY

BENNETT, N. G., and GARSON, L. K. "Extraordinary Longevity in the Soviet Union: Fact or Artifact?" *Gerontologist* 26 (1986): 358–361.

FRANCESCHI, C.; BONAFÈ, M.; VALENSIN, S.; OLIVIERI, F.; DE LUCA, M.; OTTAVIANI, E.; and DE BENEDICTIS, G. "Inflamm-aging: An Evolutionary Perspective on Immunosenescence." *Annals of the New York Academy of Sciences* 908 (2000): 244–254.

McMURDO, M. E. T. "A Healthy Old Age: Realistic or Futile Goal?" *British Medical Journal* 321 (2000): 1149–1151.

PERLS, T. T.; BOCHEN, K.; FREEMAN, M.; ALPERT, L.; and SILVER, M. H. "Validity of Reported Age and Centenarian Prevalence in New England." *Age and Ageing* 28 (1999): 193–197.

RITCHIE, K. "Mental Status Examination of an Exceptional Case of Longevity: J. C. Aged 118 Years." *British Journal of Psychiatry* 166 (1995): 229–235.

SCHÄCHTER, F. "Human Genetics '98: Causes, Effects, and Constraints in the Genetics of Human Longevity." *American Journal of Human Genetics* 62 (1998): 1008–1014.

SCHÄCHTER, F. "Genetics of Survival." *Annals of the New York Academy of Sciences* 908 (2000): 64–70.

TULJAPURKAR, S.; LI, N.; and BOE, C. "A Universal Pattern of Mortality Decline in the G7 Countries." *Nature* 405 (2000): 789–792.

An elderly man on Beijing, China, reads a newspaper story detailing China's military build-up due to supposed increased tensions with neighboring Taiwan in 2000. (AP/WideWorld)

VAUPEL, J. W.; CAREY, J. R.; CHRISTENSEN, K.; JOHNSON, T. E.; YASHIN, A. I.; HOLM, N. V.; IACHINE, I. A.; KANNISTO, V.; KHAZAELI, A. A.; LIEDO, P.; LONGO, V. D.; ZENG, Y.; MANTON, K. G.; and CURTSINGER, J. W. "Biodemographic Trajectories of Longevity." *Science* 280 (1998): 855–860.

WESTWENDORP, R. J. G., and KIRKWOOD, T. B. L. "Human Longevity at the Cost of Reproductive Success." *Nature* 396 (1998): 743–746.

WILMOTH, J.; SKYTTHE, A.; FRIOU, D.; and JEUNE, B. "The Oldest Man Ever? A Case Study of Exceptional Longevity." *Gerontologist* 36 (1996): 783–788.

CHINA

Fertility in China has declined dramatically from more than six children per woman in the 1950s and 1960s to about 1.8–2.0 children per woman today, which is roughly the same as in the United States. Average life expectancy at birth for both sexes combined in China has increased from about 41 years in 1950 to 68.4 years in 1990, and 71 years in 2000, and will continue to increase (United Nations, 1999 vol. 1). The large cohorts of baby boomers, those born in the 1950s and 1960s, will become elderly in a couple of dec-

ades. Such demographic regimes have determined that the population of China, the most populous country in the world with about 1.3 billion people in 2000, is aging at an extraordinarily rapid speed and on a large scale. This article summarizes the demographic trends of aging, living arrangements, economic status, retirement patterns, and access to health and long-term care of the elderly in China.

Increase in proportion and number of elderly

The proportion of elderly (defined as those aged sixty-five and above in this article) of the Chinese population was 5.6 percent in 1990 and 7.0 percent in 2000. However, this proportion will climb quickly to 15.7 percent in 2030 and 22.6 percent in 2050, under medium fertility and medium mortality assumptions (United Nations, 1999, vols. 1 and 2). Note that the medium fertility assumes that the Chinese fertility level will be about 1.9 children per woman in the first half of the twenty-first century, and the medium mortality assumes that life expectancy at birth in China will increase from 71 years in 2000 to 78.7 years in 2050. Under such assumptions, the average annual rate of increase in the proportion of the

China has the largest elderly population in the world, as one out of every ten people was aged sixty or older in 2000. Several elderly men practice Wushu martial arts near the Forbidden City on September 4, 2000. (AP photo by Chien-min Chung.)

elderly population between 2000 and 2050 will be 2.4 percent, while the average annual growth rate of the total population of China during the same period will be only 0.3 percent. In 2000, China's population consists of 21.1 percent of the total world population, and the Chinese elderly population is about 20.8 percent of all elderly living in the world. By 2050, China is projected to have 16.6 percent of the total world population, but will have 22.9 percent of the world's elderly (United Nations, 1999, vol. 2).

In Western societies, the aging transition has been spread over a century or more. In China, however, this change will take place within a few decades and will reach a level of population aging similar to that of most developed countries by the middle of the twenty-first century. It will take about twenty years for the elderly population to increase from 10 percent to 20 percent in China (2017–2037), compared with twenty-three years in Japan (1984–2007), sixty-one years in Germany (1951–2012), sixty-four years in Sweden (1947–2011), and fifty-seven years in the United States (1971–2028) (United Nations, 1999, vol. 2). By the middle of the twenty-first century, the proportion of elderly persons in China will be higher than that in the United States by 0.9 percentage points, and the average annual increase between 1990 and 2050 in China will be 2.6 times as high as that in the United States.

The very large size of the elderly population is another unique feature of population aging in China. In 1990 there were sixty-seven million, and in 2000, eighty-eight million, elderly persons aged sixty-five and over. Under the medium mortality assumption, there will be 235 million elders in China in 2030 and 334 million in 2050. China's elderly population will be fairly close to the total population size of the United States, and 4.4 times as large as the U.S. elderly population, by the middle of the twenty-first century. In 2050 China's elderly population will outnumber India's by 103 million, whereas the total Chinese population will be smaller than that of India by 51 million (United Nations, 1999, vol. 2).

Increase of those aged eighty and above

The oldest old persons, aged 80 and above, are most likely to need help, and most of the younger elderly persons, aged sixty-five to seventy-nine, are relatively healthy. There were about 7.7 million oldest old in China in 1990 and 11.5 million in 2000; their number will climb extremely [SPC1] rapidly, to about 27 million in 2020, sixty-four million in 2040, and one hundred million 2050, under the medium mortality assumption. The average annual increase of the oldest old between 2000 and 2050 will be 4.4 percent. The percent share of the oldest old among the elderly population in 2050 will be 2.3 times as high as that in 2000 (United Nations, 1999, vol. 2), as China's baby boomers, those born in the 1950s and 1960s, become oldest old after 2030.

Aging problems in rural and urban areas

Although fertility in rural China is much higher than in urban areas, aging problems will be more serious in rural areas because of the continuing massive rural-to-urban migration, the large majority of which is young people. Under the medium fertility and medium mortality assumptions, the proportion of elderly will be 26 percent in rural areas and 22 percent in urban areas by the middle of the twenty-first century. The proportions will be 31 percent in rural areas and 26 percent in urban areas under medium fertility but low mortality assumptions (Zeng and Vaupel, 1989). It is also important to note that the extremely rapid and large-scale population aging in China is accompanied by a per capita GNP that is considerably lower (especially in rural areas) than that in many other developing countries. Thus, resources for addressing the serious problems caused by rapid population aging are limited.

Economic status

Income data collected in a survey are not reliable because people usually do not wish to reveal how much money they actually make. For this reason, we will use only self-reported economic status in the following discussion, based on such questions as "Do you feel that your monthly income is enough for payment of living costs?" and the ownership of some household facilities. According to a national survey on China's support systems for the elderly, conducted by the China Research Center on Aging in 1992, 12.7, 53.1, 22.7, and 11.6 percent of the rural elderly reported that their monthly income was enough with savings, roughly enough, a little bit difficult, and rather difficult, respectively. The corre-

sponding figures for the urban elderly were 15.3, 63.9, 15.9, and 5.0 percent, respectively. About 0.8, 47.4, 14.7, and 7.3 percent of the rural elderly had a telephone, a television set, a washing machine, and a refrigerator in their home, in contrast to 7.5, 88.2, 51.5, and 46.6 percent for the urban elderly (CRCA, 1994). Obviously, the economic status of the rural elderly is substantially worse than that of their urban counterparts.

Access to health services and long-term care

Based on the 1992 survey, 66.6 percent of the urban elderly had their medical expenses paid entirely or partially by the government or collective enterprises in 1991. However, this figure was only 9.5 percent for the rural elderly (CRCA, 1994). According to a national survey on healthy longevity of the oldest old conducted by China Research Center on Aging and by Peking University in 1998, around 80 percent of the Chinese oldest old reported that they could get adequate medical care when they were sick. Note that the term "medical care" used in the survey includes traditional Chinese medicine, which is cheap and widely available even in poor and remote areas. As a result, we should not interpret the 1998 survey figures as an indication of good and modern health service facilities in China today.

The census data show that the proportions of elderly men and women who lived in nursing homes in 1990 in the urban areas were 2.1 and 0.8 percent, respectively. The corresponding figures for rural elderly men and women were 0.8 and 0.2 percent, respectively. Given the extremely limited long-term care facilities available and that a large majority of the elderly live with children, especially those in rural areas, perhaps the major cause of institutionalization of elderly persons in China in 1990 was childlessness (or absence of children). Therefore, the percent of the elderly living in nursing homes was extremely low, compared with that in developed countries, where the most common reason for an elderly person to move into an institution is disability. Chinese elderly women's lower social and economic status made them less likely to be able to access long-term care facilities. This is another social disadvantage faced by elderly women in Chinese society, and merits the attention of both society and the government.

Retirement patterns

In China the pension system, which was introduced in 1952, supports only employees of state-owned enterprises in urban areas; its coverage now includes about 140 million persons (Poston and Duan, 2000). Farmers do not have a retirement pension, but continue to work until their health fails. In general (with extent depending on location), China provides the "Five Guarantees" of food, clothing, shelter, medical care, and a funeral for old persons who are childless, disabled, and have no close relatives to rely on (Poston and Duan, 2000). According to the 1992 survey of the elderly, only 5.9 percent of the rural elderly age sixty and over were pension recipients, in contrast to 73.7 percent in the urban areas (CRCA, 1994). The rural elderly have almost no social security coverage. This is a strategically important issue to be considered by policy makers; the old age insurance system should be made universal and strengthened as soon as possible.

Living arrangements and family support

Among the elderly, 37.4 percent of men and 66.5 percent of women do not have a surviving spouse. The proportion of those not living with a spouse increases tremendously with age, due to high rates of widowhood at advanced ages (the divorce rate in China is very low). Many more elderly women are widowed than men because of the gender differential in mortality at old ages. The proportion of old men and women living alone is 8.0 and 10.2 percent, respectively. Elderly women are more likely to be widowed and thus live alone. On the other hand, elderly women are economically more dependent. Therefore, the disadvantages of women in marital life and living arrangements are substantially more serious than those of men at old ages (Zeng and George, 2000).

On the basis of 1990 census data, a large majority of old men (68.8 percent) and women (74.8 percent) live with their children ("children" includes grandchildren hereafter). Female elderly persons are more likely to live with their children, because elderly women are more likely to be economically dependent and widowed. Among the elderly who live with offspring, a majority (68.5 percent of men and 80.1 percent of women) live with both children and grandchildren. Multigeneration family households are one of the main living arrangements for the elderly.

In the cultural context of Chinese society, the philosophy regarding the support of one's older parents is quite different from that of modern Western societies. Filiality (*xiao*) has been one of the cornerstones of Chinese society for thousands of years, and it is still highly valued. The philosophical ideas of filiality include not only respect for older generations but also the responsibility of children to take care of their old parents, which is stated clearly in the Chinese constitution and in laws protecting the rights of elderly persons (Zeng, 1991). Families have been playing, and will continue to play, crucial roles in bearing the costs of caring for the elderly, given limited pensions and health service facilities, especially in rural areas.

ZENG YI

See also JAPAN; POPULATION AGING; SOUTH ASIA.

BIBLIOGRAPHY

CHINA RESEARCH CENTER ON AGING (CRCA). *A Data Compilation of the Survey on China's Support Systems for the Elderly*. Beijing: Hua Ling Press, 1994.

OGAWA, N. "Aging in China: Demographic Alternatives." *Asia-Pacific Population Journal* 3, no. 1 (1988): 21–64.

POSTON, D. L., and CHENGRONG, C. D. "The Current and Projected Distribution of the Elderly and Eldercare in the People's Republic of China." *Journal of Family Issues* 21, no. 6 (2000): 714–732.

UNITED NATIONS. POPULATION DIVISION. *World Population Prospects: The 1998 Revision* Volume 1: *Comprehensive Tables*. Volume 2: *Sex and Age*. New York: United Nations, 1999.

ZENG Y. *Family Dynamics in China: A Life Table Analysis*. Madison: University of Wisconsin Press, 1991.

ZENG Y., and GEORGE, L. "Family Dynamics of 63 Million (in 1990) to More than 330 Million (in 2050) Elders in China." *Demographic Research* 2, no. 5 (2000).

ZENG Y., and VAUPEL, J. "Impact of Urbanization and Delayed Childbearing on Population Growth and Aging in China." *Population and Development Review* 15 (1989): 425–445.

CHOLESTEROL

Cholesterol, cholesterol esters, and triglycerides are fats, or lipids. On their own these would not be soluble enough to circulate, so to circulate in blood, these lipids are combined with phospholipids and protein in particles called lipoproteins. Generally, only three lipoproteins—very low density lipoproteins (VLDL), low density lipoproteins (LDL), and high density lipoproteins (HDL)—are found in the serum of fasting persons.

Cholesterol is absorbed from the intestine and transported to the liver where it is taken up by the LDL receptors. Cholesterol from the liver enters the circulation as VLDL and is metabolized to remnant lipoproteins after an enzyme (lipoprotein lipase) removes triglycerides. The remnant lipoproteins are removed by LDL receptors or further metabolized to LDL and then removed by LDL receptors. Cholesterol also is transported from peripheral cells to the liver by HDL. Cholesterol is recycled to LDL and VLDL or is taken up in the liver by an enzyme known as hepatic lipase. Cholesterol is excreted in bile.

LDL is the major cholesterol-containing lipoprotein, the major lipoprotein implicated in the development of atherosclerosis, and the primary target of therapeutic interventions. LDL cholesterol may be increased because of increased dietary saturated fat and cholesterol, obesity, or genetic disorders, or because of other secondary causes such as hypothyroidism, a kidney disorder known as nephrotic syndrome, biliary cirrhosis, and renal failure.

HDL is synthesized in both the liver and intestine and exerts a protective effect on the development of atherosclerotic vascular disease, a condition also sometimes referred to as "hardening of the arteries." HDL reverses cholesterol transport and removes cholesterol from cells to be delivered directly to the liver or indirectly via transfer of other lipoproteins for catabolism (breakdown into simpler substances with the release of energy). HDL also prevents oxidation and aggregation of LDL in the arterial wall. Low HDL cholesterol may be genetically determined or associated with nutritional habits, cigarette smoking, and lack of exercise.

VLDL is a triglyceride-rich lipoprotein synthesized and secreted by the liver. Hypertriglyceridemia is associated with genetic disorders, obesity, heavy alcohol intake, diabetes mellitus, renal failure, and drugs such as estrogens.

The measurement of levels of LDL cholesterol, HDL cholesterol, and triglycerides in the serum is used to assess risk for atherosclerotic vascular disease. Serum total cholesterol = LDL cholesterol + HDL cholesterol + 1/5 triglycerides. Hypercholesterolemia is a serum total cholesterol of 200 mg/dL or higher. An elevated serum LDL cholesterol is 130 mg/dL or higher. An abnormally low serum HDL cholesterol is 35 mg/dL or lower. Hypertriglyceridemia is serum triglycerides of 190 mg/dL or higher.

An elevated serum total cholesterol, an elevated serum LDL cholesterol, and a low serum HDL cholesterol are risk factors for coronary artery disease, stroke, and peripheral arterial disease in older and younger men and women. The higher the serum total cholesterol, the higher the serum LDL cholesterol, and the lower the serum HDL cholesterol, the greater the incidence of atherosclerotic vascular disease in older and younger men and women.

Elevated serum triglycerides is associated with an increased risk of atherosclerotic vascular disease. However, except for being a weak independent risk factor for new coronary events in elderly women, hypertriglyceridemia is not an independent risk factor for atherosclerotic vascular disease in older or younger men and women.

Because the incidence of atherosclerotic vascular disease is much higher in older men and women than in younger men and women, hypercholesterolemia, an elevated serum LDL cholesterol, and a low serum HDL cholesterol contribute more to the absolute incidence of atherosclerotic vascular disease in older than in younger men and women.

In addition to dyslipidemia, cigarette smoking, hypertension, and diabetes mellitus are major risk factors for atherosclerotic vascular disease. The greater the number and severity of major risk factors, the higher the incidence of atherosclerotic vascular disease.

Persons with dyslipidemia should have secondary causes of dyslipidemia treated, lose weight if obese, and begin dietary treatment. A Step II American Heart Association diet should be used if drug therapy is being considered. The Step II diet contains no more than 30 percent of calories from fat, less than 7 percent of calories from saturated fatty acids, and less than 200 mg of cholesterol daily. Other major risk factors for atherosclerotic vascular disease must be treated.

Increased plasma homocysteine is also an independent risk factor for atherosclerotic vascular

Figure 1
The effects of high cholesterol on the human body.

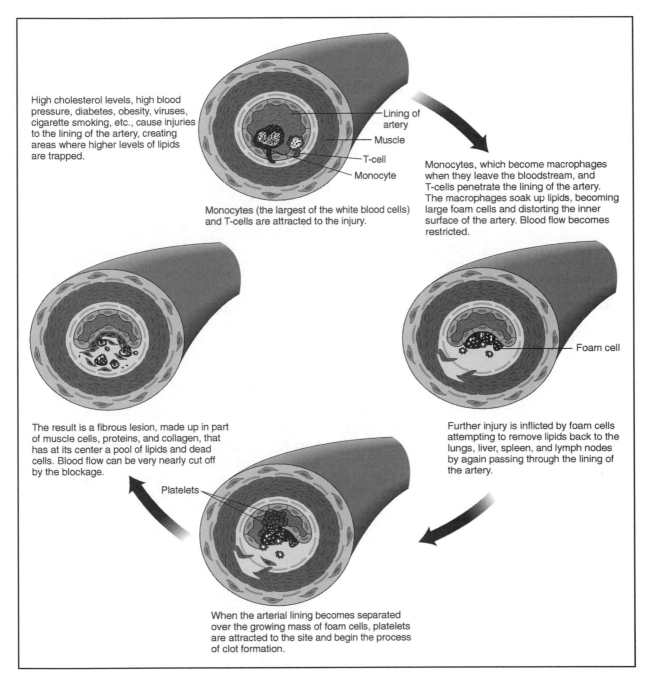

High cholesterol levels, high blood pressure, diabetes, obesity, viruses, cigarette smoking, etc., cause injuries to the lining of the artery, creating areas where higher levels of lipids are trapped.

Lining of artery

Muscle

T-cell

Monocyte

Monocytes (the largest of the white blood cells) and T-cells are attracted to the injury.

Monocytes, which become macrophages when they leave the bloodstream, and T-cells penetrate the lining of the artery. The macrophages soak up lipids, becoming large foam cells and distorting the inner surface of the artery. Blood flow becomes restricted.

Foam cell

The result is a fibrous lesion, made up in part of muscle cells, proteins, and collagen, that has at its center a pool of lipids and dead cells. Blood flow can be very nearly cut off by the blockage.

Platelets

Further injury is inflicted by foam cells attempting to remove lipids back to the lungs, liver, spleen, and lymph nodes by again passing through the lining of the artery.

When the arterial lining becomes separated over the growing mass of foam cells, platelets are attracted to the site and begin the process of clot formation.

SOURCE: Drawing by Hans and Cassidy for the Gale Group.

disease in older and younger men and women. The presence of both increased plasma homocysteine and dyslipidemia increases independently the incidence of atherosclerotic vascular disease.

Statins are drugs that reduce the synthesis of cholesterol and the secretion of VLDL and in-crease the activity of LDL receptors. Bile acid–binding resins increase the secretion of bile acids. Nicotinic acid reduces the secretion of VLDL and the formation of LDL and increases the formation of HDL. Fibrates reduce the secretion of VLDL and increase the activity of lipoprotein lipase, thereby increasing the removal of triglycerides.

Older and younger men and women with atherosclerotic vascular disease and a serum LDL cholesterol greater than 125 mg/dL despite dietary treatment should be treated with statin drugs to lower the serum LDL cholesterol to below 100 mg/dL. Statins will decrease serum total and LDL cholesterol and triglycerides, increase serum HDL cholesterol, and reduce in these patients all-cause mortality, cardiovascular mortality, major coronary events, stroke, heart failure, angina pectoris, and peripheral arterial disease. Because mortality rates and cardiovascular events increase with age, statins will reduce all-cause mortality, cardiovascular mortality, and cardiovascular events approximately twice as much in men and women sixty-five years of age and older than in men and women younger than sixty-five years.

Older and younger men and women with atherosclerotic vascular disease and a normal serum LDL cholesterol but a low serum HDL cholesterol should be treated with nicotinic acid or gemfibrozil to reduce cardiovascular events.

Older and younger persons without atherosclerotic vascular disease with a serum LDL cholesterol of 160 mg/dL or higher and two other coronary risk factors (including older age, male gender, smoking, hypertension, diabetes mellitus, low serum HDL cholesterol, and family history), or with a serum LDL cholesterol of 130 mg/dL or higher and a low serum HDL cholesterol, or with a serum LDL cholesterol of 190 mg/dL or higher and no other coronary risk factors should be treated with statins to reduce cardiovascular events.

WILBERT S. ARONOW

See also HEART DISEASE; HIGH BLOOD PRESSURE; STROKE.

BIBLIOGRAPHY

ARONOW, W. S. "Treatment of Hypercholesterolemia in Older Persons with Coronary Artery Disease." Clinical Geriatrics 7 (1999): 93–100.
ARONOW, W. S. "Risk Factors for Coronary Artery Disease, Peripheral Arterial Disease, and Atherothrombotic Brain Infarction in Elderly Persons." In Vascular Disease in the Elderly. Edited by W. S. Aronow, E. A. Stemmer, and S. E. Wilson. Armonk, N.Y.: Futura Publishing Co., 1997. Pages 81–103.
DOWNS, J. R.; CLEARFIELD, M.; WEIS, S.; WHITNEY, E.; SHAPIRO, D. R.; BEERE, P. A.; LANGENDORFER, A.; STEIN, E. A.; KRUYER, W.; and GOTTO, A. M., JR. "Primary Prevention of Acute Coronary Events with Lovastatin in Men and Women with Average Cholesterol Levels. Results of AFCAPS/TexCAPS." Journal of the American Medical Association 279 (1998): 1615–1622.
LAROSA, J. C. "Hyperlipidemia in the Elderly." In Cardiovascular Disease in the Elderly Patient, 2d ed. Edited by D. D. Tresch and W. S. Aronow. New York: Marcel Dekker, Inc., 1999. Pages 129–137.
MIETTINEN, T. A.; PYORALA, K.; OLSSON, A. G.; MUSLINER, T. A.; COOK, T. J.; FAERGEMAN, O.; BERG, K.; PEDERSEN, T.; and KJEKSHUS, J. "Cholesterol-Lowering Therapy in Women and Elderly Patients with Myocardial Infarction or Angina Pectoris. Findings from the Scandinavian Simvastatin Survival Study (4S)." Circulation 96 (1997): 4211–4218.

CIRCADIAN RHYTHMS

Circadian rhythms (from circa [approximately] and dies (day)) are internally generated, near-24-hour fluctuations in physiology, performance, and behavior. Circadian rhythms have been identified in nearly every species in which they have been examined, from unicells to plants to mammals. Circadian rhythms are thought to provide an adaptive advantage to the organism by providing it a means to anticipate regular periodic changes in the environment, and such daily oscillations are thought to have arisen through the process of natural selection that took place in the presence of a regular 24-hour environmental alteration of day and night.

In the early 1970s, the neural structure responsible for synchronizing circadian rhythms in mammals was localized to the suprachiasmatic nucleus (SCN), a small structure located in the brain's hypothalamus. This structure was first identified in studies in which the SCN was lesioned. SCN lesions, resulted in behavior that no longer occurred at regular, near-24-hour intervals but instead was arrhythmic. After the SCN was identified, additional studies in which the electrical activity of the SCN was recorded revealed that part of the brain has a 24-hour cyclicity in electrical activity. A series of elegant studies in which the SCN from mutant animals was transplanted into SCN-lesioned wild-type animals, and vice versa, resulted in the host animals exhibiting the circadian characteristics of the donor animals, further evidence of the role of the SCN as the circadian pacemaker. Since that time, further studies have demonstrated that the near-24-hour pattern of electrical activity is a property of individual SCN neurons.

In the 1990s, great progress in understanding the molecular and cellular basis for near-24-hour rhythmicity was made. The production of 24-hour rhythms from much shorter biochemical events within the cell results from the interaction of several genes and their protein products. Rising levels of proteins interact and then bind to DNA to halt further protein production. As the levels of these clock component proteins fall, the genes are no longer inhibited, and begin production of these proteins again. In some cases, levels of particular proteins are suppressed by exposure to light, adding another feature to the variation of gene and protein levels between day and night that might be related to the mechanism of photic resetting of the circadian clock. The genes and proteins involved in generating circadian rhythmicity have now been identified for a number of species, and while some details differ from species to species, the general mechanism of transcriptional-translational feedback loops is highly conserved—meaning that the general mechanism of having a transcription-translation feedback loop to produce near-24-hour rhythms is quite similar across a wide array of species, from lower to higher organisms.

The primary source of environmental information to this internal pacemaker is the light-dark cycle, which is transmitted along a monosynaptic pathway (the retinohypothalamic tract, or RHT) from the retina to the SCN. There are other, non-photic, rhythmic factors from the environment that have been shown to provide information to the circadian pacemaker in some species, including cycles in environmental temperature or food availability. Rhythmic alterations in behavior can also provide timing information to the circadian system in certain situations.

Circadian rhythms are endogenously generated, and not simply a reflection of daily changes in light and darkness, ambient temperature, or patterns of rest and activity. As such, circadian rhythms continue to be expressed when the organism is studied in constant conditions, although the exact period (cycle length) of the rhythm is usually no longer precisely 24 hours, but instead is slightly shorter or longer than 24 hours. The actual cycle length of a circadian rhythm when studied under constant environmental conditions is termed the free-running period. Under normal conditions, these non-24-hour rhythms are synchronized to the 24-hour day by periodic exposure to signals from the environment, a process called entrainment. For most mammals, regular exposure to the light-dark (LD) cycle entrains the circadian timing system to the 24-hour solar day. In order to maintain entrainment, an organism with a slightly shorter than 24-hour circadian period must have its circadian system reset slightly later each day, while an organism with a longer than 24-hour period must have its circadian system reset earlier each day.

The time of a particular event within the circadian cycle is referred to as the phase of that event. For example, the nadir of the endogenous circadian rhythm of core body temperature is often used as a circadian phase marker. The time at which the core body temperature phase occurs can then be compared with respect to the timing of the sleep-wake cycle, can be compared between individuals, or can be compared before and after an intervention. Thus, the term phase refers to a reference point within the near-24-hour rhythm.

Another key feature of the circadian timing system is that it typically has a phase-dependent response to many types of stimuli. This means that the time within the circadian cycle that a stimulus is applied will affect the magnitude and direction of the response to that stimulus. For example, the resetting response of the circadian system of most organisms to light is phase-dependent. A light stimulus applied in the early night will cause a phase delay shift of the animal's circadian rhythms (the timing will be shifted to a later hour), a light stimulus applied in the late night will cause a phase advance shift (to an earlier hour), and a light stimulus applied in the middle of the day will cause a very small change in phase. The phase-dependent response of the circadian system to a stimulus is typically summarized in a phase-response curve (PRC).

Under entrained conditions, the phase of a circadian rhythm has a fixed relationship to the signal from the environment (in most cases, the light-dark cycle) that synchronizes, or entrains, the circadian timing system to the 24-hour day. This phase relationship is termed the phase-angle of entrainment.

Another feature of a circadian rhythm is its amplitude, or the size (magnitude) of the oscillation.

The study of circadian rhythms in the laboratory

While circadian rhythms are endogenously (internally) generated, they can also be directly affected by changes in the environment or by changes in behavior. For example, nocturnal rodents typically are inactive during the light portion of the light-dark cycle. If bright lights were turned on during the animal's normal dark time (when it would typically be active), the animal may cease activity. Thus, the endogenous component of the animal's circadian activity rhythm is acutely altered by exposure to light. This can also occur when human circadian rhythms are studied, and the endogenous circadian component of many physiologic and behavioral rhythms can be affected by things such as ambient light, activity, sleep-wake state, food intake, postural change, and emotional state. Thus, it is important that studies of circadian rhythmicity be conducted under controlled conditions in which the endogenous component of circadian rhythms can be measured.

Studies of circadian rhythms in humans began as early as the 1930s. Nathaniel Kleitman studied human subjects in Mammoth Cave in Kentucky, an environment where temperature, humidity, and darkness were constant. While the experimental subjects in those studies were allowed access to artificial lighting, Kleitman's studies revealed that humans, like other organisms, continue to exhibit near-24-hour physiological rhythms even when living in constant conditions. In the 1960s, JÎrgen Aschoff and colleagues began a series of circadian rhythm studies in Germany. They studied their subjects in underground bunkers, which, like the cave used by Kleitman, were shielded from information from the external environment. In the 1970s and later, special laboratories were developed for the study of circadian rhythms in humans. Those laboratory study rooms were typically shielded from outdoor light, were soundproof, and contained no obvious means of telling the time of day (e.g., they did not have clocks, radios, televisions).

Results of studies from humans living in those special laboratory conditions have revealed that there are circadian rhythms in many aspects of human behavior and physiology. Those rhythms include daily oscillations of hormone levels (including such hormones as cortisol, melatonin, thyroid stimulating hormone, and prolactin); core body temperature; EEG activity; alertness and vigilance; sleep tendency; and many aspects of performance. Neuroanatomical studies have also found that the same structures that comprise the circadian timing system in mammals, the SCN and RHT, are present in the human brain.

The particular methods used for studying human circadian rhythms depend on the aspect of circadian physiology that is of interest. The constant routine is an effective protocol to assess phase, amplitude, or the effect of a particular stimulus on the endogenous output of the human circadian system. In this protocol, subjects' circadian rhythms are measured for at least one complete circadian cycle while they remain awake, in a constant posture, in constant dim light, and with food and fluid intake distributed across day and night. In constant routine studies, often multiple variables controlled by the circadian timing system are measured simultaneously, so the phase and amplitude of each of those rhythms can be assessed. In studies in which the influence on the circadian timing system of a particular stimulus is of interest, an initial assessment of circadian phase and amplitude is made, the stimulus is applied, and then a reassessment of phase is done. Thus, the change in phase and amplitude as a result of the stimulus can be estimated.

Initial studies attempting to measure the period of the human circadian system used the free-running protocol. This protocol required subjects to live in an environment without time-of-day information, but allowed them to self-select their light exposure. As described above, it is now understood that light is the primary signal from the environment that affects the human circadian system, and light has phase-dependent effects on circadian timing. Experts also know that when subjects are allowed to choose when to go to sleep and wake without knowledge of what time it is, they prefer to go to sleep several hours later than they do under normal, entrained conditions. In doing so, they remain awake, exposed to light, throughout much of the time in the circadian cycle when light causes phase delay shifts.

Figure 1

Circadian variation of objective (lower panel) and subjective (middle panel) sleep quality and neurobehavioral performance (upper panel) in young and older subjects during forced desynchrony. For a complete description of this figure and its source, please see the section called "Figure legend" near the end of this essay.

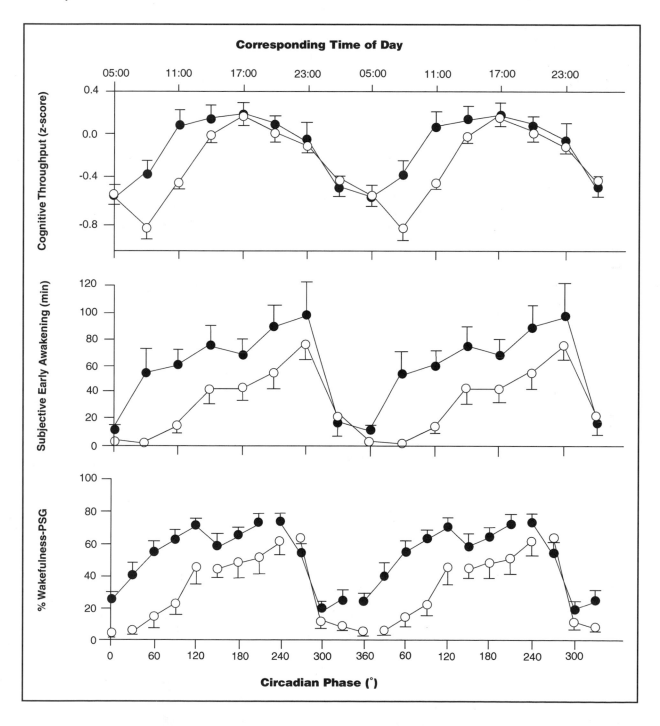

In addition, they remain asleep several hours beyond when they would wake up under normal entrained conditions, shielding themselves from light exposure during the time when light causes phase advance shifts. Thus, in free-running studies, allowing subjects to self-select their own light-dark exposure leads to cumulative phase delay shifts each day, and an observed free-running period that is consequently longer. It was widely reported based on results from free-running studies that the period of the human circadian system was near 25 hours, substantially longer and much more variable than the periods reported from most other species.

In more recent studies carried out in the 1990s, the forced desynchrony protocol was used to assess circadian period in humans under conditions that minimizes the influence of the light-dark cycle on the observed period. In this protocol, subjects are scheduled to live on a sleep-wake cycle length that is much shorter (typically ü20 hours) or longer (ü28 hours) than 24 hours. Furthermore, ambient light levels during the entire time one is awake are kept to a low level to minimize the phase-shifting effect of such light exposure. Using such protocols, it has been reported that the period emanating from the human circadian pacemaker is very close to 24 hours, with much less interindividual variability, similar to that found in most other mammalian species.

Relationship of sleep to circadian rhythmicity

The circadian timing system is a major determinant of daily variations in subjective alertness, neurobehavioral performance, and sleep. The early evidence for this was derived from long-term sleep deprivation experiments carried out in the 1970s. In those experiments, alertness and performance exhibited rhythmic variations over the course of the sleep deprivation, with a period close to 24 hours, superimposed on a steady deterioration of alertness and performance, attributable to sleep loss. The notion that sleep, alertness, and neurobehavioral performance are determined by the interaction of two processes, a circadian and a sleep-wake dependent process (sometimes referred to as a homeostat), is now widespread.

Studies carried out in the late 1970s found that spontaneous sleep duration depends primarily on the phase of the circadian timing system at bedtime, rather than on the length of prior wakefulness. Those studies involved young subjects free-running in temporal isolation, with the subjects allowed to self-select their bed and wake times. Results from such studies consistently documented that spontaneous sleep duration was longest when bedtime occurred near the circadian phase at which temperature peaks, and spontaneous sleep duration was shortest when bedtime occurred closer to the circadian phase of the temperature nadir (which under normal entrained conditions occurs 2-3 hours before usual wake time). Thus, the spontaneous self-selected duration of sleep episodes begun at the peak of circadian sleep tendency (at or after the temperature nadir) were actually cut short by the rising portion of the wake propensity rhythm (the variation in the likeliness of waking up or of remaining awake), whereas those begun at the nadir of circadian sleep tendency (near the temperature crest) were extended by the rising portion of the sleep propensity rhythm. Ironically, this occurred because sleep propensity was greatest just after the endogenous circadian temperature nadir and minimal near the endogenous circadian temperature peak. In fact, results from forced desynchrony studies carried out on young adults during the 1990s suggest that proper alignment between the timing of sleep and the timing of circadian rhythms is even more important for sleep consolidation than previously thought.

Circadian rhythms in older subjects.

One prominent age-related change in the organization of daily behavior is the advance of bed and wake times to an earlier hour. Associated with this is an age-related increase in two specific sleep complaints, early morning awakening and difficulty maintaining sleep. Early morning awakening and difficulty maintaining sleep in the latter part of the night have been shown in a number of studies to affect up to 40% of the older population. It has also been reported that age-related sleep disturbances are associated with increased mortality and with increased usage of sleeping pills.

Given the role played by the circadian system in sleep-wake timing, age-related changes in circadian rhythms have been hypothesized to underlie the shift of sleep-wake timing and the increase in circadian rhythm sleep disorders in older people. Numerous reports that daily physiologic rhythms occur at an earlier hour in older people than in young adults seem to support the idea that there is a change in the circadian timing system with age. In fact, circadian entrainment theory predicts that a shortening of the period of the circadian pacemaker would result in a phase advance of circadian rhythms with respect to the light-dark cycle, the main environmental signal synchronizing circadian rhythms to the 24-hour day. Studies of animal circadian rhythms carried out in the 1970s and 1980s supported the idea that the period of the circadian system shortened with age. Those studies compared separate groups of young and older animals. In the 1990s, studies were carried out in which the circadian period of animals was monitored throughout their entire life span. Those more recent studies found that the average period in when the animals were old was not significantly different from when the same animals were young, thus refuting the idea that circadian period shortens with age.

Early studies of human circadian rhythms had also suggested that circadian period shortened with age, but those studies were confounded by allowing the subjects to self-select their sleep-wake and light-dark times. During the 1990s, a series of forced desynchrony studies were carried out in very healthy young and older human subjects to compare circadian period lengths between the two age groups. Those studies found no significant difference in circadian period with age. Thus, a key feature of the circadian timing system, its intrinsic period, does not appear to change with age.

Interaction of sleep and circadian rhythmicity in aging

Despite consensus on the significance of both the rhythmic circadian and the sleep-wake dependent processes in the regulation of sleep in young adults, attempts to quantify the extent to which each process contributes to sleep in older people are scarce. The forced desynchrony studies of human circadian rhythms described above, in which it was found that circadian period is not significantly different with age, revealed several new findings about the relationship between the circadian timing system and the sleep-wake cycle in aging. Despite the fact that the older subjects in that type of study were extremely healthy, had no sleep complaints, and were screened to rule out the presence of sleep disorders, they slept much more poorly than did the young subjects. On the baseline nights in that study when all subjects were sleeping at their habitual times, the older subjects had a sleep efficiency of only 77 percent compared with a greater than 90 percent sleep efficiency in the young subjects. During the forced desynchrony segment of the study when sleep episodes were

scheduled at all different circadian phases, even small changes in the timing of sleep with respect to the phase of the circadian pacemaker resulted in substantial self-perceived and objectively-measured sleep disruption. This sleep disruption was greater in the older subjects, especially when the latter part of the sleep episode was scheduled to occur after the temperature minimum, which occurred on average in those same subjects at 5:15 a.m. Finally, there was a much narrower range of circadian phases when older subjects could maintain high sleep efficiency at the end of their scheduled sleep episodes. It therefore seems that the circadian drive for sleep is reduced in the early morning hours in even very healthy older individuals. This finding suggests that there is a crucial relationship between the circadian timing system and the timing of the sleep episode, and that if the alignment between these two regulatory systems is altered, the sleep of older individuals is much more vulnerable to disruption. Two additional studies support the notion that the alignment between the circadian timing system and the timing of the sleep-wake cycle may be altered in aging. Those studies used different experimental designs, but both found that the relative timing of the habitual sleep-wake cycle with respect to the timing of circadian rhythms is significantly different in older subjects.

Melatonin, sleep, and aging

Melatonin is a hormone produced by the pineal gland at night in both nocturnal and diurnal mammals. The circadian pacemaker imposes rhythmicity onto the pineal gland through a well-characterized neural pathway, thus driving the rhythm of melatonin secretion. In addition to this control by the circadian pacemaker, melatonin production can be suppressed by light. In seasonally breeding mammals, the nightly duration of melatonin secretion is used as an endocrine signal of day length, and seasonal changes in the duration of melatonin secretion times reproduction to the optimal time of year.

Because melatonin is produced at night, it was thought to be causally related to sleep in humans (although it should be noted that melatonin is produced at night in nocturnal animals, who sleep during the day). In fact, studies of exogenous melatonin administration have shown that melatonin can facilitate sleep onset at certain times of day, although not at all times of day.

Because there is increased sleep disruption with age and because of reports of exogenous melatonin's sleep promoting effects, there have been suggestions that an age-related reduction in melatonin level or a decrease in the duration of melatonin secretion might be associated with the age-related decrease in sleep quality. While some older people may secrete less melatonin, a study published in 1999 reported that nocturnal plasma melatonin concentrations in most very healthy older subjects was not significantly reduced when compared to those of healthy young men and women, nor was there a significant difference in the duration of the nightly melatonin secretion time between young and older subjects. Thus, neither decreased plasma melatonin levels nor a shorter duration of melatonin secretion can fully explain the age-related changes in sleep timing and consolidation that have been observed in even healthy older individuals.

There have been conflicting reports of whether exogenous melatonin administered to older individuals with insomnia improves sleep quality. In one study in which sleep (brain waves, eye movements, muscle activity) was recorded, of older insomniacs, exogenous melatonin administration did not affect total sleep time, sleep efficiency, or subjective sleep quality, and there was no correlation between endogenous melatonin level and sleep quality. However, another similar study reported that older insomniacs had low endogenous melatonin levels. That same study also reported that a low dose (0.3 mg) of melatonin improved sleep efficiency in those older insomniacs with low melatonin levels, although it did not affect the sleep in older control subjects. Thus, there is conflicting information about how endogenous melatonin levels in aging are related to sleep quality and whether melatonin replacement will improve sleep.

Summary

The circadian timing system is a major organizing feature of human physiology and behavior. Great progress in understanding the molecular and genetic basis of circadian rhythmicity in mammals was made in the 1990s. While it was once hypothesized that age-related changes in the circadian timing system led to an increase in disorders of sleep timing with age, recent studies have indicated that many aspects of circadian rhythmicity are not significantly different between young and healthy older individu-

als. There are, however, age-related changes in sleep, and also age-related changes in the interaction between the timing of sleep and the output of the circadian pacemaker, resulting in age-related sleep disruption in the latter half of the night. While the neurobiological basis of age-related changes in the interaction between sleep and circadian rhythmicity are not yet known, continued research promises better understanding of how these systems change with age and how knowledge of such changes can lead to development of chronobiological treatment for age-related sleep disruption.

Figure legend

(A basic description of Figure 1 on page 233 is listed with the figure. This is a more detailed description.)

Filled symbols refer to the older subjects; open symbols to the young subjects; means = standard errors. Data are double plotted and shown with respect to circadian phase (lower axis) derived from core body temperature data (nadir temperature waveform = 0¤). The corresponding time of day under normal conditions for the older subjects is shown in the upper axis. Lower panel: percent of wakefulness during scheduled sleep. Middle panel: subjective early awakening. Upper panel: normalized cognitive performance.

There are prominent circadian variations in objective and subjective sleep quality and performance, with all showing a nadir at the circadian phases corresponding to the early morning hours. Older subjects show greater objective and subjective sleep disruption at all circadian phases, and there is a much narrower range of circadian phases when older subjects can remain asleep; young subjects can maintain high sleep quality for many hours after their typical wake time, while older subjects experience increasing levels sleep disruption when scheduled to sleep at or just after the time of their circadian temperature nadir (0¤, on average at 5:15 a.m.). This is also reflected in the circadian performance rhythm, where young subjects show impaired performance at and just after the circadian phases corresponding to their usual wake time, while the performance of the older subjects is improving at these phases.

These measures of sleep and wake indicate that there is a change in the interaction between the circadian timing system and sleep with age, and that there appears to be a decreased drive for sleep in older subjects in the early morning hours.

The figure was adapted from the following sources: Duffy, J. F.; D. F. Dijk; E. B. Klerman; and C. A. Czeisler. "Later Endogenous Circadian Temperature Nadir Relative to an Earlier Wake Time in Older People." *American Journal of Physiology* 275 (1998): R1478–R1487; and Dijk, D. J.; J. F. Duffy; E. Riel; T. L. Shanahan; and C. A. Czeisler. "Ageing and the Circadian and Homeostatic Regulation of Human Sleep During Forced Desynchrony of Rest, Melatonin and Temperature Rhythms. *Journal of Physiology (London)* 516 2 (1999): 611–627.

BIBLIOGRAPHY

Aschoff, J. "Circadian Rhythms in Man: A Self-sustained Oscillator with an Inherent Frequency underlies Human 24-hour Periodicity." *Science* 148 (1965): 1427–1432.

Brainard, G. C.; Rollag, M. D.; and Hanifin, J. P. "Photic Regulation of Melatonin in Humans: Ocular and Neural Signal Transduction." *Journal of Biological Rhythms* 12 (1997): 537–546.

Czeisler, C. A.; Duffy, J. F.; Shanahan, T. L.; Brown, E. N.; Mitchell, J. F.; Rimmer, D. W.; Ronda, J. M.; Silva, E. J.; Allan, J. S.; Emens, J. S.; Dijk, D. J.; and Kronauer, R. E. "Stability, Precision, and Near-24-hour Period of the Human Circadian Pacemaker." *Science* 284 (1999):2177–2181.

Czeisler, C. A.; Weitzman, E. D.; Moore-Ede, M. C.; Zimmerman, J. C.; and Knauer, R. S. "Human Sleep: Its Duration and Organization Depend on Its Circadian Phase." *Science* 210: 1264–1267, 1980.

Czeisler, C. A., and Wright, K. P., Jr. "Influence of Light on Circadian Rhythmicity in Humans." In F. W. Turek, and P. C. Zee eds., *Regulation of Sleep and Circadian Rhythms.* New York: Marcel Dekker, Inc. 1999.

Daan, S.; Beersma, D. G. M.; and Borbély, A. A. "Timing of Human Sleep: Recovery Process Gated by a Circadian Pacemaker." *American Journal of Physiology* 24 (1984): R161–R178.

Dijk, D.-J., and Czeisler, C. A. "Paradoxical Timing of the Circadian Rhythm of Sleep Propensity Serves to Consolidate Sleep and Wakefulness in Humans." *Neuroscience Letters* 166 (1994): 63–68.

Dijk, D.-J.; Duffy, J. F.; and Czeisler, C. A. "Age-related Increase in Awakenings: Impaired Consolidation of Non-REM Sleep at All Circadian Phases." *Sleep* 5 (2001): 565–582.

Duffy, J. F. "Constant Routine." In M. A. Carskadon ed., *Encyclopedia of Sleep and Dreaming.* New York: Macmillan, 1993.

Duffy, J. F.; Dijk, D. J.; Klerman, E. B.; and Czeisler, C. A. "Later Endogenous Circadian Temperature Nadir Relative to an Earlier Wake Time in Older People." *American Journal of Physiology* 275 (1998): R1478–R1487.

Foley, D. J.; Monjan, A. A.; Brown, S. L.; Simonsick, E. M.; Wallace, R. B.; and Blazer, D. G. "Sleep Complaints among Elderly Persons: An Epidemiologic Study of Three Communities." *Sleep* 18 (1995): 425–432.

Klein, D. C., and Moore, R. Y. "Pineal N-Acetyltransferase and Hydroxyindole-O-Methyltransferase: Control by the Retinohypothalamic Tract and the Suprachiasmatic Nucleus." *Brain Research* 174 (1979): 245–262.

Klein, D. C.; Moore, R. Y.; and Reppert, S. M. *Suprachiasmatic Nucleus: The Mind's Clock.* New York: Oxford University Press, 1991.

Kleitman, N. *Sleep and Wakefulness.* Chicago: University of Chicago Press, 1939.

Miles, L. E., and Dement, W. C. "Sleep and Aging." *Sleep* 3 (1980): 119–220.

Monk, T. H. "Circadian Rhythms in Subjective Activation, Mood, and Performance Efficiency." In M. H. Kryger, T. Roth, and W. C. Dement eds., *Principles and Practice of Sleep Medicine.* Philadelphia: W. B. Saunders Company, 1994.

Moore, R. Y. "Circadian Rhythms: Basic Neurobiology and Clinical Applications." *Annual Review of Medicine* 48 (1997): 253–266.

Pittendrigh, C. S. "Temporal Organization: Reflections of a Darwinian Clock-Watcher." *Annual Review of Physiology* 55 (1993): 17–54.

Pittendrigh, C. S., and Daan, S. "Circadian Oscillations in Rodents: A Systematic Increase of Their Frequency with Age." *Science* 186 (1974): 548–550.

Prinz, P. N.; Vitiello, M. V.; Raskind, M. A.; and Thorpy, M. J. "Geriatrics: Sleep Disorders and Aging." *New England Journal of Medicine* 323 (1990): 520–526.

Reppert, S. M., and Weaver, D. R. "Molecular Analysis of Mammalian Circadian Rhythms." *Annual Review of Physiology* 36 (2001): 647–676.

Turek, F. W., and Czeisler, C. A. "Role of Melatonin in the Regulation of Sleep." In F. W. Turek and P. C. Zee eds., *Regulation of Sleep and Circadian Rhythms.* New York: Marcel Dekker, 1999.

Van Cauter, E.; Plat, L.; Leproult, R.; and Copinschi, G. "Alterations of Circadian Rhythmicity and Sleep in Aging: Endocrine Consequences." *Hormone Research* 49 (1998): 147–152.

Weaver, D. R. "Melatonin and Circadian Rhythmicity in Vertebrates: Physiological Roles and Pharmacological Effects." In F. W. Turek and P. C. Zee eds., *Regulation of Sleep and Circadian Rhythms*. New York: Marcel Dekker, 1999.

Wever, R. A. *The Circadian System of Man: Results of Experiments under Temporal Isolation*. New York: Springer-Verlag, 1979.

JEANNE F. DUFFY
CHARLES A. CZEISLER

CLINICAL NURSE SPECIALIST

See NURSE PRACTITIONER

COGNITIVE-BEHAVIORAL THERAPY

Cognitive-behavioral therapy (CBT) is a combination of cognitive and behavior therapies that are directive, time-limited, structured, and place great emphasis on homework exercises. While cognitive therapy emphasizes the role of cognitive processes in the origin and maintenance of psychological disorders, behavior therapy focuses on principles of learning theory and the role of reduced reinforcement in the creation and maintenance of these disorders. In cognitive therapy, individuals learn to identify and monitor distorted, negative thinking, to become aware of the relationship between such thoughts and negative assumptions about oneself—and of the association between thoughts and feelings. Individuals also learn to apply techniques to challenge these thoughts. In behavior therapy, individuals are taught to track the frequency of targeted behaviors and to understand the relationship between these behaviors and their antecedents and consequences. Furthermore, individuals learn techniques to increase or decrease particular events, and are taught skills such as problem solving, relaxation, and assertiveness. Both cognitive therapy and behavior therapy assume that psychological problems can be alleviated by teaching individuals new skills to identify negative thoughts, form adaptive thoughts, and alter maladaptive behavior patterns.

CBT is effective in treating the psychological problems of older adults. In a review of empirically validated psychological treatments for older adults (Gatz et al., 1998) reported that behavioral and environmental interventions can help older adults with dementia, sleep disorders, and depression.

Potential sources of change in psychotherapy with older adults

Potential modifications to psychotherapeutic regimens may be necessary due to the various changes inherent in the aging process as a result of development, cohort differences, and the social context of older adults. It is important to keep in mind that these changes represent hypotheses in need of empirical investigation. Outcomes of psychological interventions with older adults indicate that maturational changes with aging have no negative impact upon the use of CBT with older adults.

Development. Slowing in cognitive processes and memory changes may require changes in cognitive-behavioral therapy. For instance, therapeutic conversation may need to be slower and simpler with older clients. Furthermore, it may be necessary for therapists to repeat new material, to ask the client to summarize the information to make sure that he or she understands it, and to ask the client to take notes on important points to increase recall of information and the effectiveness of the therapeutic intervention.

Changes in therapy may also arise as a result of the more positive aspects of maturation. Older adults have many useful strengths and existing skills as a result of the stability of crystallized intelligence and the development of expertise in several life domains. Rediscovering these skills, rather than teaching new ones, may frequently occur in therapy. It is also important to note that the normal decline in fluid intelligence suggests that the therapist may need to guide the older adult to certain conclusions, rather than giving suggestions and expecting the client to infer them.

Emotional changes that come with maturity may also affect the presentation of problems, requiring an adjustment of cognitive interventions. Research on emotion suggests that young adults experience pure and intense emotions, whereas older adults experience both sad and happy emotions in response to the same environmental or cognitive stimulus. Instead of replacing a negative, distorted thought with a more neutral or positive thought, it may be more strategic to have the older client focus on both the positive and negative emotions experienced.

A tendency for older adults to reminisce may make it difficult to focus on the present in CBT. Keeping an exclusively present-oriented focus when working with older adults who want and need to talk about the past is likely to be counterproductive. It is important to allow time for reminiscence, which may be perceived as reinforcement for other therapeutic work.

Cohort differences. In working with older adults, it is important to be aware of cohort differences that may influence the process of therapy. Cohort differences refer to an individual's membership in a birth-year group and the socialization process that shapes the abilities, beliefs, attitudes, and personality aspects of individuals born in a specific cohort. The attributes of a cohort are believed to be stable as the cohort ages, and thus differentiate it from those born earlier and later. For example, later-born cohorts (people who are now younger) have more years of formal education, are superior in reasoning ability and spatial orientation, and are more extroverted. Consequently, it may be necessary to change the wording of scales or assignments to adjust to different education levels of earlier cohorts and to adapt to cohort-specific values or examples in order to increase comfort with written assignments given in CBT. Thus, younger therapists working with older adults need to learn what it was like to grow up before the therapist was born because cohort differences in education level, intellectual skills, and personality may influence the process of therapy.

Social environment. Knowledge of the social context of older adults is crucial for appropriate interventions within both classic behavioral and social learning models of therapy because reinforcement contingencies that create or maintain maladaptive behavior or negative affect often arise from the environmental context. Staff in nursing homes, for example, may reward older adults for passively conforming to scheduled routines, a passivity that may result in reduced activity levels, lowered sense of control, and worsened mood. In order to improve the client's mood, the environment will need to be changed or staff will need to be consulted about possible environmental changes in the client's highly structured residential setting.

Cognitive-behavioral interventions for late-life problems

Many older adults who seek help in therapy deal with problems that threaten their well-being, including chronic illness, disability, and the death of loved ones. These problems are not unique to late life, but they are likely to occur more frequently at older ages. Furthermore, the usual difficulties of life, such as disappointments in love, arguments with family, and failure to achieve goals, can also take place in late life. Finally, many persons who struggle with depression, anxiety, substance abuse, or psychosis in their younger years continue to do so in their later years.

Chronic illness and disability. Conducting CBT with distressed older adults often means working with a population that is chronically ill, physically disabled, or both, and that struggles to adjust to these problems. In working with this population, it is important to learn about chronic illnesses and their psychological impact, control of chronic pain, adherence to medical treatment, rehabilitation strategies, and assessment of behavioral signs of medication reactions.

A frequent element of treating chronically ill or disabled elders is addressing concurrent depression, since up to 59 percent of this population experiences depression. Although there have been few studies examining the effectiveness of cognitive-behavioral therapy with medically ill older adults, results are encouraging for both outpatient and inpatient populations. Rybarczyk et al. (1992) have identified five important issues in applying CBT to chronically ill older adults: (1) solving practical barriers impeding participation, (2) acknowledging that depression is a separate and reversible problem, (3) limiting excess disability, (4) counteracting the loss of important social roles and autonomy, and (5) challenging the thought of being a "burden." For instance, in challenging the belief of being a burden on a family caregiver, the therapist may help the client to recall things he or she has done for the family caregiver in the past, thereby providing the client with a greater sense of equity in the relationship. Breaking down the issues facing the chronically ill older adult is helpful to the therapist in developing a strategy using both cognitive-behavioral techniques and practical considerations.

In addition to treating depression in medically ill or disabled elders, cognitive and behavioral techniques are also effective in managing pain associated with rheumatoid arthritis and delayed healing from injuries. Cognitive pain-management methods include distracting oneself from the pain, reinterpreting pain sensations, using pleasant imagery, using calming self-statements, and increasing daily pleasurable activities.

Depression. As mentioned previously, depression is prevalent in older adults who are chronically ill, disabled, or grieving; although the prevalence of depression in older adults is less than in young adults. Cognitive and behavioral approaches are effective in relieving depression in older adults. In treating depression, CBT focuses on teaching new coping strategies to deal with problems and on challenging those thoughts that interfere with effective coping. The client's participation in daily events that affect mood may also be addressed in therapy. By using a chart to monitor the frequency of these events, the therapist enables the client to see the relationship between pleasant events and moods, so that the frequency of pleasant events can be increased while the frequency of unpleasant events is reduced during the course of therapy. The therapist may also use the *dysfunctional-thought record*, a technique showing self-talk and negative interpretation of events, to enable the client to recognize distorted thoughts and replace negative and irrational thoughts with more adaptive ones.

Anxiety. Anxiety is fairly common in late life, but it is an understudied problem. Results from various studies indicate that brief courses (less than twenty sessions) of cognitive-behavioral therapy may be effective in treating late-life anxiety. In cognitive therapy, distorted thoughts that may exacerbate anxiety, such as "My heart is beating faster, which means I am about to have a heart attack" are challenged (Wetherell, 1998). Other cognitive restructuring techniques consist of making more accurate risk estimates; "decatastrophizing" by determining ways to cope with the feared situation; stopping thoughts by noticing and eliminating anxiety-provoking thoughts; and replacing automatic, anxious thoughts with positive thoughts. Relaxation training is often combined with diaphragmatic breathing and cognitive restructuring. For a review of treatment of anxiety in older adults, see Wetherell (1998).

Alcohol abuse. Even though alcoholism rates are lower for older adults than for younger adults, older problem drinkers often drink in response to loneliness, depression, and poor social-support networks. Consequently, CBT for the treatment of alcoholism in older adults focuses on improving the client's life in various ways in addition to just abstaining from drinking. Studies indicate that CBT models are effective in treating alcoholism in older adults, although further research is needed because not all studies have included a control group.

Stopping drinking completely, or at least achieving a period of abstinence followed by very limited and controlled drinking is a mandatory goal in treatment. Analysis of the drinking behavior itself also takes place to figure out the maladaptive purpose underlying the drinking behavior. Coping skills and behavior alternatives are then developed and practiced in therapy to handle situations in which the urge to drink arises. Irrational thoughts associated with the drinking are also challenged during therapy to increase the mood and self-esteem of the client, which in turn helps to control drinking behavior.

Conclusion

CBT may be effectively adapted for use with older adults by applying minor modifications to clinical techniques, since the principles of cognitive and behavioral theory are assumed to be similar for older and younger adults. Deciding which modifications to make, and how to conduct them, relies on a complete understanding of the various changes inherent in the aging process as a result of development, cohort differences, and the social context of older adults. Applying CBT to older clients entails several challenges, including learning about the social environment of older adults, working with clients whose experiences may be different from and prior to those of the therapist, and dealing with the interplay of physical and psychological problems on a frequent basis. Those who take on the challenge are likely to discover that their ideas about therapy and about aging will be transformed by working with older clients.

BOB G. KNIGHT
GIA S. ROBINSON

See also ALCOHOLISM; ANXIETY; BEHAVIOR MANAGEMENT, BEREAVEMENT, DEPRESSION; GERIATRIC PSYCHIATRY; INTELLIGENCE; PSYCHOTHERAPY.

BIBLIOGRAPHY

AREAN, P., and MIRANDA, J. "The Treatment of Depression in Elderly Primary Care Patients: A Naturalistic Study." *Journal of Clinical Geropsychology* 2 (1996): 153–160.

BALTES, M. M. "Dependency in Old Age: Gains and Losses." *Current Directions in Psychological Science* 4 (1995) 14–18.

CARSTENSEN, L. L.; EDELSTEIN. B. A.; and DORNBRAND, L., eds. *The Practical Handbook of Clinical Gerontology.* Thousand Oaks, Calif.: Sage Publications, 1996.

COOK, A. J. "Cognitive-Behavioral Pain Management for Elderly Nursing Home Residents." *Journal of Gerontology: Psychological Sciences* 53B (1998): P51–P59.

DUFFY, M. *Handbook of Counseling and Psychotherapy with Older Adults.* New York: John Wiley, 1999.

FINCH, E.; RAMSAY, R.; and KATONA, C. "Depression and Physical Illness in the Elderly." *Clinics in Geriatric Medicine* 8 (1992): 275–287.

GALLAGHER-THOMPSON, D., and THOMPSON, L. W. "Applying Cognitive-Behavioral Therapy to the Psychological Problems of Later Life." In *A Guide to Psychotherapy and Aging.* Edited by S. Zaret and B. G. Knight. Washington, D.C.: American Psychological Association, 1996: Pages 61–82.

GATZ, M.; FISKE, A.; FOX, L. S.; KASKIE, B.; KASL-GODLEY, J.; MCCALLUM, T.; and WETHERELL, J. "Empirically-Validated Psychological Treatments for Older Adults." *Journal of Mental Health and Aging* 4 (1998): 9–46.

KNIGHT, B. G. *Psychotherapy with Older Adults,* 2d ed. Thousand Oaks, Calif.: Sage Publications, 1996.

KNIGHT, B. G., and SATRE, D. D. "Cognitive-Behavioral Psychotherapy with Older Adults." *Clinical Psychology: Science and Practice* 6 (1999): 188–203.

LICHTENBERG, P. A. *A Guide to Psychological Practice in Geriatric Long-Term Care.* New York: Haworth Press, 1994.

LOPEZ, M. A., and MERMELSTEIN, R. J. "A Cognitive-Behavioral Program to Improve Geriatric Rehabilitation Outcome." *The Gerontologist* 35 (1995): 696–700.

RYBARCZYK, B.; GALLAGHER-THOMPSON, D.; RODMAN, J.; ZEISS, A.; GANTZ, F. E.; and YESAVAGE, J. "Applying Cognitive-Behavioral Psychotherapy to the Chronically Ill Elderly: Treatment Issues and Case Illustration." *International Psychogeriatrics* 4 (1992): 127–140.

SCHONFELD, L., and DUPREE, L. W. "Treatment Approaches for Older Problem Drinkers." *The International Journal of the Addictions* 30 (1995): 1819–1842.

TERI, L.; CURTIS, J.; GALLAGHER-THOMPSON, D.; and THOMPSON, L. W. "Cognitive-Behavior Therapy with Depressed Older Adults." In *Diagnosis and Treatment of Depression in Late Life.* Edited by L. S. Schneider, C. F. Reynolds, B. Liebowitz, and A. J. Friedhoff. Washington, D.C.: American Psychiatric Press, 1994. Pages 279–292.

WETHERELL, J. L. "Treatment of Anxiety in Older Adults." *Psychotherapy* 35 (1998): 444–458.

WIDNER, S., and ZEICHNER, A. "Psychological Interventions for the Elderly Chronic Pain Patient." *Clinical Gerontologist* 13 (1993): 3–18.

ZARIT, S. H., and KNIGHT, B. G., eds. *A Guide to Psychotherapy and Aging: Effective Clinical Interventions in a Life-Stage Context.* Washington, D.C.: American Psychological Association, 1996.

ZEISS, A. M., and STEFFEN, A. "Behavioral and Cognitive-Behavioral Treatments: An Overview of Social Learning." In *A Guide to Psychotherapy and Aging.* Edited by S. Zarit and B. G. Knight. Washington, D.C.: American Psychological Association, 1996. Pages 35–60.

COHORT CHANGE

The concept of *cohort change*, which is an attempt to link the "biological rhythm of human existence" (Mannheim, 1952) with the "evolution of the social order" (Parsons, 1951), is a prime example of a tool designed to analyze linkages between the micro (i.e., individual) and macro (i.e., societal) levels of human reality. The phenomena of cohort replacement creates opportunities for societies to rethink, and perhaps redefine, individuals' roles, rights, responsibilities, and rewards. This connection between changes in culture and the gradual and continuous processes of individual aging, birth, and death has led sociologists to investigate how these demographic processes may intersect with personality development.

Although cohorts can be defined in a variety of ways (e.g., a new cohort of graduate students, a new cohort of employees), questions of cohort change, cohort replacement, and cohort succession are primarily about birth cohorts—people born within a given time period. Ryder (1965) described the process of cohort change as an illustration of "demographic metabolism." Social change and population processes are interdependent because the composition of society (aggregate characteristics of the set of individual members) is always in flux. Fertility and in-migration infuse a society with new members, while mortality and out-migration deplete a society of its members. The continuing change in a society's membership creates a dynamic at the macro level that is different from the micro-level dynamic of individual aging. Aging as an individual, biological process also has social implications, because as people age they move from one set of roles or positions to another. In addition, aging is connected to population dynamics through fertility, mortality, and in- and out-migration. Therefore individual aging creates connections between the pace of demographic change and societal transformation. Cohort continuity through the life span provides the element of stability, whereas the perpetual entry, aging, and exit of successive cohorts provide flexibility.

Although initially framed as "the problem of generations" (Mannheim, 1952), the issue under consideration was essentially that of cohort succession—the entry, aging, and exit of successive cohorts—and how it is linked to social change. In 1965, Norman Ryder formulated one answer to this question by describing how cohort characteristics (e.g., size, race/ethnic composition, average level of education) could provide the impetus for social change. The impetus for social change in his demographic approach concentrated on an easily observable feature, the equilibration of supply and demand. For example, an unusually large cohort (e.g., the baby-boom cohort) would require building more schools, hiring more teachers, and perhaps the development of community activities for children. In contrast, an unusually small cohort might motivate an emphasis on small classroom size or changes in immigration policy. Although these stimulus-response pairings seem logical, they represent a subset of a much larger number of possible pairings. Why was the response to the baby boom a school construction program rather than a massive shift to home schooling? And if a small cohort cannot satisfy the demand for labor, why not change expectations and policies governing the average workweek, the frequency of vacations, and/or the child labor laws? These questions illuminate the heart of the puzzle. For it is not only the objective features of a cohort—by itself or relative to those of adjacent and/or coexisting cohorts—that determine the societal response to the demograph-

ic stimulus. Subjective factors are also important, for it is here that the link between the perceived importance of the stimulus and the appropriate response (e.g., relative to constraints, expectations) is forged.

That the biological process of aging is embedded in a social context creates variability in the experience of aging. This variability can be expressed as the difference between individuals, between cohorts, and over time. But it is not simply time (or historical location) that accounts for this variability, for shared experiences require a common framework of perception, interpretation, and reaction. The methodology of cohort analysis requires that people be classified into groups initially based on quantitative markers such as age, date of birth, date of marriage, or date of hire. Group boundaries are created relative to start dates and similar to any grouping exercise, boundary problems are encountered. If it is a birth-year cohort that is of interest, should that year run from January 1 through December 31, from September 1 through August 31, or some other start and end date? How is it sensible to assign two people born on consecutive dates to different cohorts?

While birth cohorts are often used to organize individuals, for analytic purposes the subjective experiences of cohort members must also be considered. The fact that each cohort is defined by a unique intersection of biography and history provides the possibility for commonality of subjective experience, but this potential is actualized only if the subjective experience of history is the same or similar across cohort members. Events must arouse the same kind of outrage or celebration; ideas must elicit similar levels of inspiration or aversion; public figures must be viewed with similar levels of admiration or revulsion.

Early development of the concept of cohort

Cohort approaches to the study of aging and social change have historically focused on the relationship between theoretical and empirical uses of the concept. During the 1970s, researchers continued to struggle with an operationalization of cohort study that did not invite ambiguities in the interpretation of research findings. For example, when comparing people of different ages at one point in time, cohort (based on year of birth) and age (the difference between current year and year of birth) cannot be distinguished.

When extending the information across time—such as comparing people of the same or different ages at different points in time—cohort, age, and year (as the measure of historical time) are intertwined. Age equals current year (history) minus birth year (cohort). Irving Rosow argued in 1978 that focusing attention on methodological solutions to the confounding of age, period, and cohort resulted in the neglect of conceptual and empirical development of the concept of cohort. His question, "What actually is a cohort?" pointed to uncertainties in the definition of cohort and the difficulties inherent in measuring and modeling the complex processes and historical circumstances that cohort members collectively experience. Nevertheless, Rosow conceded that until the mechanisms that translated cohort characteristics into different attitudes and behaviors could be specified in models, cohort, measured simply as shared birth year, remained a useful proxy measure.

Norval Glenn, an early proponent of cohort analysis, conducted much research on social change in attitudes and behaviors. He also warned of the dangers of complete reliance on technical expertise at the cost of careful theoretical development in cohort analyses (see Glenn and Grimes, 1968; Glenn and Zody, 1970; Glenn, 1974)—sophisticated statistical techniques alone would not solve the linear restrictions of age, period, and cohort effects in quantitative analysis. Glenn maintained that while Ryder's classic essay developing the connection between cohort succession and social change was extremely influential, it contained few specifics on the techniques of research.

In addition to this emphasis on cohort analyses, a second branch of cohort literature attempted to ground cohort research more firmly in a consideration of social structural constraint and facilitation. Age stratification theory, an attempt to link a structural perspective to the study of individual behavior, emphasized the manner in which the age structure of societal roles organized members into hierarchies (see Riley, 1973; Riley, Johnson, and Foner, 1972; Riley, 1987). Matilda White Riley combined a cross-sectional approach to age group differences with a longitudinal perspective that considers what happens to particular cohorts as they move through time.

From age stratification theory grew the life-course perspective, which is now the dominant approach in social gerontology. The life-course perspective draws on diverse intellectual sources to study differences in aging across cohorts by capturing individual biography within the context of social structure and historical circumstance. Glen Elder was one of the first to conduct micro-level research using longitudinal data on children's lives to systematically study change in families and children over time. Since then, the use of the life-course perspective to connect trajectories of individual lives to larger societal changes has been fueled by the development of new analytic techniques. These techniques allow researchers to represent underlying dynamics of aging, to assess the multilevel contextual impact of environments on individual level outcomes, and to model the individual-level processes that correlate individual outcomes with individual characteristics over time (see Tuma and Hannan, 1987; Kreft and de Leeuw, 1998).

Examples of cohort diversity

Compared to cohorts who lived in the 1800s, cohorts who came of age during the 1900s had a different experience of aging. In 1900, the median age for men was 23 years old; for women 22. By 1999, the median age had risen to 34 for men and 37 for women, in part a reflection of changes in fertility rates, but also linked to changes in life expectancy. In 1900, life expectancy for men was 46 years, for women, 48 years—compared to 74 and 79, respectively, in 1999. The proportion of men and women aged 65 and older more than tripled (from 4 to 13%) during the twentieth century. Compared to earlier cohorts of 40 year olds, the cohorts of today's 40 year olds do not view their lives as almost over: the expectation of longevity has allowed people to contemplate second careers, and retirement is often viewed as an enjoyable time of life.

Increased life expectancy not only adds years to life; the anticipation of living to older ages transforms the subjective experiences of younger people as well. So, with regard to fertility, for example, not only did the fertility rate drop from an early 1900s high of 3.6 births to 2.1 births in 2000, but the timing of births moved to somewhat older ages. Comparisons of relatively recent fertility behavior demonstrates this point: in the 1960s, most childbearing occurred among women in their early twenties; while in 2000, birth rates for women in their early twenties and late twenties are almost equal, declining only among women in their thirties. The lives of contemporary women are organized much differently than the lives of their mothers and grandmothers. Women are bearing more children out-of-wedlock, marrying later, staying in school longer, becoming increasingly active in the labor force, and working in a wider variety of positions.

Net change and gross change

Studies of cohort change emphasize a dynamic different from that employed by studies of individual change and development. As an example, consider polls that measure approval ratings for elected officials. To examine change at the individual level, it is necessary to interview and reinterview the same respondents. Each time a respondent registers an approval level, the question of change requires a comparison to that individual's previous responses. Changes can be linked to respondents' experiences during the interval. Respondents could alternate between positive and negative reactions to an elected official as the official's actions in turn pleased and then displeased them. Although this type of volatility in approval ratings may carry certain disadvantages, so long as an equal number of people are switching directions, they cancel each other out. The official could therefore enjoy a majority approval rating on a continuous basis, even though the vast majority of people voiced disapproval sometime during the measurement period. In other words, the balanced magnitude and direction of gross change (change at the individual level), results in no change in the approval rating (zero net change). While the composition of those citing favorable versus unfavorable opinions may change, at any given time the official may continue to do a "good" job according to the majority of constituents. *Gross change*, therefore, refers to the volume of change at the individual level (how often individual evaluations shift from positive to negative or vice versa), whereas *net change* refers to a change at the aggregate level (i.e., whether the overall approval rating is higher or lower).

Under conditions of relative stability, these two measures of change may not be very different. For example, if one assumes that retirement is an absorbing state (i.e., a state that, once entered, cannot be vacated), then once a member of a particular cohort shifts from employment to retirement, no subsequent shifts occur. As a consequence, the labor-force participation rate char-

acterizing that cohort progressively declines. However, if retirement (at least within certain age ranges) is a temporary status, then the labor-force participation rate for a given cohort can remain stable, even though individual members of the cohort are regularly moving in and out of employment. In contrast, comparing different cohorts who occupy the same age range at different points in time may reveal the impact of cohort replacement. If the average age of retirement is gradually declining, then comparing different cohorts at ages sixty to sixty-four, for example, will also show a decline in labor-force participation rates, as progressively more members of successive cohorts move into retirement at younger ages, demonstrating that the timing of the retirement transition is changing.

Challenges in studying cohort change

In trying to disentangle the various clocks that govern aging, careful conceptualization, rich data, and advanced analytic techniques are all essential. Because of the tendency to use chronological time as the measure for all the various clocks, ambiguous results are often produced: Cohort and period differences become confounded in trend data because different cohorts are compared in different historical periods; age and cohort differences are confounded in cross-sectional data because people who share cohort membership are also the same age; and age and period effects are confounded in intra-cohort trend data because people age into new historical periods.

The key to understanding the linkage between cohort change and social change will be an explanation of how a shared common understanding—a shared social consciousness—is created by cohort members, and how this understanding resembles or contradicts that of earlier cohorts or same-aged people of a different mind.

MELISSA HARDY
ANDREA E. WILLSON

See also AGE; AGE-PERIOD-COHORT MODEL; BABY BOOMERS; LIFE COURSE; POPULATION AGING; THEORIES, SOCIAL.

BIBLIOGRAPHY

ELDER, G. H., JR. *Children of the Great Depression: Social Change in Life Experience*. Chicago: University of Chicago Press, 1974.

ELDER, G. H., JR. "Age Differentiation and the Life Course." *Annual Review of Sociology*, 1 (1975): 165–190.

ELDER, G. H., JR. "Perspectives on the Life Course." In *Life Course Dynamics: Trajectories and Transitions 1968–1980*. Edited by G. H. Elder, Jr. Ithaca, N.Y.: Cornell University Press, 1985. Pages 23–45.

FIREBAUGH, G., and HAYNIE, D. L. "Using Repeated Surveys to Study Aging and Social Change." In *Studying Aging and Social Change: Conceptual and Methodological Issues*. Edited by M. A. Hardy. Thousand Oaks, Calif.: Sage, 1997. Pages 148–163.

GLENN, N. D. "Aging and Conservatism." *Annals of the American Academy of Political and Social Science* 415 (1974): 176–186.

GLENN, N. D. "Cohort Analysts' Futile Quest: Statistical Attempts to Separate Age, Period, and Cohort Effects." *American Sociological Review* 41 (1976): 900–904.

GLENN, N. D., and GRIMES, MICHAEL. "Aging, Voting, and Political Interest." *American Sociological Review* 33 (1968): 563–575.

GLENN, N. D., and ZODY, R. E. "Cohort Analysis with National Survey Data." *The Gerontologist*, 10 (1970): 233–240.

KREFT, I., and DE LEEUW, J. *Introducing Multilevel Modeling*. Thousand Oaks, Calif.: Sage, 1998.

MANHEIM, K. "The Problem of Generations." In *Essays in the Sociology of Knowledge*. Edited by P. Kecskemeti. Boston: Routledge and Kegan Paul, 1952. (Original work published in 1927).

MARSHALL, V. W. "The State of Theory in the Social Sciences." In *Handbook of Aging and the Social Sciences*, 4th ed. Edited by R. H. Binstock and L. K. George. New York: Academic Press, 1996.

PARSONS, T. *The Social System*. New York: Free Press, 1951.

RILEY, M. W. "Aging and Cohort Succession: Interpretations and Misinterpretations." *Public Opinion Quarterly* 37 (1973): 35–49.

RILEY, M. W. "On the Significance of Age in Sociology." *American Sociological Review* 52 (1987): 1–14.

RILEY, M. W.; JOHNSON, M.; and FONER, A. *Aging and Society, Vol. 3: A Sociology of Age Stratification*. New York: Russell Sage, 1972.

ROSOW, I. "What is a Cohort and Why?" *Human Development* 21 (1978): 65–75.

RYDER, N. B. "The Cohort as a Concept in the Study of Social Change." *American Sociological Review* 30 (1965): 843–361.

TUMA, N. B., and HANNAN, M. T. *Social Dynamics: Models and Methods*. San Diego: Academic Press, 1984.

U.S. Bureau of the Census. *Statistical Abstract of the United States: 1999*. Washington, D.C.: U.S. Bureau of the Census, 1999.

COMORBIDITY

See GERIATRIC MEDICINE

COMPETENCY

The determination of competency is a critical one in a liberal democracy as it tries to balance the values of self-determination and the protection of innocents from harm. This determination becomes particularly important in elderly persons for whom chronic illness and mental disability both necessitate and frustrate decisions about medical treatment, about institutional placement, and, sometimes, about the quality of life itself. While there is no "Holy Grail" by which to judge competency (Roth et al.), careful consideration of this important social construct is necessary to maximize patient independence and well-being.

Although American society highly values freedom and autonomy, there are competing values. In the provision of health care, patient autonomy has been a relatively new arrival, coming of age in the rights movements of the 1960s and 1970s. More tried and true for health professionals are the principles of beneficence (to help) and nonmaleficence (to do no harm). Usually these old and new values do not come into conflict. Patients seek the care of physicians in order to relieve or prevent suffering. They voluntarily go to physicians because the latter are professionals with special technical knowledge and practical wisdom about the relief of suffering. In most instances patients exercise their autonomy by asking physicians for advice and then following it. (Youngner).

Sometimes, however, patients and their physicians do not agree about what is best for the patient. Physicians often deal with such conflicts by overriding patients' wishes directly, by force, or indirectly, by manipulation or deceit. This is paternalism; the physician acts unilaterally in what he or she perceives as the patient's best interest. Today paternalism has been, for the most part, rejected. The notion of competence, however, offers a way out of the impasse: in order to exercise freedom of choice and accept responsibility for that choice, a person must have the mental ability to do so. Although freedom of choice is valued, society wants to prevent harm to persons who are inherently unable to make choices.

Competency is one of five elements of the legal and moral doctrine of informed consent that governs the complicated exchange of information about treatment options and the decisions that result from it (Meisel et al.). The other elements are voluntariness, provision of adequate information, understanding, and the making and expression of an actual decision. Competency refers to mental and decision-making capacities inherent in the patient.

Competency is decision- and situation-specific. One person may be competent to make medical decisions but incompetent to handle finances; another may be competent to consent to a chest X-ray but incompetent to agree to complicated surgery. Competency can fluctuate over time. For example, a patient may become very confused when experiencing a high fever, but be quite clear when his or her temperature returns to normal (Appelbaum et al.). Some patients may be found globally incompetent—they lack the capacity to make any important decisions in their lives. In such cases a guardian of person must be appointed.

Competency and capacity

Although the terms "competency" and "capacity" are often used interchangeably, they differ in a critical manner. "Competency" is a legal term. People are presumed competent until proven otherwise. Competency is also a threshold concept—one is either competent or not competent. (Buchanan et al.). If a person is competent, he or she has the right and the responsibility to make decisions in life, including medical decisions. If a person is incompetent, he or she loses those rights and responsibilities. Someone else must make the decisions for that person.

"Decision-making capacity," on the other hand, is a clinical term that is used to describe varying degrees of mental ability, ranging, for example, from none to slight, moderate, or excellent. Unlike competency, decision-making capacity describes a spectrum of ability (Youngner). Clinicians know that people's inherent ability to make decisions, unlike their legal right to do so, is not an all-or-nothing phenomenon. At one end of the spectrum is the comatose patient, totally unable to make decisions; at the

other end is the totally calm, intelligent, rational, decisive, and self-aware person. In reality most patients fall someplace in between. Inherent qualities such as character (e.g., difficulty making decisions), neurosis (e.g., fears and anxieties), and illness-imposed qualities (e.g., pain, fear, isolation, diminished self-image, or dementia) attenuate decision-making capacity to some degree. The critical question, then, is when, on this spectrum of ability, society is willing to take away a person's right and responsibility to make his or hers own decisions.

Drawing the line between competency and incompetence

Except at the extremes (the comatose patient or the ideally rational one), wherever one draws the line on the decision-making capacity spectrum, persons with some degree of capacity will be denied the legal right to make decisions while others with some degree of impairment will be allowed that right. For example, a patient with severe dementia may be judged incompetent but still have credible opinions about the quality of his or her care. Similarly, a patient may be judged competent despite some forgetfulness and confusion.

In order to be judged incompetent, patients must have evidence of mental illness that demonstrably affects their judgment about the matter at hand. Neither mental illness nor disturbed judgment alone is sufficient to prove incompetence. Patients with depression, dementia, or even schizophrenia may have adequate decision-making capacity to take responsibility for medical, financial, or other personal decisions. However, poor judgment alone is not adequate for a legal determination of incompetence. Neurosis, character flaws, and situational upset generally do not qualify as reasons to excuse persons from, or deprive them of, responsibility for their choices.

To demonstrate incompetence, then, one must show that mental illness has disrupted a person's judgment about a particular decision or set of decisions to the point where he or she cannot have, and no longer should have, that decision-making responsibility. What type of criteria and tests can be applied to make this determination?

Alan Buchanan and Daniel Brock have suggested three fundamental attributes necessary for adequate decision making: (1) understanding and communication, (2) reasoning and deliberation, and (3) a stable set of values (Buchanan). "Understanding" includes the abilities "to receive, process and make available for use the information relevant to particular decisions." "Relevant" means the information that is necessary for making a specific decision—that is, recommended treatment, alternative treatments (including no treatment at all), and the benefits and burdens of each alternative. Patients must also be able to communicate their questions, concerns, and decisions. Paul Appelbaum and Thomas Grisso argue that communications must be stable "long enough for them to be implemented."

The ability to reason and deliberate requires the patient to understand the consequences of making certain choices in terms of how they further one's good or promote one's values. It also includes some ability to use probabilistic reasoning and to understand the implications of current decisions for future outcomes (Appelbaum and Grisso). While rational thinking is an important consideration, few decisions in life are entirely rational. Appelbaum and Grisso note that "Rational manipulation involves the ability to reach conclusions that are logically consistent with the starting premises. . . . Assessing the relevant capacities requires examining the patient's chain of reasoning."

Finally, patients must have a stable set of values and a notion of well-being that is minimally consistent and stable. That is, they must have a sense of the good that is authentic to them and against which they can judge the outcomes of their decisions.

There is no unique or consistent correspondence between various organic or psychological states and specific loss of these fundamental attributes. For example, dementia might disrupt the ability to retain relevant information, but delirium or severe anxiety also could produce such a deficit. One must remember that each of the attributes necessary for decision making—the ability to understand and communicate, the ability to reason, and a stable set of values—is most often partially, rather than completely, compromised. This leaves the evaluator in the position of making a weighty decision as to whether the compromise is sufficient to declare the patient incompetent.

There are, however, some objective guidelines for making this judgment. First, a caveat is in order. Because competency is such a multidimensional concept and because the tests for measuring it vary according to the circumstances of the case, there is no single, correct test. No specific psychometric or clinical tests exist to operationalize the determination of competency. Tests such as the Mini-Mental State Exam, which attempt to quantify cognitive ability, and more general tests, such as the comprehensive mental status examination, do not in themselves provide the answer. A low score on a quantitative test or deficits detected on clinical examination (e.g., loose associations, memory deficits, and pressured speech) will certainly raise suspicions about competency. The key question remains, however, Do these deficits impair the patient's capacity enough that the authority to make decisions should be assigned to someone else? Various tests for evaluating competency have been suggested in the literature.

Buchanan and Brock identify three tests of competence that are "more or less stringent" and "strike different balances between the values of patient well-being and self-determination."

1. The first test is that the patient is merely able to express a preference. This is a minimal standard and leaves unexamined the patient's capacities for understanding, reasoning, and whether or not the decision conforms with the patient's own values.
2. A somewhat more stringent test relies on the outcome of patients' decisions—that is, patients are competent if their decisions seem reasonable to others. Although such a standard can often be expected to protect patient well-being, it does so in a manner that may not, in fact, reflect the values of the patient. It also makes inferences about patients' ability to understand and deliberate about their choices, inferences that may be mistaken. Therefore, this standard may fail to respect patient self-determination and, consequently, well-being.
3. The most stringent standard examines the process of reasoning that precedes and results in the specific decision in question. Of the three tests, the process test alone makes an attempt to evaluate decision-making attributes directly. Here, one examines the actual ability to understand, reason, and hold a stable set of values.

Should the standard for determining competence be the same in all cases, or should it vary with each decision and clinical context? With few exceptions (Culver and Gert) most people reject the notion of one standard, endorsing instead a sliding scale that demands a more stringent standard when patients' choices seem to threaten their well-being. (Roth et al.). This decision-relative approach is the one most often used in the clinical setting, and reflects health professionals' and society's effort to reach an acceptable compromise when patients' decisions seem to threaten their well-being. When patients agree to recommendations for treatment that have an excellent chance of restoring health and without which they are likely to die, their competence is rarely called into question. For example, if a mildly demented male patient were to agree to lifesaving but relatively risk-free surgery for acute appendicitis, it is unlikely that his physicians would call in a psychiatrist to examine the reasoning behind his decision more deeply. On the other hand, if the same patient refused the surgery, the test for competency would likely become more stringent.

Similarly, when patients refuse treatments that are unlikely to benefit them and carry great risks (e.g., a highly invasive experimental therapy), their competence will rarely be challenged. Under these circumstances it is the decision to accept the risky treatment that will be subjected to greater scrutiny.

Who should evaluate competency?

Although competency is at root a legal determination, physicians routinely make competency judgments in the acute care setting. While these determinations could theoretically be challenged in court retrospectively, they rarely are. For non-urgent competency evaluations, such as competency of a person for nursing home placement, a court hearing must be held and a formal guardian appointed. Physicians' opinions are rarely challenged in these more formal legal settings. What type of physician should make competency evaluations? The answer is relative to the situation. Psychiatrists and clinical psychologists are the most trained to recognize and treat mental illness. Many of these specialists are experienced in competency evaluations. However, if a patient is comatose, severely demented, or wildly psychotic, and the situation is urgent, an expert opinion may be superfluous; the competency de-

termination may be readily handled by the primary physician.

STUART YOUNGER, M.D.

See also ADVANCE DIRECTIVES FOR HEALTH CARE; ASSESSMENT; AUTONOMY; MENTAL STATUS EXAMINATION.

BIBLIOGRAPHY

APPELBAUM, P. S., and GRISSO, T. "Assessing Patients' Capacities to Consent to Treatment." *New England Journal of Medicine* 319 (1988): 1635–1638.

APPELBAUM, P. S., and ROTH, L. H. "Clinical Issues in the Assessment of Competency." *American Journal of Psychiatry* 138 (1981): 1462–1467.

BUCHANAN, A. E., and BROCK, D., W. *Deciding for Others: The Ethics of Surrogate Decision Making*. Cambridge, U.K.: Cambridge University Press, 1989.

CULVER, C. M., and GERT, B. "The Inadequacy of Incompetence." *The Millbank Quarterly* 68 (1990): 619–643.

DRANE, J. F. L. "The Many Faces of Competency." *The Hastings Center Report* 15 (1985): 17–21.

MEISEL, A.; ROTH, L. H.; and LIDZ, C. W. "Toward a Model of the Legal Doctrine of Informed Consent." *American Journal of Psychiatry* 134 (1977): 285–289.

ROTH, L. H.; MEISEL, A.; and LIDZ, C. W. "Tests of Competency to Consent to Treatment." *American Journal of Psychiatry* 134 (1977): 279–284.

YOUNGNER, S. J. "Competence to Refuse Life-Sustaining Treatment." *In End of Life Decisions: A Psychosocial Perspective*. Edited by M. D. Steinberg and S. J. Youngner. Washington D.C.: American Psychiatric Press, 1998. Pages 19–54.

COMPRESSION OF MORBIDITY

As people live longer, some fear that they will spend additional years in poor health, disabled, and demented. In contrast, the compression of morbidity hypothesis (1980) posits that people can have both a longer life and a healthier old age. To do so, it is necessary to postpone the onset of morbidity (e.g., disability), through healthy preventive practices, more rapidly than death is postponed.

Figure 1

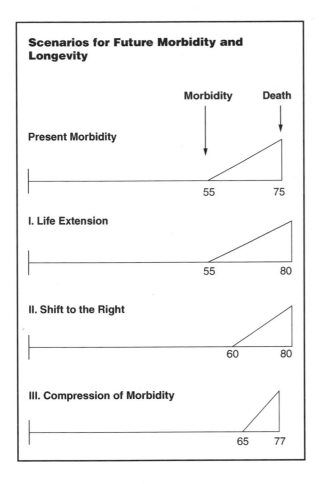

SOURCE: Author

Figure 1 depicts three future scenarios for morbidity and longevity. At present, disability begins to be detectable around age fifty-five in the average individual, and death occurs, on average, a bit after seventy-five years of age. Most disability occurs between these points, and the level of disability increases with time, as shown by the areas of the triangles. At some future time there could be (I) extended life expectancy but no change in the time of first disability. If that would be the case, each typical life would have more morbidity than at present. This scenario has been termed the "failure of success." Or there could be (II) extended life expectancy and postponed morbidity by about the same amount, so that everything happens the same but a bit later. Or there could be (III) more emphasis on postponing disease than on increasing life expectancy, thereby compressing morbidity between a later age of onset and a more slowly rising age at

death. Morbidity and disability then would decrease for the typical person, and medical care costs might decline as well, providing relief for cost pressures on Medicare.

Data support the view that compression of morbidity is occurring, and can be made to occur more rapidly. First, life expectancy at advanced ages has plateaued rather than having increased markedly, as previously predicted. In the United States the life expectancy of women at age sixty-five, for example, has increased only 0.7 years since the 1980s. Second, epidemiologic studies have documented the ability to postpone the onset of disability by eight years through exercise, weight control, and not smoking. Over the period from 1982 to 1999, disability rates in the United States decreased at 2 percent per year while mortality rates declined only 1 percent per year. Third, randomized trials of health enhancement programs in seniors have shown reductions in health risks and medical care costs of 10 to 20 percent.

There are three stages in developing documentary evidence to support health policies directed at improving senior health: (1) a theoretical framework, as represented by the compression of morbidity hypothesis; (2) the epidemiologic data to establish proof of the concept; (3) randomized trials to establish the ability to intervene successfully. These data are now abundant.

The paradigm of a long, healthy life with a relatively rapid terminal decline represents an attainable ideal. Health policies must be directed at modifying those health risks which precede and cause morbidity if this ideal is to be approached for a population.

JAMES F. FRIES, M.D.

See also FRAILTY; LIFE SPAN; OLDEST OLD.

BIBLIOGRAPHY

FRIES, J. F. "Aging, Natural Death, and the Compression of Morbidity." *New England Journal of Medicine* 303, no. 3 (1980): 130–135.

FRIES, J. F.; KOOP, C. E.; SOKOLOV, J.; BEADLE, C.E.; and WRIGHT, D. "Beyond Health Promotion: Reducing Need and Demand for Medical Care." *Health Affairs* 17, no. 2 (1998): 70–84.

GRUENBERG, E. M. "The Failure of Success." *Milbank Memorial Fund Quarterly: Health and Society* 55, no. 1 (1977): 3–24.

Rolland Digre (right) delivers a meal to homebound Dolly Bogen in May 2001 in Hendricks, Minnesota. The local Meals on Wheels program in Hendricks delivers quality meals to to the city's growing senior citizen population. (AP/Wide World photo.)

MANTON, K. G., and GU, XI LIANG. "Changes in the Prevalence of Chronic Disability in the United States Black and Nonblack Population Above Age 65 from 1982 to 1999." *Proceedings of the National Academy of Sciences* 98 (2001): 6354–6359.

VITA, A. J.; TERRY, R. B.; HUBERT, H. B.; and FRIES, J. F. "Aging, Health Risks, and Cumulative Disability." *New England Journal of Medicine* 338, no. 15 (1998): 1035–1041.

CONGREGATE AND HOME-DELIVERED MEALS

The Nutrition Program for the Elderly (NPE), part of the Older Americans Act (OAA) grants for state and community programs on aging, helps ensure a healthy, well-balanced diet for older Americans. Through this program, seniors who might otherwise be isolated and lonely, or who cannot afford to buy or prepare meals for themselves, do not have to go without food. They can eat a meal and socialize with their friends in a neighborhood setting, or they can have nutritious meals delivered to their home, often by a volunteer.

The NPE is administered by the Administration on Aging of the U.S. Department of Health and Human Service through the national network of state and area agencies on aging. The U.S. Department of Agriculture (USDA) Food and Nutrition Service contributes cash and commodity foods to support the NPE.

Congregate and home-delivered meals are available to seniors free of charge, though participants are encouraged to contribute toward their costs. Any senior who is at least age sixty is eligible for the program, and so are spouses, regardless of age. Seniors do not have to meet any income test or other requirements to receive meals under the program.

Community nutrition programs are especially important for the very old, people living alone, people at or near the poverty line, minorities, and people with failing health or physical or mental impairments. NPE therefore tries to locate meal sites where vulnerable and at-risk frail older persons live.

During the 1960s senior citizen advocates began to push for a national program to protect the nutritional health of seniors. Their advocacy was spurred, in part, by a 1965 USDA nutrition study that attracted attention with its finding that 95 million Americans did not consume an adequate diet, including 6 to 8 million older persons. In response, Congress appropriated $2 million in 1968 for nutrition demonstrations and research. These groundbreaking demonstrations led to the creation of community nutrition programs for the elderly. The federal legislation authorizing the NPE was sponsored by Senator Edward M. Kennedy and signed into law March 1972 by President Richard M. Nixon.

For the fiscal year 2000, Congress appropriated $512 million for the NPE. The federal government uses a population-based formula to apportion NPE funds to states. State Units on Aging transfer the funds to Area Agencies on Aging (AAA), which in turn contract with community nutrition providers. In some cases, the AAAs also provide services themselves. Community nutrition programs have various other sources of funding that include state and local government, in-kind contributions, private donations, and voluntary contributions from participants. In 1997 these additional resources totaled $621 million.

A similar nutrition program for Native American elders is authorized by Title VI of the OAA. The Administration on Aging awards funds directly to federally recognized Indian tribal organizations and nonprofit private organizations serving Native Hawaiians. Indian tribal organizations may select an age below sixty for defining an "older" person for their tribes.

Good nutrition and healthy aging

Good nutritional health is vital to healthy aging, and a proper diet provides the energy and nutrients the body and mind need. Experts agree that the risk for malnutrition is high among specific groups of elder Americans, especially those with inadequate income to purchase food, those who are isolated, and those who suffer from illness, disease, and other conditions affecting independence.

The dangers of poor nutrition have been well documented. Risks include: decreased life span, premature nursing home admission, increased disease incidence and chronic disability, increased hospitalization, and longer hospital stays. In addition to severe health problems, seniors who are malnourished are more likely to need home care or to be placed in an institution.

Community nutrition programs are a first line defense against hunger and can change older people's lives. The following list (Nutrition Screening Initiative; *Older Americans 2000*) shows why:

- Four out of five older adults have chronic diseases that are affected by diet.
- Only 13 percent of older adults eat the minimum amount of fruits and vegetables they need.
- Older persons living in poverty are nearly twice as likely to have a poor diet (21 percent) as those at or above the poverty level (11 percent).
- One of every five older people has trouble walking, shopping, and/or buying and cooking food, especially as they get older.

Warning signs of poor nutritional health

The Nutrition Screening Initiative, a multifaceted national health initiative led by the American Academy of Family Physicians, the American Dietetic Association, and the National Council on the Aging, has developed a screening tool to identify signs of malnutrition in older adults. Some of the risk factors are the following:

- Eating too little or too much
- Tooth or mouth problems that make it hard to eat
- Poverty (not enough money to buy food)
- Eating meals alone (social isolation)
- Taking three or more different prescription or over-the-counter drugs a day
- Involuntary weight loss/gain (ten pounds in the last six months)
- Alcohol abuse (three or more drinks almost every day)
- Acute/chronic illness or recent hospitalization

Help in staying healthy

Across the country, in neighborhoods small and large, community nutrition programs serve over 1 million meals a day to seniors at least once a day, five or more days a week. In 1997, more than 116 million meals were served to about 2 million older persons in congregate settings and over 123 million meals were served to about 890,000 homebound older persons.

Congregate meals. Congregate meal sites are located in senior centers, senior housing projects, schools, churches, and other community settings. Community nutrition programs also deliver supportive services other than a meal, including nutrition and health screening, and nutrition education. When possible, transportation is offered to and from meal sites for those who need it. Many meal sites have outreach programs and linkages with other community agencies to locate hard-to-reach, isolated, or underserved older people. As a result, the NPE helps provide access to many other health, housing, and social services.

The costs of a congregate meal in 1997 averaged $4.60. While many elders drop in at community meal sites quite frequently (60 percent usually participate four or five days a week), others participate only occasionally.

Home-delivered meals. The first Meals on Wheels program was established in 1954, in Philadelphia. Today, home-delivered meals are available throughout the country. They are provided by congregate meal sites, affiliated and nonaffiliated food service establishments, and other community organizations.

In 1997, the cost of preparing a home-delivered meal averaged $3.65. The use of volunteers to deliver the meals and provide friendly visiting helps keep the costs low. Persons may be homebound because of illness, disability, or isolation. Some homebound elders may need meals delivered for only a short while, following a hospital stay. People with more extensive needs may require home-delivered meals in addition to other community-based long-term care and social support services. For these people, home delivery of meals is crucial to their ability to remain independent.

Where to go for more information

To learn more about community nutrition programs, contact the local office on aging, go to www.aoa.gov, or call (in the United States) the Eldercare Locator at 800-677-1116. More information about nutrition and aging can be obtained from the organizations listed below.

Food and Nutrition Information Center, Room 304, National Agriculture Library Building, U.S. Department of Agriculture, Beltsville, MD 20705-2351; Tel (301) 504-5719; Fax (301) 504-6409; E-mail fnic@nalusda.gov; Web site www.nalusda.gov/fnic/ The Food

and Nutrition Information Center provides information to professionals and the general public on human nutrition, food service management, and food technology.

Meals on Wheels Association of America (formerly the National Association of Meal Programs), 1414 Prince Street, Suite 202, Alexandria, VA 22314; Tel. (703) 548-5558; Fax (703) 548-8024; E-mail mowaa@ tbg.dgsys.com; association's web site is at www.projectmeal.org MOWAA is the oldest trade association in the United States for nutrition services providers. It offers training and technical assistance to those who plan and conduct congregate and home-delivered meal programs.

National Association of Nutrition and Aging Services Programs, P.O. Box 9007, Grand Rapids, MI 49509-0007; Tel. (616) 531-9909 or (800) 999-6262; Fax 616-531-3103; E-mail NANASP@mindspring.com. NANASP is a membership and advocacy organization for professionals working in or interested in the fields of aging, community-based services, and nutrition and the elderly.

National Policy and Resource Center on Nutrition and Aging, Department of Dietetics and Nutrition, Florida International University, University Park, OE200, Miami, FL 33199; Tel (305) 348-1517; Fax (305) 348-1518; TTY (800) 955-8771; E-mail nutrelder@ solix.fiu.edu; Web site www.fiu.edu The National Policy and Resource Center on Nutrition and Aging works with the Administration on Aging to improve the nutritional status of older Americans.

The Nutrition Screening Initiative, 1010 Wisconsin Avenue, NW, Suite 800, Washington, DC 20007. E-mail nsi@gmmb.com; Web site www.aafp.org/nsi/index.html

Robert C. Ficke
Susan Coombs Ficke

See also Area Agency on Aging: State Unit on Aging; Malnutrition; Nutrition Program for the Elderly (NPE); Older Americans Act; Senior Centers; Social Services.

BIBLIOGRAPHY

Administration on Aging. *Administration on Aging State Program Report: A Summary of State and Community Programs Under Title III of the Older Americans Act of 1965, as Amended, Federal Fiscal Year 1997.* Washington, D.C.: Administration on Aging. U.S. Department of Health and Human Services, 2000.

CODISPOTI, C. L., and BARTLETT, B. J.. *Food and Nutrition for Life: Malnutrition and Older Americans. Report by the Assistant Secretary for Aging, Administration on Aging, Department of Health and Human Services.* Washington D.C.: 1994.

Nutrition Screening Initiative. *Keeping Older Americans Healthy at Home: Guidelines for Nutrition Programs in Health Care.* Washington, D.C.: Greer, Margolis, Mitchell, Burns & Associates, 1996.

Older Americans 2000: Key Indicators of Well-Being, Hyattsville Md.: Federal Interagency Forum on Aging-Related Statistics, 2000.

PONZA, M.; OHLS, J. C.; and MILLEN, B. E. *Serving Elders at Risk. The Older Americans Act Nutrition Programs: National Evaluation of the Elderly Nutrition Program, 1993–1995*, 3 vols. Princeton, N.J.: Mathematica Policy Research, 1996.

CONGREGATE HOUSING

The term *congregate housing* has both generic and specific meanings. Generically, it refers to multiplex-unit, usually planned, supportive housing for older people (and younger people with disabilities) who need or want assistance with daily activities. Seen as a more independent option than an assisted living or skilled nursing facility, congregate housing typically provides services such as housekeeping, meal preparation, and personal care, and frequently offers the opportunity for a congregate meal. Settings vary, however. For example, the site may have few or many units. It may be freestanding or part of a larger complex. Units may be fully equipped apartments or single rooms. Property management may be separate from or linked to services management. Services may be available to all residents or to a subset. Costs for housing or services, or both, may be publicly subsidized or require a fee.

In its more specific form, the term refers to certain federal- and state-funded programs for people with low incomes and significant needs for assistance with daily activities. These programs are typically located in rent-subsidized housing, follow specific procedures for assessing residents' needs and delivering or arranging services, and limit residents' costs (usually capped at 30 percent of income for rent and 20 percent for services).

This entry discusses supportive housing generally, then highlights the federal Congregate

Housing Services Program (CHSP). The entry focuses on residential options for people with low incomes—because their needs are greatest and their options most limited. However, it should be noted that middle-income older people have few supportive housing options. They have too many resources to qualify for publicly subsidized programs, and too few to afford the $2500-plus per month costs of the more upscale supportive housing options (many of which could be described as assisted living facilities or retirement communities). Some private-pay retirement homes, often owned and operated by municipalities or nonprofit organizations, are relatively affordable, with monthly costs averaging $900 to $1500 for rent and a supportive services package that usually includes meals and housekeeping. Since nearly three-quarters of older people have incomes under $32,000 per year, even these "affordable" options are too expensive for many.

Why supportive housing?

Supportive housing for people with low incomes is one reasonable response to the following intertwined factors (among others):

- The number of people who need assistance with daily activities is increasing. The population is aging and younger people with disabilities are living to older ages. In addition, long hospital stays are increasingly discouraged.
- People strongly prefer to live in community rather than institutional settings.
- Policymakers and individuals are interested in cost-effectiveness and flexibility. Settings with large numbers of older residents, such as senior housing, offer unique service delivery opportunities through service "clustering." Clustering can reduce service costs, improve efficiency, and increase flexibility by reducing the number of workers on-site and the minimum hours workers must spend with one person.

Stephen Golant, in his excellent report *The Casera Project: Creating Affordable and Supportive Elder Renter Accommodations*, put it this way: "Not considering the elder-occupied rent-subsidized facility as a major service delivery target is a badly missed opportunity" (p. 37).

At its best, supportive housing offers accessible environments, well-functioning communities, social support, choices, control, access to flexible, cost-effective health care and supportive services, and social activities. Many observers believe that the setting, with its flexibility and balance between support and challenge, promotes health and functional independence, prevents or slows the progress of disability, prevents or tempers accidents, helps residents adhere to medical regimens, and responds creatively and effectively to diversity (the older population is, on almost any measure, more diverse than any other age group).

Although most older Americans live in single-family housing, about 12 percent—nearly four million—live in multiple-unit housing developments. About twenty thousand of these developments are federally subsidized and built specifically for older people. Many thousands more have been built with federal and state assistance. As residents age in place, these developments and community-based service providers have increasingly responded to residents' service needs. Often residents, families, professionals, and property managers arrange services as best they can (a "patchwork" approach). A more organized and effective strategy is on-site service coordination (also known as "resident service coordination" or "resource coordination").

The goal of service coordinators is to improve residents' quality of life and delay or avoid institutionalization by helping residents to obtain services they need and want. Coordinators play multiple roles, including service broker, community builder, educator, advocate, quality monitor, mediator, investigator, and counselor. Before 1990 the Department of Housing and Urban Development (HUD) and others in the housing realm prohibited service-related activity. Today, thousands of managers and residents depend on coordinators, who are often considered the key to successful supportive housing. The American Association of Service Coordinators was founded in 1999. Many states have active coordinators' associations.

The Federal Congregate Housing Services Program

HUD administers the Congregate Housing Services Program (CHSP). Designed to assist older people and younger people with disabilities to live independently in their own apartments, the CHSP provides housing combined with professional service coordination and supportive services, such as housekeeping, personal care, congregate meals, and transportation. It aims to encourage maximum resident independence in a home environment, improve management's ability to assess eligible residents' service needs, and ensure delivery of needed services.

The CHSP has about one hundred sites across the United States. Some are from the original CHSP, authorized in 1978; the rest have been funded since a new version was authorized in 1990. (The new version mainly increases the amount of financial support required from the housing sponsor and community.) No new CHSP sites have been funded since 1995. CHSP participants pay 30 percent of their (adjusted) income in rent and up to 20 percent for services. HUD, state home- and community-based services programs, Medicaid, and donations cover the remaining costs.

Several studies have documented the original CHSP's overall effectiveness. The following description of the Portland, Oregon, CHSP may help illustrate the model. Four Housing Authority of Portland (HAP) apartment complexes have thirty CHSP slots each, representing about 30 percent of their total population. Each complex has an on-site service's coordinator who works with participants, CHSP staff, and local service providers to arrange and monitor services, recruit and oversee volunteers, and help participants strengthen informal supports. CHSP also employs homemakers and meal service staff. The Professional Assessment Committee, including health and social service professionals, consults with the coordinator on assessment, care planning, and troubleshooting.

Portland CHSP participants are encouraged and assisted to take an active role in advocating and caring for themselves. The program is voluntary, and participants decide what services they will use. Available services include on-site daily meals in a group setting, assistance with housekeeping and personal care, transportation, health and wellness promotion, Senior Companions, affordable foot care clinics, and daytime check-ins by CHSP staff. Trained HAP staff, contracted home health agencies, a nearby nursing school, and many volunteers provide services. Since service coordinators assign service providers to an entire site, workers often shop and do laundry for more than one person at a time, thus keeping costs low.

The Portland CHSP serves five main types of residents: frail older people who live in the

CHSP building, at-risk older people from outside the CHSP complexes, deinstitutionalized people, younger people with disabilities, and people with temporary disabilities. Participants generally must be able to be on their own at night and for much of the day, and to be independent in transferring (moving from one position to another [e.g., from wheelchair to bed]) and toileting. The CHSP can often support a person who can transfer but is unstable for some tasks, or who has a temporarily higher level of need.

Looking to the future

Although there has been an increase in supportive housing innovations and initiatives since the late 1980s, supportive housing is still not readily available, and many complexes have long waiting lists. Golant, in *The Casera Project*, recommends several strategies to expand the availability and quality of supportive housing (pages 33–36), including the following:

- Increased funding for service coordinators
- Incentives for complexes to provide services
- Strengthened partnerships among state agencies, service providers, housing complexes, and others
- Assistance to property managers
- Continued research.

Other strategies include the following:

- Applying the lessons learned from planned supportive housing—especially in terms of service coordination, service delivery, and balancing support and challenge—to buildings or neighborhoods with disproportionate numbers of older people (sometimes known as naturally occurring retirement communities.
- Developing more options for middle-income older people, such as supportive cooperative housing.

SUSAN C. LANSPERY

See also CONTINUING CARE RETIREMENT COMMUNITIES; GOVERNMENT ASSISTED HOUSING; HOUSING.

BIBLIOGRAPHY

GOLANT, S. M. *Housing America's Elderly: Many Possibilities, Few Choices.* Newbury Park, Calif.: Sage, 1992.

GOLANT, S. M. *The Casera Project: Creating Affordable and Supportive Elder Renter Accommodations.* Gainesville: University of Florida, 1999.

HEUMANN, L. F. "A Cost Comparison of Congregate Housing and Long-Term Care Facilities for Elderly Residents with Comparable Support Needs in 1985 and 1990." In *Congregate Housing for the Elderly: Theoretical, Policy, and Programmatic Perspectives.* Edited by Lenard W. Kaye and Abraham Monk. Binghamton N.Y.: Haworth Press, 1991. Pages 75–98.

HOLLAND, J.; GANZ, L.; HIGGINS, P.; and ANTONELLI, K. "Service Coordinators in Senior Housing: An Exploration of an Emerging Role in Long-Term Care." *Journal of Case Management* 4, no. 3, (Fall 1995): 25–29.

MILBANK MEMORIAL FUND, in cooperation with the American Association of Homes and Services for the Aging. *Linking Housing and Health Services for Older Persons.* New York: MMF, 1997.

PYNOOS, J. "Supportive Housing for the Elderly: Past, Present, and Future." *The Public Policy and Aging Report* 8, no. 2 (Spring 1997): 14–15.

SCHULMAN, A. "Service Coordination: Program Development and Initial Findings." *Journal of Long-Term Home Health Care* 15, no. 2, (Spring 1996): 5–12.

U.S. DEPARTMENT OF HOUSING AND URBAN DEVELOPMENT. *Evaluation of the Service Coordinator Program.* 2 vols. HUD-1614-PDC. Washington, D.C.: Office of Policy Development and Research, HUD, 1996.

CONSTIPATION

Constipation is a very common presenting symptom in elderly people. There are two reasons for this: (1) bowel function and defecation become less satisfactory with advancing years, since emptying may be incomplete and the presence of a small residue of feces may cause continuing discomfort; and (2) uncertainty as to what constitutes a normal bowel pattern may create anxieties about disease or other aspects of aging. Physicians often find that if they ask an elderly patient if he or she suffers from constipation, the answer will be "yes," even if the number of motions a week is within the normal range.

By constipation, patients may mean one of several things:

- bowel motions are less frequent than they used to be
- bowel motions are less frequent than they think that they ought to be

Figure 1
Diagram of the colon. a. Cecum—junction between small and large bowel, also the appendix. b. Ascending colon. c. Transverse colon. d. Descending colon. e. Sigmoid colon. f. Rectum. g. Anus.

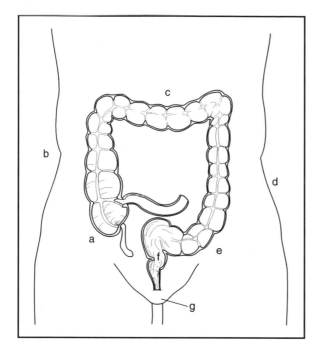

SOURCE: Author

fluid, flatus, and feces, thus allowing a sampling of contents if the rectum is suddenly distended—an important social safeguard. The main functions of the colon are storage of feces and reabsorption of water and some electrolytes. The colon looks like a series of small bladders joined together to form a wide tube. Circular bands of muscle serve to move the contents back and forth between the bladder-like segments (known as shuttling motility) which promotes absorption, and a number of longitudinal muscle bands the whole length of the colon cause onward movement of feces into the rectum (mass peristalsis). This movement occurs several times a day, prompted particularly by food entering the stomach and by a person moving about. Thus, it occurs particularly after breakfast and is less likely to occur in immobile people (e.g., those who are bedridden).

Filling, and thus distention, of the rectum produces the desire to void, which may be responded to or, if inconvenient, may be voluntarily suppressed and the feces may then be returned to the colon. This effect of food entering the stomach is called the gastrocolic reflex. This used to be regarded as a neural reflex via the spinal cord and colonic nerves, but is now regarded as a chemical reaction to substances secreted by the stomach as it is filled with food.

Continence mechanisms

There are several anatomical arrangements that prevent feces spilling out of the rectum at inappropriate times. The anal canal is surrounded by two circular muscle bands, known as the sphincter muscles. One of these (the internal anal sphincter) is not under voluntary control, but maintains constant contraction except when bowel emptying is occurring. The external anal sphincter can be contracted voluntarily for a very short time to prevent an unwanted catastrophe. It also contracts automatically when abdominal pressure is suddenly raised (as in coughing or sneezing) A third continence mechanism is the anorectal angle, maintained at less than 90 degrees by a sling-like muscle, the puborectalis (see Figure 2), which arises from the back of the pubic bone and divides into two parts to encircle the anorectal junction—the two parts then fusing together posteriorly. Fecal incontinence may occur if the anal sphincters are damaged (e.g., in childbirth) or if the anorectal angle is maintained at more than 90 degrees—as by a constipating mass

- bowel motions are hard and more difficult to pass

The first of these is important and requires some investigation. The second is problematical, since the normal range of frequency of defecation varies between three times daily and twice weekly. In general, this does not change with aging, though it may increase. The third is an effect of constipation itself.

Anatomy and physiology

The colon, or large bowel, is configured like an inverted U and comprises three parts: the ascending colon, starting from the cecum where it is connected to the small bowel; the transverse colon; and the descending colon, which ends in an S shaped part known as the sigmoid colon (see Figure 1). The sigmoid connects to the rectum, which terminates in the anus.

The upper end of the anal canal contains nerve endings, which can distinguish between

Figure 2
The ano-rectal angle maintained by the sling effect of the pubo-coxygeus muscle.

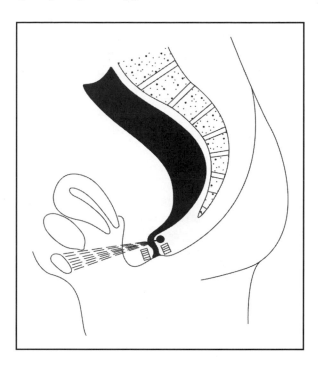

Figure 3
Loss of ano-rectal angle due to constipating mass of feces in the rectum.

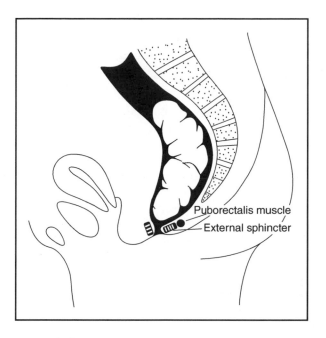

of feces lying in the rectum (see Figure 3). This may also impair awareness of the nature of rectal contents, particularly in confused elderly persons, and feces may be expelled when the individual simply attempts to pass flatus (gas).

Causes of constipation

Constipation may be a symptom of disease in the lower bowel, most commonly irritable colon or diverticular disease. Cancer is also a possibility, though it is likely to be of recent onset and associated with other symptoms such as diarrhea or bleeding. Constipation is occasionally due to a lack of coordination between an attempt to empty the bowel and the contracted sphincter muscles and the puborectalis, which fail to relax appropriately. Another possible cause is trauma in the anal canal—such as a fissure or painful hemorrhoids—which can result in an individual avoiding defecation. Management of all these conditions requires medical investigation and appropriate treatment.

Constipation may also be caused by a number of medications that increase shuttling motili-ty. These include morphine and its derivatives, especially codeine, or drugs that prevent mass peristalsis, such as other antidiarrhea drugs. The character of the diet (especially if it becomes low in bulky and fibrous foods such as vegetables) may cause constipation. Other causes include a change of living conditions (e.g., moving into a communal living environment), a toilet that is not easily accessible, and a loss of the ability to walk far, and constipation may be associated with a number of general diseases such as depression, hypothyroidism, and diabetes.

The most common cause of constipation, however, is called *dyschezia*, or *ideopathic constipation* (*ideopathic* means that the cause is unknown). This condition occurs at all ages and is not necessarily associated with aging. Various life-long and lifestyle features may be responsible, including inappropriate toilet training or possible abuse in childhood; deliberate suppression of defecation over a long period in situations that are perceived as embarrassing; lack of exercise; a diet low in fiber; or overuse of laxatives. Counseling and explanation may be sufficient in managing dyschezia. Occasionally, keeping a diary of bowel motions, measuring transit time (e.g., time for a number of swallowed markers to appear in the feces), and the exclusion of diseases mentioned above are required. Correction of diet and exercise are important, and laxatives may be used with discretion (see below).

Laxatives, suppositories and enemas

There are three main types of laxatives. One consists of the so-called stimulant or irritant laxatives, which promote mass peristalsis. These include cascara, senna, bisacodyl, phenolpthalein, docusate, and picosulphate. The second group promote an outpouring of fluid from the bowel washing out the fecal mass; these are generally known as osmotic laxatives. They include magnesium sulfate, magnesium hydroxide, and lactulose (whose main ingredient is a semisynthetic disaccharide). Either of these types may cause colic or fecal incontinence.

The third type—bulk laxatives—include substances that swell when mixed with water. They include ispaghula, sterculia, methyl cellulose, and bran. They are generally available in powder form and taken in water, and may need to be taken for a few days before becoming effective.

Other miscellaneous laxatives include mineral oil and docusate sodium. The former should be avoided in elderly people because of its possible side effects, which include anal leakage, absorption of fat-soluble vitamins (especially vitamin D, which if long continued may diminish bone density (see osteo malacra), and inhalation pneumonia. Docusate sodium, which is really a stool softener, is useful to prevent the accumulation of hard fecal masses.

Finally, suppositories or enemas may be used, particularly where a fairly speedy result is desired, though few people have difficulty in retaining them. Suppositories may increase bulk in the rectum by their hygroscopic, or osmotic, effect (e.g., glycerin), or they may stimulate mass peristalsis (e.g., bisacodyl). Prepacked enemas generally contain hypertonic phosphates which have a hygroscopic effect.

JOHN BROCKLEHURST

See also URINARY INCONTINENCE.

BIBLIOGRAPHY

BARRETT, J. A. *Fecal Incontinence and Related Problems in the Older Adult*. London: Edward Arnold, 1993.

BROCKLEHURST, J. C. "Constipation and Fecal Incontinence in Old Age." In *Brocklehurst's Textbook of Geriatric Medicine and Gerontology*, 5th ed. Edited by R. Tallis, H. Fillit, and J. Brocklehurst. Edinburgh: Churchill Livingstone, 1998. Pages 1329–1342.

KAMM, M. A., and LENNARD JONES, J. E. *Constipation*. Petersfield, U.K.: Wrightson Biomedical Publishing. 1994.

CONSUMER DIRECTED CARE

According to the definition developed by the National Institute on Consumer-Directed Long-Term Services, consumer direction of long-term care services, or consumer-directed care, is both a philosophy and a practice model for home care. As a philosophy, it emphasizes consumer choice and control, recognizing that service recipients themselves are the ones who best know their needs and preferences and, as such, should have primary authority and responsibility for making decisions about those services. In practice, consumer direction means that consumers make concrete choices about their care and ultimately manage the delivery of their services to the extent that they are willing and able to do so.

While people ordinarily associate consumer direction with hiring and firing workers, there is more to it than that. It also involves consumers: having good information about the service network in order to make informed decisions; being involved in the care planning process; selecting home care agencies and workers; training workers; and monitoring the quality of services by providing performance feedback to workers and provider agencies (Eustis and Fischer). However, with the additional information and authority over services also comes increased responsibility for consumers to understand their service needs and preferences and to manage the delivery of their care.

In addition to increased consumer control over service management, consumer-directed care also often allows for more flexibility in terms of who delivers the services. Many consumer-directed care programs offer consumers the opportunity to hire those who are most familiar to them—family members, friends, and neighbors—to serve as independent (nonagency) providers of home care services.

Which services do consumers direct?

The term *personal assistance services* is often used by younger adults with disabilities to describe what is known in the field of aging services as home care. These refer to "tasks. . .that individuals would normally do for themselves if they did not have a disability" (Litvak, Zukas, and Heumanm).

Specifically, these tasks relate to personal care/activities of daily living (i.e., bathing, dressing, toileting, mobility, and transfer), instrumental activities of daily living (i.e., housekeeping, chore services, laundry, meal preparation, menu planning, transportation, and money management), communication (i.e., reader services for those with visual impairments and interpreter services for those with hearing impairments), and paramedical services (i.e., administration of medication, injections, catheterization, and ventilator care). Also included may be home modifications, assistive devices and technologies, and care management. Depending on the program, some or all of these services may be directed by consumers.

What does service management involve?

Managing home care services involves many responsibilities. These include, but are not limited to: recruiting, screening, interviewing, hiring, scheduling, training, supervising, paying, withholding taxes, providing performance feedback to workers and, if necessary, firing workers. Other tasks that may be associated with service management include conflict resolution and self-advocacy. Many consumer-directed care programs allow consumers to select surrogates or authorized representatives such as family members or friends to handle these responsibilities on their behalf, and some programs provide support and assistance with these tasks for consumers (Flanagan and Green).

History of and trends toward consumer-directed care

The underpinnings of consumer-directed care can be found in the independent living movement that started in the 1970s, which was led by persons with disabilities who demanded their rights to live independently and participate fully in mainstream society. The idea behind this model is that persons with disabilities are hindered or impaired by barriers in their environment rather than by their physical or cognitive disabilities. One such barrier has been a lack of appropriate long-term care services mostly in the form of personal assistance services (Litvak, Zukas, and Heumann; Batavia, DeJong, and McKnew).

Consumer-directed care has been much slower in developing in the field of aging services, only gaining prominence during the 1990s. A 1996 survey of state administrators found 103 consumer-directed care programs throughout the United States (Lagoyda et al.). In some states (such as Oregon, California, Maine, and Wisconsin), these programs have been well-established parts of the long-term care system; however, in other states (such as Arkansas, New Jersey, and Ohio), these programs are relatively new or still under development.

In the movement toward increased consumer choice and control, disability communities (those with physical disabilities, cognitive and developmental disabilities, and psychiatric disabilities) have taken a much broader approach, emphasizing self-determination—individuals' overall control over their lives and ability to participate fully in society. However, in the aging community, the focus has been limited to consumer direction of long-term care services. And while in the disability communities consumers have led the movement toward self-determination and self-direction, in the field of aging services, the impetus toward consumer direction has come largely from professionals.

Within the field of home care in general, there has been much movement toward consumer direction. During the 1980s and 1990s the Medicaid Personal Care Services Benefit Option, which offers more flexibility for consumer-directed care than traditional Medicaid home and community-based services waiver programs, expanded greatly as a source of funding for personal assistance services. As of 2000, more than thirty states participated in this program. Typically, however, the home services programs that offer the most flexibility and choice in their consumer-directed care options rely on state funds due to the more restrictive rules under Medicaid (Scala and Mayberry).

The 1990s saw increased commitment on the part of the federal government to explore consumer-directed care as a service option. The long-term care proposal developed in 1992 by the Clinton Administration Task Force on

Health Care Reform included a consumer-directed option. With funding from the Administration on Aging and the Office of the Assistant Secretary for Planning and Evaluation, the National Council on the Aging, Inc., and the World Institute on Disability established the National Institute on Consumer-Directed Long-Term Services, which has helped to define the concept of consumer direction and that provides information and technical assistance to states about consumer-directed care. In addition, in the late 1990s, two major grant initiatives by the Robert Wood Johnson Foundation, the Cash and Counseling Demonstration Program (which is also supported by the Office of the Assistant Secretary for Planning and Evaluation) and the Independent Choices program, have examined consumer-directed care through various research and demonstration projects.

Barriers to consumer direction

There are several reasons why consumer-directed care has taken so long to develop in the field of aging services. First, the overarching goal of home care for older adults has been simply to keep seniors out of nursing homes, rather than to foster choice and self-determination. A second reason is the general paternalistic bias in long-term care toward the safety and protection of clients, as evidenced by current regulatory practices, which assumes that consumer autonomy—including the right to make poor choices—is of lesser importance (Scala and Mayberry).

However, underlying some of professionals' concerns about consumer-directed care are legitimate tensions between the balance of autonomy and risk for their clients. Most professionals generally respect consumers' desires and preferences for choice and autonomy; however, they also feel very real professional responsibility to assure their clients' well-being and quality of care as well as to protect their agencies/states from liability in the event that consumers make poor choices (Scala, Mayberry, and Kunkel; Micco, Hamilton, Martin, and McEwan).

Finally, one of the biggest barriers to consumer-directed care is concern on the part of professionals and states about quality assurance—especially about fraud and abuse. This is especially the case in programs that allow the use of independent providers who are trained and monitored by consumers, rather than by home care agencies. In their survey of state administrators, Robert Lagoyda and colleagues found this to be a leading concern.

Rationale for consumer direction

A number of other factors have combined to bring consumer-directed care to the forefront within the world of aging services at the beginning of the twenty-first century. The 1990s brought increased emphasis on consumer preferences and autonomy (and how these relate to consumers' quality of life) within the field of aging services. Consumers have become more involved in all aspects of their care, from participating in the care planning process to expressing their opinions about their care through consumer satisfaction surveys administered through home care programs and nursing facilities alike. In addition, there has been increasing concern over the quality of agency-provided services received by home care consumers. The need to cut the rising costs of long-term care has also contributed to the current interest in consumer-directed care (Simon-Rusinowitz et al.).

Another driving factor behind the movement toward consumer-directed care has been the dramatic shortage of frontline workers, which plagues the field of long-term care. By allowing consumers to hire family and friends as independent providers, consumer-directed care may be able to infuse new workers into the system and alleviate this shortage. Also contributing to the increased emphasis on consumer-directed care is the aging of the baby boomers, who are viewed as more likely than the current generation to demand more autonomy and control over the management and delivery of their long-term care services when they eventually need them.

Finally, legislative efforts and judicial decisions have also fueled the drive toward consumer-directed care. In 1998 the MiCASSA (Medicaid Community Attendant Services and Supports Act) was introduced in Congress. This bill offered Medicaid-eligible persons with disabilities the option of choosing personal assistance services and supports in their own communities, rather than placement in a long-term care facility. The year 1999 brought even more attention to the issues of consumer choice and control with the Supreme Court decision in *Olmstead v. L.C.*, which stated that "unnecessary segregation of persons in long-term care facilities constitutes discrimination under the Americans with Disabilities Act" (Rosenbaum). This decision is leading many states to examine (and potentially to expand) their home and community-based options. In the event of increases in home and community-based options, disability advocates will likely argue for such options to incorporate consumer direction.

Models of consumer direction

Not surprisingly, several different models of consumer-directed care have been developed over the years in order to accommodate consumers' differing needs, abilities, and preferences regarding their involvement in the management of their services. These models, going from most to least consumer-directed, are described below.

In the *direct pay/cash and counseling* program, consumers manage both the funding and the delivery of their services. Consumers may receive an actual check or vouchers to use to pay for their care, and they handle all the employer-related responsibilities. Consumers also are the *employer of record*, accepting all liability for personal injury (to themselves and their workers) and for employment tax and benefits for their workers.

In the *supportive intermediary* model, consumers handle as many of the employer-related responsibilities as they want to or are capable of and are the employer of record. An intermediary agency (either the state/program or a third-party agency contracted by the state/program) provides support or assistance with the tasks the consumer is unable or unwilling to assume. Most often this assistance takes the form of doing payroll, taxes, and paperwork for consumers. However, other supports include recruitment assistance, criminal background checks on workers, training workers, and more.

In the last model, *self-directed care management/agency with choice*, the state/program (or the home care agency) handles the money and most of the service management responsibilities (recruiting, interviewing, hiring, training, paying, and firing workers) and is the employer of record. Consumers may interview and select workers (who are sent out from agencies) and provide performance feedback to workers and agencies.

Finally, relatively few programs offer consumers a range of these models to choose from within a single home care program—what is known as a *spectrum intermediary model* (Flanagan and Green). This allows consumers to choose the level of responsibility that they wish to assume, rather than force them into a traditional home care program if they do not wish to handle all of the responsibilities associated with one consumer-directed model.

Implications and future issues

Consumer-directed care provides a long overdue opportunity for consumers to have more control over their management and delivery of their home care services and for home care programs to become more responsive to clients' needs and preferences. Nevertheless, it is not without significant implications for both consumers and state administrators wishing to implement consumer-directed care.

For consumers, this model offers them the chance for increased autonomy and choice with regard to their services. This may include more hours of service, more flexibility in scheduling those hours, more input into who provides those services, and possibly better quality of care. However, with this autonomy also comes responsibility. First and foremost, consumers must know what they want and need in terms of services and providers and must have realistic expectations about these. In addition, the employer-related responsibilities associated with consumer-directed care can take a great deal of time and energy. Recruiting and hiring care providers are difficult tasks, especially in this era of worker shortages and low wages for workers. And while the option of hiring family members or friends may alleviate this problem, consumers who do so may also be faced with the uncomfortable prospect of combining a business relationship (i.e., employer to employee) with their personal relationship. Consumers must also have reliable back-up plans for when independent providers are unable to show up for work.

For state officials, consumer-directed care also has some significant implications. Consumer-directed care has the potential to ease the provider shortage through the use of independent providers, but with the low wages and lack of benefits that are still likely to exist in such programs, retaining quality workers will remain a challenge. Enabling consumers to hire independent providers may also allow for better matches between clients and workers and consequently improved consumer satisfaction for both consumers and workers. However, as in the present long-term care system, the potential for fraud and abuse still exists, particularly if the state has a more limited role in quality monitoring.

Consumer-directed care also has the potential to reduce home care costs by utilizing independent providers, which cuts out the administrative overhead charged by home care agencies. Such savings may allow home care programs to serve additional clients. However, these cost savings may be offset by other costs associated with consumer-directed care, such as the cost of training clients as to their service management responsibilities. Many consumers may not have prior experience with such responsibilities, and thus may require some type of training or guidance.

Finally, there is the issue of liability. Despite the fact that there has been very little in the way of litigation against agencies or privately hired providers, this nonetheless is a significant concern for states (Lagoyda et al.; Kapp). States thinking about implementing consumer-directed care may also need to revisit their Nurse Practice Acts in order to allow for the delegation of nursing tasks to unlicensed personnel such as independent providers.

Consumer direction is still in its infancy within the world of aging services. There is still much research to be done, especially with regard to cost effectiveness and quality of care. The results of demonstrations such as the Cash and Counseling Demonstration and Independent Choices Programs are likely to provide some results that may provide further evidence of the viability of consumer-directed care as a long-term care policy option.

MARISA A. SCALA

See also AUTONOMY; HOME CARE AND HOME SERVICES; LONG-TERM CARE; PERSONAL CARE.

BIBLIOGRAPHY

BATAVIA, A. I.; DEJONG, G.; and McKNEW, L. B. "Toward a National Personal Assistance Program: The Independent Living Model of Long-Term Care for Persons with Disabilities." *Journal of Health Politics, Policy, and Law* 16 (1991): 523–545.

EUSTIS, N. N., and FISCHER, L. R. "Common Needs, Different Solutions? Younger and Older Home Care Clients." *Generations* 16 (1993): 17–22.

FLANAGAN, S. A., and GREEN, P. S. *Consumer-Directed Personal Assistance Services: Key Opera-tional Issues for State CD-PAS Programs Using Intermediary Service Organizations.* Washington, D.C.: MEDSTAT, 1997.

KAPP, M. B. "Improving Choices Regarding Home Care Services: Legal Impediments and Empowerments." *St. Louis University Public Law Review* 10 (1991): 441–484.

LAGOYDA, R.; NADASH, P.; ROSENBERG, L.; and YATSCO, T. *Survey of State Administrators: Consumer-Directed Home and Community-Based Services.* Washington, D.C.: The National Council on the Aging, Inc., 1999.

LITVAK, S.; ZUKAS, H.; and HEUMANN, J. E. *Attending to America: Personal Assistance for Independent Living.* Berkeley, Calif.: World Institute on Disability, 1987.

MICCO, A.; HAMILTON, A. C. S.; MARTIN, M. J.; and McEWAN, K. L. "Case Manager Attitudes Toward Client-Directed Care." *Journal of Case Management* 4 (1995): 95–101.

National Institute on Consumer-Directed Long-Term Services. *Principles of Consumer-Directed Home and Community-Based Services.* Washington, D.C.: The National Council on the Aging, Inc., 1996.

ROSENBAUM, S. *Olmstead v. L.C.: Analysis and Implications for Medicaid Policy.* Princeton, N.J.: Center for Health Care Strategies, 2000.

SCALA, M. A.; MAYBERRY, P. S.; and KUNKEL, S. R. "Consumer-Directed Home Care: Client Profiles and Service Challenges. *Journal of Case Management* 5 (1996): 91–98.

SCALA, M. A., and MAYBERRY, P. S. *Consumer-Directed Home Services: Issues and Models.* Oxford, Ohio: Scripps Gerontology Center, 1997.

SIMON-RUSINOWITZ, L.; MAHONEY, K. J.; DESMOND, S. M.; SHOOP, D. M.; SQUILLACE, M. R.; and FAY, R. A. "Determining Consumer Preferences for a Cash Option: Arkansas Survey Results." *Health Care Financing Review* 19 (1997): 73–96.

CONSUMER PRICE INDEX AND COLAS

The U.S. Consumer Price Index (CPI) is a measure of the average change in the prices paid by consumers living in urban areas for a bundle of consumption goods and services. Average price changes can be driven by changes in consumer income, population and demographic changes, and changes in consumer preferences, as well as by the introduction of new product distribution patterns and marketing techniques. The CPI is updated on a regular basis to respond to such changes. In addition, technological and methodological improvements are introduced into the CPI to improve accuracy.

The CPI is not designed to compare prices between areas. For example, one could say that the prices in Chicago increased by 2 percent from one period to another, while they increased by 5 percent in Washington, D.C. But it would be incorrect to say that prices in Washington, D.C., are higher than they are in Chicago, based on the CPI for these cities.

The official CPI is calculated and published by the Bureau of Labor Statistics (BLS), part of the U.S. Department of Labor. CPIs are published for metropolitan areas in the United States (thirty-eight in 2001), as well as for the four census regions and other areas. National indexes, known as the U.S. City Average, are also produced. Not all indexes are published monthly. Indexes are produced for over 200 basic item categories (for example, bananas, prescription drugs, electricity, women's dresses) and eight major groups or item aggregations. The major groups are food and beverages, housing, apparel, transportation, health care, recreation, education and communication, and other goods and services. The CPI includes government-charged user fees, such as water and sewerage charges, and automobile registration fees, along with taxes such as sales and excise taxes, but excludes income and Social Security taxes. The CPI does not include investment items such as stocks, bonds, real estate, and life insurance. For most of the basic items, the BLS chooses a sample of several hundred specific items within selected business outlets (including stores, mail order firms, and the Internet) frequented by consumers, using scientific sampling procedures, to represent the thousands of items available in the marketplace.

Over time, improvements in the CPI have been introduced. The primary and most visible change has been the introduction of a new "market basket" of goods and services upon which to base the indexes. This market basket is a reflection of what consumers (specifically consumer units, also referred to here as households; consumer units share major expenditures, while a group of people in a household may not) buy; data are collected using household expenditure surveys (also known as consumer expenditure surveys). Shares of total expenditures for items in the market basket are produced from the survey data. Shares are produced over all households within an area, and thus the market basket is considered to be "representative" of the purchases by households within an area. These shares are known as "expenditure weights" or "relative importances," and are attached to prices collected by the BLS to produce the CPI. Consumer expenditures from 1999 to 2000 are used (as of 2002) for expenditure weights for items in every CPI index area. To maintain accuracy, the CPI has historically updated the expenditure patterns approximately every ten years. Beginning in 2002, the expenditure weights are to be updated every two years.

The BLS officially produces an index for two population groups; other indexes are also produced, but are referred to as "experimental." The two official indexes are the Consumer Price Index for All Urban Consumers (CPI-U) and the Consumer Price Index for Urban Wage Earners and Clerical Workers (CPI-W). The CPI-U is based on the experience of consumers living in urban areas of the United States only. This population accounted for about 80 percent of the total U.S. noninstitutionalized population in 1978, when the index was introduced. The CPI-W is a subset of the CPI-U population and is based on the experience of wage earners and clerical workers living in urban areas in the United States. To be included in this population, more than half of the household's income must come from a clerical or wage occupation and at least one of the household's earners must have been employed for at least thirty-seven weeks during the previous twelve months. The CPI-W's population represented about 32 percent of the total U.S. population in 1978.

Uses of the CPI

The CPI is the primary source of information concerning trends in consumer prices and inflation in the United States. As a measure of inflation, it is one of the nation's most important economic indicators, and affects nearly all people living in the United States as well as many Americans living abroad. It is also used to create "constant dollar" key economic indicators. Such indicators include, but are not limited to, estimates of income, earnings, productivity, output, and poverty. The index is also widely used for economic analysis and policy formation in the public and private sectors.

The CPI is often employed as a cost-of-living adjustment (COLA), even though it is not a cost-of-living index. It is used to adjust wages and benefit payments to account for the erosion of consumer purchasing power due to price increases faced by consumers. The CPI is the best measure for adjusting wages and payments when the goal is to allow consumers to purchase, at today's prices, a market basket of goods and services equivalent to one that they could have purchased at an earlier time. This is the type of adjustment often called for when the CPI is applied to meet statutory obligations. Such obligations include payments to Social Security beneficiaries and federal and military retirees—all of which are tied to the CPI-W—and those for a number of entitlement programs, including food stamps and school lunches. The impact on the finances of the federal government is quite significant when such adjustments are made. Annual escalation adjustments in the federal income tax brackets, as well as personal exemption and standard deduction amounts, are made using the CPI-U. With regard to the impact on federal taxes, it has been estimated that in the fiscal year 1996, each 1 percent increase in the CPI resulted in a $5.7 billion increase in outlays and a $2.5 billion decline in tax revenues.

Difference between the CPI and COLI

The BLS uses a cost-of-living framework in making practical decisions about constructing the CPI, but the CPI differs in important ways from a complete cost-of-living index (COLI), as noted above. A COLI would measure changes over time in the amount that consumers need to spend to reach a certain level of living ("utility level," in economics terminology). Like the CPI, a COLI would reflect changes in the prices of goods and services, such as food and clothing, that are directly purchased in the marketplace. However, a complete COLI would go beyond this to take into account changes in governmental or environmental factors that affect consumers' well-being. It is very difficult to determine the correct treatment of public goods, such as safety and education, and other broad concerns, such as health, water quality, and crime, that would be in a complete cost-of-living framework.

History of improvements in the CPI

The CPI was begun during World War I. At this time, prices were increasing rapidly, particularly in shipbuilding centers. To deal with the fact that these price increases were eroding the

buying power of wages, the federal government decided that an index on which to base cost-of-living adjustments was necessary. To create such an index, household patterns of expenditures needed to be identified in order to create expenditure weights that would be used to compile the index. These data were collected in ninety-two industrial centers in 1917–1919. The BLS began the periodic collection of prices in 1919, and published indexes for thirty-two cities. Regular publication of the U.S. City Average began in 1921. At this time, indexes were estimated back to 1913. The first indexes were for wage earners and clerical workers.

As would be expected, the buying habits of consumers change substantially over time. In order to account for these changes, several household or consumer expenditure surveys have been conducted. After the 1917–1919 survey, others were conducted in 1934–1936, 1950, 1960–1961, and 1972–1973. In October 1979, continuous consumer expenditure surveys were introduced. A reason for continuous collection of these data is to have data available to update the CPI expenditure weights more frequently.

During these time periods many improvements in pricing and calculation methods were introduced. A Point of Purchase Survey was introduced in 1978. This survey made it possible for the BLS to collect prices directly, based on a new store-specific approach to select items. At this time, the BLS introduced a new index, the more broadly population-based CPI for All Urban Consumers (CPI-U). The CPI-U population included professional and salaried workers, part-time workers, the self-employed, the unemployed, and retired consumers in addition to wage earners and clerical workers.

The last two major revisions in the CPI took place in 1987 and 1998. With the 1987 revision, improvements were made in sampling, data collection, processing, and statistical estimation. Data from the consumer expenditure surveys of 1982–1984 were used for the expenditure weights. The 1980 census was the sample base, and the ongoing Point of Purchase Survey was used to select new item and outlet samples.

With the 1998 revision, another new market basket was introduced, along with methodological changes, a new system for data collection and processing, and a new sample base (the 1990 census). This is the sixth major revision in the CPI's history, and includes changes in the selection and classification of areas, items, and outlets. Several other improvements reflected in the current CPI were not part of a major CPI revision. For example, in 1983, a major change was introduced to separate shelter costs from the investment component of home ownership.

Issues in constructing an appropriate index

The CPI is the aggregate, representative measure of price change as experienced by households. In order to compute the index, one needs to know who buys, where they buy, what they buy, what an item costs (for example, the price of a loaf of bread is $1.00), and what in total is spent for an item (for example, $5.00 is spent for five loaves of bread purchased by the consumer). Statistical samples of household expenditures, prices, and area populations for urban areas provide the inputs for the calculation. Information is collected from a sample of urban households or consumer units to determine their expenditure patterns by using the consumer expenditure survey. Information on prices is collected from a sample of outlets and products based on their likelihood of being patronized and purchased, respectively. The overall CPI is then constructed in two stages by taking a weighted average of household information. At the first stage, prices within CPI item categories are averaged (using appropriate statistical techniques) to form basic item indexes. At the second stage, these indexes are averaged together.

Limitations of the CPI

There are several limitations of the CPI. Two sets of limitations of the CPI are discussed here: application and measure. The CPI may not be applicable to all population groups. Since it is designed to measure the experience of people living in urban areas, it may not accurately reflect the experience of people living in rural areas. Also, the CPI does not separately reflect the inflation faced by subgroups of the population, such as older persons, the poor, various ethnic groups, and males versus females. As noted earlier, the CPI measures only time-to-time changes in relative prices within an area. A higher index would not necessarily mean that prices are higher in one area compared with another area with a lower index value. The CPI cannot be used as a measure of the total change in living costs because social and environmental changes

and changes in income taxes, which are beyond the scope of the CPI, are excluded.

Limitations on measure include sampling errors and nonsampling errors. Since the CPI is based on a sample of items, the index will differ from one based on all goods and services purchased in the United States. Nonsampling errors can be the result of problems in data collection, logistical lags in conducting surveys, difficulties in defining basic concepts and their operational implementation, and difficulties in handling the problems of quality change. Such errors can lead to persistent bias in the index.

Critiques, research, and experimental CPIs

There have been many improvements in the CPI over the years, a number of them resulting from research conducted within the BLS. The latest major external review of the CPI followed Senate Finance Committee hearings in the spring of 1995. As a result of the hearings, the committee appointed an advisory commission to study the CPI and make recommendations for methodological improvements. The commission's report, *Toward a More Accurate Measure of the Cost of Living*, informally referred to as the "Boskin Commission Report," did not identify new issues but did result in focusing greater attention on known limitations of the index.

The CPI program has developed experimental indexes of consumer prices. Only two are described here.

The one most relevant to this volume is referred to as the Experimental Consumer Price Index for Americans 62 Years of Age and Older (CPI-E). The question addressed with this index is how price increases faced by older persons living in urban areas of the United States differ from those faced by all consumers living in urban areas.

The other is the Consumer Price Index Research Series Using Current Methods (CPI-U-RS). This index incorporates most of the improvements in the CPI-U that have been made since 1978. A question that could be addressed with this experimental index is what would have been the measured rate of inflation since 1978 if the methods currently used in calculating the CPI-U had been in use since 1978. When consistent CPIs are preferred for deflating, this measure gives somewhat different results than the official CPI-U. Such applications include the Bureau of Economic Analysis's use of the CPI-U-RS in its 1999 comprehensive revision of the National Income and Product Accounts; the BLS Office of Productivity's use of the index in its measure of real hourly compensation for its quarterly measure of labor productivity and costs; and the Bureau of the Census's use of the CPI-U-RS for its estimates of historical real income.

The CPI-E

In 1988 the BLS first produced monthly and annual experimental CPIs for Americans age sixty-two and over, with the series going back to December 1982. The index is referred to as the CPI-E. The creation of the index evolved from the 1987 amendments to the Older Americans Act of 1965, in which the BLS was directed to develop an index for older Americans.

The older population, upon which the experimental index is based, is identified as being age sixty-two or older and living in urban areas. Specifically this population includes the following:

1. Unattached individuals who are at least sixty-two years of age
2. Members of families whose reference person (as defined in the consumer expenditure surveys) or spouse is at least sixty-two years of age
3. Members of groups of unrelated individuals living together who share living expenditures, and whose reference person is at least sixty-two years of age.

About 22 percent of urban consumer units (upon which the CPI-U is based) meet the above definition, using data from the consumer expenditure survey data collected in 1993–1995.

Expenditures of some older people are excluded, while those of people younger than age sixty-two are included. For example, older people who are living in institutionalized housing are not included in the sample, nor are older people who are living with adult children. However, expenditures of children or other related individuals living in an older person's household are included.

Over the period 1983–2000, the CPI-E rose by an annual average of 3.5 percent, while the CPI-U averaged 3.3 percent. The CPI-W, the index to which Social Security is tied, increased an average of 3.2 percent.

As noted above, the CPI-W is used to adjust Social Security payments and many retirement payments. However, there are problems with both the experimental index and the CPI-W in terms of applicability to Social Security beneficiaries and to the older population specifically. With regard to the CPI-W, the population upon which this index is based does not include most Social Security beneficiaries, since by definition the population is composed of wage earners and clerical workers. The CPI-E also has several limitations as a potential index for escalating Social Security benefits. First, the group of persons age sixty-two and older is not likely the most appropriate population. Many people younger than sixty-two receive Social Security benefits. About 25 percent of all Social Security beneficiaries are younger people who receive benefits because they are surviving spouses and/or minor children of covered workers, or because of disability. The expenditure experience of this group is not included in the weights for the CPI-E. In addition, a sizable number of people age sixty-two and over do not receive Social Security benefits. In 1988, over 40 percent of the population age sixty-two to sixty-four did not collect Social Security retirement benefits. One might question whether such people's expenditures ought to be included in the calculation of an index for older persons if the goal is to adjust the Social Security benefits.

In addition, the outlets, items, and prices used for calculating the CPI-E are the same as those used for the CPI-U. This means that the way the CPI-E population shops and the prices they pay are not being accounted for separately in the experimental CPI-E. Older people not only may shop at different outlets than people in the CPI-U population, but also may use discounts that are not available to other consumers. Without the development of a series of household surveys for the older population, for example, that obtains detailed descriptions of items purchased by this group and the identification of the outlets where the items were purchased, a full-scale CPI for older persons is not possible within the BLS. To provide such an index would be costly and likely would take years to implement. Much research and development must be done.

THESIA I. GARNER
KENNETH J. STEWART

See also CONSUMPTION AND AGE; MEDICARE; PENSIONS; SOCIAL SECURITY; SUPPLEMENTAL SECURITY INCOME.

BIBLIOGRAPHY

AMBLE, N., and STEWART, K. J. "Experimental Price Index for Elderly Consumers." *Monthly Labor Review* 117, no. 5 (May 1994): 11–16.

BOSKIN, M. J.; DALBERGER, E.; GORDON, R. J.; GRILICHES, Z.; and JORGENSON, D. W. *Toward a More Accurate Measure of the Cost of Living. Final Report of the Advisory Commission to Study the Consumer Price Index.* S.Prt. 104-72. Washington, D.C.: U.S. Government Printing Office.

Bureau of Labor Statistics. "Frequently Asked Questions." World Wide Web document, April 2001. *stats.bls.gov/cpifaq.htm*

Bureau of Labor Statistics. "Home Page." World Wide Web document, April 2001. *stats.bls.gov/cpihome.htm*

Consumer Price Index. Hearings before the Committee on Finance, U.S. Senate. Washington, D.C.: U.S. Government Printing Office, 1995.

DIEWERT, W. E. "Index Numbers." In *The New Palgrave: A Dictionary of Economics.* Edited by John Eatwell, Murray Milgate, and Peter Newman. Volume 2. London: Macmillan, 1987. Pages 767–779.

GREENLEES, J. S., and MASON, C. C. "Overview of the 1998 Revision of the Consumer Price Index." *Monthly Labor Review.* 119, no. 12 (December 1996): 3–83.

Handbook of Methods. Bulletin 2285. Washington, D.C.: Bureau of Labor Statistics, 1997. Pages 167–231.

MASON, C. C. "An Analysis of the Rates of Inflation Affecting Older Americans Based on an Experimental Reweighted Consumer Price Index." Report prepared by the Bureau of Labor Statistics for presentation to the Senate Select Subcommittee on Aging, June 1988.

SCHOLL, K. K. "Cost-of-Living Adjustments (COLAs)." *Encyclopedia of Financial Gerontology.* Edited by Lois A. Vitt, Jurg K. Siegenthaler, et al. Westport, Conn.: Greenwood Press, 1996, Pages 98-102.

STEWART, K. J., and REED, S. B. "Consumer Price Index Research Series Using Current Methods, 1978–1999." *Monthly Labor Review* 122, no. 6 (June 1999): 29–38.

U.S. Senate, Special Committee on Aging. *Developing a Consumer Price Index for the Elderly.* Washington, D.C.: U.S. Government Printing Office, 1987.

CONSUMER PROTECTION

Older consumers are just like all other consumers in many ways. They want to get fair treatment in the market place and avoid unscrupulous or sharp business dealings.

Consumer expectations

A fair marketplace supports several general rights. An important right is the opportunity to make informed choices among a variety of goods or services. To make informed choices, consumers need to receive complete and accurate information about their purchases. This information might include the product's content (for example, if the product contains nuts for those who may have an allergic reaction), safety warnings (the flammability of a garment), and product care instructions (temperature for safely storing an aerosol product). Obviously, this information needs to be written in plain language that will inform, rather than confuse, the consumer. It should be printed in a readable type size.

All consumers also expect a fair price. A price is fair if it reflects the actual cost of manufacture or providing the service without exorbitant mark up. They also want to be able to buy the item in the store at the price mentioned in an advertisement. They want to know if online price comparison services accept payment from advertisers to list their products more prominently. Consumers have a right to know all costs associated with a purchase, such as shipping and handling, and to get the same price as other consumers without discrimination.

Consumers also expect to be able to get someone to pay attention to their concerns about a product or service. Older consumers are particularly concerned about receiving personal service and individual attention from shopkeepers and financial institutions. They need to know with whom they are dealing, how to communicate with a company, and how to obtain refunds. They want access to effective remedies, such as enforcement of regulations, prosecution of criminal violations, and adjudication of private and class action lawsuits.

With the advent of new marketing media, from the telephone to the Internet, and the capacity of computers to collect and store massive amounts of information, consumer privacy is a growing concern. All consumers have a right to personal privacy. Older consumers especially

Nellie, who did not wish to give her last name, speaks to fellow support group members in Philadelphia in 1995. The eighty-year-old was a victim of a consumer scam, which she reported to the Crimes Against the Elderly and Retired Unit (CARE) of the Philadelphia police department. At the time, the unit was the only one in the United States to focus solely on crimes against the elderly. (AP photo by Nanine Hartzenbusch.)

want to be able to reject intrusive marketing practices, such as unsolicited contact by telephone, fax, or e-mail, and to control how and to whom personal information is given.

Older consumers at risk

The older population is growing rapidly. The aging of the "baby boomers," those born between 1946 and 1964, will accelerate this growth. The thirty-five million persons who were age sixty-five or older in 2000 make up a substantial force in the marketplace and have a significant impact on the economy. The economic status of older people has improved markedly over the past few decades. Compared to their parents, they have greater net worth and financial security. Between 1984 and 1999, the median net worth of households headed by older persons increased by about 70 percent. Fifteen percent of householders age fifty-five to fifty-nine have annual household incomes of $100,000 or more, as do 11 percent of those age sixty to sixty-four.

Householders age fifty-five to sixty-four, who generally are still working and enjoying peak earnings, spend more than young adults in most product and service categories. As better-educated and more affluent generations of Americans reach retirement age, they are projected to be more willing to spend in their older age than their Depression-era parents.

Moreover, several characteristics of the older population put them at special risk as consumers. Retirees living on Social Security or savings have less opportunity to recover financially if they lose their savings to an investment scam. A poor financial decision can have a greater impact on the older person than on a younger wage earner who can get another job and has time to replenish savings. Unfortunately, memory impairment or other cognitive losses for older adults can make them especially vulnerable to financial exploitation.

With money to spend, invest, and possibly leave to heirs, older consumers are at risk that someone will try to take advantage of them financially.

Controlling 70 percent of the nation's household net worth, persons over the age of fifty are prime targets for financial exploitation. Among the most vulnerable consumers are those over age seventy-five. Studies of consumer behavior of persons over fifty by the AARP (formerly American Association of Retired Persons) show that they expect honesty in the marketplace, are less likely to take action when they are defrauded, and are less knowledgeable about their rights in an increasingly complex marketplace (AARP, 1999). Frequently retired, they are more likely to be at home when a home repair contractor, who just happens to be in the neighborhood, knocks on the door. Telemarketers know they are home during the day to answer telephone solicitations.

The list of potential exploiters is long. They can be telemarketers, door-to-door salespersons, home repair contractors, finance companies, funeral directors, and financial advisors, as well as friends and family. All means of deception can be used to separate older consumers from their money. Con artists work their trade at the front door, on the street, in the office, or over the phone. Wherever they meet their victims, they rely on psychology, rather than force, to control their victims. Typically, the best players of these mind games have perfected the basic techniques of a confidence crime. First, they grab the potential victim's attention through some promise to make or save money. Using fast talk and impressive wording, they build confidence and trust. Next, to keep the victim's attention, they demonstrate an authoritative manner, pleasing personality, and empathy for the victim's needs or concerns. By playing on the victim's emotions and moving quickly through the pitch, the clever con artist gains control. Once the victim loses control of the transaction, or the conversation, they are likely to be rushed into making decisions, so they cannot check with others or use common sense.

Seventeen percent of consumers age eighteen and over report in the 1999 AARP survey of consumer behavior that they were the victim of a major consumer fraud or swindle. In AARP studies of telemarketing fraud more than half (57 percent) of persons over age fifty report getting at least one telemarketing call each week. And those calls work. Fourteen percent of respondents said that they had sent money, given their credit card number, entered a contest, made an investment, or donated to a charity in response to a phone solicitation.

Because of appreciation in home values and paid-off mortgages, the home is where the money is for older consumers. More than 80 percent of households headed by persons age fifty and older own their homes. Almost 60 percent of that group owns those homes free of any mortgage. Older homeowners are more likely to live in an older home that needs repairs, but less likely to be able to do the repairs on their own or to have money on hand for major repairs. This combination of factors puts them at risk for home repair fraud. To further compound the fraud, the contractor may steer the homeowner to a high cost home loan. Predatory mortgage lending practices in some communities threaten the stability of home ownership for older Americans. When loans are based on the equity in a home, rather than the homeowner's ability to repay the loan, the risk of foreclosure is greatly increased. The number of foreclosures in the United States has tripled since 1980, from over 150,000 to almost 459,000 in 1995. The consequences of foreclosure for an older homeowner can be shattering. It represents more than a loss of shelter; it could be the loss of the home a family has occupied for decades. As a result of foreclosure, some older homeowners may have to move into a nursing home.

Older persons who are concerned about passing their estates on to heirs may fall prey to investment counselors, insurance sales presentations, and living trust purveyors who falsely promise risk-free investments and exaggerate the costs of probate. Parties on both sides of a viatical settlement can be exposed to fraud. A viatical settlement is the sale at a discount of a life insurance policy. Insured persons, called viators, can obtain cash by selling a life insurance policy to a viatical settlement company. The viatical settlement company, in turn, sells the policy to a third-party investor. The investor continues to pay the premiums on the policy and collects the face value of the policy after the original policyholder dies. While in some instances this financial transaction can produce much needed money for medical or nursing home expenses, unscrupulous promoters can defraud both the viator and investor.

Protections available

Legislative and regulatory protections are provided when abuse occurs in the marketplace. Most consumer protections are available to all consumers, regardless of age. The major group of consumer protection laws falls within state statutes called generically "unfair and deceptive acts and practices" (UDAP). Most UDAP statutes are very broad, and can be used to challenge a wide range of fraudulent, abusive, or deceptive activities. Some state statutes apply generally to the sale of goods and services. Other statutes target specific commercial activities, such as mobile home parks or timeshare properties. State UDAP statutes can vary in the specifics of who can sue, who can be sued, what practices are prohibited, and what relief is available. Most allow many different types of relief, including actual, treble, or punitive damages, injunctive relief, class actions, and in some cases, attorney fees. A public librarian could be of assistance in locating UDAP provisions in a state code.

UDAP statutes might be used to challenge billing practices of nursing homes that charge residents extra money for services covered by Medicaid payments or provide substandard care. The statute could be used to contest unfair terms in an assistive living facility's admission contract or misleading advertising about costs. These laws could be useful obtaining an injunction against a scam artist who tried to steal the equity from a senior homeowner.

Federal laws protect all consumers by requiring specific disclosures in credit transactions through the Truth in Lending Act (TILA). TILA provisions mandate that credit card companies have a process to correct billing errors and allow borrowers to get out of loans if lenders do not make certain disclosures about the cost of the loan. TILA protections can be particularly valuable to the older homeowner who becomes the victim of predatory home mortgage lending practices. Similarly, the Home Ownership and Equity Protection Act (HOEPA) is a useful tool to protect older homeowners. HOEPA was enacted in an effort to crack down on the use of high-interest, high-fee loans that strip the equity an older homeowner has built up. TILA and HOEPA are used to halt foreclosures. Under TILA, when the loan is secured by the equity in a home, the borrower's three-day unconditional right to get out of the loan can be extended to three or possibly more years, if the lender failed to make required disclosures. Violation of the HOEPA protections gives the homeowner the right to sue for damages, as well as to seek cancellation of the loan in certain circumstances.

Other consumer protection laws are of special interest to older consumers.

- The Consumer Leasing Act, created to address abuses in car leasing, and the FTC Used Car Rule, requiring a prominent sticker describing the car's warranty terms, protect older consumers on the go.
- The Fair Debt Collection Practices Act curbs harassing practices by debt collectors. The older debtor, who may fall prey to misleading statements or scare tactics by creditors, can use this provision to obtain damages for personal humiliation, embarrassment, mental anguish, and emotional distress.
- The Equal Credit Opportunity Act specifically protects against discrimination in the granting of credit because of age. This protection may come into play when a recently widowed person first applies for credit in her own name after her husband dies.
- The Federal Telephone Consumer Protection Act and the Telemarketing and Consumer Fraud and Abuse Prevention Act require callers to give consumers basic information identifying who is making the call. Telemarketers cannot make calls before 8:00 a.m. or after 9:00 p.m. They may not call persons who have asked to be placed on the calling company's "do not call" lists.
- The Federal Trade Commission Mail or Telephone Merchandise Rule requires merchants to deliver items ordered by phone or mail within thirty days. Older consumers who may have difficulty getting out to do their shopping need this protection to make sure what they order from home will be delivered as promised.
- The Federal Trade Commission Regulation for Door-to-Door Sales specifically gives relief to consumers pressured into buying something at home. The salesperson must tell consumers they can change their mind and cancel the entire transaction. By notifying the company within three business days of the sale, consumers can cancel and get a refund of any purchases made at their home or other temporary locations.

Sources of help

At the federal level, the Federal Trade Commission (FTC) has the primary responsibility to protect the interests and rights of consumers. Through enforcement actions, the commission can order parties to stop practices that violate federal consumer protection statutes and to pay fines. The FTC encourages people to file complaints about problems with deceptive or unfair practices through its online complaint process at www.ftc.gov/. While it cannot resolve individual complaints, the commission relies on its complaint database to track problems and initiate investigations. Other federal agencies involved with consumer issues include the Consumer Product Safety Commission and the Consumer Information Center. The United States Postal Inspectors investigate mail fraud and work closely with U.S. Attorneys in prosecuting cases.

At the state level, the attorney general has similar enforcement responsibility over state consumer protections. The attorney general may have a staff of investigators and prosecutors who concentrate on elder consumer issues. Many states have consumer protection offices either within the attorney general's office or as a separate state agency. These offices receive complaints, investigate and prosecute state fraud violations, and provide consumer education.

Many other state agencies have consumer protection responsibilities. The utilities commission may regulate the cost of residential gas and electricity. The department of weights and measures checks grocery store scanners and gasoline pumps for accuracy. Licensing of home contractors, hearing aid dispensers, and funeral directors offers a measure of protection when a service problem develops. Insurance commissioners determine what insurance products can be sold in the state.

As with any other type of legal problem, consumers can go to court with consumer claims. However, private litigation in the consumer area is not that commonplace. With claims involving smaller amounts of money, small claims courts may offer a practical solution for the individual consumer. A group of aggrieved consumers can band together to bring a class action suit, particularly if a company's practice has affected a large number of people. In between small claims court and class actions, the individual consumer may have difficulty finding a private attorney to handle the consumer dispute. The cost to bring the case may be higher than the potential recovery. The losing party generally does not have to pay the other side's attorney's fees unless the consumer protection statute expressly authorizes recovery of attorneys fee to the successful consumer. The consumer runs the chance of losing the case and having a large bill from legal counsel, if the lawyer will take the case in the first place. The American Bar Association reports that the number of private lawyers with a strong practice focus in consumer law may stand at about two thousand. Many of these attorneys built their practice on prior experience handling consumer matters as legal services attorneys or assistant state attorneys general.

The future

The emerging global economy presents many opportunities and challenges for consumers. Computer and communications technology advances place powerful tools in the hands of consumers. While online, consumers can access a brokerage account, buy a clock directly from a German artisan, compare the prices of cell phone service, and research eighteenth-century passenger manifests—all from the home computer. These same technologies allow businesses to collect an unprecedented amount of information about the purchase patterns and financial holdings of consumers. As e-commerce becomes a driving market force, new problems will need to be addressed about how best to protect consumers of all ages. At the same time, all consumers need to be alert that frauds and scams can just as easily, and certainly more rapidly, happen electronically.

SALLY BALCH HURME

See also CONSUMPTION AND AGE; RETAIL AND OLDER ADULTS.

BIBLIOGRAPHY

American Association of Retired Persons (AARP). *Consumer Behavior, Experiences and Attitudes.* Washington, D.C.: AARP, 1999.

American Association of Retired Persons (AARP). *Consumer Home Equity/Home Improvement Lending Survey.* Washington, D.C.: AARP, 2000.

American Association of Retired Persons (AARP). *Findings from a Baseline Omnibus Survey on Telemarketing Solicitations.* Washington, D.C.: AARP, 1996.

Federal Interagency Forum on Aging Related Statistics. *Older Americans 2000: Key Indicators of Well-Being*, 2000.

LOONIN, D. "Consumer Law and the Elderly: Using State Unfair and Deceptive Practices Statutes to Protect and Preserve the Financial Independence of Seniors." *Bifocal* 20, no. 3 (fall 1999): 1–10.

WASIK, J. "The Fleecing of America's Elderly." *Consumers Digest* 39, March Report (2000): 77.

YNTEMA, S., ed. *Americans 55 and Older: A Changing Market.* 2d ed. Ithaca, N.Y.: New Strategist Publications, Inc., 1999.

INTERNET RESOURCES

American Association of Retired Persons:
www.aarp.org
Consumer Information Center:
www.pueblo.gsa.gov
Consumer Product Safety Commission:
www.cpsc.gov
Federal Trade Commission:
www.ftc.gov
National Association of Consumer Advocates:
www.naca.net
National Consumer Law Center:
www.consumerlaw.org
National Senior Citizens Law Center:
www.nsclc.org
United States Postal Inspectors:
www.usps.com/postalinspectors

CONSUMPTION AND AGE

Simply defined, consumption is household spending on consumption goods and services. However, consumption can also be defined as the satisfaction obtained by consumers from the use of goods and services. A person's life-cycle stage is usually regarded as the most important predictor of consumption. Households headed by young people usually spend less than average on products and services because their households are small and their incomes are low. In middle age, spending reaches a maximum as family size increases and incomes peak. Spending then declines in older age as household size and income decline.

The changing demographics of the American population are likely to affect consumption in the future. There were 34.4 million persons age sixty-five or older in the United States in 1998, and by 2030 there will be about 70 million persons age sixty-five or older. In 1998 this age group represented 12.7 percent of the U.S. population; in 2030 the comparable figure will be 20 percent. Diversity within the older population, and how it changes, will also influence consumption of goods and services.

Theoretical framework

Theories that attempt to explain how income and consumption vary over the life cycle include the life-cycle hypothesis, the permanent-income

Table 1

Percent Change in Average Household Spending Between 1987 and 1997 by Selected Categories: Consumer Expenditure Surveys, 1987 and 1997

Category	Food Away from Home	Entertain-ment	Health Care
Total	-13.1	7.6	14.8
Under 25	-22.3	-0.1	-11.0
25-34	-15.1	1.5	14.2
35-44	-23.1	-10.4	4.7
45-54	-8.4	16.4	9.7
55-64	-12.7	18.3	11.9
65-74	-3.4	5.4	21.6
75+	0.3	97.9	24.1

SOURCE: Consumer Expenditure Surveys, 1987 and 1997

hypothesis, and precautionary savings. The life-cycle hypothesis (Ando and Modigliani, 1963) suggests that consumers try to maintain a relatively stable level of consumption over their lifetime. In practice, this means that younger people borrow to meet consumption needs, middle-aged people save as large a proportion of income as possible, and older people spend down their assets when their income is reduced in retirement. The permanent-income hypothesis (Friedman, 1957) suggests that consumers adjust their spending level to their perceived level of future income and that they dissave in retirement. The precautionary-saving model (Deaton, 1992) suggests that older people are extremely cautious about spending down their assets because they are uncertain about how long they will live, about the cost of health care in the future, and about the possibility of becoming impoverished.

Diversity among older persons

The diversity of the older population contributes to a broad range of consumption needs and preferences. The sex ratio is an example: in 1998, there were 20.2 million older (65+) women and 14.2 million older men, or a sex ratio of 143 women for every 100 men. This ratio increases in older age groups: in 1998, it ranged from 118 women per 100 men for the 65 to 69 age group, to 241 women per 100 men for persons aged 85 and over. Marital status presents another example of the diversity of the older population—older men are much more likely to be married than older women. In 1998, 75 percent of older men and 43 percent of older women were married. There were four times as many widows as widowers in 1998.

Living arrangements of older persons are also diverse. In 1998 the majority of older noninstitutionalized persons lived in a family setting; that is, with a spouse or relatives. Approximately 80 percent of older men and 58 percent of older women lived in a family setting. Further, living alone was found to increase with advanced age. Three of every five women age 85 and older lived outside of a family setting in 1998. The percentage of persons 65 and older who lived in nursing homes in 1996 increased dramatically with age; only 1.1 percent of persons age 65 to 74 lived in nursing homes while 19.8 percent of persons 85 and over did so.

Participation of older persons in the labor force shows diversity as well. Twelve percent of older Americans were in the labor force in 1998, and older men were twice as likely to be employed as older women. Just over half (54 percent) of the workers over 65 were employed part-time: 48 percent of men and 62 percent of women. Twenty-three percent of older workers were self-employed, compared to 7 percent of younger workers. Over two-thirds (71 percent) of the self-employed were men.

The amount of income and the sources of income of older persons are also diverse. The median income of older persons in 1998 was $18,166 for males and $10,504 for females. The major sources of income in 1996, as reported by the Social Security Administration, were Social Security benefits (reported by 91 percent of older persons), income from assets (reported by 63 percent), public and private pensions (reported by 43 percent), earnings (reported by 21 percent), and public assistance (reported by 6 percent). In 1996, Social Security accounted for 40 percent of the aggregate income of the older population. The remainder consisted of earnings (20 percent), pensions (18 percent), assets (18 percent), and 4 percent from other sources. In summary, with advancing age, the population of older persons in the United States is more likely to be female, living alone, and to have less income than middle-aged people.

Overview of household spending

The Consumer Expenditure Survey (CEX), sponsored by the U.S. Bureau of Labor Statistics, is the primary source of information on U.S. consumption at the household level. Through in-depth interviews with a large representative sample of U.S. households, the survey gathers spending data on nearly one thousand different products and services, focusing on consumer units, which are defined as all members of a particular housing unit related by blood, marriage, adoption, or other legal arrangement. The survey collects data only from consumer units that have independent living status. Residents of retirement communities are included in the survey, but long-term-care facility residents are excluded. There are thirteen major expenditure categories in the CEX: food at home, food away from home, alcohol and tobacco, housing, apparel and apparel services, transportation, health care, entertainment, personal care, reading materials and education, cash contributions, personal insurance, and miscellaneous.

Geoffrey Paulin used CEX data from 1984 to 1996 to analyze expenditure trends for different age groups and to test whether tastes and preferences changed over time for older consumers. He found that the change in average annual expenditures between 1984 and 1997 (in 1997 dollars) was as follows: for families under age 65 there was a 1.5 percent increase; for families 65 to 74 there was a 13.6 percent increase; and for families 75 and older there was a 18.0 percent increase. In other words, younger families had relatively stable expenditure levels, but real expenditures rose substantially for those over 65. Paulin also analyzed the change in income before taxes between 1984 and 1997 (in 1997 dollars) and found that families under age 65 had a 10.9 percent increase, families 65 to 74 had a 13.2 percent increase, and families 75 and older had a 7.4 percent increase.

Paulin investigated whether older consumers had different tastes, preferences, or physical needs than younger consumers by analyzing trends for several of the thirteen major expenditure categories. He found that older consumers purchased different amounts than younger consumers, but in most cases the trend of expenditures was similar for older and younger consumers. There was one interesting exception: recreation. All age groups exhibited a real decrease in spending for recreation during the 1990–1991 recession. In 1997, however, the recreation expenditures for younger consumers were down about 1 percent from their 1991 value, but they had risen substantially for older consumers. In fact, they had risen 19 percent for those age 65 to 74 and 28 percent for those at least 75 years old.

In another study, three of the thirteen CEX categories (food away from home, entertainment, and health care) were selected by Cheryl Russell to highlight changes in average spending by the various age categories between 1987 and 1997 for all households. The data show that most households, especially younger households, reduced spending on food away from home in 1997, compared to 1987. Households 65 to 74 and over 75 had increases of 21.6 percent and 24.2 percent, respectively, for health care expenditures when 1987 and 1997 were compared. Households 75 and over showed greatly increased spending on entertainment—almost double the 1987 level (up 97.9 percent). It is important to note that Russell compared spending in two different years, 1987 and 1997, while Paulin analyzed the period from 1984 to 1997.

Differences in consumption among older persons

Some researchers have focused more specifically on older households. For example, Mohamed Abdel-Ghany and Deanna Sharpe compared expenditures of households with 65 to 74 year olds and households with members 75 and over using the 1990 CEX data. They found that expenditures for food at home, housing, transportation, and health care made up the largest share of expenses for both groups. Housing was the largest expenditure for each group. Transportation was the second highest expenditure for the 65 to 74 age group, and health care was the second highest expenditure for households 75 and over. In general, urban residents spent relatively more than rural households for food at home, housing, entertainment, and personal care, and relatively less for transportation and health care. The investigators suggested that rural residents may grow some of their own food, reducing expenditure for food at home, and urban residents may use public transportation and have a shorter distance to travel, reducing transportation costs.

Abdel-Ghany and Sharpe also found that households headed by college graduates spent relatively more than households headed by those who did not complete high school on items associated with an active social life: food away from home, alcohol and tobacco, apparel and apparel services, entertainment, and personal care. The results suggest that education influences consumers' tastes and preferences. Racial differences were observed as well. Compared to older white households, older African-American households spent significantly more on personal insurance and significantly less on food away from home and entertainment.

Compared to married-couple households, households headed by unmarried females spent significantly more for apparel and apparel services and significantly less on food at home, food away from home, alcohol and tobacco, health care, and personal care. Spending by households headed by unmarried males varied by age. The 65 to 74 year old unmarried-male households spent relatively more on food away from home, entertainment, and personal insurance; and significantly less on food at home, health care, and personal care, than did married couples age 65 to 74. Households headed by unmarried males age 75 and over spent significantly more on alcohol and tobacco and personal insurance than did married-couple households of the same age.

Based on their results, Abdel-Ghany and Sharpe concluded that households of 65 to 74 year olds had higher marginal propensities to spend for food at home, food away from home, alcohol and tobacco, transportation, entertainment, and personal insurance, compared to the 75 and over group. The 65 to 74 age group had a lower propensity to spend for housing, apparel and apparel services, health care, and personal care, compared to the 75 and over group.

In his study of CEX data from 1984 and 1997, Paulin observed that health care expenditures rose substantially for all groups during this period. His findings showed that those 65 and older, who made up about 20 percent of the sample being studied, accounted for nearly one-third of total health expenditures. He noted that health expenditure shares were most volatile for those age 75 and older. All groups spent a larger share of their health care dollars on health insurance in 1997, compared to 1984. Expenditures for drugs appeared to trend upward slightly as a share of the health care budget, at least for those 65 and older, but shares were most volatile for the 75 and older group.

Differences in consumption by the vulnerable elderly

Using 1990 CEX data, Rose Rubin and Michael Nieswiadomy compared consumption of older households that received cash assistance (food stamps or Supplement Security Income [SSI]) with those that received no cash assistance. The latter group was further subdivided into three income categories: poor (income less than 125 percent of the poverty level), low income (between 125 and 200 percent of the poverty level), and higher income (more than 200 percent of the poverty level). The results suggest that poor and low-income recipients were less well-off than cash assistance recipients. Overall, as income increased, the percentage of the budget spent on food decreased for all income categories. A 1 percent increase in income generated approximately a 1 percent increase in spending on housing for all three income groups. For health care, a 1 percent increase in income generated about a 1 percent increase in spending for the poor, no significant change for the low-income group, and a 0.37 percent increase for those with higher income. Overall, Rubin and Nieswiadomy concluded that poor and low-income older households that did not receive cash assistance were even more financially distressed than those receiving financial assistance: "Their reported current income is substantially lower than their expenditures, so they dissave at unsustainable rates. This annual dissaving, combined with their relatively low levels of financial assets, indicates continuing financial exigency" (Rubin and Nieswiadomy, 1997, pp. 96–97).

Differences in consumption by work status

The expenditure patterns of workers and nonworkers were also studied by Thomas Moehrle, who drew his sample of people age 62 to 74 from the 1986–1987 CEX. Moehrle found that two-thirds of the sample was not working while one-third was still employed. The sample was further subdivided into low-, middle-, and high-income groups. Moehrle found that the head of household of the working households was younger and had attained higher levels of education than their nonworking counterparts. Across all income groups, those not working were more likely to own their homes without mortgages and to spend more on food prepared at home and on health care. Transportation expenditures were higher for the working households, and the working households had notably higher expenditure shares for retirement, pension, and Social Security contributions across all income levels.

Rubin and Nieswiadomy (1994) studied retired and nonretired households headed by those age 50 and older using 1986–1987 CEX data. Their sample was further subdivided into married couples, single men, and single women. They found that nonretired married couples spent 45 percent more than retired couples, while nonretired single men spent 65 percent more than retired men, and nonretired women spent 50 percent more than retired women. The retired households spent a significantly greater share on food at home, housing, rent, utilities, household operations, and health care. The nonretired households allocated a greater share to food away from home, alcoholic beverages, owned and other dwellings, home furnishings, apparel and services, all transportation categories (except public), entertainment, education, miscellaneous gifts, and insurance. Rubin and Nieswiadomy found that spending on health care was positively correlated with education levels. Retired single women, nonwhites, and those over 75 were given larger shares of cash gifts and contributions.

Volunteer service: time use and consumption

Consumption may also take the form of time used for services that provide for well-being and personal satisfaction. Time-use studies are based on the premise that time outside of work can be used either to earn more money to purchase goods or for volunteer services that provide services to others. Volunteering can be done outside of the home (e.g., Red Cross, church). Caregiving is another example of using time to provide services.

Volunteer service by older persons is a valuable resource. Data from the 1991 Commonwealth Fund Productive Aging Survey (see Caro and Bass, 1995) showed that about one-quarter of persons over 55 were currently doing volunteer work. Volunteering was found to be more common among women, those with education beyond high school, those with professional or technical skills, those in good health, and those active in religion. The proportion of volunteers was highest for older adults age 55 to 59 among whom 31 percent were volunteers. Interestingly, almost one-tenth (9.4 percent) of persons age 85 and over were volunteers, according to the survey.

When the characteristics related to volunteer assignments were analyzed, the following associations were observed by Caro and Bass: Younger respondents were more likely to be engaged in fund-raising. Older respondents were more likely to drive a vehicle. Women were more likely than men to work in an office. Higher-income people were more likely to serve on a board or a committee. Higher levels of education were associated with service on a board or committee, office work, and fund-raising. Better health was associated with direct-service assignments.

Further analysis of the 1991 Commonwealth Fund Productive Aging Survey revealed that those active in religious organizations were more often female, younger, well-educated, and active in religion than the sample as a whole. Older people were more likely to volunteer for a health organization or a senior citizen center. Those with higher levels of education were more likely to volunteer for religious and health organizations, and being in good health was linked to volunteering in the health sector.

Caregiving: time use and consumption

Another important use of time by older persons is the time spent providing care to others. Although studies report somewhat different statistics on caregiving, this is likely to be a reflection of the manner in which caregiving is defined. For example, the Senate Select Committee on Aging (1988) reported that about 80 to 90 percent of elder care is informally provided by the family. The average caregiver is a 57-year-old female, but 36 percent of caregivers are over 65.

Slightly more than one-fourth of those 65 and over who participated in the 1991 Commonwealth Fund Survey reported providing informal assistance to a sick or disabled relative, friend, or neighbor during the previous week (Doty, 1995). About 15 percent of Commonwealth Fund Survey respondents age 65 and older who reported providing care to sick or disabled persons during the previous week reported providing more than twenty hours of care. Forty percent of persons age 65 and older with children reported that they had provided informal assistance of a nonfinancial nature to children, grandchildren, or great-grandchildren during the previous week, and 11 percent reported providing twenty or more hours of help.

According to the 1989 National Long-Term Care Survey (NLTCS), 53 percent of the primary caregivers of the disabled elderly were themselves 65 or older, and 18.7 percent of the caregivers of the disabled elderly were 75 or older. Primary caregivers are defined as individuals who bear most of the responsibility for providing long-term care for a disabled elder.

Data collected for the Assets and Health Dynamics Among the Oldest Old (AHEAD) study on respondents age 70 and older revealed the amount of help provided for people age 70 years and older with activity limitations. Some 51 percent of paid and unpaid caregivers provide help every day, 21 percent provide help several times a week, 14 percent provide help once a week, and 14 percent provide help less than once a week. When help given to people aged 70 and over was measured by hours-per-day, 34 percent received 1 hour of help, 46 percent received 2 to 5 hours, 9 percent received 6 to 10 hours, 4 percent received 11 to 23 hours, and 7 percent received care 24 hours per day. The pool of family caregivers is dwindling, however. In 1990 there were eleven potential caregivers for each person needing care. In 2050 the ratio will be four to one.

The demography of the U.S. population is changing in many ways. The increasing average age of the population is important. As the proportion of older consumers continues to increase, they are likely to account for an increased share of total expenditures. An examination of trends revealed that older consumers were similar to younger consumers in what was purchased. However, Paulin points out that the population of older consumers in 2000 were not members of the baby boom generation. He speculates that there may be more diversity in tastes and preferences as the baby boomers age.

SHARON A. DeVANEY

See also CONSUMER PROTECTION; ECONOMIC WELL-BEING; LIFE CYCLE THEORIES OF SAVINGS AND CONSUMPTION; POVERTY; RETAIL AND OLDER ADULTS.

BIBLIOGRAPHY

ABDEL-GHANY, M., and SHARPE, D. L. "Consumption Patterns Among the Young-Old and Old-Old." *Journal of Consumer Affairs* 31, no. 1 (1997): 90–112.

ANDO, A., and MODIGLIANI, F. "The Life Cycle Hypothesis of Saving: Aggregate Implications and Tests." *The American Economic Review* 53, no. 1 (1963): 55–84.

CARO, F. G., and BASS, S. A. "Increasing Volunteering Among Older People." In *Older and Active: How Americans Over 55 Are Contributing to Society*. Edited by S. A. Bass. New Haven, Conn.: Yale University Press, 1995. Pages 71–96.

DEATON, A. *Understanding Consumption*. Oxford: Oxford University Press, 1992.

DEVANEY, S. A. "Economic Status of Older Adults in the United States: Diversity, Women's Disadvantage, and Policy Implications." In *Gerontology: Perspectives and Issues*, 2d ed. Edited by K. Ferraro. New York: Springer Publishing Company, 1997. Pages 285–304.

DOTY, P. "Older Caregivers and the Future of Informal Caregiving." In *Older and Active: How Americans Over 55 are Contributing to Society*. Edited by S. A. Bass. New Haven, Conn.: Yale University Press, 1995. Pages 97–102.

FRIEDMAN, M. *A Theory of Consumption Function*. Princeton, N.J.: Princeton University Press, 1957.

HARRISON, B. "Spending Patterns of Older Persons Revealed in Expenditure Survey." *Monthly Labor Review*, 109, no. 10 (1986): 15–17.

HITSCHLER, P. B. "Spending by Older Consumers: 1980 and 1990 Compared." *Monthly Labor Review*, 1116, no. 5 (1993): 3–13.

Institute for Health and Aging. *Chronic Care in America*. University of California-San Francisco for the Robert Wood Johnson Foundation, 1996.

JACKSON, M. E. *Informal Care of the Disabled Elderly: A Research and Policy Initiative*. Final report to the Office of the Assistant Secretary for Planning and Evaluation, U.S. Department of Health and Human Services. Lexington, Mass.: SysteMetrics, 1992.

MOEHRLE, T. "Expenditure Patterns of the Elderly: Workers and Nonworkers." *Monthly Labor Review* 113, no. 5 (1990): 34–41.

National Academy on an Aging Society. "Caregiving: Helping the Elderly with Activity Limitations." Washington, D.C.. May, no. 7 (2000): 1–6.

PAULIN, G. D. "Expenditure Patterns of Older Americans, 1984–1997." *Monthly Labor Review* 123, no. 5 (2000): 3–28.

RUBIN, R., and NIESWIADOMY, M. L. "Expenditure Patterns of Retired and Nonretired Persons." *Monthly Labor Review* (1994): 10–21.

RUBIN, R., and NIESWIADOMY, M. L. *Expenditure of Older Americans*. Westport, Conn.: Praeger Publishers, 1997. Volume 117, no. 4.

RUSSELL, C. "The New Consumer Paradigm." *American Demographics* April (1999): 50–58.

Select Committee on Aging, U.S. House of Representatives. *Exploding the Myths: Caregiving in America*. Washington, D.C.: U.S. Government Printing Office, 1988.

STONE, R. "Defining Family Caregivers of the Elderly: Implications for Research and Public Policy." *The Gerontologist* 27 (1991): 616–626.

CONTINUING CARE RETIREMENT COMMUNITIES

Where a person lives directly impacts that person's quality of life. While most older people continue to live in private homes or apartments, some older people choose to live in an organized community such as a continuing care retirement community (CCRC).

Definition and history

The American Association of Homes and Services for the Aging (AAHSA) defines a CCRC as an organization that provides individuals a combination of housing options, accommodations, and health care services, depending on the level of care needed. Thus, within a single setting, an individual can move from an independent to a more restrictive housing environment as his or her needs increase. A CCRC organization typically has a formal contract or agreement with an individual or couple entering the community that includes the costs and level of services that will be provided (Sherwood, Ruchlin, Sherwood, Morris, 1997).

CCRC organizations are not a new phenomena, but have been around for more than a century. Beginning in Europe as a means to shelter and care for the aged, early CCRCs were affiliated with religious organizations. By the 1900s there were seven CCRCs in the United States. As the older population experienced growth during the 1960s, there was a corresponding increase in CCRC development, and since that time the number of CCRCs in the United States has steadily grown. In the year 2001 there were almost 2,000 CCRCs located in the U.S. with the average resident population of these facilities around 300 (AASHA, 1999). Pennsylvania, California, Florida, and Virginia have higher concentrations of CCRCs, with the Philadelphia/Delaware Valley area recognized as the "CCRC capital of the world" due to the high concentration (45) of CCRCs in that area. The total number of residents in CCRCs make up roughly 2 percent of the older population.

A majority of CCRCs are not-for-profit organizations (AAHSA, 1999), and they generally have religious affiliations. Since the mid 1980s there has been a slow push away from nonprofit to for-profit CCRCs, and large corporations such as Marriot and Hyatt have entered the industry. However, the majority of CCRCs are still not-for-profit organizations.

CCRCs today

CCRCs vary in size, accommodations, and services provided. However, most CCRCs have several basic housing levels on one campus setting. Providing residents with a range of care options is termed the *continuum of care*.

Independent living unit (ILU).   This type of housing, which is common to almost all CCRCs, may include apartments, cottages, one- or two-story houses, or luxury high-rises. Usually, amenities such as transportation to outside community events, meals, laundry service, housekeeping, security, and maintenance are included in the cost. An individual can choose to have more amenities, but extras come with an additional price. Health care services are available, but a resident living in an ILU is usually healthy and requires little health care assistance.

Personal care unit. (PCU)   An individual living in a personal care unit usually has some trouble performing specific activities of daily living. This level of care entails help in such areas as personal assistance or medication monitoring, allowing a person to continue to live independently.

Assisted-living facility.   A next step in the continuum between independent living units and nursing homes is the assisted-living facility. This type of housing is relatively new, and is designed for those individuals who do not require the level of care and supervision provided in a nursing home. In this type of facility, which is provided by most CCRCs, personal assistance with everyday activities such as dressing, eating, medication administration, RN staff, serving meals, rehabilitation, and bathing are common services available.

The nursing home.   This type of facility is common to all CCRCs. Residents of a CCRC can utilize the nursing home to recover from a short-term illness or as a means of treatment for a chronic illness. In this type of housing, residents receive round-the-clock care from nurses and nurse's aides.

This continuum of care allows the individual to receive all necessary health care services within one campus. However, it is important to note that the progression is not always linear—residents can move to any one of these housing arrangements and then back to the previous type of facility. For instance, an individual living in an ILU might receive care within the nursing home to recover from a short-term illness. After recovery, that individual could return to a less restrictive location.

Programs and activities.   One of the CCRCs main objectives is to keep residents healthy. Although research is limited, some studies report that CCRC residents live one and a half to two years longer than other older adults. This may be because CCRCs take a more active approach to maintaining health than individuals living in the community might. There are different types of programs that have been established at CCRCs in this regard. Although not all CCRCs offer such programs, many encourage exercise by providing swimming pools, tennis courts, golf courses, and walking paths, and many promote proper nutrition. Most CCRCs provide comprehensive meal options, promote proper medical care, and have health and dental facilities on the campus. In addition, they promote social involvement through a range of social and educational programs.

The contract

The contract that individuals sign when entering a CCRC determines the amount that their stay will cost and the type of amenities and health care services that will be provided. There are three main types of contracts: extended, modified, and fee-for-service.

About four out of ten CCRCs use an extended contract (AAHSA, 1999), in which individuals agree to pay an entry fee up front and a monthly fee for the rest of their life. Monthly fees usually only increase due to inflation or increased operating costs. This type of contract covers almost all of the health care needs of residents throughout their stay.

Three out of ten CCRCs provide a modified contract, which generally has a lower entry and monthly fees than an extended contract. However, there is a set limit on the number of days of health care per year that an individual can receive, and each resident is responsible for all costs beyond that limit. Like an extended contract, the costs of this agreement can only go up based on inflation and increased operating costs.

A fee-for-service contract is used by about three out of ten CCRCs. Individuals utilizing this option typically come from outside the organization to access the nursing home facility and are willing to pay as they receive care. Costs for this type of care can increase with inflation, operating costs, and with the amount of long-term care usage.

Cost and fees

It is relatively expensive to live in a CCRC. Data show that most individuals choosing CCRC's are in the middle- or upper-income bracket. Cost can be based on the type of contract negotiated, the size of apartment, and the services and amenities received. According to AARP, entry fees can range from $20,000 to $400,000, with monthly payments ranging from $200 to $2,500. AAHSA (1999) found that entry fees ranged from $34,000 for a studio apartment to $439,000 for a two bedroom home. The range of monthly fees was $1,383 for a single resident to $4,267 for a couple.

Whether or not one receives a refund of the entry fee, either for choosing to leave the community or upon one's death (in which case, a person's estate would receive the refund) depends on the particular CCRC. Organizations usually establish one of three types of refunds: declining scale, partial refund, or full refund. With a declining scale refund, the longer an individual stays at a facility, the more the entry fee refund decreases. With the partial refund option, a percentage of the fee will be refunded within a particular time period, after which there will be no refund. Full refunds are not generally available, though some CCRCs with high entry fees do offer them.

Requirements for entry

CCRC facilities can have different requirements for entry. Most typically require entering individuals to have physical and mental examinations, and they also stress the importance of having full Medicare coverage. It is important for the individual to demonstrate the ability to pay the entry and monthly fees.

Regulations governing CCRCs

Due to past occurrences of bankruptcy in the CCRC community, different regulatory methods have been established to protect the consumer and help bolster the image of CCRCs. As of 1997, there were thirty-seven states that had specific regulatory requirements for CCRCS—up from twenty-eight in 1988 (Brod, 1997). Each state has different requirements for licensing and accreditation. These requirements include financial disclosure, consumer protection, refund provisions, and resident contracts (Somers and Spears, 1992). The federal government has little involvement in the regulatory process, but does regulate those nursing homes located within CCRCs that rely on Medicaid and Medicare reimbursement.

Fearful that increased federal regulations will potentially raise costs, the industry has also established its own regulatory and accreditation system—the Continuing Care Accreditation Commission, established in 1985, has set standards "focusing on finance, governance, residential life, and health care" within CCRCs (Sanders, 1997, p. 16).

Current issues

One of the most challenging issues faced by CCRC organizations is whether such an option is affordable to most older people. Many people cannot afford high entry and monthly fees. Certain communities have used government subsidies through HUD to help low income individuals afford CCRC housing (Sanders, 1997). This suggests that unless government dollars are placed towards CCRCs, the only older individuals able to afford high entry fees will continue to come from the middle or upper class.

Another issue is whether individuals within CCRCs are truly "aging in place." By aging in place, older individuals expect to reside at home throughout the remainder of their lives. However, residents must still make the transition from home to the CCRC setting. This transition can be hard for some older individuals who find themselves having to adjust to a new setting and lifestyle with rules and restrictions (Sanders, 1997). Furthermore, as health issues increase they will need to move again.

Age segregation is another important issue faced by the CCRC industry. There has been an attempt in American society to move away from age segregation and to develop programs that keep older individuals involved in the community. Some researchers estimate that almost 10 percent of the older population might come to live in a CCRC. It is not known what affect this separation from other age groups might have, and the question of whether this might cause problems across generations needs to be addressed.

The issue of financial solvency must also be addressed. In the past there have been problems with CCRCs going out of business or going bankrupt, leaving individuals out in the cold. There needs to be a system in place to ensure financial security for individuals living in these facilities.

Research has shown that the different activities and programs promoting a healthy lifestyle help to reduce the risk of disease and disability in the CCRC population (Scanlon and Layton, 1997). Yet, its effectiveness on lowering health care costs has not been shown. Until research is conducted that controls for differences in income, education, health, and other factors it will be difficult to get an accurate idea on CCRC's cost effectiveness (Scanlon and Layton, 1997).

Regardless of these issues, CCRCs have the potential to be a very important option for older adults in the future. Already CCRSs have shown that they promote healthy lifestyles. Further research will strengthen this position. Policy changes that help make CCRCs more affordable could also increase the number of residents and also the number of communities. What is not clear is exactly what path the industry will follow.

IAN NELSON

See also FINANCIAL PLANNING FOR LONG-TERM CARE; HOUSING; LONG-TERM CARE.

BIBLIOGRAPHY

AARP. "Continuing Care Retirement Communities." World Wide Web document, 2001. www.aarp.org

SANDERS, J. "Continuing Care Retirement Communities: A Background and Summary of Current Issues." World Wide Web document. 2001. http://aspe.os.dhhs.gov

SCANLON, W., and LAYTON, B. D. *Report to Congressional Requesters: How Continuous Care Retirement Communities Manage Services for the Elderly.* Washington, D.C.: U.S. General Accounting Office, 1997. Available online at: http://frewebgate.access.gpo.gov

SOMERS, A. R., and SPEARS, N. L. *The Continuing Care Retirement Community.* New York: Springer, 1992.

CONTROL, PERCEIVED

Healthy and successful individuals often have a strong sense that they are in control of their lives and the world around them. Likewise, men and women who feel that they are in control of their lives tend to be healthy and successful. An individual's perception of his or her ability to be effective in the world, what psychology textbooks refer to as *perceived control,* is widely studied because it has such an important, and sometimes obvious, impact on an individual's physical and mental health. Perceived control reflects the degree to which an individual believes that a situation is controllable and that he or she has the skills necessary to bring about a desired (or avoid an undesired) outcome. There are two fundamental aspects: contingency (i.e., does the person believe that this outcome is controllable?) and competence (i.e., does the person perceive himself or herself as capable of producing the desired, or suppressing the undesired, event?).

Perceived control differs from objective control in that it focuses on a person's subjective perception (i.e., what the person believes is accepted as the reality for that individual, regardless of the actual control available). When people perceive themselves to be in control, but are not, it is called an illusion of control. A number of studies have investigated illusions of control. However, because the amount of control actually available is often not known, the practicality of examining this aspect of control has been questioned. Overall, research points to a fundamental difference between the actual control available in a situation and a person's perception of control; the perception of control (whether accurate or not) influences people's behaviors and emotions more strongly than actual control.

Historically, control beliefs, studied as locus of control, were conceived of as unidimensional, with internal control on one end of the continuum and external control on the other. Deriving his work from social learning theory, Dr. Julian Rotter developed the Internal-External scale in the 1960s. The Internal-External Scale utilized a forced-choice format questionnaire, and individuals were divided into those with either internal or external control beliefs. Those with an internal orientation believed that their own actions could produce desired outcomes, whereas those with an external view expected external forces (e.g., chance) to produce outcomes. This traditional conceptualization focused on what people believed caused events, irrespective of their perceived abilities to bring forth or prevent the events. In other words, this conceptualization lacked the component of competence.

Locus of control has since been expanded, and is now called by many different names, including primary/secondary control, sense of control, control beliefs, decisional control, control motivation, self-efficacy, self-directedness, self-determination, choice, decision, mastery, autonomy, helplessness, and explanatory style (see Skinner for a thorough compilation of terms falling under the rubric of control). Researchers now believe control beliefs are multidimensional, with internal and external beliefs independent. In Dr. Hanna Levenson's model (developed in 1972), there are three dimensions related to how a person views the cause of an event: internal or personal mastery ("It's due to me"), chance ("It's luck"), and powerful others ("It's due to others").

Rather than simply assessing beliefs about the controllability of a situation, modern conceptualizations also measure competence. That is, if people have a strong sense of control, they will likely believe not only that the outcome is dependent on their behavior but also that they have the ability to engage successfully in relevant actions. Further, perceived control is measured in both general (e.g., control over life in general) and specific domains (e.g., control over health, intellectual functioning, memory, and interpersonal relations). Domain-specific measures have helped to clarify complex relationships; for example, while there are typically no age differences on generalized measures of control, age differences have been found in domain-specific control beliefs in the areas of health and intelligence, with older adults showing decrements in these domains.

Control and self-efficacy

Domain-specific control beliefs are often studied under the term *self-efficacy*. Self-efficacy is the most studied component of Dr. Albert Bandura's social cognitive theory, originally formulated as the unifying theory of behavior change (1977). This theory states that behavior is governed by expectancies and incentives, and includes aspects of both contingency (outcome expectations) and competence (efficacy expectations). Efficacy expectations are influenced by four primary sources of information: performance accomplishments, vicarious experience, verbal persuasion, and motivational arousal. Performance accomplishments are the most effective type of information in forming efficacy beliefs. Successes will increase beliefs, and once an individual has a strong sense of efficacy, occasional failures will not be processed as negatively. Individuals with many performance accomplishments will persist in the face of defeat, and a failure that is later overcome will greatly strengthen efficacy beliefs.

Self-efficacy is measured in a specific and graduated fashion rather than on a general and global level. For example, an item measuring perceived control in the domain of health may read "How much control do you have over your health these days?," and the respondent rates his or her perceived control on a scale ranging from "No Control" to "Very Much Control." An item on a self-efficacy scale measuring perceived ability to exercise would read "How confident are you that you would exercise if you were in a bad mood?," and the respondent would give a confidence rating ranging from 0 to 100. Self-efficacy is frequently measured in studies examining behavior change, such as smoking cessation, exercise adherence, and phobia reduction. Most theories explaining human behavior include a self-efficacy component, and many researchers have called for an integration of the prominent theories. However, the social cognition theory, often referred to as simply the self-efficacy theory, is probably the most straightforward and popular framework, although it is not without its critics (see Maddux for a discussion of conceptual issues, and Smedslund for criticisms related to definitions and theoretically necessary versus empirically testable constructs within the theory).

Correlates of perceived control

Researchers examining diverse outcomes, and using various definitions of control, repeatedly find a relationship between perceived control and numerous positive outcomes. For example, individuals who possess a strong sense of control are wealthier and more educated, have better memories and higher intellectual functioning, are more physically active, enjoy better health, and live longer than those with a weak sense of control. Control is also associated with positive psychological outcomes, including greater life satisfaction, a more positive self-concept, greater well-being, and feeling young for one's age. Cross-sectional research cannot exclude the possibility that the above correlates produce a sense of perceived control; for example, greater wealth may lead to stronger control beliefs. Studies that do offer evidence for control as a causal agent indicate that a strong sense of perceived control is beneficial to an individual; however, little is known about possible negative effects of control.

Negative outcomes associated with control occur when there is a lack of fit between the person and the environment. For example, people who want low control may be dissatisfied with a situation that encourages them to take control. Further, encouraging perceptions of control may have harmful effects (e.g., frustration or helplessness) if a person lacks ability or if the situation does not allow control (as in some institutional settings).

It may be that global control beliefs are generally adaptive, whereas domain-specific control beliefs may or may not be adaptive, depending on the controllability of the domain. For example, interpersonal relationships at a minimum involve two people (and, when considering an entire social network, consist of an intricate web of social ties); thus the controllability over these relationships will vary, with control shared across the network. In this case, it would be reasonable to expect that a person with a moderate sense of perceived control could build and utilize a successful network, whereas someone holding strong beliefs about his or her control over other people in the network—for example, a partner or family member—may be exposed to social conflict or disappointment. While it may be harmful to exert efforts to control an event that is truly uncontrollable, a strong sense of control will be adaptive if it is assumed that most of the situations people face throughout their lives, as well as their responses to them (i.e., how one copes), are to some extent controllable or of unknown controllability (e.g., illness and disease).

Processes of control

There are two primary mechanisms through which perceived control may produce beneficial outcomes: direct (main-effect model), or indi-

rect, through a reduction in stress (stress-buffering model; see Cohen).

The main-effect model suggests that having a strong sense of control has a direct positive effect on health through various mediators, or mechanisms. These mediators include cognitive, behavioral, and physiological factors. For example, control may lead to positive psychological states, such as high self-esteem and positive affect. This in turn may lead to favorable physiological responses as well as to participation in health-promoting behaviors. Together, these produce health-relevant biological influences (e.g., immune effects) resulting in good health. This model does not explicitly include alternative paths, which also likely exist. For example, it is plausible that a health-promoting behavior like exercise would influence health, physiological responses, and subsequent feelings of control.

There is evidence for a main-effect model. For example, an internal health locus of control has been related to the importance placed on good health, and both of them are predictors of engaging in preventive health behaviors. Thus, control beliefs can help explain why some people abstain from risky behaviors (e.g., smoking) and participate in healthy ones (e.g., exercise).

In the psychological domain, perceived control has been associated with increased levels of self-esteem, optimism, vigor, and social support, and decreased levels of depression and anxiety. While many of the studies in this area are correlational, growing numbers of experimental manipulations of objective control and interventions enhancing efficacy beliefs have produced beneficial results, suggesting that the causal direction is from feelings of control to health and well-being.

While the main-effect model assumes that there are effects of control on health and well-being (through cognition, behaviors, and/or physiology), an alternative and equally plausible view suggests that a strong sense of control may aid in the buffering of stress. Stress is assumed to have negative effects on health and well-being. In the stress-buffering model, a potentially stressful event is tempered by feelings of control at multiple points. For example, control may lead a potentially stressful event to be appraised as less so, or, once a stressful event is perceived, control may ward off feelings of helplessness.

Studies in which outcomes depend upon an interaction between stress and control support a stress-buffering model (e.g., control moderates the effects of stress on physical and mental health). Research also supports interactions between control and physiological aspects of stress; physiological responses to stressful events are lessened in those with strong control beliefs. For example, when people believe they have control over an aversive event like noise, or that they can successfully overcome a stressor, they show lower levels of stress-related hormones.

Perceived control in aging

A desire to exert control over the environment is implicit in theories of control, and evidenced in early life. Whether described as an effectance drive, mastery motivation, or the need for competence, research indicates that perceiving control over the environment is a basic need in humans (see Heckhausen and Schulz for a review).

Personal control beliefs (internal control) increase during childhood. In middle childhood, concepts of control become more differentiated, and there appears to be an increase in internal control beliefs as people age. Several studies have shown that general control beliefs remain relatively stable, decreasing only slightly, well into older adulthood. However, age-related changes in domain-specific control beliefs have been found, with older adults showing declines in areas of health, physical appearance, and intellectual functioning. In addition there is evidence that beliefs about constraints increase markedly in later life.

Control beliefs in older adults are especially important subjects of study; normative beliefs about aging include an increase in the risk for losses (social, personal, and physical) and a corresponding decrease in opportunities for gains. Thus, developmental changes in later life present challenges for an individual's actual, as well as perceived, control. However, studies have indicated that older adults can maintain a sense of control through accommodation processes. A theory that incorporates accommodation, termed selective optimization with compensation (Baltes and Baltes), explains a person's ability to maintain beliefs in control by selecting high-efficacy domains, taking measures to optimize functioning in these areas, and, when necessary, compensating when requisite skills or resources are no longer available. For example, an aging pianist may give up other activities and reduce

her repertoire (selection), practice more often (optimization), and slow down the playing of the song before a fast section to give the impression of speed (compensation). Thus, while general internal control beliefs remain stable in adulthood, external control beliefs increase in later life, and domain-specific decreases in control are likely to occur in areas that are susceptible to age-related loss.

The modifiability of control beliefs has also been studied from a life span perspective. Interventions designed to affect control beliefs in adulthood have demonstrated that while control beliefs are more malleable in younger adults, once older adults are convinced of their ability, they devote more time and effort to relevant tasks and therefore attain further gains in both performance and efficacy beliefs.

Implications for research in aging

Because strong control beliefs have been related to so many positive outcomes, there have been many attempts to enhance such feelings through interventions. Researchers have attempted to modify or enhance control beliefs in regard to memory, rehabilitation from physical impairments, cancer treatment, dealing with chronic diseases such as osteoarthritis or rheumatoid arthritis, as well as to facilitate control beliefs in the face of losses associated with aging. These studies indicate that control beliefs can be influenced well into late life. Such findings grow in importance as models of health behavior move from the treating of acute illnesses in a physician-directed environment to long-term symptom management associated with chronic diseases in a patient-directed environment.

For example, a number of nursing home studies have reported that when people are given opportunities to exercise control, they show significant improvements on a number of measures, ranging from memory tasks and activity to overall health and psychological adjustment. In an often cited study by Drs. Ellen Langer and Judith Rodin, conducted in 1996, nursing home residents who were given more control over their environment (e.g., when to watch a movie, taking care of a house plant) were happier, more active, and more alert at a follow-up conducted months later. Also, only 15 percent of the group with enhanced control had died, compared with 30 percent in the group of residents who were told the hospital staff was responsible for their care (see also Banziger and Roush; Schulz and Hanusa for other interventions in institutional settings). The research in this area indicates that strong beliefs in perceived control may reverse, delay, or protect against functional declines associated with aging.

The success of interventions seeking to increase control beliefs (especially in later life) presumably will hinge on the assessment of relevant components of control: desire, ability/ perception, and actual control available. Efficacious interventions will likely be those that first determine which aspects should be changed and then successfully produce the desired changes. For example, if nursing homes are designed to discourage control, attempting to enhance control in such a setting could lead to frustration for the individual as well as for the staff. Accordingly, interventions designed with a multilevel focus that balance an individual's needs and abilities with the adaptability of the environment may be the most effective.

Summary

The finding that perceptions of control and feelings of self-efficacy are beneficial and adaptive is robust. People with a strong sense of perceived control generally fare better (both mentally and physically) than do those who do not hold such beliefs. However, the relationships between health and aspects such as desire for control and maladaptive control beliefs are less studied. Some research suggests that there may be an adaptive level of control for certain situations, and that an individual's desire for control should be considered when explaining positive or negative outcomes. Research that aims to increase and/or maintain high levels of perceived control in adulthood and later life becomes an increasingly fertile area of investigation as the population ages. Whether effecting change directly in an individual, an entire social group, or through the restructuring or developing of institutions, hospitals, or communities, innovative ideas from a collection of fields (e.g., psychology, medicine, architecture) may change the way people age.

HEATHER R. WALEN

See also INTERVENTIONS, PSYCHOSOCIAL BEHAVIOR; LIFE SPAN THEORY OF CONTROL; SELECTIVE OPTIMIZATION WITH COMPENSATION THEORY; STRESS AND COPING.

BIBLIOGRAPHY

BALTES, P. B., and BALTES, M. M. "Psychological Perspectives on Successful Aging: The Model of Selective Optimization with Compensation." In *Successful Aging: Perspectives from the Behavioral Sciences.* Edited by Paul B. Baltes and Margret M. Baltes. Cambridge, Mass.: Cambridge University Press, 1990. Pages 1–34.

BANDURA, A. *Self-Efficacy: The Exercise of Control.* New York: W. H. Freeman, 1997.

BANZIGER, G., and ROUSH, S. "Nursing Homes for the Birds: A Control-Relevant Intervention with Bird Feeders." *The Gerontologist* 23 (1983): 527–531.

BURGER, J. M. "Negative Reactions to Increases in Perceived Personal Control." *Journal of Personality and Social Psychology* 56 (1989): 246–256.

COHEN, S. "Control and the Epidemiology of Physical Health: Where Do We Go from Here?" In *Self-Directedness: Cause and Effects Throughout the Life Course.* Edited by J. Rodin, C. Schooler, and K. W. Schaie. Hillsdale, N.J.: Lawrence Erlbaum, 1990. Pages 231–240.

FREUND, A. M., and BALTES, P. B. "Selection, Optimization, and Compensation as Strategies of Life Management: Correlations with Subjective Indicators of Aging." *Psychology and Aging* 13, no. 4 (December 1998): 531–543.

FRY, P. S. *Psychological Perspectives of Helplessness and Control in the Elderly. Advances in Psychology, 57.* Amsterdam: North-Holland, 1989.

GATZ, M. "Stress, Control and Psychological Interventions." In *Stress and Health among the Elderly.* Edited by M. Wykle and E. Kahana. New York: Springer, 1992. Pages 209–222.

HECKHAUSEN, J., and SCHULZ, R. "A Life-Span Theory of Control." *Psychological Review* 102, no. 2 (1995): 284–304.

LACHMAN, M. E. "Locus of Control in Aging Research: A Case for Multidimensional and Domain-Specific Assessment." *Journal of Psychology and Aging* 1, no. 1 (1986): 34–40.

LACHMAN, M. E., and BURACK, O. R. "Planning and Control Processes Across the Life Span: An Overview." *International Journal of Behavioral Development* 16, no. 2 (1993): 131–143.

LANGER, E. J. "The Illusion of Control." *Journal of Personality and Social Psychology* 32 (1975): 311–328.

LANGER, E. J. *Mindfulness.* Reading, Mass.: Addison-Wesley, 1989.

LANGER, E. J., and RODIN, J. "Long-term Effects of a Control-Relevant Intervention with the Institutionalized Aged." In *Readings in Social Psychology: The Art and Science of Research.* Edited by S. Fein and S. Spencer. Boston: Houghton Mifflin, 1996. Pages 175–180.

LEVENSON, H. "Differentiating among Internality, Powerful Others, and Chance." In *Research with the Locus of Control Construct: Assessment Methods.* Vol. 1. Edited by H. M. Lefcourt. New York: Academic Press, 1981. Pages 15–63.

MADDUX, J. E. "Social Cognitive Models of Health and Exercise Behavior: An Introduction and Review of Conceptual Issues." *Journal of Applied Sport Psychology* 5 (1993): 116–140.

RODIN, J. "Control by Any Other Name: Definitions, Concepts, Processes." In *Self-Directedness: Cause and Effects Throughout the Life Course.* Edited by J. Rodin, C. Schooler, and K. W. Schaie. Hillsdale, N.J.: Lawrence Erlbaum, 1990. Pages 1–18.

ROTTER, J. B. "Generalized Expectancies for Internal Versus External Control of Reinforcement." *Psychological Monographs* 80, whole no. 609 (1966).

SCHULZ, R., and HANUSA, B. H. "Long-Term Effects of Control and Predictability-Enhancing Interventions: Findings and Ethical Issues." *Journal of Personality and Social Psychology* 36 (1978): 1194–1201.

SKINNER, E. A. "A Guide to the Constructs of Control." *Journal of Personality and Social Psychology* 71, no. 3 (1996): 549–570.

SMEDSLUND, J. "Bandura's Theory of Self-Efficacy: A Set of Common Sense Theorems." *Scandinavian Journal of Psychology* 19 (1978): 1–14.

WEISZ, J. R. "Can I Control It? The Pursuit of Veridical Answers Across the Life Span." In *Life-Span Development and Behavior.* Edited by P. B. Baltes and O. G. Brim. New York: Academic Press, 1983. Pages 233–300.

CORESIDENCE

Over the course of the twentieth century, dramatic changes occurred in the coresidential patterns of older Americans. Between 1900 and 1998, the percentage of elderly persons living alone increased five-fold, rising from 5 percent to 26 percent. This historical rise in living alone has been attributed to three basic mechanisms that reflect a long-term change in the status and well-being of older people and their families: (1) increasing levels of economic resources available to the older population, (2) an increased preference for privacy and residential independence,

and (3) demographic changes affecting the availability of potential residential partners.

Economic resources. Scholars have attributed the increasing pursuit of independent living and economic security among widows to the growth in public entitlement programs. In the past, widows were more compelled to rely on family support. Evidence of an economic basis for the historical rise in living alone has been documented by McGarry and Schoeni (2000), who demonstrated that income growth in the personal incomes of older citizens, particularly through Social Security benefits, have allowed the elderly to live apart from family. This finding echoes Anderson's (1977) research showing how the introduction of pensions in nineteenth-century England enabled greater residential independence of older people. Although pensions increased the propensity for older adults to live alone, having wealthier offspring may dampen this effect. Another version of the economic model, however, is advanced by Steven Ruggles (1996), who connected burgeoning household wealth during the late nineteenth century to the growth in the proportion of people living in extended family households. Economic resources accumulated by younger families enabled them to coreside with elderly family members, which did little to enhance the economic (and residential) freedom of the older generation.

Preferences. Another factor influencing historical patterns of coresidence among older Americans has been the increasing preference for single living. Personal preferences often reflect the changing norms of a modernizing society as it moves from a more collectivistic to a more individualistic orientation, stressing autonomy and privacy. Although most scholars acknowledge that preference or taste has played a role in the growing residential independence of the aged, they disagree over its relative contribution and timing. Some researchers have identified the preference to live apart from kin as a persistent, but latent, desire among the elderly that only recently—through public entitlement programs—has become economically feasible. Preferences for intergenerational coresidence also appear to be perpetuated through generations as an aspect of family culture. Having lived in a three-generational household as a child appears to strengthens one's willingness as an adult to provide housing for an older parent.

Demographic change. The availability of suitable household partners is another key dimension determining coresidency patterns of older adults. Among the demographic transitions altering such availability are fertility, divorce, and widowhood. Fertility rates were particularly low during the Great Depression (1930s) and World War II periods, resulting in relatively smaller families among the current cohort of the oldest old. R. T. Gillaspy (1979) cites lower fertility rates among women born at the turn of the twentieth century as a main reason for the 16 percent increase between 1970 and 1998 in the proportion of women 75 years and older living alone. Sharp fertility increases during the post–World War II years (1946–1964) increased the pool of potential residential partners for the current young-old, while a decline in the fertility rates of the baby boomers themselves portends a deficit of such partners in future elderly cohorts.

Even though fertility rates fluctuated somewhat over the last half of the twentieth century, there was an overall decline in such rates between 1940 and 1998. There was also a decline (from 71 percent to 20 percent) in the percentage of women living with their children during this period. However, an important factor that mitigated the impact of fertility reductions on kin-supply was the dramatic increase in life expectancy resulting from mortality declines during the twentieth century. As children are able to spend more of their adult years with their parents, they have greater opportunities for sharing a residence with them.

Changing marriage patterns have also contributed to the growing trend among elderly persons to live alone. Janet Wilmoth (1998) found that transitioning to living alone increases with marital dissolution, whether due to death, separation, or divorce. While separation and divorce are relatively less common than widowhood in the older population, this pathway to living alone has grown increasingly more prevalent among the young-old. Baby boomers will present an older cohort with relatively high representations of never-married, divorced, and childless individuals. These trends may well signal a future decline in the proportion of elderly persons who coreside with family members.

Diversity in living arrangements

Variations in the propensity to live alone or with others are found by age, gender, race, and ethnicity. As age increases, older people are more likely to live alone or with a relative other than a spouse—a product of increasing widowhood rates in later life. In general, rates of coresidence with sons and daughters are higher for older women than for older men, though this differential diminishes with increasing age. Gender differences in coresidence have much to do with spouse availability patterns that are linked to widowhood. Relatively fewer older men live alone, as compared to older women, because they are less likely to be widowed. In 1990, 79 percent of men between the ages of sixty-five and seventy-four, and 70 percent of those seventy-five and older, lived with a spouse, as compared to 54 percent and 25 percent of older women in these respective age categories. However, among the unmarried, older men were 17 percent more likely than older women to coreside with a relative (84 percent for men vs. 67 percent for women).

Patterns of coresidence among older parents vary by both their own age and the gender of their adult children. The young-old (age sixty-five to seventy-five) are more likely to live with a son, while the old-old (age seventy-five to eighty-five) are more likely to live with a daughter. The preference for daughters as household partners is found particularly among women who are over age eighty and living without a spouse. This is likely due to the fact that daughters are more likely than sons to become caregivers for an older parent. Indeed, scholars have expressed some concern that fertility reductions, combined with labor-force participation among women, may limit the availability of middle-aged daughters to serve as coresident caregivers for their very old parents.

There are striking racial and ethnic differences in the living arrangements of older adults. Relatively fewer older Asian (21.2 percent) and Hispanic (27.4 percent) women live alone than older white women (41.3 percent) and African American women (40.8 percent). However, in 1998 an estimated 42 percent of older white women were coresiding with a spouse, as compared with 24 percent of older black women. Older African American women are more likely than older white women to live with other relatives—a result of the higher rates of nonmarriage among African Americans. Older Hispanic women are also more likely than whites to coreside with other relatives, especially adult children. Similar coresidential patterns by race and ethnicity are found among older American men.

Differences in coresidence of the elderly by race and ethnicity have been attributed both to socioeconomic need and cultural traditions. Some evidence points to economic need as a more salient reason for coresidence in African American families, and cultural values are a more prominent reason for coresidence in Hispanic families. Asian Americans age fifty-five and older are more likely than white non-Hispanics of the same age to live with their grandchildren (21.9 percent vs. 4.5 percent). This difference has been attributed to traditional Confucian ideals of filial piety—the unquestioning obligation to respect and care for elders in old age. In addition, higher rates of marriage give Asian Americans a greater likelihood of having children and grandchildren with whom to live. Healthy and able grandparents are reported to play an active role in providing baby-sitting and housekeeping services to their coresident working adult children, saving them both time and resources.

Advantages and disadvantages of coresidence

In reviewing research on coresidence and solitary living, results show that there are both costs and rewards for older individuals. Although sharing a household enhances the ability of older adults to receive needed instrumental services, such as help with activities of daily living, it has been shown to have little relation to emotional support from family and others. Older individuals who make the transition to the household of a child or other relative tend to be in poorer health and more likely to be widowed. In addition, older people who have greater limitations in physical functioning, often in conjunction with widowhood, enhance their likelihood of coresiding with an adult child or other relative. Given these findings, it is likely that health improvements in the older population has increased their functional independence and suppressed the need to live with others.

From another point of view, independent living may produce psychological benefits for older adults. Some scholars have argued that living independently from children allows older adults to enjoy more privacy and greater autonomy. All things considered, older parents generally appear to be satisfied living with their adult children, as this arrangement enhances their experience of closeness with the coresident adult child. However, the quality of the relationship sometimes suffers when adult children—especially in middle age—remain or become economically dependent on their parents.

Changing patterns in coresidence

In spite of historical increases in living alone, the large majority of elderly persons—about seven out of ten—still live with others. According to the Census Bureau's 1998 *Population Reports*, slightly more than half (54 percent) of the older population live with a spouse, 13 percent live with at least one relative other than a spouse, and 2 percent live with a nonrelative. However, these statistics belie recent shifts in the types of households in which older people tend to reside. There are two important historical changes in the intergenerational household circumstances of the aged: (1) generational reversals in household headship, and (2) a rise in older adults raising grandchildren.

One of the most striking changes in the residential circumstances of elderly persons is their gain of power within multigenerational households. Between 1940 and 1990, older adults cohabiting with members of other generations contributed an increasingly larger share to their total household incomes and were gradually more likely to assume household headship. Today, older parents are more likely to provide a home for their middle-aged adult children than their children are to provide a home for them. In part, this trend is due to the changing needs of the younger generation as divorce rates have accelerated. Children's marital status is a strong predictor of coresidence, as parents with unmarried adult children have an appreciably greater risk of having an adult child at home. While separated and divorced daughters are more likely than married daughters to move in with their parents, these unmarried daughters tend to offer less financial and social support, suggesting that it is the daughters' needs that precipitated the shared living arrangement.

Another growing phenomenon is the increase in the number of grandparents who raise grandchildren. In 1999, 5.6 percent of grandchildren under the age of eighteen—5.5 million children—lived with at least one grandparent, representing a 76 percent increase since 1970. It is estimated that between 10 percent and 16 percent of grandparents have had the experience of housing a grandchild for at least six months.

Often, in such households, the parent is not present due to economic difficulties, divorce, or single parenthood. Between 1990 and 1994, the number of children being raised in these skipped-generation households increased by 45 percent (from 935,000 to 1,359,000). Most of these households are the product of parental characteristics, behaviors, or conditions (such as incarceration, substance abuse, teen pregnancy, divorce, mental and physical illnesses, child abuse and neglect, and HIV/AIDS) that inhibit their ability to parent effectively.

The phenomenon of grandparents coresiding with grandchildren is most common among minority group members. In 1995, 13.5 percent of African-American grandchildren were living with a grandparent or other relatives, compared with 6.5 percent of Hispanic children and 4.1 percent of white children. An estimated 30 percent of African-American grandmothers have been responsible for raising a grandchild for at least six months, compared with 10.9 percent of all grandparents. This difference is attributed to cultural values and the pooling of limited economic resources between generations. In the decades of the 1980s and 1990s, African-American grandmothers between fifty and sixty-nine years of age were 6 to 8 percent more likely than white grandmothers to live in a skipped-generation household. At least some of this growing racial disparity has been attributed to the crack-cocaine epidemic, as well as the growth of the African American underclass in the 1980s, which resulted in grandparents (and great grandparents) being primary caregivers for grandchildren whose parents were in crisis.

Within a long-term historical framework a different picture emerges, as the recent rise in grandparent-headed households appears to be a historical anomaly. Evidence shows that over the twentieth century there was a decline in the percentage of American grandparents who coreside with their grandchildren. According to Peter Uhlenberg (2000), between 1900 and 1990 the proportion of white grandmothers sixty to sixty-nine years of age coresiding with a grandchild declined from 24 percent to 6 percent. The proportion of African-American grandmothers in the same age category who coresided with a grandchild declined from 40 percent to 17 percent over the same period. Thus, the recent upturn in grandparent-grandchild coresidence is only a slight reversal of a long-term downward trend. However, the social implications of this re-

cent change are vast, given the sheer number of grandchildren involved, and have caused fundamental changes in family life, with grandparents increasingly being given the opportunity to serve as filial "safety nets."

The age of grandparents coresiding with grandchildren has become younger over time. Before 1980, the majority of grandparents living with grandchildren were over sixty years old, after which the majority were under sixty years of age. This trend is the result of changes in the nature and type of household structure of coresiding grandparents, with increasingly more grandparents as providers of support to others in the household. There are sometimes emotional costs for grandparents who provide extraordinary forms of care by assuming parenthood for the second time. Adopting such a role may induce distress if it is unanticipated and involuntary. Grandparents who raise grandchildren have less time for their spouses, friends, and hobbies. Fuller-Thompson and Minkler (2000) found that grandparents raising grandchildren suffer from increased psychological and physical distress when compared to grandparents who do not have grandchildren in their households. Many caregiving grandparents have adult children struggling with serious difficulties, leading to feelings of self-blame, betrayal, and helplessness, as well as accentuated experiences of physical health symptoms.

Conclusion

Social, economic, health, and demographic changes have influenced the propensity of elders to live alone, with culture, values, and personal preferences playing a role in the decision whether to coreside with others or to live alone. However, factors that have enhanced the propensity of the elderly to live alone, such as gains in economic resources, declining fertility, and improving health, may be mitigated by the other factors, such as increasing ethnic diversity and the growing need for housing among younger adults. As can be seen from the phenomenon of grandparents raising grandchildren, it is important to consider the needs of all generations of the family in order to fully appreciate the dynamics of coresidence among the elderly.

Sharing a residence in later life enables the exchange of crucial services within and across generations. Increases in immigration and the swelling number of minority elders may continue to fuel the recent growth in multigenerational coresidence as the fulfillment of filial responsibility. However, young and middle-aged adults may enter old age possessing fewer filial, financial, and housing resources than earlier generations, limiting their potential for coresidence and testing the resilience of older adults to adapt to changing contingencies in their informal networks.

MERRIL SILVERSTEIN
FRANCES YANG

See also GRADNPARENTHOOD; INTERGENERATIONAL EXCHANGES; LIVING ARRANGEMENTS; PARENT-CHILD RELATIONSHIP.

BIBLIOGRAPHY

ANDERSON, M. "The Impact on the Family Relationships of the Elderly of Changes since Victorian Times in Governmental Income-Maintenance Provision." In *Family, Bureaucracy and the Elderly*. Edited by Ethel Shanas and M. Sussman. Durham, N.C.: Duke University Press, 1977.

ANGEL, R. J., and TIENDA, M. "Determinants of Extended Household Structure: Cultural Pattern or Economic Need?" *American Journal of Sociology* 87 (1992): 1360–1383.

AQUILINO, W. S. "The Likelihood of Parent-Adult Child Coresidence: Effects of Family Structure and Parental Characteristics." *Journal of Marriage and the Family* 52 (1990): 405–419.

BRODY, E. M.; LITVIN, S. J.; HOFFMAN, C.; and KLEBAN, M. H. "Marital Status of Caregiving Daughters and Co-residence with Dependent Parents." *The Gerontologist* 35, no. 1 (1995): 75–86.

BURTON, T. "African-American Grandparents." In *Handbook on Grandparenthood*. Edited by Maximiliane Szinovacz. Westport, Conn.: Greenwood Press. 1998.

CRIMMINS, E.; SAITO, Y.; and INGEGNERI, D. "Changes In Life Expectancy and Disability-Free Life Expectancy in the U.S." *Population and Development Review* 15, no. 2 (1989): 235–267.

FULLER-THOMPSON, E., and MINKLER, M. "African American Grandparents Raising Grandchildren: A National Profile of Demographic and Health Characteristics." *Health and Social Work* 25, no. 2 (2000): 109–118.

GIARRUSSO, R.; SILVERSTEIN, M.; and BENGTSON, V. "Family Complexity and the Grandparent Role." *Generations* 20 (1996): 17–23.

GILLASPY, R. T. "Older Population: Considerations for Family Ties." In *Aging Parents*. Edited by P. K. Ragan. Los Angeles: Ethel Percy Andrus Gerontology Center, University of Southern California. Pages 11–26.

GOLDSCHEIDER, C., and JONES, M. B. "Living Arrangements among the Older Population: Constraints, Preferences and Power." In *Ethnicity and the New Family Economy*. Edited by Frances K. Goldscheider and Calvin Goldscheider. Boulder, Colo.: Westview, 1987. Pages 75–91.

GOLDSCHEIDER, F. K., and LAWTON, L. "Family Experiences and the Erosion of Support for Intergenerational Coresidence." *Journal of Marriage and the Family* 60, no. 3 (1998): 620–632.

HIMES, C. L. "Future Caregivers: Projected Family Structures of Older Persons." *Journal of Gerontology: Social Sciences* 47, no. 1 (1992): S17–S26.

HIMES, C. L.; HOGAN, D. P.; and EGGEBEEN, D. J. "Living Arrangements of Minority Elders." *Journal of Gerontology: Social Sciences* 51, no. 1 (1996): 42–52.

KAMO "Asian-American Grandparents." In *Handbook on Grandparenthood*. Edited by Maximiliane Szinovacz. Westport, Conn.: Greenwood Press, 1998. Pages 56–79.

MCGARRY, K., and SCHOENI, R. F. "Social Security, Economic Growth, and the Rise in Elderly Widows' Independency in the Twentieth Century." *Demography* 37, no. 2 (2000): 221–236.

MUTCHLER, J. E., and BURR, J. A. "A Longitudinal Analysis of Household and Nonhousehold Living Arrangements in Later Life." *Demography* 28, no. 3 (1991): 375–390.

PEZZIN, L. E., and SCHONE, B. S. "Intergenerational Household Formation, Female Labor Supply and Informal Caregiving: A Bargaining Approach." *The Journal of Human Resources* 34, no. 3 (1999): 475–503.

PYNOOS, J., and GOLANT, S. "Housing for the Aged." In *Handbook of Aging and the Social Sciences*, 4th ed. Edited by K. Warner Schaie and Linda K. George. San Diego: Academic Press, 1996.

RUGGLES, S. *Living Arrangements and Well-Being of Older Persons in the Past*. New York: Population Division, Department of Economic and Social Affairs, United Nations Secretariat, 2000.

RUGGLES, S. "Prolonged Connections: The Rise of the Extended Family in Nineteenth-Century England and America." In *Social Demography*. Edited by Doris P. Slesinger, James A. Sweet, and Karl E. Taeuber. Madison: University of Wisconsin Press, 1996.

SOLDO, B.; WOLF, D.; and AGREE, E. "Family, Households, and Care Arrangements of Frail Older Women: A Structural Analysis." *Journal of Gerontology: Social Sciences* 45 (1990): S238–S249.

SPEARE, A., JR.; AVERY, R.; and LAWTON, L. "Disability, Residential Mobility, and Changes in Living Arrangements." *Journal of Gerontology: Social Sciences* 46, no. 3 (1990). 133–142.

SZINOVACZ, M. "Grandparenthood in the United States." In *Handbook on Grandparenthood.* Edited by Maximiliane Szinovacz. Westport, Conn.: Greenwood Press, 1998.

UHLENBERG, P., and KIRBY, J. B. "Grandparenthood Over Time: Historical and Demographic Trends." In *Handbook on Grandparenthood.* Edited by Maximiliane Szinovacz. Westport, Conn.: Greenwood Press, 1998. Pages 23–39.

U.S. Bureau of the Census. *Current Population Reports, 1998.* Washington, D.C.: U.S. Government Printing Office.

U.S. Bureau of the Census. "Household and Family Characteristics: March 1998 (Update) and Earlier Reports." *Current Population Reports.* 2001: P20–515.

WILMOTH, J. M. "Living Arrangement Transitions among America's Older Adults." *Gerontologist* 38, no. 4 (1998): 434–444.

WILMOTH, J. M. "Unbalanced Social Exchanges and Living Arrangement Transitions among Older Adults." *Gerontologist* 40, no. 1 (2000): 64–74.

CORONARY BYPASS

See REVASCULARIZATION: BYPASS SURGERY AND ANGIOPLASTY

COST OF LIVING

See CONSUMER PRICE INDEX AND COLAS

CREATIVITY

Creativity is most often defined as the individual capacity to generate ideas that are both original and useful. Thus, those who have highly novel but clearly maladaptive ideas are not considered creative. An example would be paranoid psychotics whose delusions of grandeur and persecution prevent them from leading normal lives. By the same token, in everyday life there are numerous solutions to problems that work just fine but are totally routine, such as a motorist's decision to take an alternate route to the grocery store when an automobile accident blocks the habitual route. Of course, the two defining components of creativity—originality and utility—are not discrete characteristics—there are varying degrees of these elements in a creative idea. Hence, a measure of originality can vary from utterly conventional ideas (the zero point) to ideas that can be considered extremely surprising or even revolutionary. Similarly, a measure of utility can range from an idea that proves completely impractical or unworkable (the zero point) to an idea that solves a problem perfectly. As a necessary consequence, their joint product, creativity, can also vary along some implicit scale. At the lower end of this scale is everyday creativity. This category includes successful and novel solutions to the problems that people often encounter during the course of their lives. At a higher level on this scale is creativity that actually results in some discrete product, such as a poem published in a regional literary magazine or a painting displayed at a local gallery or exhibit. Higher still are those products so creative that they exert a more lasting and pervasive impact on a discipline, culture, society, or civilization. At this extreme it is common to speak of "creative genius."

Yet it is critical to stress that genius-grade creativity is not necessarily superior to more ordinary forms of creativity. Although the influence of an artistic or scientific masterpiece is more impressive in the long run, such masterworks are also relatively rare. In contrast, ideas that appear at the middle levels of creativity, because of their frequency, play a bigger role in daily affairs, whether in the home, school, or workplace. Indeed, everyday creativity often plays a crucial role in making life more enjoyable. The amateur cooks who delight in devising and testing new recipes, the do-it-yourselfers who enjoy designing and building furniture for their homes, and the "Sunday painters" who derive joy from expressing their feelings and images on canvas all illustrate some of these commonplace forms of creative activity.

From the standpoint of aging, there are two fundamental questions that must be addressed. The first question concerns how creativity changes across the life span, particularly in the final years of a person's life. The second question regards the best explanations for any developmental changes. In short, the first question is empirical, the second theoretical.

Empirical findings

The first task in assessing longitudinal trends is to decide on an appropriate measure of creativity. For the most part, researchers have adopted one of two assessment methods: psychometric tests and productivity indicators.

Psychometric tests.   A large number of psychometric instruments exist that purport to assess creativity. Some measures assess personality characteristics, others cognitive style, and yet others biographical background factors. Nonetheless, research on the relation between age and creativity has been almost exclusively confined to one particular set of tests, namely, those that purport to assess a person's capacity for "divergent thinking." Such measures determine whether an individual can generate an impressive number of novel responses to test stimuli. Typical is the *unusual uses* test that requires the respondent to conceive all of the potential uses for a paper clip. These tests can be scored for fluency (number of responses), flexibility (number of distinct categories to which the responses belong), and originality (how rare the response is relative to others taking the test). Moreover, some divergent-thinking tests use verbal stimuli, whereas other tests use visual stimuli. The underlying assumption behind these measures is that they tap the cognitive processes that are essential to creative thought. In any case, investigators who have applied such divergent-thinking tests have consistently found that divergent thinking tends to exhibit an inverted-U shape with regard to age over the life course, with a clear tendency for scores to drop off in the latter half of life. Optimum creativity usually appears around the fortieth year of life.

Even so, caution must be exercised in interpreting these findings. It cannot be confidently inferred from these results that creativity must decline after a person attains middle age. First of all, most of these empirical investigations depend exclusively on cross-sectional data, a methodological tactic that conflates the effects of aging with those of birth year (i.e., age versus cohort effects). Hence, special care must be taken to gauge aging effects from truly longitudinal data (within, rather than across, individuals). In addition, the specific shape of the longitudinal trajectory is contingent on the particular types of tests that are used. Because divergent-thinking tests constitute only one possible type of creativity assessment, different age curves can emerge when different measures are applied. Most tellingly, instruments that assess problem-solving abilities in more practical situations can actually yield scores that fail to decline with age, and may even increase. Lastly, not all experts in the area of creativity assessment accept the validity of so-called creativity tests. Most validation studies reveal that such tests exhibit small correlations with direct behavioral measures of creativity, such as achieved eminence in a creative domain.

Productivity indicators.   The best single predictor of achieved eminence as a creator is lifetime creative output. Therefore, it appears reasonable to adopt productivity as a behavioral measure of creativity. Because scientific inquiries into age changes in creative productivity began in 1835, with the work of Adolphe Quételet (1796–1874), this topic can be considered the oldest in life-span developmental psychology. Yet the first truly important figure in this area was Harvey C. Lehman, whose work was summarized in his 1953 book *Age and Achievement*. Although Lehman's research was plagued with many methodological problems, later investigations that introduced more advanced methods have confirmed his central conclusion: the generation of products tends to increase with age until a maximum output level is attained, with productivity declining thereafter. Indeed, the age where output peaks corresponds approximately with the age where performance on divergent-thinking tests usually maximizes.

Nevertheless, research using productivity measures also have positive implications for the expected level of creativity in the later years of life. This optimism follows from seven empirical results:

1. The age-curve specific form—especially the placement of the peak and the slope of the postpeak decline—depends on the domain in which creativity takes place. In some domains the optimum will occur much later in life, and the drop will be very slow, or even negligible.
2. Creative productivity seldom declines to zero. On the contrary, in most creative domains, persons in their seventies will display higher output rates than they did in their twenties. Furthermore, those in their seventies will usually be generating ideas at a rate only 50 percent below what they achieved during their productive peaks.
3. Individual differences in lifetime productivity are far more substantial than longitudinal

changes in productivity within any particular creator's career. In other words, cross-sectional variation in output accounts for more variance than does age. Accordingly, highly prolific creators in their seventies and eighties are more productive than are less prolific creators during their career acme.

4. Longitudinal fluctuations in creative output are a function of career age, not chronological age. Hence, "late bloomers" who begin their careers much later in life will not reach their career optima until much later in life. The same pattern holds for those who switch fields, thereby resetting the longitudinal clock.

5. A respectable amount of the productivity loss in the last half of life is not necessarily inevitable, insofar as it can be ascribed to various extrinsic factors, such as declining health or increased professional or personal responsibilities. By the same token, certain settings can sustain creativity well into the later years. In the sciences, for instance, those creators who are enmeshed in a rich network of colleagues and students are prone to exhibit longer creative careers.

6. If one looks at the *quality ratio* of successful works relative to total works produced in consecutive age periods, one discovers that this ratio does not change systematically over the course of a creative career. Most notably, this success rate does not diminish as a creator ages. As a result, although creative elders may produce fewer masterpieces in their final years, they also generate fewer inferior works. On a work-for-work basis, there is absolutely no reason to speak of any age-related decrement.

7. Quantitative declines in creative productivity across the life span are often accompanied by qualitative changes in the nature of the output—changes that frequently operate in a compensatory manner. For instance, as creators mature, they will tend to focus on more ambitious products, such as epics, operas, novels, and monographs. More critically, creators in their concluding years often greatly alter their approach to their creative endeavors. In the visual arts, this longitudinal shift is called the *old-age style,* while in music this change is styled the *swan-song* phenomenon.

The foregoing considerations imply that psychometric measures may underestimate the creativity of older persons.

Theoretical explanations

Several researchers in several disciplines have attempted to explain the observed declines in creativity. These explanations can be assigned to the following four categories:

Psychobiological theories. These strive to explicate developmental changes in terms of the physical and neurological changes that attend the aging process. For instance, individuals entering the latter part of life may exhibit declines in sensory acuity, reaction time, and memory retrieval. To the extent that these perceptual and cognitive functions underlie the creative process, such decrements can have negative consequences for creativity.

Psychological theories. In contrast to psychobiological theories, psychological theories attempt to explain any age declines in terms of cognitive processes more directly tied to the creative process. According to one information-processing theory, for example, the career trajectory is a function of an underlying two-step cognitive process by which potential creativity is converted to actual creativity. The theory obtains a postpeak decline without assuming the intrusion of any psychobiological decrements.

Economic theories. These theories treat creativity as another form of productive behavior. As a consequence, economists will speak of creativity as the consequence of sufficient investment in "human capital" and the existence of incentives that give output high utility. Thus, any age decrements in creativity will be ascribed to the obsolescence in the accumulated capitol or to the decreased incentive to maintain productivity in the final years.

Sociological theories. These place the causal locus of any developmental changes outside the individual. In particular, longitudinal changes in creativity may result from corresponding shifts in the norms and role expectations that a society associates with distinct age groups. For instance, poets may produce their best works at younger ages than philosophers because that is most consistent with societal expectations about the romanticism of youth versus the wisdom of maturity. In addition, declines in creativity in the later years might simply reflect shifts in the number and kinds of roles that people are expected to occupy as they get older.

Each of these theoretical accounts can be shown to be inconsistent with certain empirical facts about how creativity changes in the later years. For instance, psychobiological explanations predict that creative productivity should vary according to chronological age, whereas the research shows that career age accounts for more longitudinal variance. Likewise, economic interpretations predict that creativity must decline in the last years, due to the higher cost-benefit ratio, in contradiction to the observation that creativity can resuscitate in the final years. Such empirical inadequacies imply that creativity in the latter part of life is probably the complex function of numerous distinct factors, some beneficial and others detrimental to continued creative activity.

DEAN KEITH SIMONTON

See also INTELLIGENCE; WISDOM.

BIBLIOGRAPHY

ADAMS-PRICE, C. E., ed. *Creativity and Successful Aging: Theoretical and Empirical Approaches.* New York: Springer, 1998.

COHEN, G. D. *The Creative Age: Awakening Human Potential in the Second Half of Life.* New York: William Morrow, 2000.

LEHMAN, H. C. *Age and Achievement.* Princeton, N.J.: Princeton University Press, 1953.

LEVY, B., and LANGER, E. "Aging." In *Encyclopedia of Creativity,* Vol. 1. Edited by M. A. Runco and S. Pritzker. San Diego: Academic Press, 1999. Pages 45–52.

LINDAUER, M. S. "Old Age Style." In *Encyclopedia of Creativity,* Vol. 2. Edited by M. A. Runco and S. Pritzker. San Diego: Academic Press, 1999. Pages 311–318.

SIMONTON, D. K. "Age and Outstanding Achievement: What Do We Know After a Century of Research?" *Psychological Bulletin* 104 (1988): 251–267.

SIMONTON, D. K. "Creative Productivity: A Predictive and Explanatory Model of Career Trajectories and Landmarks." *Psychological Review* 104 (1997): 66–89.

SIMONTON, D. K. "Creativity and Wisdom in Aging." In *Handbook of the Psychology of Aging,* 3d ed. Edited by J. E. Birren and K. W. Schaie. New York: Academic Press, 1990. Pages 320–329.

CREUTZFELDT-JAKOB DISEASE

Creutzfeldt-Jakob disease is one of the transmissible spongiform encephalopathies, a family of diseases affecting humans and animals (see Table 1). They are transmissible, in that susceptible animals inoculated with diseased tissue will develop a similar disease; spongiform, in that, under a microscope, small spaces (vacuoles) in brain tissue are invisible, giving the appearance of a sponge; and encephalopathies, in that they affect the brain.

The disease was first reported by Hans Creutzfeldt in 1920 and Alfons Jakob in 1921. A related, exclusively familial disease, Gerstmann-Sträussler-Scheinker syndrome, was reported in 1928. Creutzfeldt-Jakob disease is a dementia characterized by a rapid progression and a multitude of varying cognitive and motor deficits.

The first advance in understanding the diseases occurred with the recognition that kuru, a disease afflicting only the Fore people of New Guinea, caused similar changes in brain tissue. Kuru is a rapidly progressive dementia (over months) characterized by cerebellar degeneration, causing clumsiness and difficulty walking (ataxia), tremor, and slurred speech. It has been linked to the Fore's practice of eating the brains of deceased relatives. Dr. D. C. Gadjusek, of the National Institutes of Health, hypothesized that ingestion of brain tissue caused the disease, and demonstrated in 1966 that inoculation of brain tissue from kuru patients into chimpanzees' brains caused the disease. Shortly afterward transmissibility was also demonstrated for Creutzfeldt-Jakob disease and Gerstmann-Str;äussler-Scheinker syndrome. Gadjusek and a colleague, Baruch S. Blumberg, were awarded the 1976 Nobel Prize in Medicine for this work.

Prions

The demonstration of transmissibility produced a search for the infectious agent. Initially researchers believed that a virus must be involved, but by the early 1980s the prion hypothesis had been proposed. "Prion" is a term coined by Dr. Stanley Prusiner in 1982 to indicate that the agent is both a protein and infectious. Prusiner, a University of California neurologist, received the 1997 Nobel Prize in medicine for his work on this new class of infectious agent.

The prion protein is a normal constituent of the human body, and although the exact function is unknown, it is involved in neuron development and prevention of neuronal cell death. The abnormal form of the protein has an insoluble conformation; that is, the protein folds in such a way that it can not easily interact with other body molecules. Since the abnormal form is resistant to degradation by normal body enzymes, it is termed protease-resistant prion protein. The abnormal protein can both accumulate into plaques and induce normal prion protein, in a chain reaction, to transform into the abnormal conformation. The prion protein is concentrated in nervous tissue but can also be found in other tissues, particularly white blood cells and the lymphatic system.

The prion hypothesis explains many of the characteristics of the Transmissible Spongiform Encephalopathies: how a familial disease could be infectious (the inheritance is due to a mutation in the prion gene, but the resultant abnormal protein can induce the conformational chain reaction in people without the mutation); why the agent is so resistant to disinfection (most viruses or bacteria are more susceptible to heat or detergents than insoluble proteins are); and how a disease can be infectious without the involvement of any DNA. The best evidence for the prion hypothesis comes from work on self-propagating prions of yeast.

Clinical features

Creutzfeldt-Jakob disease occurs worldwide, with an incidence rate of one per million, most commonly between the ages of fifty and seventy. There are familial forms of the disease, due to mutations in the prion protein gene, best studied in populations in Slovakia and among Libyan Jews. The disease can be iatrogenic, caused by exposure to infectious tissue, such as corneal transplants, dura mater grafts, contaminated surgical instruments, and medications made from human brain tissue, most notably human growth hormone. The time between exposure and onset of the disease can be many years. Most cases, however, are sporadic, or random. There has never been a known case of person-to-person infection. Although it can theoretically be transmitted by blood transfusion, no such case has been identified. There was much interest in the 1970s and 1980s in dietary risk factors, particularly ingestion of animal brains, but this has not been supported by more recent studies. Preliminary data reported in September of 2000 suggest

Table 1

Transmissible Spongiform Encephalopathies

Syndrome (year of first report)

Human

Creutzfeldt-Jakob disease (1920)
Gerstmann-Sträussler-Scheinker syndrome (1928)
Kuru (1957)
Fatal familial insomnia (1986)
Variant Creutzfeldt-Jakob disease (1996)

Animal

Scrapie (c. 1750)
Transmissible mink encephalopathy (1947)
Chronic wasting disease of elk (1980)
Bovine spongiform encephalopathy (1987)
Spongiform encephalopathy of exotic ungulates (1988)
Feline spongiform encephalopathy (1990)
Spongiform encephalopathy of captive primates (1996)

SOURCE: Author

that variant Creutzfeldt-Jakob disease can be passed on through blood transfusions and from a mother to her fetus.

The diagnostic criteria for Creutzfeldt-Jakob disease are presented in Table 2, and are self-explanatory. Often patients with Creutzfeldt-Jakob disease, particularly those with myoclonus, have a typical pattern of sharp waves on their electroencephalograph. Elevated levels of the 14-3-3 protein, a neuronal protein of unknown function, have been found in the cerebrospinal fluid of patients with Creutzfeldt-Jakob disease, and occasionally other cerebral diseases. If Creutzfeldt-Jakob disease is suspected, testing for this protein can help confirm the diagnosis.

Creutzfeldt-Jakob disease progresses rapidly, with a median duration from onset to death of four and a half months. There is no effective treatment for any of the Transmissible Spongiform Encephalopathies. Treatment is limited to comfort care and, if appropriate, genetic counseling. The search for possible therapies involves agents that may stimulate the body to break down the abnormal prion protein, that may disrupt the conformational chain reaction, or that may prevent spread of the prion to the nervous system in an exposed individual.

The epidemic of Bovine Spongiform Encephalopathy in the United Kingdom in the

Table 2
World Health Organization diagnostic criteria for Creutzfeldt-Jakob disease

Sporadic Creutzfeldt-Jakob disease

Definite: One of the following:
Standard neuropathological techniques

Immunocytochemical or Western blot confirmed protease-resistant prion protein

Scrapie-associated fibrils

Probable
Progressive dementia

At least two of the following four clinical features:
Myoclonus

Visual or cerebellar disturbance

Pyramidal/extrapyramidal dysfunction

Akinetic mutism

and both
A typical electroencephalograph during an illness of any duration and/or a positive 14-3-3 cerebrospinal fluid assay and a clinical duration to death of less than 2 years

Routine investigations do not suggest an alternative diagnosis

Possible
Same as for Probable, except

    No electroencephalograph or atypical electroencephalograph

    And duration less than 2 years

Iatrogenic Creutzfeldt-Jakob disease
Progressive cerebellar syndrome in a recipient of human cadaveric-derived pituitary hormone or

Sporadic disease with a recognized exposure risk

Familial Creutzfeldt-Jakob disease
Definite or probable disease in the patient and a first-degree relative

and/or

Neuropsychiatric disorder plus disease-specific prion protein gene mutation.

SOURCE: Author

1980s produced fears that this disease might enter the food chain, and affect humans and other species. This fear has proven true, although the eventual magnitude is as yet unknown. New diseases with prions identical to that causing bovine spongiform encephalopathy have been found in humans, cats, and zoo animals, most likely from prion-contaminated food. This new human disease, variant Creutzfeldt-Jakob disease, differs in that it typically affects people in their twenties and thirties; psychiatric symptoms are prominent; and the pathological appearance is different, with many prion protein-containing plaques found throughout the cortex. Only people with a prion protein gene coding for the amino acid methionine at codon 129 on both gene copies (homozygous for methionine) are susceptible to the disease. People homozygous for valine, or heterozygous for both valine and methionine, are not known to be susceptible to the new variant. Cases have occurred only in Great Britain and France. It is difficult to know if an epidemic will occur, but the incidence increased by 33 percent between 1994 and 2000. Some of this increase may reflect new diagnostic methods.

Not all scientists support the prion hypothesis. They hypothesize that a cofactor, probably a virus, is also present. The works by Manuelidis and Balter cited in the bibliography present these alternative views.

CHRIS MACKNIGHT

See also DEMENTIA.

BIBLIOGRAPHY

BALTER, M. "Prions: A Lone Killer or a Vital Accomplice." *Science* 286 (22 October 1999): 660–662.

CAUGHEY, B. "Transmissible Spongiform Encephalopathies, Amyloidoses and Yeast Proteins: Common Threads?" *Nature Medicine* 6 (2000): 751–754.

COLLINGE, J. "Variant Creutzfeldt-Jakob Disease." *Lancet* 354 (24 July 1999): 317–323.

MACKNIGHT, C. "Clinical Implications of Bovine Spongiform Encephalopathy." *Clinical Infectious Diseases* 32 (2001): 1726–1731.

MANUELIDIS, L. "Dementias, Neurodegeneration, and Viral Mechanisms of Disease from the Perspective of Human Transmissible Encephalopathies." *Annals of the New York Academy of Sciences* 724 (1994): 259–281.

PRUSINER, S. B., ed. *Prion Biology and Diseases.* Cold Spring Harbor Monograph Series, no. 38. Cold Spring Harbor, N.Y.: Cold Spring Harbor Laboratory, 1999.

SOTO, C.; KASCSAK, R. J.; SABORIO, G. P.; AUCOUTURIER, P.; WISNIEWSKI, T.; PRELLI, F.; KASCSAK, R.; MENDEZ, E.; HARRIS, D. A.; IRONSIDE, J.; TAGLIAVINI, F.; CARP, R. I.; and FRANGIONE, B. "Reversion of Prion Protein Conformational Changes by Synthetic B-sheet Breaker Peptides." *Lancet* 355 (January 15, 2000): 192–197.

SUPATTAPONE, S.; NGUYEN, H.-O. B.; COHEN, F. E.; PRUSINER, S. B.; and SCOTT, M. R. "Elimination of Prions by Branched Polyamines and

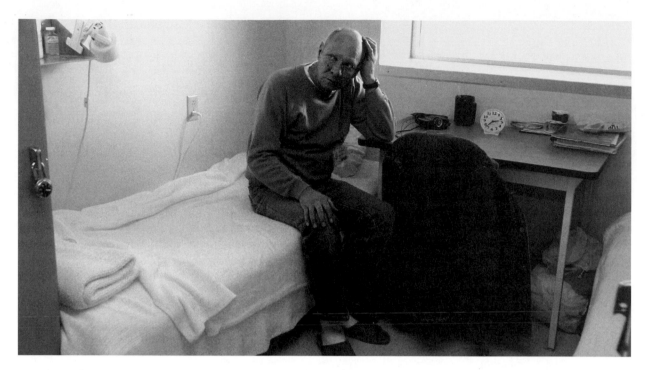

Joseph Fowler, sixty-six, is a prisoner at the Ahtanum View Assisted Living Facility in Yakima, Washington, where he is serving a sentence of twenty years to life for second-degree murder. Beginning in 1997, the state of Washington began housing elderly and disabled prisoners in a minimum security, assisted-living environment that is designed to save money and better serve prisoners. (AP photo by Jackie Johnston.)

Implications for Therapeutics." *Proceedings of the National Academy of Sciences* 96 (1999): 14529–14534.

WILSON, K.; CODE, C.; and RICKETTS M. N. "Risk of Acquiring Creutzfeldt-Jakob Disease from Blood Transfusions: Systematic Review of Case-Control Studies." *British Medical Journal* 321 (1 July 2000): 17–19.

World Health Organization. "Transmissible Spongiform Encephalopathies." World Wide Web document. www.who.int

CRIMINAL BEHAVIOR

An eighty-year-old man is convicted of second-degree criminal solicitation for offering a substantial sum of money to have his business partner of forty years murdered. A woman, seventy-two years old, robs a female acquaintance, age ninety-one, at gunpoint. A restaurant supply delivery man argues with a bank security guard after double-parking his truck and blocking three of the bank's parking spaces and is shot to death by the sixty-seven-year-old security guard.

Why do these events seem so out of place? Should such violent acts by older adults surprise us? In fact, real-life incidents such as these are somewhat unusual, but there are more and more of them in the news. Probably the most widely accepted truism in the field of criminology is that criminal activity declines sharply as age increases. According to Uniform Crime Report data compiled for 1997, only 0.2 percent of the U.S. population 65 years of age and older was arrested for any criminal offense, compared to 7.7 percent of those age 25 to 29 and 2.5 percent of those age 45 to 49.

However, number of arrests may be a particularly poor indicator of actual criminal activity taking place among the older population. Anecdotal evidence exists to suggest that older individuals are less likely than younger people to be arrested, at least for minor offenses. Police may exercise considerable discretion and choose not to make any arrest out of deference—or pity—for older persons. Such "special" treatment could change, of course, as older persons form a larger segment of the population in coming decades. Be that as it may, the proportion of crimes committed by older adults will grow as the ranks of older individuals increase from 12.6 percent of the total U.S. population in 2000 to 13.2 percent in 2010 and to approximately 20 percent by 2030.

The substance abuse factor

Another reason that the portion of total crimes that involves arrests of older persons seems destined to grow is that future cohorts of older adults will include a significantly larger number of individuals who have a history of moderate to heavy drinking (and problem drinking) than has been the case in the past. Indeed, alcohol misuse already appeared more frequently in the older population in 2000 than in previous cohorts. Although the exact role played by alcohol is not well understood, it is clearly associated with the commission of a significant proportion of crimes. The prevalence of illicit drug use, while not as strongly associated by itself with criminal acts as is alcohol, will also almost certainly be higher among future cohorts of older persons, as they will be more likely to have been at least recreational users of these drugs when young. The combination of illicit drugs and alcohol, especially if used in combination with medications, may increase the number of serious criminal acts committed by older individuals.

Crimes older adults commit

Despite their very low profile among those who commit crimes, older adults have proven themselves capable of committing the full spectrum of criminal offenses, from misdemeanors to heinous violent acts. Fortunately, the relative frequency of offenses committed by older adults follows essentially the same pattern as that of younger offenders: the less serious crimes occur far more frequently. Period effects, at least those in the 1990s, also seem to apply equally across generations—the fairly dramatic downturn in serious crime in the U.S. between 1995 and 1999 occurred among those sixty-five and older just as it did among those age eighteen to twenty-nine.

Specifically, then, what types of crime are older adults most likely to engage in? National Uniform Crime Report data covering 1998 indicate that the ten offense categories for which older adults are most likely to be arrested, in descending order of frequency, are: DWI/DUI; larceny/theft; drunkenness; assault; aggravated assault; disorderly conduct; white-collar crime; drug offenses; liquor violations; and sex offenses.

Explanations for criminal behavior

Four of these categories are directly alcohol- or drug-related, and four others (assault, aggravated assault, disorderly conduct, and sex offenses) are behaviors in which alcohol abuse is often found to be involved. Other potential explanations of older adult criminality include: misuse or interaction of prescription and over-the-counter medicines, sometimes yielding behavioral results similar to those from alcohol or dementia; cerebral degeneration, such as Alzheimer's disease or other forms of dementia; and depression, social isolation, and boredom, which can all lead to alcohol abuse or other reckless behavior. Anecdotal evidence suggests that (for older men, at least) getting into trouble with the law for the first time may follow an emotionally traumatic event (such as the death of a spouse) or a deterioration in physical health. These possible explanations apply principally to late-onset criminal behaviors. Older offenders who have been "career criminals" commit crimes, undoubtedly, for many of the same reasons that recidivists of any age do.

Sentencing of older offenders

Overall, older adults receive more lenient sentences than younger persons for the same offenses. Exceptions to this pattern occur for drug offenses, where sentencing disparities are far narrower. A study of sentencing outcomes in Pennsylvania covering the 1991–1994 period revealed that those sixty and older sentenced for nondrug offenses were 26 percent less likely to receive a prison sentence than were offenders age twenty to twenty-nine, and the terms of those sentenced to prison averaged nearly eleven months less than the sentences of those age twenty to twenty-nine (Steffensmeier and Motivans, 2000).

The reasons for this disparity remain unclear, but they undoubtedly include a perception that older adults pose a lesser danger to society and that they have fewer years of life remaining, so a harsher sentence imposes a greater burden on older than on younger individuals.

Given the disparity between older and younger offenders in sentencing, it is little wonder that the most common offenses of older adults who are sentenced to probation, jail, or prison differ somewhat from the most common charges filed against older adults at the point of arrest and booking. In Florida, for example, the state with the highest proportion of residents sixty and older, nearly one-quarter (24 percent) of those under correctional supervision but not incarcerated in 1999–2000 were being supervised for sexual offenses; 21.5 percent were being supervised for theft, forgery or fraud; 18.0 percent for violent personal offenses; and 13.8 percent for drug offenses. While the order of primary offense categories was similar among Florida prison inmates sixty years of age and older during this same period, the second highest proportion (19.5 percent), was incarcerated for drug offenses, which was the top category (28.5 percent) among inmates under sixty years of age. These figures do not distinguish inmates according to criminal history or age when they committed the crime for which they were imprisoned. Those admitted to state prisons for the first time as older adults typically have been sentenced for very serious crimes.

The older prisoner population is growing rapidly, in part due to stiffer sentencing and reduced use of parole in most states in the late twentieth century. This very substantial expansion of the older prisoner population, which tends to be significantly less healthy than older adults in the noninstitutionalized population, is a cause for growing concern among state policymakers. The cost of caring for a chronically ill prisoner is estimated to be about three times higher, on average, than that for a similar patient outside of prison.

BURTON DUNLOP
MAX B. ROTHMAN

See also ALCOHOLISM; CRIMINAL VICTIMIZATION; DRUGS AND AGING.

BIBLIOGRAPHY

Florida Department of Corrections Bureau of Research and Data Analysis. Tallahassee, Fla.: Florida Department of Corrections.

KERBS, J. J. "The Older Prisoner: Social, Psychological, and Medical Considerations." In *Elders, Crime, and the Criminal Justice System: Myth, Perception, and Reality in the 21st Century*. Edited by Max B. Rothman, Burton D. Dunlop, and Pamela Entzel. New York, N.Y.: Springer Publishing Company, Inc., 2000. Pages 207–228.

National Institute on Alcohol Abuse and Alcoholism (NIAAA). *Ninth Special Report to the U.S. Congress on Alcohol and Health*. NIH Pub. No. 97-4017. Bethesda, Md.: NIAAA, 1997.

National Institute on Alcohol Abuse and Alcoholism (NIAAA). *Tenth Special Report to the U.S. Congress on Alcohol and Health*. NIH Pub. No. 00-1583. Bethesda, Md.: NIAAA, 2000.

PASTORE, A. L., and MAGUIRE, K., eds. *Sourcebook of Criminal Justice Statistics*. World Wide Document. www.albany.edu

STEFFENSMEIER, D., and MOTIVANS, M. "Sentencing the Older Offender: Is There an Age Bias?" In *Elders, Crime, and the Criminal Justice System: Myth, Reality and Perception in the 21st Century*. Edited by Max B. Rothman, Burton D. Dunlop, and Pamela Entzel. New York, N.Y.: Springer Publishing Company, Inc., 2000. Pages 185–205.

CRIMINAL VICTIMIZATION OF THE ELDERLY

Criminal victimization

One of the most unequivocal findings in the social science literature is the negative relationship between age and the probability of violent victimization (for review, see Fattah and Sacco, 1989). That is, older individuals are significantly less likely to become victims of violence than younger age cohorts. This reality is perhaps one of the reasons why the needs of elderly victims of crime have been virtually ignored in American society. Research, however, has revealed that behind this backdrop of decreased risk, elderly citizens in the United States experience unique patterns of vulnerability to victimization. Thus, though the elderly are less likely to experience a criminal victimization compared with younger individuals, patterns of vulnerability across age groups are very different. This essay we will provide an epidemiological assessment of victimization against the elderly based on U.S. statistics and show how this victimization varies across the life course.

Homicide victimization. Table 1 presents average annual rates of homicide by age group, gender, and race for 1992-1997. As can be seen, individuals sixty-five or older were much less likely to be victims of homicide across both gender and racial categories. The gender differential between males and females diminishes, however, for the elderly. For example, males under the age of sixty-five were four times more likely to become the victims of homicide, compared with their female counterparts, where as males age sixty-five or older were only twice as likely as fe-

Table 1

Average annual homicide rates per 100,000 persons by age category, sex of victim, and race/ethnicity of victim.

	Persons 12-64 Years of age	Persons 65 or older
Gender		
Male	17	4
Female	4	2
Race/Ethnicity		
Caucasian	6	2
African-American	43	12
Other	7	3

SOURCE: Klaus, P. A. *Crimes Against Persons Age 65 or Older, 1992–1997* NCJ 176352. Washington: Bureau of Justice Statistics, U.S. Department of Justice, 2000.

Table 2

Relationship of the victim to the offender in murders by age of the victim, 1992

Relationship	Persons 12-64 Years of age	Persons 65 or older
Nonstranger total	50.1	45.8
Relative, Intimate	26.4	13.5
Other Known	23.7	32.3
Stranger	14.6	14.3
Relationship Not Identified	35.3	39.9

SOURCE: Klaus, P. A. *Crimes Against Persons Age 65 or Older, 1992–1997* NCJ 176352. Washington: Bureau of Justice Statistics, U.S. Department of Justice, 2000.

males age sixty-five or older to be victims of homicide. African-Americans in both age groups had significantly higher rates of homicide compared with both Caucasians and individuals of other racial and ethnic backgrounds.

Table 2 presents the relationship between homicide victims and offenders during 1992-1997, by age group. While the absolute rates of homicide were lower for those sixty-five years of age or older, individuals in this age group were a unique vulnerability to intimates (spouses, exspouses, boy/girlfriends, ex-boy/girlfriends) and other relatives compared to younger individuals. However, they were 50 percent less likely than victims between the ages of twelve and sixty-four to have been killed by intimates.

Nonlethal violent and property victimization. Average annual rates of nonlethal violent and property crime victimization by age of victim and type of crime from the National Crime Victimization Survey (NCVS) are presented in Table 3. The probability of experiencing all types of crime was significantly lower for those sixty-five years of age or older compared with those sixty-four and younger. The exception to this is for personal theft victimizations such as purse snatching and pocket picking. Individuals both under and over the age of sixty-five had similar rates of victimization for this type of personal theft.

Since robbery and assault victimizations are the most common type of violence experienced by all age groups, it is important to examine

these crimes in greater detail. Table 4 presents the average annual rates of robbery and assault by gender and age group. The probability of experiencing either a robbery or an assault decreases with older age among both males and females. The risk differential is, however, clearly more marked for assault victimization compared with robbery. For example, females younger than twenty-five were more than thirty times more likely to experience an assault than females older than sixty-five. However, females age twenty-five and younger were seven times more likely, compared with those sixty-five and older, to experience robbery. Another pattern that emerges from Table 4 is the differential vulnerability to robberies between males and females across the life course. Males younger than the age of sixty-five were at least 1.5 times more likely to experience a robbery compared with their female counterparts. However, for those older than sixty-five, the ratio of male to female robbery victims dropped to approximately 1.2 Men and women older than sixty-five, therefore, appear to have a roughly equivalent risk of being a robbery victim. This is unlike any other period during the life course.

Table 5 examines the contextual characteristics of robbery and assault victimizations of the elderly in greater detail by specifying the place of occurrence, weapon presence, injury status, and victim/offender relationship by age and gender of victim. Several vulnerabilities emerge from this table. First, elderly women were more likely to sustain injuries as a result of both robbery and assault. Further, while elderly men were less likely to sustain injuries compared with other victims, both elderly men and women who were

Table 3

Average annual rates per 1,000 persons for violent and property crime victimization, by age of victim or household head. National Crime Victimization Survey, 1992–1997.

Type of Crime	Persons 12-64 Years of age	Persons 65 or older
Rape	2.4	0.1
Robbery	6.4	1.3
Aggravated Assault	12.3	1.1
Simple Assault	35.3	2.8
Personal Theft (Purse Snatching, etc.)	1.9	1.5
Household Burglary	58.5	29.5
Motor Vehicle Theft	19.2	5.9

SOURCE: Klaus, P. A. *Crimes Against Persons Age 65 or Older, 1992–1997* NCJ 176352. Washington, D.C.: Bureau of Justice Statistics, U.S. Department of Justice, 2000.

Table 4

Average annual age and gender-specific robbery and assault victimization rates per 1,000 population. National Crime Victimization Survey, 1992–1994.

Age Group	Robbery Rate Females	Robbery Rate Males	Assault Rate Females	Assault Rate Males
12–24	7.3	14.9	71.3	105.8
25–34	5.8	9.4	44.1	54.3
35–49	3.1	5.8	27.8	39.1
50–64	1.6	3.5	9.4	15.5
65 and older	1.0	1.2	2.4	4.7

SOURCE: Source: Adapted from: Bachman, R., Dillaway, H., & Lachs, M.S. "Violence Against the Elderly: A Comparative Analysis of Robbery and Assault Across Age and Gender Groups." *Research on Aging* 20 no. 2 (1998): 183–198.

injured were more likely to require medical care compared with younger victims who were injured. It is also important to note that the elderly were more vulnerable to being robbed and assault at or near their private residences, compared with younger victims.

Trends in personal victimization. Figure 1 displays average annual rates of violent crime by age group for 1992-1997. Included are incidents of murder, rape, robbery, and assault. While rates of violence for all age groups declined during this period, the rate decline was more dramatic for younger individuals compared with those between the ages of fifty and sixty-four or those sixty-five and older.

Rates of personal theft (e.g., pocket-picking and purse snatching) are displayed in Figure 2 (see page 303). This graphically illustrates that, except for those under the age of twenty-four, those sixty-five and older have been equally vulnerable to personal theft compared with their younger age cohorts. In fact, during 1992-1994 individuals aged sixty-five and older experienced rates of personal theft higher than those between the ages of twenty-five and sixty-four.

Conclusions

In general, individuals older than sixty-five are significantly less likely than younger individuals to experience a crime victimization. The ex-

ception is for personal theft, such as pocket picking and purse snatching, in which the elderly are just as vulnerable as those younger than sixty-five years of age. In addition, elderly women are just as likely as elderly men to experience a robbery victimization. This is important. At no other time in the life course are men and women equally vulnerable to becoming the victims of robbery. Thus, the elderly appear particularly vulnerable to crimes of economic predation.

These patterns of victimization have important implications related to issues of quality of life for many elderly citizens. While victimization undoubtedly has dramatic consequences for people's health and sense of security, fear of victimization is also inextricably related to feelings of well-being. By 2030 the United States will become a nation in which those older than the age of sixty-five will represent 20 percent of the total population. While government officials strive to consider what this growth will do to such programs as Social Security and Medicare, very little attention has been given to issues regarding the quality of life older Americans can come to expect, including feelings of safety. Of the policy initiatives directed at crime, virtually all have ignored crime against the elderly, including the Omnibus Crime Prevention and Control Act implemented by Congress in 1994. Clearly, more research is needed to understand and explain the unique vulnerabilities to crime that older

Table 5

Percentage distribution of place of occurrence, weapon presence, injury and medical treatment required, number of offenders, and victim/offender relationship for robbery and assault victimizations by age and gender of victim. National Crime Victimization Survey, 1992–1994.

	12–64 Years of Age		Age 65 and older	
	Females	Males	Females	Males
Robbery Victimizations				
Occurred in private location	41	22	39	49
Weapon was present	39	49	25	66
Victim was injured	33	29	45	24
Victim required medical care	48	55	73	88
Lone offenders	69	48	61	54
Known offenders	48	28	13	21
Assault Victimizations				
Occurred in private location	47	24	67	44
Weapon was present	18	26	25	33
Victim was injured	27	21	30	13
Victim required medical care	42	44	56	50
Lone offenders	86	79	93	80
Known offenders	78	57	79	60

SOURCE: Source: Adapted from: Bachman, R., Dillaway, H., & Lachs, M.S. "Violence Against the Elderly: A Comparative Analysis of Robbery and Assault Across Age and Gender Groups." *Research on Aging* 20 no. 2 (1998): 183–198.

Figure 1

Average Annual Rate of Violent Crime by Age Group, 1992–1997

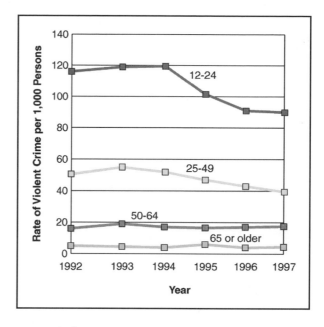

SOURCE: Author

KLAUS, P. A. *Crimes Against Persons Age 65 or Older, 1992-1997.* NCJ 176352. Washington, D.C.: Bureau of Justice Statistics, U.S. Department of Justice, 2000.

CRITICAL GERONTOLOGY

Generally speaking, the term "critical gerontology" can be used to describe a rather broad spectrum of theoretical interests, ranging from constructions and deconstructions of aging (Gubrium, 1986; Hazan; Katz) to the issue of power and control in contemporary society (Estes; Moody, 1988, 1993; Phillipson and Walker). What ties these different perspectives together is that all of them, in one form or another, have been critical of "a theoretical self-understanding of gerontology, which is dominated by an idealized concept of natural science as the representative of 'objective' knowledge" (Baars, p. 220). In contrast, critical gerontologists argue that the nature of scientific data cannot be separated from the approach, interest, orientation, and other subjective aspects of the researcher. The issues raised have focused primarily on the ideological and socially constructive features of age conceptualizations. Three theories in particular—

persons in our society face. Only through such empirical assessments can policies aimed at preventing such violence be responsibly enacted.

RONET BACHMAN

See also CRIMINAL BEHAVIOR; ELDER ABUSE AND NEGLECT

BIBLIOGRAPHY

BACHMAN, R., H. DILLAWAY; AND LACHS, M. S. "Violence Against the Elderly: A Comparative Analysis of Robbery and Assault Across Age and Gender Groups" *Research on Aging* 20, no.2 (1998): 183–198.

FATTAH, E. A.; AND SACCO, V.F. *Crime and Victimization of the Elderly.* New York: Springer-Verlag, 1989.

Figure 2
Average Annual Rate of Personal Theft Victimization, 1992–1997

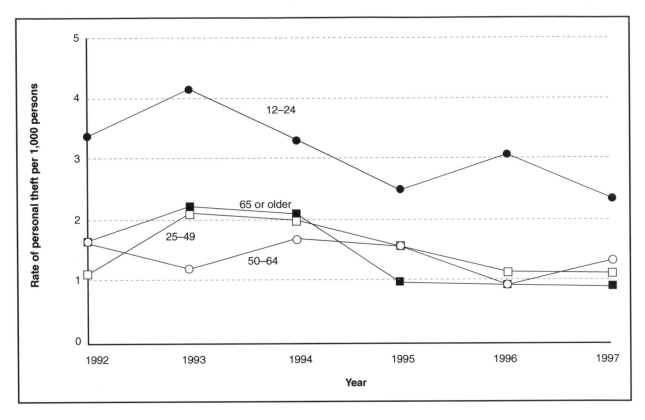

SOURCE: Author

critical theory, political economy, and social phenomenology—are exemplary in this regard. We discuss each in turn.

Critical theory

Drawing on the tradition of the Frankfurt school of thought (see Held), Harry Moody (1988) has attempted to apply critical theory to the study of aging. He relies, in particular, on the work of Jürgen Habermas, especially his book *Knowledge and Human Interests* (1971). In it, Habermas distinguishes three kinds of cognitive interest toward any world of concern. Cognitive interests are the general intellectual task orientations taken in describing a world of objects. Asking, in effect, "For what purpose is this knowledge?" Habermas specifies three answers: cognitive interests in control, understanding (*verstehen*), and emancipation. Our discussion will focus on the interests in control and emancipation. (For a description of all three interests as they relate to aging, see Lynott and Lynott.)

Consider first a cognitive interest in control, which underlies conventional theories of aging. From this point of view (with this tacit interest), social objects and events are believed to be *things* in their own right, separate from those who experience them. This understanding makes it reasonable to raise questions about the relationship between individuals, on the one hand, and a real, objective world that they encounter, on the other. For example, if one feature of an individual's world is that it is organized around a life span or a life course with distinct stages, cohorts, or points of transition, then one might reasonably ask what sort of impact these "things" have on the characteristics of the individuals who are located within, or proceeding through, them, and how this affects adjustment in old age. The knowledge obtained by empirically testing various hypotheses in this regard would then allow one to effectively intervene in human affairs, or at least to suggest alterations, in order to bring about desirable changes (control) of some sort, as a consequence of policymaking.

In contrast, a cognitive interest in emancipation does not take for granted the separate and objective existence of objects—separate, that is, from those for whom they are objects. Thus, for example, the life course, as a thing, is not treated as an entity that is ontologically distinct from those who experience it. It would make no sense, with this interest, to ask how persons proceed through the life course, since the procedure itself, in some critical sense, produces the life course. (Murphy and Longino, [p. 147] have pointed out in this regard that the term "life course" itself conjures up an image of a person's life as having "a natural or evolutionary course," which glosses over the "pervasiveness of interpretation" in everyday life.) The emancipation of concern to critical theorists is to reveal to the subject that the objects of his or her experiences (things like stages, cohorts, and transitions in later life) are products of his or her labor.

An interest in emancipation arises out of the understanding that, on the one hand, the objects of the world get produced by meaningful action, and yet, on the other hand, in the course of human affairs the source of the objects gets lost. The research task for this cognitive interest is critique, and thus theory becomes critical. What is critiqued by critical theorists is not the objective state of objects per se; what is critiqued are transformations of the relationship between subjects and objects from being genuine to being alienated (ideologically distorted). Thus, a major concern for critical theorists, with respect to age conceptualizations and theories of aging in general, would be how they represent a language serving to reify experience as something separate from those doing the experiencing. In the final analysis, critical theorists would argue that treating age-related concepts as depicting things separate from their human origins allows for their use as a means of social control. In other words, ignoring the possibility that objects are objects-for-someone, thereby being in someone's interest, can lead "not to freedom. . .[for elderly persons]. . .but to new domination, perhaps a domination exercised ever more skillfully by professionals, bureaucrats, or policymakers" (Moody, 1988, p. 26).

Following this line of reasoning, Moody (1993, p. xvi) states that a cognitive interest in control "can never provide a rational foundation for purpose, value, or meaning in [late] life." It can only serve "to reify the status quo and provide new tools to predict and control human behavior" (Moody, 1988, p. 33). What is missing in theories of aging, for Moody, is a form of "emancipatory knowledge" that offers "a positive vision of how things might be different or what a rationally defensible vision of a 'good old age' might be" (Moody, 1993, p. xvii). To achieve this, he argues, gerontologists must move beyond their attempts to study aging based upon the natural-science model, and explore contributions toward theory development from a more reflective mode of thought derived from disciplines within the humanities, such as history, literature, and philosophy (see, e.g., Cole et al.).

However, it is unclear how Moody's vision of emancipation can be realized, given that, as Michel Foucault's work (1980) has demonstrated, knowledge and power are always inextricably intertwined. Foucault's sober message cuts short attempts to provide new, more truthful discourses. Moody (1988, p. 27) himself has acknowledged that "we still have no clear account of where that emancipatory ideal is to be found." Nonetheless, the incorporation of critical theory into gerontological thinking has expanded critical awareness in the field, adding to the ideological and epistemological concerns raised earlier by political economists and social phenomenologists (see Lynott and Lynott; Passuth and Bengtson). We discuss each of these perspectives in turn.

Political economy

The political economists (Estes; Estes et al.; Guillemard; Minkler and Estes, 1991, 1999; Myles; Olson; Walker) argue that to understand the problems of elderly people, one should attend to the political and economic conditions surrounding them. This turns attention away from the problems of elders as largely lying, according to gerontological theorists, in "their private troubles" and toward the political economy of growing older. To apply C. Wright Mills's (1959) language further, attention is centered on (1) the public issue of age and (2) the relationship between public issues and private troubles.

For political economists, the sources of private troubles, such as social isolation and role loss in old age, are found in the relations between the state and a capitalist economy. (Marxists [e.g., Olson] give signal governance to the economy; Weberians [e.g., Myles] provide for relatively independent state influence in social relations.) This view stands in stark contrast to the notion that older people have problems for which they are virtually blamed—blaming the victim. The solution, for the latter, is for elderly persons to "do something about it" or, as actually happened, for an army of experts to help them with the task. However, the political economists maintain that "Older persons individually are powerless to alter their social status and condition" (Estes, p. 15), positing that the structure of society itself has created the problem of old age.

Consider, for example, the Older Americans Act of 1965 (OAA) as a state-supported means of perpetuating the private troubles of elderly persons (Estes; Estes et al.; Olson). While OAA had the ideal of establishing the independence and well-being of older people, its welfare-oriented articulation further transformed them into a state-dependent class, a welfare class. The program saw the solution to the problems of aging, in application, largely in local planning for the coordination of fragmented, recreation-like programs. For example, rather than make elderly persons economically solvent, the strategy was to keep them happy in the confines of places like senior centers. Rather than make them independent, individual managers of their affairs, their very sustenance became bound to a system of dependence, perhaps best symbolized by nutrition programs (hot meals and Meals on Wheels).

Such programs, Carroll Estes (p. 22) argues, "ignore the widespread poverty of the aged and provide no direct economic relief. Instead the aged become consumers of services that simply feed the expanding service economy." The army of experts, professionals, and service providers that has arisen to dole out benefits of various kinds to the elder population has expanded the service sector of the American economy. A tremendously complex welfare bureaucracy that both controls and presumably benefits elders also provides an ever-expanding job market for the young. The process results in a large discrepancy, on income grounds alone, when comparing the income of bureaucrats servicing the elders with the income of the elders they service. In effect, the political economy of aging serves those who serve the state more than it serves those who are troubled by its conditions.

The political economists shift the focus of attention from attempting to explain the existing conditions of old age in terms of individual adjustment to a class explanation for the helplessness of the position of older people (Olson). While the argument presented raises important questions concerning "individualistic" thinking in gerontological theory—asking, in effect, "Whose interests are served by thinking of age in particular ways?"—at the same time, it tends to overstate the extent to which elderly persons, as a whole, are impoverished and disenfranchised (see Harris and Associates). Indeed, some researchers have suggested that the majority of elderly people in American society constitute a "new old" who are healthier and live in relative economic well-being (Cain; Neugarten). Political economists, however, increasingly have attempted to include issues of gender, race, and ethnicity as part of their class analysis (Minkler and Estes, 1991, 1999). Another problem with the political economy perspective is that it is overly deterministic. Political economists tend to treat private troubles as direct distillations of public issues, as if individuals automatically realize in their personal experiences what is defined at large. This ignores problems of meaning and interpretation in the everyday lives of elderly people, something that is of primary concern for the social phenomenologists, to whom we now turn.

Social phenomenology

The social phenomenologists (Gubrium, 1986, 1993; Gubrium and Buckholdt; Gubrium and Lynott, 1983, 1985; Lynott; Starr) turn their attention from causal explanations of human behavior to a concern for the reality-defining labor of practitioners of everyday life. Drawing primarily from the works of Alfred Schutz (1970) and Harold Garfinkel (1967), they "bracket," or set aside, one's taken-for-granted belief in the reality of age and age-related concepts in order to examine the process by which they are socially constructed. The analysis focuses on membership in various communities of discourse (professional and lay alike), showing how members collectively negotiate a sense of age and aging through talk and interaction.

Social phenomenologists have criticized theories of aging for taking the existential status of age for granted. While the theories look at variations in the meaning of age and aging behavior along, for example, historical, cohort, and exchange lines, the variations are accepted as background factors or outside forces operating upon older people. Thus, the interpretation of the so-called forces and their subsequent reinterpretation, in the ongoing practice of everyday life, is ignored. (This criticism also applies to the concept of social class, as was noted above.) The social phenomenologists, on the other hand, focus attention on the process by which age, agedness, and age-related "facts" are produced and reproduced in the first place. Their concern lies with the issue of how the objects of and ideas about aging are understood by people who experience them, and how these experiences serve to produce and reproduce themselves along certain lines.

The social construction of fact has been concretely demonstrated in an analysis of the Alzheimer's disease experience (Gubrium, 1986; Gubrium and Lynott, 1985; Lynott). The study examined the social organization of two types of discourse—aging and disease—by which to reference, describe, and explain the "symptoms" of aging. It was clear that those affected by the variety of conditions experienced considerable suffering. The existence of the objects of turmoil—neurofibrillary tangles and senile plaques in the brain and their erratic behavioral correlates, including memory loss and confusion—were equally empirically validated, as was the alarm they generated. Their meaning, however, was problematic, with all the existing evidence, from neuropathological to psychological, being garnered on behalf of both a disease entity and the aging process itself.

Yet, in the final analysis, it was not the "facts" per se that secured the disease distinction, but the practical usages they served. In this regard, the desire to ameliorate the conditions observed were part and parcel of Alzheimer's assigned factual status, for the disease interpretation allowed medical researchers to search for treatments and possible cures that aging itself did not. Likewise, the Alzheimer's Disease and Related Disorders Association's instrumental efforts in spreading the word about what was increasingly presented as the devastating effects of a disease served to transform the meaning of the conditions dealt with. The result was that "Alzheimer's disease [was] not normal aging." The telltale signs of aging became a disease, the "disease of the century." By implication, a reality meaningfully came to possess its own concrete facts.

The transformation, however, was not a linear and progressive process of redefinition from old age to disease. It was clear that the ongoing assignment and descriptive practices of those concerned were continually producing what the sense of this thing—aging/disease—was to be for the practical purposes at hand. For example, in the support groups for caregivers of Alzheimer's patients, the condition of a patient could be interpreted as a sign of a given stage of the disease against a background of certain comparisons with others. That "same" condition could shift, with a change in framework, to an interpretation of old age when lamenting the lack of any "rhyme or reason" to the course of illness. In this respect, there were no straightforward facts concerning any aspect of the disease experience; rather, the facts entered into ongoing practical experiences as more or less useful ways to understand the condition and related experiences under consideration.

The social phenomenological analysis reveals that the potential realities assigned to the aging experience are the products of an ongoing process of social construction, descriptively organized by prevailing stocks of knowledge (Schutz). Even so, the issue of power is never fully addressed by this perspective. The reason is that while the approach generates important data about the process of social production, at the same time it tends to ignore its structure. That is, it tends to conclude its analysis when the human products of the process have been produced, considering the product not as a configuration of social conditions independent of and perhaps confronting members, but rather in terms of its interpretive resources and production and reproduction—a concern for structuration rather than structure as such (Giddens).

Conclusion

While the theories discussed (critical theory, political economy, and social phenomenology) have very different orientations to the study of aging, the analytic challenges they pose represent something new—new modes of self-consciousness—in terms of the nature and practice of gerontological inquiry (Lynott and Lynott). This does not mean to suggest, however, that a paradigm shift in definitions of and thoughts about age and aging is developing (Kuhn). On the contrary, as Jan Baars (p. 220) has pointed out, the theories, in large part, "have been excluded by the established 'mainstream.'" Each of these approaches, in its own fashion, takes issue with conventional theorizing in the field, providing new insights into, and critical self-reflection on, the continuing effort to understand the aging experience.

ROBERT J. LYNOTT
PATRICIA PASSATH LYNOTT

See also LIFE COURSE; THEORIES, SOCIAL.

BIBLIOGRAPHY

BAARS, J. "The Challenge of Critical Gerontology: The Problem of Social Constitution." *Journal of Aging Studies* 5, no. 3 (1991): 219–243.

CAIN, L. D. JR. "Age, Status, and Generational Phenomena: The New Old People in Contemporary America." *The Gerontologist* 7 (1967): 83–92.

COLE, T. R.; ACHENBAUM, W. A.; JAKOBI, P. L.; and KASTENBAUM, R., eds. *Voices and Visions of Aging: Toward a Critical Gerontology.* New York: Springer, 1993.

ESTES, C. L. *The Aging Enterprise: A Critical Examination of Social Policies and Services for the Aged.* San Francisco: Jossey-Bass, 1979.

ESTES, C. L.; LINKINS, K. W.; and BINNEY, E. A. "The Political Economy of Aging." In *Handbook of Aging and the Social Sciences,* 4th ed. Edited by R. H. Binstock and L. K. George, San Diego, Calif.: Academic Press, 1996. Pages 346–361.

FOUCAULT, M. *Power/Knowledge: Selected Interviews and Other Writings, 1972–1977.* Translated by C. Gordan, L. Marshall, J. Mepham, and K. Soper. Edited by C. Gordan. New York: Pantheon, 1980.

GARFINKEL, H. *Studies in Ethnomethodology.* Englewood Cliffs, N.J.: Prentice-Hall, 1967.

GIDDENS, A. *The Constitution of Society: Outline of the Theory of Structuration.* Berkeley: University of California Press, 1984.

GUBRIUM, J. F. *Oldtimers and Alzheimer's: The Descriptive Organization of Senility.* Greenwich, Conn.: JAI Press, 1986.

GUBRIUM, J. F. *Speaking of Life: Horizons of Meaning for Nursing Home Residents.* Hawthorne, N.Y.: Aldine de Gruyter, 1993.

GUBRIUM, J. F., and LYNOTT, R. J. "Alzheimer's Disease as Biographical Work." In *Social Bonds in Later Life: Aging and Interdependence.* Edited by W. A. Peterson and J. Quadagno, Beverly Hills, Calif.: Sage, 1985. Pages 349–367.

GUBRIUM, J. F., and LYNOTT, R. J. "Rethinking Life Satisfaction." *Human Organization* 42, no. 1 (1983): 30–38.

GUBRIUM, J. F., and BUCKHOLDT, D. R. *Toward Maturity: The Social Processing of Human Development.* San Francisco: Jossey-Bass, 1977.

GUILLEMARD, A.-M., ed. *Old Age and the Welfare State.* Beverly Hills, Calif.: Sage, 1983.

HABERMAS, J. *Knowledge and Human Interests.* Translated by J. J. Shapiro. Boston: Beacon Press, 1971.

HARRIS, L., and Associates, Inc. *The Myth and Reality of Aging in America.* Washington, D.C.: National Council on the Aging, 1975.

HAZAN, H. *Old Age: Constructions and Deconstructions.* Cambridge, U.K.: Cambridge University Press, 1994.

HELD, D. *Introduction to Critical Theory: Horkheimer to Habermas.* Berkeley: University of California Press, 1980.

KATZ, S. *Disciplining Old Age: The Formation of Gerontological Knowledge.* Charlottesville: University Press of Virginia, 1996.

KUHN, T. S. *The Structure of Scientific Revolutions.* Chicago: University of Chicago Press, 1962.

LYNOTT, R. J. "Alzheimer's Disease and Institutionalization: The Ongoing Construction of a Decision." *Journal of Family Issues* 4, no. 4 (1983): 559–574.

LYNOTT, R. J., and LYNOTT, P. P. "Tracing the Course of Theoretical Development in the Sociology of Aging." *The Gerontologist* 36, no. 6 (1996): 749–760.

MILLS, C. W. *The Sociological Imagination.* New York: Oxford University Press, 1959.

MINKLER, M., and ESTES, C. L., eds. *Critical Gerontology: Perspectives from Political and Moral Economy.* Amityville, N.Y.: Baywood, 1999.

MINKLER, M., and ESTES, C. L., eds. *Critical Perspectives on Aging: The Political and Moral Economy of Growing Old.* Amityville, N.Y.: Baywood, 1991.

MOODY, H. R. "Overview: What is Critical Gerontology and Why is it Important?" In *Voices and Visions of Aging: Toward a Critical Gerontology.* Edited by T. R. Cole, W. A. Achenbaum, P. L. Jakobi, and R. Kastenbaum, New York: Springer, 1993. Pages xv–xli.

MOODY, H. R. "Toward a Critical Gerontology: The Contribution of the Humanities to Theories of Aging." In *Emergent Theories of Aging.* Edited by J. E. Birren and V. L. Bengtson, New York: Springer, 1988. Pages 19–40.

MURPHY, J. W., and LONGINO, C. F., JR. "What is the Justification for a Qualitative Approach to Ageing Studies?" *Ageing and Society* 12, no. 2 (1992): 143–156.

MYLES, J. *Old Age in the Welfare State: The Political Economy of Public Pensions,* Rev. ed. Lawrence: University Press of Kansas, 1989.

NEUGARTEN, B. L. "Age Groups in American Society and the Rise of the Young Old." *Annals* of the American Academy of Political and Social Science 415 (1974): 187–198.

OLSON, L. K. The Political Economy of Aging: The State, Private Power, and Social Welfare. New York: Columbia University Press, 1982.

PASSUTH, P. M., and BENGTSON, VERN L. "Sociological Theories of Aging: Current Perspectives and Future Directions." In Emergent Theories of Aging. Edited by J. E. Birren and V. L. Bengtson, New York: Springer, 1988. Pages 333–355.

PHILLIPSON, C., and WALKER, A. "The Case for a Critical Gerontology." In Social Gerontology: New Directions. Edited by S. Di Gregorio. London: Croom Helm, 1987. Pages 1–15.

SCHUTZ, A. On Phenomenology and Social Relations: Selected Writings. With an introduction by H. R. Wagner. Chicago: University of Chicago Press, 1970.

STARR, J. M. "Toward a Social Phenomenology of Aging: Studying the Self Process in Biographical Work." International Journal of Aging and Human Development 16, no. 4 (1982–1983): 255–270.

WALKER, A. "Towards a Political Economy of Old Age." Ageing and Society 1, no. 1 (1981): 73–94.

CULTURAL DIVERSITY

Cultural diversity, as it relates to aging, connotes variety among the older adult population in racial, gender, social, economic, religious, health, and other characteristics. The present discussion focuses primarily on the demographic characteristics of race, ethnicity, and national origin as they relate to selected aspects of the aging process. The U.S. Bureau of the Census recognizes four distinct race/ethnicity groups—whites, African Americans, Native Americans (including Eskimos and Aleuts), and Asian/Pacific Islanders—as well as one national origin group, Hispanics (whose members can be of any race). Unless otherwise noted, population statistics cited below come from Census Bureau sources.

Like the United States, other nations of the world have expanding older populations that are growing culturally more diverse. These trends challenge governments to provide all qualifying individuals with an income stream that is continuous and adequate, sustains purchasing power, and maintains the socioeconomic position of older, retired persons. This is certainly true for the more industrialized countries of the world, yet the greatest increases in the elderly popula-tion are occurring in less developed countries—many of which are less prepared and less able to address the needs of multiple racial and ethnic groups within their borders.

Within the United States, in 1980 non-Hispanic whites comprised 88 percent of all persons age sixty-five and older. By 2000, this percentage had dropped to 83.5 percent, and by 2050 it is expected that no more than 64.2 percent of the older adult population within the United States will be non-Hispanic whites.

These figures point to the increasing proportion of older adults who will come from minority populations. The largest gain is projected to occur among Hispanics. Currently estimated to number 1.9 million persons, by 2050 Hispanic older adults are expected to exceed 13 million. Minorities will constitute a larger proportion of the older population in the future because minorities have had higher fertility than whites and because a disproportionate number of immigrants have been members of minority populations.

Lifelong processes

The United States is peopled by groups that arrived in search of economic opportunity or political refuge, as well as by populations who were conquered, enslaved, or subordinated. To understand the social position and characteristics of today's minority elders, one must appreciate the lifelong processes and historical experiences that have brought them to their current stage of life. A life course perspective highlights the ways in which earlier life circumstances significantly channel people's later opportunities, outcomes, and quality of life decades later. For instance, the persistent racism, economic inequality, and residential segregation experienced by many African Americans early in life have had harmful effects on later development and life chances. These effects accumulate over the life span and can widen disadvantages in health, survival, and economic well-being (Jackson et al., 1993).

Today's elders have been shaped by their membership in birth cohorts that have lived through particular historical periods. Contemporary minority elders, born in the United States prior to 1940, have experienced a very different social context than those who will be elders in the future, born after the mid-1950s. For one thing, these later cohorts have had the benefit of more

Chef David Qiang Dai uses a wok to prepare a traditional Chinese meal at the Aegis Gardens assisted living facility in Fremont, California. When it opened in late 2001, the retirement community was thought to be the first for-profit company to target Asian senior citizens. Qiang Dai also prepares other cultural dishes upon request. (AP photo by Julie Jacobson.)

education than earlier cohorts, who often came from poor, rural backgrounds. Later, younger cohorts not only have had more years of formal education, but also have had a better quality of education by receiving part, if not most, of their education in desegregated schools. Later cohorts have had the historical benefits of better health care, and more economic and employment opportunities in the wake of the civil rights movement.

Lifelong processes produce racial differences in survival to older ages. Members of minority groups who live to be old are more highly "selected" than their white peers. For example, for every 100,000 black and white men born alive, 17,000 more white men than black men will reach age sixty-five. Similar differences are found for women, though not as dramatic—10,100 fewer black women will reach age sixty-five (Williams and Wilson, 2001). Exposure to risk factors and stress hastens the early onset of chronic disease and premature death, which lower the probability that African Americans will live to be old.

Observers have speculated that inequalities over the life course are further compounded when adults reach later life. A "double jeopardy" hypothesis posits that minority elders face the dual burden of racial and age discrimination The result is that these elders are doubly disadvantaged in their health and economic well-being, and this accentuates the disparities between minorities and whites. One can even conceive of multiple jeopardy, such as being a women and old and a minority. An alternative hypothesis is that age acts as a "leveler," narrowing differences between majority and minority elders. Minorities may become relatively less disadvantaged as they age because, having dealt with racial discrimination over their entire lives, they are prepared to cope with age discrimination; because health problems in later life cut across racial lines; and because welfare state programs such as Social Security and Medicare have given minority elders greater access to health care and income security. Research has not settled whether either of these two perspectives—double jeopardy and age-as-leveler—is a more accurate depiction than a state of persistent inequality for minority elders (Ferraro and Farmer, 1996; Pampel, 1998).

Mortality patterns of African Americans support a leveling hypothesis. Over most of the life span, age-specific death rates for African Americans are higher than those of their majority group counterparts. But mortality rates increase more slowly with age for African Americans than for whites in later life, and after the late eighties there is a "crossover" so that white majority group members have higher mortality rates than African Americans. However, this apparent crossover pattern is controversial. Some argue that it is a function of selective survival, in which the hardiest African Americans reach late life. Others argue that the observed phenomenon is an artifact of age misreporting for African Americans whose births went unregistered in the South early in the twentieth century (Williams and Wilson, 2001).

Elders from minority groups are likely to have benefited from remarkable extended family support networks (Stoller and Gibson, 2000). Racial and ethnic groups are characterized by family-centered cultures with traditions of mutual aid in the form of practical, emotional, and material exchanges. Closer kin bonds also foster affection across age groups. The patterns of giving and receiving in these social support "convoys" are born of ethnic cultures and rural backgrounds where family remains a strong feature of social organization. The nature of family is also a strategy for meeting economic need, sharing scare resources of time and money. African Americans have tended to have open kin networks that allow both blood relatives and non-kin within the family. Asian and Hispanic groups tend to limit family support to persons with close blood ties (Dilworth-Anderson and Burton, 1999). An often noted feature among Asian peoples is the norm of filial piety or children's duty, a tradition of respect and deference toward parents and grandparents that is rooted in Confucian culture.

Strong familism can aid elders when they need physical assistance, help with household chores, or a place to live. Minority elders have thus been less likely to turn to formal support systems, such as government services or nursing homes. At the same time, familism does not excuse elders from giving when other dependent family members are in need, for example, accepting grandchildren into their households. Elders also assume an obligation to be the conservators of cultural heritage for younger kin. As economic forces and acculturation threaten to dissolve the solidarity of extended family networks, one important question is whether the next generation will continue to maintain family support for tomorrow's elders.

Hispanics

Looking forward to the middle of the twenty-first century, it will become more difficult to characterize any racial or ethnic group with a simple description. Such is the case for Hispanics and Latinos, the nation's largest minority group, numbering one of every eight Americans in 2000. Most Hispanics are of Mexican (58 percent), Puerto Rican (10 percent), or Cuban descent (4 percent); the remainder are from Central and South America. Hispanics made up 5.6 percent of the older adult population in 2000, but are projected to be 16.4 percent of the older adult population by 2050. Sometime before 2030, the Hispanic population age sixty-five and older will likely outnumber African-American elders.

The diversity of the Hispanic population is mainly due to different immigration histories of the various national-origin groups. Some Mexican Americans' residence in the Southwest predates the formation of the United States. Many others migrated to the United States in order to harvest crops, encouraged by the bracero program of the 1940s and 1950s. These native-born and earlier immigrant Mexicans are now the majority of those reaching old age. The future growth of the Hispanic and Latino elderly population (it will triple by 2050 as a share of all minority elders) will be propelled by larger, recent cohorts of immigrants from Mexico.

If Mexican Americans are still a comparatively young group, the population of Cuban Americans is considerably older. Comprising only 4 percent of the Hispanic population overall, they are 17 percent of the population of older Hispanics. Older Cubans now include the cohort of political refugees who fled the Castro regime in the 1960s. Elderly Puerto Ricans add other special circumstances to the mix of Hispanic seniors. They are a substantial population (11 percent of all Hispanic elders) that does not reside primarily in the South or the West, and their U.S. citizenship allows them to move easily back and forth between the island and the mainland United States (Siegel, 1999).

African Americans

According to the 2000 census, African Americans are the second largest minority group, making up 12.3 percent of the resident population of the United States. (The Census Bureau changed its method of reporting racial categories for the 2000 census. Figures presented here count those who reported only one race. Individuals had the option of choosing more than one racial category. Adding those who chose African American in combination with some other category, the total African-American population was 12.9 percent.) African Americans in 2000 made up 8.4 percent of all persons age sixty-five and older, and are projected by 2050 to be 13.2 percent of older adults.

Studies of African-American older adults are now forsaking habitual black/white comparisons in favor of studies that explore the variety and depth of experience among people of African descent. All too often, researchers have taken a simplistic view of older African Americans and failed to note the considerable heterogeneity that exists among this population. A comparative disadvantage to whites is one legacy of generations of social, economic, political, and legal discrimination, but there are also traditions of cultural strength and resilience in kinship networks and black churches. At present, it is clear that African-American older adults tend to have higher morbidity and mortality rates than those of non-Hispanic whites. For many this is an outcome of lifelong poverty, poor educational resources, underemployment or unemployment, and inadequate access to health care. The cumulative effect is that many have reached older age with poor health and inadequate resources.

Yet, there is also considerable and growing variation among African-American older adults. Improvements in health care access since the 1960s and the emergence of a viable African-American middle class have produced a diversity among African Americans that parallels the variety observed in other population groups within the United States. Older African Americans display a wide range of social, economic, and cultural patterns.

Native Americans, Aleuts, and Eskimos

Native Americans make up just less than 1 percent of the total population and only about 0.50 percent of older adults within the United States. Small population size and a shifting self-identification of race have made it difficult to obtain stable demographic estimates for these peoples. The Native American population is distributed among several hundred federally recognized tribes and entities (including American Indians, Eskimos, and Aleuts). Many of these subgroups have different cultures, histories, and degrees of self-identification, and a wide range of economic and social characteristics. Two-thirds of Native American older adults reside in ten states, and there is a further divide along rural-urban lines. Considerable American Indian migration to cities during and following World War II has left roughly half of these people dispersed among the U.S. urban population. Elders in cities forgo the support of tribal communities that is available to their rural and reservation counterparts who live in cultural enclaves (John, 1999).

Asian and Pacific Islanders

The Asian/Pacific Islander (API) grouping was 3.7 percent of the total population in 2000 and 2.4 percent of the older adults in the United States. This population includes Chinese, Filipino, Japanese, Vietnamese, Asian Indian, and Korean Americans; as well as native Hawaiians and other Pacific Islanders. The API population has considerable linguistic and cultural variation in addition to different histories of immigration. The comparative recency of immigration strongly influences the composition of groups of Asian elders. Chinese and Japanese people have a longer history of migration to the United States. Today's elders from these ethnic groups (they make up over half of all API elders) are more likely to be the native-born children of earlier immigrants or were young immigrants themselves. They have had a lifetime of acculturation and participation in the American economy. In 1965 changes in federal law governing national origin quotas allowed new Asian migration streams of Korean, Asian Indian, and Vietnamese people, often in a family context that brought older relatives to the United States. These immigrants are now taking their place in the older population (Siegel, 1999).

Poverty

There is considerable variation in socioeconomic status among the different racial/ethnic and national origin groups. One way to measure this is to examine the proportion of elders who fall below federal poverty thresholds. Although poverty rates have fallen for all groups since 1980, comparison of historical poverty rates for adults age sixty-five and older by race reveals that non-Hispanic white older adults have consistently had the smallest proportion of older adults in poverty, with Asian/Pacific Islanders having a slightly larger proportion who are poor. African Americans and Hispanics consistently have proportions that are much larger. In fact, Hispanics tend to have poverty rates twice as large as non-Hispanic whites, and poverty rates for African Americans have historically been triple those for non-Hispanic whites.

Several characteristics of older minority populations partially explain why they have higher poverty rates. In general, married people are less likely than unmarried people to be poor, and high school graduates are less likely than those who did not complete high school to be poor. Older minorities are less likely than older whites to be married and to be high school graduates. When examining the educational patterns of older adults, one finds that 28 percent of whites and 35 percent of Asian/Pacific Islanders have less than a high school education. Among older African Americans, 56 percent have failed to complete high school; among Hispanic older adults, 71 percent have not completed high school (Federal Interagency Forum on Aging Related Statistics, 2000). These disparities in educational attainment stem from minority elders' origins in social backgrounds with fewer educational opportunities, whether in the rural South or the underdeveloped nations from which they migrated. Following a life course perspective, lower education has adverse effects on the prospect for better jobs and pay, promotions, and wealth building.

Health

As noted earlier, minority older adults who survive to age sixty-five and beyond tend to be in poorer health than age peers who are white (though it is important to note that some ethnic subgroups have a higher life expectancy than the undifferentiated category of whites). Minority older adults are also more likely to suffer from multiple illnesses that further complicate treatment regimens (Markides and Miranda, 1997). Yet there are some commonalities across racial and national origin groups for adults age sixty-five and older. For instance, for both men and women across all groups, heart disease and cancer are the two leading causes of death. Strokes and chronic obstructive pulmonary disease

(COPD), also known as lung disease, tend to be either the third or fourth leading cause of death, with the exception of Native Americans and Hispanics, both of whom have diabetes mellitus as the fourth leading cause of death. Alzheimer's disease is the eighth leading cause of death among white men, and the sixth leading cause among white women, age sixty-five and older. Alzheimer's disease is also the tenth leading cause of death among African-American women, the ninth leading cause of death for Native American women, and the seventh leading cause death among Hispanic women.

Older adults on the lower rungs of the socioeconomic ladder often lack adequate private insurance to supplement Medicare, and do not have resources to meet out-of-pocket costs. This especially affects African-American and Hispanic older adults, who experience high rates of poverty. Without adequate resources to pay for medical care, they tend to receive inferior services. They must depend on Medicaid and hospital emergency rooms, rather than a regular physician, for care.

VIRGIL H. ADAMS III
DAVID J. EKERDT

See also GENETICS: ETHNICITY; IMMIGRANTS; LIFE COURSE; POVERTY.

BIBLIOGRAPHY

DILWORTH-ANDERSON, P., and BURTON, L. "Critical Issues in Understanding Family Support and Older Minorities." In *Full-Color Aging: Facts, Goals, and Recommendations for America's Diverse Elders.* Edited by T. P. Miles. Washington, D.C.: Gerontological Society of America, 1999. Pages 93–106.

Federal Interagency Forum on Aging Related Statistics. *Older Americans 2000: Key Indicators of Well-Being.* Washington, D.C.: U.S. Government Printing Office, 2000.

FERRARO, K. F., and FARMER, M. M. "Double Jeopardy: Aging as Leveler, or Persistent Health Inequality? A Longitudinal Analysis of White and Black Americans." *Journal of Gerontology: Social Sciences* 51B (1996): S319–S328.

JACKSON, J. S.; CHATTERS, L. M.; and TAYLOR, R. J., eds. *Aging in Black America.* Newbury Park, Calif.: Sage, 1993.

JOHN, R. "Aging among American Indians: Income Security, Health, and Social Support Networks." In *Full-Color Aging: Facts, Goals, and Recommendations for America's Diverse El-*

ders. Edited by T. P. Miles. Washington, D.C.: Gerontological Society of America, 1999. Pages 65–92.

MARKIDES, K., and MIRANDA, M. R. *Minorities, Aging, and Health.* Thousand Oaks, Calif.: Sage, 1997.

PAMPEL, F. C. *Aging, Social Inequality, and Public Policy.* Thousand Oaks, Calif.: Pine Forge Press, 1998.

SIEGEL, J. S. "Demographic Introduction to Racial/Hispanic Elderly Populations." In *Full-Color Aging: Facts, Goals, and Recommendations for America's Diverse Elders.* Edited by T. P. Miles. Washington, D.C.: Gerontological Society of America, 1999. Pages 1–19.

STOLLER, E. P., and GIBSON, R. C. *Worlds of Difference: Inequality in the Aging Experience,* 3d ed. Thousand Oaks, Calif.: Pine Forge Press, 2000.

WILLIAMS, D. R., and WILSON, C. M. "Race, Ethnicity, and Aging." In *Handbook of Aging and the Social Sciences,* 5th ed. Edited by R. H. Binstock and L. K. George. San Diego: Academic Press, 2001. Pages 160–178.

D

DAY HOSPITALS

Geriatric day hospitals have been part of the health care of older adults for many years. The global increase in the number of older adults has combined with fiscal pressures to decrease lengths of stay in acute care facilities and resulted in shortages of long-term care space in most developed countries. Day hospitals are intended to serve as a midpoint between acute care and outpatient rehabilitation, and to not only delay institutionalization but also to improve quality of life and independence in the patients who attend.

First introduced in the United Kingdom in the early 1960s, when long-term care beds were even more limited than at present, day hospitals were designed to provide interdisciplinary assessment and management of chronic health problems for older persons. They were initially developed in association with geriatric inpatient services to allow access to diagnostic facilities, but many are now sited with ease of access for older persons in mind. There are day hospitals in community centers and in shopping malls in some parts of the world. Day hospitals are even known as community rehabilitation centers in some parts of Australia. Several programs in the United States use centralized day programs to provide integrated assessment and therapy for frail older persons (Program for the All-Inclusive Care of Elders, or PACE). The key feature is the interdisciplinary assessment and management provided. Staffing usually consists of a geriatrician or physician with special training in the care of the elderly, nurses, nurse practitioners, physiotherapists, occupational therapists, social workers, and sometimes a speech pathologist or nutritionist. Often there is a recreational therapist. Case management models are usually used and day hospitals work in liaison with other community caregivers, such as home care services.

Patients who attend day hospitals benefit from both the therapy and the company of other peers. Most have individual therapy with specific treatment but will also participate in group activities such as exercise and usually some recreation. Some day hospitals provide more acute assessment and management. Persons usually attend for two days per week, although more often in some cases (PACE), and usually for about four hours each day. The geriatric program often arranges transportation.

Day hospitals should be distinguished from day centers, which do not provide specific therapy. Day centers are designed to maintain function and to provide not only activity and socialization but also respite for caregivers. They do not have the rich staffing of the geriatric day hospitals.

Reasons for attendance at a day hospital

The patients appreciate the interdisciplinary framework of a day hospital, which allows them to return to their own home the same day. The usual reason for admission is a complication of a chronic disease that has lead to a functional disability. A few persons are reluctant to come initially, preferring the security and comfort of their own home, but once they have become used to the staff and other patients, they are equally reluctant to leave! Older persons become deconditioned quickly after a serious illness or prolonged period of functional loss and as a result may have lost a considerable amount of muscle strength. They may be recovering from a stroke, an acute illness, a fractured hip, or have arthritis, or Parkinson's disease. For some reason they have become less independent and need physical therapy, adjustment of medications, and help in arranging their daily activities as efficiently as possible. Hypertension and diabetes are common conditions in day hospital patients. The staff of the day hospital spends much time educating the patients and families about the health problems and usually allows them a leading role in establishing the treatment goals. Once those goals have been met, the person is discharged from the day hospital.

Evidence of effectiveness

There is much controversy as to the effectiveness of day hospitals. A recent systematic review concluded day hospital care to be an effective service for elderly people who need rehabilitation, but it did not have any advantage over other comprehensive care, such as home therapy. It may be more expensive. There is little favorable published evidence from randomized controlled trials.

No difference was shown in the rate of hospitalization or degree of disability for patients who attend day hospitals compared to those who receive home care in either a Finnish or a British day hospital. An earlier Canadian study showed no difference in mortality between GDH and usual specialized geriatric care. Randomized controlled trials of geriatric day hospitals have generally failed to show any benefit in terms of either patient outcomes or cost savings, although those patients with the greater degree of disability have seemed to improve in some trials. These disappointing results may have been due to heterogeneity of physical and mental function in the patients who come to day hospitals or the wrong outcomes may have been measured. There may have been too much of a variation in the health status of the persons admitted to the day hospitals. The measurement instruments may not have been the best ones to measure important changes. Instruments that are designed to discriminate between persons who have a condition and those who do not may not be the best ones to measure change in that condition. If a woman has had a stroke, she may not improve the paralysis of the leg involved by attending the day hospital but after attending she may be able to walk a little further with an aid and feel much better

about going out in a car or even public transport. She may also enjoy life more. Measuring her muscle power or the degree of weakness would not have shown much improvement.

On the other hand, it is possible that day hospitals are not effective ways of managing health problems in the frail older adult and other approaches, such as increased home care, need to be better evaluated. There is, however, a high acceptance of this approach from day hospital attendees and staff. Increasing evidence shows targeting patients most likely to benefit may improve outcomes in both physical function and reduction of caregiver stress. In several published studies, patients with the highest degree of physical disability seemed to benefit the most. Better selection of patients in the future may improve the effectiveness of these popular programs, but this would require evaluation in further rigorous research studies.

IRENE TURPIE

See also ASSESSMENT; FRAILTY; GERIATRIC MEDICINE; HEALTH AND LONG-TERM CARE PROGRAM INTEGRATION; MULTIDISCIPLINARY TEAM; OCCUPATIONAL THERAPY; SOCIAL WORK.

BIBLIOGRAPHY

BROCKLEHURST, J. C. "Geriatric Services and the Day Hospital." In *Textbook of Geriatric Medicine and Gerontology*. 2d ed. Edinburgh: Churchill-Livingstone, 1978.

ENG, C.; PEDULLA, J.; ELEANOR, G. P.; et al. "Program for All-Inclusive Care of Elders (PACE): An Innovative Model of Geriatric Care and Financing." *Journal of American Geriatrics Society* 45 (1997): 223–232.

FORSTER, A.; YOUNG, J.; and LANGHORNE, P. "Systematic Review of Day Hospital Care for Elderly People." *British Medical Journal* 318 (1999): 837–841.

TURPIE I. "The Geriatric Day Hospital." In *The Oxford Textbook of Geriatric Medicine*. Edited by J. Grimley Evans. Oxford, U.K. Oxford University Press, 2000. Pps. 1076–1086.

DEATH AND DYING

Dying and death are profound aspects of the human experience. Social science research documents the fact that defining someone as "dying" is a social process. Although critical medical conditions certainly have a physiological basis, disease states are given significance through interpretation (Muller and Koenig). Perceptions that dying has begun and the meanings associated with those perceptions are contingent on a range of such social and cultural factors as the state of biological knowledge, the value of prolonging life or accepting finitude, the relative roles of religion, science, and medicine in creating meaning in everyday life, and personal familiarity with the dying transition. Dying today is shaped by particular notions of therapeutic possibility as well as ideals about approaching the end of life. The distinguishing feature about the process of dying today is that, to some degree, it can be negotiated and controlled depending on the preferences of the dying person, the goals of particular medical specialties, the organizational features of technology-intensive medical settings, and the presence and wishes of family members. It is impossible to think about death today except in language informed by institutionalized medicine.

A century ago, the leading causes of death in the United States were communicable diseases, especially influenza, tuberculosis, and diphtheria, and more than half of deaths occurred among individuals age fourteen or younger. During the twentieth century average life expectancy increased and the chance of dying in childhood was greatly diminished (Quadagno). Since the Second World War, heart disease, cancer, and stroke have become the leading causes of death. In 1995 they accounted for 67 percent of deaths for persons age sixty-five and older. The fact that more people than ever before are dying in advanced age of chronic conditions creates unprecedented challenges—for individuals as they confront the dying process of relatives and friends, for the health care delivery system, and for American society as its members struggle to define and implement the idea of a "good death."

Medicalization of dying

In 1900 most Americans died at home, often surrounded by multiple generations of family members. By 1950 approximately half of all deaths occurred in hospitals, nursing homes, or other institutions. By the mid-1990s, 80 percent of Americans died in medical institutions, attended by paid staff. Persons over age sixty-five comprised less than 13 percent of the population, yet they represented 73 percent of all deaths in the United States in the mid-1990s. At the beginning of the twenty-first century, 55 to 60 percent of persons over the age of sixty-five die in the acute-care hospital, though patterns vary considerably across the nation (Institute of Medicine). Those persons fall into two distinct groups. The first includes elderly who were functioning independently until they were struck by a serious illness such as heart attack, stroke, or fractured hip. Most of those patients receive relatively intensive care. The second group includes people who are older, frail and debilitated, have multiple degenerative and chronic conditions, but are not clearly dying. The second group is larger, comprising 70 percent to 80 percent of elderly patients in the hospital. Individuals in that group may require repeated hospitalizations for supportive or intensive care, to stabilize conditions and treat acute problems (Scitovsky and Capron).

As the place of death has shifted from the home to the hospital, medicine, as a system of knowledge, has become the dominant cultural framework for understanding death, the process of dying, and how to act when death approaches. Health professionals have the assumed responsibility, once held by family and community, for the care of persons at the end of life, and they now widely influence how that care is understood and delivered. Physicians have become the gatekeepers of the dying transition in the United States. They, rather than the dying person or family, define when the dying process has begun. This is most obvious in the hospital intensive care unit (ICU), where the inevitability of death frequently is not acknowledged until the end is very near, and the discontinuation of life-sustaining treatments often signifies the beginning of the dying process. Moreover, in the ICU, medical staff members are able to orchestrate and control the timing of death (Slomka).

A growing elderly population, cultural ambivalence about the social worth of the frail and very old, medical uncertainty about whether or not to prolong frail lives, and rising health care costs contribute to controversy both among health professionals and the wider public about decision-making and responsibility at the end of life. The costs of medical care, and especially the costs of intensive care, are high in the last months of life. Those rising costs have been the source of debates about rationing health care to elderly persons in order to reduce health care costs. For many people both within and outside of medicine, the value of prolonging life by technological means competes with the value of allowing death to occur without medical intervention. That cultural tension has given rise to a vast array of seemingly insoluble dilemmas about the management of dying. A vast literature in bioethics illustrates dilemmas in treatment and care for the dying elderly for which there are competing claims and no distinct solutions. Common dilemmas about technologically prolonging life include the following: whether or not to artificially feed (through a feeding tube) a person who can no longer feed him or herself; whether or not to place a person who has difficulty breathing on a mechanical ventilator; and whether or not to admit a dying person to an intensive care unit.

As more technological and clinical innovations become available, there is more that can be done to postpone death. The technological imperative in medicine—to order ever more diagnostic tests, to perform procedures, to intervene with ventilators, medications, and surgery in order to prolong life or stave off death whenever there is an opportunity to do so—is the most important variable in contemporary medical practice, influencing much decision-making at the end of life. There are no formulas that health professionals, patients, or families can use to decide between life-extending treatments and care that is not aimed at prolonging life. It is very common for patients, family members, and health professionals to feel obligated to continue aggressive medical treatment even though they do not wish to prolong the dying process.

The largest study ever conducted on the process of dying in the hospital was carried out in five university hospitals across the United States over a four-year period beginning in 1989 (SUPPORT Principal Investigators). In the first two-year phase of the project, 4,300 patients with a median age of sixty-five who were diagnosed with life-threatening illnesses, were enrolled. The SUPPORT investigators concluded that the dying process in the hospital was not satisfactory. For example, only 47 percent of physicians knew when their patients wanted to avoid cardiopulmonary resuscitation (CPR); 38 percent of patients who died spent ten or more days in an ICU preceding death; 46 percent of *Do Not Resuscitate* (DNR) orders were written within two days of death even though 79 percent of the patients had a DNR order; and for 50 percent of the conscious patients, families reported moderate to severe pain at least half the time in the three days preceding death. Even when a focused effort was made to reduce pain and to respect patient wishes regarding end-of-life care, no overall improvement in care or outcomes was made.

The technological imperative shapes activities and choices in the hospital even though death without high-technology intervention is valued by many in principle. One survey of nurses and physicians revealed that health professionals would not want aggressive life prolonging treatments for themselves, and many would decline aggressive care on the basis of age alone (Gillick, Hesse and Mazzapica). Approximately half of physicians and nurses interviewed in another study stated they had acted contrary to their own values by providing overly aggressive treatment (Solomon et al.).

Philosopher Daniel Callahan has noted that American society, including the institution of medicine, has lost a sense of the normal or natural life span, including the inevitability of decline and death. Callahan and other critics challenge the medical imperative of considering death as an option, one of several available to practitioners and consumers of health care (Callahan). Medicine pays little credence to the biological certainty of death; the tendency instead is to believe that dying results from disease or injury that may yield to advances in technology (McCue). Yet there is a lack of clarity about what constitutes normal aging and decline and what distinguishes them from disease.

Family members are sometimes confronted with the choice of prolonging the life of a person who they consider to have died already as the result of a stroke, a coma, or other serious condition that destroys or masks the personality of the individual. Such *social death*, when the person can no longer express the same identity as before the health crisis, occurs days, weeks, months, or years before *biological death*, when the physical organism dies. The discrepancy between social and biological death is one of the most difficult features of contemporary medical decision-making.

The use of hospice programs, in which clinical, social, and spiritual support are given to dying persons and their families without the intention of prolonging life, began in the United States in 1974. Hospice embodies a philosophy, originating with Dr. Cicely Saunders in Great Britain, that pain control, dignity, and the reduction of spiritual and psychological suffering are the most important goals of patient care as death approaches. Hospice care, delivered both in the home and institutional setting, has been growing steadily since the 1980s. Yet in 1995 only about 17 percent of all deaths (all ages) took place in a hospice setting. The notion of *palliative care*, medical care that seeks to reduce and relieve symptoms of disease during the dying process without attempting to effect a cure or extend life, is gaining support and acceptance among health care practitioners and the public, but the desire to control and conquer end-stage disease still strongly influences most medical thought and action (Institute of Medicine 1997).

Cultural diversity

There is not just one attitude or approach toward dying and death among Americans. Studies in the social science and health literatures on how cultural diversity influences patient, family, and provider responses to end-of-life treatments and decision-making have been appearing slowly but steadily since the mid-1980s. Two themes emerge from this research. First, health workers are trained in particular professional cultures and bring their own experiences to bear on the dying process. Physicians, nurses, social workers, chaplains, and other health care professionals hold different assumptions from one another about how death should be approached as a result of their different types of training, and those sets of assumptions differ from the experiences of patients and families (Koenig). Second, the relationships among ethnic identification, religious practices, ways of dying, and beliefs and priorities about care, autonomy, and communication are complex and cannot be neatly organized along ethnic, class, or professional lines. In assessing cultural variation in patient populations, for example, cultural background is only meaningful when it is interpreted in the context of a particular patient's unique history, family constellation, and socioeconomic status. It cannot be assumed that patients' ethnic origins or religious background will lead them to approach decisions about their death in a culturally specified manner (Koenig and Gates-Williams).

In an increasingly pluralistic society, there is growing diversity among health care workers as well as among patient populations. Especially in urban areas, the cultural background of a health professional is often different from that of a dying patient to whom care is being given. It is impossible and inappropriate to use racial or ethnic background as straightforward predictors of behavior among health professionals or patients. In their study of ethnic difference, dying, and bereavement, Kalish and Reynolds found that although ethnic variation is an important factor in attitudes and expectations about death, "individual differences within ethnic groups are at least as great as, and often much greater than, differences between ethnic groups" (p. 49). The impact of cultural difference on attitudes and practices surrounding death in the United States cannot be denied. The challenge for society is to respect cultural pluralism in the context of an actively interventionist medical system.

SHARON R. KAUFMAN

See also BEREAVEMENT; HOSPICE; MEDICALIZATION OF AGING; MORTALITY; PALLIATIVE CARE; REFUSING AND WITHDRAWING MEDICAL TREATMENT.

BIBLIOGRAPHY

CALLAHAN, D. *The Troubled Dream of Life: Living with Mortality*. New York: Simon and Schuster, 1993.

GILLICK, M.; HESSE, K.; and MAZZAPICA, N. "Medical Technology at the End of Life: What Would Physicians and Nurses Want for Themselves?" *Archives of Internal Medicine* 153 (1993): 2542–2547.

Institute of Medicine. *Approaching Death: Improving Care at the End of Life*. Washington, D.C.: National Academy Press, 1997.

KALISH, R. A., and REYNOLDS, D. K. *Death and Ethnicity: A Psychocultural Study*. New York: Baywood, 1976.

KOENIG, B. "Cultural Diversity in Decision Making about Care at the End of Life." In *Approaching Death: Improving Care at the End of Life*. Institute of Medicine. Edited by M. Field and C. K. Cassel. Washington, D.C.: National Academy Press, 1997. Appendix E. Pages 363–382.

KOENIG, B., and GATES-WILLIAMS, J. "Understanding Cultural Difference in Caring for Dying Patients." *Western Journal of Medicine* 163 (1995): 244–249.

McCUE, J. D. "The Naturalness of Dying." *Journal of the American Medical Association* 273 (1995): 1039–1043.

MULLER, J., and KOENIG, B. "On the Boundary of Life and Death: The Definition of Dying by Medical Residents." In *Biomedicine Examined*. Edited by M. Lock and D. Gordon. Boston: Kluwer, 1988. Pages 351–374.

QUADAGNO, J. *Aging and the Life Course: An Introduction to Social Gerontology.* Boston: McGraw-Hill, 1999.

SCITOVSKY, A. A., and CAPRON, A. "Medical Care at the End of Life." *An American Review of Public Health* 7 (1986): 59–75.

SLOMKA, J. "The Negotiation of Death: Clinical Decision Making at the End of Life." *Social Science & Medicine* 35 (1992): 251–259.

SOLOMON, M., et al. "Decisions Near the End of Life: Professional Views on Life-Sustaining Treatments." *Journal of Public Health* 83 (1993): 14–23.

SUPPORT Principal Investigators. "A Controlled Trial to Improve Care for Seriously Ill Hospitalized Patients." *Journal of the American Medical Association* 274 (1995): 1591–1634.

DEATH ANXIETY

Although humans have always thought about death, empirical research on death anxiety did not begin in earnest until the late 1950s. Over one thousand articles have now appeared on the topic, and death anxiety remains an important issue in thanatology (the study of psychological and social aspects of death and dying).

What is death anxiety?

There have been substantial changes in the way Western scientists have interpreted or understood the concept of death anxiety. Early writings, which were heavily influenced by psychodynamic theory, stressed that fear and anxiety about death were universal, and, in an attempt to deal with their neurotic concerns about death, most individuals repressed or denied their true, negative feelings. In other words, everyone feared or was anxious about death, no matter what they said or how they acted. As death research matured, however, investigators discovered not only that some people actually had little or no anxiety about death, but also that the term *death anxiety* was really a misnomer for a variety of related negative reactions to death. These reactions include elements of fear, anxiety, concern, threat, worry, and confusion, and they can be focused on different death-related issues. For instance, distinctions should be made regarding anxiety about one's own death or the deaths of others, reactions to a painful dying process, uncertainties about when and how one will die, and concerns about an afterlife.

Another major transformation that occurred in thanatological theory and research involved the recognition that individuals can also have positive views and feelings about death. Death is not always viewed completely negatively. For instance, death can give life meaning and can accentuate a positive philosophy of life. People can view death positively, for instance, if it brings relief of pain and suffering, gives loved ones a chance to come together and express their care and concern for each other, or if death and dying helps to refocus attention on important personal values and needs. Finally, dealing with death can reveal strengths in terminally ill individuals, their family members and friends, and health care professionals. In sum, attitudes and feelings about death are multidimensional, and people can simultaneously have both positive and negative sentiments about a broad array of death-related phenomena.

Correlates of death anxiety

Although there are exceptions, it is possible to summarize the association between death anxiety and several demographic and experiential factors. For instance, both gender and age are often related to death anxiety. Females tend to report higher death anxiety than males, and a negative relationship is often seen between age and death anxiety. Younger populations (primarily high school and college age students) tend to report higher levels of death anxiety than elderly persons. The reasons for these differences are not clear.

The effect of contact or experience with death is not straightforward. On the one hand, some workers, such as firefighters and police, whose duties places them at heightened risk for injury and death may have heightened concerns or thoughts about death, which is realistic given their jobs. On the other hand, those working directly with dying or bereaved individuals, such as physicians, nurses, funeral directors, or hospice and AIDS volunteers, do not, as a rule, demonstrate heightened death anxiety and may, in fact, show greater sensitivity and acceptance of death than other groups. Bereavement does not seem to have any direct impact one way or another on feelings about death.

As one might expect, religion and death have often been studied together. Belief in an afterlife or having a religious affiliation seems to have no specific effect on death anxiety, however, though one's religious orientation is important. Individuals whose religious and spiritual beliefs have been internalized, and therefore have an influence on their general behavior, values, and personal world view (a construct often identified as *intrinsic religiosity*) tend to report less death anxiety, while those whose religion serves a more social than ideological function (called *extrinsic religiosity*) report greater death anxiety.

Assessing and changing death anxiety

The most common method used to assess death anxiety is the self-report questionnaire, which has been employed in over 95 percent of all studies. Several of the more carefully validated measures, including those assessing positive feelings about death are reviewed in Robert Neimeyer's *Death Anxiety Handbook* (1994). Projective instruments (e.g., the Rorschach inkblot test or Thematic Apperception Test), which were once popular assessment methods, are no longer in favor due to the inability of researchers to document the reliability and validity of projective techniques.

Feelings about death can be modified, although there is still much to learn about causal factors. There is information about two types of events: near-death experiences and death-education programs. Near-death experiences are situations in which individuals feel their death is imminent as a result of an accident, a near-accident, a medical condition, or some other event. Near-death experiences often have a salutary effect by reducing negative feelings and increasing positive feelings about death.

Death education can also influence death anxieties, but it depends on the type of program. *Experiential* death education refers to classes or workshops that help participants examine and discuss their personal views and feelings about death. This is usually achieved through a combination of readings, movies, videos, experiential exercises, and frank discussions. In contrast, *didactic* death education is primarily educational in nature and tends to include lectures and readings, but little or no exploration and disclosure of personal feelings. Whereas experiential death education significantly reduces death anxiety, didactic programs have no significant impact.

Death anxiety and behavior

The few studies relating death anxiety and behavior suggest that caregivers who are comfortable with death are more likely to interact positively with the terminally ill, to speak directly and honestly about death, and to be emotionally comforting and supportive to others in need. In contrast, high levels of death anxiety may influence people to avoid seeking needed medical attention or to plan appropriately for their own and others' medical care (e.g., by refusing to consider or execute *advanced directives,* which are documents such as living wills or a Durable Power of Attorney for Health Care that provide a person some control about how terminal features of their medical care should be handled). High death anxiety can also create missed opportunities to help others, such as someone who is bereaved and needs to speak about their feelings or children struggling to understand and cope with death-related experiences.

JOSEPH A. DURLAK

See also ANXIETY; DEATH AND DYING.

BIBLIOGRAPHY

DURLAK, J. A., and RIESENBERG, L. A. "The Impact of Death Education." *Death Studies* 15 (1991): 39–58.

NEIMEYER, R. A., ed. *Death Anxiety Handbook: Research, Instrumentation, and Application.* Washington, D.C.: Taylor and Francis, 1994.

NEIMEYER, R. A., and VAN BRUNT, D. "Death Anxiety." In *Dying: Facing the Facts,* 3d ed. Edited by H. Wass and R. A. Neimeyer. Washington, D.C.: Taylor and Francis, 1995. Pages 49–88.

RING, K. *Life at Death: A Scientific Investigation of the Near-Death Experience.* New York: Quill, 1982.

SPELDER, L. A., and STRICKLAND, A. L. *The Last Dance: Encountering Death and Dying,* 5th ed. Mountain View, Calif.: Mayfield Publishing.

TOKUNUGA, H. T. "The Effect of Bereavement upon Death Related Attitudes and Fears." *Omega* 16 (1985): 267–280.

DECONDITIONING

Deconditioning can be defined as the multiple, potentially reversible changes in body systems brought about by physical inactivity and disuse. Such changes often have significant functional and clinical consequences in older people. Deconditioning commonly occurs in two situations: (1) a sedentary lifestyle, which is common in older people even in the absence of significant disease or disability and may result in a slow, chronic decline in physical fitness; and (2) bed or chair rest during an acute illness, which can lead to disastrously rapid physical decline.

Decline in muscle strength and muscle bulk is the most important and consistent feature of deconditioning. Reduced maximal oxygen uptake during exercise, impairment of balance responses, and decreased cardiac output during exercise have also been linked to deconditioning but may primarily result from the reduction in muscle bulk.

Aging or deconditioning?

Many people, and even some health care professionals, often see much of the disease and loss of function found with aging as a normal and inevitable consequence of aging. However, it is now clear that such changes are in fact due to a combination of true age-related decline, disease (whether overt or hidden), and disuse. It is often difficult in practice to determine the relative contribution of each of these factors.

Muscle mass declines steadily with increasing age. This results in a loss of muscle strength of 1 to 2 percent per year. It is important to note, however, that reduced muscle mass (or *sarcopenia*) with age cannot be entirely due to inactivity, as it is also found in highly trained elderly athletes. The patterns of muscle loss do appear to differ between the two. While aging results in a reduced number of muscle fibres, disuse primarily causes a reduction in muscle fibre size. Sustained muscular activity requires the delivery of an adequate supply of oxygen to the muscles and utilization of the oxygen in the mitochondria of the muscle cells. Cross-sectional studies (comparing people of different ages) and longitudinal studies (serial examinations of people as they age) have found a decline in maximal oxygen uptake with age. The most important factor in this decline may be the changes in muscle mass due to either age or disuse, since maximal oxygen uptake is almost independent of age when expressed relative to fat-free mass (mass mainly composed of muscle). Similarly, cardiac output shows little change with age when related to fat-free mass.

The degree to which decreased physical activity with increasing age is a cause, rather than an effect, of reduced muscle bulk is uncertain. Jackson and colleagues have argued that about

half of the decline in exercise capacity over the adult life span can be attributed to chronic physical inactivity and the resultant changes in body composition (increased body fat and reduced muscle bulk). The beneficial effects of exercise training programs on muscle strength, exercise capacity, and balance suggest, but do not prove, that the decline in physical fitness with old age is at least partially preventable.

Effects of acute illness

Major trauma, sepsis, or surgery lead to the breakdown of skeletal muscle in order to provide nitrogen and amino acids essential to immune function and tissue repair. While this response can be ultimately beneficial, the resultant loss of muscle mass and strength may impede recovery of normal function after surgery. This is particularly likely if breakdown of muscle is compounded by unnecessary immobilization (as often happens in a hospital) or if prior deconditioning has led to preexisting muscle weakness and a smaller reserve of muscle for consumption.

Functional consequences of deconditioning

Muscle strength of itself matters little; what is important is how changes in muscle strength affects the ability to perform daily activities. As the strength of a muscle decreases with age, activities relying on that muscle require a greater proportion of the maximum strength of the muscle. Eventually, a threshold is reached where the maximum strength available to an individual for a particular action is the minimum strength required for that action. Any further decline in muscle strength will make the activity impossible. If that activity is essential to an independent existence, a small decline in muscle function, such as following a brief period of inactivity due to acute illness, may be sufficient to cause dependence. For example, the quadriceps (thigh muscle) is the most important muscle used in rising unaided from a toilet or from a low chair. The threshold for quadriceps contraction needed to perform these activities is reached at about the age of eighty in women, and a few years later in men.

Appropriate patterns of muscle contractions in the leg (and trunk) are used to adjust and maintain balance (following a stumble, for instance). Deconditioning can adversely affect balance in a number of ways. Disuse atrophy will reduce the functional reserve of muscles needed to maintain balance. For example, loss of strength in the muscles that flex the ankle joint (dorsiflexors) has been associated with falls in nursing-home residents. Prolonged bed rest may cause the brain to adapt to the recumbent position and hence lead to imbalance when the patient eventually tries to walk.

Risk factors for deconditioning

The cumulative effects of multiple chronic diseases such as dementia, depression, stroke, osteoarthritis, heart failure, incontinence, respiratory disease, and diabetes mellitus contribute to physical inactivity and disability in older people. Inadequate dietary intake and nutritional deficiencies exacerbate age-related decline in muscle mass. Psychosocial factors—such as the attitudes of older people themselves, and of caregivers and relatives—are also important. For example, an attitude that physical decline is inevitable in old age can lead to a delay in seeking medical attention for treatable problems. The end result is a reduction in functional reserve, which increases the risk of clinically significant decline during intercurrent acute illness. People with increased susceptibility to disability and deconditioning are often described as *frail*.

Acute illness in older people is often complicated by development of acute confusion (delirium), incontinence, immobility, or instability. Indeed, these may be the presenting features of acute illness—myocardial infarction may present with confusion rather than chest pain. An atypical presentation may result in delayed presentation by the patient and delayed diagnosis and treatment by the doctor and is a predictor of a poor outcome.

Hospitalization of older people may have deleterious effects distinct from the effects of acute illness. The unusual environment and routine of hospitals and complications of polypharmacy and of therapeutic and diagnostic procedures may worsen or precipitate problems like confusion or incontinence. Use of urinary catheters in incontinent patients or treatment of delirium with physical restraints or with sedative medications will exacerbate immobility and functional impairment. Functional dependency may be reinforced if hospital staff are overly concerned about the risk of falls or if they perform, rather than supervise, daily activities. In addi-

tion, social networks may disappear during a long illness, and patients may become demoralized and depressed.

Prevention and treatment of deconditioning

The adage "use it or lose it" is true at all ages, but it is a fundamental tenet of the care of older people. Given the difficulties of reversing deconditioning and its functional effects once established, prevention is the best option. This requires a variety of strategies.

Regular physical exercise in middle age protects against many conditions common in old age, including late-onset diabetes mellitus, osteoporosis, hypertension, and cardiac disease. The role of exercise in older life in combating these conditions is less clear. However, Roy Shephard has noted that physical training can lead to the equivalent of a twenty to thirty year reversal of the usual age-associated decline in aerobic power. Maintenance of physical fitness and avoidance of a sedentary lifestyle with increasing age must therefore be an important goal of community health programs, reinforced whenever possible by advice from doctors to individual patients. In particular, patients and caregivers must be educated about the importance of maintaining physical activity even in the face of significant chronic illness, as well as the importance of early intervention during acute decline or illness.

Prevention of deconditioning in hospitals during acute illness requires a multifaceted approach that includes physical therapy, maintenance of nutrition, medical management, and psychological support. Activity and independence should be promoted from the time of admission. Education of health care staff about the dangers of deconditioning is vital, since bed rest continues to be recommended during acute illness despite the lack of evidence showing benefits and the considerable evidence showing potential adverse effects from this advice. Sedative medications and restraints should be used sparingly, if at all.

Exercise programs can be beneficial for older people regardless of their disability. In randomized controlled trials of both healthy and frail elderly subjects, including people over eighty years of age, exercise has been shown to improve lower-limb muscle strength, exercise endurance, balance, speed of walking, and overall levels of physical activity. Practice of specific skills is required if improved muscle strength is to translate into functional benefits. Exercises including a balance component (e.g., tai chi) may be useful in preventing falls. Physical exertion has potential dangers, and exercise programs for older people should be tailored to the needs and capacity of the individual person.

Restoration of physical function and independence in a frail and deconditioned hospital patient is particularly difficult. Comprehensive clinical, functional, and psychosocial assessment is mandatory. It is important to set measurable, attainable goals and to monitor progress carefully. This is aided by the use of standardized tools to measure important areas such as cognitive function and the ability to perform daily activities. An active multidisciplinary rehabilitation program is essential, and should include nutritional and psychologic support.

SHAUN O'KEEFFE

See also EXERCISE; FRAILTY; GERIATRIC MEDICINE; PHYSIOLOGICAL CHANGES; PHYSIOLOGICAL CHANGES, ORGAN SYSTEMS: SKELETAL MUSCLE; SURGERY IN ELDERLY PEOPLE.

BIBLIOGRAPHY

BROWN, M.; SINACORE, D. R.; EHSANI, A. A.; BINDER, E. F.; HOLLOSZY, J. O.; and KOHRT, W. M. "Low-Intensity Exercise As a Modifier of Physical Frailty in Older Adults." *Archives of Physical Medicine and Rehabilitation* 81 (2000): 960–965.

BUCHNER, D. M., and WAGNER, E. H. "Preventing Frail Health." *Clinics in Geriatric Medicine* 8 (1992): 1–17.

FIATARONE, M. A.; O'NEILL, E. F.; RYAN, N. D.; et al. "Exercise Training and Nutritional Supplementation for Physical Frailty in Very Elderly People." *New England Journal of Medicine* 330 (1994): 1769–1774.

HUNTER, G. R.; TREUTH, M. S.; WEINSIER, R. L.; et al. "The Effects of Strength Conditioning on Older Womens' Ability to Perform Daily Tasks." *Journal of the American Geriatrics Society* 43 (1995): 756–760.

JACKSON, A. S.; BEARD, E. F.; and WIER, L. T. "Changes in Aerobic Power of Men Ages 25–70." *Medical Science of Sports and Exercise* 27 (1995): 113–120.

KENNIE, D. C.; DINAN, S.; and YOUNG, A. "Health Promotion and Physical Exertion." In *Brockle-hurst's Textbook of Geriatric Medicine and Gerontology*, 5th ed. Edited by R. Tallis, H. Fillit, and J. C. Brocklehurst. Edinburgh: Churchill Livingstone, 1998. Pages 1461–1472.

PROVINCE, M. A.; HADLEY, E. C.; HORNBROOK, M. C.; et al. "The Effects of Exercise on Falls in Elderly Patients: A Preplanned Meta-Analysis." *Journal of the American Medical Association* 273 (1995): 1341–1344.

SHEPHARD, R. J. "Physical Fitness and Exercise." In *Principles and Practice of Geriatric Medicine*. Edited by M. S. J. Pathy. Chichester, U.K.: John Wiley & Sons, 1998. Pages 137–151.

WOLFSON, L.; WHIPPLE, R.; DERBY, C.; et al. "Balance and Strength Training in Older Adults: Intervention Gains and Tai-Chi Maintenance." *Journal of the American Geriatrics Society* 44 (1996): 498–506.

DECUBITUS ULCER

See PRESSURE ULCERS

DELIRIUM

Delirium is a derangement of mental function characterized by disturbance of consciousness and impairment of cognition. In contrast to dementia, delirium usually develops over a short period of time, it tends to fluctuate in severity over the course of the day, and it usually resolves with treatment of the underlying causes. This disturbance of consciousness results in reduced awareness of the external environment, and a reduction of the ability to focus, sustain, and shift attention. Cognitive impairments in delirium include disorientation in time and place, memory deficits, and language disturbances. Sensory perception, particularly vision, may also be disturbed, resulting in misinterpretations, illusions, and hallucinations. There may be disruption of the normal sleep-wake cycle, with individuals being drowsy during the day and active at night. The acute mental disturbances of delirium can be very frightening and upsetting for patients, who may respond with agitated and aggressive behavior. In younger adults, an episode of delirium is usually quite dramatic and florid (hyperactive delirium), and its detection and diagnosis is relatively straightforward. By contrast, the mental disturbances in elderly individuals with delirium are often much less obvious, particularly if there is a pre-existing dementia (hypoactive delirium). As a result, it is quite common for delirium in an elderly person to be overlooked by their families, by other carers, and by medical and nursing staff. This is unfortunate because, like pain and fever, delirium is an important nonspecific sign that the patient is physically ill, and requires further investigation to identify the cause. If the individual is very demented or very ill, they may be unable to complain of other symptoms, and delirium may be the first or only sign that something significant is amiss.

Age and delirium

Delirium occurs when the brain receives an external insult powerful enough to disrupt its normal functioning. It can occur at any age, but it is most commonly seen in children and elderly people. In childhood, the brain is vulnerable because it is still developing. In old age, increased vulnerability to delirium is due to factors such as dementia and sensory impairment, which become more common with increasing age. As well as being more vulnerable, elderly people are also more liable to be exposed to the external insults, such as physical illness and medication, that commonly cause delirium. The more vulnerable the individual, the less severe such insults need to be in order to precipitate a delirium. Consequently, the highest rates of delirium are to be found in high-risk populations such as elderly medical, surgical, and psychiatric inpatients. Some elderly patient groups, such as those with hip fractures, appear to be particularly prone to developing delirium. In elderly patients, it is important to distinguish delirium from other mental disorders that occur in old age. This can be difficult, not least because disorders such as dementia and depression are themselves risk factors for delirium, and may be co-morbid with it. A useful rule of thumb is that any sudden worsening of cognitive functioning, particularly if alertness and attention are impaired, should be investigated as delirium until proved otherwise.

Causes

Physical illnesses cause delirium by acutely disrupting the normal metabolism of the nerve cells in the brain. This can come about by reducing the oxygen supply (e.g., cardiac failure, a fall in blood pressure, anemia), by physiological disturbances (e.g., fever, liver or kidney failure, endocrine disorders), by the action of drugs and toxins, and by direct damage (e.g., stroke, head injury). The most common causes of delirium in elderly patients are acute infections (particularly of the chest and urinary tract), and the prescribed drugs that they are taking. Almost any drug can cause delirium in an elderly patient, but some are particularly associated with this problem, either because they act directly on the brain (e.g., tranquilizers, anticonvulsants), or because they are broken down and eliminated less efficiently by the elderly body and so accumulate, or because they have particular modes of action. Drugs with anticholinergic activity are particularly liable to cause delirium, which has led to the suggestion that disturbance of the cholinergic nerve systems in the brain is an important feature of the pathology of delirium. In practice, elderly patients are often taking many drugs, and delirium may occur as a cumulative effect of this polypharmacy rather than it being due to one drug acting alone. It is important to bear in mind that delirium can also be caused by the sudden withdrawal of a drug upon which the patient is physically dependent. The most common drug in this respect is alcohol, although in elderly patients other possibilities, such as opiate analgesics and benzodiazepines, should be considered. Although delirium usually has a physical cause, it is recognized that, in particularly vulnerable individuals, a severe psychological stress such as bereavement, relocation, or extreme sensory deprivation may be sufficient to precipitate it.

Outcome

Traditionally, delirium has been regarded as a transient disorder that terminates with either recovery or death. In the majority of cases, the delirious episode is relatively short, but about one-third of patients have prolonged or recurrent episodes. Delirium is associated with increased short-term mortality in elderly patients, due mainly to the underlying physical illness. However, delirious patients also tend to have longer hospital stays, higher rates of functional decline, and higher rates of discharge to nursing homes. Other complications of delirium include falls and fractures if the patient is hyperactive, and pressure sores if they are hypoactive. Prospective studies show that the prognosis in terms of persistent or recurrent symptoms of delirium is relatively poor in elderly patients. This is probably because those who experience delirium are a vulnerable group more likely to develop the condition whenever they become physically ill. A proportion will also be suffering from a form of dementia, which will increase their vulnerability to delirium as it progresses. It is not known if delirium is itself a risk factor for the development or exacerbation of dementia. The family and other carers should be advised of the risk of future delirium, and educated about the symptoms so that they can recognize it if and when it occurs again.

Clinical management

The most important aspect of the clinical management of delirium is prompt diagnosis and treatment of the underlying cause or (more usually) causes. Sometimes the symptoms and behaviors of the delirium itself may need to be treated. The evidence base for this aspect of management is still very limited, and current approaches are based mainly on accumulated clinical experience. These strategies involve both pharmacological and nonpharmacological approaches. Regarding use of medication, there is always a risk that giving a powerful psychoactive drug to a delirious patient will make the problem worse, so this course of action should only be considered if the associated symptoms and behaviors are distressing or potentially dangerous to the patient and/or others. The drug treatment of delirium in elderly patients is similar to that of younger adults, although it is necessary to start with much lower doses. The drugs most commonly used in the management of delirium are neuroleptics (usually haloperidol), or benzodiazepines (e.g., diazepam, lorazepam, alprazolam) if the patient cannot tolerate a neuroleptic. The effects of the drug and its dosage need to be frequently reviewed, to ensure that it is not having any adverse effects. Once the delirium has resolved, the medication should be reduced and, if possible, discontinued over a period of a few days.

Nonpharmacological interventions in delirium are aimed at reducing the confusing, frightening, and disorienting aspects of the hospital or nursing home environment that aggravate the disorder. There is little evidence to inform the use of these strategies, but features such as good lighting, low noise levels, a visible clock, a window on the outside world, and, in particular, the reassuring presence of personal possessions and familiar individuals such as relatives are all thought to be beneficial. Any invasive intervention, including personal care tasks, should be explained simply, slowly, clearly, and repeatedly before it is carried out. Holding the patient's hand while talking helps to focus their attention, and provides reassurance.

Prevention

Regarding prevention, the aim should be to minimize exposure to the various patient- and hospital-related factors that are known to predispose to delirium in elderly inpatients. The ward environment and routines should aim to avoid unnecessary sensory impairment and sleep deprivation, and support a normal sleep-wake cycle. Nonpharmacological sleep-promotion strategies should be used in preference to hypnotic drugs. It is important to ensure adequate food and fluid intake, and patients should be encouraged to be mobile whenever possible. Careful prescribing is important, avoiding where possible any drugs with known potential to cause delirium, particularly in at-risk individuals such as those with dementia. The drug chart should be regularly reviewed, with the aim of keeping the burden of medication as low as possible. In surgical patients, good pre-, peri-, and postoperative care (especially with regard to blood pressure, oxygenation, pain relief, and infection control) will reduce the risk of postoperative delirium.

JAMES LINDESAY

See also DEMENTIA; DISEASE PRESENTATION; PSYCHIATRIC DISEASE IN RELATION TO PHYSICAL ILLNESS; SURGERY IN ELDERLY PEOPLE.

BIBLIOGRAPHY

AMERICAN PSYCHIATRIC ASSOCIATION. *Diagnostic and Statistical Manual of Mental Disorders*, 4th ed. Washington, D.C.: American Psychiatric Association, 1994.

AMERICAN PSYCHIATRIC ASSOCIATION. *Practice Guideline for the Treatment of Patients with Delirium.* Washington, D.C.: American Psychiatric Association, 1999.

BYRNE, E. J. *Confusional States in Older People.* London: Edward Arnold, 1994.

CARLSON, A.; GOTTFRIES, C.; WINBLAD, B.; and ROBERTSSON, B., eds. "Delirium in the Elderly: Epidemiological, Pathogenetic, Diagnostic and Treatment Aspects." *Dementia and Geriatric Cognitive Disorders* 10 (1999): 305–430.

FRANCIS, J., and KAPOOR, W. N. "Prognosis after Hospital Discharge of Older Medical Patients with Delirium." *Journal of the American Geriatrics Society* 40 (1992): 601–606.

INOUYE, S. K., and CHARPENTIER, P. A. "Precipitating Factors for Delirium in Hospitalized Elderly Persons. Predictive Model and Interrelationship with Baseline Vulnerability." *Journal of the American Medical Association* 275 (1996): 852–857.

LEVKOFF, S.; EVANS, D.; LIPTZIN, B.; et al. "Delirium, the Occurrence and Persistence of Symptoms among Elderly Hospitalised Patients." *Archives of Internal Medicine* 152 (1992): 334–340.

LINDESAY, J.; MACDONALD, A.; and STARKE, I. *Delirium in the Elderly*. Oxford: Oxford University Press, 1990.

LIPOWSKI, Z. J. *Delirium: Acute Confusional States*. New York: Oxford University Press, 1990.

ROCKWOOD, K.; COSWAY, S.; CARVER, D.; et al. "The Risk of Dementia and Death Following Delirium." *Age and Ageing* 28 (1999): 551–556.

RUDBERG, M. A.; POMPEI, P.; FOREMAN, M. D.; ROSS, R. E.; and CASSEL, C. K. "The Natural History of Delirium in Older Hospitalized Patients: A Syndrome of Heterogeneity." *Age and Ageing* 26 (1997): 169–174.

DEMENTIA

The word *dementia* comes from Latin and means "out of the mind." It is used to describe an acquired, persistent, global impairment of cognition/intellectual processes, which is sufficiently severe to interfere with social or occupational function. Dementia, like delirium, is known as a syndrome, that is, it is a collection of symptoms and signs, whose presence can be diagnosed, but the diagnosis does not in and of itself suggest a cause. For example, the syndrome of dementia has a number of causes, including Alzheimer's disease, Lewy body dementia, and fronto-temporal dementia.

Each of the words in the definition is important both for what it says and what it leaves out. Thus "acquired" differentiates dementia, which is usually seen in late life, from lifelong conditions of diminished intellect encountered in people who have grown older. Such people would still be described by their original diagnosis (e.g., cerebral palsy) even after they have become elderly. The most common exception to this general rule is with Down's syndrome, where a genetic abnormality that gives rise to increased amounts of the protein beta-amyloid increases the likelihood that individuals will develop Alzheimer's disease as they grow older. In consequence, the designation of the syndrome describing their cognitive impairment can properly be termed, once they have developed Alzheimer's disease, as a dementia. In other cases, however, the description of the lifelong disorder, if stable, is not described as a dementia.

The word *chronic* (some definitions use the word *persistent*) is meant to distinguish dementia from delirium. While delirium is another cause of global cognitive impairment in elderly people, it typically comes on acutely, and generally resolves quickly. Note, however, that an acute onset does not rule out dementia. For example, the dementia seen following stroke can begin suddenly. Similarly, there are other dementias, particularly Creutzfeldt-Jakob disease, and dementia with Lewy bodies, which can seem as though they came on almost out of the blue. Although it is often not stated, chronic generally implies progressive, that is, it is usually the case that the dementia gets worse over time. While there are some dementias (notably the dementia following stroke) that can have prolonged periods of plateau, most dementias follow a characteristic pattern of decline. The pattern of deficits seen as the decline progresses forms the basis of staging the dementia.

The word "global" in the definition of dementia is meant to imply that the dementia cannot be diagnosed when only one aspect of higher cortical function is impaired. Thus, for example, people with language problems (aphasia), even though they typically have great difficulty in expressing themselves, would not meet the criteria for dementia as long as other functions (such as memory) were not impaired.

Impairment of cognition may seem self-evident for a diagnosis of dementia, but its demonstration sometimes is difficult, particularly where the impairment is mild. The special challenge here is the diagnosis of cognitive impairment, which may begin to meet the dementia criteria in someone who is highly educated. Most highly educated people do well on most tests of cognition until a dementia becomes established.

One way to distinguish mild cognitive impairment from the cognitive impairment that is more likely consistent of dementia is to determine the extent to which this impairment interferes with social or occupational function. For example, although many people find as they get older that their memory is not as good as it once was, this does not imply dementia unless the memory loss impairs job performance or social roles.

Impairment of function also underlies the usual method of staging the course of dementia. While a number of formal staging systems exist, most agree on a "pre-dementia" stage, followed by mild, moderate, and then severe dementia. In the pre-dementia stage, the rough rule of thumb is that the cognitive impairment, while giving rise to symptoms, does not yet impair function. By contrast, mild dementia is diagnosed with somewhat greater confidence when impairment in instrumental activities of daily living (such as driving, balancing a check book, following a recipe) is present. Moderate dementia is diagnosed when patients begin to need prompting to carry out their personal care. Typically, prompting is required for them to change their clothes or maintain their grooming. Severe dementia is heralded when, even with prompting, people are no longer able to carry out basic activities of daily living, such as dressing, grooming, and feeding.

Dementia is a common problem among older people, affecting about 10 percent of the population over age sixty. Although dementia is age-related, it is distinct from the normal aging of the brain. Dementia increases the risk of delirium, and is often seen in the face of depression. Patients with severe dementia need to be cared for in nursing homes or in long-term care institutions. Between one-third and one-half of all people with dementia are in institutional long-term care. These facilities are quite costly and make dementia among the most expensive of medical conditions.

People with dementia necessarily have impairment of their cognitive function. Given that good cognitive function is necessary to be competent, a number of ethical issues arise when a person's competence is not assured at the same time that important decisions about the future course need to be made.

While some causes of dementia can be treated, cure is rare, and many types of dementia have no effective treatment. In consequence, in each of these ways discussed above—personal, medical, social, economic, and ethical—dementia poses a considerable challenge to an aging society.

KENNETH ROCKWOOD

See also ALZHEIMER'S DISEASE; CREUTZFELD-JAKOB DISEASE; DEMENTIA: ETHICAL ISSUES; DEMENTIA WITH LEWY BODIES; FRONTO-TEMPORAL DEMENTIA; MEMORY; PSYCHIATRIC DISEASE IN RELATION TO PHYSICAL ILLNESS; RETROGENESIS; VASCULAR DEMENTIA.

BIBLIOGRAPHY

DUNITZ, M. *Clinical Diagnosis and Management of Alzheimer's Disease.* Edited by S. Gauthier. London: Martin Dunitz, Ltd., 2001.

ROCKWOOD, K., and MACKNIGHT, C. *Understanding Dementia.* Halifax: Pottersfield, 2001.

WILCOCK, G. K.; BUCKS, R.; and ROCKWOOD, K. *Diagnosis and Management of Dementia.* Oxford, U.K.: Oxford University Press, 1999.

DEMENTIA: ETHICAL ISSUES

There has been much progress in the ethics of dementia care. Dementia is a syndrome (i.e., a cluster of symptoms) that can be caused by a myriad of diseases. The most common disease cause of irreversible, progressive dementia is Alzheimer's disease, which this article will frequently allude to.

Moral progress is evident in the fact that the use of physical restraints is diminishing in nursing homes. By the mid-1990s, ample evidence had accumulated that "minimal restraint" or "no restraint" policies actually keep persons with dementia safest, for otherwise they can choke to death on strapped chairs, or fail to thrive as a direct result of physical coercion. Increasingly, architects have focused on how to design long-term care facilities that maximize the freedom to wander while minimizing environmental obstacles or hazards. Similarly, psychiatrists have become more adept at setting clear therapeutic goals for behavioral medications, monitoring for outcome, and using the smallest doses necessary. This avoids the problem of polypharmacy (prescription of large numbers of drugs, many of which are unnecessary and cause harm), which can further harm cognition in people with dementia who have problems with agitation, paranoia, hallucination, and the like. Increasing attention is being given to the fact that people with dementia can experience physical pain, especially in the end stage, and may require pain-relieving medications (palliative care). Professionals and family members are realizing that in the advanced stage of this disease, assisted oral feeding ensures a better quality of life than artificial nutrition and hydration (Post, 2000).

Dementia and moral standing

Persons with cognitive deficits such as those brought about by dementia eventually will no longer be intellectually or economically productive. The term "hypercognitivist" was coined in 1995 by Stephen Post to describe a value system that focuses on rational decisional capacity as the marker for moral standing under the protective umbrella of the principle of nonmaleficence (i.e., "do no harm"). In the absence of the ability to make plans and implement them, the person with dementia becomes a "nonperson," who, even if still treated with a degree of care, has a diminished moral standing. In contrast, focus group studies show that most family and professional caregivers hold a diametrically opposite view: they see the person with dementia in terms of remaining capacities, and in terms of emotional and relational well-being despite cognitive losses (Post and Whitehouse, 1995). The philosopher Alasdair MacIntyre (1999) points out that contrary to dominant schools of ethics, the classical Western tradition of moral thought refuses to devalue the cognitively imperiled.

In the wider culture, the criteria of rationality and productivity may blind many to other ways of thinking about the meaning of one's humanity and the nature of humane care in the context of dementia. Many people simply cannot handle being around someone who is mentally and emotionally disabled. People with the diagnosis of dementia often complain of a sense of social diminution, of a negative social psychology in which they no longer get the respect that they once enjoyed. They typically ask to be more included in conversations, decisions, and activities. A fuller attention to emotional and relational well-being may in some cases offset some of the adverse behavioral impact of neurological impairment. Any tendency to treat someone with dementia as though he or she counts less than, or has a different status than, other human beings should be discouraged (Kitwood, 1997).

Truth telling

There is a consensus among medical ethicists that patients should be told the truth about a diagnosis of Alzheimer's disease or any other dementing illness. This is also their legal right. By the late 1990s, especially with the advent of new treatments for the cognitive symptoms of Alzheimer's disease, and with more accurate diagnosis, nearly all clinicians informed patients of their diagnosis. The discovery of inheritance patterns, emerging treatments, and the general public awareness of Alzheimer's disease contributed to a noticeable swing toward diagnostic truth telling.

The question now is not whether to tell the truth, but how to tell it in a sensitive and supportive manner that does not create unnecessary despair and that, as far as possible, maintains hope. Professionals should assure patients that there are many ways to ensure good care and the treatment of the symptoms of dementia throughout its progression (Zarit and Downs, 1999).

Truth telling allows the person with the diagnosis to plan for optimal life experiences in remaining years of intact capacities, prepare a *durable power of attorney* for health care decisions—some may also prepare a *living will*—to be implemented upon eventual incompetence, and participate actively in Alzheimer's disease support groups, to which referrals should always be made.

Autonomy

Patient autonomy (i.e., self-determination) cannot exist without truth. Autonomy can be extended through advance directives (i.e., living wills and durable power of attorney for health care), and few question the importance of such documents. The durable power of attorney for health care allows the person, while still competent, to designate a trusted individual (usually a family member with whom he or she has had ample conversation) who will make medical treatment decisions once the person becomes unable to do so. This allows the surrogate decision maker to be attentive to the person's values and wishes, and to make decisions as needed. A living will, coupled with the durable power of attorney for health care, is usually recommended by lawyers. In the absence of legal documentation, all states allow the surrogate decision maker to proceed de facto, based on the sate statutes, although some states may try to interfere with surrogate control in designated areas, such as the refusal of a feeding tube.

The still competent self may not know what the experience of moderate dementia is like, nor be privy to the forms of well-being to be facilitated for such a self, but he or she surely knows the meaning of incontinence of bowel or bladder, repeated majors infections, and severe dysfunction. The best mechanism for empowering the intact self is the implementation of a durable power of attorney for health care, which is, paradoxically, the act of relinquishing control by placing oneself in the loving hands of another, with certain broad parameters spelled out as desired.

New medications

Medical science is likely to develop treatments for Alzheimer's disease and other causes of dementia that slow the progression of the disease. Patients, while competent, and surrogates will need to reflect carefully on the ethics of altering the course of progressive dementia. It is difficult to imagine that any reasonable person would want his or her disease progression slowed in the advanced stage, which is replete with severe dysfunction. Most, it can be assumed, would prefer a comfortable death in a hospice-like setting of palliative care. A drug to slow progression would, however, be most welcome prior to onset of symptoms, or in the mild and even moderate stages, in order to avoid the indignities of advanced dementia (Post, 2000). The ethical maxim is this: prevent or delay onset of symptoms, mitigate symptoms insofar as possible, but never purposefully prolong life in the advance stage of severe dysfunction.

As for the cognitive enhancing drugs, which do not slow the progression of dementia but mitigate some symptoms for limited periods of time, the absence of clear data on outcomes necessitates caution when addressing the ethical implications. Some major ethical quandaries are, however, identifiable. The introduction of acetylcholinesterase inhibitors for treatment of mild to moderate Alzheimer's disease is, on the one hand, promising. There is anecdotal evidence of its effectiveness: a mildly demented woman insisted that, with the help of donepezil, she can now find her words; a woman who was too forgetful to cook anymore regained sufficient memory to begin cooking again in relative safety. But patients and caregivers who have already navigated certain crises of cognitive decline may have to repeat the process. The individual who has lost insight into his or her losses may regain insight, along with renewed anxiety. New cognitive enhancing compounds should not be prescribed without attention to individual cases. Each patient's response must be carefully monitored with regard to quality of life. Every caregiver should know that the use of these compounds is a deeply

personal and value-laden decision requiring the careful exercise of compassion and good judgment. There is nothing wrong with withdrawing an antidementia treatment that does not seem to have a positive result. Modest improvement or temporary stabilization of cognitive decline will be viewed by some caregivers as gratifying—but certainly not by all.

A natural dying

In general terms, no caregiver should feel that the technological extension of the life of a loved one with advanced Alzheimer's disease is necessary. One clear marker of the severe stage is the loss of the capacity to swallow. Artificial nutrition and hydration are generally not a solution because such intrusion is almost invariably unwelcome to the patient. Physical discomfort and complications are equally serious considerations. No wonder the person with Alzheimer's repeatedly pulls out feeding tubes. The Alzheimer's Association guidelines for the treatment of patients with severe dementia are clear: "Severely and irreversibly demented patients need only care given to make them comfortable. If such a patient is unable to receive food and water by mouth, it is ethically permissible to choose to withhold nutrition and hydration artificially administered by vein or gastric tube. Spoon feeding should be continued if needed for comfort" (1994).

In case consultations, caregivers who have already rejected the use of a feeding tube ask how aggressively to encourage eating and drinking by mouth in patients who are losing these capacities. As long as a person retains the capacity, food and water should be offered, and the taking of them encouraged by spoon feeding. A baby bottle can be helpful because the sucking reflex is often retained. But when the person no longer is able to swallow, it is of no benefit to fill the mouth with food and water.

After the capacity for natural eating and drinking has been lost, it should be firmly understood that a decision against artificial nutrition must also be a decision against artificial hydration (a fluid IV). Families need to be informed that their loved one will likely die within one or two weeks, and that dehydration is known to have sedating effects that ensure a more peaceful dying.

The clinician should proactively clarify for caregivers the burdens of invasive treatments in order to spare them the sense of guilt associated with not doing everything to prolong life. Chaplains should advise caregivers that their love is better expressed through compassion, commitment, and humble entry into the culture of dementia.

The right to well-being

It is morally imperative to build on the remaining capacities of persons with dementia. The well-being available to people with dementia is obvious to anyone who has watched art or music therapy sessions. In some cases, a person with advanced Alzheimer's disease may still draw a valued symbol, as though through art a sense of self is retained. The abstract expressionist painter Willem de Kooning painted his way through much of his struggle with Alzheimer's disease. Some critics commented that his work, though not what it had been, was nevertheless impressive. Kay Larson, former art critic for *New York* magazine wrote, "It would be cruel to suggest that de Kooning needed his disease to free himself. Nonetheless, the erosions of Alzheimer's could not eliminate the effects of a lifetime of discipline and love of craft. When infirmity struck, the artist was prepared. If he didn't know what he was doing, maybe it didn't matter—to him. He knew what he loved best, and it sustained him" (Larson, p. 298). DeKooning, like all persons with dementia, retained some strengths and abilities that he was able to capitalize on. It is important to look at what the person with dementia can do, rather than at what he or she cannot do.

In addition to self-expression through the arts, many persons with dementia enjoy the smell and look of fall leaves, or the sounds of birds singing, and they can appreciate the "wonder of it all" through such small gratifications. The losses associated with dementia must be placed within the context of losses associated with aging in general. As horizons of experience narrow, small pleasures in life become more and more important. In dementia care, pleasures and gratifications that are small loom especially large. Many of the better assisted living facilities are single-story campuses with access to rubberized pathways in garden areas surrounded by attractive fencing to prevent wandering off.

Justice for persons with dementia

While we can all agree that services for persons with dementia should be better and more plentiful, who should pay for them, and are there limits? The American health care system is oriented to pay for "rescue" medicine that pulls persons in any condition from the jaws of death, but it provides very little to support the expense of chronic and long-term care.

It is easy to reject the notion of categorical age-based rationing of life-extending health care associated with Daniel Callahan (1987), for age alone is never a fair basis for allocating lifesaving. Elderly persons are remarkably heterogeneous, and age is a notoriously poor indicator of outcome in almost all medical circumstances (Binstock and Post, 1991). Yet Callahan succeeded in forcing the question and spurring a moment of debate among intellectuals. On his side of the argument is the reality that overtreatment of older adults is rampant in American medicine, and a source of wide public concern. If the autonomy model cannot solve the problem of overtreatment, then perhaps rationing must. It might be possible for society, by some means of consensus, to arrive at the notion of categorically limiting purposeful efforts to extend the lives of persons in the advanced stage of Alzheimer's disease. This would not be based on age, however, but on the gravity of the condition and its discomforts and burdens to the patient. It would be altogether fitting for policymakers, in dialogue with informed constituencies and through democratic action, to determine that while hospice-oriented long-term care will be paid for with public funds, efforts to rescue a person in advanced and terminal dementia would not be, nor would the protracted expense of long-term care that results from such rescue. In essence, if there were a practical trade-off possible within the health care system, emphasis should be placed on everything but technological rescue efforts for persons beyond the moderate stage of Alzheimer's disease and for whom quality of life, but not quantity of life, should be enhanced.

American society is still not quite at the point of consensus. Yet in the future, policies may be constructed on a majority basis that would in fact limit rescue efforts, at least with respect to dialysis, mechanical ventilators, and cardiopulmonary resuscitation. Perhaps artificial nutrition and hydration in the terminal stage could also be deleted from public funding once the society realizes the burdens this creates (Gillick, 2000).

STEPHEN G. POST

See also ADVANCE DIRECTIVES FOR HEALTH CARE; ALZHEIMER'S DISEASE; AUTONOMY; COMPETENCY; DEMENTIA; REFUSING AND WITHDRAWING MEDICAL TREATMENT.

BIBLIOGRAPHY

ALZHEIMER'S Association Public Statement on Tube Feeding (press release). Chicago, 1994.

BINSTOCK, R. H., and POST, S. G., eds. *Too Old for Health Care? Controversies in Medicine, Law, Economics, and Ethics.* Baltimore: Johns Hopkins University Press, 1991.

CALLAHAN, D. *Setting Limits: Medical Goals in an Aging Society.* New York: Simon and Schuster, 1987.

GILLICK, M. R. "Rethinking the Role of Tube Feeding in Patients with Advanced Dementia." *New England Journal of Medicine* 342 (2000): 206–210.

KITWOOD, T. *Dementia Reconsidered: The Person Comes First.* Buckingham, U.K., and Philadelphia: Open University Press, 1997.

KLEPPER, H., and RORTY, M. "Personal Identity, Advance Directives, and Genetic Testing for Alzheimer Disease." *Genetic Testing* 3 (1999): 99–106.

LARSON, K. "DeKooning and Alzheimer's." *The World & I* 12 (1997): 297–299.

MACINTRYE, A. *Dependent Rational Animals: Why Human Beings Need the Virtues.* Chicago: Open Court Press, 1999.

POST, S. G. *The Moral Challenge of Alzheimer Disease.* Baltimore: Johns Hopkins University Press, 1995.

POST, S. G. *The Moral Challenge of Alzheimer Disease: Ethical Issues from Diagnosis to Dying,* 2d ed., rev. Baltimore: Johns Hopkins University Press, 2000.

POST, S. G., and WHITEHOUSE, P. J. "Fairhill Guidelines on Ethics of the Care of People with Alzheimer's Disease: A Clinician's Summary." *Journal of the American Geriatrics Society* 43 (1995): 1423–1429.

ZARIT, S. H., and DOWNS, M. G., eds. *Generations: State of the Art for Practice in Dementia* (a special issue of *Generations*) 23, no. 3 (Fall 1999).

DEMENTIA WITH LEWY BODIES

Dementia with Lewy bodies is a comparatively new diagnostic entity. Formal criteria for its diagnosis have existed only since 1992. Even now, changes in neuropathological techniques for its recognition are changing the understanding of how commonly this disease occurs. Depending on the study, it may vie with fronto-temporal dementia as the next most common neurodegenerative cause of dementia after Alzheimer's disease.

By definition, patients with Lewy body dementia have progressive cognitive impairment that interferes with their social or occupational functioning. What makes the diagnosis distinctive on a clinical basis is the presence of several features that, though seen in patients with Alzheimer's disease, are seen earlier in patients who have dementia with Lewy bodies. These features include mild, spontaneous Parkinsonism (usually muscle rigidity together with slowness, a tendency to fall, and, less commonly, tremor) and hallucinations. There is also some suggestion that the cognitive features in dementia with Lewy bodies differ subtly from those in Alzheimer's disease, more often showing earlier difficulties with visuospatial function, and attention and concentration.

The pathological hallmark of dementia with Lewy bodies is, of course, the Lewy body, named after the physician who first identified these spherical inclusions within the bodies of neurons. Once comparatively underappreciated, careful observation and development of new techniques have allowed these to be seen more readily. Lewy bodies were long a pathological hallmark for the diagnosis of Parkinson's disease, and in that context were found in neurons deep in the brain known as the substantia nigra. Lewy bodies are not the only abnormal proteins seen in dementia with Lewy bodies, and their exact origin and role are not yet well understood. Of some interest has been the finding that, in neuropathological examination of the brain, pure Lewy body disease remains uncommon. Most cases of dementia with Lewy bodies are seen in patients who also have neuropathological evidence of Alzheimer's disease, and many show injury from the effects of hypertension and stroke.

Clinical features of dementia with Lewy bodies that are more specific for the diagnosis include fluctuation both in the level of arousal and consciousness and in the severity of the symptoms. In these patients, arousal can be so impaired as to mimic stupor or even coma. More commonly, the picture resembles delirium with so-called "clouding of unconsciousness" and fluctuation (i.e., patients can seem vary drowsy, but within several minutes can again become alert, and even hyperalert, before cycling). Whereas in delirium these symptoms are commonly more subtle, in dementia with Lewy bodies they can persist for weeks, months, or longer. Another important and tragic aspect of the clinical picture in dementia with Lewy bodies is the presence of a neuroleptic sensitivity syndrome. Neuroleptics are drugs that typically are used to treat hallucinations, delusions, and other psychotic features. In general, they work by blocking the brain chemical dopamine. In some patients with dementia with Lewy bodies, however, the result of using even modest doses of neuroleptics can be catastrophic. Such patients can experience profound worsening of their Parkinsonism in ways from which they sometimes never recover.

There have been encouraging results, however, in the treatment of dementia with Lewy bodies with the class of drugs known as acetylcholinesterase inhibitors. Originally used for the treatment of Alzheimer's disease, these drugs can sometimes have a particularly favorable response in patients who have dementia with Lewy bodies. As with other dementia patients, there is an important role for symptomatic and supportive treatment, both of the patients and of their caregivers.

It is not yet clear how to interpret the prognosis of dementia with Lewy bodies. In the era prior to cholinesterase inhibitor therapy, particularly when the neuroleptic sensitivity syndrome was poorly understood or uncommonly recognized, the prognosis appeared to be worse than for Alzheimer's disease. How this plays out with the advent of better recognition and treatment is not yet clear.

The recognition and elaboration of the diagnosis of dementia with Lewy bodies is a tribute to careful cooperation among physicians, scientists, patients, and caregivers. Through systematic observation, what was until recently unrecognized as a disease is now seen to be a common form of treatable cognitive impairment in older adults.

KENNETH ROCKWOOD

See also ALZHEIMER'S DISEASE; DELIRIUM; DEMANTIA; FRONTO-TEMPORAL DEMENTIA; PARKINSONISM; VASCULAR DEMENTIA.

BIBLIOGRAPHY

BALLARD, C.; O'BRIEN, J.; MORRIS, C. M.; BARBER, R. SWANN, A.; NEILL, D.; and McKEITH, I. "The Progression of Cognitive Impairment in Dementia with Lewy Bodies, Vascular Dementia and Alzheimer's Disease." *International Journal of Geriatric Psychiatry* 5 (2000): 499–503.

McKEITH, I.; BALLARD, C.; PERRY, R.; INCE, P.; O'BRIEN, J.; NEILL, D.; LOWERY, K.; JAROS, E.; BARBER, R.; THOMPSON, P.; SWANN, A.; FAIRBAIRN, A.; and PERRY, E. "Prospective Validation of Consensus Criteria for the Diagnosis of Dementia with Lewy Bodies." *Neurology* 54, no. 5 (2000): 1050–1058.

McKEITH, I.; DEL SER, T.; SPANO, P.; EMRE, M.; WESNES, K.; ANAND, R.; CICIN-SAIN, A.; FERRARA, R.; and SPIEGEL, R. "Efficacy of Riva-stigmine in Dementia with Lewy Bodies: A Randomised Double-Blind, Placebo-Controlled International Study." *Lancet* 356, no. 9247 (2000): 2031–2036.

DENTAL CARE

A functional dentition—well-maintained and efficiently chewing teeth—is essential to good health and nutrition in the older adult. Demographic estimates indicate that by 2020, approximately 85 percent of adults over the age of sixty-five years will have retained some or all of their natural teeth (Douglass and Furino). By contrast, year 2020 projections suggest that nine million older adults will suffer from edentulism, the loss of all permanent teeth (Douglass and Furino). In general, individuals lose teeth as a result of trauma, tooth decay, or gum disease. The replacement of all permanent teeth is accomplished by the fabrication of complete dentures, prosthetic teeth that are fixed to plastic bases. The factors associated with tooth loss, the effect of total tooth loss, problems associated with complete dentures, and prevention of tooth loss are extremely relevant to the maintenance of good health and nutrition in the older adult.

Factors associated with tooth loss

Although trauma, tooth decay, gum disease, and aging are associated with tooth loss, most older adults in the United States lose teeth from gum disease, not through aging. Factors specifically related to the older adult that may facilitate tooth decay, gum disease, and tooth loss include lack of preventive dentistry in childhood and adolescence; limited access to dental care; lack of financial resources or dental insurance; low level of dental education; multiple medical conditions such as diabetes, osteoarthritis, stroke, Parkinson's disease, and cognitive disorders; and residence in a nursing home or long-term care facility.

Many preventive dental measures designed to maintain teeth for a lifetime were not available or accessible to today's older adults. Regular visits to the dentist, oral hygiene instruction, and the use of fluoride are commonplace today. These measures are the basis of dental awareness and education, and foster willingness to invest in programs that will prevent dental disease. Lack of dental insurance programs for the older adult and limited financial resources also may negatively impact oral health. Research with seventy-five-year-olds indicates, however, that age alone is not a good predictor of self-perceived dental needs and dental care utilization (Wilson and Branch). Rather than income or level of education, the presence of teeth appears to be the most powerful predictor of perceived dental need (Branch et al.).

The presence of multiple medical conditions in the older adult usually necessitates prescription drugs in addition to over-the-counter preparations the individual may already be taking. The potential for adverse drug interactions and side effects increases to 50 percent when five drugs are administered (Sloan). A common side effect of multiple medications in the older adult is xerostomia, or dry mouth (Paunovich et al.). Older adults with dry mouth often complain of mouth soreness, burning tongue, difficult chewing, problems with swallowing, and discomfort when wearing complete dentures (Felder et al.).

Research studies have proposed links between systemic illness and oral health status. Relevant to the issue of gum disease with resulting tooth loss are two studies that have investigated type II (adult onset) diabetes. One study suggests that individuals with poorly controlled blood sugar are at significantly greater risk for severe, progressive gum disease than are those with controlled blood sugar (Taylor et al.). A clinical study aimed at controlling blood sugar levels by treating gum disease has shown that standard gum disease treatments can result in significant blood sugar reductions (Grossi et al.). These studies are encouraging in view of the fact that type II diabetes and tooth loss to gum disease are common among older adults. Proper medical control of adult onset diabetes and proper dental control of gum disease help to prevent the loss of permanent teeth.

If permanent teeth are neglected as a result of poor, inadequate, or no oral hygiene procedures such as brushing and cleaning between the teeth, the oral health of the individual may be placed at risk. Bacteria within the mouth can initiate the disease processes responsible for tooth decay and gum disease. Daily removal of bacteria is essential to the health of the mouth. The frail older adult may not have enough strength to perform adequate oral hygiene. Individuals with cognitive impairment such as Alzheimer's disease often forget to perform basic oral hygiene. Older adults recovering from stroke may have paralysis of the dominant hand and be incapable of daily oral hygiene. Toothbrushing and other oral hygiene techniques can be very difficult to perform for older adults suffering from osteoarthritis, and Parkinson's disease. Hand and finger deformities common with osteoarthritis, and lack of muscle control in Parkinson's disease, may prevent these individuals from performing tasks often taken for granted.

Studies of residents of long-term care facilities and nursing homes suggest that they experience significant dental decay, bleeding of the gums, loose and uncomfortable complete dentures, and soft tissue sores attributed to wearing dentures (Weyant et al.; Kiyak et al.). In a study of 263 elderly subjects, 74 percent experienced difficult chewing, 72 percent reported oral discomfort, 54 percent reported functional dental handicaps, and 22 percent complained of oral pain (Lester et al.). Residents in assisted living facilities also appear to have more oral health problems.

Effect of total tooth loss

Removal of all teeth has immediate effects in the bone and soft tissue that formerly supported the teeth. These tissues undergo dramatic and irreversible changes. The bone connected to the roots of teeth (alveolar bone) anchors the teeth; as soon as the teeth are removed, it begins to dissolve and disappear. After removal of all permanent teeth, an individual is left with residual ridges of alveolar bone in the upper and lower jaws. The disappearance of these ridges (residual ridge resorption), has been described as chronic, progressive, irreversible, and disabling (Atwood). Not only does the bone resorb and shrink in size and shape, but the soft tissues over the bone collapse. The definitive scientific investigation of alveolar bone resorption concluded that the process is very aggressive in the first year, occurs four times more extensively in the lower jaw than the upper jaw, and may result in one centimeter of vertical bone loss in the lower jaw after twenty-five years of wearing complete dentures (Tallgren). The resorption process compromises successful denture wearing.

The loss of all teeth creates other problems. An individual loses essential support for the muscles of facial expression. Typically, one observes sunken cheeks, unsupported lips, and a facial profile on which the nose and chin appear to be too close together. The profile is altered because teeth support the jaws and the vertical dimension of the face; therefore, in the absence of teeth, the facial structures collapse upon themselves. Because front teeth help to pronounce many sounds and words, speech is affected when the teeth are removed. Functionally, most older adults attempt to wear complete dentures in order to chew food effectively. In addition, many adults will not venture into a public or social setting without teeth. Consequently, it is not surprising that edentulism has been associated with a reduction in quality of life, self-image, and daily functioning (Gift and Redford).

Problems with complete dentures

Although teeth are important to proper speech and to a pleasing smile, chewing food is the main function of a complete and healthy dentition. In the absence of all permanent teeth, a dental professional may be asked to make upper and lower complete dentures. Complete dentures consist of specially manufactured plastic, prosthetic teeth that are processed to high-impact plastic bases. The process of complete denture fabrication consists of five steps. The first two are patient assessment and making impressions or molds of the residual alveolar ridges. These steps result in upper and lower casts of the ridges upon which the complete dentures are constructed. At the third step, the patient's correct occlusion or bite is recorded. Prosthetic teeth are chosen to satisfy the patient's aesthetic and functional needs. At the fourth appointment, the patient previews the complete dentures before the dental laboratory processes the prosthetic teeth to the base. At the final appointment, the patient receives the complete dentures and begins to function with them.

In the process of complete denture fabrication, three areas can be the source of frustration and failure for both the dental professional and the patient. First, the dental professional must communicate effectively with the patient, and vice versa. Promises made by the dental professional may be untrue for a specific patient. Such promises include the following: Patients adapt easily to complete dentures; complete dentures are as functional and efficient as natural teeth; and dentures are comfortable to wear. Likewise, patients whose expectations of complete dentures equal or exceed those of natural teeth need to be educated to the contrary. Second, making the impression is critical. Complete dentures that are constructed on inadequate casts from poor impressions are too small and lack essential features for retention and stability within the mouth. A functionally stable and retentive denture must utilize all available support tissues within the mouth. A shortcut in this step may lead to an unstable, painful denture. Third, a proper occlusion or bite is essential to acceptable functioning and comfortable wearing. When the occlusion is disregarded, complete dentures may create soreness in multiple areas of the mouth. Neglect in any or all of these critical areas results in unhappy denture wearers and frustrated dental professionals.

It is important to note that medically compromised patients who suffer from xerostomia may have difficulty adjusting to and functioning with complete dentures. Saliva is responsible not only for the retention of complete dentures but also, in part, for a comfortable fit. With a substantial lack of saliva, the denture wearer's ability to function comfortably is seriously compromised.

A traditional belief is that wearers of complete dentures alter their food choices because of compromised chewing and, therefore, are not well nourished. The chewing efficiency of complete dentures and their impact on nutrition have been studied extensively. A study of 1,106 individuals of differing ages and with various numbers of natural teeth clearly demonstrated that number of teeth, not age, best explained chewing ability (Carlsson). Refitting old dentures or fabrication of new dentures should improve chewing efficiency for denture wearers; however, none to only slight chewing improvement was found when individuals were evaluated for eighteen months (Carlsson). Another study reported that, compared to those with natural teeth, subjects wearing complete dentures required greater chewing time and more chewing strokes to complete chewing tests (Wayler and Chauncey).

In addition, wearers of complete dentures selected food largely on the basis of texture and tactile characteristics, preferring soft, easy-to-chew foods (Wayler and Chauncey). Investigators in a Veterans Administration study concluded that individuals wearing at least one complete denture may have self-imposed dietary restrictions that could compromise nutritional well-being (Chauncey et al.). Functionally, the maximum biting force that complete denture wearers can demonstrate is approximately 33 percent of the force generated with natural teeth (Carlsson). Thus, the traditional belief that denture wearers may have compromised nutrition appears to have been validated by research. The most carefully fabricated complete dentures, made by the most experienced dental professional, and worn by the most adaptable, proficient older adult can never deliver the performance of well-maintained natural dentition.

Prevention of tooth loss

An important strategy for maintaining a healthy, natural dentition is regular dental visits with oral hygiene instruction. Depending upon the medical and dental condition of the individual, older adults should visit the dentist every three to six months. This frequency enables the dentist or dental hygienist to diagnose potential tooth decay and gum disease before it can become a major problem. Because both decay and gum disease are caused by accumulations of mouth bacteria (dental plaque), proper oral hygiene instruction is crucial.

Aimed at preventing both gum disease and tooth decay, oral hygiene begins with mechanical plaque removal. This is best accomplished with brushing the teeth and cleaning between the teeth. Dental floss, between-the-teeth brushes, and toothpicks can be used to remove plaque from between the teeth. Daily, effective removal of dental plaque is critical in preventing dental disease. For those with physical handicaps, a caretaker may be required to assist in daily oral hygiene.

The role of saliva in maintaining dental health is crucial. Saliva is essential in controlling and clearing bacteria from the mouth. For older adults who suffer from dry mouth, the protective action of saliva is compromised. Regimens to replace or stimulate salivary flow include sips of water, chewing sugarless gum, and using sugarless mints. Sugar-free gums and mints are crucial for individuals with natural teeth, because disease-producing bacteria readily metabolize sugar to end products that cause tissue destruction.

Another strategy to control the levels of mouth bacteria is the use of antibacterial mouth rinses. Numerous over-the-counter preparations are available, and one phenolic rinse has been shown to significantly reduce oral bacteria for short periods of time (Moran et al.). If indicated, the dentist may prescribe a more powerful oral rinse, chlorhexidine. Chlorhexidine rinse at 0.12 percent strength is the most effective, sustained antibacterial agent available (Persson et al.).

While saliva and antibacterial rinses target both gum disease and tooth decay, fluoride preparations are specifically used to fortify and strengthen tooth structure, a process called remineralization. Older adults should be encouraged to use fluoride-containing toothpaste. Remineralization with fluoride toothpaste has been well documented (Wefel et al.).

Over-the-counter 0.05 percent fluoride rinses have been shown to reduce tooth decay and remineralize tooth structure (Ripa et al.). Fluoride gels, applied at home or in the dental office, have been shown to prevent decay and significantly remineralize tooth structure in extremely susceptible cancer patients (Dreizen et al.; Katz).

The loss of all permanent teeth and the wearing of complete dentures is not without serious functional and social limitations. Research indicates that a healthy, functional, natural dentition is important to good general health, adequate nutrition, and a sense of well-being in the older adult. The maintenance of a permanent, natural dentition can be accomplished through tested and verified strategies that are available from the dental professional.

JEFFREY D. ASTROTH

See also NUTRITION.

BIBLIOGRAPHY

ATWOOD, D. A. "The Reduction of Residual Ridges. A Major Oral Disease Entity." *Journal of Prosthetic Dentistry* 26 (1971): 266–279.
BRANCH, L. G.; ANTCZAK, A. A.; and STASON, W. B. "Toward Understanding the Use of Dental Services by the Elderly." *Special Care in Dentistry* 6 (1986): 38–41.
CARLSSON, G. E. "Masticatory Efficiency: The Effect of Age, the Loss of Teeth and Prosthetic

Rehabilitation." *International Dental Journal* 34 (1984): 93–97.

CHAUNCEY, H. H.; MUENCH, M. E.; KAPUR, K. K.; and WAYLER, A. H. "The Effect of the Loss of Teeth on Diet and Nutrition." *International Dental Journal* 34 (1984): 98–104.

DOUGLASS, C. W., and FURINO, A. "Balancing Dental Services Requirements and Supplies: Epidemiologic and Demographic Evidence." *Journal of the American Dental Association* 121 (1990): 587–592.

DREIZEN, S.; BROWN, L. R.; DALY, T. E.; and DRANE, J. B. "Prevention of Xerostomia-Related Dental Caries in Irradiated Cancer Patients." *Journal of Dental Research* 56 (1977): 99–104.

FELDER, R. S.; MILLAR, S. B.; and HENRY, R. H. "Oral Manifestations of Drug Therapy." *Special Care in Dentistry* 8 (1988): 119–124.

GIFT, H. C., and REDFORD, M. "Oral Health and Quality of Life." *Clinical Geriatric Medicine* 8 (1992): 673–683.

GROSSI, S. G.; SKREPCINSKI, F. B.; DeCARO, T.; et al. "Treatment of Periodontal Disease in Diabetes Reduced Glycated Hemoglobin." *Journal of Periodontology* 68 (1997): 713–719.

KATZ, S. "The Use of Fluoride and Chlorhexidine for the Prevention of Radiation Caries." *Journal of the American Dental Association* 104 (1982): 164–170.

KIYAK, H. A.; GRAYSTON, M. N.; and CRINEAN, C. L. "Oral Health Problems and Needs of Nursing Home Residents." *Community Dentistry and Oral Epidemiology* 21 (1993): 49–52.

LESTER, V.; ASHLEY, F. P.; and GIBBONS, D. E. "The Relationship Between Socio-dental Indices of Handicap, Felt Need for Dental Treatment and Dental State in a Group of Frail and Functionally Dependent Older Adults." *Community Dentistry and Oral Epidemiology* 26 (1998): 155–159.

MORAN, J.; ADDY, M.; WADE, W.; et al. "The Effect of Oxidizing Mouthrinses Compared with Chlorhexidine on Salivary Bacterial Counts and Plaque Regrowth." *Journal of Clinical Periodontology* 22 (1995): 750–755.

PAUNOVICH, E. D.; SADOWSKY, J. M.; and CARTER, P. "The Most Frequently Prescribed Medications in the Elderly and Their Impact on Dental Treatment." In *The Dental Clinics of North America*, vol. 41, no. 4. Philadelphia: W. B. Saunders, 1987. Page 702.

PERSSON, R. E.; TRUELOVE, E. L.; LeRESCHE, L.; and ROBINOVITCH, M. R. "Therapeutic Effects of Daily or Weekly Chlorhexidine Rinsing on Oral Health of a Geriatric Population." *Oral Surgery, Oral Medicine, Oral Pathology* 72 (1991): 184–191.

RIPA, L. W.; LESKE, G. S.; FORTE, F.; and VARMA, A. "Effect of a 0.05% Neutral NaF Mouthrinse on Coronal and Root Caries of Adults." *Gerodontology* 6 (1987): 131–136.

SLOAN, R. W. "Drug Interactions." In *Practical Geriatric Therapeutics*. Oradell, N.J.: Medical Economics, 1986. Page 39.

TALLGREN, A. "The Continuing Reduction of the Residual Alveolar Ridges in Complete Denture Wearers: A Mixed Longitudinal Study Covering 25 Years." *Journal of Prosthetic Dentistry* 27 (1972): 120–132.

TAYLOR, G. W.; BURT, B. A.; BECKER, M. P.; et al. "Severe Periodontitis and Risk for Poor Glycemic Control in Patients with Non-Insulin-Dependent Diabetes Mellitus." *Journal of Periodontology* 67 (1996): 1085–1093.

WAYLER, A. H., and CHAUNCEY, H. H. "Impact of Complete Dentures and Impaired Natural Dentition on Masticatory Performance and Food Choice in Healthy Aging Men." *Journal of Prosthetic Dentistry* 49 (1983): 427–432.

WEFEL, J. S.; JENSEN, M. E.; TRIOLO, P. T.; et al. "De/Remineralization from Sodium Fluoride Dentifrices." *American Journal of Dentistry* 8 (1995): 217–220.

WEYANT, R. J.; JONES, J. A.; HOBBINS, M.; et al. "Oral Health Status of a Long-Term Care, Veteran Population." *Community Dentistry and Oral Epidemiology* 21 (1993): 227–233.

WILSON, A. A., and BRANCH, L. G. "Factors Affecting Dental Utilization of Elders Aged 75 Years or Older." *Journal of Dental Education* 50 (1986): 673–677.

DEPRESSION

Various forms of clinical depression are defined by the American Psychiatric Association's *Diagnostic and Statistical Manual of Mental Disorders, Fourth Edition* (DSM IV). According to this classification scheme, five or more symptoms (see Table 1) must be present during the same two-week period, and they must represent a change from previous functioning, in order for a person to receive a diagnosis of *major depressive disorder* (MDD). At least one of these symptoms must be either depressed mood or loss of interest or pleasure (i.e., anhedonia). The symptoms must cause distress or impairment in social, occupational, or other important areas of functioning, and they must not be clearly and fully accounted for by the direct physiological effects of a substance or a general medical condition. The average episode

Table 1

Symptoms of a Major Depressive Episode

1. Depressed mood most of the day, nearly every day
2. Markedly diminished interest or pleasure in all, or almost all activities most of the day, nearly every day
3. Significant weight loss when not dieting or weight gain, or decrease or increase in appetite nearly every day
4. Insomnia or hypersomnia nearly every day
5. Psychomotor agitation or retardation nearly every day
6. Fatigue or loss of energy nearly every day
7. Feelings of worthlessness or excessive or inappropriate guilt nearly every day
8. Diminished ability to think or concentrate, or indecisiveness, nearly every day
9. Recurrent thoughts of death, recurrent sucidal ideation without a specific plan, or a suicide attempt or a specific plan for committing suicide

SOURCE: Author

length for major depression is approximately seven months.

In addition to major depressive disorder, *dysthymic disorder* is a less severe, but more chronic form of depression. Dysthymia is indicated by the presence of a depressed mood occurring on most days for a period of at least two years. Average episode length is approximately ten years, and the disorder often lasts for up to twenty or thirty years. To meet criteria for dysthymic disorder, a person must display, in addition to depressed mood, at least two of the following symptoms: poor appetite or overeating, insomnia or hypersomnia, low energy or fatigue, low self-esteem, poor concentration or difficulty making decisions, and feelings of hopelessness. The person must have these symptoms for more than two months to meet the criteria for diagnosis. As with major depression, these symptoms must cause distress or impairment in social, occupational, or other important areas of functioning, and must not be clearly and fully accounted for by the direct physiological effects of a substance or a general medical condition.

Individuals who do not meet criteria for a major depressive episode or dysthymic disorder may nonetheless display symptoms of depression. Estimates in the late 1990s indicated that approximately 10 percent of elderly primary-care patients display such subsyndromal depression. Research in the late 1990s and early 2000s suggests that subsyndromal depression among elderly persons is best viewed as a less intense form of major depressive disorder. That is, el-derly persons with subsyndromal depression experience distress and impairment, but to a lesser degree than those who meet the full criteria for MDD. Two symptoms that may distinguish MDD from subsyndromal depression among elderly persons are suicidal thoughts and feelings of guilt or worthlessness.

A specific category of subsyndromal depression, bereavement, may be particularly likely to occur among elderly individuals due to higher mortality rates among this population. Bereavement is a normal reaction to the loss of a loved one. Bereaved individuals frequently display symptoms characteristic of MDD, although a diagnosis of MDD should not be made unless the symptoms persist for more than two months after the loss. The presence of any of the following symptoms may be indicative of MDD, as opposed to bereavement: guilt unrelated to actions taken at the time of death; thoughts of death other than a desire to have died with the deceased person; marked feelings of worthlessness; marked psychomotor retardation; marked functional impairment; and hallucinations that do not involve the deceased person.

One-year prevalence rates of depression among elderly persons vary depending on where they live and if they have a medical condition. For adults age sixty-five and older who live in the community and do not have a medical condition, the prevalence rate of MDD ranges from 1 to 6 percent. This prevalence rate is less than that for younger adults. However, when considering the prevalence rate for those that experience depressive symptoms but do not meet criteria for diagnosis, the rate for older adults increases to 20 to 30 percent. The one-year prevalence rate for individuals with dysthymia averages between 1 and 2 percent.

The one-year prevalence rates of MDD is higher for elder persons who live in nursing homes, compared to those who live in the community. For older adults who live in a nursing home, the prevalence rate for MDD ranges from 6 to 25 percent. When just considering depressive symptoms, the prevalence rate increases to between 16 and 30 percent. The one-year prevalence rate for older adults in nursing homes with dysthymia ranges from 16 to 30 percent, which is substantially higher than the rate for older adults in the community.

Depressive symptoms are common among individuals with medical conditions. One-year prevalence rates for elderly persons with medical conditions range from 6 to 44 percent. The rates can be higher among individuals with severe illnesses, such as cancer, or with more functional disabilities.

Depression can be usefully conceptualized within a diathesis-stress framework, where an individual will have certain factors that predispose him or her to depression. When these predisposing factors combine with a stressor, depression can result. There are various factors that can predispose someone to depression, some of which are biological. For example, having low or dysregulated levels of certain neurotransmitters, such as serotonin or norepinephrine, has been associated with depression. It has also been found that as people get older their levels of norepinephrine, as well as other neurochemicals, decrease. Another biological factor associated with depression is brain abnormalities similar to those seen with Alzheimer's disease or dementia. These brain abnormalities include enlargement of the ventricle areas and changes in white matter. Thus, changes in the neurochemistry, neurophysiology, and neuroanatomy can make one more vulnerable to depressive symptoms.

Other factors that can predispose an individual to depression are social and psychological in nature. Depressed individuals tend to have thought patterns that can distort reality and emphasize negative aspects of a situation. In addition, depressed individuals may view themselves, their future, and others in a negative light. These thought patterns produce behaviors that can predispose and exacerbate the individual's depression. For example, depressed individuals might seek reassurance or positive feedback from others. However, due to their negative views about themselves, they do not believe the feedback they receive and seek it again. This leads into a cycle of continuously seeking feedback, which eventually tires the other person and leads the depressed individual to eventually receive negative feedback. This pattern of thoughts and behaviors not only predisposes individuals to depression, but also helps maintain the depression.

Stressors and negative life events can also trigger and impact the severity of depression. Elderly persons may encounter various stressors in their lives, such as the death of loved ones, loss of physical agility and ability, loss of ability to work, caregiving for other individuals, physical

disability, and medical illness. Diagnosing depression in the presence of physical disability and medical illness can be difficult. Numerous medical conditions, including cardiovascular, pulmonary, endocrine, infectious, malignant, metabolic, and neurological disorders, may lead elderly persons to present with symptoms of depression. For instance, hypothyroidism often presents as sadness, disinterest, fatigue, decreased appetite, and poor concentration. Certain medications may also produce side effects mimicking depressive symptoms. For example, cancer treatments may induce depression-like symptoms of fatigue, insomnia, and decreased appetite. Such disorders and medications should be ruled out before a mood-disorder diagnosis is made and treatment is implemented.

Older adults with medical illnesses and physical disabilities are more susceptible to depression, even when taking into account those symptoms that overlap. Approximately 60 to 85 percent of depressed older persons report a physical illness that preceded their depression. However, not all medically ill older adults suffer from depression. Other factors, such as social support and coping styles, can prevent older adults from having depression.

Treatment of depression

Three methods of treatment have been demonstrated to be effective among elderly persons: antidepressant medications, psychosocial interventions, and electroconvulsive therapy (ECT). Antidepressant medications can be divided into four classes. The first class, heterocyclic antidepressants (HCAs), includes medications such as nortriptyline (Pamelor, Aventyl), desipramine (Norpramin), bupropion (Wellbutrin), and trazedone (Desyrel). HCAs tend to produce unpleasant side effects such as dry mouth, constipation, and mild cognitive impairments. Moreover, they sometimes lead to orthostatic hypotension (low blood pressure that occurs when an individual stands upright) and cardiotoxic affects, which may be especially problematic among individuals with existing heart or blood pressure conditions. In general, bupropion and trazedone produce fewer adverse side effects than other HCAs.

Monoamine oxidase inhibitors (MAOIs) are the second class of antidepressant medications. Similar to HCAs, these medications often produce a number of unpleasant side effects. Moreover, they have potentially lethal interactions with other medications and foods, which may make treatment more difficult among persons who take other medications or who have trouble maintaining dietary restrictions. As a result, MAOIs are rarely used among elderly individuals. Examples of MAOIs include moclobemide (Aurorix), phenelzine (Nardil), and selegiline (Eldepryl).

The third class of antidepressants, serotonin reuptake inhibitors (SRIs), include medications such as paroxetine (Paxil), fluoxetine (Prozac), and sertraline (Zoloft). SRIs typically produce fewer side effects than HCAs and MAOIs, are less reactive with other medicines, and are less lethal in overdose. Consequently, they may be preferable to the other classes. Evidence suggests that HCAs, SRIs, and MAOIs are comparably effective, producing improvement in 50 to 80 percent of depressed, elderly persons.

The fourth group of antidepressant medications is referred to as *atypical* because their chemical properties do not fit into any of the other classes. These medications have not yet been adequately studied among depressed, elderly persons. Thus, it is not currently known how effective they may be for this population. Examples of atypical antidepressants include nefazodone (Serzone) and venlafaxine (Effexor).

The duration of antidepressant treatment must be considered when treating depressed, elderly persons. Elderly persons typically respond to antidepressant medications more slowly than younger persons; twelve weeks of treatment may be required to achieve maximum response. Furthermore, treatment should be continued at the same dosage for a minimum of six months after remission to prevent relapse.

In addition to antidepressant medications, five psychosocial interventions have demonstrated efficacy for treating depressed, elderly persons: cognitive-behavioral therapy (CBT), brief psychodynamic therapy, interpersonal psychotherapy (IPT), reminiscence therapy, and psychoeducational approaches. A brief description of these therapies is presented in Table 2. CBT, IPT, and brief psychodynamic therapy all appear to be comparably effective to antidepressant medications, with improvement rates near 70 percent. Reminiscence therapy has been shown to be effective for mild and moderate cases of depression, but does not appear to be as effective as CBT for more severe cases of depression. Psychoeducational interventions are effective in re-

ducing depressive symptoms among elderly persons with subsyndromal depression. Psychosocial interventions may be superior to antidepressants and electroconvulsive therapy at reducing the risk of future depression.

Electroconvulsive therapy (ECT) is a third form of treatment for depressed, elderly individuals. ECT involves passing electrical current through an individual's brain, and is typically used only in severe cases of depression that have not responded to other treatments. ECT appears to be as effective (and perhaps more effective) than antidepressant medications for the short-term treatment of MDD, particularly in severe and psychotic cases of depression. It typically produces a more rapid response than either antidepressants or psychosocial interventions. Nevertheless, the majority of individuals who receive ECT relapse into depression if they do not receive additional treatment. In addition, roughly one-third of elderly persons who receive ECT experience complications such as memory impairment, delirium, and arrythmias.

Although combinations of the three forms of treatment have not been researched thoroughly, a limited amount of data and common clinical practice indicate that antidepressant treatment combined with psychosocial interventions may be superior to either form of treatment administered alone. If the increased cost associated with a second form of treatment is feasible, and if combined treatment is not contraindicated for medical reasons, combined antidepressant and psychosocial interventions may provide the optimal treatment for depression among older adults.

THOMAS E. JOINER, JR.
JEREMY W. PETTIT
MARISOL PEREZ

See also ALZHEIMER'S DISEASE; ANTIDEPRESSANTS; ANXIETY; BEREAVEMENT; COGNITIVE-BEHAVIORAL THERAPY; DIAGNOSTIC AND STATISTICAL MANUAL OF MENTAL DISORDERS-IV; ELECTROCONVULSIVE THERAPY; NEUROTRANSMITTERS; PSYCHOTHERAPY.

BIBLIOGRAPHY

American Psychiatric Association. *Diagnostic and Statistical Manual of Mental Disorders*, 4th ed. Washington, D.C.: APA, 1994.
GEISLEMANN, B., and BAUER, M. "Subthreshold Depression in the Elderly: Qualitative or Quantitative Distinction?" *Comprehensive Psychiatry* 41, no. 2, supp. 1 (2000): 32–38.

Table 2
Effective Psychosocial Interventions for Depression among the Elderly

Treatment	Focus	Typical Duration
Cognitive Behavioral Therapy	Dysfunctional and irrational cognitions, as well as deficits in behavior and motivation	10-20 weeks
Interpersonal Psychotherapy	Interpersonal functioning as it relates to current depression and the onset of depression; development of interpersonal skills for dealing with problems such as grief, role issues, and interpersonal deficits	12-16 weeks
Brief Psychodynamic Therapy	Unresolved grief, self-integration, existential concerns	16-20 weeks
Reminiscence Therapy	Recalling and reinterpreting the meaning of past life events	12-16 weeks
Psychoeducational Approaches	Explain what depression is and strategies to cope with depression	Varies

SOURCE: Author

LYNESS, J. M.; KING, D. A.; COX, C.; YOEDIONO, Z.; and CAINE, E. D. "The Importance of Subsyndromal Depression in Older Primary Care Patients: Prevalence and Associated Functional Disability." *Journal of the American Geriatrics Society* 47, no. 6 (1999): 647–652.

NIEDEREHE, G., and SCHNEIDER, L. S. "Treatments for Depression and Anxiety in the Aged." In *A Guide to Treatments that Work*. Edited by Peter E. Nathan and Jack M. Gorman. New York: Oxford University Press, 1998. Pages 270–287.

WOLFE, R.; MORROW, J.; and FREDRICKSON, B. L. "Mood Disorders in Older Adults." In *The Practical Handbook of Clinical Gerontology*. Edited by Laura L. Carstensen and Barry A. Edelstein. Thousand Oaks, Calif.: Sage Publications, 1996. Pages 274–303.

ZARIT, S. H., and ZARIT, J. M. *Mental Disorders in Older Adults: Fundamentals of Assessment and Treatment*. New York: Guilford Press, 1998.

DESIGN

See HUMAN FACTORS

DEVELOPMENTAL PSYCHOLOGY

Developmental psychologists are interested in time- and age-related changes in cognitive and intellectual functioning, personality, and social relationships from birth to death. Theory and research deal with three core phenomena: general principles of developmental change, individual differences in development, and intervention possibilities. Two research designs are used to examine these phenomena: cross-sectional and longitudinal studies. Consider, for example, the study of intelligence across the life span. In order to determine general principles of age-related change in intelligence, a cross-sectional design that compares the performance of various age groups (e.g., children, adolescents, young and older adults) on the same test could be used. If children and older adults show a lower test performance compared with the other age groups, one could infer that intelligence increases with age in early life and declines in old age. However, other factors, such as historical changes in education, could also explain the low performance of older adults. Age group differences observed in cross-sectional studies are confounded with cohort differences in life experience and life contexts. Longitudinal studies in which the same individuals are repeatedly measured over time on the same test provide the best assessment of how performance changes with age.

Both cross-sectional and longitudinal research designs are used to investigate individual differences in development. Developmental psychologists ask, for example, whether family backgrounds are linked to individual differences in intellectual development, why some children show delayed or slower growth in intellectual abilities compared with their age peers, and why some adults remain cognitively fit into old age and others show cognitive decline. In addition, developmental researchers are interested in the extent to which cognitive performance (e.g., memory, reasoning, knowledge) can be enhanced at different points in the life course. Carefully designed intervention and training studies are important tools in this respect. Learning about the modifiability (reserve capacity or plasticity) of the cognitive system at different ages helps in better understanding the processes underlying intellectual and cognitive functioning across the life span.

There is general consensus about the importance of investigating three systems of influence on development: age-graded, history-graded, and nonnormative. Each of these systems involves biological and environmental components that contribute to similarities in development as well as to subgroup variations. Age-graded influences include biological and physical changes (e.g., puberty, menopause) as well as exposure to age-related social factors (e.g., schooling, family life cycle, retirement). History-graded influences imply changes in societal structure and function (e.g., economic depression, medical and technical modernization, periods of war or political oppression). Longitudinal research on the developmental trajectories of men and women who were either young children or adolescents during the 1930s economic depression in North America exemplifies this approach (e.g., Elder). Nonnormative influences are conditions that are not associated with chronological age or historical time, but affect an individual's development in important ways (e.g., a lottery win, loss of a leg in an accident).

There is no unified theoretical framework of developmental psychology. Major metatheoretical positions emphasize cognitive structural, biogenetic, psychoanalytical, action-theoretical, social learning, transactional, contextualist, dialectical, and dynamic systems perspectives (for reviews see Bornstein and Lamb; Cairns).

Concepts of change and development

There has been a long-standing debate in the psychological literature about what aspects of change define development and whether or not development occurs across the life span or only in early life (for reviews see Bengtson and Schaie; Cairns; Valsiner). Traditionally, developmental psychology focused primarily on the description and explanation of positive changes (e.g., increased adaptive capacity or growth) in the structure and function of mind and behavior. Change, within this tradition, is considered to reflect development if one or more of the following criteria are met: (1) it is directed toward a state of maturity; (2) it is quantitative and qualitative (stagelike) in nature; (3) it is relatively robust or irreversible; and/or (4) it moves toward greater complexity and differentiation. Using these criteria to define development encourages theoretical precision but also restricts the concept primarily to growth in early life. Is change observed during adulthood and old age associated with development or with processes of aging?

The life-span approach outlined by Paul B. Baltes (1997; Baltes, et al.) proposes that development is not completed at young adulthood (maturity) but extends across the entire life course. Each age period (e.g., infancy, adolescence, adulthood, old age) has its own developmental tasks. When viewed together, however, these age-specific phenomena contribute to continuous (cumulative) and discontinuous (innovative) change throughout life. The great regularity of development observed in infancy and childhood may be attributed to the fact that the biological and cultural influences that shape childhood are more programmed (genetically and societally) than is true for late adulthood. In old age, the conjoint dynamics of biological and cultural influences are less well-orchestrated, in part because the culture of old age is still evolving.

The life-span approach of Baltes and colleagues alerts researchers to the fact that development can be multidirectional in that it involves trajectories of positive growth, stability, and negative change (loss) across the life span. A classic example of this concept is longitudinal research on the trajectories of fluid versus crystallized intelligence during adulthood and into old age (e.g., Schaie). Dimensions of fluid intelligence (e.g., spatial ability, reasoning, perceptual speed) generally show decline beginning in middle age, whereas aspects of crystallized intelligence (e.g., knowledge) remain relatively stable up to at least age eighty.

Expanding the concept of development from a growth model to a multidirectional model led to the insight that development is likely always a combination of gains and losses. A gain in one direction, for example, may exclude alternative pathways of development. The search for gains and losses across the life span has led to much recent research on the plasticity of mind and behavior; the fundamental role of processes of selection, optimization, and compensation in development; and profiles of successful aging.

JACQUI SMITH

See also DEVELOPMENTAL TASKS; LIFE COURSE; LIFE-SPAN DEVELOPMENT; SELECTIVE OPTIMIZATION WITH COMPENSATION THEORY.

BIBLIOGRAPHY

BALTES, P. B. "On the Incomplete Architecture of Human Ontogeny: Selection, Optimization, and Compensation as Foundation of Developmental Theory." *American Psychologist* 52 (1997): 366–380.
BALTES, P. B.; LINDENBERGER, U.; and STAUDINGER, U. M. "Life-Span Theory in Developmental Psychology." In *Handbook of Child Psychology.* Vol. 1, *Theoretical Models of Human Development,* 5th ed. Edited by R. M. Lerner. New York: Wiley, 1998. Pages 1029–1143.
BENGTSON, V. L., and SCHAIE, K. W., eds. *Handbook of Theories of Aging.* New York: Springer, 1999.
BORNSTEIN, M. H., and LAMB, M. E., eds. *Developmental Psychology: An Advanced Textbook,* 4th. ed. Mahwah, N.J.: Erlbaum, 1999.
CAIRNS, R. B. "The Making of Developmental Psychology." In *Handbook of Child Psychology.* Vol. 1, *Theoretical Models of Human Development,* 5th ed. Edited by R. M. Lerner. New York: Wiley, 1998. Pages 25–106.
ELDER, G. H. "The Life Course and Human Development." In *Handbook of Child Psychology.* Vol. 1, *Theoretical Models of Human Development,* 5th ed. Edited by R. M. Lerner. New York: Wiley, 1998. Pages 939–991.
SCHAIE, K. W. *Intellectual Development in Adulthood: The Seattle Longitudinal Study.* New York: Cambridge University Press, 1996.
VALSINER, J. "The Development of the Concept of Development: Historical and Epistemological Perspectives." In *Handbook of Child Psychology.* Vol. 1, *Theoretical Models of Human Development,* 5th ed. Edited by R. M. Lerner. New York: Wiley, 1998. Pages 198–232.

DEVELOPMENTAL TASKS

A developmental task is one that arises predictably and consistently at or about a certain period in the life of the individual (Havighurst, 1948, 1953). The concept of developmental tasks assumes that human development in modern societies is characterized by a long series of tasks that individuals have to learn throughout their lives. Some of these tasks are located in childhood and adolescence, whereas others arise during adulthood and old age (see also Heckhausen, 1999). Successful achievement of a certain task is expected to lead to happiness and to success with later tasks, while failure may result in unhappiness in the individual, disapproval by the society, and difficulty with later tasks.

Developmental tasks arise from three different sources (Havighurst, 1948, 1953). First, some are mainly based on physical maturation (e.g., learning to walk). Another source of developmental tasks relates to sociostructural and cultural forces. Such influences are based on, for instance, laws (e.g., minimum age for marriage) and culturally shared expectations of development (e.g., age norms; Neugarten, Moore, and Lowe, 1965), determining the age range in which specific developmental tasks have to be mastered. The third source of developmental tasks involves personal values and aspirations. These personal factors result from the interaction between ontogenetic and environmental factors, and play an active role in the emergence of specific developmental tasks (e.g., choosing a certain occupational pathway).

Childhood and adolescence

Early childhood is characterized by basic tasks such as learning to walk, to take solid food, and to control the elimination of body wastes. In addition, young children have to achieve more complex cognitive and social tasks, such as learning to talk, to form simple concepts of reality, and to relate emotionally to other people. In middle childhood, developmental tasks relate to the expansion of the individual's world outside of the home (e.g., getting along with age mates, learning skills for culturally valued games) and to the mental thrust into the world of adult concepts and communication (e.g., skills in writing, reading, and calculating). Achieving adolescent developmental tasks requires a person to develop personal independence and a philosophy of life. Adolescents are confronted, for example, with learning to achieve new forms of intimate relationships, preparing for an occupation, achieving emotional independence of parents, and developing a mature set of values and ethical principals. The peer group plays a major role in facilitating the achievement of adolescents' developmental tasks by providing a context in which some of these tasks can be accomplished.

Adulthood and old age

The concept of developmental tasks describes development as a lifelong process. Thus, it is also an early and significant contributor to the emerging field of lifelong human development (e.g., life-span psychology and life-course sociology; Setterstery, 1999).

In young adulthood, developmental tasks are mainly located in family, work, and social life. Family-related developmental tasks are described as finding a mate, learning to live with a marriage partner, having and rearing children, and managing the family home. A developmental task that takes an enormous amount of time of young adults relates to the achievement of an occupational career. Family and work-related tasks may represent a potential conflict, given that individuals' time and energy are limited resources. Thus, young adults may postpone one task in order to secure the achievement of another. With respect to their social life, young adults are also confronted with establishing new friendships outside of the marriage and assuming responsibility in the larger community.

During midlife, people reach the peak of their control over the environment around them and their personal development. In addition, social responsibilities are maximized. Midlife is also a period during which people confront the onset of physiological changes (Lachman, 2001). Developmental tasks during midlife relate to, for example, achieving adult responsibilities, maintaining a standard of living, assisting children with the transition into adulthood, and adjusting to the physiological changes of middle age (e.g., menopause).

Old age has often been characterized as a period of loss and decline. However, development in any period of life consists of both gains and losses, although the gain-loss ratio becomes increasingly negative with advancing age (Heckhausen, Dixon, and Baltes, 1989; Baltes, 1987). A central developmental task that characterizes the transition into old age is adjustment to retirement. The period after retirement has to be filled with new projects, but is characterized by few valid cultural guidelines. Adaptation to retirement involves both potential gains (e.g., self-actualization) and losses (e.g., loss of self-esteem). The achievement of this task may be obstructed by the management of another task, living on a reduced income after retirement.

In addition, older adults are generally challenged to create a positive sense of their lives as a whole. The feeling that life has had order and meaning results in happiness (cf. ego-integrity; Erikson, 1986). Older adults also have to adjust to decreasing physical strength and health. The prevalence of chronic and acute diseases increases in old age. Thus, older adults may be confronted with life situations that are characterized by not being in perfect health, serious illness, and dependency on other people. Moreover, older adults may become caregivers to their spouses (e.g., Schulz and Beach, 1999). Some older adults have to adjust to the death of their spouses. This task arises more frequently for women than for man. After they have lived with a spouse for many decades, widowhood may force older people to adjust to loneliness, moving to a smaller place, and learning about business matters.

Other potential gains in old age relate to the task of meeting social and civic obligations. For example, older people might accumulate knowledge about life (Baltes and Staudings, 2000), and thus may contribute to the development of younger people and the society. The development of a large part of the population into old age is a historically recent phenomenon of modern societies. Thus, advancements in the understanding of the aging process may lead to identifying further developmental tasks associated with gains and purposeful lives for older adults.

CARSTEN WROSCH

See also DEVELOPMENTAL PSYCHOLOGY; LIFE-COURSE; LIFE-SPAN DEVELOPMENT.

BIBLIOGRAPHY

BALTES, P. B. "Theoretical Propositions of Life-Span Developmental Psychology: On the Dynamics Between Growth and Decline." *Developmental Psychology* 23 (1987): 611–626.

ERIKSON, E. H. *Identity: Youth and Crisis.* New York: Norton, 1968.

HAVIGHURST, R. J. *Developmental Tasks and Education.* Chicago: University of Chicago Press, 1948.

HAVIGHURST, R. J. *Human Development and Education*. New York: Longmans, Green, 1953.

HECKHAUSEN, J.; DIXON, R. A.; and BALTES, P. P. "Gains and Losses in Development Throughout Adulthood as Perceived by Different Adult Age Groups." *Developmental Psychology* 25 (1989): 109–121.

NEUGARTEN, B. L.; MOORE, J. W.; and LOWE, J. C. "Age Norms, Age Constraints, and Adult Socialization." *American Journal of Sociology* 70 (1965): 710–717.

SCHULZ, R., and BEACH, S. "Caregiving as a Risk Factor for Mortality: The Caregiver Health Effects Study." *Journal of the American Medical Association* 282 (1999): 2215–2219.

DHEA

Dehydroepiandrosterone (DHEA) and dehydroepiandrosterone-sulfate (DHEA-S) are the most abundant steroids produced by the human adrenal gland. DHEA-S, sometimes considered as a plasma "reservoir" for the hormone, appears in the circulation at about one thousand times the concentration of DHEA, is water soluble, and is capable of being bound to albumin. Although it is DHEA that has been identified as having biological activity, the cellular receptor for, and molecular mode of action of, DHEA and DHEA-S remains uncertain. Depending upon the species and tissue, the possibilities for the former seem to include the NMDA sigma receptor, the GABAA receptor, the estrogen receptor, and the PPAR alpha receptor. In addition, and further complicating the situation, is the possibility that DHEA and DHEA-S work indirectly on target tissues, either following conversion into more potent steroids (including estrogen and testosterone), through another mediator, or as an antagonist to still another potent steroid, cortisol.

DHEA and DHEA-S are synthesized in large amounts by the fetal adrenal gland, with the levels dropping dramatically in newborn and in children. Beginning in about middle -adolescence, and coincident with the development of the zona reticularis in the adrenal cortex, the levels begin to rise sharply again. This onset of heightened activity of the adrenal gland is referred to as adrenarche. At about puberty, the blood hormone levels in boys and girls are similar; thereafter the serum concentration in males begins to exceed that of females. In both sexes, the levels of circulating DHEA and DHEA-S reach their peak during young adult life. Subsequently, in humans and other higher primates, the levels of DHEA and DHEA-S undergo, on average, a steady decline with advancing age. In humans, this decline in circulating hormone reaches about 30 percent of young adult levels by about age 65 years and about 10 percent by age 85 and older. The reduction in DHEA/DHEA-S is thought to result, at least in part, from an involution of the zona reticularis. The latter, age-associated change in adrenal gland structure and DHEA production is referred to as adrenopause.

In spite of the substantial individual-to-individual variation in hormone levels, the progressive decline of these levels with age has led to consideration of DHEA and DHEA-S as biomarkers of the aging process; that is, as chemical indicators useful in tracking age-related senescent change, morbidity, and mortality. More importantly, the decline in levels of these two closely related steroids has also been implicated as being responsible, at least in part, for many of the senescent changes seen in advanced-aged individuals and in individuals with chronic illness. These changes include, but are not limited to, body composition, some forms of cancer, type II diabetes, atherosclerosis and ischemic heart disease. At least some of these associations are sex specific, though not always in a readily understood manner. For example, DHEA-S appears to be related to body composition (fat and lean body mass) in men but not in women. On the other hand, a similar association of DHEA to body composition may be present in women (17). Whatever the limitations and contradictions in the existing literature, it is the notion that diminished hormone levels in older persons are causally linked to age-related functional decline and structural change that has provided the rationale for the well-promoted use of DHEA as an "anti-aging" intervention. In the United States, DHEA is readily available without prescription. However, clinical data documenting the usefulness of DHEA supplementation in humans is limited to very few examples. As of 2001, most of the impressive findings reported on the effects of DHEA treatment have come from studies in rodent models of aging and senescent change; not from human subjects.

Systemic lupus erythematosus (SLE) appears to be one circumstance where taking DHEA benefits the patient. Using the steroid has been reported to reduce the symptoms of SLE and to permit lowering the dose of corticosteroid used to treat the disease. The latter is important because of the potential negative side effects associated with the chronic use of corticosteroids. DHEA may also be useful in the treatment of major depression. Barrett-Conner et al. (1995) found endogenous DHEA-S levels to be significantly and inversely associated with depressed mood. This finding compliments an earlier report that modest doses of DHEA over four weeks improves depression ratings in patients with major depression and low plasma DHEA-S values.

Even though hormone replacement seems a rational approach for ameliorating the possible negative consequences of naturally occurring, age-related declines in hormone levels, the only circumstance in which there is clear documentation supporting such a strategy is estrogen replacement in postmenopausal women. Even here, however, the approach remains controversial because of the risk of increasing the incidence of cancer in estrogen sensitive tissues. The justification for using DHEA in hormone replacement is (as of 2001) much weaker, with the prevailing view being that more long-term, carefully controlled, and larger clinical trials are needed before such action can be justified. In particular, more work is needed to confirm those special circumstances where initial findings are promising, such as the treatment of major depression. In addition, there appears to be growing support for the idea of using DHEA to help mitigate the negative side effects of corticosteroids (e.g., prednisone) in patients where the latter are an essential part of therapy (e.g., for chronic inflammatory disease and SLE). Thus, while no compelling reasons can be found for recommending DHEA supplementation to the healthy elderly, there may well be clinical circumstances where such supplementation will ultimately prove of significant value.

ARNOLD KHAN

See also ANDROGENS; ESTROGEN; LIFE SPAN EXTENSION; NUTRITION, DIETARY SUPPLEMENTS.

BIBLIOGRAPHY

ABBASI, A.; DUTHIE, E. H., JR.; SHELDAHL, L.; WILSON, C.; SASSE, E.; RUDMAN, I.; and MATTSON, D. E. "Association of Dehydroepiandrosterone Sulfate, Body Composition, and Physical Fitness in Independent Community-Dwelling Older Men and Women." *Journal of the American Geriatrics Society* 46 (1998): 263–273.

BARRETT-CONNOR, E.; VON MUHLEN, D.; LAUGHLIN, G. A.; and KRIPKE, A. "Endogenous Levels of Dehydroepiandrosterone Sulfate, But Not Other Sex Hormones, Are Associated with Depressed Mood in Older Women: The Rancho Bernardo Study." *Journal of the American Geriatrics Society* 47 (1999): 685–691.

EBELING, P., and KOIVISTO, V. A. "Physiological Importance of Dehydroepiandrosterone." *Lancet* 343 (1994): 1479–1481.

HINSON, J.P., and RAVEN, P. W. "DHEA Deficiency Syndrome: A New Term for Old Age?" *Journal of Endocrinology.* 163 (1999): 1–5.

LANE, M.; INGRAM, D. K.; BALL, S. S.; and ROTH, G. S. "Dehydroepiandrosterone Sulfate: A Biomarker of Primate Aging Slowed by Calorie Restriction." *Journal of Clinical Endocrinology and Metabolism* 82 (1997): 2093–2097.

PARKER, C.R. JR. "Dehydroepiandrosterone and Dehydroepiandrosterone Sulfate Production in the Human Adrenal During Development and Aging." *Steroids* 64 (1999): 640–647.

VAN VOLLENHOVEN, R. F.; MORABITO, L. M.; ENGELMAN, E.G.; and MCGUIRE, J. L. "Treatment of Systemic Lupus Erythematosus with Dehydroepiandrosterone: 50 Patients Treated Up to 12 Months." *Journal of Rheumatology* 25 (1998): 285–289.

WATSON, R.R.; HULS, A.; ARAGHINIKUAM, M.; and CHUNG, S. "Dehydroepiandrosterone and Diseases of Aging." *Drugs and Aging* (October 9, 1996): 274–291.

YEN, S. S., and LAUGHLIN, G. A. "Aging and the Adrenal Cortex." *Experimental Gerontology* 33 (1998): 897–910.

DIABETES MELLITUS

Diabetes mellitus is a failure to control blood sugar levels so that they become too high. It is classified into two categories. Type 1 diabetes (also called juvenile diabetes) is characterized by an acute destruction of insulin-secreting beta cells in the pancreas by autoantibodies. Insulin is a hormone essential to maintaining *blood sugar* at a normal level. Diabetes results in the abolition of insulin secretion by the pancreas, severe hyperglycemia (*high blood sugar*) and production of ketones. Type 2 diabetes (also called adult onset diabetes) is characterized by a gradually increasing blood sugar level resulting from a combination of resistance to the action of insulin at the cellular level and a gradual decline of insulin secretion by the pancreas.

Diabetes mellitus is a common disease in the older population. The vast majority of elderly subjects have type 2 diabetes, which means that the degree of hyperglycemia is variable and rarely results in the production of ketones. Since the degree of hyperglycemia is variable and elderly subjects are often not aware of the symptoms of high blood sugar (see below), there may be a few years of asymptomatic disease before a diagnosis of diabetes is made.

Prevalence

The most recent health and nutrition survey in the United States demonstrated that the prevalence of diabetes approaches 20 percent in Caucasian persons over age seventy, and may be as high as 50 percent in certain ethnic groups (Harris et al.). Canadian data suggest a similar picture with about 12 percent of people age sixty-five and older affected (Roc et al.). As of 2000 in North America, the group of people over sixty-five represents about 13 percent of the total population. Assuming that the trend of aging persists, this group will likely represent around 21 percent of the population by 2020. If the prevalence of diabetes remains the same, there is likely to be a marked increase in the absolute number of elderly diabetic patients by the middle of twenty-first century.

Clinical presentation and diagnosis

At least half of elderly individuals with diabetes are unaware that they have the disease, and often the diagnosis is made after the complications of the disease are established (Harris et al.). Although the reasons for late diagnosis of diabetes are unclear, it may be related to a lack of awareness of the diagnostic criteria on the part of physicians, lack of interaction by elderly patients with a physician, and the fact that elderly patients frequently do not manifest the classic symptoms of hyperglycemia: excessive secretion of urine, excessive thirst, and excessive appetite. Symptoms do not generally occur until blood glucose levels are substantially elevated, possibly because the level at which sugar spills into the urine increases with age. When patients do have symptoms, they are often nonspecific (e.g., failure to thrive, low energy, confusion, frequent urination, with or without incontinence, various

infections), and may not always trigger the measurement of a plasma glucose level or a consultation with a physician. This phenomenon, along with the fact that identification and management of diabetes can relieve many of these symptoms, improve the quality of life, and prevent or delay subsequent chronic illnesses, highlights the importance of screening for diabetes in elderly individuals.

The diagnosis of diabetes may be accomplished by measuring fasting plasma glucose. It is currently recommended that fasting glucose be measured every three years in elderly persons and yearly in persons with risk factors for the development of diabetes, such as obesity, hypertension, and a strong family history of diabetes. The diagnosis of diabetes is made by a fasting plasma glucose of at least 7.0 millimol/liter on two occasions. A diagnosis can also be made when a patient is found to have a glucose of at least 11.1 millimol/liter two hours after a 75 gram oral glucose load (American Diabetes Association, 1997), but for practical reasons a glucose tolerance test is not generally performed.

Complications

As a result of high blood sugar levels; abnormalities of lipid levels, blood pressure regulation, and blood coagulation; and oxidative stress, elderly patients with diabetes develop a number of complications. The long-term complications of diabetes are classified as microvascular (mainly kidney and eye problems) and macrovascular (vascular problems related to heart, brain, and lower limbs). Diabetes is a leading cause of blindness, kidney failure leading to hemodialysis, heart problems (angina and infarction), and limb amputation in the elderly diabetic population.

Treatment

All clinicians agree that blood glucose levels should be controlled sufficiently well to reduce the symptoms of hyperglycemia. There is less consensus regarding the optimal degree of blood sugar control in elderly diabetic patients. This is due in part to the fact that no randomized controlled trials involving elderly subjects have definitively assessed whether tight blood glucose control reduces the risk of disease and disability in this age group. The United Kingdom Prospective Diabetes Study (UKPDS) recruited middle-aged patients with type 2 diabetes and randomized them to either intensive blood glucose control with metformin, sulfonylurea, or insulin or a control group with conventional treatment. The UKPDS data did demonstrate that improved glycemic control reduces the risk of microvascular complications related to diabetes, and perhaps macrovascular complications in middle-aged patients. Furthermore, in observational studies of elderly subjects, improved glycemic control is associated with a reduced risk of microvascular and macrovascular complications related to diabetes (Kuusisto et al.; Morisaki et al.), as well as with improved cognitive function (Meneilly et al.). Based on these data, it is recommended that goals for control in elderly patients should be less than 7 millimol/liter before meals and less than 10 millimol/liter after meals.

Nonpharmacological intervention. Achieving optimal blood sugar control in elderly persons with diabetes is challenging. These patients take numerous medications, have multiple comorbidities, and often live in challenging social situations. Because of the complex nature of these patients and the need for lifestyle modifications, a team approach is essential. A structured diabetes teaching program will improve blood sugar control, compliance with therapy, and quality of life in older patients. Self-monitoring of blood sugar level at home is possible with a portable device called a glucometer. The self-monitoring of blood sugar constitutes a key aspect of diabetic management. Levels of HbA1c (glycosilated hemoglobin) and/or fructosamine are the standard laboratory measures of long-term glycemic control in older individuals, and should be assessed at regular intervals (Meltzer et al.).

Exercise programs have been shown to improve the sense of well-being, glucose levels, and lipid levels in elderly patients with diabetes (Agurs-Collins et al.). Unfortunately, concomitant health problems often prevent elderly patients from participating in exercise programs, and optimal activity levels may be difficult to achieve. Thus exercise programs of even low and moderate intensity are of value in selected elderly patients.

Elderly patients with diabetes have diets that are too low in complex carbohydrates and too high in saturated fats, and they frequently do not comply with a diabetic diet. As noted above, multidisciplinary interventions have been shown to improve compliance with dietary therapy in aged diabetics. For community-dwelling elderly subjects, weight loss programs have been shown to result in substantial improvements in blood sugar control (Reaven et al.). In contrast, for frail elderly nursing home residents, diabetic diets complicate and increase the cost of care, and do not improve blood sugar control.

Pharmacological intervention. The principal metabolic defect in lean elderly patients with diabetes is profound impairment in glucose-induced insulin secretion. Medications that stimulate insulin secretion, such as sulfonylureas, have been widely used for the treatment of diabetes in elderly patients that is not controlled with dietary therapy. This kind of medication is associated with an increased risk of hypoglycemia, especially in the elderly. Chlorpropamide and glyburide are the sulfonylureas associated with the greatest risk of hypoglycemia in the elderly. Observational studies and small, randomized controlled trials suggest that glipizide and gliclazide are associated with a lower risk of hypoglycemia in the older population with diabetes (Brodows; Tessier et al.). In general, initial doses of these drugs should be half those for younger people, and should be increased more slowly. The role of newer insulin-stimulating drugs, such as repaglinide, remains to be determined for elderly patients with diabetes.

The UKPDS suggests that metformin, a member of the biguanide family, is an effective agent in obese middle-aged patients, and may be more beneficial than sulfonylureas in reducing the risk of morbid events. The main effect of metformin is to reduce insulin resistance. This drug results in substantial improvements in blood sugar control in obese elderly patients (Lalau et al.). Metformin should not be given to patients with creatinine values (blood indicator of kidney function) above 180 microns/liter, chronic liver disease, or significant congestive heart failure. Based on clinical experience, sulfonylureas and metformin can often be given in combination to elderly patients with diabetes to improve blood sugar control.

Because of their ability to improve insulin resistance, thiazolidinediones (pioglitazone and rosiglitazone) may also be a useful class of drugs for obese elderly patients. This class of drug improves insulin resistance. Pending the results of further studies in the elderly, this class of drugs should be reserved for the treatment of obese elderly patients whose blood sugar is not optimally controlled with another kind of antidiabetic medication. When thiazolidinediones are prescribed for the elderly, liver function should be monitored at regular intervals.

Alpha glucosidase inhibitors are a class of drugs that interfere with the action of the enzymes responsible for the digestion of complex carbohydrates and disaccharides at the brush border of the intestine. This class of drugs slows the absorption of glucose through the small intestine. Acarbose is the first of these drugs released for clinical use. A study has been published on the efficacy of this drug for elderly diabetes patients (Meneilly et al.). At present, acarbose should be considered as first-line therapy for lean elderly patients with a modest increase in fasting glucose levels.

Insulin therapy substantially improves blood sugar control with no adverse effect on the quality of life in patients who are inadequately controlled by oral agents (Tovi and Engfeldt). Elderly patients can make substantial errors when trying to mix different kinds of insulin in the same syringe (e.g., the rapid-acting R or Toronto insulin with the intermediate-acting N or NPH insulin). For this reason, insulin preparations that do not require mixing are preferable for them. In type 2 diabetes, insulin therapy is usually started ". . .with one dose of intermediate acting insulin in addition to pills given at different times of the day such as metformin and glyburide." However, many patients who are started on one daily dose of insulin need a second injection in order to control blood sugar.

Management of hypertension and excess lipids

Traditional risk factors for cardiovascular disease, such as smoking, hypertension, and excess lipids, are associated with an increased risk of diabetes-related complications in the elderly. Modification of these risk factors may reduce the risk of these complications.

Studies suggest that treatment of hypertension with drugs such as the thiazide diuretics and calcium channel blockers reduces mortality and the risk of vascular complications related to diabetes in the elderly (Tuomilehto et al.; Curb et al.). In the Systolic Hypertension in the Elderly Patient study (SHEP), patients with systolic hypertension and type 2 diabetes who were treated with a thiazide diuretic, had a significantly lower incidence of cardiovascular events than subjects receiving a placebo. The absolute risk reduction with active treatment compared with the placebo was twice as great for diabetic as for nondiabetic patients who participated in this study. The Systolic Hypertension in Europe Trial (SystEur) undertook a similar subgroup analysis of older patients with both hypertension and type 2 diabetes. Among the nondiabetic participants who were started on a calcium-channel blocker, nitrendipine, a 55 percent reduction of mortality was observed compared to the placebo group. In the group receiving active treatment, reduction of overall mortality was significantly higher among the diabetic patients than among the nondiabetic ones.

There are no data from randomized trials in the elderly diabetic population to determine the benefits of treatment of excess lipids. Subgroup analysis of middle-aged patients with diabetes (Pyorala et al.; Goldberg et al.) and subjects sixty-five or older (LIPID Study Group) who enrolled in prevention trials suggesting that reduction of low-density lipoprotein (LDL) cholesterol can significantly decrease vascular events in this population.

Perspective

Considering the aging trend in American society, an increased prevalence of diabetes is expected among the elderly population. The economic and sociological impacts of this health problem will dramatically increase by the middle of the twenty-first century. More research will be necessary to understand the disease and the mechanisms involved in the progression of associated complications.

DANIEL TESSIER
TAMAS FÜRLÖP
GRAYDON S. MEINELLY

See also CHOLESTEROL; DIET; DISEASE PRESENTATION; HEART DISEASE; HIGH BLOOD PRESSURE.

BIBLIOGRAPHY

AGURS-COLLINS, T. D.; KUMANYIKA, S. K.; TEN HAVE, T. R. et al. "A Randomized Controlled Trial of Weight Reduction and Exercise for Diabetes Management in Older African-American Subjects." *Diabetes Care* 20 (1997): 1503–1511.

American Diabetes Association. Expert Committee on the Diagnosis and Classification of Diabetes Mellitus. "Report of the Expert Committee on the Diagnosis and Classification of Diabetes Mellitus" 20 (1997): 1183–1197.

BRODOWS, R. G. "Benefits and Risks with Glyburide and Glipizide in Elderly NIDDM Patients." *Diabetes Care* 15 (1992): 75–80.

CURB, J. D.; PRESSEL, S. L.; CUTLER, J. et al. "Effect of Diuretic Based Antihypertensive Treatment on Cardiovascular Risk in Older Diabetic Patients with Isolated Systolic Hypertension." *Journal of the American Medical Association* 276 (1996): 1886–1892.

GOLDBERG, R. B.; MELLIES, M. J.; SACKS, F. et al. "Cardiovascular Events and Their Reduction with Pravastatin in Diabetic and Glucose-Intolerant Myocardial Infarction Survivors with Average Cholesterol Levels: Subgroup Analyses on the Cholesterol and Recurrent Events (CARE) Trial." *Circulation* 98 (1998): 2513–2519.

HARRIS, M. I.; FLEGAL, K. M.; COWIE, C. C. et al. "Prevalence of Diabetes, Impaired Fasting Glucose, and Impaired Glucose Tolerance in U.S. Adults. The Third National Health and Nutrition Examination Survey, 1988–1994." *Diabetes Care* 21 (1998): 518–1924.

KUUSISTO, J.; MYKKANEN, L.; PYORALA, K. et al. "NIDDM and Its Metabolic Control Predict Coronary Heart Disease in Elderly Subjects." *Diabetes* 43 (1994): 960–967.

LALAU, J. D.; VERMERSCH, A.; HARY, L. et al. "Type 2 Diabetes in the Elderly: An Assessment of Metformin." *International Journal of Clinical Pharmacology and Therapeutic Toxicology* 28 (1990): 329–332.

LIPID Study Group. "Prevention of Cardiovascular Events and Death with Pravastatin in Patients with Coronary Heart Disease and a Broad Range of Initial Cholesterol Levels." *New England Journal of Medicine* 339 (1998): 1349–1357.

MENEILLY, G. S.; CHEUNG, E.; TESSIER, D. et al. "The Effect of Improved Glycemic Control on Cognitive Functions in the Elderly Patient with Diabetes." *Journal of Gerontology* 48 (1993): M117–M121.

MENEILLY, G. S.; RYAN, E. A.; RADZUIK, J. et al. "Effect of Acarbose on Insulin Sensitivity in Elderly Patients with Diabetes." *Diabetes Care* 23 (2000): 1162–1167.

MELTZER S.; LEITER, L.; DANEMAN, D.; GERSTEIN,HJ. C. et al. "1998 Clinical Practice Guidelines for the Management of Diabetes in Canada." *Canadian Medical Association Journal* 159 (8 suppl) (1998): S1–S29.

MORISAKI, N.; WATANABE, S.; KOBAYASHI, J. et al. "Diabetic Control and Progression of Retinopathy in Elderly Patients: Five-Year Follow-up Study." *Journal of the American Geriatric Society* 42 (1994): 142–145.

PYORALA, K.; PEDERSEN, T. R.; KJEKSHUS, J. et al. "Cholesterol Lowering with Simvastatin Improves Prognosis of Patients with Coronary Heart Disease: A Subgroup Analysis of the Scandinavian Simvastatin Survival Study (4S)." *Diabetes Care* 20 (1997): 614–620.

REAVEN, G. M., and STAFF OF THE PALO ALTO GRECC AGING STUDY UNIT. "Beneficial Effects of Weight Loss in Older Patients with NIDDM." *Journal of American Geriatric Society* 33 (1985): 93–95.

ROCKWOOD, K.; TAR, M. H.; PHILLIPS, S.; and MCDOWELL, I. "Prevalence of Diabetes Mellitis in Elderly People in Canada." *Age Ageing* 27 (1998): 573–577.

TESSIER, D.; DAWSON, K.; TETRAULT, J. P. et al. "Glibenclamide vs. Gliclazide in Type 2 Diabetes of the Elderly." *Diabetic Medicine* 11 (1994): 974–980.

TOVI, J., and ENGFELDT, P. "Well-being and Symptoms in Elderly Type 2 Diabetes Patients with Poor Metabolic Control: Effect of Insulin Treatment." *Practical Diabetes International* 15 (1998): 73–77.

TUOMILEHTO, J.; RASTENYTE, D.; BIRKENHAGER, W. H. et al. "Effects of Calcium-Channel Blockade in Older Patients with Diabetes and Systolic Hypertension. Systolic Hypertension in Europe Trial Investigators." *New England Journal of Medicine* 340 no. 9 (1999): 677–684.

United Kingdom Prospective Diabetes Study. "Intensive Blood Glucose Control with Sulphonylureas or Insulin Compared with Conventional Treatment and Risk of Complications in Patients with Type 2 Diabetes (UKPDS33)." *Lancet* 352, no. 9131 (12 September 1998): 837–853.

DIAGNOSTIC AND STATISTICAL MANUAL OF MENTAL DISORDERS-IV

The fourth edition of the *Diagnostic and Statistical Manual of Mental Disorders*, DSM-IV published by the American Psychiatric Association (APA) in 1994, acts as a comprehensive guide to the nomenclature, classification, and diagnostic criteria for mental disorders in the United States. Used widely for research, clinical, and statistical purposes, the DSM-IV provides a systematic method to form psychiatric diagnoses and facilitates communication by providing general and universally used definitions and descriptions of mental disorders, and possible courses of action for each diagnosis.

The lack of an adequate statistical measure of mental illness in U.S. censuses in the nineteenth century sparked the formation of a systematic nomenclature system for mental illness in 1917. This new system, developed by the APA and the National Commission on Mental Hygiene, was devised mainly for clinical and statistical use. The APA developed the first edition of the DSM (DSM-I) in 1952 after mental illnesses were included in the World Health Organization's sixth edition of the *International Classification of Diseases* (ICD-6). Sixteen years later, DSM-II appeared, with few changes. In 1978 DSM-III—including more specific diagnostic criteria, a multiaxial system, and unbiased descriptions—helped the efforts of clinicians and researchers. The revised edition (DSM-III-R) was published in 1987. DSM-IV is notably more culture sensitive than DSM-III-R.

DSM-IV uses five axes to diagnose mental illness. Each axis considers a different component of a patient's overall physical and mental health. The axial system allows clinicians and researchers to better gauge how a mental illness fits with a patient's overall health and lifestyle. Axis I consists of current mental disorders; some of the disorders classified on Axis I are learning disorders, dementias, schizophrenias, and mood, anxiety, eating, and sleep disorders. Personality disorders (e.g., obsessive-compulsive personality disorder) in adults and developmental problems (e.g., mental retardation) in children and adolescents are listed on Axis II. General medical conditions that may influence mental health are listed on Axis III. Axis IV rates an individual's psychosocial stressors, and Axis V rates an individual's level of functioning on a numerical scale (Davison and Neale).

The DSM-IV uses a categorical classification approach for assigning diagnosis, which has the advantage of simplicity and ease of communication (Widiger). However, categorical classification of psychopathology is exceedingly difficult; a psychological diagnosis is rarely defined by the presence of a single attribute. It is more typical for diagnosis instead to be based on some of several listed attributes (e.g., symptoms, course), none of which alone is sufficient for diagnosis.

In addition, the majority of psychological phenomena operate on some type of continuous distribution that categorical systems cannot precisely and reliably describe (Frances). Categorical systems also are less able to account for borderline cases and variability across clinical settings according to variables such as geographical location, socioeconomic status, and coexisting medical conditions (Finn).

Mental disorders that commonly affect older adults are generally found in the "Delirium, Dementia, Amnestic, and Other Cognitive Disorders" or the "Mental Disorders Due to General Medical Condition" sections of DSM-IV. However, a number of the diagnostic criteria for other disorders, most notably anxiety disorders, are still based primarily on studies in adolescents and younger adults and are applied primarily to these age groups.

NEETI BATHIA
THOMAS R. LYNCH

See also ANXIETY; DEPRESSION; GERIATRIC PSYCHIATRY; PSYCHOLOGICAL ASSESSMENT; PSYCHOPATHOLOGY.

BIBLIOGRAPHY

American Psychiatric Association. *Diagnostic and Statistical Manual of Mental Disorders*, 4th ed. Washington, D.C.: American Psychiatric Association, 1994.

DAVISON, G. C., and NEALE, J. M. "The Diagnostic System of the American Psychiatric Association." In *Abnormal Psychology*. New York: John Wiley and Sons, 1996. Pages 58–72.

FINN, S. E. "Base Rates, Utilities, and DSM-III: Shortcomings of Fixed-Rule Systems of Psychodiagnosis." *Journal of Abnormal Psychology* 91 (1982): 294–302.

FRANCES, A. "Categorical and Dimensional Systems of Personality Diagnosis: A Comparison." *Comprehensive Psychiatry* 23 (1982): 516–526.

WIDIGER, T. A. "Categorical Versus Dimensional Classification: Implications from and for Research." *Journal of Personality Disorders* 6 (1992): 287–300.

DIET

See NUTRITION; MALNUTRITION; VITAMINS

DISABILITY: ECONOMIC COSTS AND INSURANCE PROTECTION

Chronic conditions reduce economic activities, and the consequence may be a reduction in income and in social networking efforts and opportunities. When these chronic conditions are a cause of the inability to perform one or more necessary occupational tasks, work hours and earnings are likely to be limited, and wage growth over a person's lifetime will be less than if work were not limited. The cost of disabling conditions to the older population is due to the effect of these conditions on earnings, as well as on the timing of earlier withdrawal from the labor force. Further, the economic constraints imposed by disability reduce the probability of medical intervention. Reductions in social contact that are often associated with chronic conditions may shut off the possibilities of nonpaid assistance and make the social rewards of beneficial lifestyle changes that could mitigate the risk and progress of these conditions less evident.

The economics of disability

By the broadest definitions of disability—being limited in an activity due to a chronic health condition—about 15 percent of the noninstitutionalized population in the United States is disabled. The disabled are on average less economically well off than the nondisabled. La-Plante et al. report that 27.3 percent of persons in families with incomes below $10,000 report some activity limitation, compared to only 9 percent of those in families with incomes of $35,000 or more. If disability is defined as the inability to perform a major life activity, the respective percentages are 10.6 and 1.8. The relationship between lower economic status and having at least one chronic condition is found at all ages, over time, and across nations Older individuals with at least one of the major chronic conditions (heart disease, depression, asthma, hearing loss, arthritis, diabetes) have lower incomes and fewer assets than comparably aged individuals without those conditions. (Alzheimer's disease, more highly correlated with age than other conditions, stands alone as a chronic condition whose incidence is not correlated with economic status.)

There are two possible, not mutually exclusive, explanations for the persistent relationship between disability and economic status. Chronic conditions that occur independently of economic status are likely to lead to lower income due to subsequent reductions in work and earnings, and the higher out-of-pocket costs for medical and physical care. Persons age sixteen to sixty-four with a work-related disability less likely than the nondisabled to be either working or looking for work. Those who work are more likely to work part-time and, even if they do work full-time, to have lower earnings (Kaye). On the other hand, low income may lead to a higher incidence of chronic conditions because limited resources reduce access to medical care, in part because of the inability to pay the out-of-pocket costs of care. Even preventive lifestyle changes (e.g., weight and cholesterol management through better diet, regular exercise regime, smoking cessation program) are less likely because these require resources and social support.

Chronic and Disabling Conditions, published by the National Academy for an Aging Society as part of its Public Policy and Aging Report series, documents three important aspects of chronic conditions that influence the relationship between disability and economic status later in life.

- Early life chronic conditions have subsequent effects on economic status because young persons with chronic conditions miss more school than their healthy peers, thus slowing their educational achievements and consuming parental resources that might otherwise be spent on children's education.
- The most prevalent chronic conditions among the older population (e.g., depression, asthma, hearing loss, and heart disease) can be managed effectively with medication, therapy, and changes in lifestyle. However, the lower social and economic support associated with these chronic conditions limits the ability to obtain appropriate treatment, and the earlier the onset, the more likely are they to slow the accumulation of financial resources to pay for medical care and necessary lifestyle changes.
- Caregiving at home disrupts employment and leisure activities of family members. It is estimated that U.S. businesses lose $33 billion a year due to lost productivity and absenteeism of caregivers. Adding to the time commitments of care are the out-of-pocket costs for care.

Work withdrawal by older disabled workers

Workforce withdrawal later in life due to a work-limiting disability may have different consequences for economic well-being in retirement than does retirement at the end of a relatively healthy work life. A chronic condition that had limited job opportunities and work performance for a large share of an individual's work life will lower earnings and savings, and increase probability of employment in a job not covered by a pension or health benefits. Thus individuals with lifelong disabilities are more likely to enter retirement with more limited resources compared to their nondisabled peers, and to be less financially protected against the unexpected risks in the retirement period. They are also more likely to leave the workforce earlier than their nondisabled peers. However, Haveman et al. (1999) show that individuals who first received Social Security disabled-workers benefits at age fifty-five or older have lower family income and assets than do their nondisabled peers, even as the latter entered the retirement. This difference is a consequence of their less favorable work histories and their consequent lower earnings-related retirement benefits, their lower likelihood of retirement employment, and the lower probability of being married (and having a second earner or pensioner).

Some disabled persons surely have such severe work limitations that they have few labor market "choices." However, for the majority of older workers with work-limiting conditions, the decision to continue paid labor force work will be determined in part by the financial advantage of continuing the work they are able to do, compared to receiving private or public benefits for which they are eligible. (For a fuller discussion on the labor market choice of men with disabilities, see Haveman et al. [1991], Haveman and Wolfe [1984], Bound [1989], and Leonard [1986].) These disability benefits may be linked to retirement benefits (e.g., from Social Security or employer-provided pensions). A work-related disability must be substantiated, however, and benefits may be received at an earlier age than allowed for receipt of retirement benefits. In making this choice, disabled workers assess the future trajectory of labor market opportunities and earnings, and compare this with the trajectory of income flows if they receive disability benefits. The lower market earnings because of a work-limiting disability and disability benefits that may

be structured to reduce the penalty for "early" retirement (often coupled with coverage by employer-provided or public-sector health plans) are theorized to encourage work withdrawal. There is evidence that for some older disabled workers, disability benefits do encourage early retirement (Haveman et al. 1988; Berkowitz).

Disability insurance: general policy features

Because chronic or sudden-onset health conditions are known to limit or prevent paid work, public and private disability programs are in place to provide income for persons who cannot work. Such programs typically provide benefits for disabled persons of all ages, but have an eligibility cap at an age when individuals are expected to rely on retirement-related savings and transfer programs.

Disability insurance that compensates for the loss in earnings due to a work-limiting disability may be obtained through the employer or through the private purchase of insurance, and is provided by the Social Security Administration to workers in covered employment. The eligibility of a person for disability payments depends on how the policy defines a compensable disability, whether there is a waiting period (or elimination period), and the benefit period.

A policy or program typically defines a compensable disability as total or partial and by the type of occupation whose performance the disability prevents. Benefits may be paid only after a waiting (or elimination) period, and the duration of payments may be limited. Work-related disability programs pay benefits based on prior wages, although the calculation of replacement varies across programs.

Disability is typically defined as the inability to perform occupational duties; that occupation may be specified as the insured's own occupation at the time of disablement, any occupation for which the insured is trained, or any gainful occupation. This distinction is critical to whether a person unable to perform his or her usual occupation is expected to seek other employment. The distinction between total and partial disability is important to the payment amount when a person is deemed eligible for disability payments. Total disability will qualify an individual for full payments, whereas partial disability, or the inability to perform one or more important tasks of a person's occupation, leads to a partial payment of disability benefits.

Policies typically have waiting periods during which benefits are not paid. A longer period reduces the costs of policies to the individual, employer, and (in the case of Social Security) society. It is also expected that employed individuals will have access to sick leave or other short-term disability benefits, or their own savings. In addition, policies limit the duration of benefits to either a specific number of years or to an age at which retirement benefits are expected to be accessed. Finally, disability programs, even those that require documentation that the disability is total and expected to be permanent, may require some type of rehabilitation or retraining.

The cost of disability policies to individuals and employers has risen substantially in recent years due to an increase in the number of claims, in part the result of the recognition that mental health and alcohol and drug problems are legitimate causes of work disability. This has changed the distribution of reported disabilities among disability income recipients and has led to changes in policy provisions that are likely to make disability policies more restrictive and more difficult for individuals to obtain.

Social Security disability insurance benefits

In 1956 legislation added disability insurance (SSDI) to the U.S. Social Security program. Benefits are calculated approximately like retired worker benefits, based upon average indexed monthly earnings over a period defined by the individual's year of disablement. Currently about 5 million individuals are SSDI beneficiaries, receiving an average of about $787 per month.

To be eligible for disability benefits, in general a person needs to have been employed in covered work for forty quarters, as is the case for retired-worker benefits. However, for disability benefits, twenty of those quarters must be earned in the 10-year period ending in the year in which the person became disabled, and younger workers may qualify with fewer quarters. Disability applications are considered up to age sixty-five, after which applicants are considered for retired-worker benefits. Persons who received disability benefits prior to age sixty-five are administratively converted to retired-worker status with no change in benefit amount. They are then subject to retired-worker benefit rules.

Eligibility for SSDI benefits requires total disablement—the inability to work either in the job performed prior to disability or in any other job the individual would be able to perform given his or her marketable skills. Disablement is determined either by a person having a listed medical condition that is considered so severe that it leads to automatic determination of eligibility or by a person's nonlisted condition being determined to be so severe as to prohibit employment in any work for which he or she is qualified. The disability must be expected to last at least one year. While disablement typically is medically determined, earnings of more the $780 a month (in 2002, adjusted annually by the average rise in wages) is evidence of a person's being able to work, and therefore not sufficiently disabled for SSDI benefits. This level of earnings is also considered evidence that a person already receiving SSDI no longer has a work-limiting disability. In order not to discourage reentry into the workforce by younger disabled persons, the SSDI program allows a period of earnings and continued Medicare coverage.

Disability benefits are based on average indexed monthly earnings (AIME), which are equal to total indexed covered earnings averaged over the number of years between 1956 or age twenty-five (whichever is later) and the year prior to the disablement. Average indexed monthly earnings are converted to a primary benefit amount using the same formula used for calculating the primary benefit amount for retired workers. There are several important distinctions between disabled-worker and retired-worker status. First, in calculating benefits, the earnings averaging period ends at the date of disablement, and thus can be of different length for persons of the same age. For retired workers, that period remains the same for individuals in the same birth cohort, regardless of date of retirement. Second, disabled-worker benefits are payable to individuals below age sixty-two, the minimum age of eligibility for retired-worker benefits. Third, individuals receiving disability benefits before age sixty-five are not assessed an early retirement penalty. Thus, a person applying for SSDI between ages sixty-two and sixty-four will not have his or her benefits lowered by the actuarial reduction that would be imposed for receipt of retired-worker benefits. Fourth, SSDI brings eligibility for Medicare at an age younger than sixty-five, the age at which retired-worker beneficiaries become eligible for Medicare.

Thus a worker who ceased paid work (voluntarily or involuntarily) at age fifty-five and applied for Social Security retirement benefits at age sixty-two would have an AIME calculated over a period that included seven years of zero earnings (between ages fifty-five and sixty-two) and a benefit that was reduced by 20 percent for early receipt. If the same worker were able to qualify for disability at age fifty-five, the averaging period would be reduced by those seven years, and no actuarial reduction would be imposed. Thus, older workers able to meet the Social Security disability criteria—which are somewhat relaxed at ages above fifty (Ycas)—may assess early SSDI application to be a better option than (1) later application for SSDI benefits or (2) delaying receipt until becoming eligible for retired-worker benefits.

Additional benefits are payable to the spouse, children, and survivors of disabled workers under eligibility rules identical to those for spouses, children, and survivors of retired workers. Benefits are payable to a spouse who is sixty-two or older (or at any age if he or she is caring for a child who is under age sixteen, or is disabled), although the spouse may receive only the higher benefit for which she or he is eligible from Social Security. Survivor benefits are payable at age sixty, although if the survivor is disabled, they may be received as early as age fifty. However, the disability must have started before the worker's death or within seven years after the death.

Employer-provided disability benefits

These programs can be divided into those which address short-term disability and long-term disability. Short-term disability coverage is most often paid sick leave. Although sick leave is a benefit widely offered by U.S. employers, duration of benefits is limited to the accumulated sick days. Some firms offer sickness and accident insurance, typically with a service requirement for eligibility.

Long-term disability coverage may be provided through separate disability policies or by provisions in an employer-sponsored pension plan. The Employee Benefit Research Institute (www.ebri.org) estimates that about one-third of U.S. workers are covered by long-term disability policies other than Social Security. This percentage has actually declined, as has the percentage of persons who are covered by pension plans that offer a disability benefit.

While these accounts are not necessarily linked to employment, early withdrawals without income tax penalty from Individual Retirement Accounts and 401(k) and 403(b) accounts are allowed when due to disability.

Health care cost coverage

Disability presents an additional disadvantage for security in retirement in that it is likely to be associated with extraordinary (compared to nondisabled individuals of the same age) medical care expenses and to require costly physical care that a nondisabled retiree does not face. If these additional expenses were incurred during working years but were not covered by health insurance, the individual's ability to save for retirement would have been further limited. When other family members provide unpaid services, these added responsibilities may reduce the caretaker's market earnings, and consequent savings that the disabled individual could share in retirement. Further, disabled workers not covered by employer-provided health insurance are forced into the individual insurance market, where coverage may be denied, premiums may be higher because of their greater health risks, or coverage may be limited by preexisting condition clauses.

Health insurance is important for the treatment and management of chronic conditions; its absence may contribute to the association between chronic conditions and economic status. SSDI beneficiaries are covered by Medicare following 24 consecutive months of benefit receipt. These individuals may purchase "Medigap" insurance, although out-of-pocket costs for these supplementary policies may limit purchase. Clearly, health insurance coverage is important to the treatment of chronic conditions, yet health insurance coverage is less likely among the disabled than among their healthy peers. Absence of coverage reduces the probability of effective treatment and management of work-limiting chronic conditions. Consider two of the most common chronic conditions among the elderly: arthritis, affecting almost half of all elderly people in the United States, and hearing loss, affecting 22 million people. Among persons between the ages of forty-five and sixty-four with arthritis, only 46 percent have private insurance, compared to 80 percent of those without arthritis. Hearing loss can be effectively treated with hearing aids, yet two out of three persons who are sixty-five or older and have hearing loss do not use hearing aids, in part a consequence of Medicare not covering hearing aids.

KAREN HOLDEN

See also AMERICANS WITH DISABILITIES ACT; EMPLOYMENT OF OLDER WORKERS; FUNCTIONAL ABILITY; JOB PERFORMANCE; RETIREMENT, DECISION MAKING; RISK MANAGEMENT AND INSURANCE; SOCIAL SECURITY, HISTORY AND OPERATIONS.

BIBLIOGRAPHY

BERKOWITZ, M. "Linking Beneficiaries with Return-to-Work Services." In *Disability: Challenges for Social Insurance, Health Care Financing and Labor Market Policy.* Edited by Virginia Reno, Jerry Mashaw, and Bill Gradison. Washington D.C.: National Academy of Social Insurance, 1997. Pages 41–83.

BOUND, J. "The Health and Earnings of Rejected Disability Insurance Applicants." *American Economic Review* 79, no. 3 (1989): 482–503.

HAVEMAN, R.; HOLDEN, K.; WOLFE, B.; SMITH, P.; and WILSON, KATHRYN. "The Changing Economic Status of U.S. Disabled Men: Trends and Their Determinants, 1982–1991." *Empirical Economics* 24 (1999): 571–598.

HAVEMAN, R., and WOLFE, B. "Disability Transfers and Early Retirement: A Causal Relationship?" *Journal of Public Economics* 24, (1984): 47–66.

HAVEMAN, R.; DE JONG, P.; and WOLFE, B. "Disability Transfers and the Work Decisions of Older Men." *Quarterly Journal of Economics* 106 (1991): 939–949.

HAVEMAN, R.; WARLICK, J.; and WOLFE, B. "Labor Market Behavior of Older Men: Estimates from a Trichotomous Choice Model." *Journal of Public Economics* 36 (1988): 153–175.

HOLDEN, K. "Chronic and Disabling Conditions: The Economic Costs to Individuals and Society." *Public Policy and Aging Report* 11, no. 2 (2001): 1–6.

KAYE, H. S. *Is the Status of People with Disabilities Improving? Disability Statistics.* Abstract no. 21. San Francisco: Disability Statistics Center, University of California at San Francisco, 1998. Also available at www.dsc.ucsf.edu/UCSF and www.ed.gov

LAPLANTE, M. P.; CARLSON, D. H.; KAYE, S.; and BRADSHER, J. E. *Families with Disabilities in the United States. Disability Statistics.* Report no. 8. San Francisco: Disability Statistics Center, University of California at San Francisco, 1996. Also available at www.dsc.ucsf.edu/UCSF

LEONARD, J. "Labor Supply Incentives and Disincentives for Disabled Persons." In *Disability and the Labor Market: Economic Problems, Policies, and Programs.* Edited by M. Berkowitz and M. A. Hill. Ithaca, N.Y.: Industrial and Labor Relations Press, 1986.

National Academy for an Aging Society. "Challenges for the 21st Century: Chronic and Disabling Conditions." www.agingsociety.org

YCAS, M. A. "Patterns of Return to Work in a Cohort of Disabled-Worker Beneficiaries." In *Disability, Work and Cash Benefits.* Edited by Jerry L. Marshaw. Kalamazoo, Mich.: W. E. Upjohn Institute for Employment Research, 1996.

DISEASE PRESENTATION

Much was learned in the twentieth century about disease and how it presents in children and adults. Traditional medical teaching emphasizes specific disease symptoms and signs that point to a specific diagnosis. However, in the last several decades it has become apparent that common diseases often present differently in older adults. This has lead to the concept of so-called atypical disease presentation in older adults. The exact prevalence of atypical disease presentation in the elderly is unclear in the medical literature but some researchers report that as many as 50 percent or more of older adults, particularly those who are frail, primarily present with disease atypically.

As people age, many bodily changes occur, but two have major consequences for disease presentation. The first is the inevitable alterations that occur within the various body systems that represent normal physiological changes of aging. Many are unavoidable and alone do not fully explain why older adults often present atypically. However, some of these changes certainly set the stage for increased susceptibility both to illness and to the way in which the disease presents itself. A classic example is alteration in thermoregulation with age, so that many older people do not have a fever when infected. Other examples are the increased risk for hyperthermia, hypothermia as well as dehydration due primarily to the changes in the body's ability to control body temperature and detect thirst. These normal consequences of aging coupled with concomitant disease and medications often together help set the stage for atypical disease presentations.

The second change that occurs with aging is related to the pathophysiological changes associated with aging, or the *accumulation of disease*. Many of the most common diseases that affect people increase in frequency and severity as the body ages. The likelihood of developing major diseases such as heart disease, diabetes, osteoporosis, stroke, and dementia all increase with age.

Another evolving concept that contributes to atypical disease presentations in older adults is the syndrome of frailty, understood as a vulnerable state arising from multiple interacting medical and social problems. The syndrome of frailty is critical to the understanding of disease presentation in the older adult. It is the frail elderly who most often present atypically.

Traditional disease presentation

Learning how disease presents in adults is the cornerstone of traditional teaching of those in the medical profession and other health care professionals. Health care practitioners learn that each disease has a specific set of signs and symptoms and are trained to sort through all of this information to come up with the most likely diagnosis for each set of signs and symptoms. Different diseases are classified and subsequently taught according to the different body systems and the symptom complexes in which they present. Scanning any medical textbook would confirm this method of organization, as each chapter usually deals with different body systems and the diseases that affect it.

Using this model of diagnosis would suggest that if an older adult is having difficulty walking, the health care professional would most likely assume that the causative disease should be related to the bones, muscles, or nerves that allow them to walk. In this scenario an accurate diagnosis of a broken hip may be made using traditional diagnostic approaches. However, in the older frail adult the diagnosis could as easily be heart failure or influenza as a broken hip. This emphasizes the importance of the need for an understanding of atypical disease symptoms in older adults, particularly those who are frail.

Atypical disease presentation

The concept of atypical disease presentation has been described by many in the literature. The phrase *geriatric giants* has long been recognized and taught in geriatric medicine and refers to the usual way in which disease presents itself in aging individuals. The commonly cited geriatric giants include *immobility*, *instabilty* (falls), *incontinence*, and *intellectual impairment*. These four syndromes are often the way in which disease presents itself. Other terms have also been used to describe the way older adults present with disease and these include *silent presentation* and *nonspecific presentation*.

Several studies conducted in the 1980s and 1990s have shown that atypical disease presentation may indeed be the most common type of disease presentation in the older adult. One study found that 36 percent of all elderly persons admitted to hospital presented atypically. When the population was stratified for frailty, 60 percent of those who were frail at the time of admission presented atypically, compared to 25 percent of those that were previously well. This emphasizes the interaction between frailty and atypical disease presentation.

Types of atypical disease presentation

The most common form of atypical disease presentation is with one or several of the geriatric giants listed above. It is important to recognize that one of the geriatric giants may be the presenting complaint but often many coexist. The key to recognizing the geriatric giants as a presentation of disease is to understand that a new appearance of a geriatric giant in an older individual is often a sign of a new illness. Likewise, a worsening of any of these giants equally signifies a problem worthy of assessment. Therefore, it is important to understand how an older person was functioning when they were well in order to notice the new onset of a geriatric giant or worsening of one.

Understanding an individual's level of function is key to understanding the importance of the geriatric giants for picking up disease in older adults. An older person may have difficulties getting around inside and outside their home due to underlying diseases such as osteoarthritis and require a walker. This may be their normal level of function. However, if this same individual is now unable to get up from bed and stand this should indicate that something is wrong and should be considered an atypical presentation of some disease (immobility).

Likewise, when an individual begins to fall (instability) for no apparent reason, the body may be saying that it is sick and this may be the way in which an acute illness is presenting. A new onset of incontinence (either urinary or fecal) is often a marker of an underlying recent illness that also deserves attention.

Acute confusion in an older person is nearly always associated with a new underlying illness. An illness presenting this way would be presenting as one of the geriatric giants-intellectual impairment. In medical terminology this is referred to as delirium, which is an acute change in cognition often associated with inattention. Dementia is also a cause for intellectual impairment but is chronic in nature and slowly progressive. Those with an underlying diagnosis of dementia are at increased risk of developing delirium if ill for any reason.

Any change in an individual's normal level of function requires consideration in order to rule out any possible new illness that may be contributing to the problem. It was found in one study that delirium was the most common form of an atypical disease presentation, being the presenting symptom in 50 percent of those presenting atypically. Falls and immobility combined accounted for 21 percent of the atypical presentations and nonspecific functional decline for another 20 percent.

Implications of atypical disease presentation

While atypical disease presentation may indeed be the norm for older frail adults presenting with disease, the implications of this type of presentation are less well understood. Those adults who present atypically tend to do worse in terms of adverse hospital outcomes, particularly in terms of admission to long-term care facilities following discharge from an acute care hospital. They are more often restrained in hospital, given nighttime sedation, and wind up with pressure ulcers than those who present typically. These older adults, particularly those who are frail, tend to have a poorer prognosis than those who present with typical disease symptoms.

Differential diagnosis of atypical disease presentations

The differential diagnosis of atypical disease presentations in older adults is as encompassing as the entire spectrum of medicine. Virtually any disease, either acute or the worsening of a chronic illness, may be the precipitating cause for any atypical disease presentation in an older adult. However, there are a few common illnesses that account for the majority of these cases. The more common illnesses to consider would be:

1. Infection (urinary, pneumonia, sepsis, other)
2. Ischemic heart disease (congestive heart failure, myocardial infarction, other)
3. Medications (alcohol, prescription and non-prescription)
4. Metabolic abnormalities (dehydration, electrolyte imbalance, other)

This is by no means meant to be an exhaustive list but will certainly assist in formulating a management plan for further assessment and subsequent treatment for these individuals. Investigations targeted to identify these common causes of disease in the elderly will yield positive results the majority of the time.

Management

The management of elderly patients who present with atypical disease presentations begins with initial recognition of their illness. All too often recognition that the person is sick goes unnoticed. It is not uncommon for health care providers, patients, and their families to attribute some of the symptoms as synonymous with aging, and they may not even seek medical attention. It is of paramount importance to recognize when illness is present and to seek medical attention. It is then the responsibility of the health care providers to recognize this call for help, investigate appropriately, and treat reversible causes.

It is important to target investigations in order to identify the most common cause for the atypical presentation of an illness. Simple investigations including blood work, cultures, and x-rays are often invaluable in pinpointing a cause. It is also important to review all medications that the individual is taking including prescription drugs, over-the-counter preparations, and alcohol use. Inquiring about compliance with medications is also prudent, because missing some medications or taking too many of an other can equally be the cause of the atypical disease presentation. Once the cause is found, appropriate medical management can proceed.

Of paramount importance in the treatment of older, frail adults, particularly in hospital, is appropriate treatment strategies to prevent further complications of hospitalization. It is well known that elderly adults, once hospitalized, are at increased risk of complications from both the treatment as well as bed rest. It is important to be cognizant of this and promote early mobilization, adequate nutrition, and appropriate maintenance of physical functioning to try to avoid these complications.

Conclusion

Atypical disease presentation in older adults is very common and in fact is the most common presentation of illness in the frail older adult. It is merely the body's way of indicating that it is unwell and that it requires attention and treatment. The underlying cause for these disease presentations is often a common medical problem such as infection, congestive heart failure, or medications (too much or too little). A comprehensive review of a person's medical history and functional history is required along with a detailed review of all medications. Targeted investigations will often reveal the underlying cause and treatment of this is often successful. However, older adults presenting with atypical disease presentations may have poorer health outcomes then those who present with typical disease symptoms. The understanding that disease presents differently in older adults is one of the main reasons why specialties such as geriatric medicine and geriatric psychiatry have evolved into the disciplines that they are today.

PAMELA G. JARRETT, M.D., F.R.C.P.C.

See also ASSESSMENT; BALANCE AND MOBILITY; DELIRIUM; EMERGENCY ROOM; FLUID BALANCE; FRAILTY; HEART DISEASE; PNEUMONIA; SWALLOWING; URINARY INCONTINENCE.

BIBLIOGRAPHY

BERMAN, P.; HOGAN, D. B.; and FOX, R. A. "The Atypical Presentation of Infection in Old Age." *Age and Aging* 16 (1987): 201–207.

EDDY, D. M., and CLANTON, CHARLES H. "The Art of Diagnosis." *New England Journal of Medicine* 306, no. 21 (1982): 1263–1268.

EMMETT, K. R. "Nonspecific and Atypical Presentation of Disease in the Older Patient." *Geriatrics* 53, no. 2 (1998): 50–60.

FRIED, L. P.; STORER, D. J.; KING, D. E.; and LODDER, F. "Diagnosis of Illness Presentation in the Elderly." *Journal of the American Geriatrics Society* 39 (1991): 117–123.

GRAHAM, J. E.; MITNITSKI, A. B.; MOGILNER, A. J.; and ROCKWOOD, K. "Dynamics of Cognitive Aging: Distinguishing Functional Age and Disease from Chronologic Age in a Population." *American Journal of Epidemiology* 150, no. 10 (1999): 1045–1054.

HAMERMAN, D. "Toward an Understanding of Frailty." *Annals of Internal Medicine* 130, no. 11 (1999): 945–948.

JARRETT, P. G.; ROCKWOOD, K.; CARVER, D.; STOLEE, P.; and COSWAY, S. "Illness Presentation in Elderly Patients." *Archives Internal Medicine* 155 (1995): 1060–1064.

LEVKOFF, S. E.; CLEARY, P. D.; WETLE, T.; and BESDINE, R. W. "Illness Behaviour in the Aged. Implications for Clinicians." *Journal of the American Geriatrics Society* 36 (1988): 622–629.

ROCKWOOD, K. "A Brief Clinical Instrument to Classify Frailty in Elderly People." *The Lancet* 353 (1999): 205–206.

ROCKWOOD, K. "Medical Management of Frailty: Confessions of a Gnostic." *Canadian Medical Association Journal* 157, no. 8 (1997): 1081–1084.

ROCKWOOD, K.; FOX, R. A.; STOLEE, P.; ROBERTSON, D.; and BEATTIE, N. L. "Frailty in Elderly People: An Evolving Concept." *Canadian Medical Association Journal* 150, no. 4 (1994): 489–495.

SAMIY, A. H. "Clinical Manifestations of Disease in the Elderly." *Medical Clinics of North America* 67, no. 2 (1983): 333–344.

TAFFET, G. E. "Age-Related Physiological Changes." In *Geriatric Review Syllabus*, 4th ed. Edited by E. L. Cobbs, E. H. Duthie, Jr., and J. B. Murphy. New York: Kendall/Hunt Publishing Company, 1999. Pages 10–22.

WINOGRAD, C. H.; GERETY, M. B.; CHUNG, M.; GOLDSTEIN, M. K.; DOMINGUEZ, F.; and VALLONE, R. "Screening for Frailty: Criteria and Predictors of Outcomes." *Journal of the American Geriatrics Society* 39 (1991): 778–784.

DISENGAGEMENT

The year 1961 was a watershed in the emergence of theory in the field of aging. That year saw the publication of Elaine Cumming and William Henry's book *Growing Old,* in which the term *disengagement* was introduced. This was the first time a distinct theory of aging emerged in scientific form, signaling the beginning of theoretical consciousness in social gerontology and setting the stage for the development of a range of alternative theoretical challenges.

Cumming and Henry described disengagement as "an inevitable mutual withdrawal . . . resulting in decreased interaction between the aging person and others in the social systems he belongs to." Their study was based on data generated from the Kansas City Study of Adult Life, wherein age comparisons of levels of various kinds of social involvement and ego investment, as well as attitudinal changes, provided evidence of the disengagement process. Informed by Talcott Parsons' social systemic theorizing, Cumming and Henry argued that aging could not be understood separately from the characteristics of the social system in which it is experienced. In turning to the social system for clues to the aging process, the authors explained a person's actions in terms of the ongoing operations of the system of which he or she is a part. For example, in modern societies, with the emphasis placed on standards of achievement and efficiency, the social system, in order to be a viable one, requires its work to be done effectively and expeditiously. Elderly persons, they argued, do not contribute to the system with the comparative efficiency of younger adults, and thus present a burden to it. The functional maintenance of social systems, therefore, requires some mechanism for systematically disengaging older persons from major life roles, roles critical to social system maintenance.

While people make decisions concerning their life course, the choices they make are normatively defined. By internalizing the norms and values of society (thus becoming fully socialized), the individual becomes part of the social order, carrying out the needs of the social system of which he or she is a part. The individual, in disengagement theory, in effect takes it as his or her obligation to disengage for the benefit of the social system. The extent to which one actualizes disengagement will determine how well one is adjusted or happy in old age. As Cumming and Henry state, "The factor with the greatest bearing on morale seems to be the ability to disengage" (p. 209).

The ultimate form of disengagement is death. As aging persons withdraw from more and more social roles, they come closer to a final preparation for separation from the social order. By gracefully removing oneself from society and making room for others, one is "free to die" (Cumming and Henry, p. 227), without disrupting the equilibrium of the system. Dying, therefore, is the final contribution one makes to societal functioning. Death, in time, sustains the ultimate efficiency of the social system.

Disengagement theory analyzes individual adjustment in old age by focusing on the needs and requirements of the social system. The process of disengagement is a gradual one, with continued withdrawal in later life being the hallmark of success. Cumming and Henry compared persons age eighty and over with those in their seventies; the former are described as more adjusted because of their greater degree of disengagement. Individuals, in effect, must aim toward becoming more and more "settled" in old age. To the extent this is achieved, society remains in a state of equilibrium. However, when the process fails—when persons remain engaged well into later life—it represents a dysfunctional infringement on system maintenance. These "late-life engagers" represent the problem of old age in disengagement theory. By disrupting "social necessity," they present a burden to system efficiency. As such, the system is responsible for either providing room for their quirks or forcing them to disengage along with others, who, by and large, typify disengagement. In the disengagement process, it is eventually system adjustments and readjustments that sustain the norm. In effect, the system's long-term equilibrating needs stand as its own system of adjustment.

Critical assessment of disengagement theory

Disengagement theory generated considerable controversy in the field of aging (see Hochschild, 1975, 1976, for a review of this debate). Activity theorists, especially the symbolic interactionists (e.g., Rose, 1964), referred to the idyllic, unreal qualities of the disengagement argument. They also brought to bear data showing that individuals resented forms of disengagement such as mandatory retirement and other age-related exclusionary policies. Furthermore, data were marshaled to show that older workers were not necessarily less efficient than younger ones.

Responding to the controversy, Cumming and Henry offered separate revisions of their theory. In her article entitled, "Further Thoughts on the Theory of Disengagement" (1963), Cumming reacted to the problem of differential adjustment or individual variations in the disengagement process by offering a psychobiological explanation for it. According to this approach, those who are temperamentally "impingers" are most likely to remain engaged, while "selectors" are most likely to disengage in later life. Aside from this amendment, the theory remains essentially the same. Henry's (1965) more extreme revision of disengagement theory practically abandons it in favor of a more expressly developmental perspective.

Arlie Hochschild (1975, 1976) also presented both a theoretical and empirical critique of Cumming and Henry's argument, addressing vaguely defined concepts and logical flaws in the approach. She summarized these as the "escape clause," "omnibus variable," and "assumption of meaning" problems. The "escape clause" refers to the fact that the theory is unfalsifiable. Hochschild presented evidence, obtained from Cumming and Henry's own data, showing that a significant proportion of elderly persons do not systematically withdraw from society. Yet, Hochschild pointed out, Cumming and Henry's descriptions of these kinds of older people as being "unsuccessful" adjusters to old age, "off time" disengagers, or members of "a biological and possibly psychological elite" (Hochschild, 1975, p. 555) provide a means for "explaining" virtually any type of continued engagement in later life, making the theory impossible to refute empirically.

The "omnibus variable" problem refers to the over-inclusiveness of the variables *age* and *disengagement* in Cumming and Henry's approach. Hochschild described age and disengagement as "'umbrella' variables that crowd together, under single titles, many distinct phenomena." For example, while an elderly person may experience disengagement from former work associates, he or she may, at the same time, be more community-involved, church-centered, or family-oriented. Hochschild argued that the use of these two variables to explain adjustment in old age ignores the diverse and complex processes involved in growing older.

The "assumption of meaning" problem refers to the theory's preference for inferring compliance from behavior. Cumming and Henry argued that elderly individuals willingly withdraw from society; yet, they did not provide data to adequately address this issue. For Hochschild, "What is missing is evidence about the *meaning* of the daily acts that constitute engagement or disengagement" (1976, p. 66).

The disengagement approach also has been criticized for ignoring the impact of social class

on aging experiences. Laura Olson (1982) argued, for example, that the theory's "free-market conservative" view leaves unquestioned how the class structure and its social relationships prevent the majority of older people from enjoying a variety of opportunities or advantages. Disengagement theory precludes virtually any type of social conflict. Indeed, when one confronts his or her society or has some self-investment in it, he or she is considered to be maladjusted, a form of deviance from this perspective.

Cumming and Henry's social systemic theorizing painted a very deterministic picture of human behavior. Their approach ultimately depicts the individual as being fused with society, becoming what Alvin Gouldner (1970) called an "eager tool" of the system. Lacking the freedom to act "on their own," persons exist within the system only by virtue of carrying out behavior that is normatively prescribed. There is no sense, from this point of view, that persons can recognize their own interests as members of society. What they do recognize is the realization of an internal social program that moves them along. And, since it's the systematically normative movement of members that disengagement theory is concerned with, individual aging experiences disappear altogether. The details, the circumstantial contingencies, and the variety of ongoing situations, wherein persons experience their social lives, are treated as nuances on common systemic themes. Thus, we're left with little understanding of how members of a social system grow older in it, except for a very general conception of socialization.

Despite the limitations of disengagement theory, it has had a profound effect on the field of aging. Its emergence marked the first time formal theoretical concerns had gained the attention of gerontologists. This set the stage for the development of a number of alternative theoretical viewpoints, including exchange theory, subculture theory, the age stratification approach, modernization theory, and the political economy perspective. Disengagement theory continues to influence research that examines the place of older adults in society at large (e.g., Johnson and Barer, 1992; Tornstam, 1989; Uhlenberg, 1988).

PATRICIA PASSUTH LYNOTT
ROBERT J. LYNOTT

See also LIFE COURSE; PRODUCTIVE AGING; THEORIES, SOCIAL.

BIBLIOGRAPHY

CUMMING, E. "Further Thoughts on the Theory of Disengagement." *International Social Science Journal* 15, no. 3 (1963): 377–393.

CUMMING, E., and HENRY, W. E. *Growing Old: The Process of Disengagement.* New York: Basic Books, 1961.

GOULDNER, A. W. *The Coming Crisis of Western Sociology.* New York: Basic Books, 1970.

HENRY, W. E. "Engagement and Disengagement: Toward a Theory of Adult Development." In *Contributions to the Psychobiology of Aging.* Edited by R. Kastenbaum. New York: Springer, 1965. Pages 19–35.

HOCHSCHILD, A. R. "Disengagement Theory: A Critique and Proposal." *American Sociological Review* 40, no. 5 (1975): 553–569.

HOCHSCHILD, A. R. "Disengagement Theory: A Logical, Empirical, and Phenomenological Critique." In *Time, Roles, and Self in Old Age.* Edited by J. F. Gubrium. New York: Human Sciences Press, 1976. Pages 53–87.

JOHNSON, C. L., and BARER, BARBARA M. "Patterns of Engagement and Disengagement among the Oldest-Old." *Journal of Aging Studies* 6, no. 4 (1992): 351–364.

LYNOTT, R. J., and LYNOTT, P. P. "Tracing the Course of Theoretical Development in the Sociology of Aging." *The Gerontologist* 36, no. 6 (1996): 749–760.

OLSON, L. K. *The Political Economy of Aging: The State, Private Power, and Social Welfare.* New York: Columbia University Press, 1982.

PARSONS, T. *The Social System.* New York: Free Press, 1951.

PASSUTH, P. M., and BENGTSON, VERN L. "Sociological Theories of Aging: Current Perspectives and Future Directions." In *Emergent Theories of Aging.* Edited by J. E. Birren and V. L. Bengtson. New York: Springer, 1988. Pages 333–355.

ROSE, A. M. "A Current Theoretical Issue in Social Gerontology." *The Gerontologist* 4, no. 1 (1964): 46-50.

TORNSTAM, L. "Gero-Transcendence: A Reformulation of the Disengagement Theory." *Aging: Clinical and Experimental Research* 1, no. 1 (1989): 55–63.

UHLENBERG, P. "Aging and the Societal Significance of Cohorts." In *Emergent Theories of Aging.* Edited by J. E. Birren and V. L. Bengtson. New York: Springer, 1988. Pages 405–425.

DIVORCE: ECONOMIC ISSUES

Divorce is a major stage in life for large numbers of older men and women in the United States (and many other countries). For example, in the United States in 2000, there were more than a million women over the age of sixty-two who were either divorced or separated. Until now this group of women has been relatively invisible within the elderly population.

Difficult as it is to believe, few statistics have been published on divorced older persons and their economic situation. It is common practice in statistical tabulations published by the U.S. Bureau of the Census to combine divorced persons with those who "never married" and/or those who are "widowed." The result is that we know relatively little about this important subgroup of the elderly population. Yet this group is destined to become much more important in years to come, given the fact that divorce rates in the United States have soared to record high levels.

The economic well-being of many older persons has improved over the years. At the same time, there has been increasing concern about those elderly persons whose economic situation remains poor. Numerous studies have documented that poverty among older persons is increasingly concentrated among older women and minorities. Also, there is growing agreement among researchers and policymakers that more attention must be given to understanding why poverty persists among these groups and the feasibility of alternative policies that would effectively respond to the problems.

The economic situation of divorced older women

Overall, the income situation of older divorced women is not very good. Many are poor, and most of the rest have very low incomes. For example, survey data for 1998 indicate that almost one-quarter of older divorced women had yearly total incomes below the poverty line (Social Security Administration).

There are also large differences in the sources of income by poor and nonpoor divorced older women. The poor women receive almost al of their income (86 percent) from Social Security programs. In contrast, income form work, employer-sponsored pensions, and interest plays a much more important role for those with incomes above the poverty level.

Table 1
Poverty among Older Women Age 45 or Over in 1989

	Age 45-61	Age 62-74	Age 75+	All
Married	5%	5%	9%	6%
Widowed	22	16	21	19
Never Married	24	17	22	19
Divorced	17	23	28	24
Separated	36	38	NA	42

NA = Not available due to insufficient sample size

SOURCE: Crown, W. H.; Mutschler, P.; Schultz, J. H.; and Loew, R. *The Economic Status of Divorced Older Women.* Waltham, Mass.: Policy Center on Aging, Heller Graduate School, Brandeis University, 1993.

A team of researchers at Brandeis University (including this author) focused on the economic situation of older divorced women in the late 1980s. It is widely known that the rate of poverty among all older women is very high, and much higher than for older men. Among older women, however, poverty rates vary greatly. Table 1 shows the 1989 rates for various subgroups of older women. It indicates that, based on a national sample of the U.S. population, poverty rates are significantly higher for women who are divorced or separated than for the other subgroups of older women. If the divorced group is broken down further by ethnic status (not shown in the table), the poverty rates in that year were even higher for minority women: 43 percent for Latino and 46 percent for nonwhite divorced older women.

What about the future?

Social Security benefits are a basic source of income at later ages for most Americans. The federal government's Social Security Administration, in conjunction with several nonprofit research institutions (the Brookings Institution, the Urban Institute, and the RAND Corporation), has developed a projection model to estimate future differences in Social Security benefits by marital status. The model focuses on men and women born between 1931 and 1960.

Not surprisingly, the Social Security model projects that total income at retirement will be larger for men that for women, regardless of when they were born. However, Social Security benefits are projected to differ greatly for men and women of different races, marital statuses, and educational attainments. Women are projected to receive the largest share of their total income from Social Security benefits. And looking only at older divorced persons, the model estimates that divorced men will receive 12 to 17 percent higher monthly Social Security benefits than divorced women.

Two key developments

Two developments over recent years help to explain those projections, which will have an important impact on the economic situation of divorced persons:

- Changes in the divorce laws with regard to the switch in most states to "no fault" divorce (especially regarding alimony and child support payments) have important implications for the economic welfare of divorced women in their later years.
- As employer-sponsored pensions grow in importance as a source of retirement income, older women are likely to be in an increasingly disadvantaged position if current practices and laws do not change.

The "divorce revolution" was launched in 1970, the year that California passed no-fault divorce legislation. No-fault divorce laws have shifted the focus of the legal process from moral questions of fault and responsibility to economic issues of ability to pay and financial need. Ironically, although divorce reform was not intended to create fewer equitable settlements for women, in many cases that has been their precise effect. The no-fault divorce laws promised the abolition of all sexist, gender-based rules that failed to treat wives as equals in the marital partnership. However, a problem arises when the legal system ignores the very real economic inequalities that still exist between women and men in the larger society. Those inequalities are largely a function of the primary responsibility still assigned to women for the care of their husbands, children, and frail elders. The economic discrepancies between the sexes also reflect society's hesitancy to assign a monetary value to women's domestic work. Thus, by treating women and men "equally" at divorce, the legal system largely ignores the very real economic inequalities that marriage creates as a result of the division of labor within marriage.

The no-fault standards for alimony and property awards may be shaping radically different economic futures for divorced men and women. However, research to date on this issue is inconclusive. While some research indicates that the resulting financial situation of women under no-fault settlements is worse than for men, the study reported by Jacob concluded that the effects of no-fault divorce legislation on the economic status of divorced women may be neutral or even positive.

The second new factor affecting women is the evolution of pensions in the workplace. Employer-sponsored pensions play an increasingly important role in providing adequate retirement incomes for significant numbers of Americans. However, data show that large numbers of divorced women will not be covered by these plans, either through their own work or based on the pension plans of their former spouses. For example, in 1998 only 22 percent of unmarried women over the age of 64 received a private pension, compared with 31 percent of all aged units (Social Security Administration).

This situation is likely to have important financial consequences if it continues. Today pension accruals for many workers represent substantial personal wealth. This results primarily from growth since the 1960s in pension plan coverage and improvements in both pension benefit levels and vesting provisions (i.e., the years of service required before the worker obtains a legal right to his or her benefit).

Such accruals have become the subject of greater attention from attorneys and the courts, especially with regard to the question of a spouse's financial interests in pension wealth upon the dissolution of a marriage. How spousal rights to pensions are treated legally depends to a large extent on whether a particular state embraces community-poverty rules for a husband and wife, subscribes to common-law rules modified by the adoption of the Universal Dissolution of Marriage Act, or accepts the pure common-law concept of the property of husband and wife. For instance, in pure common-law jurisdictions, separate property remains such upon a marriage dissolution, and only jointly held property is divided and distributed. In New York (a common-law state), for example, pension benefits or expectations would normally be classified as separate property, and therefore no subject to distribution on divorce. In contrast, in the California case of *Smith* v. *Lewis* (California is a community-property state), a wife successfully sued her divorce attorney for malpractice because he neglected her interest in her husband's pension.

Social Security provisions relating to divorce

The Social Security program provides more than twelve different types of benefits—each with its own unique set of eligibility rules and often with different benefits structures. To understand the different benefits provided by the program, it is useful first to distinguish the difference between primary and secondary beneficiaries. A primary beneficiary is a person who receives a benefit based on his or her own work in Social Security-covered employment. In contrast, a secondary beneficiary is a person who receives a benefit because of his or her relationship to a retired worker, a disabled worker, a deceased insured person, or an insured ex-spouse not yet receiving benefits.

One group of secondary beneficiaries relates to spouses: the aged spouse benefit, the child in care spouse benefit, and the divorced spouse benefit. Regarding the last, someone who is sixty-two years old (or older) and was married to a person for ten or more years is eligible to receive a divorced spouse benefit if he or she is divorced from that person and the person is a retired or disabled worker or is a living insured person sixty-two years old or older.

Another type of eligibility arises from being the survivor of a deceased insured person. A divorced person who is at least sixty years old and whose ex-spouse is deceased is eligible to receive a surviving divorced spouse benefit if the marriage to the ex-spouse lasted ten years or more. In addition, divorced persons who survive their ex-spouses can qualify for child in care benefits or disabled survivor benefits.

The amount paid to a secondary depends on a complex calculation of lifetime average earnings, determining what is called the "primary insurance amount" (PIA). The PIA is calculated from the lifetime earnings record of either the retired/disabled person or the insured person. The benefit amount of an aged spouse or a divorced spouse retiring at the "normal retirement age" (currently age sixty-five but scheduled to rise gradually to age sixty-seven) is equal to 50 percent of the calculated PIA. Thus, generally the worker receives an amount twice as large as the worker's spouse or ex-spouse. However, an aged widow(er) or a surviving divorced spouse can receive a benefit equal to 100 percent of the PIA if the benefit received at the "normal retirement age." All benefits before the "normal retirement age" (regardless of marital status) are reduced on the basis of actuarial calculations using estimates of average life expectancy at any particular "early retirement age."

To receive secondary benefits, a person cannot be married to a new partner. A new marriage generally makes a person ineligible to receive, for example, a divorced spouse benefit. Also, a remarried person cannot collect a surviving divorced spouse benefit (unless his or her current marriage occurred after the age of sixty).

Another complexity of the benefit calculation arises when the divorced person is also eligible for a primary benefit, that is, a benefit based on his/her own work history. When a person's primary benefit exceeds his or her secondary benefit, only the primary benefit is paid. Thus, most aged women who are divorced do not receive divorced spouse benefits because of their own work history that entitles them to higher primary benefits. However, the benefit determination is not either-or decision. In many cases a person may receive both a primary benefit and part of a secondary benefit. The primary benefit is paid in full but, if relatively small, is supplemented by the spouse benefit up to the amount the person would have received as a spouse without any work history. And if an individual is eligible for two or more secondary benefits, generally only the highest secondary benefit is paid. Thus, the general operative principle is that an individual cannot pyramid benefits based on two or more eligibility statuses but can receive only a (combination of) benefits(s) equal to the largest of the eligible benefits.

Employer-sponsored pensions and divorce

As indicated above, an employer-sponsored pension is often an important asset that becomes part of the discussions that occur with regard to the disposition of marital property during a divorce. The federal Retirement Equity Act of 1984 provides for the issuance of a "qualified domestic relations order" that can be used by a court to split a pension benefit or account between divorcing spouses, effectively dividing the pension without the need to place a monetary value on it.

There are situations, however, where a division of the pension equally between both parties in a divorce may not be in their best interests. In some cases, for example, other assets within the marriage cannot be easily split (such as a home, trusts, or other real property). In these cases it may be best to determine the monetary value of a future pension benefit so that it may be offset against the value of other marital property.

In the case of "defined contribution" pension plans, the value of benefits accruing to a particular worker can be determined quite easily. Defined contribution plans establish separate accounts for each worker that are valued periodically—often daily.

The benefits of "defined benefit" pension plans cannot be valued so easily, and the benefits generally cannot be assigned or transferred to some other person. There are nearly forty-two million working men and women in about fifty-five thousand, private-sector defined benefit pension plans. The most distinguishing characteristic of these plans is that they promise to deliver a clearly specified (i.e., defined) benefit amount based on a formula that typically relates the worker's benefit to years of service and (somewhat less frequently) to the earnings level of the worker. Thus, the value of these pensions in the future depends on the evolving work history of each worker and any changes in the benefit promise made by the employer in future years. This means that in the case of divorce, it is not a straightforward exercise to place a lump-sum monetary value on defined benefit plan assets held by a worker at any moment in time.

Possible Social Security changes

It is often suggested that Social Security benefits paid to divorced spouses are two low. The 50 percent of the ex-spouse's Social Security PIA received by many divorced spouses is typically below the poverty index used by the federal government to assess income adequacy. Thus it has been suggested, for example, that the divorced spouse benefit be increased to, say 75 percent of the PIA. This would bring the benefit level roughly into line with the levels received by other beneficiary groups composed primarily of unmarried women (e.g., disabled widows and child in care widows). However, this benefit level would still be below the regular widow's benefit of 100 percent of the PIA.

Some people fear that raising divorce benefit levels will encourage divorce relative to the current law. Such a reform, however, is unlikely to have a significant effect on young or middle-aged persons who are not apt to be thinking about their retirement years when divorce is considered. Even at later ages, however, such a change is unlikely to have a major effect, given the many other considerations that go into such decisions.

With a continuing focus on federal budgetary matters and the possible "privatization" of Social Security benefits, benefit level reform has received little political attention. Because of this and the lack of information, it is not likely that the economic issues related to divorce and its impact in old age will be addressed in the near future.

JAMES H. SCHULZ

See also DIVORCE: TRENDS AND CONSEQUENCES; MARRIAGE AND REMARRIAGE; PENSIONS; SOCIAL SECURITY; WIDOWHOOD: ECONOMIC ISSUES.

BIBLIOGRAPHY

CHOUDHURY, S., and LEONESIO, M. V.. "Life-Cycle Aspects of Poverty among Older Women." *Social Security Bulletin* 60, no. 2 (1997): 17–36.

JACOB, H. "Another Look at No-Fault Divorce and the Post-Divorce Finances of Women." *Law and Society Review* 23, no. 1 (1989): 95–115.

MOSS, A. *Your Pension Rights at Divorce*. Washington, D.C.: Pension Rights Center, 1991.

SCHULZ, J. H. *The Economics of Aging*, 7th ed. New York: Auburn House, 2000.

Social Security Administration. *Income of the Population 55 or Older, 1998*. Available at www.ssa.gov/statistics

DIVORCE: TRENDS AND CONSEQUENCES

Divorce is the voluntary, legal termination of a marriage. To understand how divorce influences the aging experience, a life-course perspective is particularly informative. A major tenet of this approach is that history shapes an individual's life experience. In terms of divorce, this is certainly true, as documented by the variations in divorce statistics by historic period and birth cohort. The life-course perspective also contends that the timing of life transitions influences how they are experienced. Thus, divorcing in early adulthood is likely to constitute a very different experience than divorcing later in life. Young and old adults face different developmental challenges, and they differ in the types and amount of resources they possess for dealing with life changes like divorce.

Even when divorce occurs in early adulthood, it can affect one's later years. This may occur as a result of individuals divorcing in their twenties, thirties, or forties, and then remaining divorced throughout their lives. Timothy Brubaker has labeled these persons the *career divorced*, and, as a result of declining remarriage rates, their numbers are growing (see Uhlenberg, Cooney, & Boyd). However, even for those who remarry, divorce may have a cumulative and lasting impact, as some consequences of divorce are not easily reversed. The life-course perspective emphasizes how events such as divorce differ in their impact depending on the life experiences that preceded them. Finally, this perspective considers individuals within their family and social systems. Because of family interdependencies, individuals may be affected by events such as divorce even when they occur to someone other than themselves. These principles of the life-course perspective shed light on the interplay of aging and divorce.

Divorcing in middle and late life

Although most divorces occur in early adulthood to couples whose marriages have lasted less than a decade, divorcing is not unheard of in the second half of life. According to the National Center for Health Statistics, 12 percent of divorces granted in 1988 in the United States involved persons in marriages of over twenty years duration. About one-third of the half-million divorces granted that year were to men age forty and over, and 25 percent involved women in midlife or beyond. After age sixty-five, only two out of one thousand married men are likely to divorce in a given year, and fewer than two of every one thousand women age sixty-five and over divorce.

Yet, many more middle-aged and older adults divorce in early adulthood and reach later life in that status. Between 12 and 18 percent of individuals between forty-five and sixty-four years old reported their marital status as divorced in 1998 (depending on sex and age). In addition, 6.1 percent of men and 7.1 percent of women age sixty-five and older were divorced.

This compares to 3.6 percent of older men and 3.4 percent of older women were divorced in 1980. The rapid growth in the rate of divorce for older adults has led demographers to project that the likelihood of divorce may be as high as 11 to 18 percent for baby boomers who reach midlife (age 40) in an intact first marriage.

What leads couples to divorce in later life, after many years of marriage? A 1970s Canadian study of over two hundred individuals divorcing after twenty or more years of marriage found that adultery, alcoholism, and incompatibility were frequently given as causes. In this sample, 75 percent of the middle-aged and older adults noted long-term marital unhappiness, and about half claimed to have postponed divorce until their children were adults. Research done in the 1990s comparing predictors of divorce for persons of different marital durations indicated that personality factors (e.g., neuroticism, disagreeableness) were not linked to a heightened risk of later-life divorce, although they predicted divorce earlier in marriage. Thus, situational factors and incompatibility appear more predictive of divorce in later life than individual personality factors.

The impact of a recent midlife or later-life divorce on individual well-being varies by gender. One study of individuals age fifty and over who had ended long-term marriages found that women reported more feelings of guilt, confusion, anger, avoidance, and helplessness, postdivorce, than did men. Compared to widows, however, neither sex appeared markedly disadvantaged emotionally or psychologically. Similarly, Walter Gove and Hee-Cheen Shin (1989) found that the only significant difference in adjustment between divorced and widowed women was that the former felt more "trapped" after marital disruption; while divorced men actually reported better adjustment than widowed men. Studies also indicate that the effects of divorce on emotional adjustment are no worse for persons divorcing in middle or late life than those ending marriages voluntarily in younger adulthood. In fact, a longitudinal study conducted in the 1990s revealed positive outcomes for women divorcing in midlife. Paul Costa and Ilene Siegler (1999) found that women who divorced between ages forty and forty-nine became more active and outgoing, whereas men in this age range who divorced exhibited reductions in their sociability and achievement strivings. According to the life-course perspective, role experiences in marriage may shed some light on these outcomes. A positive adjustment to divorce could be explained by considering the distress experienced by persons in their in marital role prior to divorce. For example, women who are able to escape an abusive marriage after years of violence may have fewer physical and psychological symptoms after divorce.

Personal well-being following divorce also depends on social support, with some types of support being more helpful than others. Having a confidant who provides emotional and social support has been linked to reduced depression following divorce, while receiving material support can have a negative psychological effect. In addition, specific sources of support may vary based on age and gender. Middle-aged and older adults who divorce may not consider their parents as useful sources of help, while offspring may be more significant sources of support for this age group. In Carol Wright and Joseph Maxwell's 1991 study of persons divorcing after an average of twenty-eight years of marriage, women were more likely than men to rank grown children as the most helpful source of support. They received more advice, services, and financial, social, and emotional support from offspring than did men. In contrast, friends and parents reportedly provided more support than offspring to men.

The fact that adult offspring are more available to and supportive of their mothers than their fathers following later-life divorce is consistent with findings regarding relations between adult children and parents who have divorced years earlier. Both Teresa Cooney (1994) and William Aquilino (1994) reported that when the parents of young adults divorced after long-term marriages, rates of intergenerational visitation and contact were significantly reduced, especially with fathers, compared to rates for still-married parents and their adult children. Divorce also seems to result in a more voluntary relationship between adult children and parents. In divorced families, contact between young adults and their parents was associated with the younger generation's feelings of closeness to parents, whereas contact appeared to be motivated by something other than, or in addition to, affection, perhaps obligation, in families with married parents. Aquilino also found that older, recently divorced parents provide less emotional, practical, and financial support to their sons (but not their daughters) than parents who are still married.

The career divorced

Divorce early in adulthood has been linked to both advantages and disadvantages in later life. Some outcomes associated with divorce have cumulative, negative effects, so that, as time passes, the disadvantages precipitated by the divorce actually increase—or at least are not relieved. For example, the economic setback many women experience with divorce may not be dramatically reversed unless they remarry.

Similarly, the effects of earlier divorce on family relations can be especially enduring. As with recent divorce, both career divorce and earlier divorce followed by remarriage result in poorer quality relations between older parents and their adult offspring. Previously divorced parents, especially fathers, have less contact with their adult offspring than married parents, with reductions in interaction being particularly strong for those who divorced when their children were very young. Regarding affective relations, adults whose parents have divorced feel less loved and listened to by their older fathers than those with continuously married parents. Reduced contact and affection also translate into reduced support for aging parents who have divorced at some point in adulthood, as older men who have been divorced perceived significantly less potential support from their adult offspring than do continuously married men. Adults in general, however, believe offspring bear some responsibility for the care of their aging parents, even when parents have divorced. But most people consider the level of responsibility to be highly contingent on the parents' contact and commitment to their children over the preceding years. Support to aging parents, therefore, may be seriously jeopardized by divorce, especially when marital disruption occurred relatively early and substantially altered the ongoing relationship between parent and child.

Divorcing in earlier adulthood has been shown to have some long-term positive consequences for older adults. By coping with the divorce transition during one's earlier years, some individuals appear to gain important survival skills and character strengths that pay off in late life. One study found that women who had experienced divorce early in their life course demonstrated better adjustment to widowhood after age sixty. These previously divorced older women were more self-sufficient, and they adapted to the widowhood transition more effectively than did continuously married women.

Effects of divorce in the family system

Because older adults are heavily involved in exchange relationships with members of their families, divorce may affect their lives even when it occurs to someone else in the family. Colleen Johnson (1988) reported that two-thirds of the adults she studied turned to aged parents for instrumental support, especially childcare and other services, following divorce. In addition, emotional support and practical advice are frequently offered. According to Raeann Hamon (1995), however, older parents struggle with finding a balance between offering support and avoiding interference in their children's postdivorce lives.

The grandparent-grandchild relationship also is subject to dramatic change when adult offspring divorce. Whether these relationships are intensified or weakened clearly depends on the custodial status of the divorcing offspring. Because mothers still maintain primary custody of children in the majority of divorces, maternal grandparents often experience heightened involvement with their grandchildren following an adult child's divorce. This intensified grandparental role typically results from the increase in assistance they are providing to the single, custodial mother (their daughter). In contrast, paternal grandparents are often delegated to a more distant position, characterized by ritualistic contact on special occasions.

Finally, the flow of support to aging parents may be threatened by the divorce of adult offspring. As grown children experience greater vulnerability and need during and after their divorces, they may be less able to assist the older generation. In addition, the reduction in involvement with former children-in-law may reduce the size of the potential support system for older adults.

TERESA M. COONEY
JEONG SHIN AN

See also DIVORCE: ECONOMIC ISSUES; LIFE COURSE; MARRIAGE AND REMARRIAGE; PARENT-CHILD RELATIONSHIP.

BIBLIOGRAPHY

AQUILINO, W. S. "Later Life Parental Divorce and Widowhood: Impact on Young Adults' Assessment of Parent-Child Relations." *Journal of Marriage and the Family* 56 (1994): 908–922.

BULCROFT, K. A., and BULCROFT, R. A. "The Timing of Divorce: Effects on Parent-Child

Relationships in Later Life." *Research on Aging* 13 (1991): 226–243.

CHERLIN, A. J., and FURSTERNBERG, F. F., JR. *The New American Grandparent*. New York: Basic Books, 1986.

COONEY, T. M. "Young Adults' Relations with Parents: The Influence of Recent Parental Divorce." *Journal of Marriage and the Family* 56 (1994): 45–56.

COONEY, T. M., and UHLENBERG, P. "The Role of Divorce in Men's Relations with Their Adult Children after Midlife." *Journal of Marriage and the Family* 52 (1990): 677–688.

COSTA, P., and SIEGLER, I. "Why Women Fare Better than Men After Middle-Age Divorce." *Jet* 96 (1999): 46–47.

DECKERT, P., and LANGELIER, R. "The Late-Divorce Phenomenon: The Causes and Impact of Ending 20-Year-Old or Longer Marriages." *Journal of Divorce* 1 (1978): 381–390.

FARNSWORTH, J.; PETT, M. A.; and LUND, D. A. "Predictors of Loss Management and Well-Being in Later Life Widowhood and Divorce." *Journal of Family Issues* 10 (1989): 102–121.

GANONG, L. H., and COLEMAN, M. *Changing Families, Changing Responsibilities*. Mahwah, N.J.: Lawrence Erlbaum Associates, 1999.

GOVE, W. R., and SHIN, H.-C. "The Psychological Well-Being of Divorced and Widowed Men and Women." *Journal of Family Issues* 10 (1989): 122–144.

HAMON, R. R. "Parents as Resources When Adult Children Divorce." *Journal of Divorce and Remarriage* 23 (1995): 171–183.

JOHNSON, C. L. "Postdivorce Reorganization of Relationships Between Divorcing Children and Their Parents." *Journal of Marriage and the Family* 50 (1988): 221–231.

MILLER, N. B.; SMERGLIA, V. L.; GAUDET, D. S.; and KITSON, G. C. "Stressful Life Events, Social Support, and the Distress of Widowed and Divorced Women." *Journal of Family Issues* 19 (1998): 181–203.

National Center for Health Statistics. "Advanced Report of Final Divorce Statistics, 1988." *Monthly Vital Statistics Report* 39, no. 12, Supplement (1991).

O'BRYANT, S. L., and STRAW, L. B. "Relationship of Previous Divorce and Previous Widowhood to Older Women's Adjustment to Recent Widowhood." *Journal of Divorce and Remarriage* 15 (1991): 46–67.

SMYER, M. A., and HOFLAND, B. F. "Divorce and Family Support in Late Life: Emerging Concerns." *Journal of Family Issues* 3 (1982): 61–77.

TUCKER, J. S.; KRESSIN, N. R.; SPIRO, A., III; and RUSCIO, J. "Intrapersonal Characteristics and

The Timing of Divorce: A Prospective Investigation." *Journal of Social and Personal Relationships* 15 (1998): 211–225.

UHLENBERG, P.; COONEY, T.; and BOYD, R. "Divorce for Women After Midlife." *Journal of Gerontology: Social Sciences* 45 (1990): S3–S11.

U.S. Census Bureau. *Statistical Abstract of United States*, 119th ed. Washington, D.C.: U.S. Government Printing Office, 1999.

WEBSTER, P. S., and HERZOG, A. R. "Effects of Parental Divorce and Memories of Family Problems on Relationships Between Adult Children and Their Parents." *Journal of Gerontology: Social Sciences* 50 (1995): S24–S34.

WRIGHT, C. L., and MAXWELL, J. W. "Social Support During Adjustment to Later-Life Divorce: How Adult Children Help Parents." *Journal of Divorce and Remarriage* 15 (1991): 21–48.

DIZZINESS

Dizziness is a common medical problem. Thirty percent of people over age sixty-five complain of dizziness and 20 percent of all older persons experience dizziness severe enough to seek medical advice.

The syndrome of dizziness is varied and encompasses a wide range of symptoms. Getting a precise and accurate description of the individual's symptoms is therefore essential for making an accurate diagnosis and helps to differentiate between the four medical subtypes traditionally considered to be the most common causes of dizziness: vertigo, presyncope, dysequilibrium, and light-headedness.

Causes of dizziness

Vertigo is the illusion of movement of either the body or environment. This symptom is often described using terms such as spinning, turning, reeling, or any other depiction of movement. Most commonly, vertigo is due to a problem within the inner ear or the vestibular nerve, which is the nerve that helps to maintain balance. Benign positional vertigo, an illness caused by free-floating particles within the inner ear, can be diagnosed by its characteristic symptoms. With this illness, vertigo is provoked by changing position or moving the head, and symptoms usually last thirty seconds to several minutes. On the other hand, vestibular neuronitis, also called acute labyrinthitis or vestibulitis, usually causes a single episode of vertigo that may last from one day to several months. Vestibular neuronitis is thought to be caused by a viral infection. Another illness of the inner ear, Meniere's disease, can be differentiated by its long duration and associated hearing loss. Sometimes, vertigo can be caused by a central problem within the brain, such as a stroke.

The term presyncope refers to near fainting. People describe this as "blacking out" or "nearly fainting." There are many causes of presyncope, such as abnormal heart rhythms, medication, problems with internal blood pressure control (carotid hypersensitivity), and volume depletion. Not uncommonly, presyncope will occur without an identifiable underlying medical illness or specific cause.

The two remaining subtypes of dizziness, dysequilibrium and light-headedness, are less specific and in many cases the cause of these complaints cannot be accurately determined. The term dysequilibrium refers to a feeling of imbalance. The subtype of light-headedness is reserved for symptoms of dizziness that do not fit into any of the three other categories.

Although these subtypes of dizziness account for some causes of dizziness, it is not always possible to classify symptoms in a given individual. Often, one simple cause cannot be found to explain why dizziness is occurring and frequently there are several contributing causes, none of which alone would pose a problem. In combination, however, these factors produce the sensation of dizziness. Common contributors to dizziness include medication, impaired balance, heart disease, visual impairment, hearing loss, blood pressure that drops upon standing (i.e., orthostatic hypotension), decreased sensation in the feet, and chronic medical problems. Other cited causes of dizziness include psychiatric problems, hyperventilation, seizures, and disorders of the neck.

Evaluation

The tests needed to evaluate dizziness will depend on the information gathered during the clinical interview. Confirmation of the clinical diagnosis through physical examination and laboratory testing is necessary. In order to document whether there is a fall in blood pressure as the person stands up, examination should include blood pressure measurement in the lying and standing positions. Checking for vestibular ab-

normalities, examining vision, observing gait, and looking for neurologic abnormalities can be helpful. Important laboratory tests include measures of blood cell counts, thyroid function, blood chemistry (such as sodium), kidney function, calcium, and liver function. Sometimes additional tests may be needed to clarify the diagnosis. These could include tests of hearing and vestibular function, monitoring heart rhythm, evaluation of hearing, or CT or MRI scanning of the head.

Treatment

Management of dizziness will depend upon the subtype and causes identified. Antivertigo medications, such antihistamines and others, can be used to treat the debilitating symptoms of vestibular neuronitis, such as nausea, vomiting, and the sensation of movement. These treatments should be used for short periods of time and withdrawn as soon as symptoms improve. Side effects of these medications include stomach upset, fatigue, and confusion. For benign positional vertigo, there is evidence that antivertigo medications may delay improvement. In this circumstance, vestibular desensitization, such as rapidly tilting the body from one side to the other, may alleviate symptoms. Meniere's disease is treated with salt restriction, diuretic therapy, surgery, or antivertigo medications. Most of these treatments have uncertain benefits and are generally recommended only for short-term use. Aspirin, or another medication with antiplatelet effect, is recommended for stroke-related vertigo.

Treatment of dizziness caused by presyncope involves identifying whether or not there is an underlying cause. Presyncope may be caused by medications that lower blood pressure or cause dehydration (diuretics), or by medical illnesses, such as blood loss or arrhythmias. In these cases the identified problem should be appropriately treated. Information about treating presyncope that is associated with a drop in blood pressure when standing can be found in the section on fainting.

In many instances, a single cause of dizziness will not explain the symptoms and the focus of treatment will involve correcting as many contributing problems as possible. Offending medications should be stopped, gradually decreased, or replaced. Correcting vision and optimizing health status may be helpful. Exercise and walking aids may ameliorate problems of balance.

Conclusion

Dizziness is a common and challenging problem for an elderly person, which requires a systematic and detailed approach. Once medical problems are identified, treatment requires careful management of each difficulty identified, with fastidious follow-up to determine whether treatment is effective or producing side effects. In some circumstances, dizziness will not respond to treatment, in which case supportive therapy will be necessary.

LAURIE HERZIG MALLERY

See also BALANCE AND MOBILITY; FAINTING; HEARING.

BIBLIOGRAPHY

COLLEDGE, N. R.; WILSON, J. A.; MACINTYRE, C. C. A.; and MACLENNAN, W. J. "The Prevalence and Characteristics of Dizziness in an Elderly Community." *Age and Ageing* 23 (1994): 117–120.

FURMAN, J. M., and CASS, S. P. "Benign Paroxysmal Positional Vertigo." *The New England Journal of Medicine* 341, no. 21 (1999): 1590–1596.

SLOANE, PHILIP; BLAZER, DAN; and GEORGE, LINDA K. "Dizziness in a Community Elderly Population." *Journal of the American Geriatric Society* 37 (1989): 101–108.

DNA DAMAGE AND REPAIR

DNA is the master molecule and serves as the blueprint for the formation of all proteins and enzymes in every organism. The proteins then generate all the other substances in our cells. Thus, it is essential for reproduction, growth, and maintenance, and for sustaining normal living, that the DNA remains intact so that the genetic code can be read correctly. The stability and intactness of the DNA is a prerequisite for normal cellular functions, and there is good evidence that damage to the DNA can lead to cellular dysfunction, cancer and other diseases, or cell death. A major theory of aging holds that much of the aging phenotype (changes that can be observed) is caused by the gradual accumulation of DNA damage over a life span. DNA damage occurs at a high frequency due to metabolic processes and environmental factors such as various types of exposures and the intake of food and drugs. The prevention or repair of DNA damage is thus a major concern in biology and medicine.

DNA damage

The long, thin DNA molecules contain three components: nitrogen-rich bases, sugar groups, and phosphate groups. The composition of the four types of bases—adenine, guanine, cytosine, and thymidine—makes up the genetic code. Damage to DNA can occur to any of its three components. The bases are the most reactive, and there is far more knowledge about changes to them than to the sugar or phosphate components of DNA. Also, many chemicals or carcinogens form adducts (lesions) with new chemical groups being attached to existing DNA bases.

Base modifications in DNA after exposures

Living organisms are constantly exposed to stress from environmental agents and from endogenous metabolic processes. An important factor is exposure to oxidative reagents or oxidative stress. The resulting reactive oxygen species (ROS) attack proteins, lipids and DNA. Since proteins and lipids are readily degraded and re-synthesized, the most significant consequence of oxidative stress is thought to be DNA modifications, which can become permanent via the formation of mutations and other types of genomic instability.

Many different DNA base changes have been observed following oxidative stress, and these lesions are widely considered to instigate the development of cancer, aging, and neurological degradation. The attack on DNA by ROS generates a low steady-state level of DNA adducts that have been detected in the DNA from human cells. More than one hundred oxidative base modifications in DNA have been detected in human cells (Dizdaroglu), and a few of these are shown in Figure 1. The best-known and most widely studied oxidative DNA base adduct is 8-hydroxyguanosine (8-oxoG).

Oxidative DNA damage is thought to contribute to carcinogenesis, and studies have shown that it accumulates in cancerous tissue. Furthermore, the cumulative risk of cancer increases dramatically with age in humans (Ames), and cancer can in general terms be regarded as a degenerative disease of old age. There is evidence for the accumulation of oxidative DNA damage with age, based on studies mainly measuring the increase in 8-oxoG, the best-known and most widely studied oxidative DNA base lesion.

Figure 1
Examples of DNA base modifications observed in human tissue.

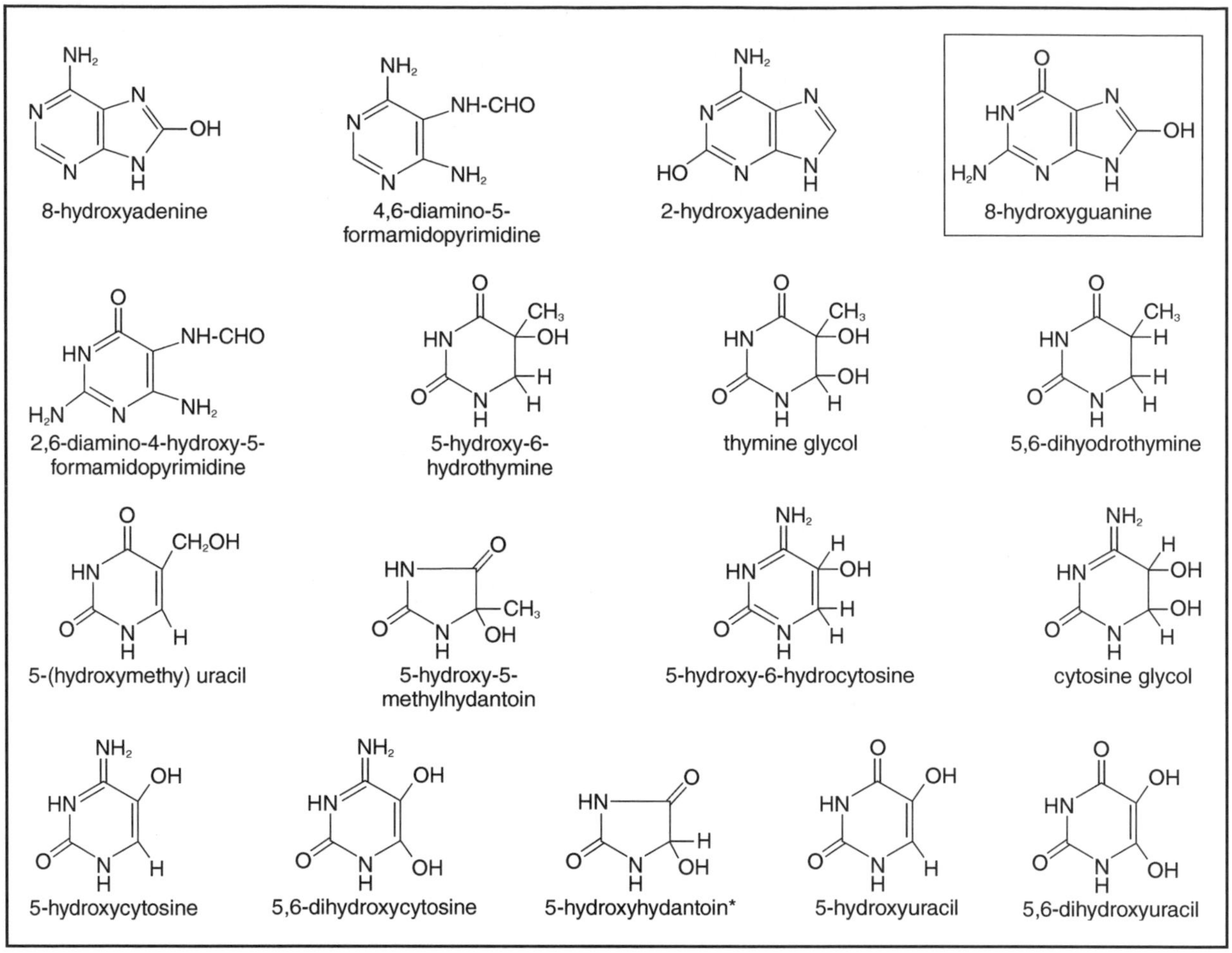

SOURCE: Modified from: Dizdaroglu, M. "Chemical Determination of Free Radical-Induced Damage to DNA." *Free Radical Biology and Medicine* 10 (1991): 225–242.

DNA base damage also can occur after direct attack by external sources. Irradiation from various sources can directly damage bases in DNA. For example, ultraviolet irradiation from exposure to sunlight creates certain DNA lesions. Irradiation from γ-ray sources, such as X-rays, leads to many different kinds of lesions in DNA, including base modifications, sites with a loss of base, and breaks in the DNA strand. Since DNA contains two strands running in parallel but opposite directions, breaks can be either single-stranded or double-stranded. A large number of components of food intake can directly damage DNA. These include carcinogens and chemicals that cause DNA damage, either by direct reactions or via metabolic modification. For example,

aromatic amines are found in variety of foods and are known to cause DNA damage and to be highly mutagenic. A number of poisons work by attacking the DNA and damaging it. An example of this is the poisonous gas nitrogen mustard, which causes modification of DNA bases and also can link DNA bases on opposite DNA strands. These cause serious havoc in the cell by completely blocking the progression of polymerases.

Detection of DNA damage

DNA can be extracted from human cells or tissues and then analyzed chemically for its components. There are various assays to detect DNA modifications. Some of these techniques are very sensitive and can detect rare changes in DNA. They include a number of chemical analyses and chromatographic measurements of DNA. A hotly debated issue is the choice of method to purify DNA from cells or tissues. Many of the available extraction procedures introduce new DNA damage in the process of purification. A number of enzymatic methods have been used in which specific enzymes or antibodies detect certain kinds of DNA base modifications and/or adducts formed in DNA. These enzymes become molecular "probes" for the damage, an approach that can be very sensitive. Radioactive labeling procedures can be a simple and easy way to measure several modifications in DNA.

The free radical theory of aging was first put forward by Denham Harman in 1956. He proposed that free radicals would be produced in the utilization of molecular oxygen by animal cells, and that as a consequence of free radical reactions with nucleic acids and other cellular components, the animal would develop mutations and cancer. He also suggested that damage by endogenous free radicals was the fundamental cause of aging. A second theory, proposed in 1959 by Leo Szilard, postulated specifically that time-dependent changes in somatic DNA, rather than other cellular constituents, were the primary cause of senescence. Both authors based their theories in large part on the belief, common at the time, that radiation accelerated aging independently of its effects on carcinogenesis.

Consequences of DNA damage

Figure 2 shows some of the consequences of DNA damage. As mentioned above, DNA damage can be induced by external or internal sources. Ultraviolet (UV) irradiation and ionizing irradiation are examples of exogenous sources of stress. Reactive oxygen species generated by the oxidative phosphorylation that occurs in mitochondria, and thus via cellular metabolism, is an example of an endogenous type of stress. Mutations in DNA can occur via replication of the damaged DNA whereby they become "fixed." Lesion bypass or replication errors can give rise to other forms of genomic instability. A lesion in DNA can block transcription (conversion of DNA to RNA) completely, it may truncate the transcript, or it may cause errors in the transcription. Alternatively, the DNA damage may induce new transcripts, and a number of genes have been shown to be inducible by vari-

ous forms of cellular stress. These changes in transcription patterns that are caused by DNA damage may be part of the origin of the malignant phenotype; many changes in transcription have been reported in cancers. They are also likely to be a cause of some of the changes seen in aging, where reductions, or in some cases increases, in transcriptional activity are well established (Bohr and Anson). Lesions in DNA also can lead to cell cycle arrest, or they can cause strand breaks in DNA.

It is estimated that there are several thousand DNA alterations in each cell in the human organism per day (Lindahl), caused by both endogenous and exogenous stresses. Were it not for an efficient DNA repair process, genetic material would be destroyed by these processes over a normal human lifetime.

DNA repair

Mammalian cells can make use of a variety of DNA repair pathways. An overview of these is presented in Figure 3. Most studies over the years have been based on the assumption that the DNA repair pathways listed were confined to the removal of specific lesions within certain categories. For example, nucleotide excision repair (NER) was the system that removed bulky lesions in DNA that dramatically changed the DNA structure. In contrast, base excision repair (BER) was the process responsible for the removal of simple lesions in DNA, which are considered to cause only small structural changes in DNA and may not represent major blocks to transcription and replication. This concept has changed somewhat in recent years as it has become evident that many of the DNA repair pathways listed in Figure 3 are overlapping and share components. Thus, although it is useful to think of repair pathways as confined to the removal of different types of DNA lesions, that distinction is of limited validity. It would be much too ambitious to review all the pathways listed in Figure 3. Two of the most predominant pathways are NER and BER, and these will be discussed in more detail. The mismatch repair pathway is of particular interest in relation to cancer.

In general terms, the DNA repair process consists of a number of steps that act in concert to accomplish the complete repair of DNA damage. The first step is the recognition of the DNA lesion, and this is accomplished by proteins that constantly survey the DNA for any unwanted

Figure 2

Some consequences of DNA damage. Lesions in DNA can instigate a number of DNA related transactions, discussed in the text, that ultimately lead to genomic instability and other features of cancer and aging.

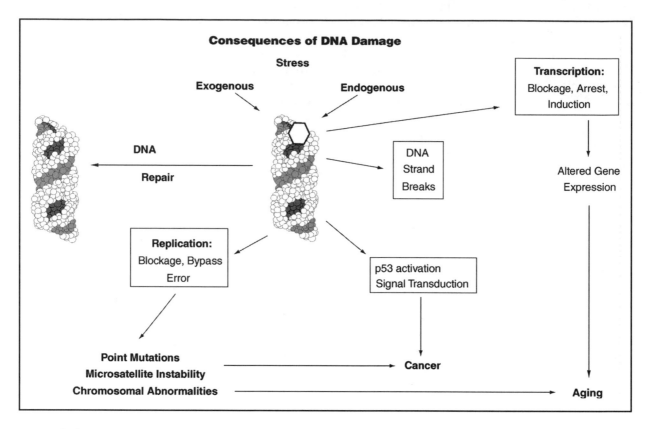

SOURCE: Author

modifications. In the next step, incision, enzymes are cut into the DNA to remove the damaged DNA base. This step is complex and involves many proteins. When the damaged base has been removed, there is a step of resynthesis, in which new DNA is made to replace that which was removed in the incision step. This is accomplished by proteins called DNA polymerases, and there are several kinds of these in each mammalian cell. Since the DNA damage was in one strand of DNA, the other strand has the information required to copy itself. After the DNA synthesis, there is a ligation process in which the gaps in the DNA are sealed and a new, intact double helix is formed.

Base excision repair. Base excision repair (BER) of oxidative DNA damage is initiated by DNA glycosylases, a class of enzymes that recognize and remove damaged bases from DNA by hydrolytic cleavage of the base-sugar bond, leaving an abasic site (AP site). There are at least two

pathways for further processing of the AP site. One of these is catalyzed by AP endonuclease, and results in a single-nucleotide gap that is then filled and sealed.

An alternative pathway, long patch BER, has been reported. In addition to a DNA glycosylase and AP endonuclease, it also involves a single-strand flap structure that is recognized and excised, and then the DNA is ligated (Klugland and Lindahl). These repair events result in a repair patch two to seven nucleotides long. There has been much research activity in the BER area (see Krokan et al.; Friedberg et al.).

Nucleotide excision repair. Most of the understanding of the nucleotide excision repair (NER) pathway has come through the study of the human disorder xeroderma pigmentosum (XP). There are seven genetically different types of this disease, designated A–G. XP proteins are designated after the cell line in which they are

Figure 3

Some of the major pathways of DNA repair in mammalian systems such as humans. These pathways can operate independently, but also are interactive. (TCR is the abbreviation for transcription coupled repair.)

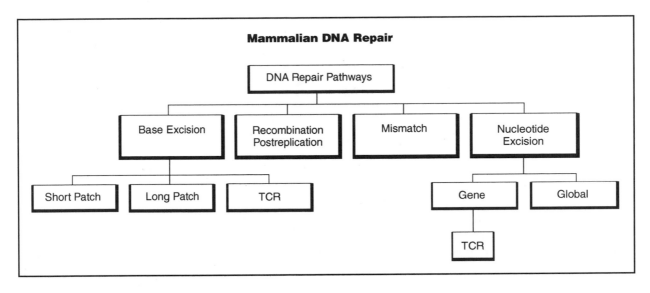

SOURCE: Author

mutated (e.g., the XPA protein is the one mutated in XPA cells). The individuals afflicted with this condition suffer from high incidences of skin and internal cancers, hyperpigmentation, and premature aging (Friedburg et al.). Cells from XP patients cannot incise their DNA at a site of a UV-induced lesion, and thus are in general deficient in the incision process of NER. The enzymatic steps involved in NER are recognition of the lesion, incision of the DNA, excision of the damaged DNA template, resynthesis of new DNA based on the intact template, and ligation of the newly formed DNA repair patch into the reconstructed double helix. A number of reviews have discussed NER in much more detail (see, e.g., Friedberg).

Genomic heterogeneity of NER. A major advance in the study of DNA repair has been the insight that NER and possibly other repair pathways operate with considerable heterogeneity over the mammalian genome. The NER pathway can thus be subdivided into pathways relating to the functional and structural organization of the genome. Only about 1 percent of the genome is transcriptionally active, and a repair pathway called transcription coupled repair (TCR) operates here. The remainder of the genome, the 99 percent that is inactive, has a separate pathway, general genome repair (GGR). Much work has

been dedicated to the further delineation and clarification of these pathways. For a more thorough review and discussion of the repair in genes, see Balajee and Bohr, which also discusses the human premature aging syndrome, Cockayne syndrome (CS), where TCR is deficient. CS is a rare and severe clinical condition in which patients appear to be much older than their chronological age. It is a premature aging disorder because many of the clinical signs and symptoms are those seen in the aging process in normal individuals.

Mitochondrial DNA repair in mammalian cells

Mitochondria are the energy stations inside the cells. Here, oxidative phosphorylation occurs, generating adenosine triphosphate (ATP). In this process, reactive oxygen species are formed at high frequencies, and the mitochondrial DNA (mtDNA) is directly exposed. The mitochondrial DNA does not have a recognized chromatin structure and thus is particularly exposed to formation of oxidative DNA base lesions.

There are about one thousand mitochondria per mammalian cell. Each mitochondrion has four to five DNA plasmids. This means that about

2 percent of total human DNA is in the mitochondria. All mtDNA is transcribed, whereas only about 1 percent of the nuclear DNA is transcribed. Thus the mtDNA makes up a large fraction of the total transcribed DNA in a mammalian cell.

MtDNA does not code for any DNA damage-processing enzymes. Thus, all repair enzymes functioning in the mitochondria need to be transported into them. It has been shown that mitochondria do not repair UV-induced lesions; this observation provided the basis for the notion that there is no DNA repair capacity in mtDNA. There have been many observations indicating the presence of BER in mitochondria. BER enzymes have been identified and characterized, and studies have shown that a number of oxidative DNA base lesions are efficiently removed from mtDNA. Other repair processes have also been detected (see Croteau et al. and other articles in the same issue of *Mutation Research*). An important question remaining is whether mitochondria possess any capabilities to repair bulky lesions via the NER pathway.

Knowledge about mtDNA repair is limited because it has been very difficult to study. Experimental techniques and methods have not been nearly as well developed as those for the study of nuclear DNA repair. Whereas in vitro repair studies have been performed with great success on nuclear or whole cell extracts from cells, this kind of biochemical approach has only very recently become available for mtDNA. Recent advances suggest that mtDNA repair can now be studied using more sophisticated biochemical analysis (Stierum et al.), and this should provide great advances in the near future.

Oxidative phosphorylation in mitochondria (which produces ATP) results in the production of reactive oxygen species (ROS). Other processes that contribute significantly to the pool of ROS include heat, ultraviolet light, drugs such as those used in the treatment of HIV, and ionizing radiation. Hydrogen peroxide, singlet oxygen, and hydroxyl radicals are among the ROS produced. The interactions between ROS and mtDNA result in oxidation of specific mtDNA bases, and such base modifications have been detected in human cells. Thus, insufficient mtDNA repair may result in mitochondrial dysfunction and thereby cause degenerative diseases, loss of energy formation, and pathophysiological processes leading to aging and cancer.

Identification of BER enzymes in mitochondria. Early indications for a BER mechanism in mitochondria came with the isolation of a mammalian mitochondrial endonuclease which specifically recognizes AP sites and cleaves the DNA strand. Later, it was demonstrated that a combination of enzymes purified from *Xenopus laevis* (a frog) mitochondria efficiently repair abasic sites in DNA.

The isolation of mitochondrial glycosylases has provided further evidence for a BER mechanism in mitochondria. Endonucleases specific for oxidative damage (mtODE), and for thymine glycols have been purified from rat mitochondria (Croteau et al., 1999).

The molecular mechanisms that lead to aging in multicellular organisms are still unclear. Many theories have arisen to explain the aging process, and among them the mitochondrial theory of aging, described earlier, has received much attention.

Age-related changes in DNA repair

There has been a great deal of interest in the question of whether DNA repair declines with age. Investigators have looked at many conditions of premature and normal aging, and many different types of assays have been used. In general, there seems to be a growing consensus that DNA repair declines slightly with age (see Bohr and Anson). One study reported a 1 percent decline in DNA repair capacity per year with advancing age in individuals (Wei et al.). Attempts to correlate DNA repair capacity of different organisms with maximum life span have been made. Hart and Setlow (1974) demonstrated a linear correlation between the logarithm of life span and the DNA repair capacity in cells from different mammalian species, suggesting that higher DNA repair activity is associated with longer life span. Although these studies document a connection between DNA repair capacity and age, there are also a large number of studies in which no connection between these two parameters were found.

Changes in mitochondrial function with age have been observed in several organisms. Experimental data from many laboratories suggest that the mitochondrial genome indeed accumulates DNA damage with age (Bohr and Anson, 1995).

Since oxidative DNA damage accumulates in mitochondria, changes in mtDNA repair with age have been studied. Initially, mtODE activity in mitochondrial extracts obtained from livers and hearts of rats six, twelve, and twenty-three months old was compared. In contrast to the common notion that DNA repair decreases with age, an increase in mtODE activity with increasing age was found. In both organs, activities at twelve and twenty-three months were significantly higher than at six months (p< 0.01) (Souza-Pinto et al.). These results suggest that the changes observed in mtODE activity reflect a specific upregulation of the oxidative DNA damage repair mechanisms. Similar results were obtained when investigating mtODE activity in extracts from mouse liver mitochondria. The activity increased from six to fourteen months of age.

Perspectives

DNA repair is a complex and fascinating process, and it is very interactive with other DNA metabolic processes. It is tightly linked to the transcription process and also to DNA replication and a number of signal transduction pathways. An age-associated decline in DNA repair could explain why older individuals suffer from age-associated diseases and become highly susceptible to cancer. This understanding could also lead to therapeutic interventions in the future where DNA repair activities could be enhanced.

VILHELM BOHR

See also BIOLOGY OF AGING; CANCER, BIOLOGY; CELLULAR AGING: BASIC PHENOMENA; CELLULAR AGING: DNA POLYMORPHISMS; MOLECULAR BIOLOGY OF AGING; MUTATION; THEORIES OF BIOLOGICAL AGING: DNA DAMAGE.

BIBLIOGRAPHY

AMES, B. N. "Endogenous Oxidative DNA Damage, Aging and Cancer." *Free Radical Research Communications* 7 (1998): 121–128.

BALAJEE, A. S., and BOHR, V. A. "Genomic Heterogeneity of Nucleotide Excision Repair." *Gene* 250 (2000): 15–30.

BOHR, V. A., and ANSON, R. M. "DNA Damage, Mutation and Fine Structure DNA Repair in Aging." *Mutation Research* 338 (1995): 25–34.

CROTEAU, D. L.; STIERUM, R. H.; and BOHR, V. A. "Mitochondrial DNA Repair Pathways." *Mutation Research* 434 (1999): 137–148.

DIZDAROGLU, M. "Chemical Determination of Free Radical-Induced Damage to DNA." *Free Radical Biology and Medicine* 10 (1991): 225–242.

FRIEDBERG, E. C.; WALKER, G. C.; and SIEDE, W. *DNA Repair and Mutagenesis.* New York: ASM Press, 1995.

HARMAN, D. "Aging: A Theory Based on Free Radical and Radiation Chemistry." *Journal of Gerontology* 11 (1956): 298–300.

HART, R. W., and SETLOW, R. B. "Correlation Between Deoxyribonucleic Acid Excision Repair and Life Span in a Number of Mammalian Species." *Proceedings of the National Academy of Sciences of the United States of America* 71 (1994): 2169–2173.

KLUNGLAND, A., and LINDAHL, T. "Secondary Pathway for Completion of Human DNA Base Excision-Repair: Reconstitution with Purified Proteins and Requirement for DNase IV (FEN1)." *EMBO Journal* 16 (1997): 3341–3348.

KROKAN, H. E.; STANDAL, R.; and SLUPPHAUG, G. "DNA Glycosylases in the Base Excision Repair of DNA." *Biochemical Journal* 325 (1997): 1–16.

LINDAHL, T. "Instability and Decay of the Primary Structure of DNA." *Nature* 362 (1993): 709–715.

SOUZA-PINTO, N. C.; CROTEAU, D. L.; HUDSON, E. K.; HANSFORD, R. G.; and BOHR, V. A. "Age-Associated Increase in 8-Oxo-Deoxyguanosine Glycosylase/AP Lyase Activity in Rat Mitochondria." *Nucleic Acids Research* 27 (1999): 1935–1942.

STIERUM, R. H.; DIANOV, G. L.; and BOHR, V. A. "Single-Nucleotide Patch Base Excision Repair of Uracil in DNA by Mitochondrial Protein Extracts." *Nucleic Acids Research* 27 (1999): 3712–3719.

WEI, Q.; MATANOSKI, G. M.; FARMER, E. R.; HEDAYAT, M. A.; and GROSSMAN, L. "DNA Repair and Aging in Basil Cell Carcinoma: A Molecular Epidemiology Study." *Proceedings of the National Academy of Sciences of the United States of America* 90 (1993): 1614–1618.

DRIVING ABILITY

Transportation is a critical link for independent living and healthy aging; and for many people in the United States, transportation is defined as driving. Whether it is a trip to the grocery store, to volunteer, to see a doctor, to visit a friend, or to simply experience the joy of getting out, the automobile is the means for most people to remain active and healthy contributors to society.

Moreover, there is often no viable alternative to driving. The majority of older adults in the United States live in suburban and rural locations where public transportation services are either modest or nonexistent. Other transportation services, often provided by faith-based organizations, community centers, or those that are part of a regional transportation system, typically provide only basic service to doctors and food stores.

Future generations of older adults are likely to place an even greater demand and reliance on driving. For the rapidly aging baby boom generation (those born between 1946 and 1964), life has been based on and built around the mobility of the automobile. Research suggests that the majority of the baby boomers will choose to age-in-place in the suburban and rural communities that make safe walking a challenge and where distances to stores and other activities can be many miles.

Moreover, as this group ages, they are likely to travel more than their parents and grandparents. Improvements in health, greater incomes, and higher education levels lead to a greater desire to get out and participate in an active lifestyle of part-time work, volunteering, social and entertainment activities, and recreation. Sarah Bush (2001) has suggested that the changing role of women may also place additional demands on the car. Women are likely to drive more in the future due to independent lifestyles developed at a younger age, including professional careers, greater income, and more education. Lifestyle factors, housing patterns, and socioeconomic factors suggest that the next wave of retirees will want to lead an active and mobile life—which, for now, only the automobile can support.

There are a number of safety concerns about the ability of older adults to continue to drive safely in their advanced years. Transportation statistics indicate that drivers between the ages of sixteen and twenty-four have the highest fatality rate, with drivers age seventy-five and older having the second highest rates. Those arguing that older drivers present a risk to themselves and others on the road cite these data as supporting their concern that older drivers are unsafe, or that they should be tested more often than younger drivers. The statistics are not as clear as their argument would suggest, however. Researchers are uncertain about why adults over seventy-five experience high fatality rates. Many argue that older people are more likely to die in a crash, not because they are the cause of such an accident, but because they are more fragile than younger drivers and are more likely to die from an injury. The ambiguity surrounding driving ability, who can drive safely, and what an older driver is presents a continuing personal and public policy dilemma—one that is made more complex by the importance of transportation to people's lives, the uncertainty of how age affects driving skills, the lack of accepted testing technology, and the absence of viable alternatives to the car.

The natural aging process and driving ability

Nowhere is the ambiguity surrounding the older-driver issue better demonstrated than in attempts to identify who is old. As people age, their physical, mental, and cognitive capacities begin to change. In addition, age-related diseases, and the medicines used to treat those conditions, may also affect capacity. Figure 1 illustrates some of the systematic changes that tend to affect people, to varying degrees, as they age. Within this context, the discussion of older-driver safety arises. Are older people mentally and physically capable to drive? In most cases, the answer is a resounding "yes."

Physical, perceptual, and cognitive function

Over time, one may expect to experience weaker (or somewhat diminished) physical, perceptual, and cognitive function. These changes, which can occur as early as age forty, include reduced capacity of vision at night and weaker contrast sensitivity, which makes signage along roadways more difficult to read. Most people also experience an increased sensitivity to glare during night driving, and many have difficulty recovering from bright lights. Hearing loss usually accompanies aging. Most people compensate for both visual and auditory changes as they happen, and do not realize that their abilities have declined over time.

Decreased strength and flexibility also typically accompany aging. While these may be offset with regular exercise and strength training, most people exercise less frequently as they age, when they should be exercising more to compensate for weakening muscle and bone mass. These problems lead to more problematic neck and

Figure 1
Age-related changes in different parts of the information processing system.

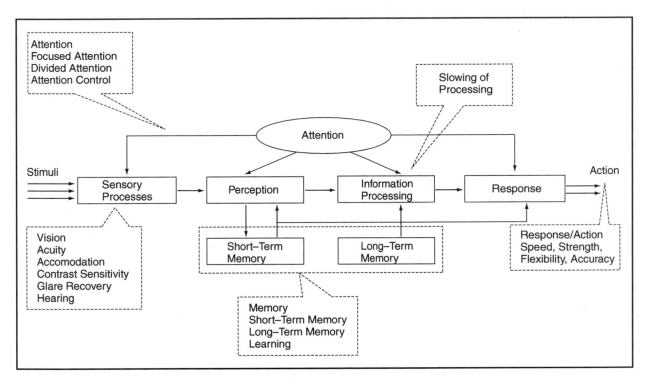

SOURCE: Based on data from: Wickens, C. D. *Engineering Psychology and Human Performance*. New York: Prentice Hall, 1993.

trunk rotation, in addition to difficulty accessing a vehicle or turning the head to compensate for natural blind spots in the car to view oncoming traffic or pedestrians. For some, these physical changes may contribute both to a reduced desire to travel and more difficulty in concentrating on the entire situation of driving. The speed with which most people perform routine and simple tasks slows as they age because movement is more difficult as muscle strength and flexibility decrease.

Individual perceptions change over time as well. For example, some research indicates that capacity for judgment of velocity and distance of approaching vehicles becomes reduced with age. This judgment is a crucial component in the driving process, and when it is impaired it may cause an accident. The driver who cannot accurately determine the distance and speed of an oncoming vehicle risks an accident when making a left turn at an intersection.

People begin to react more slowly to stimuli as they age because response times begin to slow. While driving, a split-second decision can be the difference between an accident and a close call. Reaction time is an important feature of driving because a driver must see a problem, think about it, and then react—apply the brake, steer, or take another action as necessary. As shown in Figure 1, *attention* is made up of many linear subtasks that lead to action. The stimulus affects the sensory processes in the brain, which affect perception, information processing, and response, all of which are key components of attention. The longer it takes for each response, the longer it takes for the intended action. This leads to problems concentrating on the many subtasks that must be considered while driving. Synthesizing multiple pieces of information and conducting the many actions of driving may sometimes overwhelm the older driver who cannot react quickly to a stimulus.

Self-regulation

Age-related restrictions on the relicensing of older drivers in the United States is an issue that affects millions of people. While it affects the driver directly, it affects many people indirectly.

Someone's ability to continue driving affects the people who may depend on that person for transportation; it affects that person's spouse, family and friends, who are concerned both for the person's happiness and quality of life, and it affects public safety officials, who must remain vigilant of potential problems.

Most older drivers are safe drivers. Although a popular public policy debate, regulating older drivers is done principally by the individual, not government, and with great success. In other words, older drivers routinely practice self-regulation—they choose not to drive in conditions that they believe are difficult or may present a dangerous situation. For example, most older drivers begin to drive less in the evening to compensate for diminished night vision and problems with glare. Other drivers feel less comfortable on busy highways, or driving in poor weather; choosing, therefore, routes and schedules that allow them to avoid troublesome conditions. Self-regulating driving behavior allows older adults to maintain their mobility and independence while optimizing their safety and the safety of others.

Government regulation of the older driver

Typically sparked by an accident involving an older driver, combined with the ensuing media coverage, the issue of what age is too old to drive has often become a debatable policy problem. While policymakers want drivers on the roadways to be safe drivers, they are not inclined to pass legislation limiting the driving of older adults. The issue is emotionally charged, as many older drivers in the United States have been driving for forty or more years and do not want to give up their privileges, and in most instances this is neither appropriate nor necessary. This fact, combined with uncertainty about defining *old*, deciding how best to assess driving skills, and a general lack of organizational capacity to implement such regulation, usually results in little if any regulatory change.

Ambiguity surrounds the definition of *old*. While some people in their fifties might have severe physical impairments caused by aging, others in their eighties might be perfectly capable of driving as safely as they were many years previous. Each state that regulates older drivers has determined the age at which the licensing laws change. The youngest age at which a state implements restrictions is fifty (in Oregon), while the oldest age at which point changes are mandated is seventy-five (in Illinois, Montana, New Hampshire, and New Mexico).

Typical relicensing restrictions on older drivers involve the length of time between renewals. In some states the duration of a valid license is reduced by some amount for older drivers. For example, Iowa allows drivers to possess a license for four years before renewal, but when a person reaches age seventy, his or her license is only valid for two years. These regulations provide the states more frequent control if drivers' abilities are slipping.

Another regulatory tool for older drivers is in the form of testing procedures. A few states that do not require periodic vision testing have implemented testing after a certain age, but most states require vision testing every few years for all drivers. A handful of states require a driving test at a certain age, and others require a driving test if the examiner at the Division of Motor Vehicles feels that the applicant should be tested. Tests for mental competency are not required by any state, but most allow the examiner the discretion of requiring further testing if necessary. Most states, however, at least suggest, if not mandate, that physicians must report individuals who are not competent to drive to the state licensing bureau.

One problem with testing older drivers is the lack of understanding surrounding the issue. No clear scientific study or policy consensus exists on the type of testing that would produce the most accurate results regarding the abilities of an older driver. Additional constraints include the budgets of licensing organizations, along with the question of what type of person would be the most qualified to give a test. While some people feel that anyone qualified should administer such a test, others question what makes a person qualified.

Summary

Many characteristics work together to contribute to a person's ability to drive safely. Physical capacity, mental acuity and competency, adequate reaction time, and appropriate skills are only a few of the abilities that must be considered when evaluating driving ability. Chronological age alone is not an appropriate predictor of how someone will function behind the wheel. Most older drivers are safe drivers, and they choose to drive when they are most capable. Moreover, the important role of driving to an older person's independence and quality of life makes the issue of driving ability, relicensing, and the search for viable alternatives to the car (when driving may no longer a choice) a critical and enduring challenge for an aging society.

JOSEPH COUGHLIN
MEREDITH COLEY

See also AGING IN PLACE; HEARING; MEMORY; REACTION TIME; VISION AND PERCEPTION.

BIBLIOGRAPHY

BURKHARDT, J. E.; BERGER, A. M.; CREEDON, M.; and MCGAVOCK, A. T. *Mobility and Independence: Changes and Challenges for Older Drivers.* Bethesda, Md.: Ecosometrics, 1998: 25–33.

BUSH, S. "Does Future Elderly Transportation Demand Pose a Pending Crisis?" *Public Policy and Aging Report* 11, no. 4 (2001): 15–19.

COBB, R. W., and COUGHLIN, J. F. "Are Elderly Drivers a Road Hazard?: Problem Definition and Political Impact." *Journal of Aging Studies* 12, no. 4 (1998): 411–427.

COLEY, M., and COUGHLIN, J. F. "State Older Driver Re-Licensing: Conflict, Chaos and the Search for Policy Consensus." *Elder's Advisor: Journal of Elder Law* 3, no. 4 (spring 2002).

WICKENS, C. D. *Engineering Psychology and Human Performance.* New York: Prentice Hall, 1993.

DRUG REGULATION

The road to drug development is a long and demanding process that can take up to 15 years. Before a substance is deemed "safe" it must go through the series of phases shown in Figure 1. These phases are called: discovery; preclinical testing (in animals); phase I; phase II; phase III; review by the U.S. Food and Drug Administration (FDA); and phase IV.

Discovery

A new drug may be "discovered" by numerous methods, as listed below.

Testing traditional or folk medicine. The root of the plant *Podophyllum peltatum* was traditionally used by North American aboriginal people to treat warts. The active chemical, called podophyllotoxin, was isolated in 1940, and was found to have anticancer activity. Etoposide, a semisynthetic chemical made from podophyllotoxin, is used in the treatment of some cancers.

Accident or serendipity. The anticancer activity of the chemicals found in the rosy periwinkle (*Catharanthus roseus*) was discovered accidentally. Native people in Africa, Australia, India, and South Africa traditionally used the rosy periwinkle to treat diabetes. Two scientists tested the extract to find out whether it was useful in lowering blood sugar, and found that it was not. Something in the extract was found to reduce the number of white blood cells in test animals, however, and two chemicals, called vincristine and vinblastine, were isolated and are still used as anticancer agents in the treatment of leukemia today.

Random sampling of chemicals. After the discovery of penicillin by Dr. Alexander Fleming in 1928, the screening of chemicals found in nature became an important way to find new drugs.

Rational drug design. Cimetidine is a chemical that is used to treat stomach ulcers. It is not known how ulcers start, but it is known that the amount of acid in the stomach makes the ulcer worse. To design cimetidine, chemists first had to understand how the stomach produces acid. They then had to design a chemical that blocks the acid production so that the stomach has a chance to heal. Cimetidine was the result of rational drug design.

Preclinical testing

To find out whether a substance that is thought to have medicinal values is safe to use and effective, information on how it affects the body must be gathered. It therefore enters a phase called *preclinical testing*. Here, scientists from many disciplines must study the chemical and biological properties of the substance. *Pharmacology*, in its broadest sense, includes the study of how a substance is absorbed, distributed, metabolized or processed, and excreted by the body. These studies are done on small animals in the laboratory.

Substances can be given by mouth (oral), applied to the skin (topical), or be injected or inhaled (parenteral). Absorption studies determine how much of a compound is *absorbed* after it is given. Some compounds may be destroyed in the stomach by stomach acid so that very little reaches the site where it is needed. How quickly a compound gets to the part of the body where it exerts its effect is called *absorption* and *distribution*.

Different substances produce different effects on different parts of the body. Some sub-

Figure 1
The path a drug takes from its discovery until it is approved by the Food and Drug Administration.

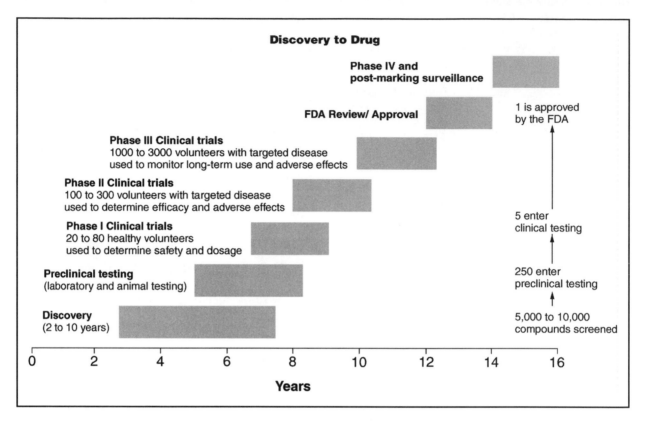

Discovery to Drug

SOURCE: Author

stances affect only the heart; some, the muscles; and some, the kidneys. This depends on the shape and size of the substance. Correlation between the size and shape of a substance and its effect on the body is called its *structure-activity relationship*.

Drug *metabolism* is the study of how a substance is altered or processed in the body so that it can be removed or *eliminated* (excreted) by the body in the urine or feces.

This information is obtained by giving the substance to a test animal. Samples of blood, urine, and feces are collected at specific times, and the amount of substance present is recorded. All of this information is called the *pharmacologic profile* of the substance. An autopsy is also done to examine all organs and tissues to give more data. Special studies are also done to see whether the substance is found in the milk of nursing animals. In pregnant animals, studies are done to see if it reaches the developing baby.

Toxicology deals with the unwanted effects of substances. Toxicological studies determine whether a substance can cause nausea, vomiting, changes in eating or drinking habits, weight change or changes in behavior. Work is also done to see if the it can cause cancer (carcinogenic) or produce birth defects (teratogenic).

The manufacture of a substance into a tablet, capsule, or liquid preparation is called *formulation*. For a substance to be formulated into a suitable dosage form for human use, requires consideration of whether the compound is a solid or liquid, whether it is stable at room temperature, and whether it smells or tastes bad.

Phase I

Once a substance has completed preclinical testing, the manufacturer files an Investigational New Drug (IND) Application with the U.S. Food and Drug Administration (FDA). The IND becomes effective if the FDA does not disapprove of it within thirty days. The IND allows scientists investigating the drug to distribute it to responsible investigators for use in clinical trials that will involve humans. All clinical trials must be reviewed and approved by the Institutional Review Board (IRB) of the medical institution that will be conducting the clinical trial.

Normal, healthy volunteers are used in Phase I clinical trials. Phase I studies are several months in duration, and the size of the group can range from twenty to eighty subjects. The purpose of these trials is to determine the *safety profile* or benefit to risk assessment for use in humans, including the safe dosage range; and absorption, distribution, metabolism, and excretion in humans.

Phase II

In Phase II, one hundred to three hundred subjects with the targeted disease are selected. These patients cannot have other medical conditions that might complicate the assessment. For example, if a drug is being tested to reduce blood pressure, the subject cannot have high blood pressure and diabetes.

Phase II trials are randomized, double-blind, placebo-controlled, clinical trials. *Randomization* is the process of assigning the subjects in the trial into two groups, the control group and the treatment group, in a random manner. This helps to eliminate bias when assigning patients to each group. *Double-blind* means that neither the subjects nor the people giving the drug know to which group each subject has been assigned. *Placebo-controlled* means that the control group receives a placebo—a pill that does not contain the drug—while the test group receives a pill with the drug. All these provisions help to eliminate bias that may skew the results of the trial.

Phase II clinical trials are several months to two years in duration. They are carried out to determine the best dosage for the drug, look for unwanted effects (adverse effects), and to evaluate the efficacy of the drug; that is, whether it is useful to treat the target disease.

Phase III

This phase involves 1,000 to 3,000 subjects with the targeted disease. The disease condition can range from being mild to severe, and the subjects may have other complicating medical conditions. These trials are done in different locations across the country (multicentre). Phase III clinical trials are one to four years in duration, and are done to confirm dosage, monitor unwanted or adverse effects, look for unwanted effects from long-term use, establish the safety profile of the drug, and confirm the efficacy of the drug.

Review by the U.S. Food and Drug Administration

The FDA evaluates the data presented from the clinical trials in the New Drug Application (NDA) submitted by the manufacturer. The application consists of the application form and data from preclinical testing, chemistry and manufacturing data, clinical trials, samples and product labeling, and relevant publications.

The FDA evaluates the safety and efficacy of the drug and the quality of the data supporting the claims being made by the manufacturer. If approved, the product goes to market and enters Phase IV clinical trials.

Phase IV

During Phase IV the drug becomes available for physicians to prescribe, but the manufacturer must continue to submit reports to the FDA that evaluate the effectiveness of the drug, monitor drug interactions, provide data that compare the drug with other drugs that are used for the same purpose, evaluate the cost-effectiveness of the drug, and provide long-term safety and efficacy data. This ongoing monitoring is called *postmarketing surveillance*.

Age factors

When a new drug enters clinical trials, special attention is given to older adults (65 years or older) because they often develop unwanted effects to drugs at levels that are well-tolerated by younger persons. This may be caused by age-related sensitivity to the drug, or because the metabolism and excretion of the drug is slower in the older adult.

In all phases of clinical trials, the risks and benefits to susceptible populations must be evaluated. These populations include infants, young children, pregnant women, nursing mothers, and older adults.

Clinicians who are experts on the disease being treated are used as investigators during

Phase I and Phase II clinical trials. In Phase III, the usefulness of the drug in an expanded patient base is evaluated and adverse effects that may not have appeared in the previous two phases may become apparent during this period. The drug may be withdrawn from testing at any time if the risk to patients outweigh the benefits.

When the drug enters Phase IV, any adverse event reported to the manufacturer must be reported to the FDA within fifteen days after initial receipt of the information. This allows for continued evaluation and, if necessary, warnings to be issued by the FDA to prescribing physicians, pharmacists, and the public. In extreme cases, it may warrant the removal of the drug from the market.

The FDA requires that postmarketing adverse drug events be reported at quarterly intervals for three years from the date of approval of the NDA, and then at annual intervals. This provides an ongoing evaluation of the benefit-to-risk ratio of new drugs. It also gives recognition to the rights of all patients who participate in clinical drug studies in all stages of development.

Time and cost

From discovery to FDA approval of a drug takes about fifteen years and costs about $500 million. From the 5,000 to 10,000 new chemicals that are screened, about two hundred and fifty enter preclinical testing. Of this 250, only five enter clinical testing, and only one is approved and marketed.

M. B. THADANI

See also DRUGS AND AGING; EVIDENCE-BASED MEDICINE; HERBAL THERAPY.

BIBLIOGRAPHY

ANSEL, H. C.; ALLEN, L. V.; and POPOVICH, N. G. *Pharmaceutical Dosage Forms and Drug Delivery Systems*, 7th ed. Philadelphia, Pa.: Lippincott, Williams & Wilkins, 1999.
GENNARO, A. R., ed. *Remington: The Science and Practice of Pharmacy*, 20th ed. Philadelphia, Pa.: Lippincott, Williams & Wilkins, 2000.
GUARINO, R. A., ed. *New Drug Approval Process*, 3d ed. New York: Marcel Dekker, 2000.
PATRICK, G. L. *An Introduction to Medicinal Chemistry*. Oxford, U.K.: Oxford University Press, 1995.
THADANI, M. B. *Medicinal and Pharmaceutical Uses of Natural Products*, 2d ed. Winnipeg: Cantext Publications, 1998.

DRUGS AND AGING

Medication use by older people continues to receive attention in the lay media and in medical literature. People age sixty-five and over make up approximately 13 percent of the total population, yet they consume about 40 percent of all medications (Jones-Grizzle et al.). This rate of medication use among seniors coincides with the rate of many chronic diseases, which rise sharply with age. For example, arthritis, high blood pressure, and angina are reported by 47 percent, 43 percent, and 31 percent, respectively, by people age sixty-five years or older.

Patterns of medication use by seniors living at home or in nursing homes have previously been described (Avorn et al.; Chrischilles et al; and Cooper). In general, seniors living at home consume three to eight medications, with an increase in use with increasing age, for females, and for those with poor self-reported health (Chrischilles and Cooper). In the nursing home the number of ordered medications ranges from four to nine (Beers 1992).

The most commonly used classes of medications generally reflect the types of diseases that seniors have (Table 1). For example, the most commonly used medication classes are drugs for high blood pressure, arthritis, and stomach or intestinal diseases, and blood thinners and drugs such as antidepressants or tranquilizers (Chrischilles et al.).

Adverse drug reactions

Unfortunately, medication use carries an inherent level of risk, particularly when people are taking multiple medications concomitantly. One risk is the occurrence of adverse drug reactions. An adverse drug reaction is defined as a response to a drug that is harmful or unintended, which occurs at doses used in humans for the prevention, diagnosis, or treatment of disease. They can range from minor symptoms such as stomach upset, to conditions requiring hospitalization, such as gastrointestinal bleeding, or in some cases to death (Hanlon et al., 1995).

It has been estimated that 10 to 25 percent of community-dwelling seniors and 54 to 67 per-

Table 1
Drug classes most commonly used by older people.

Cardiovascular drugs
Analgesics/antipyretic drugs
Gastrointestinal drugs
Central nervous system drugs
Anti-rheumatic-drugs
Nutritional supplements

SOURCE: Author

cent of seniors living in nursing homes suffer from an adverse drug reaction (Gurwitz and Avorn; Cooper). Among community dwellers, heart/blood pressure medications and analgesics (pain killers) are the most commonly implicated medications. In the nursing home, heart/blood pressure drugs and psychiatric drugs are usually responsible.

The risk of adverse drug reactions is related to many factors, some of which are modifiable. Important predictors of adverse drug reactions include the number of medications that a patient consumes and the number of diseases that a patient has. Although some researchers have suggested that seniors and females are at higher risk, this remains controversial (Gurwitz and Avorn; Hanlon et al.).

Adverse drug reactions and health care utilization

Approximately 10–16 percent of hospital admissions result from adverse drug reactions from which approximately two-thirds of patients recover (Colt and Shapiro; Col). Inappropriate prescribing is a leading cause of adverse drug reactions. Fifty percent of adverse drug reactions detected on admission to hospital in one study were from absolutely contraindicated or unnecessary medications (Lindley et al.). Furthermore, there were 0.34 adverse drug reactions for each unnecessary medication and only 0.08 per necessary medications. In a study of nursing home patients, 61 percent of adverse drug reactions were felt to have resulted from inappropriate prescribing (Cooper).

Adverse drug reactions have an important impact on health care use. Of seniors who report experiencing adverse drug reactions, 63 to 75 percent need to contact their physician, 50 per-

cent have laboratory tests ordered, 10 percent visit the emergency room, and 7 to 11 percent are hospitalized (Chrischilles et al., "Self-reported Adverse Drug Reactions"; Hanlon, 1997). When projected to the entire community-dwelling older population, this translates into two million annual physician visits, one million laboratory tests, and 146,000 hospitalizations from adverse drug reactions (Chrischilles et al., "Self-reported Adverse Drug Reactions").

Increases in health care utilization can also be measured in the length of hospital stay or in dollar costs. For patients admitted to hospital who suffered an adverse drug reaction, this occurrence was associated with an increased length of stay of two days and a cost increase of $2,263 (Classen). Results from another study highlights this point: for every dollar spent on medications in nursing facilities, $1.33 is spent in the treatment of medication-induced problems that can be prevented (Bootman et al.).

Medication use in the older population

It is not clear why medication use in the older population is so challenging, however, multiple interacting factors complicate medication use in seniors. Important issues include: increased disease burden; changes in physiology, pharmacokinetics, and pharmacodynamics with aging; patient and family expectations; poor patient-physician communication; over-the-counter medication use; using other people's medications; and the use of multiple physicians, to name a few. Lastly, seniors are often excluded from clinical trials that are conducted when drugs are being studied. Therefore when these drugs are marketed, they have not been extensively studied in older people, even though these are generally the patients most likely to receive them.

Pharmacokinetics, pharmacodynamics, and aging

These are two areas that are well understood, and can be taken into account by clinicians in every day practice.

Pharmacokinetics. Pharmacokinetics is a biological science concerned with the characterization and mathematical description of the absorption, distribution, metabolism, and excretion of drugs, their by-products, and other substances of biologic interest.

These processes determine the amount and rate of appearance of drugs in the body, distribution throughout the tissues, and elimination of the drug from the body. In other words, pharmacokinetics is the study of how the drugs move into and out of the body.

It is simplest to begin with the first event that occurs when a patient takes a medication: *absorption*. Most drugs that are commonly used are given by mouth (although some medications can be applied to the skin, eyes, or by other means). Absorption of the medication takes place at the lining of the stomach or small intestine, depending on the drug. Although there are various age-related changes in the physiology of the gut, as a whole they do not result in any clinically significant age-related changes in drug absorption.

Distribution.   After a drug is absorbed, it is distributed into the bloodstream and various tissues and/or fluids (e.g., skin, lungs, brain, urine, etc.) where the drug will exert its therapeutic action (see below, pharmacodynamics). The degree to which a drug distributes into different tissues varies, and depends on physicochemical properties of the drug: the drug's relative solubility in fat as opposed to water, its affinity for various tissues, and the drug's binding to plasma proteins. Directly relevant to distribution are the following age-related changes in body composition: there is an increase in body fat (about 15–30 percent) accompanied by a decrease in total body water (about 10–15 percent). These alterations can result in an altered drug distribution profile, which may affect the response to the drug. For example, if a patient is given a drug that is mainly water-soluble, its concentration, and thus its effect, may be greater. This is explained by the fact that the older person has less body water in which the drug would distribute into, leading to a higher drug concentration. In most cases however, this will not be clinically significant, and can be accounted for by proper drug dosing (see below, general principles of drug therapy).

Metabolism.   Cytochrome P450 refers to a group of enzymes located on the membrane of the endoplasmic reticulum. The ancestral genes for the P-450 proteins have been estimated to have existed as far back as 3.5 million years ago, suggesting that drug metabolism is a secondary role. The original role for these enzymes likely is to: (1) metabolize endogenous compounds (e.g., cortisol); and (2) detoxify exogenous compounds (e.g., especially after oral ingestion). Conse-

quently, the highest concentrations of these enzymes are in the liver and small intestine, with very small quantities found elsewhere, and the liver is the major site where drugs are metabolized.

Metabolism of a drug produces substances that are called metabolites. This process is called *biotransformation*. Biotransformation may occur via two major groups of reactions (or through a combination of the two) called phase I and phase II reactions. Phase I reactions typically convert a drug to a more polar compound. Phase II reactions generally involve coupling of the parent compound with a substance found in the body to produce a drug conjugate. Most conjugates are inactive and very water soluble, allowing for rapid excretion by the kidneys (Matzke and Milikin). Metabolites may be biologically inactive, just as active as the parent drug, or more or less active than the parent drug. A drug may be metabolized to a number of metabolites, each with potentially different properties. Although some drugs are metabolized by phase I, followed by phase II reactions, many are metabolized by only one these types of reactions.

Various age-related liver changes impair drug metabolism. Liver mass decreases, as does liver blood flow. The metabolic capacity of phase I reactions also decrease. This is illustrated by a decreased clearance (i.e., the drug remains in the body for a longer period of time) of various drugs such as triazolam, diazepam, alprazolam, warfarin, and others (Sotaniemi et al., 1997). Unfortunately, there are no markers that help determine how well the liver is metabolizing drugs. Nonetheless, this reduced clearance has important clinical implications (Gordon et al.).

In contrast, phase II reactions are largely unaffected by aging. Thus, one factor considered by clinicians in drug selection is whether a drug's metabolism is affected by aging. If so, an alternative drug is selected. If this is not possible, alternative strategies are used to avoid problems.

Elimination.   The kidneys play a major role in eliminating drugs and other substances from the body. The last step in the movement of drugs is elimination, which is accomplished by the kidneys. Elimination occurs via two (or a combination of the two) mechanisms: drugs can be filtered or actively secreted through the glomerulus (functional unit of the kidney). The rate the glomerulus filters drugs is called the glomerular filtration rate. As people age, this rate, and thus the ability to eliminate certain drugs, decreases (meaning that the drug will persist in the body for a longer period of time) starting at about age forty (Mayersohn). The glomerular filtration rate, unlike liver enzyme activity, can be estimated by using mathematical equations. This estimate is used to help select appropriate drug doses for seniors, since many commonly used drugs are largely eliminated by the kidney. By doing so, drug build-up in the body is prevented that may otherwise lead to side effects.

Pharmacodynamics. Pharmacodynamics is defined as the study of the biological effects resulting from the interaction between drugs and biological systems. More simply stated, it is what the drug does to the body. Aging often results in different responses to the same amount of drug.

Aging and the brain: drug effects

The brain has millions of brain cells called neurons (i.e., its working units). Neurons operate using various substances called neurotransmitters, examples of which include acetylcholine and dopamine. For proper brain function there needs to be a balance of these neurotransmitters. Imbalances in or marginal deficits in certain neurotransmitters can lead to symptoms or disorders that could have serious consequences.

In older people, two major changes in neurotransmitters are of importance. There is a decrease in the number of cholinergic and dopaminergic neurons, which leads to a relative state of deficiency of acetylcholine and dopamine (Drachman). This reduces the reserve capacity of the brain and makes the balance between neurotransmitters more delicate. The end result is that medication-related problems are more common, and of serious consequence in seniors. Commonly used medications that can be problematic include antipsychotics (e.g., haloperidol), benzodiazepines (e.g., diazepam), and medications with anticholinergic properties (e.g., diphenhydramine or Benadryl). For example, the incidence of drug-induced Parkinsonism (a condition that mimics Parkinson's disease) is much higher in seniors. This condition can cause significant problems due to problems in moving, walking, performing every day tasks with their hands, and can lead to falls, which can have disastrous consequences. Seniors who take benzodiazepine drugs are also at risk for drug-induced cognitive impairment. This means that they may suffer from memory loss, decreased

ability to think, and present with other characteristics that may mimic Alzheimer's disease. Lastly, medications with anticholinergic effects such as diphenhydramine (Benadryl, Tylenol PM), dimenhydrinate (Dramanine), and other commonly used medications present a particular problem in older people. In older people they should be avoided, as they are a common cause of cognitive impairment and delirium.

General principles of drug therapy

Many useful strategies exist that simplify drug use in seniors (Gordon et al.). The two most useful tips are generally (1) Start low, go slow, and (2) Do one thing at once.

The "start low, go slow" principle is how clinicians globally account for the aforementioned changes in the way that the seniors handle drugs. For example, if the normal dose of sertraline (antidepressant) is 50mg daily, 25mg daily commonly would be prescribed. Then, as is common for many drugs, the drug dose is increased to a specific amount. If sertraline is normally increased to 100mg in one week, it would be increased in one and one-half to two weeks by an increment of 25mg. This lessens the chance of severe side effects from using a dose that is too high for an older person that may lead to the patient becoming sick and stop taking the drug or, worse yet, that may lead to hospitalization.

"Do one thing at once" refers to making one medication change at a time. People with more than one medical problem must often take more than one medication. After the patient has been interviewed and examined, the clinician will have ideas as to what the problems are that need to be addressed. This may involve adding, adjusting the dose, or stopping drugs that may be contributing to the problems. Whenever possible, it is essential that only one drug be added or removed (or its dose changed) at a time. Otherwise, if the patient improves or worsens after adjusting more than one drug, the clinician will not be able to determine which drug was of benefit (or detrimental). For example, consider a patient with arthritic knee pain who is prescribed aspirin and ibuprofen together for pain. If the patient's pain improves the question is: which drug helped? Which drug should they continue to take? In order to ascertain which drug was useful, the patient would have to stop one drug, see what happens, and go from there (in other words, if the pain returns, add the second drug, then see if the first drug helped at all). Such an approach is time consuming and complicated. Similarly, if the patient suffers from side effects, they will not know which drug is the offending agent. This is an undesirable scenario that could be avoided by starting with one drug, using it properly, and assessing whether or not the drug worked before adding a second drug. Furthermore, situations like this can result in a patient incorrectly being labeled as "unresponsive" to both drugs, or "allergic" or "intolerant" to both drugs.

Conclusion

The older population is growing rapidly, bringing various challenges to the health care system. One of the major challenges is that of ensuring safe and effective medication use in older people. The unique needs and characteristics of this population must be taken into account by health care professionals involved in the care of older people in order to prevent drug-related problems.

CARLOS H. ROJAS-FERNANDEZ

See also ALCOHOLISM; ARTHRITIS; BRAIN; DRUG REGULATION; HERBAL THERAPY; KIDNEY; AGING.

BIBLIOGRAPHY

AVORN, J., and GURWITZ, J. H. "Drug Use in the Nursing Home." *Annals of Internal Medicine* 123 (1995): 195–204.

BEERS, M. H.; OUSLANDER, J. G.; FINGOLD, S. F.; MORGENSTERN, H.; REUBEN, D. B.; ROGERS, W., et al. "Inappropriate Medication Prescribing in Skilled-Nursing Facilities." *Annals of Internal Medicine* 117 (1992): 684–689.

BOOTMAN, J. L.; HARRISON, D. L.; and COX, E. "The Health Care Cost of Drug Related Morbidity and Mortality in Nursing Facilities." *Archives of Internal Medicine* 157 (1997): 2089–2096.

CHRISCHILLES, E. A.; SEGAR, E. T.; and WALLACE, R. B. "Self-Reported Adverse Drug Reactions and Related Resource Use. A Study of Community Dwelling Persons 65 Years of Age and Older." *Annals of Internal Medicine* 117 (1992): 634–640.

CHRISCHILLES, E. A.; FOLEY, D. J.; WALLACE, R. B.; LEMKE, J. H.; SEMLA, T. P.; HANLON, J. T., et al. "Use of Medications by Persons 65 and Over: Data from the Established Populations for Epidemiologic Studies of the Elderly." *Journal of Gerontology* 47 (1992): M137–M144.

CLASSEN, D. C.; PESTOTNIK, S. L.; EVANS, R. S.; LLOYD, J. F.; and BURKE, J. P. "Adverse Drug Events in Hospitalized Patients. Excess Length of Stay, Extra Costs, and Attributable Mortality." *Journal of the American Medical Association* 277, no. 4 (1997): 301–306.

COL, N.; FANALE, J. E.; and KRONHOLM, P. "The Role of Medication Non-compliance and Adverse Drug Reactions in Hospitalization of the Elderly." *Archives of Internal Medicine* 150 (1990): 841–845.

COLT, H. G., and SHAPIRO, A. P. "Drug-induced Illness as a Cause for Admission to a Community Hospital." *Journal of the American Geriatrics Society* 37 (1989): 323–326.

COOPER, J. W. "Probable Adverse Drug Reactions in a Rural Geriatric Nursing Home Population: A Four Year Study." *Journal of the American Geriatrics Society* 44 (1996): 194–197.

DRACHMAN, D. "Aging and the Brain: A New Frontier." *Annals of Neurology* 42 (1997): 819–828.

GORDON, J.; ROJAS-FERNANDEZ, C.; and ROCKWOOD, K. "Practical Solutions to Polypharmacy Problems in the Elderly." *Canadian Journal of Diagnosis* 15, no. 4 (1998): 78–90.

GURWITZ, J. H., and AVORN, J. "The Ambiguous Relation Between Aging and Adverse Drug Reactions." *Annals of Internal Medicine* 114 (1991): 956–966.

HANLON, J. T.; SCHMADER, K. E.; and LEWIS, I. K. "Adverse Drug Reactions." In *Therapeutics in the Elderly*. Edited by J. C. Delafuente and R. B. Stewart. Cincinnati: Harvey Whitney Books, 1995. Pages 212–227.

HANLON, J. T.; SCHMADER, K. E.; KORONKOWSKI, M. J., et al. "Adverse Drug Events in High Risk Older Outpatients." *Journal of American Geriatrics Society* 45 (1997): 945–948.

JONES-GRIZZLE, A. J., and DRAUGALIS, J. R. "Demographics." In *Geriatric Pharmacology*. Edited by R. Bressler and M. D. Katz. New York: McGraw-Hill, 1993. Pages 1–8.

LINDLEY, C. M.; TULLY, M. P.; PARAMSOTHY, V.; and TALLIS, R. C. "Inappropriate Medication is a Major Cause of Adverse Drug Reactions in Elderly Patients." *Age and Aging* 21 (1992): 294–300.

MATZKE, G. R., and MILIKIN, S. P. "Influence of Renal Function and Dialysis on Drug Disposition." In *Applied Pharmacokinetics: Principles of Therapeutic Drug Monitoring*. Edited by W. E. Evans, J. J. Schentag, and W. J. Jusko. Vancouver, Wash.: Applied Therapeutics, 1992. Secs. 8.1–8.49.

MAYERSOHN, M. B. "Special Considerations in the Elderly." In *Applied Pharmacokinetics: Prin-*

ciples of Therapeutic Drug Monitoring. Edited by W. E. Evans, J. J. Schentag, and W. J. Jusko. Vancouver, Wash.: Applied Therapeutics, 1992. Secs. 9.1–9.43.

SOTANIEMI, E. A.; ARRANTO, A. J.; PELKONEN, O., et al. "Age and Cytochrome P450-linked Drug Metabolism in Humans: An Analysis of 226 Subjects with Equal Histopathologic Condi-tions." *Clinical Pharmacology and Therapeutics* 61 (1997): 331–339.

DURABLE POWER OF ATTORNEY

See ADVANCE DIRECTIVES FOR HEALTH CARE

ISBN 0-02-865468-4